THE

AN ILLUSTRATED HISTORY OF THE NEW ENGLAND PATRIOTS

PATS

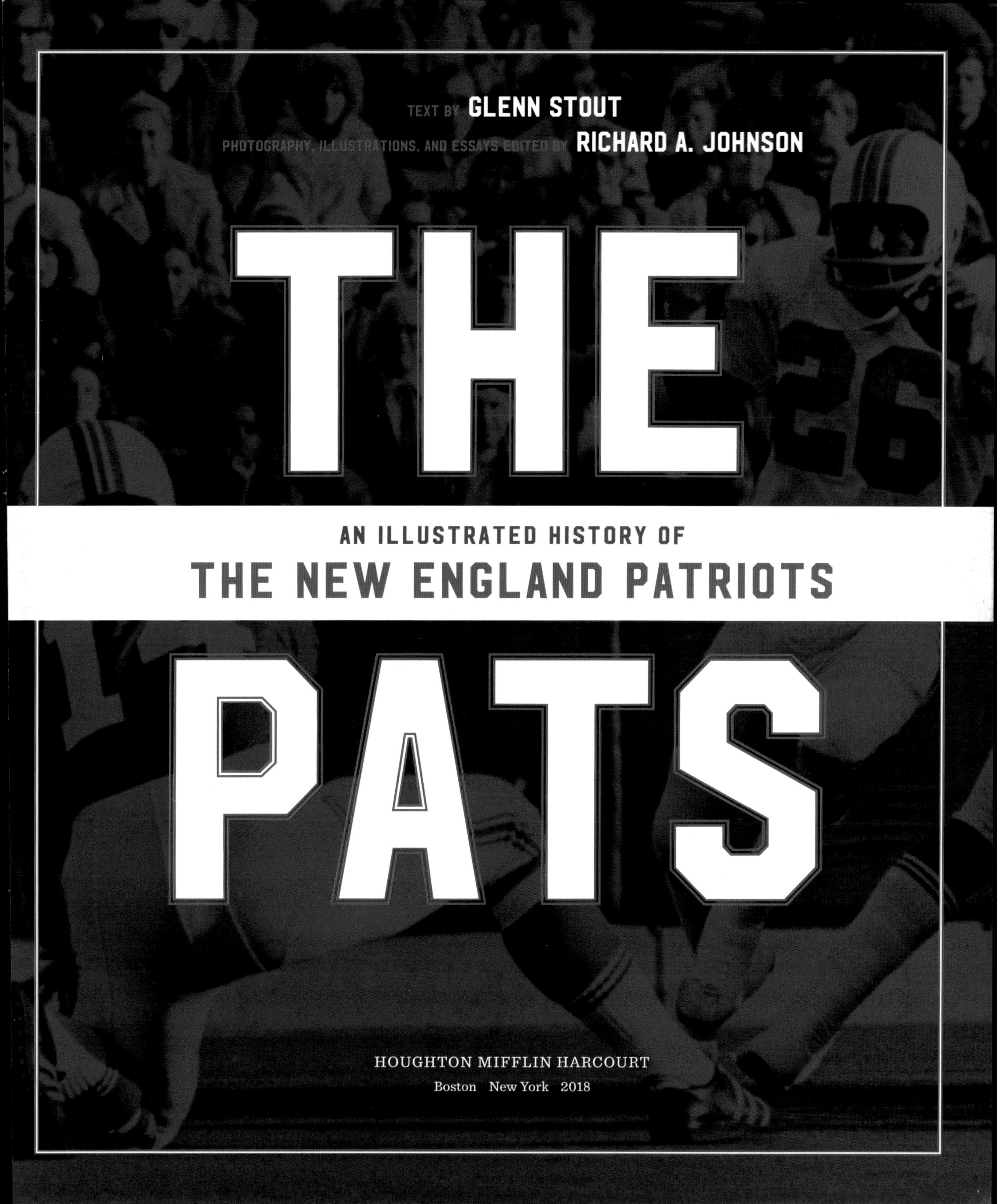

TEXT BY **GLENN STOUT**

PHOTOGRAPHY, ILLUSTRATIONS, AND ESSAYS EDITED BY **RICHARD A. JOHNSON**

THE

AN ILLUSTRATED HISTORY OF
THE NEW ENGLAND PATRIOTS

PATS

HOUGHTON MIFFLIN HARCOURT

Boston   New York   2018

RICHARD A. JOHNSON:

To my uncle Red McDonough, who played football at Brown in the leather

helmet days; Patriot QB/punter Tom Yewcic, a great sportsman and friend;

Al Coulthard, loyal friend and Phillips Academy trainer in the days of two

prodigies named Bill Belichick and Ernie Adams; my dear friend Jack Grinold,

who worked for the first Patriots team; cartoonist Phil Bissell, the father

of Pat and one of the all-time great sports cartoonists; our beloved Patriot

and NFL warrior and Hall of Famer Junior Seau; Ron Marshall;

Kathryn Maynes; and my home team of Mary, Lizzy, Bobby, and Brenna.

GLENN STOUT:

To all those who give so much of themselves to play a game for the

enjoyment and entertainment of others; to all those who play in

backyard Thanksgiving Day games everywhere; to my family; and

to every member of the Patriots, past, present, and future.

For information about permission to reproduce selections from this book, write to
trade.permissions@hmhco.com or to Permissions, Houghton Mifflin Harcourt
Publishing Company, 3 Park Avenue, 19th Floor, New York, New York 10016.

hmhco.com

Library of Congress Cataloging-in-Publication Data is available.

ISBN 978-1-328-91740-9

Book design by Vertigo Design NYC

Printed in China

SCP 10 9 8 7 6 5 4 3 2 1

CONTENTS

ACKNOWLEDGMENTS

THANKS TO editor Susan Canavan and Jenny Xu of Houghton Mifflin Harcourt; Peter Oyegun and Sarah Johnson of Getty Images; cartoonist Phil Bissell; artist-archivist Walter Pingree; historian Bob Hyldburg; Patriots publications director Fred Kirsch; Patriots vice president of media relations Stacey James; Hall at Patriots Place executive director Bryan Morry; Sports Museum executive director Rusty Sullivan; *Boston Globe* sports editor Joe Sullivan; *Boston Globe* librarian Rosemarie McDonald; and to Pam Schuyler Cowens, Eric Adler, the New England Patriots, Eddie Andelman, Alfred Coulthard, Bob Walsh, Jack Grinold, Billy Sullivan, Mark Waitkus, Dan Kraft, Ed "Moose" Savage, Leigh Montville, George Plimpton, Lesley Visser, Lisa Olsen, Mike Raphael, Upton Bell, Ron Borges, Robert Flynn Johnson, Robert Hamilton Johnson, Mary Hamilton Johnson, and Elizabeth Hamilton Johnson.

—RAJ

IN ADDITION to many of those cited above, I also would like to thank the men and women of the Boston press, both print and broadcast, and those other reporters around the country who reported so well and for so long on the Boston Patriots, the American Football League, the New England Patriots, and the National Football League. Their reporting forms the spine and flesh of this book, and such an undertaking would have been impossible without them. The authors of the many previous books on the Patriots—and in particular Larry Fox's *The New England Patriots: Triumph and Tragedy* and Jeff Miller's history of the AFL, *Going Long*—were extraordinarily helpful. Thanks also to my colleague in this project and so many others, Richard Johnson and the Sports Museum of New England; to book designer Alison Lew and copy editor Cynthia Buck; to agent John Taylor "Ike" Williams and to Katherine Flynn and Hope Denekamp of Kneerim & Williams; to Howard Bryant for his informative and illuminating insights; to journalist Stephanie Kuzydym for her studious fact-checking; and to my circle of writing friends around the country who put up with late-night phone calls and early morning emails—you know who you are and how much you mean to me—and my many friends who are Patriots fans who shared their stories, in particular Paul and Linda Valiquette and Scott Bortzfield. The Patriots and NFL websites and ProFootballReference.com were also invaluable, as were the Boston Public Library and the many YouTube videos uploaded by fans and other parties that make it possible to see the Patriots on the field across nearly six decades. My early work with *Boston* magazine also helped inform this project—little did I know that thirty years after writing about the Patriots for the first time I would find myself still telling their story. And thanks also to my family, Siobhan, Saorla, and my brother Gary, for allowing me the time and space that writing a book requires.

—GS

INTRODUCTION

OVERTIME

ALL ACROSS NEW ENGLAND—from Bangor to Hartford, Alburgh to Block Island, Manchester to Uxbridge, Amherst, Concord, Worcester, Providence, and Burlington, to Boston and Lowell and everywhere in between, it seemed as if everyone, *everyone*, in numbers never before imagined, was glued to the TV: watching, hoping, and some even praying. One team, a dynasty. The other an upstart. And now, in the season finale, a ball tumbling through the air . . . three, two, one . . . and sudden death. Empty beer bottles were abandoned for full ones, fingers scratched at the bottom of bowls of chips, betting slips were fondled and blessed, favored chairs fought over, bars filled to the breaking point, waitresses stuck in the crush.

First the coin toss . . . *YES!*

A kickoff and a failed third down, a punt, and then, the slow shredding of hopes and dreams, the excitement deflating with each tough yard, the air slowly leaking from the ball. And then it was over.

Bottles broke, men cursed, dogs hid behind the davenport, and women and children screamed and cried. New England's team had lost.

It did not seem possible. When the Baltimore Colts defeated the New York Giants 23–17 in sudden-death overtime for the NFL championship on December 28, 1958, a game that would be described for decades as the greatest football game ever played, no place in the country mourned more than New England.

Sure, the Giants played in New York, in a chilled Yankee Stadium where most of the 65,000 fans that day now slumped back in their seats, exhausted and spent after sixty-eight minutes and fifteen seconds of grind-it-out, hard-nosed football. But elsewhere in New York the game had not been seen, blacked out by a league that did not understand exactly what it had—or more important in the long run, what had just happened.

DAILY NEWS
NEW YORK'S PICTURE NEWSPAPER

FINAL

48   New York 17, N.Y., Monday December 29, 1958   5 CENTS

COLTS WIN TITLE

Giants Beaten in 'Sudden-Death' Game, 23-17

—Story on Page 44

(By Associated Press)

The golden coach turns into a pumpkin, the white stallions revert to mice and the Cinderella story that the N. Y. Giants had been living these past weeks comes to a crashing end as Alan (The Horse) Ameche slams through a gaping hole in the Giant line to score from the one in in sudden-death overtime. Giants' Patton (right) moves in.

Holing Up For the Winter

[←] Ameche barrels over the fallen Patton as he blasts through for winning score. Official signifies TD.
—*Story on page 44; other pictures in centerfold*

(NEWS foto by Walter Kelleher)

The *New York Daily News* back-page headline of December 29, 1958, is the perfect showcase to announce the result of the most significant game in pro football history and the game that helped inspire the founding of the American Football League: "COLTS WIN TITLE, Giants Beaten in 'Sudden—Death' Game, 23–17."

This early photograph of football at Braves Field in Boston captures the gritty nature of the sputtering fortunes of the pro game in the Hub, which saw the failure of five franchises prior to the founding of the Patriots in 1960.

Earlier that morning and the previous night, thousands of Giant fans had headed north and east in caravans of cars winding down unfamiliar two-lane roads into New England, stopping at roadside taverns or motels that touted FREE TV to fight locals over bar stools or to find a place to stand in a cramped room with a twin bed. Everyone jockeyed to watch the dancing shadows in shades of gray and hear a tinny voice over a too-small

loudspeaker call out the names: Kyle Rote, "Big Daddy" Lipscomb, Sam Huff, Raymond Berry, Pat Summerall . . . and Frank Gifford, the California Golden Boy, who fumbled and stumbled and, on that day, fell short. And Johnny Unitas, the name cut from Americana, who carved the air in overtime with pass after pass, calling plays like a chess master until Alan Ameche barreled through the exhausted New York defense from one yard out, ending a game still talked about almost sixty years later, when another team gave New England a chance at retribution.

In 1958, the Giants were New England's team as much as they were also Manhattan's and New Jersey's and Long Island's, the only professional football team north and east of Philadelphia. Just as the St. Louis Cardinals were also the team of Oklahoma and Colorado and the rest of the West before baseball expanded to the coast, the Giants owned every football fan's heart east of the Catskills and Adirondacks. In New England, college football lagged behind the pros in popularity. The established college football powers of old—Ivy League Harvard, Dartmouth, Yale, and Brown, and the Catholic rivals Boston College and Holy Cross—were no longer national powers, and state college alma maters meant little.

Yet football was embedded in the region's DNA. The first high school game had been played in 1862 on Boston Common, and the Ivies made the game a mandatory part of college life. High school football was just as important, a long-established Thanksgiving Day tradition in many places where rivalries between the big schools—Lowell and Lawrence, Leominster and Fitchburg, or Fall River and New Bedford—drew tens of thousands of fans.

Then there was pro football. The National Football League (NFL) had been founded in 1920 as the American Professional Football Association (APFA). Centered in the upper Midwest, the APFA had ten teams in four states, playing in metropolises like Chicago and Detroit but also places like Decatur and Akron and Muncie. For the next thirty years, pro football struggled to become established, and what eventually became the NFL had to fend off challenges from several rival circuits before the league more or less achieved stability and success in the 1950s following the collapse of the All-America Football Conference.

But no pro team had ever managed to last in New England, at least not for very long. At various times, Boston hosted the Pere Marquettes, Bears, Bulldogs, Yanks, Redskins, and Shamrocks (a club that also gave Providence a try), but no matter how well they played on the field, none survived for more than a few seasons. The problem was usually a combination of financial and stadium issues, often made worse by underfinanced

ownership that called someplace else home. The last of those teams, the NFL Boston Yanks, left Boston in 1948.

By the time the Colts and Giants met in the 1958 NFL championship game, New England had gone a decade without a major league pro football team. Without even trying, the Giants had become New England's de facto home team, their games broadcast most Sundays on TV and radio throughout the region. Because of the blackout rule, which prevented broadcasts of home games, fans in Boston, Rhode Island, eastern Connecticut, and the rest of the region actually had more access to the Giants on TV than New Yorkers. The Giants recognized this and overtly courted New England, even holding training camp at St. Michael's College in Winooski, Vermont. And after winning an NFL championship in 1956, the club was poised to embark on the most successful run in franchise history.

Then came the 1958 title game. Broadcast nationwide by NBC, that game would prove to be a watershed moment. Although only 9 percent of all households had a TV in 1950, by 1958 that number had risen to more than 80 percent: as broadcast quality and screen size improved, more than 40 million American households now had TVs. Pro games looked better on TV than college games, which still featured mostly line lunges and feints off the single wing, or wing-T, formation, making the ball hard to follow. Pro football was less conservative: the players spread out, and they passed far more often—you didn't need to squint to see what was happening. And on that gray December afternoon in 1958, with quarterback Johnny Unitas carving apart the Giants defense beneath the stadium lights with pinpoint accuracy, the game jumped out of the screen.

When the ratings came out and it was announced that some 45 million people—almost one out of every three Americans old enough to read—had stayed inside to watch *a football game*, everyone noticed. That meant 45 million people also saw every commercial. All of a sudden, a lot of guys with a lot of money (and a lot of guys who didn't have money but knew people who did) wanted to own a pro football team.

The NFL was a closed community of only twelve teams: the Rams and 49ers on the West Coast; the

In the wake of the landmark 1958 NFL championship game, the American Football League was formed by a group of businessmen who branded themselves "the Foolish Club," in recognition of their far-fetched ambitions. This picture from 1961 includes seven of the eight original members: (*seated from left*) K. S. "Bud" Adams (Houston), Joe Foss (AFL commissioner), (*standing from left*) Billy Sullivan (Boston), Cal Kunz (Denver; the Broncos' original owner, Bob Howsam, sold his interests to a syndicate headed by Kunz in 1961), Ralph Wilson (Buffalo), Lamar Hunt (Dallas), Harry Wismer (New York), Wayne Valley (Oakland), and Barron Hilton (San Diego).

Into this void would come a new league: the American Football League. The Patriots were the last franchise to join the AFL. A confluence of history, luck, and, to be honest, greed finally resulted in a professional football team for Boston and New England . . . or at least a rough facsimile of it.

The irony is that for much of the Patriots' history, they were hardly beloved, apart from a small knot of partisans surrounding Massachusetts Bay. Most football fans in and around Boston were, if not indifferent toward them, at least suspicious. That was because whenever the Pats did finally manage to win a few games and turn a head or two, there was always something that exposed the folly of expecting an enduring relationship to result. The Pats were the suitor that always left the date standing at the threshold, forgot the anniversary, neglected to make the reservation, or called their lover by the wrong name. Every time the Pats seemed to earn fans' love,

Chicago Bears and Cardinals, Detroit Lions, Cleveland Browns, Green Bay Packers, and Pittsburgh Steelers in the upper Midwest; and four teams on the East Coast: Baltimore, Washington, Philadelphia, and New York. That left vast portions of the country without a team— from Chicago to the West Coast and south of a line drawn from the Windy City to Baltimore . . . and New England. With money to be made, people soon started knocking on the door of the NFL, asking to join the party. For most NFL franchise owners, however, football was their main business. They were not anxious to expand and share their suddenly more valuable product.

they let them down, time and time again, in ways that were ever more implausible and bizarre, ranging from coaches fired in the midst of the playoffs to players lying about injuries, prisoners earning a game ball, and fans being electrocuted by the goalposts. And every time fans thought they'd seen it all, well, the Patriots showed them something even more difficult to believe. Oh, interest sometimes spiked when they won, but fans recognized such rare occurrences as anomalies, temporary illusions to be greeted by heads nodding in agreement, raised eyebrows, beers slammed on the bar, and the unspoken lament: "Well, whaddya think would happen? It's the Patriots, for God's sake. We shoulda known better."

CRADLE OF THE GAME: THE ORIGINS OF FOOTBALL AND THE PRO GAME IN BOSTON

RICHARD A. JOHNSON

And then the suits of armor, together with the presence of the ready surgeon and the waiting stretcher (and, for all I know, the undertaker), made it all savor a little too strongly of the Roman amphitheater to be compatible with what football was intended for, namely a healthy and invigorating pastime.

—*James D'Wolf Lovett,* Old Boston Boys and the Games They Played, *1907 (Lovett was a member of America's first football team, the Oneidas of Boston, 1861–1863)*

It's safe to say that Boston, and greater New England, is the cradle of American football, for within a two-hour (non–game day) drive of Gillette Stadium lie the environs of Boston, Cambridge, and New Haven, whose practice fields were the incubator of most—if not all— of the rules and language that define the game.

Long before all those glittering Super Bowl trophies, Duck Boat parades, and shiny rings, the game of American football was created as a vehicle for the expression of rugged masculinity by a legion of local schoolboys.

If one looks carefully today one will find a stone monument

The Oneida Football Club of Boston, which played its games on Boston Common, is credited with being America's first such team while playing a version of the game that included elements of both rugby and soccer.

This monument was erected in honor of the Oneida Football Club in 1925, alongside the field on Boston Common where they were undefeated for all of their four seasons.

Not long after most of the Oneidas left to join the Union Army, a hybrid version of their game became a staple of Harvard's budding intercollegiate athletic calendar. The Crimson claim to have played the first genuine intercollegiate game in 1874 against McGill.

Soon after, Yale's Walter Camp, generally regarded as "the Father of American Football," devised the modern gridiron, gave names to each position, and publicized the sport by naming the first collegiate All-American teams.

Although the college game enjoyed a robust local heritage—capacity crowds filled Harvard Stadium for teams such as their 1920 Rose Bowl champs and jammed either Fenway Park or Braves Field for the ecclesiastical

tong war between BC and Holy Cross—the pro game in Boston mostly played to empty seats.

Witness the fact that the Hub gained and lost five pro football franchises prior to Billy Sullivan plunking down $25,000 to secure the last franchise awarded in the fourth and final incarnation of the American Football League in 1959.

The origins of the pro game in Boston involved a historic and well-attended match between the Providence Steam Rollers and the George Halas–led Chicago Bears, featuring Red Grange, at Braves Field in December 1925. Providence not only won, 9–6, but in a contest that surely could have only been conjured from the imagination of a Hollywood scriptwriter, knocked Grange out of the game

tucked alongside a shaded path on Boston Common honoring America's first football team. Dating back to 1861, the team was known as the Oneidas, and its members were mostly blue-blooded adolescents from Boston Latin School and local prep schools who played a primitive version of the game that was part soccer and part rugby, not unlike the scrums that later evolved on the playing fields of Princeton, Rutgers, and Harvard. Over a period of three years, their goal was never crossed, and in November 1925 their monument was dedicated with seven surviving members of the team in attendance.

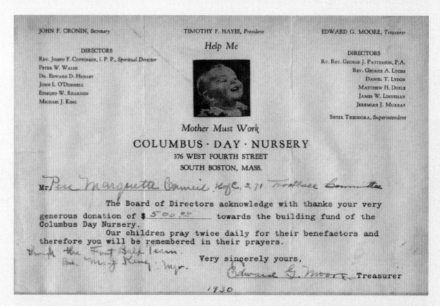

The Pere Marquette football team of South Boston was decades ahead of its time in donating proceeds from its semipro games to charities—such as this day care center, which now operates as the Laboure Center.

The Pere Marquettes made history in 1927 when they played the reigning NFL champion New York Giants at Fenway Park. They're shown here in action at Braves Field.

and provided evidence there was some interest in the pro game in Boston.

Two years later, on November 17, 1927, the longshoremen, shipping clerks, and graduate students who made up the semipro football squad of South Boston's Pere Marquette Knights of Columbus sports lodge trekked to Fenway Park to play the NFL champion New York Giants in a game that was nothing less than Boston's dress rehearsal for joining the fledgling National Football League. A crowd of between 8,000 and 10,000 cheered their neighbors in a heroically fought 34–7 loss on an afternoon when most pigskin fans were across town watching Yale play Harvard.

The effort inspired a local group led by South Boston native George Kenneally to purchase the Pottsville Maroons NFL franchise for $2,500, a sum that today might get you two seats with parking for a single regular-season game in the EMC Club at Gillette Stadium.

The new team, known as the Bulldogs, lasted for a single season in 1929—winning and losing four games against opponents such as the Staten Island Stapletons, Orange Tornadoes, Dayton Triangles, Buffalo Bisons, and Providence Steam Rollers.

Three years later, George Preston Marshall and two partners founded the Boston Braves NFL franchise, so named because they played their inaugural season at Braves Field. Touted on the team letterhead as "Playing Post Graduate Foot Ball at Braves Field in Boston," the Braves were led by

quarterback "Honolulu" Hughes and future Hall of Famers Turk Edwards and Cliff Battles.

To save money in the pre–college draft era, the ownership had rented a bus on the West Coast and had Turk Edwards, a former Washington State star, drive the rig across country picking up free agent signees at various stops. The team discovered the gem who was Cliff Battles at little-known West Virginia Wesleyan, where the running back was also a member of Phi Beta Kappa and an aspiring concert pianist.

During their five years in Boston, the Braves would adopt the controversial moniker of "Redskins" after the team left Braves Field at the end of the '32 season some $46,000 in debt and in need of a new name while

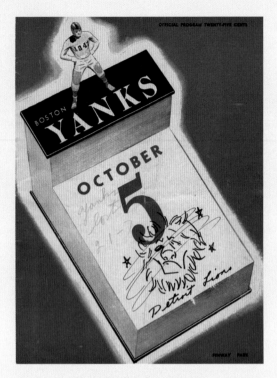

The Yanks, the third NFL team and fifth pro football team to call Boston home, played their home games at Fenway Park from 1944 to 1948.

decamping to Fenway Park. Then, following four seasons of mostly indifferent fan and media interest, owner George Preston Marshall made the bold and unprecedented move of relocating the 1936 NFL title game versus the Green Bay Packers from Fenway Park to New York's Polo Grounds as his angry parting gesture prior to relocating the franchise to Washington.

Much as fans missed seeing Henry Aaron in a Boston Braves baseball uniform in 1954, football fans missed the arrival of quarterback extraordinaire Sammy Baugh by a single season that could well have kept the Boston Redskins in Boston and helped preserve pro football in the region.

When the Redskins captured their NFL division title, they were sharing Fenway Park with the Boston Shamrocks, an entry in what was then the second version of the American Football League. Led by former Providence College star and future American League umpire Hank Soar, the Shamrocks were among the first teams to play night football in Boston, stringing up temporary klieg lights at Fenway a decade before Tom Yawkey mounted light towers.

Following the Shamrocks' demise in 1937 as the result of the Great Depression, Fenway Park played host to the Boston Bears (of the third version of the AFL), who played their first and only season in 1940.

The demise of Boston's Bears was followed by two very successful war charity exhibitions played by the Chicago Bears to capacity crowds at Fenway in 1942 and '43. And it was the success of these games that inspired the forming of Boston's third NFL franchise, the improbably named Yanks, who played at Fenway from 1944 to 1948.

The Yanks, despite showcasing the talent of former Notre Dame star and Lynn native Boley Dancewicz, lost owner Ted Collins a small fortune. He was forced to move the team to New York, where they became the football Yankees before ultimately relocating to Baltimore. There, known as the Colts, they achieved iconic status with Johnny Unitas before Robert Irsay unceremoniously moved them to Indianapolis in the middle of the night in 1984.

So, whether tossing a football on the same Boston Common playing fields once trod by the Oneidas or tuning in to a Patriots contest versus the Redskins or Colts, never forget that the seeds of the game itself were planted in the rocky soil now often littered with confetti blown skyward by yet another Patriots victory parade.

RICHARD A. JOHNSON, curator of Boston's Sports Museum since 1982, has collaborated on eight books with Glenn Stout.

Sixty years later, reality has trumped fiction. Today the Patriots are both the most loved and hated team in the game, something that seems almost unimaginable and makes the more recent incarnation of their story so compelling. A team that was underfinanced and almost homeless at the start, a near-perennial also-ran, and an occasional laughingstock for much of its first three decades is now the NFL's dominant franchise. As of this writing, they have made the playoffs in nine straight seasons and fourteen of their last sixteen, played in a total of ten Super Bowls (more than any other team), and appeared in the title game seven times since 2002, winning five Super Bowls. If professional football has a dynasty today, they are it, relegating previous dynasties—the Browns, Packers, Steelers, 49ers, and Cowboys—to history.

Almost out of nowhere (but not, as the reader will learn, for no reason), the Patriots have been utterly transformed. They made a region that only six decades ago had no enduring legacy of professional football and a fading presence in the collegiate game into what is considered the center of the professional football universe, a hard-earned and inarguably deserved status when measured by championships and passion. And in that category, Patriots fans are the most rabid in the game. Every game they have played at home since 1994, whether exhibition, regular-season, or postseason, has been a sellout. According to various surveys, the Patriots are not only one of the two or three most beloved NFL franchises, with a fan base that extends to every region of the country, but

simultaneously one of the most detested. That love-hate relationship is both the prize and the price of winning, one that fans wear with pride.

Few football fans of any kind are indifferent to the team that today calls all of New England home. Babies are named Brady and dogs are called Gronk. College students come to Boston from Chicago and Philadelphia wearing the jerseys of the Bears and Eagles and go back home wearing Patriots hats and sporting Super Bowl tattoos. The uncle with the funny accent who everyone used to pity during the holiday visit now gloats and tells stories about Bourbon Street while the rest of the family moans. Public allegiance to the Patriots is as commonly mentioned in obituaries as a commitment to God, and upheld with the same pride that Boston's Brahmins once placed in membership in the Mayflower Society. From Eisenhauer to Gronkowski, Holovak to Belichick, Songin to Brady, Nance to Lewis, Cappelletti to Gostkowski, from Braves Field to BU, Harvard to BC, and Fenway Park to Foxborough—the story created by the Pats from their very first season has been as unique and memorable in New England as the Boston Tea Party, the Great Molasses Flood, the Impossible Dream, or the Blizzard of '78.

You couldn't make it up if you tried. And now, fortunately, you don't have to. It's all here, or most of it. The story of the Pats has become part of the story of a people—as much yours as it is theirs.

Glenn Stout
Alburgh, Vermont

CHAPTER ONE

WHERE FOOLS RUSH IN

The story of the Patriots begins with the creation of the American Football League, a story of "no room left at the inn" that resulted in the most accidental, most improbable of teams. Their birth is for the most part well documented if not well known. The team began not in Boston but in Texas and the Massachusetts mill town of Lowell, built from wealth pulled from the earth by oil derricks and from the sweat off the brow of the millworker—an appropriate start for a game and a league built in equal parts from lucre and labor.

IN THE FALL OF 1958, Lamar Hunt, the twenty-four-year-old son of millionaire Texas oilman H. L. Hunt, tried and failed to purchase a controlling interest in the NFL Chicago Cardinals, which had long struggled as the less successful neighbor of the powerhouse Bears. He wanted to move them to Dallas, his hometown. But Cardinals' owner Harry Wolfner and his wife rejected Hunt's bid and those of several others who wanted to move the franchise to their home cities, including Houston oilman Bud Adams; Bob Howsam, the owner of the minor league baseball Denver Bears; and Max Winter, part-owner of the Minneapolis Lakers of the NBA. But Hunt was not deterred.

Just a few days after the 1958 NFL championship, Hunt had a final, unfruitful meeting with Wolfner in Florida. As he flew back to Texas, Hunt later recalled, "the thought just occurred to me" to start his own league. There was already half a league's worth of interest from those trying to buy the Cardinals, and although Hunt did not quite realize it yet, the NFL championship game had planted the same idea in people of means in other cities.

As the World Football League, United States Football League (USFL), and XFL have all learned, starting a new league in the shadow of an established NFL is fraught with peril, but it wasn't that way in 1958. Ticket sales mattered, not television deals. Salaries were so low that NFL commissioner Bert Bell regularly warned NFL rookies "not to give up the day job." Rosters were small and expectations even lower. Owning an NFL team was more like owning a minor league baseball club than a major league franchise. While starting anything from nothing was certain to prove costly, all a franchise really needed was a place to play, a coach, and a roster of willing combatants. Most

Patriots owner Billy Sullivan called on his former Boston College and Notre Dame colleagues to help establish his new team. Included in their ranks were the legendary Frank Leahy (*left*) and Ed McKeever (*right*).

NFL rosters were stagnant, with a turnover of only three or four players a year per team, and not every college football player talented enough to play in the NFL cared to try. In short, there were plenty of guys talented enough to play pro football who were not—maybe even more than the number who were. All they needed was opportunity and some incentive, and after the 1958 championship game, when Gifford and Unitas and other Sunday heroes were suddenly all over the magazines selling cigarettes and convertibles and shown in the newspapers escorting beautiful girls, incentive was easier to come by.

Lamar Hunt convinced Bud Adams to join him—Houston and Dallas had a natural rivalry—and they were off. Hotel magnate Barron Hilton backed a Los Angeles franchise, and broadcaster Harry Wismer, who already owned a small stake in the Redskins and Lions, was eager to place a team in New York. Bob Howsam wanted a fall tenant for his ballpark in Denver, and there was also interest in Minneapolis. Sensing a threat to its virtual monopoly, the NFL let Hunt and Adams know that it might be amenable to new clubs in Dallas and Houston, but by then it was too late. On August 14, 1959, in Chicago, Hunt and Adams announced the formation of the six-team American Football League. They planned to start play in 1960. All that was required to join was an initial investment of $25,000.

At first, they thought six teams were enough. After all, the National Hockey League (NHL) had operated successfully for years with only six teams, and it was easy to envision a ten-game season, each team playing a home-and-away series against every other member of the league. But now that the league was public knowledge, cities without competition from big collegiate programs, like St. Louis, Cincinnati, Buffalo, Atlanta, and Louisville, began to show interest. Ralph Wilson, a Detroit native and wealthy industrialist, was rebuffed by Miami before deciding, somewhat reluctantly, on Buffalo.

In November 1959, the investors from Minneapolis got cold feet and accepted an expansion offer from the suddenly cooperative NFL, but Barron Hilton now insisted on a second West Coast franchise to provide a rival for his team in LA. A group of eight investors eventually emerged to back a franchise in Oakland. Now the seven-team league needed an eighth member. Which meant they needed an eighth guy who could either finance a franchise outright or put together a group willing to take a chance.

That guy was Billy Sullivan. Like so many others, his interest had been sparked by the 1958 championship game. According to Harold Kaese of the *Boston Globe*, Sullivan told him: "It must have been the greatest game ever played. Until then, I'd been pretty casual about pro football, but last season I didn't miss a game."

• • •

That was a lie, but the PR man already knew how to spin a tale. During his tenure with the Patriots, Sullivan spun so many of them that it made everyone else's head spin.

But have no doubt—in the almost sixty years that have passed since the Patriots were nothing more than a twinkle in Sullivan's eye, no figure in the history of the franchise has been as important . . . or as controversial. Without Sullivan, pro football might not have come to New England for another eight or ten years. With Sullivan, though . . . well, some would argue that might not have been such a bad thing.

To understand Patriots history, you have to understand Billy Sullivan. Few other NFL owners started with so little, yet of all Boston sports team owners, perhaps no one else has ever had such a direct impact on a Boston team. He was, after all, the Patriots' "father." And for better or worse, the first few decades of the Patriots' existence were made in his image. Even today, from their nickname to the location of their home stadium, signs of Sullivan's DNA are everywhere. As Sullivan himself once observed, "I hate being called a 'non-entity.'" The Patriots were Sullivan's way to ensure that would never happen. Over the years he would be many things to many people, some of them unprintable, but he was never, ever, a non-entity. For the remainder of his life, the Patriots and Billy Sullivan would be almost indistinguishable from one another.

He was, as one observer said, "equal parts Knute Rockne and Mel Brooks," sometimes at the same time.

> "I HATE BEING CALLED A 'NON-ENTITY.'"
> —BILLY SULLIVAN

Part dreamer, part schemer, Sullivan was a vat of raw ambition wrapped in a cloak of piety, a wannabe desperate to be a somebody who played angles like a veteran pool player and used a gift of blarney and bluster, family money, professional connections, and coattails to crash into a fledgling league and hang on for dear life. Compared to Adams and Hunt and Hilton, Sullivan was the bellhop who somehow ended up running the hotel. As *Globe* sportswriter Clif Keane once noted, "I don't know how to wrap him up or describe him . . . I couldn't put into a thousand words what I think of Billy Sullivan. I liked him yet at times I hated his guts." Over time most Patriots fans would know exactly what Keane meant.

Yet somehow Sullivan and his team survived despite their star-crossed history marked by decades of near-comic, sometimes tragic failure, and then the team even thrived in his wake, emerging as perhaps the game's foremost dynasty.

Few other NFL owners started with less . . . or ended with less. Sullivan is as central to the story of the Patriots as Bob Kraft, Tom Brady, Bill Belichick, or anyone else in club history.

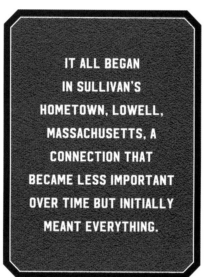

IT ALL BEGAN IN SULLIVAN'S HOMETOWN, LOWELL, MASSACHUSETTS, A CONNECTION THAT BECAME LESS IMPORTANT OVER TIME BUT INITIALLY MEANT EVERYTHING.

It all began in Sullivan's hometown, Lowell, Massachusetts, a connection that became less important over time but initially meant everything. For it was in Lowell that Sullivan learned how to access the levers of power that could make a nobody into an unforgettable somebody.

Francis Cabot Lowell, son of a member of the Continental Congress, created Lowell in northern Massachusetts on the Merrimack River to serve as a center for textile mills. At first the workers were women, girls drawn away from the farm and willing to work for a wage, but by the mid-1800s they began to be supplanted by Irish immigrants, who first got a foothold in the mills as strikebreakers.

That's what brought the Sullivans—starting with Billy's great-grandfather Eugene—to Lowell and what was known as "the Holy Acre," Lowell's Irish enclave. His son and namesake Eugene was the first Sullivan in Billy's line born there, but he would grow up on a farm in nearby East Chelmsford before returning to Lowell to work in the mills, eventually settling in at the US Cartridge Company and becoming a pioneer member of the Sacred Heart Church.

Traditionally, many Irish in America followed the same pathways to the middle class—the Church, politics, or booze, with all three often tangled up in the same twine. It was no different for the Sullivans.

In his later years, Billy liked to opine on the prejudice his family faced in Lowell, once claiming his father told him, "You know the way to beat the bigots? You've got to outwork them, out-hustle them." But by the time Sullivan was born in 1915, the era of "No Irish Need Apply" had long passed, at least for the Sullivans of Lowell. By then, the Irish ran local politics, and their place under the boot had been taken by a new generation of immigrants—mostly French Canadians and Greeks—who bore the brunt of local prejudice. Yet for the Sullivans, a healthy work ethic and the ability to hustle—literally and figuratively—had already become a family trait.

Billy's father, William, was one of the first Sullivans really to make it in America. He chose politics. Hired as the first telegraph operator at the daily *Lowell Sun*, William parlayed that job into something of a career. His connections and attention to detail earned him a place in City Hall as personal secretary to Mayor Thomas J. Corbett in 1927 and 1928. When his boss was ousted, Sullivan moved to the other side of the fence and became Lowell correspondent for the *Boston Globe*, another job that allowed him to interact with the powers that really ran the city. Eventually, he became Lowell city clerk, a position he held for fifteen years.

His brothers didn't do too badly either. When the *Sun* and other Lowell papers were unable to keep up with the growing demand for commercial printing, David and Joseph Sullivan opened their own print shop in 1916. Cultivating their family's connections with the Church, the brothers thrived, doing all manner of work for the local diocese and also began printing counterfeit-proof pari-mutuel tickets and racing programs. Working for saints and sinners alike, the Sullivans' print shop became the biggest sports printing business in the country, eventually responsible for the printing of the *Daily Racing Form*. Dave later started his own public relations firm, while Joseph became known for his close friendship with the Church and with Archbishop and later Cardinal Richard Cushing.

By the time Billy was ready to enter high school, the Sullivans of Lowell were both comfortable and connected. Billy and his twin sister, Vera, were named president and secretary of their class at Morey Junior High, where it was noted that Billy competed in the high jump for the track team and wanted to become a newspaperman. He wasn't the athlete in the family—that was his younger brother Paul, who later played football for Boston University and captained the team. Paul was the only Sullivan ever really to play the game.

It wasn't until Billy graduated from Lowell High School and went to Boston College that his future career—and his path to the Patriots—began to coalesce. At BC, Sullivan learned how valuable it was to know the right people who knew the right people and to stay as close to them as possible. Football showed him the way.

Several years before, the Catholic university, following the lead of Notre Dame, had made the decision to become a big-time football power. In 1936, BC hired coaching legend Gil Dobie, who turned BC's program around in three seasons and then retired, saying, "This game of football has become too complicated for me." An utter traditionalist, Dobie was particularly averse to the forward pass.

In his stead, BC hired Frank Leahy, who'd played tackle for the great Knute Rockne at Notre Dame before taking a series of assistant jobs at Georgetown (then a football power), Michigan State, and Fordham, where he coached the line, including a young Vince Lombardi, one of Fordham's famed "Seven Blocks of Granite." Leahy continued BC's resurgence, employing the Notre Dame box offense, a wide-open, exciting scheme. His brand of piety—selling the school's moral influence as much as the education—also proved effective: as a recruiter,

he snapped up the cream of Massachusetts schoolboys, including running back Lou Montgomery, BC's first black recruit and most electrifying back.

By then, Billy Sullivan was in the employ of the BC athletic department. Initially planning to be a journalist, Sullivan did occasional sports writing for the *Lowell Evening Leader* and, as BC's fortunes improved, helped the school out with publicity. After all, Dad knew everyone at the *Globe*. When he graduated in 1937, Billy buttonholed BC dean Joseph Maxwell, pointed out that Harvard had a full-time PR staff, and suggested that BC hire him for a similar position. The fact that Sullivan Brothers' Printing handled Boston College's printing account didn't hurt.

When Leahy arrived, the equally ambitious young PR man found his perfect boss. Sullivan became Leahy's shadow. He idolized the coach, calling him "the best friend I ever had," and worked overtime burnishing the brand of both the coach and the college as BC went to back-to-back bowl games. They lost in the Cotton Bowl to Clemson in 1939, but then won the Sugar Bowl over Tennessee in 1940 to claim the national championship.

Sullivan did a brilliant job of convincing the local and national press that the ambitious Leahy was a coaching genius, becoming so close to the coach that it was sometimes hard to see where Sullivan ended and Leahy began. Boston sportswriter Will Cloney later wrote that "you could close your eyes when he talked and hear Leahy."

The school and Sullivan's morality would be tested during his tenure. In both 1939 and 1940, Boston College bowed to pressure from southern schools when traveling there, either keeping Lou Montgomery behind or on the bench in street clothes. He didn't play in either bowl game, even though in 1939 he had averaged almost ten yards per carry as a rusher. But Sullivan used his close ties with the Boston press—he occasionally wrote for the *Globe*, usually covering Lowell sports—and adeptly managed to keep the story of a Catholic institution bowing to Jim Crow from going national, except in the black press.

One feature he wrote for the *Globe*, "The Story of Dallas' Cinderella Man," would prove particularly prescient in Sullivan's career. In advance of the Cotton Bowl, Sullivan penned a glowing profile of the bowl game's

One of Billy Sullivan's greatest legacies was his role, as public relations director of the Boston Braves, in establishing the Jimmy Fund in 1948; it would become the nation's preeminent sports-related charity. He is shown here at a Jimmy Fund gathering with former Braves Johnny Sain (*center*) and Sibby Sisti (*right*).

founder, Texas oilman J. Curtis Sanford. After attending the Rose Bowl in 1936, Sanford decided to stage a similar game in Texas and financed it himself, turning the otherwise previously unknown Fair Park Stadium into an iconic facility and essentially paving the way for the bowl season that now dominates college football.

Sullivan's portrait, which gushed for more than 2,500 words, praised Sanford for his foresight and audacity, calling him "a youthful sports visionary." Reading the profile today, one can sense the lightbulbs going off in Sullivan's head for the way Sanford used the game to make his name among the crowded field of Texas oilmen. The piece ended: "He doesn't do things half-way, this Sanford fellow, and Texas as well as the national sports scene could stand more like him." Sullivan may as well

have been writing about himself, or at least about who he wished to be, and the path forward was clear: football and football stadiums were a way to ensure that he would never be a non-entity.

Sullivan even assisted Leahy in recruiting. In one famous incident, Sullivan was enlisted to help Leahy recruit Lowell High football star Jack Kerouac, who later sparked the Beat Generation and became famous as the author of the seminal novel *On the Road*. Leahy desperately wanted Kerouac for Boston College. After Kerouac starred in the Lowell-Lawrence Thanksgiving Day game in 1938, Leahy and Sullivan had dinner at the Kerouac home; several letters from Sullivan to Kerouac now reside in the Kerouac archive in the New York Public Library. Kerouac's father, Leo, was employed by Sullivan Brothers'

Printing, and the football player faced intense pressure to attend BC—Leahy even sent the brothers a postcard that read "Get Jack to BC at all costs." But Kerouac's horizons reached far beyond stultifying Lowell, and he eventually chose to go to Columbia. When he did, Leo Kerouac was abruptly let go. Although Joseph Sullivan later claimed to like the elder Kerouac and denied that the sacking had anything to do with his son's choice of schools, Billy Sullivan was less circumspect, noting that the elder Kerouac should have been "sacked" long before. Loyalty meant everything to Sullivan. As he often admonished associates, "If you're not with me, you're against me." And when disloyalty was shown, well, there would always be consequences.

Except when he was the beneficiary. After the Sugar Bowl win, Leahy wanted to break his contract and accept an offer to coach Notre Dame, then the most prestigious coaching job in football. When BC refused to release him from his contract, Leahy, presumably with Sullivan's help, held a press conference to announce just the opposite, saying, "Gentlemen, I've called you all here today to inform you that I recently received my release from my coaching contract. With the release went the good wishes and benediction of Boston College." It was a blatant lie, but had the intended effect, and BC bid Leahy good riddance.

Billy Sullivan went along as Notre Dame's assistant athletic director, which really meant he was Leahy's secretary and personal lackey. World War II then intervened. In 1942, Sullivan enlisted in the Navy, but he never saw combat. Taking advantage of his PR experience, the Navy stationed the young officer in Washington to serve with the Navy Department and then at the Naval Academy, where he began to establish his reputation as a PR man ahead of his time. For the 1944 Army-Navy game, for instance, he produced a lavish, collectible program that set the standard for years to come. That Sullivan knew the printing business was certainly a help.

When he was mustered out, he fell back on his prewar connections to serve as Leahy's ghostwriter before deciding to go into the growing field of public relations, like his uncle Dave. But Sullivan didn't return to Lowell—he went to Boston, where his growing number of personal relationships meant a little more. He pitched himself to

the Red Sox publicity department but was rebuffed; then he approached the crosstown Boston Braves. The club had recently been purchased by three local contractors known collectively as "the Three Steam Shovels": Lou Perini, Guido Rugo, and Joseph Maney. Sullivan talked them into putting him in charge of publicity, a job usually given to an old sportswriter in need of work . . . whose main responsibility was to keep the liquor flowing in the press box.

The perennially also-ran Braves had nothing to lose, but with an infusion of cash from the Three Steam Shovels, Sullivan had free rein and a big budget to do as he saw fit. He kept the press happy by keeping the liquor flowing—former beat writer Bob Holbrook once recalled that the Braves' press box bar "put a lot of people on the wagon forever"—but Sullivan was also a genuine innovator. He produced color promotional films, talked ownership into selling unused press box space as private boxes (essentially inventing the concept of the luxury box), organized press junkets to see Braves prospects, and made sportswriters' lives easy by providing reams of press releases. In fact, he sent out so many press releases touting third baseman Bob Elliott for the 1947 MVP Award (which he won) that *New York Herald Tribune* sports writing legend Red Smith dubbed Sullivan "the Maître de Mimeograph." He also played a key role in launching the Braves-sponsored cancer charity, the Jimmy Fund (since taken over by the Red Sox).

It worked for a while. The Braves won a surprise pennant in 1948, and attendance temporarily soared. His success led the *Globe's* Jerry Nason to describe Sullivan as a "guileless looking young fellow in whose mouth butter would instantly melt," as well as a "shrewd operator." But in the end, it was all for naught. The club simply could not supplant the Red Sox. Boston wasn't big or prosperous enough to support two teams, particularly once television broadcasts started and the Braves remained saddled with an uncomfortable and cavernous ballpark featuring a grandstand that guaranteed each spectator a fabulous view of the back of the head of the person in front of them. It simply wasn't pitched correctly, something that lowering the field surface by three feet could not correct. In 1952, when his budget was cut, Sullivan departed, and the team left Boston for Milwaukee a year later.

Billy Sullivan is shown here on the far right with (*left to right*) Ken Coleman, Johnny Pesky, Jean Yawkey, and Carl Yastrzemski at a ceremony honoring the Jimmy Fund at the Patriots' former home of Fenway Park.

By then, not only had Sullivan learned a lot, but he had added a growing number of Boston and state political leaders, local scions of industry, and the local press to his retinue of pals in the worlds of football, Boston College, and the Catholic Church. He was becoming a guy who knew everybody and was someone everybody knew, a nexus between a lot of rich and powerful people. That was power. Sullivan was becoming someone very useful to know.

But because there was as yet no place for him in Boston, he turned back to Frank Leahy, who had resigned from Notre Dame after the 1953 season owing to health issues and a scandal over his controversial use of fake injuries to stop the clock. Sullivan and Leahy went into business together in California under the banner of All-Star Sports, intending to produce sports films. But the two men were out of their element in an entertainment industry that was changing too rapidly for either to catch up. Leahy later described his film ventures as "time, energy and money completely wasted." Sullivan returned

to Boston and soon found out who his friends were.

None were more important than the Catholic Church. After Sullivan announced that he was opening his own PR firm, also named All-Star Associates, on January 1, 1954, Boston College became his first client when the Catholic institution signed him on as a consultant. Then came the big break that changed everything.

In 1955, the fledgling PR flack was hired by Charles Reardon, president of Metropolitan Coal and Oil, Boston's oldest retail fuel company, to serve as a sort of executive apprentice. Reardon, nearing retirement and fearing that the parent Pittston Corporation would bring in an executive from the outside, chose Sullivan as his successor.

Precisely how and why he chose Sullivan, however, is a matter of some debate. The story Reardon and Sullivan always told was that it came about as a "chance meeting." But according to longtime Boston sportswriters, Sullivan was hired at the behest of Joseph Sullivan's old friend Cardinal Cushing—the archdiocese was one of Metropolitan's biggest clients and wielded enormous influence. Notre Dame alumnus and former end George Rohrs, a Pittston executive, also most likely played a role. Married into the Mara family, who owned the pro football Giants, Rohrs also asked Reardon to hire Sullivan, telling Reardon that Sullivan "knows everybody in town."

Sullivan was suddenly an up-and-coming young business executive and future president of a powerful local company. With his hiring came additional influence and power and, eventually, an executive's salary and entrée to the business world. In a few short years, Sullivan had gone from press hack to flack to power broker. It was all coming together.

To this point, Sullivan had evinced little public interest in professional football, but his connections were beginning to line up just as the NFL was beginning to make big money. The league was slowly becoming more popular, with television providing an influx of cash and proving to

be the magic ingredient that had been missing. Attendance would eventually prove to be less important than ratings.

In the winter of 1957, while Sullivan learned the oil business, his cousin Bob, an ad man himself whose clientele included Hampden-Harvard Brewery, approached cousin Billy. The brewery's owners, the Bissell brothers, saw an opportunity to enter sports and expand the business brand. They wanted to build a stadium, entice National League baseball back to Boston, and perhaps secure the Red Sox as tenants as well. Bob called on Billy's expertise.

Billy Sullivan rapidly squashed the notion of bringing NL baseball back to Boston—the market just could not support it, and he didn't want to betray the Three Steam Shovels. Instead, he proposed that the Bissell brothers consider building a football stadium—or better yet, a combined football/baseball venue. They could try

Work proceeds on readying Nickerson Field at Boston University shortly after the April 1, 1960, announcement that the team would play its home games there that autumn.

to secure both the Red Sox as a tenant and BC, Boston University . . . and an NFL team. Recalling good ole J. Curtis Sanford, Billy even suggested that the new stadium might one day host a collegiate bowl game. Frank Leahy retained close connections with the sport, and so did George Rohrs. In combination, they gave Sullivan some credibility and entrée to the NFL and made him a player if the NFL ever decided to expand into Boston.

Sullivan became the central figure in the scheme and tried to bring all the interested parties together. He floated the idea to Red Sox general manager Joe Cronin, who was intrigued, but who also warned that Sox owner Tom Yawkey (a man who refused his own sister's request to build a home on his South Carolina estate) didn't like to share. Besides, Yawkey liked using Fenway Park as his own private picnic ground when the Sox were out of town. Meanwhile, tentative plans for the project began to take shape. Everyone wanted to drive everywhere, so a downtown Boston location was out. Then the brewery secured an option on land in suburban Norwood just off the freeway, and an architect neighbor of Sullivan's began to work on a stadium model.

The project was nothing if not ambitious. Their plan was to build a $10 million glass-and-aluminum domed stadium with a retractable roof, featuring luxury boxes, a golf range, a massive bowling alley and parking lot, and a host of other features. At a time when most proposed stadiums were still single-function facilities, the forward-thinking plan was designed to attract attention. That it certainly did. The brewery was prominently featured in every story. Soon, so was Sullivan.

According to the story Sullivan the spinmeister later offered, the whole thing was supposed to remain a secret to appease the Red Sox, but on April 1, 1958, the brewery prematurely unveiled the project against Sullivan's wishes, scaring the Red Sox off—and forcing Sullivan to scurry to the NFL. However, like many versions of stories involving Sullivan told by the man himself, that one was incorrect.

As a number of local papers reported, the plan was actually unveiled at the end of February, when the group had to put the proposal before the Norwood board of selectmen. The infamous "accidental" unveiling of the model did take place on April 1, but by then it was no surprise. What was also no surprise was Metropolitan Oil and Coal's official announcement, on the same day the unveiling took place, that Billy Sullivan, modestly described in a press release as a "prominent Boston College alumnus and well known in the field of public relations," was the company's new president, succeeding Reardon. Sullivan had been relatively unknown to the general public to this point, but that changed overnight. A few days later, a fawning profile of Sullivan appeared in the *Globe* and made clear that the stadium was as much his idea as the brewery's. Soon the press was referring to the stadium not as Hampden-Harvard Stadium, but as "Sullivan's plan."

• • •

The Red Sox quickly distanced themselves from the project, but did manage to use it to secure a bit more parking from a city desperate to keep them in the Fenway. By then, Sullivan didn't need the ball club. He had the NFL on the line, giving lie to the tale he later spun for Kaese that his interest in the NFL was sparked by the 1958 NFL season.

Even before the plan was publicly unveiled, Leahy had provided Sullivan with an introduction to NFL commissioner Bert Bell, who was enthralled with the stadium idea, calling it "the wave of the future. . . . Imagine football with a dome over it!" He promised that the NFL would consider a Boston franchise in 1960. Boston was, after all, the largest market in the country at the time without an NFL franchise. But the stadium had to come first. Lack of a stadium had been a central reason in the failure of every previous attempt to place the pro game in Boston. Braves Field was decrepit, a football field would barely fit inside Fenway Park (and the Red Sox had no desire to share their facilities in any event), and both Harvard and Boston College were known to be loath to taint their amateur architecture with the stain of professional football.

But suddenly Sullivan was in the middle of the action. The stadium idea wasn't his, and as a newly minted executive earning in the very low five figures, he had very little money of his own. But he was a facilitator, the guy who put everything together. In Boston, where the question "who do you know?" has always been as important as "what have you done?," that had value. So far, his connections with the Church, politics, and alcohol had all worked their magic to vault him from anonymity.

Billy Sullivan and the promise of professional football in Boston were now inseparable.

Sullivan, however, wasn't the only person eyeing an NFL franchise in Boston. Braves contractor Lou Perini, one of the Three Steam Shovels, and Celtics owner Walter Brown were also intrigued by the idea of building a stadium . . . but not in Norwood.

So just as everything seemed to be lining up for Billy Sullivan and a football team for Boston—it wasn't. Perini's interest slowed down everything, leaving Sullivan's plan on the table as little more than an architectural model. Then, in October 1959, Bert Bell passed away, leaving the NFL without a singular leader. Getting the twelve NFL owners to agree on anything now was almost impossible, and the chances of Sullivan being selected to join the NFL over men with real money, like Brown and Perini, were slim. Moreover, the Hampden-Harvard Brewery's interest in the investment had gone flat, and the stadium project—without a tenant—seemed dead. Yet Sullivan was undeterred. He loved the attention and loved being in the middle of everything. He was determined to remain in the game.

In the meantime, Frank Leahy had signed on to serve as general manager for Barron Hilton's proposed Los Angeles AFL franchise. He told Sullivan that the AFL was still looking for an eighth franchise, and he let the AFL know that Sullivan might be their guy. Conveniently enough, Leahy was one of three men on the committee to select the eighth franchisee. Another committee member, Harry Wismer of the proposed New York Titans, had known Sullivan from his time serving as an announcer for Notre Dame. The third member was Lamar Hunt, who just so happened to be a friend of J. Curtis Sanford's, who thought well of Sullivan. Not only would the Cotton Bowl serve as the home field for Hunt's team, but Sanford would eventually buy the first 100 season tickets for Hunt's team and build a $3 million indoor sport facility for Hunt known as the Bronco Bowl. That sealed it.

There was just one problem—well, two problems, actually. Boston still didn't have a football stadium, and Bill Sullivan didn't have any money. Had anyone else anywhere else come up with the money—and there was interest in the eighth AFL franchise from both Atlanta and Philadelphia—Sullivan would have been boxed out.

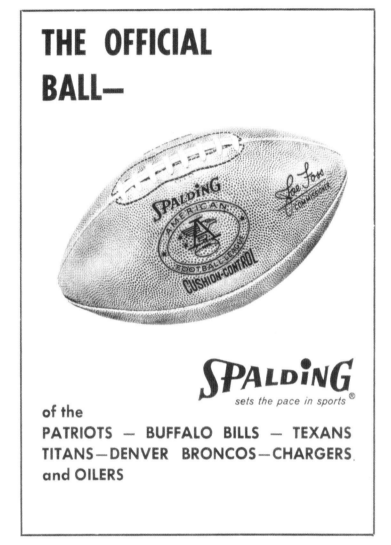

The design of the Spalding "J5-V/JV-5" football made it slightly more streamlined and cushioned than the NFL "Duke" football by Wilson. It soon became a symbol of the wide-open passing game that was an AFL trademark.

Yet interests in both cities hesitated, then eventually bowed out, giving Sullivan time. To launch a league by the fall of 1960, the AFL couldn't wait. It was overtime, and Sullivan was the last man on the field.

But with six kids, the forty-five-year-old Sullivan, who barely earned five figures a year with Metropolitan, had only managed to put about $8,000 in the bank, as a nest egg for a summer home. To secure an AFL franchise, he needed to not only raise enough money to pay the league franchise fee of $25,000 but also to locate a place to play, post a $100,000 performance bond, and find some investors. The total cost to launch the franchise was certain to push $1 million, if not more, and the idea of turning a profit was only a fantasy. Yet Sullivan was certain that if he could just get the team, one day a stadium would inevitably follow. In the meantime, there was Fenway Park, Braves Field, both BC's refurbished Alumni Stadium (for which he'd just led a fundraising effort for BC) and Harvard Stadium, plus several lesser facilities around town—White Stadium in East Boston and the Manning Bowl in nearby Lynn. He was sure he could melt enough butter or push the right buttons to find someplace.

What Sullivan lacked in funds he made up for in friends, or at least people of great influence. He wasn't shy about that. As the *Globe* reported in 2008, in midsummer of 1959, after Sullivan used his connections to get his family a guided tour of FBI headquarters, he even wrote FBI director J. Edgar Hoover: "I don't imagine the occasion will ever present itself when the sender of this note may be of any service to your dedicated group of me, yet sometimes the wheel takes strange turns, and if we can be helpful in any way . . .

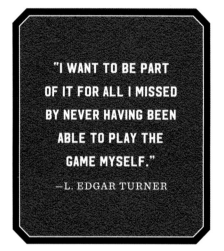

"I WANT TO BE PART OF IT FOR ALL I MISSED BY NEVER HAVING BEEN ABLE TO PLAY THE GAME MYSELF."

—L. EDGAR TURNER

we would consider it a real privilege to be of service." Hoover read between the lines and realized that Sullivan was sending more than a simple thank-you note. The FBI director initiated "a general inquiry" to see if Sullivan might prove to be of use as an SAC, or "special agent in charge." Hoover liked cultivating men of influence as soft informants to serve as liaisons to other powerful figures. Walt Disney, NASCAR founder Bill France, and Cardinal Cushing all served the FBI in that capacity. Nothing came of Sullivan's overture, but the contact between the men is emblematic of the lengths to which Sullivan would go to ingratiate himself to those in power.

It was time for Sullivan to use all his connections, all his blarney, and all his PR savvy to call in favors, pull strings, beg, cajole, plead, lie, and do whatever else was necessary to secure the backing he needed. Although

nothing he had done, by itself, gave him the credibility to launch a franchise, overall he seemed to have accumulated just enough know-how to see it through. Football, family, the Church, and business all combined to deliver the angels he needed. Already, the established owners in the AFL were referring to themselves as "the Foolish Club." In the case of the Patriots, the fools rushed right in.

Sullivan started with the usual suspects. Uncle Joe Sullivan was an obvious choice, with the added benefit of delivering another client to the printing business. Football teams needed programs, right? Edward McMann was president of Northeast Packing, owned 30,000 acres of blueberries in Maine, once owned racehorses, and was a pal of Uncle Joe's. Dom DiMaggio, the former Red Sox outfielder, brother of Joe, and president of the American Latex Corporation in Lawrence, Massachusetts, wanted to get back into sports and was a name everyone knew and trusted— who didn't like "the Lil Professor"? Bingo. Daniel Marr, a Quincy-based Notre Dame grad, had once owned a small piece of the Braves, had played football for the local semipro powerhouse Pere Marquettes, and was close to the Church—*and* his brother Joe had played fullback for BC. Check. Dean Boylan was a construction executive, a pal of DiMaggio's (the two liked to attend Harvard football games together), and also friendly with the Church hierarchy. Check again. One connection begat another. Hotel executive Paul Sonnabend had run the Hotel Shelton in Kenmore Square when Ted Williams was a seasonal guest. L. Edgar Turner was president of the local 7-Up soda distribution company and was intrigued by the marketing possibilities for his product—7-Up would be prominently featured in various team promotions. Besides, as he later said, "I want to be part of it for all I missed by never having been able to play the game myself." For flavor, and even deeper pockets, the group also included two Boston Brahmins tied to old money: George Sargent, an insurance executive and banker who played end for Virginia before contracting polio, and the banker John Ames, a heavy in the Republican Party, whose family predated the American Revolution by more than 100 years. Each of the ten men pledged to buy $100,000 worth of stock in the team at $2.50 a share, although Sullivan warned each of them that their investment might eventually grow by a factor of five before the team would prove profitable. They considered the risk, but they also remembered those 45 million fans who had tuned in the previous December to watch pro football. If the AFL could survive long enough to draw a fraction of that, it would be worth it. And it might also be fun. "If I never get a dollar back," said Turner later, "I'll still get my money's worth out of this."

For now, however, the names were all a secret, and no one had yet cut a check. Sullivan was still the only man publicly attached to the club. Some other club owners fretted over the fact that Boston had no stadium and that, compared to the others, Sullivan had no money, but the AFL had little choice—they needed that eighth team to have a balanced schedule.

Sullivan was in Hanover, New Hampshire, for Dartmouth football weekend with friends when Hunt tracked him down and told him that if he could have a check on deposit by the end of the day on Monday, Boston would have a franchise. Sullivan hustled down to Boston, borrowed money to come up with the full $25,000 franchise fee, and had the money wired to Dallas.

The check cleared, and on November 19, 1959, Sullivan put together a hastily arranged press conference to spread the news and convince the more skittish among his backers that, yes, he really did have a franchise.

The press conference was just Billy and perhaps a dozen or so reporters intrigued by a press release Billy had Uncle Joe print on the blank backside of some old football programs. Boston was a five-newspaper town— the *Globe*, the *Herald*, the *Traveler*, the *Record*, and the *American*—so eventually there would be no lack of coverage for the new venture. But there was skepticism at the start. Sullivan wouldn't name his backers, and the press speculated that the group might include people like Walter Brown or boxing impresario Sam Silverman. Sullivan wouldn't say, but assured the reporters that the investors were all men of means, "except me."

"I was asked to be president and general manager," he claimed, "but I turned it down. I'll be just a stockholder. I have a job now." That statement would be just the first of what one observer later referred to as Sullivan's "free-wheeling style of tailoring history to suit his immediate purposes" during his tenure with the Patriots. A little over two decades later, another operator, by the name of Steinbrenner, would make a similar claim when he purchased the New York Yankees—as one of the Boss's partners would note, "There is nothing in life quite so limited as being a limited partner of George Steinbrenner." So too would it be for those invested in the Patriots.

Then Sullivan announced that in a few days he would represent the fledgling club at the AFL draft of college players. For the moment, however, Billy Sullivan didn't have any players, any staff, any fans, or any place to play. Hell, the team didn't even have a name, and the league existed only on paper.

Harold Kaese of the *Globe* dubbed the new club the Boston "Un-Un-Uns"—unnamed, unlocated, and unidentified. But it was a start.

CHAPTER TWO

1960–1963

ALMOST

Ready or not—and they were not ready, not really, not even close—it was time to find out whether yet another professional football team in Boston could finally spark a lasting revolution among football fans in New England or whether interest would flare and then fade away. In ten short months, the American Football League needed to kick off.

There was no time to waste, but hardly any game plan. Unfortunately, and for many years to come, that would be true for the Boston franchise. Its early history would play out in fits and starts, steps forward and back.

ONLY HOURS AFTER THE INITIAL PRESS CONFERENCE, Billy Sullivan, as yet the only name publicly attached to the team, flew off to Minneapolis for the first-ever AFL league meeting and draft of college players. The NFL was already striking back—Minnesota would ultimately accept an expansion offer from the NFL, withdraw from the AFL, and be replaced by a franchise in Oakland. The AFL ended up holding its first draft in a city where they would never play.

Among the other AFL owners and ownership groups, Sullivan stood out. Not only did he have the smallest bank account, but Sullivan wasn't remotely qualified

Phil Bissell's "Pat Patriot" graces the cover of the program of the team's first-ever regular-season home game, though his creation wouldn't serve as the team logo for another year.

to judge talent, unless one counted his apprenticeship carrying Frank Leahy's coat. Had football acumen been required, Sullivan would have been a last-round pick. Any fan with a television had about as much experience as he did. Even though Sullivan had said at the initial press conference that "I'll just be a stockholder, I have a job now," that lasted all of about a half-minute. Sullivan, not a player or a coach, would become the face of the team.

Fortunately, his inexperience didn't matter all that much at the draft. The general concept of the player draft had been conceived of by eventual NFL commissioner Bert Bell in 1935, and in time it would be adopted by other pro leagues. The scheme was sold to the public as a way to ensure league parity—and to the league owners as a way to keep player salaries down. As Cowboys president Tex Schramm told NFL Players Association head Gene Upshaw in 1987, "You guys are cattle, and we're the ranchers." From the start, the players were almost powerless.

At that time, a career in pro football was hardly desirable, and most of the drafted players had chosen jobs in the real world rather than play for a team in a city they didn't want to live in. In 1960, the pay was poor, and only a few top NFL players earned more than $10,000 annually (the equivalent of about $90,000 in 2017). Most earned barely half that, and many far less, since most contracts weren't guaranteed: players could be cut loose at any time. Prestige was almost nonexistent. At season's end, you still needed to get a job, and many even held part-time jobs during the season. The concept of parity was also something of a lie. To waste as few picks as possible, teams traditionally negotiated contracts with the most desired players well before the draft. By draft time, at least in the first few rounds, most clubs knew who the others would select.

The AFL realized from the start that it would have to fight the NFL for fans, but it could not afford to lure established talent to the league. College players were another matter. Even though the existence of the AFL would give first-time players some bargaining power (which would eventually prove costly to both leagues), the NFL absorbed only about forty rookies a year, leaving plenty of affordable talent available.

So in that first year the AFL kept competition among themselves to a minimum. First, each team was allowed a single "territorial" pick in very rough proximity to its home city, allowing each a chance at a high-profile college star who would draw publicity even if he never signed and, if he did, would help sell tickets. This allowed the Dallas Texans to select Southern Methodist University star quarterback Don Meredith and Houston to pick the plum of the draft class, Louisiana State University halfback Billy Cannon, who would go on to win the Heisman Trophy as the best collegiate player in the country.

When it came time for Sullivan to make his pick, not only was he ill prepared, but the Boston area was hardly a hotbed of collegiate excellence—not a single New England team finished in the Associated Press's top twenty, and only one, Yale, had spent as much as a single week in the AP poll during the regular season.

Fortunately, New York and eventual national champion Syracuse also fell within Boston's allotted territory. Behind star sophomore running back Ernie Davis, Syracuse had gone undefeated, and it would secure the national title with a 23–14 victory over Texas in the Cotton Bowl. But as a sophomore, Davis was not eligible for the draft.

No matter. Davis's backfield mate Gerhard Schwedes—the son of a German soldier, he had emigrated from Germany at age twelve with his family—was considered one of the best players in college football. As defenses keyed on Davis, Schwedes had proved invaluable for Syracuse in 1959—splitting time between halfback and quarterback in Syracuse's run-oriented offense; doing a little passing, a little receiving, a lot of running, and even filling in on defense. Schwedes was the epitome of the all-purpose back at a time when many colleges still passed from the halfback position and the quarterback was sometimes a blocker.

Schwedes had excelled in this scheme, running for more than seven yards a carry and leading the Orangemen in touchdowns. But the stats didn't tell the full story. In 1959, the Orangemen, as an independent team, didn't always play the toughest schedule, and Syracuse's offense often rendered the outcome obvious by halftime. Nevertheless, as a senior, Schwedes received credit for his team's performance and was lauded for his "intangibles." Schwedes called virtually every offensive play, and his coach, Ben Schwartzwalder, said, "I may

The Patriots pinned their first-year hopes on the territorial pick of running back Gerhard Schwedes of Syracuse. In parts of two seasons with Boston, he gained only 14 yards on 10 carries.

have seen better players in my time [Jimmy Brown was a Syracuse grad], but I've never seen a greater leader." Just a few days before the draft, in a 46–0 shellacking of BU in Boston, Schwedes had the greatest game of his career, scoring three touchdowns to tie Brown's single-season school record, breaking off two runs of more than 40 yards, catching a scoring pass, throwing for another, and snagging an interception. He seemed capable of doing everything but selling tickets, a skill the Patriots would unexpectedly discover in him on their own.

RON BURTON

HALFBACK

BOSTON PATRIOTS

Northwestern graduate Ron Burton is often referred to as the "first Patriot" and was a fan favorite from 1960 to 1965. He later established a youth sports camp that remains a lasting legacy.

Sullivan was impressed—perhaps too impressed. He chose Schwedes without realizing that Schwedes really didn't have a position. The versatility he had shown in college had no place in pro football, which had better passers, faster halfbacks, tougher fullbacks, better tacklers, more sure-handed pass receivers, and quarterbacks who called their own plays. Boston essentially made a blind pick with no idea of the player's real skills.

After the territorial picks came the regular draft, although a "draw" would be a more accurate description. Primarily using All-American and All-Conference teams as a guide, a committee of general managers—Leahy, Canadian Football League veteran and Denver GM Dean Griffin, and Dallas Texan GM and former NFL referee Don Rossi—rated the best eight seniors at each position, then the next eight, and then the next eight. For each "round" the AFL put the top eight players at each position in what Lamar Hunt recalled as either a hat or a wastebasket. Each team then picked at random in alphabetical order by position, in fifty-two laborious rounds spread across several days, hoping that if they threw enough players against the wall, some would stick. In an understatement, Hunt later admitted that the league was "ill prepared" for the draft, but it served its purpose. Each player drafted resulted in news stories—in their hometown paper as well as the paper where they played collegiate ball—that spread the word that the new league was going forward better than any press release could have done.

Running back Ron Burton, a swift and shifty tailback from Northwestern and consensus All-American, was by far the best player allotted to Boston (and as he would prove by his work with at-risk youth after his career ended, one of the best people the team would ever employ). A week later, the NFL Philadelphia Eagles concurred and made him their number-one pick. Sullivan, recognizing a good story when he saw one, would later spin Burton's selection as Boston's "number one pick" when in fact the choice came by way of a random draw and the honor rightly belonged to Schwedes. Boston's draft would have been even better had they managed to sign USC tackle Ron Mix. But Mix was drafted by the NFL Colts later and made it clear that he'd sign with Baltimore unless he could play on the West Coast, so the AFL accommodated him. The league engineered a deal assigning his draft rights to Los Angeles in exchange for the rights to Holy Cross quarterback Tommy Greene, costing Boston a Hall of Fame player. As it was, of the fifty-three players Boston selected in the initial draft, only five would ever play a down for the team in a real game.

That was still a long way off. There were still the small matters of a coach, a field, a name, a logo, and just about everything else.

They had an address, a cramped 500-square-foot basement office in Kenmore Square at 522

Commonwealth Avenue, right around the corner from Fenway Park, in a building they shared with a variety of medical specialists—urologists, proctologists, and the like. For the rest, Sullivan, turning once again to his connections, went first to his alma mater, Boston College.

BC coach Mike Holovak, who had starred as a fullback and linebacker for the team under Leahy and then played professionally for the NFL Bears and Rams, had been tasked with bringing BC back to national prominence but had failed over the course of nine seasons. Although his teams were competitive, going 49-29-3, BC alums, including Sullivan, thought the Eagles should be a national power. When they weren't, BC backers, including Sullivan, who had just led a fundraising campaign to refurbish Alumni Stadium, rebelled. After Sullivan began advocating the return of Leahy, Holovak was a dead man walking.

While in Minneapolis, Sullivan sent an intermediary to Worcester, where Holovak was preparing to coach BC against rival Holy Cross. He delivered a message from Sullivan: "Win, lose or draw you can have a job on the team for as long as you want."

Although BC won, the following Monday Holovak was fired. He wasn't good enough for Boston College, but the BC pedigree was still good enough for the AFL. Sullivan snapped him up and made him the team's chief scout.

A PT boat captain in World War II, Holovak was a self-described "realistic pessimistic pessimist," a tough guy who focused on preparation, respected authority, and expected to be respected in turn. As he later wrote in his biography *Violence Every Sunday,* "The captain of the vessel usually eats alone. It avoids problems when the captain must make decisions. The same goes in pro football." His time serving Boston tested that approach.

Holovak brought some real experience and valuable knowledge to the team. A few years before, he'd nearly been named coach of the New York Giants, and coaching at BC had left him familiar with many recent collegiate players. In addition, Holovak, although a native

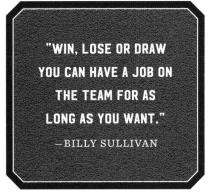

"WIN, LOSE OR DRAW YOU CAN HAVE A JOB ON THE TEAM FOR AS LONG AS YOU WANT."

—BILLY SULLIVAN

of Pennsylvania, was familiar to the Boston press and public. No other football figure in New England was better known. That was both his greatest strength and, eventually, a weakness.

As soon as Holovak signed, Sullivan sent him off in pursuit of Schwedes and several other Syracuse players the team president had fallen in love with, then to scout the bowl games and make contact with more draft picks as well as anyone undrafted who caught his mostly unsentimental eye. Holovak signed the first Patriot to a contract, inking Clemson quarterback Harvey White on December 20, 1959. The *Globe's* evening edition touted it atop page 1: "Holovak Signs First Hub Pro."

It was a start, and moving forward Sullivan turned again to BC. Ed McKeever, a gregarious Texan, had been one of Leahy's assistants at Boston College—he'd recruited Holovak—and like Sullivan he had followed the coach to Notre Dame, even filling in as head coach while Leahy was in the service. After leaving ND, McKeever served as coach and GM for the Chicago Rockets of the All-America Football Conference, the failed pro league that operated just after World War II, then joined the staff at LSU.

Sullivan named McKeever GM, and in that position he was in charge of anything Sullivan and Holovak were not: contracts and everything else. He wasn't a Boston guy—his Texas twang and high opinion of himself made him stand out—but for much of the next decade Holovak and McKeever would hold key positions in the organization.

Over the next month, McKeever signed the equivalent of more than a player a day. Although Schwedes, after starring in the Sugar Bowl and tossing an 87-yard touchdown pass to Ernie Davis in the second minute of the game, secured a two-year guaranteed contract for $25,000 to keep him away from the NFL, most players signed for far less—the league minimum was $7,500—and wouldn't be paid at all unless and until they made the team and played an official game. With a regular-season roster limited to only thirty-three players, the expected annual player payroll would barely reach $300,000.

McKeever's other job was to find a coach. Unlike most other AFL teams, Boston didn't look to pro football but to college. Sullivan was enamored with Schwartzwalder of Syracuse, but he turned down the job, as did Georgia's Wally Butts, Rip Engle of Penn State, and Otto Graham, the former Cleveland Browns quarterback who was coaching the Coast Guard. You could hardly blame them. The fledgling league just could not match the security, or salary, of a top college job.

After keeping the press guessing, Sullivan finally formally introduced the club's ten-member board of directors to the press on January 29, 1960. His explanation that they had been in place for a while but it had been difficult to get them together for an announcement fore-shadowed the difficulty this group would later have coming together on policy. As he introduced DiMaggio, Marr,

Sonnabend, and the rest, there was little doubt who was in charge. It was Billy's team.

McKeever reportedly went through some seventy coaching candidates before deciding on Lou Saban, the thirty-eight-year-old head coach of Western Illinois, then a member of the NCAA College Division, the equiv-alent of a Division II (D-II) program. For a young coach on the rise, it was an offer he could not refuse.

Saban (who was no relation to Alabama coach Nick Saban) had played quarterback at Indiana before joining the Cleveland Browns under legendary coach Paul Brown. After his playing days, he entered coaching, first as head coach at Cleveland's Case Tech, then as an assistant at Northwestern. Named to the top job there in 1955, he failed to win a game and was fired after one season, replaced by Ara Parseghian. He then served as an assistant at

Lou Saban arrived from Western Illinois as the Patriots' first head coach and led the team for just one and a quarter seasons while achieving a record of seven wins and twelve losses. He later coached both the Bills and the Broncos in the AFL.

Washington before landing the top job at Western Illinois. Apart from his failure at Northwestern, he had impressed at almost every stop and served as an assistant for Otto Graham in coaching the Collegiate All-Stars in their annual game against the defending NFL champs.

Saban was smart, confident, and not easily intimidated. His first job had been caddying for Al Capone's brother Ralph at the Acacia Country Club in Chicago, and while in the service during World War II he'd learned Chinese and served as an interpreter.

Saban looked the part of a coach: brusque, husky, and square-jawed, he already spoke in practiced coach-speak, calling the job "an opportunity," promising Boston "Paul Brown football," and touting the bona fides he'd earned while playing under the legendary Cleveland coach for four seasons. Sullivan even described him as "Paul Brown with a heart." But Saban inadvertently admitted that there were a few gaps in his résumé when he told the press that he didn't agree with Brown's "messenger system" of signal calling—sending in plays from the bench—and preferred giving that job directly to the quarterback. He admitted that at Western Illinois he had used "sort of" a pro-type offense, which even then was more spread out and far more pass-oriented than the college game, and perhaps in a tacit admission that perhaps even he realized that his background left him under-qualified for the job, Saban said that he wanted to talk to Holovak about an assistant's job. Holovak would eventually also serve as an assistant, along with Red Miller, Joe Collier, and Jerry Smith. It was a talented bunch, as all would go on to long coaching careers in the pros. Still, the new team was one of only two clubs in the league to pluck their head coach from the college ranks, the other being the Dallas Texans' Hank Stram. Other league coaches had all recently either played or coached in the NFL or Canadian football.

All the while Sullivan himself turned in double duty, going back and forth between working for Metropolitan Coal and Oil by day and spending the rest of his time in the team office or in his car dictating memos and letters to a secretary as he built a franchise from scratch. He kept the new club in the news by making just about everything, including the name and their home field, a mystery—in part because he didn't have the answers to those

The Patriots' first and most beloved logo, "Pat Patriot," was introduced to fans on the front page of the *Boston Globe*'s sports section on April 19, 1960. Billy Sullivan chose to use it for the team and later hired artist Phil Bissell to draw the team's program covers for the balance of their AFL days.

questions, and in part because the PR man knew that speculation kept the press guessing. Yet already there was some impatience with his approach, and the press was realizing that everything about the new team flowed through Sullivan first, no matter who was on the board of directors or on the field. They began to grouse that every word out of Sullivan's mouth was part of some PR plan.

As needed, Sullivan filled other front-office positions, almost always from Boston College, reinforcing his place atop the franchise and building a loyal and dedicated staff. The BC student newspaper would later publish a story entitled "Old BC Grads Never Die, They Go to Work for the Patriots," and that even included the equipment managers.

If nothing else, the board of directors agreed on one thing: the name of the new team should reflect the region's Revolutionary War roots, and they had already seized on a red-white-and-blue color scheme. Not that there were many other naming options—the city's dominant mascot animal was the cod, which was hardly more intimidating than the dominant legume, the ubiquitous Boston bean. Between the Harvard Crimson and the Red Sox, the color wheel was saturated, and Boston College had long ago scooped up the eagle, Boston University the terrier, and Northeastern the husky, so birds and dogs were out. Boston's other pro sports teams had closed the door on bears (the Bruins), the Irish (the Celtics), and Native Americans (the Red Sox), and they didn't want to duplicate the name of any other major sports team.

So the team held a contest—sort of—offering a pair of tickets for the winning moniker and, in the event of a tie, a color TV. They received hundreds of suggestions—names like the Hubs, the Beaneaters, and the Beantowners were quickly rejected, as were those that spoke to Boston's professional football past. That left the team with a portfolio of Colonials, Pilgrims, Puritans, Musketeers, Revolutionaries, and Patriots (suggested by no fewer than seventy-four fans) . . . but the most popular was the Minutemen.

Boston sportswriters actually made the final decision. When offered a choice between the Minutemen and the Patriots at a team dinner introducing Saban to the press, they overwhelmingly preferred the Patriots, no doubt pleasing the desk men responsible for writing headlines. The seventy-four fans who also favored the Patriots were then asked to write a 100-word essay to determine who would actually win the TV.

Thus, a few days later, on February 16, 1960, the new club officially became the Boston Patriots. Of course, it didn't take long for fans and scribes alike to start referring to the team as the "Pats" or to consider the alternative—the "Patsies"—if they failed to put up a good fight. A sign reading BOSTON PATRIOTS PROFESSIONAL FOOTBALL CLUB soon appeared on the sidewalk in front of the team offices, and they started selling season tickets without even knowing when the team would play or when the season would start. A few months later, Sullivan received a letter from Walter Pingree, a local railroad conductor, with a uniform design, including a tricorner hat emblem for the new team's helmets. Pingree didn't ask for any money, and Sullivan immediately adopted the design.

Meanwhile, McKeever kept signing players, not just those straight out of college, but just about anyone who'd ever shown the remotest possibility of knowing how to play—former NFL players, semipros and ex–Canadian Football League players, recent collegians who had gone undrafted, and those trying to relive their glory days. Then there were the guys coming to the team asking for a tryout: the has-beens, never-weres, schemers and dreamers, and former players who knew Holovak, McKeever, Saban, or one of the directors from their earlier stops. The club welcomed everyone—there was no risk in signing a player they might never have to pay a nickel, and in the meantime it kept him away from another AFL club.

At the same time, the AFL was trying to make some basic decisions: When should they start the season? How should they go about creating a fourteen-game schedule? And was there anything else they could do that might differentiate the AFL from the NFL?

They eschewed any blatant gimmicks, but did eventually make several decisions that helped make the new league stand out. The first was the two-point conversion option after a touchdown. The college rule had been put into effect in 1958 to cut down on tie games, and it had proven popular. The AFL chose to go with the new rule, thinking it might add excitement to the most boring scoring play in professional sports—the point after touchdown kick. AFL jerseys would also feature players' last names, and the scoreboard clock would be the official clock. Then there was the ball.

The NFL had long used a ball manufactured by Wilson, known as "the Duke." The AFL chose a version of a Spalding ball, the J5-V, that was known internally at Spalding as the J6-V. College football used the J5-V, which was one quarter-inch longer, at 11¼″, and a quarter-inch smaller in circumference, at 21¼″, had slightly different pebbling and lacing, and was tanned a slightly lighter shade of brown. But the biggest difference between the Wilson and the Spalding ball used by the AFL was even more subtle: the AFL J5-V had a thin layer of foam between the pigskin and the bladder. All these small changes made the AFL ball a bit easier to grip and throw. Quarterbacks loved it.

As the league got its act together under Commissioner Joe Foss, the Patriots still had to find a place to play. Sullivan still hoped to build his own facility. Uncle Joe Sullivan had claimed that they could do so "in a few months" simply by erecting bleacher scaffolding, presumably supplied by director Dan Marr's company, but no one really believed that, and they didn't have any property anyway. Several other parties, including former Braves partner Guido Rugo, made noise about building a stadium, but that was just talk, so Sullivan made discreet inquiries at BC, Harvard, BU, and to the Red Sox.

The Red Sox were the first to say no, and the rest quickly followed. In desperation, Sullivan began to consider other sites, including Lynn's WPA-era Manning Bowl, which could hold about 20,000, and White Stadium (now Sartori Stadium) in East Boston, a utilitarian site right next to Logan Airport.

With each passing day, the rumor that the team might have to leave Boston before ever playing a game inched closer to reality. Groups from Chicago and Atlanta expressed growing interest; one paper reported that the Atlanta group was even willing to take "their chances on the racial problem, since the Patriots have quite a few Negroes on the squad," including Burton.

In that respect, the AFL, although it failed to place a franchise in the Deep South, was far in advance of the NFL. But it is important to note that the league's progress in reflecting racial justice came about primarily through expediency, not through any overt effort to do so. By necessity, the AFL was forced to expand the scope of the player pool and look for players where the NFL did not, including at smaller schools and black colleges. During the first three years of its existence, the AFL rosters, with fewer teams, included 17 percent more black players than NFL teams, which as of 1960 still included one team, George Preston Marshall's Washington franchise, that had yet to integrate. All eight AFL teams integrated in 1960, including those in Texas, though a black player had yet to play for the University of Texas Longhorns. Over its brief existence, in almost every way, the AFL

The team's first helmet logo, used only for the 1960 season, was a tricorner hat designed by fan Walter Pingree, who worked as a conductor on the Boston and Maine railroad. Pingree was also a painter and amateur historian who was happy to share his both his designs and scrapbooks with the team.

would prove far more racially progressive than the NFL, and that alone would allow the AFL to rapidly catch up with the NFL in terms of talent.

The news from Atlanta was enough to move the political gears in Boston. Mayor John Collins interceded and convinced BU to make the old Braves Field available, although BU refused to budge from a university policy that prohibited the use of school facilities on Sundays, a "blue law" holdover from Boston's Puritan past. The Pats had a field for free for two seasons, but had to agree to absorb the cost of a quick $325,000 refurbishment: since the Braves left town, the stadium, renamed Nickerson Field by BU, had deteriorated badly. The work included bringing in stands from Shibe Park in Philadelphia, re-sodding the entire field with turf imported from Canada, and renovating the locker rooms under the stands, a press box, and the old Braves offices on Gaffney Street. It was still far from perfect, as there was virtually no parking, but the Patriots managed to boost capacity from 17,000 to 27,000.

On June 9, the Patriots—and the rest of the league—received a windfall. The AFL and ABC came to an agreement for a five-year TV deal worth $2,125,000 that gave ABC the right to broadcast a total of thirty-seven Sunday games, including the all-star and championship games. Moreover, the money would be split equally among the eight teams on an annual basis. The NFL was also televised, but its broadcast contracts varied between various outlets and teams, and the money was not shared. The Giants received $350,000 in 1960, while the small-market Green Bay Packers took in a paltry $35,000. The new deal gave the new league financial stability and in some markets, such as New York—where the Giants were blacked out—more television presence than the NFL had.

It was sheer genius and sheer desperation. ABC had overpaid, as there were no other broadcasting bidders, but the decision to spread the money equally among the eight teams in the amount of $212,500 annually, combined with ticket sales, gave the league instant solvency. If costs could be contained, it was likely to survive, if not thrive. No one would get rich right away, but neither were any of the franchises likely to go under.

Yet every solution seemed to cause yet another problem. Like the New York Titans, the Pats had no wish to go head to head against the Giants on Sunday, couldn't use their home field on Sundays anyway, and also couldn't go against BU, Harvard, and BC by playing on Saturdays. They had decided to play on Friday nights, but the Sunday TV deal left Boston home games out of the loop.

Then there was the question of training camp. After first announcing that the team would hold training camp at Saint Anselm College in New Hampshire, the Patriots found the facilities lacking and eventually settled at the University of Massachusetts in Amherst, but it was quite a haul from Boston to western Massachusetts. The Titans, following the lead of the Giants, tried to stake a claim to New England by holding camp at the University of New Hampshire.

. . .

So far the Patriots had a lot of money going out, very little coming in, and a board of directors already balking at spending more of their hard-earned cash. Yet the team was already creating some buzz among Boston sports fans. At the time, the Red Sox were in the midst of a long, slow decline that would not end until 1967's "Impossible Dream" season. The Celtics, although on the precipice of a dynasty, only half filled the Boston Garden, and the Bruins were entering the worst era in their existence: for the next eight seasons—until the arrival of Bobby Orr—they would be left out of the playoffs and fail to regularly fill the Garden. Interest in local collegiate sports had already been in decline. If ever there was a time to start a pro sports franchise in Boston, this was it. Under Mayor Collins, the city was touting "New Boston" and trying to spark development. The football team was yet another example of how Boston was changing.

The Patriots, or at least their board of directors, sensed all this and took advantage. They decided to raise money before ever playing a game by selling 120,000 shares of nonvoting stock for as much as $6 a share. They eventually sold 140,000 shares and raised, after expenses, $540,000 of capital.

Sullivan didn't like the plan himself. He was already worried about losing control to those with more money, and unlike the others, his personal investment was already based on debt. His power in the organization was political, and he served as team president only because no one else wanted the job. The rest of the investors saw running the Patriots as either a pastime or an investment; Sullivan saw it as his destiny and his shot at the big time.

After holding an open tryout in Newton, where Saban found only seven players to invite to UMass, the Pats opened camp in Amherst on July 4 with a holiday barbecue for local residents. Twelve quarterbacks and nine centers spent the next few days in drills before full camp opened on July 9. With 113 players on hand, it took all of one minute before the first casualty: tackle Ed Pitts went down with a torn knee ligament. They had only three weeks before the first scheduled exhibition, and less than two months before the start of the regular season.

The next few weeks unfolded as part boot camp, part *Animal House,* and part fire drill as players were put through their paces and sorted out. Gino Cappelletti later recalled that "there were tall fat guys and short fat guys, and mixed in among all of that was a group of pretty good athletes that had tried out for NFL teams and didn't make it, or didn't try out for NFL teams because they felt they couldn't make it. . . . Players came from every corner of the country. Some were professional wrestlers. Some had played in the NFL ten years ago and were trying to make a comeback. There were a few rookies, a few draft choices, but other than that, it was a comedy of people who showed up to play. Some guys had never played before."

Saban was sometimes forced to hold four separate training sessions just to give everyone time on the field, and it was never certain who would be there from one day to the next. Almost every day players were ferried back and forth from Boston's Logan Airport, often driven by Sullivan's son Chuck, all coming and going at a dizzying pace that only quickened as camp progressed and players cut from other AFL squads and NFL teams found their way in a conga line to the revolving door of Patriots camp. Things were so disorganized that some players hung on for days after being cut just to take advantage of the free food. They stayed in un-air-conditioned dorm rooms and often stripped off their equipment on the field for use by the next group of players. Saban later said, "I had 137 helmets and I planned to use every one." Top recent draftees and players with a Boston College pedigree, a connection to Saban, or recent pro experience had a leg up, but among the horde the Patriots did find a few gems—or at least guys who looked like gems before the tarnish of a regular season took hold.

One was thirty-six-year-old quarterback Butch Songin, who was already much older than most of his teammates. He had played quarterback for (surprise) Boston College in the late 1940s, but was better known as an All-American hockey player who led the Eagles to a national championship. He'd played a few years with the Interprovincial Rugby Football Union (the precursor to the Canadian Football League), leading Hamilton to a Grey Cup championship, and he'd played a year with

Patriots quarterback Ed "Butch" Songin, who played both pro hockey and football, meets with AFL Commissioner and WWII Medal of Honor recipient Joe Foss in the Patriots' locker room following a 1960 game.

the Eastern Hockey League's Worcester Warriors before returning to the Boston area. He was working as a parole officer in Wrentham and playing sandlot ball on weekends when he decided to give the new league a try and took leave from work. As the only quarterback with pro experience, he immediately stood out from the pack, despite his age and his insistence on wearing hockey pads instead of football shoulder pads. Songin couldn't throw long but was accurate at shorter distances, and he was more mature and more familiar with the professional game than the other players. Apart from Holy Cross rookie signal caller Tommy Greene, who arrived late to camp owing to a military commitment, Songin was never challenged. Still, the PR-savvy Patriots shaved four years off his age in the press, and everyone pretended not to notice.

Kicker and receiver Gino Cappelletti is considered by many one of the handful of great players who are *not* in the Pro Football Hall of Fame. He retired as the all-time leading scorer in AFL history and is one of only three players to have appeared in all of his team's AFL games.

Another gem was Gino Cappelletti, the AFL's leading scorer and still third on the Pats' all-time leading scoring list. At the University of Minnesota, Cappelletti had played single-wing quarterback, kicked, and played a little defensive back, but after going undrafted and failing to make the Lions as a free agent, he played several years in Canada sandwiched around a stint in the service. The thirty-year-old was tending bar for his brother in Minneapolis and playing in a rec league when he

heard about the AFL, managed to get ahold of Saban, and secured an invitation to camp.

He was just a football player who could play a little almost anywhere and wasn't afraid to hit, so he was invaluable at camp. Cappelletti told Saban, who hardly knew him, that he was a defensive back, the most undermanned position in camp. Very few guys came out of college as DBs—most were offensive halfbacks who did double duty but preferred carrying the ball. When Saban realized that the Pats, with a roster of only thirty-three, probably wouldn't be able to carry a kicker, Cappelletti announced that he could kick too, figuring that the ability to do double duty might increase his chances of making the team. He was right. Cappelletti stuck even as players faster and bigger rolled back down the Mass Pike.

The trick to sticking was to make it to the exhibition season, then do something to stand out. It was an utterly Darwinian process, and the strongest emerged after the team broke camp and began regular-season practice at Emerson Field in Concord, where neighborhood kids watched practice sitting on their bikes parked on the sidelines among the players, dads hoisted sons on their shoulders, and the line between players and fans was almost nonexistent.

On July 26, Pats made their public New England debut—not in Boston, but in Haverhill, in an intersquad tilt to benefit the local Lions Club. Songin led the first-team squad, the Whites, to a 27–6 win over the Reds in a performance that led Saban to tell him to quit his day job—he was the quarterback. BC grad and Canadian Football League refugee Jim Colclough emerged as a favorite target at end, and Ron Burton showed his speed, scoring the first touchdown. A few days later, the Pats left for Buffalo for the first exhibition game in AFL history.

One hundred thousand fans turned out for a parade to welcome the players on both teams, but only 16,474 turned out for the game in Buffalo's cavernous War Memorial Stadium, which could hold 46,500. They could hardly be blamed. The field was in what was considered a high-crime area of Buffalo, and the stadium, built with Works Progress Administration funds in 1937, had been poorly maintained. Reporter Brock Yates would later observe that it looked "as if whatever war it was a memorial to had been fought within its confines."

Behind Songin, the Patriots won easily, 28–7. Defensive end Bob Dee, another local, by way of Holy Cross and Braintree, scored Boston's first touchdown in a game with a fumble recovery in the end zone, and Songin threw for two scores, including one to Colclough, as the Patriots notched 28 first downs. Burton ran for 60 yards, and Gino Cappelletti recovered a fumble, leading John Ahern of the *Globe* to note that he was "a guy you'll be hearing from."

The one black mark was Schwedes. He'd done nothing to impress, and already the press was noting his absence, referring to him as a "mystery man" after the $25,000 player touched the ball only one time. The team quickly learned that at whatever position Schwedes played, they had someone faster or stronger. He was still on the team only because of his contract.

At this point, it was still hard to tell whether the Patriots were lucky or good. In fact, no one had any idea how good any team in the league truly was, or if they were all just varying degrees of awful.

The Pats received an answer a week later in Providence at Mount Pleasant Stadium against Denver. Although fewer than 5,000 fans turned out, the Patriots dominated in every facet of the game, with Songin and Tommy Greene both looking like Johnny Unitas while the Patriots rolled, 43–6. A few days before their home exhibition opener, the *Globe* gushed that the Pats were "the best thing ever to put on football suits." Billy Sullivan was so unimpressed with the Broncos—and impressed with his own team—that he tried to convince Joe Foss to make every team in the league donate a player to the Broncs.

Actually, the win over Denver was the worst thing that could have happened, and the first sign that Saban wasn't up to the job. Believing the score, he concluded that the team was in pretty good shape and ready to open the regular season. But what he did not know was that the Broncos had intentionally sandbagged the game, holding out their best players and not even using a playbook. They were waiting for the opening game of the regular season against Boston. Nevertheless, key Patriots players like Songin, fullback Larry Garron, Burton, Colclough, defensive end Bob Dee, and defensive backs Chuck Shonta and Fred Bruney settled in. Unlike Boston, most other teams treated the exhibition season as intended—as a test to try out new players and approaches. And with each passing week, as more players were cut from pro squads, they continued to tinker with their rosters. By the time the season started, most teams hardly resembled the ones that had taken the field in early August.

Not the Patriots. They didn't play exhibition games in college, and Saban concluded he already had a winning team that could win with virtually the same offense he had used when Western Illinois played Central Michigan—a standard split-T formation with a flanker—and he passed on newly available talent. He should have gotten the message at their home exhibition opener against

The program cover for the team's first game: a charity exhibition contest against the Dallas Texans played at Harvard Stadium on August 14, 1960.

MR. PATRIOT, GINO CAPPELLETTI

THE 310 FIGURES CURRENTLY ENSHRINED IN THE PRO FOOTBALL HALL OF FAME INCLUDE NOT ONLY SOME OF THE BEST BUT ALSO MANY OF THE MORE OBSCURE NAMES IN PROFESSIONAL FOOTBALL. FAMOUS EX-PLAYERS LIKE JERRY RICE AND BRETT FAVRE RESIDE ALONGSIDE THOSE WHO EVEN THE MOST RABID FANS HAVE TO GOOGLE—GUYS LIKE CLIFF BATTLES, RAY FLAHERTY, WAYNE MILLNER, AND TURK EDWARDS, ALL OF WHOM MADE THEIR MARK DURING PRO FOOTBALL'S EARLY DAYS IN BOSTON. EVEN GEORGE PRESTON MARSHALL, THE NOTORIOUSLY RACIST OWNER OF WASHINGTON, WHO FIRST OPERATED HIS TEAM IN BOSTON, HAS BEEN ENSHRINED.

Rather incredibly, there are only eight Patriots who spent significant time with the team with a bust in Canton: Andre Tippett (1982–1993), Bill Parcells (1993–1996), Curtis Martin (1995–1997), John Hannah (1973–1985), Junior Seau (2006–2009), Mike Haynes (1976–1982), Nick Buoniconti (1962–1968), and Randy Moss (2007–2010).

That's it. The team that is currently the league's dominant franchise is one of the most underrepresented. (By way of comparison, the Raiders have twenty-six representatives in the Hall.) And while that's certain to change with the likely addition one day of Bill Belichick, Tom Brady, Rob Gronkowski, Ty Law, Adam Vinatieri, and others, it's still surprising to learn that several other Patriots are not on that list, from Billy Sullivan for his pioneering role in the AFL to Jim Nance, one of the dominant backs of the 1960s, and more recent stars like Troy Brown and Willie McGinest.

But of all the Patriots who have been overlooked, none stands out more than Mr. Patriot, Gino Cappelletti.

Of course, for Patriots fans of a certain age, Cappelletti is an Internet search as well. So let's consider the numbers first. One of twenty AFL players active during the entirety of the league's ten-year existence, and one of only three to play in every game, he was the AFL's all-time leading scorer at the time of his retirement in 1971, with 1,130 points (42 touchdowns, 176 field goals, and 342

Coach Hank Stram and the Dallas Texans. Before 11,000 fans at Harvard Stadium, which graciously allowed the professionals to sully their field while the grass was still growing in at BU (and after the Pats promised they'd play the game for charity), the Texans, who fielded nearly twenty players with pro experience, beat Boston 24–14. Saban chalked the loss up to a couple of missed wide-open passes and the absence of Burton, who had a bad ankle and was unable to play that day. When the Patriots rebounded to win their final two exhibition contests, they seemed, at 4-1 in preseason play and the only team to finish above .500, a smart pick to win the Eastern Division. And they relished opening the season against Denver,

which after being walloped a month earlier hadn't won a game since.

Thus far, the Patriots had committed to spending nearly $1 million, most of it on player contracts and work on the field, but had sold only 6,100 season tickets for $35: seven home games for five bucks each, with single-game tickets available for $3. If the Patriots drew decent crowds at home and the other teams did as well, the 60-40 gate split with a $20,000 guarantee would serve them well. Most other teams played in stadiums with a greater capacity than Boston had, so they still figured to lose money, but they concluded that they had a fair chance of turning a profit in a few years.

points after touchdowns), as well as the Patriots' all-time scoring leader (a record he held until 2005, when it was broken by Vinatieri). Cappelletti was named AFL Most Valuable Player in 1964, led the circuit in scoring five times, and was also named an All-Pro in five seasons. On the numbers alone, Cappelletti should have placed in the Hall.

But forget the numbers, because that's not the half of it. Few players in the Hall matched his versatility: he starred at not one but two positions, as receiver and placekicker, and also played one year as a defensive back, intercepting four passes, before moving to end. He returned punts and kickoffs, threw for a TD, and would be the only player in pro football history ever to run for a two-point conversion, throw for a two-point conversion, catch a pass, intercept a pass, return a punt, and return a kickoff in the same season.

Taking into consideration his versatility along with the stats, Cappelletti's qualifications for football's highest honor should be unquestioned. But there's more to it than that. No other Patriot ever has served the franchise so well, for so long. Although born in Minnesota, Cappelletti has made New England his home, and since retirement he has served as a living ambassador for the team, the one figure able to tie the Patriots' past to their present. He also became familiar to younger generations in more than three decades of work as a broadcaster, much of it paired on the radio with Gil Santos, before retiring after the 2011 season.

Few members of the Hall ever did more for their team. Cappelletti has done everything but coach and carry the water bucket.

And let's not forget one more thing. Cappelletti lost several seasons of play before joining the AFL, and at the time of his retirement, he could have played several more years for some other team as a kicker. After eleven seasons as a Patriot, however, he had no desire to play elsewhere. He was a Patriot for life. The fact that he is not in the Hall is an omission of the highest magnitude.

Who needs the Hall anyway? If there is anyone who deserves to be thought of as "Mr. Patriot," now and forever, it is Gino Cappelletti.

It's better to be a living legend in New England than just some bust in Canton.

Oh, but there had been fiscal missteps. Clemson QB Harvey White was cut despite a $10,000 guaranteed contract, only to pass through waivers unclaimed and return to the roster. Schwedes had been conditionally traded to New York, which kept him around for a few days and then sent him back. So two of the Patriots' roster spots were an utter waste, but Saban was satisfied.

Then it was time to play for real. As with so much with this team in the early years, nothing went quite like what anyone expected. Scheduled to open AFL play with a Friday night game on September 9, the team held a workout under the lights the night before. Denver head coach Frank Filchock, taking an evening stroll from his Kenmore Square hotel, saw the lights, wandered in, and watched the whole practice from the stands, committing the Patriots' game plan to memory. It would not be the last time that spying played a role in the Patriots' fortunes.

The game started out with the usual hokey pomp: cheerleaders in pleated skirts, a marching band dressed like Revolutionary Army regulars, the Patriots sporting bright red jerseys, white pants, and white helmets, and programs for sale for fifty cents. After fans fought their way to the field—with virtually no parking, there was a forty-five-minute logjam from Kenmore Square—a surprising crowd of 21,597 settled in at Nickerson Field,

Cartoonist Vic Johnson of the *Boston Herald* drew several early Patriots program covers, including this one depicting Houston Oilers owner Bud Adams driving past a startled Paul Revere lookalike.

while the flamboyant bandleader Baron Hugo and his band entertained fans huddled in overcoats on the late summer evening. A few thousand more watched for free, hanging from the infrastructure of the new BU dorms being built across the street.

The benches were pressed up so close to the stands in the converted baseball field that fans in the first few rows could hear the players talking. But it looked like football, even though the AFL referees wore reddish-orange striped shirts trimmed in black and the Broncos wore horribly deranged-looking, vertically striped orange-and-brown socks. The Patriots started out okay, kicking

off and weathering a reverse on the return before forcing Denver to punt, then driving down to the 27, where Cappelletti lined up to kick a 35-yard field goal and score the first points in AFL history.

At least that was what he was supposed to do. But it hit him—this was for real. When the ball was snapped, he froze until placeholder Bob Dee barked, "Kick the damn thing!" Despite the belated start, Cappelletti's kick split the uprights and made history. The Patriots led 3–0.

From there, it went downhill. The Broncos anticipated every play—their coach remembered what he'd seen the night before—and scored a first-half touchdown on a short screen pass to Al Carmichael that turned into a 41-yard score as Carmichael ran around and then past every Patriot on the field. The Broncos put the game away when Gene Mingo caught a Tommy Greene punt near the right sideline at the 24-yard line, then ran straight upfield as Denver blockers toppled a succession of Patriots like dominoes. The Patriots finally managed to score after Chuck Shonta returned an interception to the 10 and Jim Colclough, despite a concussion he'd suffered in the first half catching a punt, snagged a Songin pass in the end zone to make the score 13–10. But after that, Songin couldn't connect, and without Burton, the Patriots couldn't run. The Broncos held on to win.

It suddenly became all too obvious that Boston had stood pat while the rest of the league had not. Boston looked slow, particularly on defense. Moreover, the loss shook Saban's confidence, both in himself and in his team.

A week later, in New York, after first replacing Songin with Greene at quarterback, Saban shifted gears and decided to switch back and forth between the two men.

For three quarters, it hardly mattered: the Titans moved up and down the field at will and entered the final period leading comfortably, 24–3. In only the Pats' second game, their season was already looking like a disaster, and Frank Leahy had declared the Titans the class of the division.

In the fourth quarter, the Titans started playing out the string, but Greene finally got going as halfback Dick Christy, who'd just joined the team after being cut by Pittsburgh, proved he could catch and run before Greene cashed in with a touchdown pass to Oscar Lofton.

The Patriots soon got the ball back, but Greene's TD pass was only his thirteenth in thirty tries. So now Saban turned to Songin. The old hockey player made Saban look like a genius as he moved the Pats downfield through the air for another score—this time to Colclough—while completing five of eight passes. But time was running out.

The Pats botched an onside kick, and the Titans took over at midfield, needing only to run out the clock. But after every line plunge, the Patriots lingered over the ball carrier, and each time they did, the referees, accustomed to college rules, stopped the clock to clear the pile. It cost the Titans, who were forced to run a fourth-down play. Richie Sapienza, who'd been a late cut by Boston, stood on the 35-yard line to punt. All the Titans needed to do was cover the kick, and all Sapienza needed to do was catch the snap from center Mike Hudock, but he fumbled the ball and it bounced away. Then things got weird.

First Sapienza kicked the ball to his left, away from the charging Patriots linemen. As the oblate spheroid spun and bounced sideways, all twenty-two men on the field were in pursuit.

Boston middle linebacker Tony Sardisco got to it first. He tried to pick up the ball, and then put his foot to it, accidentally or not, booting it toward the Patriot end as the clock ticked down.

He gave chase and this time fell over the ball, but as soon as his arms closed around it, he was hit by Titan Bill Mathis. The ball kept bounding toward the goal line. Five Titans were closing in on it, but Patriot Bob Dee got in the way. DB Chuck Shonta then cut through the crowd, picked the ball up on the run at the 25-yard line, and kept running even as the clock ran out, running and running until the crowd was standing in disbelief, until he was in the end zone surrounded by his teammates, until the Boston Patriots had won their first game ever in the most improbable fashion ever.

Too bad it would prove to be the highlight of the season.

The Titans protested mightily, claiming the ball had been kicked purposely toward the Patriots end. The league consulted the film and agreed, but it also showed that a Titan player had kicked the ball too. They admitted that the officiating during the entire game had been a mess, from the clock stoppages to the kicks and an earlier incident when a Titans receiver had run out of bounds to shake a defender and then came back on the field to catch a pass. All Bob Austin, the league's supervisor of officiating, could say was, "We have to give our officials time to become fully acquainted with league rules." Joe Foss disallowed the protest, and the score stood. Still, it made the league look bad.

The rest of the season followed the same improbable and preposterous script, Boston losing games they expected to win and winning games they should have lost. The Pats were shut out by the Bills at home 13–0, and then in turn snuffed out Los Angeles, 35–0. But they followed that with three straight losses, including a 45–16 loss to LA, the same team they'd shut out only a few weeks before.

When they finally returned home to face Oakland, fewer than 9,000 fans were in the stands, but the Pats responded by winning three in a row to get to .500. Suddenly they were in the race for the division title.

But it was a tease. Playing before 27,123, the first sellout crowd in AFL history (although other teams had drawn more fans in bigger stadiums), the Patriots lost a tough game to eventual division champ Houston, 24–10. Dropping its last three games as Songin battled a nagging neck injury and played like a man much older than thirty-six, the team finished a disappointing 5-9, the bottom of the division.

A final bizarre season highlight occurred during the last play of their 46–10 loss to LA, when another ball tumbled free, this time into the end zone. Thinking the play was dead, a young boy raced onto the field for the souvenir as more than a thousand pounds of humanity went for the ball. The Pats' Bob Dee saved the boy, sweeping him out of harm's way as the Chargers fell on the ball for a game-ending safety. Houston would beat LA 35–10 to become the league's first champion.

The Patriots tried to regroup for 1961. The disappointment extended to the box office, where the team had drawn only 118,269 for their seven home games, for a total gate of only $280,000—thousands of tickets had been sold at discount or given away in promotions. The club lost somewhere around $300,000. Billy Sullivan tried to spin it all by saying, "We were lucky in many ways. . . . Everything has been wonderful."

There was always a strong Boston College flavor to the Patriots. Here former Eagles quarterback Butch Songin confers with head coach Mike Holovak, himself a former BC All-American.

Except it really wasn't. Saban had lost faith in his players as the season wore on, and they in him. Increasingly, he'd adopted a "my way or the highway" posture, which looked more and more like the bluster of someone losing control. And he and McKeever didn't see eye to eye—they'd clashed early in 1960 when McKeever publicly charged Saban with favoring players from Western Illinois, saying, "There is no room for kinfolk on the squad." Boston College was presumably exempt.

The big change in the off-season came on April 4. The team traded three players, including Christy, to Oakland for veteran quarterback Babe Parilli. Although Saban referred to Parilli at the time as "capable relief," Parilli was a bona-fide pro quarterback. He had played under Bear Bryant at Kentucky, where he was a consensus All-American, before being drafted by Green Bay. In almost a decade split between the NFL and Canada, including a stint in the Air Force, Parilli had simply never

found his place on a team with a strong supporting cast. Yet he sported a strong arm and was far more mobile than Songin, who ran like a fullback.

The draft offered little help. The Patriots, with the second pick, selected Tulane halfback Tommy Mason and, with their fifth pick, quarterback Fran Tarkenton of Georgia. Although the AFL was regularly outbidding the NFL for players, that wasn't true for the Patriots, who didn't sign either player. The most notable player Boston picked up was hard-hitting defensive end Larry Eisenhauer of Boston College. He would anchor the line for much of the next decade, during which he would knock eighteen opposing quarterbacks out of action and become one of the most colorful Patriots in history. How colorful? Well, on one occasion the player his teammates nicknamed "Wild Man" nearly ran onto a snow-covered field in Kansas City wearing only his helmet, cleats, and a jock strap.

The other big change actually took place near the end of the 1960 season, when Holovak noted that while Gino Cappelletti had good hands—enough for four interceptions in the inaugural season—he didn't really have the speed needed to cover many wide receivers. He told Cappelletti that if he wanted to keep playing, he'd have to make it in 1961 as a receiver. Cappelletti seized the opportunity to become the team's most prolific and dependable pass catcher. Playing on their Italian backgrounds, and with a nudge from the Pats' PR department, the Boston press eventually dubbed the Parilli-Cappelletti connection "the Grand Opera Twins."

Still, it's not a good sign when the changing of a logo becomes one of the more notable stories in the off-season. In 1960, *Globe* sports editor Jerry Nason asked *Globe* cartoonist Phil Bissell to come up with some way to represent the team in his sports cartoons. "Pat Patriot" was the result, a cartoonish but fierce lineman hiking the ball from center and attired in a tricorner hat. Billy Sullivan saw it, liked it, and immediately adopted it for the team stationery. For the 1961 season, they decided to use it on their helmets as well, peeling off Pingree's hat-based logo and replacing it with Bissell's design. If only other changes could have been so easily accomplished.

There was open animosity between Saban and McKeever during camp, and the GM made no secret that if it was up to him, the Pats would have a new coach. Despite McKeever's title, Saban had the final authority on who to keep, who to cut, and who to sign, but from week to week he couldn't seem to decide. Roles became murky as one bad play could turn a starter into a backup and a marginal player into a starter according to Saban's whims. Meanwhile, McKeever pulled his hair out, the players threw up their hands, and Billy Sullivan looked over everyone's shoulder.

The result was chaos. The Pats opened the new season by losing to the Titans, won their next two games, and then lost to the Titans once more, after which Saban told Sullivan he wanted to dump half the players on the team. Then Sullivan heard from Lamar Hunt that Saban wanted to trade the oft-injured Ron Burton for a couple of warm bodies that the Texans planned to release anyway. It would have been a great deal for Dallas, but Hunt thought of the league first, and Sullivan vetoed the deal.

Saban's tenure was just about over. On October 1, the board of directors met and all but decided to follow Sullivan's advice and fire Saban. After the Pats fell again in their fifth game of the season, Saban was let go and the Pats had to pay off the remainder of his three-year contract—worth $16,000 a year. The only person who seemed truly surprised was Saban, who said, "The change came to me as a complete shock. . . . I think we had come to a point where we were ready to roll." In time—a very short time—Saban would receive another chance as a professional head coach, in Buffalo, and go on to become a very successful one, with one of the greatest coaching trees in league history; many of his assistants went on to become similarly successful. He simply hadn't been ready for the Boston job. Then again, the Patriots hadn't been ready either.

Make no mistake, the firing was Billy Sullivan's decision. In Boston's BC-centric front office, Saban was the odd man out, and given authority by his board, Sullivan had taken it. The other directors only knew what Sullivan told them. Unlike him, they were all focused on their day jobs.

Mike Holovak took over. He was a known quantity, a man with head-coaching experience who already knew the team's personnel and playbook. The press liked him too. And with the Patriots due to play defending champion Houston in just a few days, everyone knew that another loss would effectively end their season.

The players responded positively—they respected Holovak. He wasn't a player's coach per se, but with him you knew where you stood. Instead of bitching about the roster, he tried to get the most out of what he had.

He needed them all against the Oilers. Houston quarterback Jacky Lee passed for a league-record 457 yards as the Patriots gave up more than 500 yards in total offense, yet still almost won the game. The Oilers escaped with a 31–31 tie when George Blanda booted a late field goal. One hundred and forty yards of penalties against the Oilers helped, but the performance gave Holovak license to enact some changes.

Defensive back Ross O'Hanley entered the service, leaving the Pats outmanned, so Holovak cut the defense loose, installing a fierce blitzing attack that, when coupled with the Pats' emerging defensive line—anchored by Dee, Jim Lee Hunt, and Houston Antwine (acquired in trade)—suddenly made the Pats formidable. A 52–21 win over Buffalo followed, and the Patriots surged, going 7-1 in their next eight games as Holovak slowly turned the offense over to Parilli instead of Songin to end the season 9-4-1. In the minds of many, they finished the year as the best team in the AFL.

But it wasn't enough. That one loss came in a rematch with Houston. It kept the Pats out of the playoffs as they finished second to the defending champs.

Still, at least on the field, the Patriots entered the 1962 season in their best shape yet. The roster had settled down. Gerhard Schwedes, his two-year guaranteed contract finally over, was cut loose. Yet he had sold a lot of tickets—he ended his Patriots career helping out in the ticket office, with a career total of 35 yards of total offense to his credit. Gino Cappelletti, meanwhile, scored eight touchdowns in 1961 and led the league in scoring with 147 points. Parilli settled into the quarterback slot after Songin was traded to New York, where the Titans were a mess on the field and financially. New York fans much preferred watching the Giants in Yankee Stadium than the Titans in the decrepit Polo Grounds.

The Patriots had their own stadium issues to deal with. It was hard enough to attract talent to sign with Boston as it was, not to mention the prospect of playing

TEN YEARS OF "PAT PATRIOT"

PHIL BISSELL

I consider Pat Patriot my third son, joining Chris and Steve. He was born in my imagination and delivered to the world on the front sports page of the *Boston Globe* on April 19, 1960. As resident sports cartoonist, I needed to come up with an image to fit Billy Sullivan's newly announced football team. Therefore, I took the liberty of clothing him in colonial garb, placing him in a three-point stance, and depicting him with an Irish pug-nosed face. My Pat was a guy who got his uniform dirty and was more than happy to proclaim, "Now, to make some history around here."

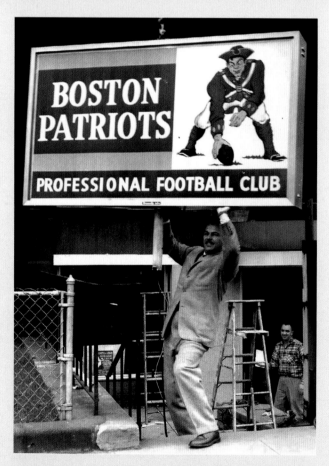

Cartoonist Phil Bissell poses with a sign bearing the image of his "Pat Patriot" at the Boston Patriots' Kenmore Square offices in 1961.

The original cartoon was conveyed to Billy Sullivan without my knowledge, but after meeting with him, we agreed to a handshake deal: the team would use the cartoon as a logo, and I would have the privilege of drawing the team's program covers for the bulk of their AFL years.

I recall asking Billy if he needed to see one of the drawings I'd done for a program cover, and he replied that he didn't because he knew he'd enjoy seeing it more while listening to the laughter of fans seeing it on game day. There's no price tag on that sentiment.

Recently I was honored by the Kraft family and team PR director Stacey James—whom I affectionately refer to as "Jesse"—when they hired me to do work for the team that included drawings for the team's fiftieth-anniversary publications. Stacey very kindly refers to me as a legend—though I always ask him to add "living" to the appellation.

Little did Pat know his original wish of making history would be granted many times over. And despite the fact that the powers that be decided to replace him as the official team logo, he endures as the people's choice, a fan's logo for the ages.

PHIL BISSELL, one of America's greatest sports cartoonists, has worked for the *Boston Globe*, the *Boston Herald*, and the *Worcester Evening Gazette*, among other publications.

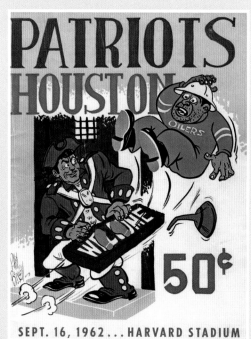

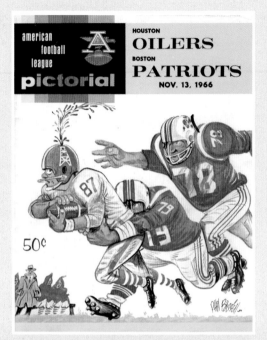

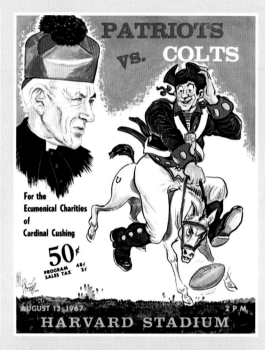

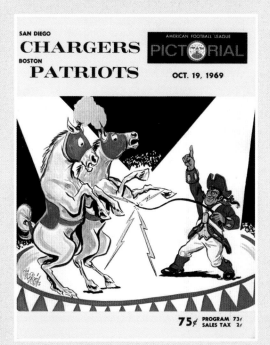

at a field less accommodating than most major college facilities. Nickerson Field wasn't big enough, and other teams complained about the poor gate returns for the Friday night contests. The Patriots sometimes made more money playing on the road than they did at home. Besides, BU was expanding and planned to dismantle the clubhouse.

The field's utter inadequacy had been underscored on November 3, 1961, in the waning moments of the Patriots game versus the Texans. A long pass left Dallas at the 2-yard line with time left for only a single play.

One of the endearing qualities of the AFL was that it didn't take itself nearly as seriously as the NFL—as witnessed by its often whimsical game programs, such as this one for an early Oilers-Patriots game.

Thinking the game was virtually over, the crowd, which included more than 5,000 standing-room ticket-holders, pressed close to the field, anticipating a celebration. By the time the whistle blew to start play, they hung over the end line and into the corners of the end zone, loosely herded behind a rope.

As Dallas quarterback Cotton Davidson barked out the signals, a fan—incorrectly described later as wearing a trench coat (as film reveals, it was a short jacket)—broke from the crowd. Ducking as if to make himself invisible, he danced toward the line, slipping in between officials like a linebacker ready to blitz. The ball was snapped, and Dallas receiver Chris Burford cut across the end zone on a slant to the middle. The Patriots were slow to react, the line held, and Burford was wide open for the winning score.

Not so fast. The intrepid twelfth man, reading the play better than anyone on the Patriot defense, slipped down the line unblocked. He found the passing lane, raised his right hand, and deflected the ball. Burford reached back to try to make the catch, but couldn't come up with it. Burford howled, but fans swarmed the field and the game ended, delivering the Patriots a victory they did not deserve. In Patriots lore, some have speculated that the fan was Billy Sullivan himself. It wasn't, but the way the Patriots were being run, it might as well have been. At season's end, the members of the board of directors were each assessed a $20,000 charge to keep the team afloat.

Boston probably should have won the AFL championship in 1962, or at least the Eastern Division, as they continued their fine play under Holovak. Only two rookies had made the team that year, one of them an undrafted, undersized, but demonstrably tough linebacker from Notre Dame, Nick Buoniconti. Only five-eleven and 220 pounds, Buoniconti was fast, tough, and smart, aptly described by one local writer as a "predatory pillager" who stuck his nose into every play. After losing their opener to Dallas, Boston went on to obliterate their next three opponents, outscoring them 118–51 with a balanced attack that featured a healthy Burton, a bulked-up Larry Garron, and Parilli's passing. In midseason they were atop the division, a stellar 6-2-1, then stumbled during a 21–17 loss to Houston. During the defeat, Houston tackle Bill Herchman blindsided Babe Parilli when he was rolling out, breaking the quarterback's collarbone.

The Patriots were eager to establish themselves in Boston by taking part in a variety of off-season promotions such as a basketball squad of team members sponsored by Hood Dairy. Here backup QB/punter Tom Yewcic [*left*] is joined by starting QB Babe Parilli [*right*].

The loss gave their rivals the division lead. Tom Yewcic, a second-year pro from Michigan State who'd seen little action except as a punter—a role in which he was particularly adept at drawing roughing calls—was forced to start the rest of the way. Yewcic, who had reached the major leagues with the Tigers as a catcher before returning to football, was adequate, but Houston didn't lose another game. In the season finale, the Patriots, with nothing to play for, lost to Oakland 20–0, giving the Raiders not only their only victory of the season but their only victory in their last nineteen games. Over the last twenty-two games, the Patriots had gone 16-5-2 but ended up with nothing to show for it except a dedicated but dwindling fan base whose enthusiasm had to overcome the difficulties of getting to Nickerson Field.

But there may have been something a little more concerning going on. Boston's last two losses to Houston and Oakland, as well as their final game against the Titans (a victory), had gotten the attention of the FBI.

In October 1962, an FBI informant indicated that "two or three members of the Boston Patriots are big betters [*sic*]." He believed that they were "shading points" and that at least one player was accepting money to do so. The tie versus Buffalo and the final contests against New York and Houston were apparently involved as well. Bureau files made public in 2016 concerning New England mobster Raymond Patriarca concurred. They included several heavily redacted memorandums citing information from an informant that at least two Patriots and perhaps as many as four or more were placing bets with the Mob on their own games—bets they won in each instance as the Patriots beat the Titans and kept the margin against Houston to less than five points. In the Oakland game, although no player was implicated in placing a bet themselves, another individual won $1,000 betting on the Raiders, despite their long losing streak and a nine-point spread in Boston's favor. Although point shaving wouldn't be a crime until the Sports Bribery Act

PATRIOTS- BUFFALO BILLS
50¢
NOV. 24, 1963 . . . FENWAY PARK

For the weekend immediately following the Kennedy assassination, the NFL decided to continue play as scheduled, while the AFL made the decision to reschedule games. The Patriots-Bills game slated for November 24, 1963, was played on December 1.

The stadium issue was finally solved—well, temporarily—when in January 1963 the Red Sox reluctantly agreed to a rental arrangement allowing the Pats to use Fenway Park. With the Red Sox in an apparently permanent slump, Tom Yawkey was spending less time in Boston. So were Red Sox fans, and the ball club could use the extra money. Still, the press reported that Yawkey didn't approve of the Patriots' "present current ownership setup," which meant Sullivan. He'd alienated Yawkey ever since he tried to strong-arm the team into supporting his stadium proposals.

The Patriots' board of directors was growing increasingly disenchanted with Sullivan as well. His act was wearing thin, and his partners were beginning to realize that Sullivan's end game was not so much creating a championship team as it was using the team to build a stadium. He'd managed to parlay his connections with the Church and local politicians to get named in 1962 to the Greater Boston Stadium Authority, which he served as its chairman, but since then had little to show for it except a series of paper plans that to some looked like schemes to enrich himself and his cronies. And he was still working full-time for Metropolitan Coal.

Dom DiMaggio had interceded with Yawkey and reportedly did "the spade work" to secure the two-year deal for Fenway, the first time the ballpark would host football since 1956. With the installation of bleachers in left and center fields, the Patriots' seating capacity would nearly double, and at Fenway they would finally have some parking—plus the ballpark was served by several streetcar lines. Although the Patriots had to defer to the Red Sox schedule and would still open the 1963 season with a game at Boston College, they could also play some home games on Sunday for the first time. As punter Tom Yewcic later noted, before the Pats secured Fenway Park, "we never knew for sure where the hell you'd be playing week to week. . . . When we got there, we felt like we'd made it."

The deal made the league happy as well, for greater attendance helped everyone. There had already been a few franchise shifts—the Chargers had moved from Los Angeles to San Diego, and the Texans, boxed out by the new NFL Cowboys, would soon move to Kansas City. The Titans were collapsing; Wismer would eventually go

of 1964, tax evasion by not reporting gambling winnings was. The FBI informed AFL commissioner Joe Foss.

There was certainly money to be made placing side bets, and Boston has a long and notorious history in regard to sports gambling—most notably the 1919 World Series fix, which was put together in Boston's Hotel Buckminster; a point-shaving scandal involving Boston College basketball that took place in the 1978–1979 season; and another point-shaving incident involving the 1996 BC football team. The opportunity for an AFL player to make an extra $500 or $1,000 at a time when most were earning only $8,000 to $10,000 annually was tempting.

bankrupt and sell out to a group led by Sonny Werblin, and the team would be renamed the Jets, but not before both New York and Oakland received some help from other teams through a redistribution of talent. As a corporate entity, the AFL was still acting for the betterment of the entire league, not for the benefit of individual teams.

That's what made the 1963 season such a surprise. The Patriots lost Ron Burton to back surgery early, and Parilli was bothered by a pinched nerve in his neck, but the power balance of the league was shifting and Boston was able to take advantage. They weren't the same powerhouse they'd been the last year and a half, but neither was anyone else in the division. With just three weeks left in the season, the Pats were 6-5-1, but those five losses had been by a combined 23 points. Houston, at 6-5, the 5-5-1 Jets, and the 5-6-1 Bills also had a shot at the division title. A scheduled bye week was responsible for the difference in games played, as the entire league had postponed action on November 24 following the assassination of President John F. Kennedy; the NFL, under heavy criticism, chose instead to play.

> "WE NEVER KNEW FOR SURE WHERE THE HELL YOU'D BE PLAYING WEEK TO WEEK. . . . WHEN WE GOT THERE, WE FELT LIKE WE'D MADE IT."
>
> —TOM YEWCIC

At 7-5-1, the Patriots controlled their own fate entering the final two weeks of the season, but were colder than the 9-degree temperature in Kansas City and fell to the Chiefs and their quarterback, Len Dawson, 35–3. They emerged banged up and bruised, with a half-dozen players in varying degrees of distress, including safety Ron Hall, who had a separated shoulder, and DB Dick Felt, who'd cracked a rib.

With a bye on the final playing date of the season, Holovak gave his team the entire week off to heal, not knowing if they'd play again or not. On Saturday, they all huddled around radios as Buffalo dumped the Jets, 19–10. On Sunday, Houston would play San Diego and could win the division outright with a victory.

Holovak watched the national broadcast from his couch in suburban Natick as the Oilers lost a heartbreaker, 20–14, narrowly missing a winning score in the final moments. "Well," he chortled afterward, "we're still playing." Buffalo and Boston ended the season with identical 7-6-1 records. The only mechanism to decide who would play San Diego for the championship was to play a tiebreaker for the division title. For the first time in their four-year history, the Patriots were in the postseason.

Before heading to Buffalo, the Patriots had some reason for optimism. Although they had split the regular-season series with the Bills, Boston had a secret weapon: Ron Burton.

• • •

Burton had hurt his back in the exhibition season, and after a misdiagnosis left him in traction for several weeks, he'd undergone surgery and had a disc removed. Doctors told him he'd be out for the year, but Burton, refusing to accept the diagnosis, had started working out and now wanted to try to play. Activating Burton from the inactive list appeared to violate league rules, but the Pats weren't about to tell him no, and the Patriot front office found a discrepancy in league rules that made it possible for him to play. Larry Garron had gained 749 yards for the year, but having Burton on the field, even as a decoy or kick returner, was invaluable.

The Bills, behind coach Lou Saban, who had taken over as Buffalo's coach a year and a half before, protested, knowing full well that Burton was a potential game-changer. Even as Burton remained uncertain if he could go—in addition to his back, his left foot was numb and he had a bad right knee—the Patriots proceeded as if he would play. Then Joe Foss ruled in the Patriots' favor, concluding that it was best for the league to have the best players on the field, no matter what the rules said.

And that was the other concern—the field. It had snowed in Buffalo and then thawed before turning frigid, leaving much of the field covered in ice. The Bills consulted with both the Bears and the Packers on what to do about it and first spread ice-melting chemicals on the surface and then covered it with straw. They were confident that, after sweeping away the hay, the ice and snow would melt and the field would be fine.

The Patriots-Chargers AFL title game at Balboa Stadium attracted a large national television audience despite the fact that the Patriots were outmatched and lost by a score of 51–10.

The Pats left for Buffalo on Friday but were delayed for nearly three hours after the bad weather required that the plane lighten its load and dump 700 gallons of fuel before landing. They worked out in the end zone of the hay-covered field, which the Bills remained convinced they could clear of snow.

That dream ended the night before the game. The hay was swept off . . . and the field was covered with ice. Oh, a few patches of something resembling a frozen patch of earth and grass showed in a few places, but virtually the entire surface was a skating rink. The Boston Bruins would have felt right at home.

Players on both teams tried every possible combination of footwear to try to gain their footing—sneakers, football cleats, one of each, street shoes, even socks worn over shoes. It hardly mattered. No one had thought of skates.

The time off had done the Patriots good. For the first time in weeks they were both fresh and well manned. At kickoff, 33,000 fans huddled in cavernous War Memorial Stadium with the temperature hovering at a chilly 21 degrees. They threw cans of beer at the Patriots for fun, who wisely kept their helmets on.

The Bills got off to a rough start. Elbert Dubenion took the kick at the 15 and sprinted upfield, but fumbled at the 33—Patriot reserve Billy Lott fell on the ball.

The Patriots got to work. Not knowing how long Burton would last, Parilli handed him the ball on the first play. He found a gap up the middle and shot toward the goal, gaining 13 yards before being brought down at the 17. A Parilli interception stopped the drive at the 7, but even though Burton would only run the ball another seven times that Sunday afternoon, and ineffectively at that, the tone was set—the Bills had to think about him, which gave fullback Larry Garron room to move.

The Patriots' defense, staunch all afternoon, soon got the ball back, and Parilli moved the team downfield by way of passes to Colclough and Cappelletti before the drive stalled, but Cappelletti's 28-yard kick gave the Patriots a 3–0 lead.

Boston got the ball back a few minutes later, and Garron made the play of the game. With the Patriots just shy of midfield, Garron took a short swing pass to the right, caught the ball in full slide on the icy surface, slipped a tackle with one swift move, then took off down the sidelines. He didn't stop for another 59 yards, giving the Patriots a 10–0 lead. As it turned out, of all the players on the field, only Garron had the right solution in footwear: he'd worn his old baseball cleats.

Buffalo was almost helpless, unable to run at all despite the presence of Cookie Gilchrist, one of the league's best backs. Boston controlled both the ball and field position as Cappelletti kicked two more field goals before the half, one of which was tipped but still managed to wobble through the goalposts. At halftime it was 16–0.

In the second half, Buffalo turned to the air, bringing in Daryle Lamonica, and he struck once, throwing a 93-yard bomb to Dubenion, but Boston came right back, scoring again on a 17-yard pass to Garron and then adding another field goal by Cappelletti, who accounted for 14 of Boston's points in the eventual 26–9 win. For the day, the Patriots intercepted four Buffalo passes and recovered two fumbles, holding the Bills to only seven yards rushing.

"That was the best my team could ever play," said Holovak years later. In another week, in San Diego against the Chargers, he would learn just how bad they could play too.

Phil Bissell captures the disheartened spirit of Patriot fans and players alike following their loss to the Chargers in the 1963 AFL title game.

CHAPTER THREE

1964–1970

PROMISES, PROMISES

South Boston native and *Boston Globe* football writer Will McDonough, a graduate of Northeastern University, covered prep sports for the *Globe* before moving to the Patriots beat in the summer of 1962 as backup to John Ahern. Like Billy Sullivan, McDonough made a career aligning with those in power.

HIS REPORTING, both with the *Globe* and later as a television analyst for CBS and NBC, focused less on the players and what took place on the field than on what went on behind the scenes, in the locker room and front office, covering the inside power struggles among the men who owned and coached the Patriots and those who ran professional football.

In quintessential McDonough fashion, he later liked to tell a story—which he never wrote—about the 1963 AFL championship game, the kind of story that enhanced his reputation as someone who knew what was *really* happening. The Chargers arranged for Boston to practice at a nearby Navy base, a presumably secure facility that

Former Boston College star running back Mike Holovak was named the second Patriots head coach partway through the 1961 season. Within a year and a half, he directed his team to a division title and an AFL championship game in San Diego.

would allow them to work out in private. Yet, according to McDonough, "the Chargers had several people dressed as Navy guys watching practice all week long," although, as a reporter who bragged he never took notes, he never provided a source for that information. According to McDonough, the Chargers thereby learned exactly what the Patriots planned to do during the game and adjusted accordingly. The Patriots were beaten before they ever took the field. Gino Cappelletti later remarked, "You know, the way the Chargers played, especially on offense, it was as if they knew just what we wanted to do."

They did, but if the Chargers had spies at the Patriots' practice, anything they learned was confirmed before the game. The fault for that lay with Mike Holovak . . . and perhaps Will McDonough.

In two earlier meetings that season, the Chargers and Patriots had played to a virtual standoff, the Chargers narrowly winning both, 17–13 and 7–6, even as the Patriots shut down the potent San Diego offense, particularly the running game led by backs Paul Lowe and Keith Lincoln. In fact, the Patriots had angered the Chargers before the game at Fenway when the home team "accidentally" forgot to cover the outfield during a rainstorm. The resulting quagmire left Lincoln and Lowe running in place. Fortunately for the Chargers, flanker Lance Alworth caught 13 passes, including the winning score. But San Diego coach Sid Gillman did not forget.

He did not just want to beat the Patriots—he wanted revenge, a victory so complete and thorough that the NFL would agree to an interleague championship game. With two weeks to prepare for Boston, Gillman, considered one of the most creative offensive coaches in the history of professional football, installed what he referred to as a "Feast or Famine" game plan, a scheme he felt would either work to perfection or fail miserably. If it failed, well, there was also the "East Formation," which put both Alworth and split end Don Norton on the strong side of the field, another wrinkle the Pats hadn't encountered. Today the schemes seem simple. In 1964, they were a revelation.

Over the course of the season, the Patriots' defense earned a reputation for what Eisenhauer called their "Ban the Bomb" defense—a gambling, near-all-out blitzing attack keyed by Buoniconti and Hall. It worked because their linemen, Dee, Hunt, and Antwine, were quick in pursuit, able to tie up runners at the line or in the backfield before they could reach the secondary and exploit any gaps abandoned by the blitzing defenders or in between the Pats' slow-footed defensive backs, whom Gillman derisively referred to as "old ladies."

The Chargers' new scheme was designed to exploit the Patriots' defensive strengths. Based on men in motion, traps, misdirection, and surprise, the new plays, some of which weren't put in place until a day or two before the game, were calculated to thwart what the Patriots planned to do and free up Lincoln and Lowe.

It wasn't the first time the surprise use of the "man-in-motion" had been used effectively in a championship game. In 1940, the Chicago Bears and Washington met for the NFL championship. Three weeks before, Washington had defeated the Bears 7–3. But in the championship game, the Bears surprised Washington by unveiling the T-formation—something that hadn't been used in decades—and putting backs in motion. Chicago rolled to a record 73–0 victory as the Washington defense spent the whole game reversing field.

As game time approached, if Gillman was wondering whether the Chargers would enjoy a scoring feast or famine, or if the Patriots would plan some changes of their own, his questions may well have been answered. A few days before the game, McDonough had interviewed Holovak about Boston's game strategy and presented it in a story with a subhead "What to Look for on TV."

Holovak may as well have handed McDonough his playbook. In a series of extensive quotes, the Patriot coach revealed his entire game plan in detail. On offense, Holovak said, the Patriots were confident they could run on San Diego, and he described one play in detail, "what we call 'a pick,'" adding, "We'll be running it all day." He noted that one San Diego defender "tips the defense," so the Pats had plans for Parilli to check off to alternative plays at the line. Thanks, Coach.

But on defense Holovak really gave away the store. He revealed that he planned to use the Patriots' blitzing reputation as a ruse, faking safety blitzes with Hall, then

LEN ST. JEAN   BOSTON PATRIOTS
GUARD

Known as the "Boston Strongboy," Len St. Jean played on both sides of the line from 1964 to 1973 as a defensive end and guard as well as playing linebacker and tackle.

having him drop back to double-cover Alworth. He said that the Patriots had drilled the defensive front to focus on pursuit and follow the flow of the play, using their speed to contain Lowe and Lincoln and then shut down Alworth deep. A confident Holovak was almost giddy with excitement.

It was as if Muhammad Ali had told Howard Cosell before "the Rumble in the Jungle" that he planned to lie against the ropes until George Foreman punched himself out. Although the *Globe* wasn't widely available in San Diego, it's hard to believe that Gillman didn't learn about the story—there were telephones, after all, and Gillman

was well connected in the football world. Whether Holovak knew McDonough was planning to run with the story or whether the information was given on background is uncertain, but at that point any trepidation Gillman had over his feast-or-famine approach would have evaporated.

Yet perhaps it wouldn't have mattered anyway. As ESPN's T. J. Quinn reported in 2009, the 1963 Chargers were the first pro football team known to supply players with steroids. After the Chargers' 4-10 finish in 1962, Gillman hired pro football's first strength coach, Alvin Roy, a man the *New York Times* later called "the guru and

Players and officials check the field, which is being cleared of snow before the game at Fenway Park on December 20, 1964. The game against the Buffalo Bills was delayed thirty-five minutes. The Patriots lost by a score of 24–14 and denied the 38,021 fans the chance to witness the clinching of a second consecutive Eastern Division championship.

godfather of the weight-training field." Roy had trained US Olympians and learned about anabolic steroids from his Russian counterparts. During camp before the 1963 season, players were ordered to lift weights and, for at least five weeks, provided with Dianabol, the first steroid developed solely to affect athletic performance, and still one of the most effective. They were given 5 milligrams of the drug three times a day, a dosage that experts agree is more than enough to impact performance. It remains the standard starting dose to this day.

The players did as they were told, and didn't know any better anyway. Neither did Gillman or Roy. No one really knew about the long-term effects of the drugs, nor did they worry much about their health impact or even whether their use was fair—US Olympians were using it too. One Charger estimated that all but 5 percent of the Chargers took the drug. As lineman Walt Sweeney told Quinn, "It was like the wild, wild West. Everything went. There was speed, painkillers, steroids." Half the league was jacked up on something, but only the Chargers had the magic steroid pills. Ron Mix recalled that "they showed up on our training table in cereal bowls." They worked too. Quarterback John Hadl said the Chargers linemen "started looking like Popeye."

Mix and a few other players eventually complained, but even though the "mandatory" program was discontinued in 1964, the drug remained available to any player who wanted it throughout the 1963 season. One thing is certain: the 4-10 Chargers of 1962 went 11-3 in 1963. And as the season went on, as other teams seemed to lag, the Chargers seemed to get stronger. Including the championship contest, they'd score a total of more than 100 points in their final two games. And let's not forget that because of the Eastern Division playoff, the Chargers had an extra week before the championship to heal and "prepare."

Or maybe the Patriots had just simply left it all on the field in Buffalo the week before . . . and then left a little more behind during a week of partying. After all, they hadn't really expected to reach the championship game, and when fans had greeted them on their return to Boston, they had suddenly found themselves popular overnight in a city that had been searching for a champion.

They continued the celebration under the warm California sun in San Diego, where the players stayed at the Stardust Inn, a *Mad Men*–era hotel that allowed patrons of the Mermaid Bar to gaze through an enormous window at bathing beauties cavorting underwater. In one famous incident, several Patriots—among them Larry Eisenhauer and Ron Hall—entered the pool themselves. Eisenhauer mooned his teammates . . . and everyone else in the bar. Suffice to say that the team's focus entering the game was not particularly sharp. Most observers installed the Chargers as narrow favorites.

Even before kickoff, the game was already something of a letdown. Despite the 71-degree temperature, Balboa Stadium, with a capacity of 34,000, looked barely half full. Though official attendance was announced to be 30,127, thousands of empty seats said otherwise. That was understandable. The uncomfortable stands featured concrete bleacher step seats and half of San Diego could pull in the TV feed from Los Angeles. It was easier to watch from the couch. Since the players' bonuses were based on attendance, by the start the Patriots knew that, win or lose, their bonus would be far less than they expected. A lot of mink coats turned to chinchilla.

The Chargers received the opening kickoff and got right to work. On the first play, San Diego quarterback Tobin Rote read an attempted blitz, then faked a toss to Lincoln and a handoff to halfback Paul Lowe. The Pats bit on both, and Rote tossed a short pass to a wide-open Lincoln for a 12-yard gain. The Patriots were playing just as expected.

The next play set the game in stone. Ron Hall faked a blitz, but Lowe went in motion. Bob Dee jumped offside, and then jumped back. As Gillman later noted, that one small change caused every Patriot player to "reset." Suddenly caught leaning, the Patriots backfield had to scramble, overloading one side of the field. Rote took the snap, the blockers went one way, the Patriots overpursued, and then Rote handed the ball off to Lincoln on an inside trap. The running back burst through the line . . . and there was no one. Fifty-six yards later, the Chargers had the ball at the 2-yard line. Rote snuck in for a touchdown.

The game was effectively over; as the *Herald*'s Joe Looney later noted, the Chargers "simply out everythinged" Boston and the Patriots couldn't adjust. Time after time Lowe went into motion, Buoniconti shifted,

Hall either backed off to double-team Alworth or burst through a hole into the backfield and tackled a phantom, while Rote either pitched to Lincoln, sent him inside in the opposite direction, or found him on a swing pass. Every so often, as if bored, Rote got the ball to Lowe, who was just as effective. The Chargers quickly scored a second touchdown on a 67-yard pitch to Lincoln, and after the Patriots came back to score on a seven-yard run by Garron after a long pass to Cappelletti, Lowe scored again on a 56-yard run.

Garron then went out with a concussion, Burton was hobbled, and that was the ball game. Five minutes after kickoff, the Patriots were as ineffective as a punched-out George Foreman. Forced to throw, Parilli spent most of the game retreating from the San Diego defense. By the end of the first quarter, the Chargers led 21–7 and Lincoln already had more than 200 yards rushing and receiving. As the *Globe*'s Bud Collins later wrote, "Every time San Diego scored, a platoon of young things in barebacked costumes threw them around in a triumphant dance . . . this kept the touchdowns from getting tedious." With a 31–10 halftime lead, Gillman was so confident that he left the locker room early to catch the end of the Grambling College band's halftime show.

The Chargers never let up in the second half, even trying a couple of onside kicks in the eventual 51–10 rout. Eisenhauer noted that "from the very first play, they were in high speed and we were in slow motion." Harold Kaese wrote that "it was the sorriest breaching of a vaunted defense since the Maginot line." Parilli said it was like "they wanted to kill us."

Gillman and the Chargers gloated after the game, and with 610 yards of offense, they deserved to. On the way back to Boston, some Pats joked about wishing their plane would be shot down, a better fate

During the 1960s, various colleges and universities supplied the Patriots with cheerleaders. Regis College did the honors for the final home game against Houston in 1965 with (*top row, left to right*) Jeanne Iandi, Amy Biagi, Joanne Valas, and (*bottom row, left to right*) Nancy Wilcox, Pat Kirk, Nancy Mozzucata, Sue Walsh, and Deidre O'Leary, with Joyce Wreiman kneeling.

than facing Patriots fans after the loss. But when asked if the defeat—which had dropped Boston's record to 7-7-1 for the season—would inspire wholesale changes on the team, Holovak indicated otherwise. "We need a touch here and a touch there," he said. "Nothing major."

• • •

The defeat, however, marked the high point of the Patriots' on-field accomplishments in the AFL. The league would last seven more seasons before merging with the NFL. The loss may have been tragic enough—and perhaps unavoidable—but the real tragedy of the ensuing seasons was that whatever success the Patriots had on the field was often blotted out by internecine front-office battles among the board and Sullivan's tortuous pursuit of a stadium. As far back as 1962, Dom DiMaggio had begun trying to oust Sullivan as team president, only to be out-voted. Since then, he had pursued a stadium plan that didn't include Sullivan. In time, referring to "the Patriots" in Boston would become something of a pejorative, a sick joke, more a metaphor for turmoil and ineptitude than a sign of excellence.

Although the NFL's Chicago Bears ignored the Chargers' challenge to a "real" championship game, the NFL was starting to pay a bit more attention to the young league. Thus far, apart from adding franchises in Minneapolis and Dallas, they'd ignored it. But competition was driving up player costs. In the meantime, things weren't exactly looking up for the new league. Although the Patriots drew better at Fenway, and the New York Jets franchise stabilized in 1964 after beginning to play at Shea Stadium, only two teams—Houston and Buffalo—were actually making money. Everyone else was hoping to merge with the NFL. Credit, which often provided operating capital, was increasingly hard to come by.

In Boston, the situation was deteriorating: team financial losses were headed toward the $2 million mark despite the influx of cash from stockholders, ticket sales, and the board of directors. If anything, as the league moved forward, the Patriots as an organization were slipping backwards, or at least not keeping pace. They now used East Boston's White Stadium as their practice field. If the planes flying low overhead on their way to Logan Airport and the gravelly turf weren't distraction enough, the Patriots were also pinching pennies whenever

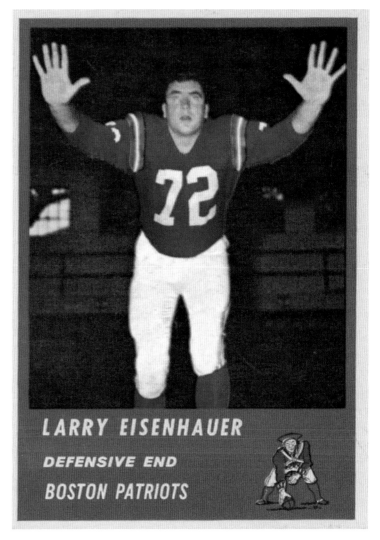

Defensive end Larry Eisenhauer was both the team "character" and a superb football player, achieving All-AFL status four times.

possible. When they held film study in the utilitarian concrete block building underneath the stands that served as a locker room, the players sat on milk crates and watched film on a bedsheet. The club skimped on hotels, meals, and air flights on the road, sometimes not flying in until the morning of a game. Or, if playing several road games in a row, they remained on the road and spent weeks staying in budget motels. Players remember one occasion when, after arriving at a motel early on the morning of a game, they were asked not to turn down the covers—the club had to pay more if they did.

The Patriots and Chargers fought many memorable battles in the mid-sixties, including a crushing 26–17 loss at Fenway in 1964 that broke Boston's four-game win streak to start the season.

The parsimony extended to the front office. In the pre-video era, scouting of college players primarily took place in person, but the Patriots didn't have a scout in the West or Midwest. As a result, the team drafted a preponderance of players from the East, where big-time college football was fading, and the still mostly segregated South. While other teams were becoming increasingly more professional, the Patriots too often seemed like a fledgling—if not floundering—franchise.

The pattern was set. For the remainder of the decade until the NFL merger, the Patriots would appear to take a step forward one year only to inexplicably fall back the next. They frustrated their fans and stressed the already financially stressed team further, leading every member of the board of directors and every sportswriter in town to feel like he had the solution to their troubles. The whole time Billy Sullivan usually blamed it all on the lack of a place to play.

There is a real question as to whether the Patriots, if not the entire AFL, would have survived past the 1964 season had it not been for television. The NFL knew it had the AFL on the ropes. Just after the first of the year, they dealt what they thought was a devastating blow: inking a two-year broadcast deal with CBS for the then-remarkable amount of $14.1 million, nearly double the amount of the NFL's last two-year deal. All of a sudden, the NFL had a revenue stream with which the AFL could not compete.

Fortunately, the NFL was too successful for its own good. Interest in pro football was skyrocketing. CBS was wiping out NBC on Sundays, and with the AFL's contract with ABC due to expire in 1965, NBC wanted in.

ABC was hesitant to open contract talks with the AFL early, so NBC jumped into the breach with an initial multiyear offer of $12 million. Sullivan and some league lesser-thans wanted to accept it, afraid the deal might be pulled off the table if Jets owner Sonny Werblin, handling the negotiations, pushed for more.

But Werblin held out, ABC finally got into the bidding, and the number just kept increasing. On January 29, the AFL agreed to a five-year deal with NBC, beginning in 1965, worth $36 million: nearly $900,000 for each team annually. Just like that, the league was solvent again, and the nearly moribund Greater Boston Stadium Authority, for which Sullivan still served as chairman, was alive. Part of the reason it had been so hard to get a stadium plan started had been the lingering questions of what would happen if the Patriots folded before it was finished. And what if the Red Sox chose to stay in Fenway Park? For the first time, the Patriots appeared to be the stable tenant a new stadium demanded.

The promise of cash suddenly made the Patriots a player in the pursuit of their 1964 number-one draft pick, quarterback Jack Concannon, whom they had traded up in the draft to select . . . and who just so happened to play for Boston College. Yet they were still outbid by the Philadelphia Eagles, who offered him a two-year, no-cut deal. That was something that the Patriots, post-Schwedes, were loath to do.

Still, they managed to pick up Holy Cross center Jon Morris in the draft, wooing him over Green Bay. He would anchor the line for the next decade.

The Patriots seemed to be on the rebound in 1964, mostly because of the strong arm of Parilli, who enjoyed his best season yet as a pro, and the toe and sure hands of Cappelletti, who scored 155 points, including seven touchdown receptions. Paired with end Art Graham, Cappelletti was often overlooked but was far more successful than he had any right to be. Boston opened the season with four straight wins, stumbled back at home, and then ripped off another five wins in a row. With a bye week before the season finale, the Patriots were a gaudy 10-2-1.

Unfortunately, under former Patriots coach Lou Saban and Cookie Gilchrist, the league's leading rusher, the Buffalo Bills started the season with nine consecutive victories. A loss to the Patriots on November 15 gave Boston a chance, and when the Bills fell again to Oakland on the last play of the game, all of a sudden the season finale on December 20 between Boston and Buffalo was the equivalent of a playoff game. Boston needed a win to earn a championship game rematch against San Diego, while the Bills needed at least a tie.

> EVERYTHING SEEMED TO BE TILTING BOSTON'S WAY—THE PATRIOTS AND THE FRANCHISE WERE POISED TO ANNOUNCE THAT THEY HAD ARRIVED IN SPITE OF THEIR STRUGGLES.

Everything seemed to be tilting Boston's way—the Patriots and the franchise were poised to announce that they had arrived in spite of their struggles. The championship would be played on the home field of the eastern champions, and Sullivan Brothers had already printed up 40,000 tickets. Babe Parilli was telling teammates that he planned to retire on top after the victory; Mike Holovak seemed likely to be named AFL Coach of the Year and was already getting feelers from the NFL; and Cappelletti would be the consensus league MVP, selected by UPI, the AP, and the *Sporting News*. Buffalo even had a quarterback crisis: Saban had grown disenchanted with the erratic Jack Kemp and was prone to pulling him in favor of Lamonica.

The game was scheduled at Fenway Park, and ABC even moved up the starting time by an hour, to 2:00 PM, hoping to draw a larger television audience. They broadcast the game everywhere but the West Coast and even allowed New England affiliates to televise it. Fenway Park was sold out—standing-room seats went quickly as Billy Sullivan licked his chops at the windfall a title might mean for the prospects of a new stadium. Here was proof that a winning team could be a huge draw. The biggest game of the day wasn't in the NFL but in Boston, where the turf at Fenway Park had been swaddled for the last month under 168 bales of salt hay and two dozen 55-by-80-foot tarps to ensure that it would remain dry and unfrozen. The forecast called for flurries, perhaps changing to rain showers, and some wind. The club planned to uncover the field as late as possible Sunday morning. Field supervisor Dan Marcotte confidently claimed, "When we finally expose the field, playing conditions should be very good."

Whoops. As Patriots fans of the era were learning, when things appeared to look very good, the opposite was often true.

After all, this was New England, where the weather forecast is often only suggestive. As Kaese speculated before the game, "If the Patriots, with all these advantages, lose to the Bills, what can we blame except the weather?"

Well, that's as good a place to start as any. The temperature dropped overnight, and the flurries expanded into something just short of a blizzard—a quick five inches that was a bigger surprise than Sid Gillman's 1963 game plan. The only people who ventured out in their cars were all headed to the same place, Fenway Park, and roads were soon choked by spinning tires and fender benders. By the time the grounds crew figured out that the snow wasn't going to stop, the tarps were buried under tons of the stuff and could not be removed.

A snow day would have been understandable, but with a near-national audience, the league wouldn't hear of it. The Bills, ensconced at the Parker House, had little trouble getting to the game, but the Patriots had a much harder time, trooping in all morning.

They all managed to make it except for Gino Cappelletti. His teammates nervously began to joke that

perhaps he'd been kidnapped by gamblers, a quip that seemed more likely with each tick of the clock. He finally made it to the locker room just before two o'clock, harried and cold after a bare-knuckle commute.

Fortunately for him, if not the viewers at home, the game was still delayed almost forty minutes. Same old Patriots. Fans expecting to see the kickoff were instead treated to a demonstration of how not to protect a field from the elements as the club called in plows to push off the snow and hay. The field rapidly froze and became snow-covered, leaving field markers and goal lines a memory. And if that wasn't bad enough, when the game started, the Bills pulled a few things out of Sid Gillman's playbook and checked off when they sensed a blitz.

Once again, the game ended almost before it started. On the Bills' first play, Gilchrist ran for seven yards and kicked Patriots cornerback Chuck Shonta in the head. Shonta was out on his feet but stayed on the field. Still groggy on the next play, he let receiver Elbert Dubenion slip past him and snag a bomb for a 57-yard score. Shonta then left the game, and there went Boston's chance of stopping the Bills in the air.

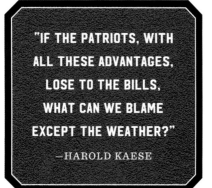

"IF THE PATRIOTS, WITH ALL THESE ADVANTAGES, LOSE TO THE BILLS, WHAT CAN WE BLAME EXCEPT THE WEATHER?"

—HAROLD KAESE

One cannot write about football in this era from a contemporary perspective without noting both the number of concussions and the utter lack of concern expressed by the teams, the players, and the press. Head injuries were considered an occupational hazard little different from an ankle sprain, something to be shaken off, played through, and ignored. And in a historical treatment such as this, one also cannot ignore the number of players who later died young or suffered health or behavioral problems that now look suspiciously like they may have been impacted by concussions. This ongoing tragedy has been part of the game from its very beginning and has grown worse over time. It is increasingly important for everyone to hold the sport accountable—players, coaches, owners, broadcasters, writers, fans, and anyone who takes enjoyment from a game that regularly leaves its athletes diminished.

When the Patriots got the ball after the touchdown, it was little better for Boston. Short on running backs apart from Larry Garron, the Pats installed what Holovak called the "Buffalo Gun" formation—an offense with one back, two tight ends, and two wide receivers—but it was ineffective. The team's last best chance came after a Parilli touchdown pass to Tony Romeo. The Patriots, going for the win, went for two. Gino Cappelletti was open but slipped on the ice trying to catch the conversion, which would have given Boston an 8–7 lead. After that, Buffalo controlled the football. The *Herald*'s Jim Carfield later noted that Boston's chances at that point of mounting a comeback "were about as good as the British trying to negotiate Bunker Hill without chains." Parilli threw, again and again and again—40 times in 51 plays—but enjoyed little success. The Bills won, 24–14, though the Pats made it look close with a meaningless late score. All the good that could have come from the game slipped away on the ice and snow. End of story. The Bills beat San Diego and became champions.

One significant but nearly forgotten incident marked the end of the season. After the championship game, the AFL was scheduled to play their postseason All-Star Game in New Orleans at Tulane Stadium. There was talk that the league might expand to the Crescent City, and city officials had promised a warm welcome. But when the players arrived, they found a segregated town. Black players, including Larry Garron and Patriots lineman Houston Antwine, faced discrimination in the French Quarter. "We couldn't go to movies," said Garron later. "If you tried to get a cab, the driver would immediately start reading an ordinance that said a Negro couldn't ride in a cab unless he was with a white associate."

So they rebelled. The seventeen black players got together at the Roosevelt Hotel and, with the support of white teammates such as Ron Mix, refused to play. After initially resisting, the league hastily agreed to

Not only was Syracuse product Jim Nance a superb fullback, but he'd also won two NCAA heavyweight wrestling titles. He is shown here posing for a publicity still shortly after signing with the Patriots in 1965.

their demands and shifted the game to Houston at the last minute. Incredibly, the 1964 incident received very little press coverage. As Antwine later noted, with some bitterness, "We didn't feel it was properly addressed." It remains one of the least-known civil rights protests in American professional sports.

Ah, but there was that TV contract, which provided a salve that healed all wounds, at least those that were

financially induced. Like every other team in the AFL, the Patriots received their first installment of the new contract at season's end and had almost $1 million to play with. They made a profit for the first time in their history.

Of course, so did everyone else in the league, and the new money spawned a bidding war for college talent. Alabama quarterback Joe Namath, the first overall pick in the AFL, secured a then-record $427,000, three-year

Boston College tight end Jim Whalen (82) was the Patriots' top receiver in the final Fenway Park season in 1968 and remains the only receiver to have caught three touchdown passes in a single game as both a collegian and a pro at BC Alumni Stadium.

deal from the Jets, a signing even more important for its symbolism—the AFL now had the resources to survive and compete on a playing field that was increasingly level.

The Patriots cashed in too. Syracuse running back Jim Nance had followed in the wake of Jim Brown and Ernie Davis to become the latest in a line of star backs from Syracuse. Nance, who nearly matched Brown's single-season school rushing record at Syracuse in his senior year, was the big back Boston desperately needed as a blocker and a runner to take the pressure off the quarterback. "We need a battleship," said Holovak. For much of the rest of the decade, Nance would be the biggest ship in the harbor, the Patriots' first truly dominant player.

It was miracle enough that he even played football. Growing up as the son of a coal miner in eastern Pennsylvania, Nance was badly burned in a fire as a young boy and carried the scars on his shoulder the rest of his life. But he grew up big and strong, as accomplished a wrestler as he was a football player. A host of colleges wanted him, but he picked Syracuse because of Jim Brown. There he played football and wrestled well enough to capture NCAA titles in the heavyweight division in his sophomore and senior years.

To try to keep bonuses down, each league was playing the same game, holding a virtual secret draft in advance of the real one, trying to tie up the best talent in advance so as not to waste a pick. The Jets wanted Nance, but they already had Matt Snell, and Nance didn't want to be a backup or get turned into a blocking back. There was also some concern that Nance, who made no secret of his goal to break Jim Brown's professional rushing record, wasn't as deferential as pro football's white power structure expected a black player to be.

In the NFL, the Chicago Bears took Gale Sayers with their first pick, and Nance went to them in the fourth round. When the "real" AFL draft was held, the Jets, certain that Nance would sign with Chicago, didn't even bother drafting him. The Patriots took a flyer in round nineteen, and then ingratiated themselves with Nance by allowing him to finish his collegiate wrestling season. When it was over, Boston swooped in and made a "take it or leave it" offer that included a $15,000 bonus. Nance, worried about playing in Sayers's shadow, turned down more money with the Bears to sign with the Patriots,

leaving Chicago fans wondering what a Sayers-Nance backfield might have done if given the chance.

He was a barrel of a runner who, when cut loose downhill, was surprisingly fast, with near-sprinter speed, and capable of big gains once he burst bowling ball–like through the line. At a time when some defensive linemen even in pro football still weighed only 230 or 240 pounds, and linebackers and backs even less, the six-two Nance—whose weight fluctuated between 230 and 260 pounds, most of it in his thighs and shoulders—was almost impossible to stop one-on-one. He wasn't particularly shifty, but he didn't have to be: he had a quick side step, and few defenders wanted to meet him head on. The smallest shift of direction often left tacklers trying to bring him down one-handed. The best way to tackle Nance was to hold on and hope for help. As Nance himself once told a writer, "Those guys in the secondary are smaller than I am . . . after I've tagged them a few times they start closing their eyes . . . and I know I've got them." Even his own blockers were afraid of Nance running over their backsides.

But Nance's size was also his weakness. He wrestled at 225, and Syracuse coach Ben Schwartzwalder warned the Patriots that Nance was most effective as a runner when he weighed less than 230 pounds. After he showed up at camp in the summer of 1965 north of that amount, he just kept getting bigger. Even though Larry Garron went down with a fractured leg, Nance ate his way out of the lineup, blaming it on "pies and cakes." With visions of Schwedes dancing in his head, Holovak finally asked Nance, "How would you like to be switched to guard?" That got the fullback's attention, and he finally dropped the weight, but it was too late to save the 1965 season. Other injuries took a toll, Parilli completed only 40 percent of his passes, and the Patriots never got going. They finished a desultory 4-8-2, and it took a three-game winning streak at the end even to reach that.

Losing once again exposed fractures in the Patriots organization as Sullivan's stadium plans continued to fall far short of groundbreaking. In 1964, the New York Jets had signed Notre Dame quarterback John Huarte to a $200,000 deal, but he barely played, and then Joe Namath made him irrelevant. But the Patriots—or at least Sullivan—were enamored of the former Fighting

Center Jon Morris was both an All-AFL selection from 1964 to 1969 and an NFL Pro Bowl choice in 1970. He was named as a starter for the team's fiftieth-anniversary All-Time Team in 2010 as one of only four team members to have spent most of his career in the AFL.

turning a profit and wanted to keep doing so. Huarte, who threw almost sidearm, never panned out.

Then came the merger.

In the spring of 1966, Joe Foss resigned as AFL commissioner, and the combative Oakland coach and part-owner Al Davis took over. Soon afterward, the NFL violated an understanding between the two leagues not to poach players from the other league when the Giants signed Buffalo kicker Pete Gogolak. To Davis, that meant war. Increasingly, the AFL was in a financial position to do the same, and AFL teams made overtures to NFL stars like Mike Ditka and John Brodie.

The emerging bidding war risked hurting everyone's bottom line. All the owners—or almost all—were making money anyway. Why mess with that?

A renegade contingent of AFL owners met with the NFL and on June 8, 1966, worked out a deal. For a cost of $20 million to the AFL to reimburse the NFL for encroaching on their territory in cities where each league had a team, the two leagues agreed to merge, beginning in 1970, after existing contractual obligations expired. In the interim, they agreed to play each other in exhibition games immediately, as well as to hold a common draft to keep costs down. Most significantly to pro football fans, they agreed to meet in a championship game at the end of the 1966 season.

At first, the never-too-inventive minds of the two leagues chose to call the game the "AFL-NFL Championship Game." Then Lamar Hunt, recalling his children's affection for their toy "Super Ball," laughingly started referring to it as the "Super Bowl." The media immediately embraced the name. Some in the two leagues were reluctant, floating alternatives such as "The Game," but the "Super Bowl" eventually became the championship game's official name, beginning with Super Bowl III.

At least in the short term, the losers in the merger were the players, or at least their salaries. Both leagues also planned to expand, costing the players leverage at contract time. The players were boxed out from having much of a say in the game they played. There was already a players' association in each league—the AFL's was led by Patriots linebacker Tom Addison—but then as now the owners considered the league "theirs" and looked upon the players as simply employees, not partners.

Irish star and increasingly dissatisfied with Parilli, so at the end of the season they swung a big trade, sending Jim Colclough and draft picks to the Jets for Huarte and his big contract. But Holovak disagreed with the deal, as did some members of the board who had been growing disenchanted with the way Sullivan was throwing around money and acting as if the team was his alone. They liked

The deal had an almost immediate impact on the Patriots. It was probably going to happen anyway, but Dom DiMaggio and Dean Boylan decided this was the sign to sell and cash out. DiMaggio, in particular, had butted heads with Sullivan for years, at least once trying to oust him as president and in another instance advocating that the group sell the team when the Westinghouse Corporation made a $5.5 million bid. DiMaggio hadn't attended a meeting of the board since helping to obtain the lease of Fenway Park, and he had run up against Sullivan again when he favored a stadium plan without the imprimatur of Sullivan's Greater Boston Stadium Authority. In February, he began negotiations to sell his shares to two outsiders, New York investors Dave McConnell and Bob Wetenhall. But the board had the right of refusal, and in August, after the current board failed to match the bid, Boylan and DiMaggio sold out for $500,000, each earning a profit of around $400,000. Of course, had they retained their stock, they'd have eventually earned even more, but both were happy to be out from under Sullivan. As Boylan said, "Our primary purpose was to bring professional football to the New England area. This purpose has been accomplished." DiMaggio was more blunt, saying, "I couldn't stand the setup." Original investors like George Sargent and Edgar Turner had passed away, and although the power still lay with Sullivan, the board was becoming ever more divided between the "Friends of Billy" and those who thought he was holding the team back.

Indeed, pro football had been brought to Boston, but that had not yet resulted in a championship. In 1966, it almost did: the Patriots could have—and maybe should have—played in the first Super Bowl. Had that happened, the history of the entire franchise might have unfolded in a very different way.

A svelte—or at least svelte-er—Nance was leading the charge, with a work ethic he credited to the opening of Jim Nance's Lounge on Parker Street in Roxbury. He told *Sports Illustrated*: "Buying the place meant my

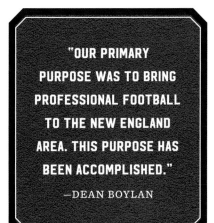

"OUR PRIMARY PURPOSE WAS TO BRING PROFESSIONAL FOOTBALL TO THE NEW ENGLAND AREA. THIS PURPOSE HAS BEEN ACCOMPLISHED."

—DEAN BOYLAN

employees had to rely on me, and I had to rely on them. If a person works for me, I expect him to do his job. I work for Holovak, and he expects me to do my job." That he did. He was tremendous all year long, not just the best back in the league but the best back in pro football, a runner who could change the game on his own and often did, chewing up great chunks of yardage, controlling the pace, pounding the line over and over again for a total of 1,458 yards in 14 games. Nance kept the ball from the opposition and freed Parilli to rebound with 20 touchdown passes. After a slow 1-2-1 start, Boston won seven of nine, once again putting itself in position for the division title. But once again, Buffalo was in its way. With one game remaining, the Pats, 8-3-2, could take the title outright with a win over the New York Jets and Joe Namath. If they lost, they'd need to see Buffalo, 8-4-1, lose as well, which didn't seem likely since the Bills were 17-point favorites over Denver.

At stake was a league championship and a possible appearance in the first Super Bowl, either of which could have, and likely would have, vaulted the Patriots to the top of the Boston sports pyramid for the first time. The Celtics, despite all those championships, rarely filled the Garden, Bobby Orr was just beginning to get untracked, and the Red Sox "Impossible Dream" was still deep in slumber. Championship hangovers in the State House might well have ushered in a state-funded stadium and made Sullivan rich—and everybody else even richer.

But Joe Namath was touched by the gods, and the Jets were everything the Patriots were not and everything they wanted to be. Joe Willie wore white shoes, grew long hair, threw longer passes, completed more of them off the field than on, packed Shea Stadium, and had all but stolen New York for the Jets—hell, he had stolen half of football with his mod swagger, brash confidence, golden right arm, and bedroom eyes. In many ways, the pro game had been stuck in the 1950s. Namath was a generation ahead, both in his grasp of the passing game and in his ability to play to the media. Pro football's last big

Before almost 60,000 New York fans, the Patriots started fast, stopping the Jets twice while Namath felt them out, then notching the first score on an 18-yard pass to Cappelletti. But Namath still concerned the Patriots, who went with a three-man line to give the secondary some help, and on their next possession the Jets countered on the ground. As Will McDonough noted later, running backs "Matt Snell and Emerson Boozer played like Nances." Namath then nailed Don Maynard on a 20-yard touchdown pass when Ron Hall went for, and missed, an interception.

Even worse, Hall took a blow to the head. Although he sat out only the next series and then returned to the game, he admitted later, "I don't remember much of the second half." Patriots fans would try to forget as well.

Namath and the Jets shredded Boston, rolling and passing downhill for the rest of the game. Although Parilli threw for almost 400 yards, playing from behind kept the ball out of Nance's hands. New York controlled the ball, taking a 31–14 lead, then winning 38–28. The ultracompetitive Namath dismissed the significance of the win to the Jets afterward, asking, "Did it do us any good? Like hell it did, we're losers," and offering that the Patriots, who had beaten Buffalo twice, deserved to win a championship, because for the third time in seven seasons they lost a chance for a title on the season's final day. The Bills defeated Denver the next day and walked off with the crown.

The Bills fell to the Chiefs in the AFL championship (the Pats had tied Kansas City in their last meeting), and the Chiefs earned the right to lose to the rugged cool efficiency of Green Bay in the Super Bowl. Losing out at the end was beginning to become a Patriot trait. The press turned on the Pats and was becoming increasingly impatient with Sullivan, who met each loss with a smile that seemed ever more disconnected from the reality of the standings. By the time the Packers defeated the Chiefs to become the first Super Bowl champions, the story in Boston was not what the Patriots had done, but how losing the championship prevented a greater humiliation.

HOUSTON ANTWINE
BOSTON PATRIOTS   DEF. END

In eleven seasons with the Patriots from 1961 to 1971, defensive tackle Houston Antwine was an All-AFL All-Star from 1963 to 1968 and a member of both the team Hall of Fame and the fiftieth-anniversary All-Time Team.

star, Jimmy Brown, had not only retired but, owing to his color and willingness to speak truth to power, had never been embraced by many fans. Stodgy old Johnny Unitas wore a flat top and looked like your dad. Namath was the guy Dad warned your sister about.

Super Pats First Super Champs, Pound Green Bay

How It Could Have Happened: A Football Fantasy

SUPER BOWL? SUPER SHOCKING?

Los Angeles, Calif., January 15—Call them the "Big Bo" Patriots. Behind the running of Jim Nance and Gino Cappelletti's delicate right foot, the Boston Patriots defeated the Green Bay Packers 23–10 in the inaugural "Super Bowl," the AFL/NFL championship game at the Los Angeles Memorial Coliseum. Nance rumbled through the Packer defense for two touchdowns and 189 hard-earned yards on a remarkable 38 carries, none for a loss, and Cappelletti converted on three field goal attempts, two from over 40 yards, as the Patriots shocked the world.

The Patriots started off slow as "super"-confident Green Bay, after winning the toss, deferred, kicking off to Boston. Jay Cunningham slipped a few tackles and returned the ball to the 42. Parilli then surprised the Packers, who, apparently keying on Nance, bit on a play-action fake. The swing pass to Garron was good for 22 yards. An incompletion and two runs by Garron, with Nance blocking, then put the

On October 30, 1966, Billy Sullivan invited a contingent of New England congressmen, led by his old Boston College friend Tip O'Neill, to Fenway Park to express his gratitude for their help in aiding the proposed merger between the AFL and NFL.

The Patriots have long been a destination for Heisman Trophy winners. Winchester, Massachusetts, native and former Navy star Joe Bellino (*right*) joined the team for limited service from 1965 to 1967. The 1960 Heisman winner was first contacted by the team while serving on a minesweeper off the coast of Vietnam.

Pats in field goal range. Cappelletti converted from the 36 to give the Patriots a 3–0 lead with ten minutes remaining in the first quarter.

Green Bay's Donny Anderson then took the return to the 28-yard line, and Bart Starr and the Packers took over. It looked at first like an exhibition game as Starr coolly and efficiently moved the Packers to midfield on a nice mix of power sweeps and short precise passes. Then came the play of the game.

Flanker Boyd Dowler turned around Ron Hall on a post-pattern and had five yards on the defensive back when Starr cut loose. Sixty thousand pairs of eyes were all focused on the ball and the prospect of the first touchdown in Super Bowl history when Dowler, forced to turn back for the pass, had it bounce off his shoulder pad and fall incomplete. What all those fans missed was big Houston Antwine setting off a chain of events that sent Green

Bay packing. His rush sent Packer tackle Forrest Gregg spinning to the ground and rolling into Starr just as he released the pass. The quarterback collapsed back, sending his helmet into Antwine's knee. Starr fell limp to the field, and although he stood a moment later and managed to trot off, he was clearly hurt. Backup quarterback Zeke Bratkowski entered the game, but a fired-up Pats defense stuffed Jim Taylor on a draw play, forcing the Packers to punt.

There was but one "Superman" on the field, and it was "Big Bo." Taking over at the 9-yard line, Nance took the ball on ten of the next twelve plays, breaking tackle after tackle at the line and then, at the 42, lowering his head against Packer middle linebacker Ray Nitschke. Both went down and only one, the man who seemed to have an "S" on his chest, bounced up. Grasping his helmet, Nitschke too was forced from the game, and the Packers later admitted that he'd suffered both a concussion and a strained neck. He would not return.

Now Parilli went to work, finding Art Graham for 22 over the middle before turning the ball back to Nance. He rumbled in from the 8—his longest run of the game—to give the Patriots a stunning 10–3 lead. More important, the drive burned nine long minutes from the game clock.

Starr returned to the field but seemed to move gingerly. Still, the Packers moved the ball, with Taylor and Anderson doing most of the work as they stuck to their

PROMISES, PROMISES | 1964–1970

pregame plan of running the ball. Boston took over after the Packers converted a 34-yard Don Chandler field goal, and the Pats were driving again at midfield when the half ended. They went to the locker room still leading 10–3.

Green Bay returned the second-half kickoff to the 36, and it was clear from the start that Starr was not himself. He spun the wrong way on a dive to Taylor and was forced to eat the ball. Then a pass to Carroll Dale fell short as Starr seemed to have trouble putting weight on his left knee, heavily taped under his uniform. The pass went off Dale's hands and into the arms of Hall, giving Boston the ball at the Patriot 46.

All week long, prognosticators had compared Taylor to Nance, and here is where Big Bo rendered the conversation moot. Apart from a screen pass to Garron that gained 15, for the next seven minutes it was all Jim Nance as he kept Green Bay off the field, pounding Green Bay's suddenly soft underbelly again and again and again, at one point converting three straight third-down plays before Holovak, gambling, called his number one more time from the 2. This time Nance didn't find any room, but he bounced back, spun, and dashed around the end, flattening Willie Wood for the score. Boston now led 17–3.

It did not seem possible, but the game was all but over. Behind Bratkowski, the Packers were forced to throw and moved the ball to midfield before Anderson lost the handle. Eisenhauer fell on

the ball and then almost jumped out of his shoes in celebration. Nance gained nine more yards on three hard runs, and as the third quarter ended, Cappelletti coolly converted a field goal from 44 yards out. The heavily favored Packers, two-touchdown favorites in Las Vegas and far more everywhere else, entered the fourth quarter trailing 20–3 and needing three scores to tie, as the AFL's two-point conversion was not in play.

After the two teams traded punts following short drives, Bratkowski, sticking to the air as the Pats rushed only three linemen, got the Packers to midfield before the drive stalled on a key holding call. Forced to punt, the Packers seemed to have a chance, pinning the Patriots at the 6. But Boston had Nance. He pounded the Packer line again and again, once breaking five tackles on a 7-yard gain, adding 65 yards to his total on the drive before Parilli, from the 28, was sacked on third down after scrambling, making it fourth and long. But for the third time Cappelletti split the uprights and the Patriots bench erupted. They were eight minutes from the most shocking upset in the history of pro football.

Bratkowski was valiant on his final drive, dodging a furious three-man rush and putting the ball in the air on almost every play before, with four minutes left in the game and fourth and goal from the 17, he found little-used Max McGee at the back of the end zone to give the Packers their only touchdown, making the score 24–10.

Needing a miracle, Green Bay tried an onside kick, but substitute defensive back Vic Purvis fell on the ball at the Patriots' 46. Holovak went helmet to helmet with Parilli on the sideline and the message was clear—don't forget how we got here.

The answer was the man with the cape—Nance, Nance, and more Nance. No other Patriot touched the ball as the Patriots worked the clock, and Green Bay was powerless to do anything but try grabbing for the ball as Nance rolled and tumbled forward again and again, twice converting on fourth down as the Pats chose to hold the ball and keep it from Green Bay.

The last play came with only forty seconds on the clock, one last hard yard at the Green Bay 9. Green Bay called its last time-out, and as Lombardi threw down his headset, half the Patriots team poured over the sideline to greet Nance, lifting him in their arms and carrying him the final five yards to the sidelines as Pats fans cheered long and hard and the last few stunned Packer fans filed out, heads down.

Parilli took a final knee and it was done. After the game, Massachusetts governor John Volpe announced that he intended to propose legislation at the next session to support a new stadium, to be called Championship City Stadium. Vince Lombardi announced his retirement from pro football.

Billy Sullivan, for once, had no comment.

Now that's a fantasy.

A 1967 *Life* magazine article on the mob named several Patriots, including quarterback Babe Parilli, as patrons of a shop near their practice field called Arthur's Farm, run by an alleged Cosa Nostra associate named Arthur Ventola (*pictured at his shop*). The story and related fallout had a negative effect on the team, which finished the season with a 3-10-1 record.

Despite the loss, Holovak was rewarded with a new contract worth $80,000 a season, but the late-season run masked a team that was starting to fall behind the times. Despite their record in 1966, they had barely outscored their opponents while playing the weakest schedule in the league. Their offense, while effective, was also predictable, and their defense was ill equipped for the deep passing game. In 1966, Nance's league MVP performance had been something of a surprise.

In 1967, Nance would again top 1,000 yards, but it wouldn't be enough, and Parilli, who'd earned the Comeback Player of the Year Award in 1966, was inconsistent. Most of the time, Boston was playing from behind.

Their window had closed, and in rushed the Red Sox, suddenly the epitome of cool, making an improbable run for the American League title behind the bat of Carl Yastrzemski in one of the closest pennant races in history. The Patriots were an afterthought before they ever took the field in 1967.

Yaz and the Red Sox were even featured on the cover of the September 8 edition of *Life* magazine, a sign that the national media was beginning to take the Red Sox seriously. But for Patriots fans, another story inside the magazine got all the attention and underscored the team's place in the pantheon of Boston pro sports.

Life had been running a series about the influence of the Mafia in American life, and in this issue writer Sandy Smith reported on the influence of the mob in sports—in particular, sports gambling. He reported that as many as twenty Patriots—including twelve currently on the team—and one coach were regular visitors to Arthur's Farm, a vegetable stand in Revere, just north of Boston and a short jaunt from the Patriots' practice field.

Nothing wrong with that—except for the fact that no one went to Arthur's Farm for the vegetables. The stand was owned by Arthur Ventola, an ex-con with known mob ties who was frequently visited by a host of local bookies, and Henry Tameleo, a top lieutenant in the

New England mob under boss Raymond Patriarca. You could buy an ear of corn and place a bet at the same time at Arthur's, and the mob used a small ramshackle building out back for meetings.

But what was inside that building was more important. Arthur's Farm was a place where those in the know could pick up all manner of stolen goods, anything from untaxed cigarettes and liquor to appliances, watches, jewelry, and furs—most of it purloined from hijacked trucks from the South Boston waterfront.

Why did that matter? Well, it wasn't like the regular guy on the street could just walk into the back building . . . unless he knew somebody. Ventola admitted that he had already been arrested more than a dozen times "for receiving stolen goods, you know, a fence," but now claimed to acquire his goods by buying retail odd lots. But the Patriots, well, they were welcome anytime, because any snippet of information—who was hurt and how badly, for instance—could affect the betting line for the next Sunday's game. And the mob took 10 percent of every bet, win or lose. Information was invaluable.

Parilli got wind of the story in advance when he was approached by Smith for a comment. He hubba-duh, hubba-duh-ed his way through it, saying he only bought "toys, razor blades, and things we get at wholesale prices." Apart from that, he knew nothing about nothing, and no other Patriot player or coach was identified by name. The AFL got wind of the story and investigated too. According to *Sports Illustrated*, league officials told the Patriots that Parilli and Holovak "were clean," and Parilli called any inference that he assisted gamblers with information "a complete lie." The Patriots didn't expect the story to have much impact.

They were wrong. Former Celtic guard and current Boston College basketball coach Bob Cousy was also implicated for his ties to gamblers in the story, and Parilli, owing to his Italian surname, seemed guilty by ethnicity. Although the Boston press downplayed the story, it got national play, including a follow-up in both *Sports Illustrated* and the *Saturday Evening Post*. Later, in his testimony before the US House of Representatives Select Committee on Crime, mob henchman Joseph Barboza, who had become an informer, suggested that Parilli and former Celtic and Red Sox pitcher Gene Conley had

knowledge of a scheme to shave points in an NBA game.

Although they denied everything, Parilli and the Patriots were shaken, and when the league failed to publicly exonerate them, well, they looked guilty. The league just wanted the story to go away as fast as possible. With the merger on the horizon, they didn't need any scrutiny. The rest of the Patriots played dumb too—only one, linebacker Tom Addison, admitted to visiting Arthur's. Mike Holovak said the players had been going there for the last four years and wondered, "How are you supposed to know if you are in a place that is run by gangsters?" Billy Sullivan was cagier, lauding Parilli for his character but neither denying the story nor expressing any shock except to blame the press and say, "It's all part of the old ball game . . . my wife has nearly had nervous breakdowns over some of the stuff written about me."

Same as it ever was. Boston and sports gambling were once again united. For years famous Boston athletes

Part of the allure of the American Football League was the fact that pro football's best broadcasting duo, Al DeRogatis (*left*) and Curt Gowdy (*right*), called their games on NBC and later called AFC games through the 1975 season.

were regularly invited to parties only to learn later that they'd met with gangsters interested in obtaining compromising information. A few decades later, NHL hockey star Chris Nilan would marry the daughter of Whitey Bulger's longtime girlfriend Teresa Stanley. Bulger even walked her down the aisle, and Bulger himself was known to own an NHL championship ring, something Nilan has always claimed to know nothing about.

No Patriot was ever charged with a crime or disciplined by the league, but the impact on the club could not have been much worse if they had. The Patriots were forced by the Red Sox's late-season run to open the season with five straight away games, and in the first game after the story broke Parilli played the worst game of his career, throwing six interceptions in a 26–21 defeat against Denver. A week later, in a 28–14 loss at San Diego, he threw two more. The Patriots tumbled to the bottom of the division, winning only three games and finishing last only one year after nearly reaching the very first Super Bowl.

After the season, the Patriots turned away from 1967 as fast as they could, earning a reputation that lasted through their remaining tenure as a member of the AFL—as a team that shifted direction every few months, drove from ditch to ditch, and ground its gears while falling further and further behind. Time and again they would pursue the latest bauble dangled before their eyes, whether it was a coach or a player, always someone they overestimated. Not only did they bury themselves at the bottom of the standings, but they also became a metaphor for ineptitude at the precise time of the impending NFL-AFL merger, a time when it would become ever more difficult to compete. In the AFL, the Patriots had depended on the insecurity of the league to reach a nominal level of success—the line between first and last wasn't very hard or fast—but as the league matured it became more difficult to make that leap. To paraphrase a later coach, they were what they were, and that was simply not very good. The era of utter ineptitude was beginning.

Parilli was sent in exile to the Jets in exchange for quarterback Mike Taliaferro, whose major qualification seemed to be that he had dressed in a locker next to Joe Namath. With poor Jim Nance starting to show some wear, the Patriots won four games in 1968, giving up 30 points or more—sometimes many more—eight times,

while scoring more than 23 points themselves only twice. The Patriots were even forced to play their "home" opener against the Jets (a 47–31 loss) at Legion Field in Birmingham, Alabama, since the Red Sox schedule took precedence. This led many to believe that it was just a matter of time before the Patriots left Boston altogether. When the Red Sox decided after the season that they didn't need a tenant anymore, the Pats were left homeless before finding temporary shelter in 1969 at Boston College and in 1970 at Harvard.

Mike Holovak, a good soldier fighting the good fight as best he could, was let go by the board over Sullivan's objection. The board was becoming ever more divided, and the new guys, McConnell and Wetenhall, increased their holdings toward a one-third stake, giving them veto power. Then came a further series of front-office snafus, like drafting defensive lineman Dennis Byrd with the first pick in the draft, oblivious to the fact that he'd just had surgery; nearly drafting a wide receiver who'd died weeks before; and time and again wasting picks on players other teams had decided were head cases. The head cases all found homes, at least for a while, in Boston. The Patriots desperately needed to knock stories like that below the fold and to the back of the sports section. The Bruins had Bobby Orr, the Celtics were a dynasty, the Red Sox mattered more than ever, and the Patriots ... did not. They hoped a new coach would change things.

Vince Lombardi was still the biggest name in coaching, and after retiring for a year he was interested in getting back in. While Joe Namath guaranteed the Jets their eventual 16–7 victory over the Colts in Super Bowl III, Billy Sullivan wooed Lombardi, promising him the biggest coaching contract in football, even throwing in 30,000 shares of nonvoting Patriots stock, enough to make Lombardi rich.

There was just one problem. Lombardi's lawyer, Edgar Bennett Williams, was also the president of the NFL Washington franchise. When he heard that his client was interested in getting back into the game, well, Washington needed a coach too. Although Washington didn't match the Patriots' package, they still gave Lombardi part of the team and the promise that he could play golf with the president and other DC bigwigs. Hanging out with Billy Sullivan didn't have the same cachet.

Rommie Loudd was a pioneer on several fronts while working for the Patriots. In 1966, he became the first African American coach in AFL history while directing the Patriots' linebacking corps. Two years later, he was named team director of player personnel, and in 1973 Loudd was appointed team director of pro scouting. He later made history as owner of the Florida Blazers of the World Football League.

Lombardi turned Boston down, took over in Washington, and left Sullivan without a date. Sullivan tried courting USC's John McKay, then turned to the flavors of the month: Baltimore assistant Chuck Noll and Jets offensive coordinator Clive Rush, both of whom were credited with their teams' recent success and identified as the best head coaching prospects in pro football.

Sullivan liked both men, Noll in particular, but was swayed by Joe Namath's effusive recommendation of Rush, whom he called "a helluva coach." Sullivan never stopped to think why Namath might want his offensive coordinator to leave just after winning the Super Bowl. (Rush had wanted the Jets to draft Craig Morton, not Namath.) And then there was the thinking of Billy the PR man: hiring a coach from a team that just won the Super

Bowl would play better in the press than hiring a coach from the team that lost. Rush got the job in Boston, and Noll would get four Super Bowl rings in Pittsburgh and a bust in Canton.

Oh boy. Sullivan should have done more homework. While Rush had a coaching pedigree that included apprenticeships under college legends Bud Wilkinson of Oklahoma and Ohio State's Woody Hayes, had briefly played in Green Bay, and had been Babe Parilli's roommate, in his only stint as a head coach, at the University of Toledo, he'd failed. More important, by the time he joined the Patriots he was battling both alcoholism and depression. In New York, where the focus was all on Namath and head coach Weeb Ewbank, that hadn't been obvious, but in Boston, where Rush was supposed to be a savior, his personal issues soon became apparent.

Or maybe he had lost a few brain cells during his initial Boston press conference, where a hot mic nearly electrocuted him. As it was, a quick execution may have

Springfield native and fan favorite Nick Buoniconti was named an All-AFL linebacker for five of his seven seasons in Boston. His trade to the Dolphins in 1969 endures as the worst deal in franchise history.

Billy Sullivan (*right*) views an architect's model of a proposed domed stadium that was to be situated along the Neponset River in Dorchester and house all four of Boston's major professional teams. He's joined by Bruins president Weston Adams Sr. (*left*) and Boston Garden president Eddie Powers (*center*).

been more humane than the protracted slow death that took a year and a half to play out—no coach in football history would have a more bizarre or, in retrospect, more tragic tenure.

Although Rush initially looked and acted the part of solid head coach, impressing players with his organizational skills and commitment to his "system," as soon as the games started it was clear to virtually everyone that they were watching a very public nervous breakdown unfurl in slow motion.

How else to explain the litany of the inexplicable during Rush's tenure, which included such bizarre episodes as the trade of Nick Buoniconti to the Dolphins for almost nothing, the "Black Power" defense, the decision to make every offensive lineman switch positions, his attempts to call NFL commissioner Pete Rozelle from the sideline phone, pulling his team off the field in protest after a bad call, repeated citations for unsportsmanlike conduct, and meandering lectures to the press about journalism? And it wasn't like he didn't have help. He led a staff of six assistants, while George Sauer Sr. served as GM and

former Patriot player Rommie Loudd, the first black NFL assistant, was director of player personnel. Team president Sullivan hired them all as he consolidated even more control over the team's day-to-day operations and held fast to his dream of somehow, some way, getting someone to build him a stadium and make him a wealthy man.

It made no difference. In 1969, Taliaferro played like Namath's locker. Nance and talented halfback Carl Garrett couldn't do everything, but they tried. Meanwhile, Rush coached like Captain Queeg investigating missing strawberries. The Clive Rush era began with seven straight losses, and the Pats finished 4-10. The highlight came during the exhibition season, when a fire broke out in the stands at BC's Alumni Field. No one was hurt and the fire was extinguished, but it seemed like the Patriots' chance at winning went up in flames that day too. At the end of the season, Rush went into the hospital to be treated for "exhaustion."

It couldn't possibly get any worse, could it?

Goodbye, AFL. Welcome to the National Football League.

CLIVE RUSH

LEIGH MONTVILLE

Clive Rush always seemed to call in the early evenings while I was still at work at the *Boston Globe*. I don't know whether the timing was by plan or happenstance. My young wife, alone at home, would answer.

The first time he called, she was excited. She was talking to the thirty-eight-year-old head coach of the Boston Patriots, someone locally famous. The excited feeling lasted about three minutes. Then she became nervous. Then she became scared. The rest of the times he called, she would be mostly annoyed.

"Who's your lawyer?" the coach would ask each time at the end of a diatribe about some alleged incivility, some alleged lack of journalistic judgment or ethics, that some twenty-six-year-old sportswriter (which was me) had exhibited in the past twenty-four hours.

"We don't have a lawyer," my wife would reply.

"Well, you'd better get one," the coach would say. "Because my lawyer is Marvin Belli, and I'm calling him to start a lawsuit against your

The Patriots greet Joe Kapp, their new quarterback as Billy Sullivan (*left*) and head coach Clive Rush (*right*) welcome the former Minnesota Vikings star to Boston.

husband. I don't want to take all of your money, but I have to."

The year was 1969. I was covering a pro football team on a daily basis for the first time. The job seemed strange. Did all coaches call sportswriters and threaten them with a lawsuit from a famous lawyer in San Francisco because of some story about a waiver-wire transaction or a change at defensive tackle? I didn't think so, but I wasn't sure.

"Is this guy different from most coaches?" I asked Will McDonough, a sportswriter veteran who also worked at the *Globe* and also received the calls.

"This guy is cuckoo," Mc-Donough said. "That's what he is."

He was a nervous man, that was for sure, nervous from the beginning. He smoked one Kent cigarette after another, seemed wary, edgy, defensive to an extravagant degree. At an early press conference, he was almost electrocuted as he touched an ungrounded microphone and 110 volts zapped through his body until someone pulled all the plugs from the wall. His nervous joke as he sat in a corner, hands and body still shaking, was a look into his nervous self.

"I heard the Boston press was tough," he said. "But I didn't know it was this tough."

He had been hired eighteen days after drawing up the offense for the New York Jets and Joe Namath in their 16–7 upset for the ages over the Baltimore Colts in Super Bowl III. If the Colts had won, Boston owner Billy Sullivan

would have tried to hire their offensive coordinator, someone named Chuck Noll, who would later win four Super Bowls as coach of the Pittsburgh Steelers. The Jets had won, so Sullivan chased and signed someone named Clive Rush.

"We got our man," Billy Sullivan boasted.

Rush had a terrific football pedigree. A graduate of Miami University in Ohio—called the "Cradle of Coaches" for the many famous coaches it had sent into college and pro football—he played tight end for a year with the Green Bay Packers and then became an assistant to Miami graduate Woody Hayes at Ohio State. He went to the University of Oklahoma for a year under Bud Wilkinson, went back to Ohio State for more time with Hayes, then became head coach at the University of Toledo for three quiet seasons. Then he became an assistant for the Jets, where he worked for Weeb Ewbank, another famous Miami alum, and had Joe Namath as his starting quarterback.

The Patriots were in their vagabond stage when he was hired, moving from college stadium to college stadium, their finances strained, hearings held every few months with city or state authorities about the latest proposed government-financed palace that would house both the Pats and the Red Sox. This new coach was their big step toward normalcy, a big-time hire to give the operation some clean air inside this ball of chaos.

Instead, he added more chaos.

"You know the reputation of the Boston press," he declared after his first team was blasted, 35–7, by the Denver Broncos to open the 1969 regular season and a bunch of stories said, well, his first team was blasted, 35–7, in the opener by the Denver Broncos. "I tried for six months. I tried."

That was the start. For the next year and a half, he simply unraveled in public and private view. His 1969 team lost its first seven games, then won four of five, then lost the last two to finish at 4-10. He did a succession of strange things. He waited outside a dressing room after a loss and tried to pick a fight with a Buffalo Bills assistant coach. He "fired" players instead of cutting them. He told players that if they didn't perform they would be "fired." He switched players from offense to defense and defense to offense, made them play positions they had never played, then switched them back. He created a "Black Power Defense"—eleven African Americans on the field at once—that he said would help solve the nation's racial ills. The problem was that he didn't have enough African American players on defense to fill out the lineup, so he switched African American players on offense to defense for this one game. The Black Power Defense died a quiet death. The racial ills remained.

Every day was an adventure. What next?

He would come off the practice field in the afternoon and pour himself a good belt of premium scotch as soon as he reached his office. He had the radio turned to WJIB, easy listening, all the time. He drummed his fingers against the desk. Smoked the Kent cigarettes. Drank the scotch. Challenged the sportswriters who appeared in front of him. The press conferences would last an hour, sometimes two. They seemed sometimes to be the biggest parts of his day.

"What are you, Fact or Flair?" he would ask a new arrival.

(I had never thought about this. What was I?)

"Flair," I had to say. "But I only use facts."

Patriots management convinced him to spend some time at Massachusetts General Hospital in the off-season for "fatigue and gastritis." He missed the draft, but was back for the preseason and seemed more in control . . . but then the regular season began and the strangeness was worse than ever.

The Patriots won the opener over the Miami Dolphins, 27–14, then went into a spiral of losing. Five losses in a row left Rush in an agitated state. He appeared at a midweek press conference at a restaurant in Dedham where he said his assistant coaches would be replaced by local sportswriters. He read a list of the jobs for different writers. (I was the coach in charge of offensive formations, dog psychology, and waiver procedures and league rules.) He left without taking questions.

On Sunday, he felt "dizzy" before the game against the Buffalo Bills at Harvard Stadium. The team doctor and Billy Sullivan encouraged him to stay in his room at the Ramada Inn, where the team dressed for games. He stayed for a half, listening to the action on the radio, but walked across the parking lots and appeared on the sidelines for the final thirty minutes of a 45–10 blowout loss.

On Monday, he met with Billy Sullivan and other officials at his home in Wellesley. They encouraged him to take a "medical leave of absence." On Tuesday at the team's Curry College training site in Milton, the Patriots announced that medical leave of absence. An hour later, Rush appeared at his office at the college and said the Patriots were wrong. He said he had resigned and never would coach the team again. He was holding a small dog as he said this and asked Ron Hobson of the *Quincy Patriot Ledger* to hold the dog for a moment. Hobson did, and Rush immediately tried to take a punch at WCVB sportscaster Clark Booth.

That was the bizarre finish to his bizarre Patriots career.

Six years later, he surfaced as the coach of the Division III football team at the United States Merchant Marine Academy in Kings Point, New York. Despite a 6-1 record, he was fired before the final two games of the season. The strangeness had returned. No details were announced, but the night he was fired he called my house again, for the first time since he left Boston. I was not home. It was as if time had not moved.

"Who's your lawyer?" he asked my wife. "You better get one."

He never called again. On August 22, 1980, he died of a heart attack at the age of forty-nine.

LEIGH MONTVILLE served as an award-winning reporter and columnist with the *Boston Globe* for twenty-one years before joining *Sports Illustrated* and then authoring many books, among them *The Center of Two Worlds*, *At the Altar of Speed*, *The Mysterious Montague*, *The Big Bam*, *Ted Williams*, and *Sting Like a Bee: Muhammad Ali vs. the United States of America, 1966–1971*. A native of New Haven, Connecticut, he lives in Massachusetts.

CHAPTER FOUR

1970–1975

WHEN YOU'RE HAVING MORE THAN ONE . . .

The next few months and seasons unfolded as an extended replay of the early years of the franchise. They encompassed not only the failed promises of what they had been, had almost been, or could have been, but also the excruciating failure the team seemed destined to experience forever. Fires had already taken place—floods and just about everything else short of pestilence would soon follow at a dizzying rate.

Schaefer Stadium

Practically lost in a snowstorm, New England Patriots quarterback Jim Plunkett looks to his bench for help during a game against the Baltimore Colts at Memorial Stadium in Baltimore on December 16, 1973. The Patriots closed a 5-9 season with an 18-13 loss.

Yet, in a funny way that is peculiar to sports, to be what they are today they had to be what they were then. After ten years of existence, the Patriots joined the NFL at the very bottom, as if they were an expansion team starting almost from scratch. They were easily the worst team in football and had the worst front office, the worst place to play, some not very good players mixed in with a few not so bad, and a coach just a phone call away from being put in a straitjacket. Sometimes being losers makes a team beloved, like the early New York Mets. Sometimes it just makes them, well, the Patriots.

Joining the NFL helped—at least financially, for the imprimatur of the league significantly raised the team's net worth—but it created many more problems in the only ways that really mattered to fans. Winning became a lot harder—and winning a championship harder still.

That, however, was the least of the Patriots' worries. Before the start of the 1970 season, Sullivan had his hands full. In a sense, it didn't even matter what

the Patriots did in 1970. Just making it to the opening kickoff required something close to a miracle. In the off-season, vultures had been circling: Seattle, Memphis, Birmingham, Jacksonville, Montreal, and Tampa all put out the welcome mat, most with ready-made stadiums sitting empty on Sundays, and most offering the Patriots—which meant the board of directors—all sorts of financial incentives in the form of free rent and tax breaks.

It kept coming back to the stadium issue, or rather, the lack-of-a-stadium issue. The Patriots didn't have one big enough to suit the NFL, which demanded that every team have a facility of close to 50,000 seats. For years other AFL teams had bemoaned Boston's paltry gate, which hurt the visiting teams' split. Now a host of cities that had a big stadium but no team hoped to pull the Patriots out of Boston and land in the NFL. Ten years of effort had sort of built a team, but it hadn't built that stadium.

The Greater Boston Stadium Authority led by Billy Sullivan had been utterly ineffective. That wasn't entirely his fault at this point, as the authorizing legislation required that a stadium be built within city limits, include a dome, and be agreeable to the Red Sox—oh yeah, and let's build a new Boston Garden while we're at it and by the way the state won't guarantee any of the bonds. This being Boston, building a stadium also meant satisfying a long line of politicians and cronies, all of whom wanted something out of the deal, preferably in cash, and then getting state government to agree with the Boston City Council, though what was good for Boston was rarely good for the rest of the state, and vice versa. Add the fact that most of the available land in Boston was built on fill, which made building anything cost twice as much.

Sullivan became Charlie Brown and the stadium the football, with local and state government sharing the role of playing Lucy as the state liked what the city did not, and what the city wanted the state hated. Everywhere else, local governments were falling all over themselves to build ballparks and stadiums. Not in Boston. Greed on both the local and state sides and a dose of "good government" that didn't buy the specious argument that sports

The Patriots played their first official NFL game, an exhibition contest at Boston College Alumni Stadium versus the Washington Redskins on August 8, 1970, against the backdrop of a fire that started at a hot dog stand and quickly spread before being contained.

facilities were good civic investments brought the issue to an impasse. In the end, the answer came at a cost less than had been spent on a decade of planning and the stadium models that ended up stored in Billy Sullivan's attic. Joining the NFL set an end date on the whole scam. It was no longer "if you build it they will come," but "if you don't build it they will go."

Sullivan had to lower his sights. As much as he wanted to be the scion of a super-duper facility with all the bells and whistles and perks, if he either lost the Patriots to another city or became a nobody in another town, well, those options were even worse.

The last straw came in March 1970: a final scheme to build a stadium in Neponset fell apart when the state said "yes" and the Boston City Council voted "no."

"As far as I'm concerned," said Sullivan, "this eliminates Boston as a home for the Patriots." The NFL thought otherwise, preferring the devil they knew—Sullivan, who in classic form had ingratiated himself with the powers that be—to one they did not. They gave him five more weeks to throw a Hail Mary before delivering last rites.

Twenty-five miles south of Boston in Foxborough, Massachusetts, the harness track originally known as the Bay State Raceway (later the New England Harness Raceway, Foxboro Raceway, and Foxboro Park) was struggling. Owned by theater impresario E. M. Loew and operated by Pres Hobson, a former sportswriter and the father of sportswriter Ron Hobson of the *Quincy Patriot Ledger*, the facility included parking and enough raw land to support a stadium. Loew donated the property—well, he was paid $1—in exchange for partial parking rights, and the town fathers of Foxborough cut a sweet deal that pleased local taxpayers.

On a map, it made sense. The site was within reach of New England's three largest cities—Boston, Worcester, and Providence—which combined were home to six million people within a fifty-mile radius. But it was serviced by only one road, four-lane US Route 1, and no other supporting government-financed infrastructure whatsoever to help with that, and no nearby public transportation. In effect, by forcing fans north of Boston to either negotiate their way through the city or take a circuitous way around it, locating the team to the south cut off nearly half the fan base.

Sullivan and investors from the local financial community—such as the Investment Bankers Association, the John Hancock Mutual Life Insurance Company, the First National Bank of Boston, the State Street Trust Company, and other New England institutions—created the Stadium Realty Trust to finance the initial $6.1 million construction cost, a plan that allowed tax-free private investment as long as 90 percent of income was returned to shareholders.

The result, a frugal no-frills facility designed by Robert M. Berg Associates Inc., was "no milestone in architecture," as engineer David Berg put it. Essentially, the stadium was a scooped-out hole in the ground, with a surrounding embankment created with the excavated dirt and fitted out with the most basic of concrete stands, requiring virtually no supporting structure. The list of what it did not have—including luxury boxes, sufficient administrative offices, a professional-grade locker room, a roof, or a modern press box—was longer than the list of what it had: 5,604 aluminum chair seats 19 inches wide and seating for another 55,363 fans on nearly 16 miles of aluminum bleachers (allotting each fan 18 inches of space). The field was low-maintenance Poly-Turf, made of polypropylene, a failed successor to Astro-Turf that turned slick in the heat and became matted. Installed over a thin pad atop asphalt, it was no longer even manufactured by 1973. Whatever.

The cost per seat of the new stadium was about $100. Stadiums elsewhere, such as in Cincinnati or Pittsburgh, were being built for between $25 million and $50 million at a cost of between $500 and $1,000 per seat. The Foxborough plan was so basic that it was more like building an enormous banked and tiered freeway interchange. The construction unions even designated it a "highway," since so little of the construction had anything to do with a building. The Patriots would get what they paid for.

Now they just had to build it. Promised that the Pats would be gone in a year, Harvard reluctantly agreed to allow them one final season in Harvard Stadium.

• • •

With the merger of the two leagues into a twenty-six-team NFL, the bar of success suddenly got a lot higher.

To retain traditional rivalries, instead of mixing the two leagues into equitable sets of divisions on roughly

Joe Kapp arrived in Boston in 1970 amid much fanfare following a stint in Minnesota that saw him lead the Vikings to the last-ever NFL championship and a berth in the Super Bowl, where his team lost to the AFL champion Kansas City Chiefs.

geographical lines, the league chose to more or less retain the AFL-NFL split through two conferences, the American Football Conference and the National Football Conference. Each was further divided into three divisions—East, Central, and West. For balance, three NFL teams, the Browns, the Steelers, and the Baltimore Colts, were moved into the AFC. The Colts were one of the best teams in football, the Browns were an established contender, and under Chuck Noll the rapidly improving Steelers were about to become a dynasty. In this new NFL, conference championships would become a consolation prize in pursuit of the only title that now mattered, the Super Bowl. It was a dramatic shift from 1969, when an AFL championship still meant something, particularly after the Jets' Super Bowl victory and Kansas City's dispatching of the Vikings the following year in Super Bowl IV.

This was not good news for Boston football fans. Now, instead of being the worst in the ten-team AFL, they were the worst in a twenty-six-team league, and certainly the worst of the thirteen teams in the AFC. The Patriots were also put in the five-team AFC East, a

placement dictating that the first-season schedule would include two games each against the four other division members (Miami, Baltimore, the New York Jets, and the Bills), three games against other teams in the AFC (the Super Bowl championship defenders, the Chiefs, as well as the Chargers and the eventual division-winning Bengals), and three games against NFC teams (the Vikings, Cardinals, and Giants, all playoff contenders).

The Patriots didn't have a chance. Half their opponents had either made the playoffs or just missed them.

Perhaps nothing was as evocative of the era as an incident in the 1970 home opener versus Miami at Harvard. Just before the game, two starting defensive backs refused to sign new contracts. Instead of exercising the reserve clause in their previous contracts, which required them to play another year at a 10 percent pay cut, Rush deactivated the men, leaving the Patriots' roster short.

A few days earlier, free-spirit backup running back and special teams player Bob Gladieux, nicknamed "Harpo" because of his Marx Brothers mop of unruly curly hair, had been cut. When the Patriots comped Gladieux a couple of tickets to the game, he and a pal spent the night on the town, then showed up at the stadium about an hour before kickoff still feeling the effects. As his buddy went to get some breakfast beer and hot dogs at the interminably long concession line, someone on the Patriots' staff remembered that Gladieux might be in the stands.

He was asked over the stadium PA system to report to the Patriots bench. He dashed down from the stands, signed a contract, got stuffed into a uniform, and minutes later was sent out with the kickoff team. Gladieux's friend returned, found an empty seat, and assumed Gladieux had become impatient and gone off to get his own beer. Then he watched the opening kickoff, saw Dolphins return man Jake Scott being taken down, heard the PA announce, "Tackle by Gladieux," and nearly choked on his red hot. The Patriots somehow won the opener, but soon found a new level to sink to. Reeling in midseason, the Patriots, as they did time after time in this era, tried a flea flicker.

Vikings quarterback Joe Kapp was determined to test the legality of the NFL's reserve clause. He had played out his option in 1970, led Minnesota to the Super Bowl, and now expected to cash in. The charismatic

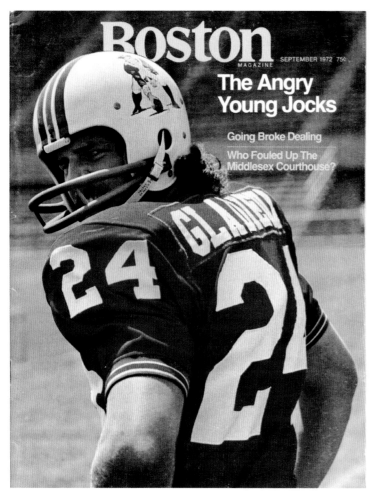

Multipurpose back Bob "Harpo" Gladieux, shown here on the cover of *Boston* magazine, will forever be remembered as the player called from the stands at Harvard Stadium and signed to a contract that allowed him to play in a game to which he'd arrived as a ticket-holder on September 20, 1970.

Kapp, a self-described "Chicano" who favored tequila and was a master of fluttering passes that somehow found their mark, should have found a market. But NFL owners looked askance at anyone trying to rock the boat, and Kapp's move was a threat to the status quo. What if everybody played out their option and became a free agent? What might that do to salaries? Kapp, who wanted $1 million for five years, received no offers.

But the losing Patriots had nothing left to lose, and in a panic move, they signed Kapp for the richest contract in NFL history, worth $600,000. Actually, it wasn't even a contract but a "memo of agreement,"

because Kapp balked at signing the standard player contract. Nevertheless, Commissioner Pete Rozelle chose to enforce the so-called Rozelle Rule, by which the commissioner could require the signing team to compensate the player's former team. Rozelle sent New England's number-one draft picks to the Minnesota Vikings. This rule, first instituted in 1962, effectively countered the "free" part of free agency. Since teams couldn't anticipate the potential compensation, they usually chose not to sign free agents at all. But in this instance, the Patriots were so desperate that they handed Kapp the keys to an offense that he didn't know and that was already sputtering.

"When will I be ready to play?" responded the brash Kapp to a question from the press. "When the time comes."

That time never came. He debuted in the second half on October 11 in relief of a terrible Taliaferro versus Kansas City, completed two of eleven passes, and was sacked twice in what McDonough called the "worst offensive performance in team history." Factoring in what they lost in sacks, the Pats netted 29 yards trying to pass. It didn't get much better in the following weeks.

In November, the erratic Clive Rush fell completely apart and was placed on a merciful "leave of absence" and replaced by assistant John Mazur. It didn't matter at that point.

• • •

Kapp finished the year alive, but with only three TD passes and 17 interceptions—a grand accomplishment after absorbing 27 sacks in 11 games. The Boston Patriots tumbled to their worst record to date, 2-12. In a season-ending 45–7 drubbing by Cincinnati, Mazur apologized for having so many "quitters" on the team and called it "the most putrid football game I've ever seen." By then, the Patriots might as well have made Billy Sullivan coach.

Ah, but they finally had a stadium—and owing to their dismal record, the number-one pick in the NFL draft. Up appeared to be the only remaining path.

With the new stadium came wholesale changes in the organization. First, the stadium got a new name. The stadium stock sale was lagging behind, threatening the whole deal as the deadline for construction to begin approached in September 1970. Sullivan was forced to hit up his New York board members for $500,000 cash and was still short when the F. & M. Schaefer Brewing Company kicked in the balance of $150,000 in exchange for naming rights. "Schaefer Stadium" became the first such brand-name facility in modern American sports history. The company, whose motto was "the one beer to have when you have more than one," would certainly get their money's worth.

Then, on February 18, 1971, Sullivan made a surprise announcement: the board had chosen to drop "Boston" from the name of the team, which would become the "Bay State" Patriots, a change he insisted had nothing to do with Boston's failure to support a stadium. "Nobody was mad at the City Council," he said, a statement absolutely no one believed. "Most of us thought 'Bay State Patriots' had a nice ring to it," he added, explaining that the name would have more appeal in New England (and it also helped E. M. Loew with the branding of the struggling Bay State Raceway).

The old PR man overlooked one thing. Just as "the Patriots" had sometimes been shortened to "the Pats"—or in times of duress "the Patsies"—the Bay State Patriots was a headline-maker's dream: "the BS Patriots" was a name wholly appropriate to their stature, recent level of play, and inept front office. Sullivan didn't notice, or pretended not to, but NFL commissioner Pete Rozelle did. Within days came an order to come up with another name, so on March 22, 1971, the BS Patriots became the New England Patriots.

Still, the team had made money in 1970, and as the 1971 season approached, fans responded to the affordable season-ticket plans and the surprisingly good sight lines touted in the press. Before the 1971 season even started, the club had sold nearly 50,000 season tickets, instantly vaulting them into the upper echelon of league earners. Now all they needed was a team.

The Patriots' front office, a mix of holdovers from Rush's tenure, was in flux. Before the 1971 season

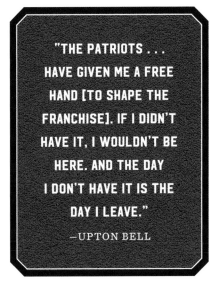

"THE PATRIOTS . . . HAVE GIVEN ME A FREE HAND [TO SHAPE THE FRANCHISE]. IF I DIDN'T HAVE IT, I WOULDN'T BE HERE. AND THE DAY I DON'T HAVE IT IS THE DAY I LEAVE."

—UPTON BELL

started, it was already going down the drain. Mazur, by default, had been named coach for the 1971 season, and soon after the draft George Sauer would be let go, the team having rapidly soured on him. Baltimore personnel director Upton Bell, son of former commissioner Bert Bell and credited with making the Colts a contender, was then named Patriots GM at thirty-three years old, the youngest in the game and the next shiny bauble to catch Sullivan's eye. The Patriots, he said at the time, "have given me a free hand" to shape the franchise. "If I didn't have it, I wouldn't be here. And the day I don't have it is the day I leave." The Patriots promised a new look, but the only problem was that they did not agree internally on what that new look should be. The "free hand" Bell was promised meant the other one was usually tied behind his back. As Bell wrote later, "The Patriots didn't have any idea what winning required."

At least they had a quarterback, and maybe even two. In addition to Kapp, with the number-one pick of the draft the Patriots now had the opportunity to add Stanford quarterback Jim Plunkett, fresh off a Rose Bowl victory over Ohio State. A player whom UCLA coach Tommy Prothro called "the best pro quarterback prospect I've ever seen," Plunkett was a sturdy six-three and 220 pounds, a classic pocket passer blessed with arm strength and precision. He was also tough. His Mexican American and Native American mother, Carmen, was blind from birth, and his father also went blind, owing to a progressive disease, so Plunkett was forced to grow up fast. What he achieved, he earned. Most teams considered him a franchise quarterback.

So did the Patriots, but Plunkett wasn't the only franchise quarterback entering the draft. Archie Manning of Ole Miss and Dan Pastorini of Santa Clara were rated just as high, a boatload of NFL teams with aging quarterbacks were desperate to hand the ball off to someone new, and the draft included a host of other intriguing quarterback prospects, such as Notre Dame's Joe Theismann, Kansas

State's Lynn Dickey, and Augustana's Ken Anderson. All six would eventually go on to long and successful NFL careers and lead their teams into the postseason. That left the Patriots with a decision: draft Plunkett or trade the pick for players and draft another quarterback.

The final decision basically came down to John Mazur. But everybody had his ear. Some wanted to draft Plunkett and trade Kapp. Others wanted to draft Plunkett and keep Kapp so the Stanford QB could learn the pro trade, a consideration that had not been shown to Pittsburgh's Terry Bradshaw, another "can't miss" quarterback who had suffered mightily with the Steelers in 1970. But with the abundance of choices available, others advocated trading the pick and reaping the benefits, reasoning that the Patriots would still end up with a top

quarterback with a later pick. Almost every team in the NFL was making an offer, most dangling their own number-one pick and anywhere from three to four solid starters, including Pro Bowlers like Baltimore's John Mackey. An influx of talent would go a long way toward making the club respectable and might make Joe Kapp Joe Kapp again, while giving a rookie time to grow.

The plan to bring Plunkett along slowly depended on Kapp, but the Pats management didn't understand that Kapp's allegiance was tenuous at best. More interested in testing the legality of the NFL contract system than in continuing to play quarterback, he refused to sign the standard NFL contract. He showed up at camp, had his picture taken, then walked out, choosing to take his battle to the courts.

(*left to right*) **Patriots president Billy Sullivan, Stadium Realty Trust president Philip David Fine, and Schaefer Brewing Company vice president Bill Schaefer examine a model of Schaefer Stadium in January 1971.**

Still, the shiny bauble had Sullivan's eye, and Mazur's as well. The Patriots probably made the worst decision possible, overlooking all evidence that indicated any rookie quarterback could turn a team as bad as the Patriots into anything. Instead, on January 28, 1971, they chose to draft Plunkett and "build a team around him." The pick satisfied fans and drove even more to buy season tickets, but in the long run drafting Plunkett was merely the latest in a series of mistakes.

The New England Patriots opened Schaefer Stadium on August 15 versus the still-popular New York Giants in a game that should have marked the rosy dawn of a new era. Instead, it provided more proof that the more things changed the more they stayed the same. The utter inadequacy of Schaefer Stadium was thoroughly exposed.

Longtime *Globe* columnist Harold Kaese's experience in getting to the game, scheduled for an 8:30 PM kickoff, was duplicated by thousands. After attending that afternoon's Red Sox game, he left Neponset Circle for Foxborough, a jaunt of only twenty-five miles. By 6:45, he was at Route 128, but by the time he reached I-95 at 7:07, traffic had come to a full stop. It took nearly another hour to crawl a mile to the Wrentham exit. By 8:12, he was still two and a half miles from the stadium and cars weren't moving. Some just pulled onto the median strip, parked, and started to walk like a flood of refugees. Other cars overheated or ran out of gas, turning the highways into parking lots. Kids were crying, fathers were cursing and slurring their words, and local residents were trying to defend their property from fans crossing their yards looking for shortcuts or just a place to pee. Kickoff time came and went, and Kaese was still stuck in traffic with thousands of fans.

At 9:15, according to Kaese, as he sat in his car, "a man passed pushing another in a wheelchair," and the columnist, who thought he'd seen it all in more than three decades in sports journalism, gave up. If a guy in a wheelchair was making more progress than he was in an automobile . . . "It now appears," he wrote later, "that while taxpayers may have been spared millions of dollars subsidizing the Patriots with a stadium, they will still be clipped millions of dollars to build access roads to this remote mecca." That would eventually prove true.

Building the Patriots' football stadium in Foxborough, Massachusetts, March 16, 1971, only eighteen weeks before the team's first exhibition game.

State police called it "a traffic holocaust," and one fan sagely noted afterward: "I've never seen anything like this in my life, but seeing as the Boston [*sic*] Patriots are involved, I would definitely believe it." The return home wasn't much better: the same fans who had trudged to the stadium now had to trudge back and find their cars in the dark. As the sun rose the next morning there were still cars stuck in traffic trying to escape.

The players, who fortunately all made it to the game, weren't impressed either. Most had played in better facilities in college. One had to explain to his wife that it wasn't a practice field but where they actually planned to play. The stadium itself and the access to it—or lack thereof—would eventually be cited by future players as a reason *not* to sign with the Patriots, or to request a trade, further hamstringing a team that was already hamstrung.

The experience of attending the inaugural game led many a Patriot fan on a decade-long bender: one would later describe it as something "like serving on an Atlantic fishing boat: lots of ups and downs, plenty of wet weather and not a lot of excitement." And that wasn't even the worst part. Sometime in the first quarter, as those who'd had many "more than one"—or had arrived at the game already five or six beers ahead—started heading to the restrooms. The toilets backed up everywhere, causing flooding several inches deep. By game's end, people were relieving themselves wherever they could—in storage rooms, in the concourses, or just up against some wall.

The cause? Well, over time any number of explanations have been offered for the cascades of sewage, including lack of consistent water pressure, the low-lying location, inadequately sized outlet pipes to the stadium's treatment plant, financial cost-cutting, even sabotage by the plumbers' union over a labor issue during construction. And if the flooding wasn't bad enough by itself, the urinals were placed so high that short fans—and kids—either had to stand back and aim up or else be lifted into position.

Foxborough town fathers were so distressed that they told the team they couldn't play there until "the deplorable plumbing conditions" were taken care of. So before the start of the regular season, the team had to spend $35,000 to install three 15,000-cubic-foot pressure tanks, pumps, and new outlet pipes, employing 52 plumbers around the clock to hook it all up. Then came the test, popularly known as "the Great Flush": as the *Herald* reported, 320 of the facility's 643 toilets were all flushed more or less at once by a collection of team personnel, players, volunteers, and even members of the press. This time the toilets worked as they should have (mostly), and the Foxborough board of health gave the team the go-ahead to play, heading off an estimated $1 million loss had the Patriots been forced to cancel their upcoming exhibition game. Plumbing continued to be a problem, however, and over time the club would spend another $500,000 to try to fix it.

The tone was set. During most of the Patriots' tenure at the stadium, the crowds were characterized by their blood-alcohol level. Early arrivals arrived *way* early to avoid the traffic, and then got hammered, while late arrivals took advantage of the interminable traffic jams to load up while stopped on the highway, which often turned Route 1 and surrounding access roads into the world's longest slowly rolling bar. The stadium gained a reputation as one that, well, wasn't the place for someone whose focus was on football. Patriots fans earned a reputation as the rowdiest and most liquid crowd in pro football—or at least east of Oakland, where the Raiders and their fans were adopting a "Wild Bunch" persona. All of it compounded the perception that the Patriots were not just a second-rate franchise but a punch line, a metaphor for ineptitude and failure.

THE NIGHT THE CARBURETORS DIED

UPTON BELL

I t was February 26, 1971. I had arrived at the Sonesta Hotel for my press conference as the general manager of the Bay State Patriots after leaving the Baltimore Colts franchise, which, in my ten years there, had gone to three championship games and two Super Bowls. Now I was coming to lead the worst team in the NFL. Ahh, how the sweet bird of youth blots out the realities of life—especially the harsh realities of the NFL.

The first question came at me from a top football writer for the *Herald Traveler*: "Mr. Bell. Why would somebody from a championship organization come to the worst team in pro football?" What was I going to say? "Because I'm a great architect of football teams"? There was no answer except to say, "The Patriots have a bright future with the drafting of Heisman Trophy QB Jim Plunkett."

In spite of my trepidation, I was thirty-three, so I took the chance. After all, how bad could it be? I soon found out.

Like Alice in Wonderland, I fell down a hole and entered a world of

An aerial view, taken March 24, 1970, of Bay State Raceway in Foxborough, Massachusetts, a possible site for the Patriots' new football stadium.

unbelievable characters and unexplained circumstances. The bizarre became the ordinary, and my first order of business was to change the name of the team from the Bay State Patriots to the New England Patriots.

Now, six months later, it's August 15, 1971, the day of the opening of Schaefer Stadium, with the Patriots facing the New York Giants. After a series of tumultuous events that included the whole team becoming free agents due to a clerical error, QB Joe Kapp refusing to sign a player contract and leaving the team, lineman Phil Olsen escaping his contract, and running back Duane Thomas being traded back to Dallas after only four days at training camp, the witching hour had arrived.

Schaefer Stadium was built in less than a year and looked like it. It

was the Aluminum Wonder of the World, built for less than $7 million in a deal arranged by Stadium Realty Trust. It encountered a number of delays and many unforeseen problems—the plumbing in particular. But the real danger was the traffic that would invade Route 1 off Interstates 95 and 495. Route 1 was not made for the avalanche of cars barreling toward Foxborough on game days.

It was still early as I looked out from the top of the stadium. All I could think of as I watched the traffic crawl down Route 1 was that, unbeknownst to the drivers, they were crossing the River Styx into Dante's Inferno. Only Mel Gibson's Road Warriors could survive the night to come.

During the week preceding the game, I had warned everyone, including the state police, that this

could be a catastrophic situation, but nobody could have anticipated how bad it really got. I thought, as I watched the scene unfold, that I'd come here to build a team, not direct traffic (or flush toilets). Oh well, you can't have it all.

I was looking at a stadium surrounded by half-finished parking lots—some of them containing potholes that hadn't been filled—and beyond the lots a traffic jam, or rather, a traffic monsoon. Add to this a plumbing problem that soon reared its ugly flush—or nonflush—by halftime. I had learned only a few weeks before that the stadium was built at the lowest point in Foxborough. What we learned during the game was that there was not enough pressure to continually flush the toilets. Holy overflow!

Cars continued to pile up on Route 1, with some making it into the parking lots by game time. Many had stalled or run out of gas. Some were on fire. By kickoff, the scene was right out of *The Last Days of Pompeii*. One of the stadium trustees had wrestled away the stadium microphone and announced that a few sightseers had caused what was a little traffic jam. Are you kidding?

We did beat the Giants that night in spite of the toilets not flushing, many people not getting to the game until the third quarter, and cars remaining stuck in the parking lots until 4:00 AM. In fact, if you look closely, there's still a belt of rust where they were parked, forty-seven years later. We

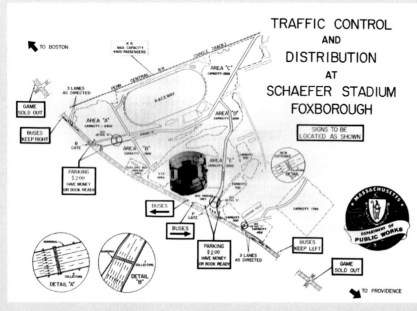

Map of Traffic Control and Distribution at Schaefer Stadium.

Boston Patriots general manager Upton Bell speaks during a press conference in Boston, February 26, 1971.

had created the biggest traffic jam in Massachusetts history.

Following the game, the stadium was closed down by the Foxborough board of health. Night games were changed to day games, and only a successful Great Flush by the media and some of the owners on a Saturday before the next game saved the season and the stadium. NFL Films was there that day and actually recorded the immortal flush for history. Schaefer Stadium reopened, and all was well in Wonderland. Then, less than two years later, I was flushed out by the owners.

Looking back now, I can say, "There was no there there." But like Alice, I had to leave Wonderland sometime.

The son of NFL commissioner BERT BELL, Upton Bell went to work for the Baltimore Colts in 1964, then joined the Patriots as general manager in 1971. Bell was co-owner of the New York Stars and the Charlotte Hornets of the World Football League before embarking on a career as a radio and television broadcaster and commentator for a number of outlets in New England. He is the author of *Present at the Creation: My Life in the NFL and the Rise of America's Game.*

Schaefer Stadium

Note the empty seats just prior to kickoff at the first New England Patriots game at Schaefer Stadium. Thousands of fans were stranded in traffic and didn't make it to the game until after the first half.

When Kapp failed to return, any chance that Plunkett had to learn his trade evaporated, making his selection even more perilous. Mike Taliaferro hung on as a backup, and even though John Mazur tried to bring Plunkett along slowly, the pressure of the season soon took over. In 1971, for the first time ever, a rookie quarterback would take every snap for an NFL team.

Plunkett was drilled, and he would continue to be drilled on almost every play for his entire tenure as Patriots quarterback—partly because of his own inexperience, partly because the Pats were trying to make something out of nothing, partly because he was staying in the pocket too long, and partly because he wasn't very mobile while players in the NFL were bigger and faster than he was accustomed to. But the bulk of the fault lay in the Patriots' mostly porous offensive line, which was more effective blocking for Carl Garrett and Jim Nance than

protecting Plunkett, and the woeful inadequacy of the Patriots' receiving corps. Plunkett's Stanford teammate Randy Vataha emerged as their only threat, catching 51 passes, but no one else caught more than 22. Plunkett, though he managed to throw for 19 TDs and 16 interceptions, topped 200 yards only once.

The rest of the time he spent being pummeled. In that inaugural season, he was sacked 36 times and took another 114 hits, a level of punishment that would stay steady over his first three seasons. And in the NFL, a sack rate above 8 percent and a hit rate above 15 percent are considered poor. In Plunkett's first season, he was sacked nearly 10 percent of the time and knocked to the ground on more than one-third of all other pass plays, meaning that every time he dropped back, there was a fifty-fifty chance he'd end up horizontal. During his time with the Patriots, as Vataha commented to a reporter in 2016, "he just got hammered—I mean hammered brutally." All the hits were made even worse by the unforgiving artificial surfaces in Schaefer Stadium and many other NFL fields.

Little wonder that today Plunkett, despite being comfortable financially, has undergone eighteen surgeries, is in constant pain, and says, "My life now sucks"—largely because of the punishment he received while prematurely playing quarterback for the Patriots during this era. It was then and is now impossible for a last-place team to "build a team around a quarterback," and Plunkett's career is evidence of that. Not until he joined the Raiders and finally got to play for an already solid team would his potential finally be fulfilled. As it was, Patriots fans never had the opportunity to really see what he could do beyond taking a punch.

It didn't help that Coach Mazur and GM Bell looked at the team in radically different ways from the start. Both men wanted to shape the franchise, but that never merged into a coherent Venn diagram. Mazur, who had served as offensive coordinator in Buffalo for seven seasons before joining the Pats, favored a slow approach, work-

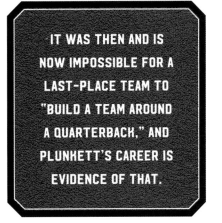

IT WAS THEN AND IS NOW IMPOSSIBLE FOR A LAST-PLACE TEAM TO "BUILD A TEAM AROUND A QUARTERBACK," AND PLUNKETT'S CAREER IS EVIDENCE OF THAT.

ing more with what he had, building on the few talented holdovers—center Jon Morris, linebacker Steve Kiner, and defensive end Julius Adams. The brash Bell, given his genealogy and the fact that he'd already played a part in building two champions in Baltimore, was super-confident; he wanted to shake things up by building up the scouting department and getting younger and stronger players. Bell also was the first member of the front office with real authority who wasn't from Boston: he hadn't come up through the organization or via the Catholic pipeline flowing from Boston College and Notre Dame.

Bell found an organization that was, in his words, "fractured and at war with itself": the board, Sullivan, and the coaches were all pulling in different directions. He also got off to a rough start by failing to send out the standard option letter to the players. That oversight, which he blamed on "my staff," cost the team the services of the previous year's number-one pick, defensive

lineman Phil Olsen. Fortunately, no other players noticed the late contracts as Bell covered his rear by handing out small surprise raises, but it was a bad beginning. His tenure would be marked by conflict.

The Duane Thomas trade epitomized that. In 1970, Thomas had joined the Cowboys and immediately stood out as the best young runner in the league, bumping star Calvin Hill from the starting lineup. After he averaged over five yards a carry and dominated in the playoffs, some were calling him the next Jimmy Brown.

But Thomas had signed a bad deal and then gotten divorced, which left him with almost nothing. He wanted to renegotiate his contract . . . which was something the Cowboys were loath to do in the first place. Moreover, he was of a generation of young black athletes emerging after the activism of the 1960s who were unafraid to speak their mind or to be themselves. This new generation wouldn't behave with the deference NFL overseers expected. Thomas chafed under the Cowboys' country club arrogance, epitomized by Coach Tom Landry, who operated with the efficiency of a corporate CEO. Thomas wanted out, calling Landry a "plastic man, actually no man at all," and team owner Tex Schramm "sick, demented and completely dishonest."

That would not do in Dallas, where Landry was considered a god and the Cowboys were worshiped with evangelical fervor. But Thomas, who had been raised in a poor Dallas neighborhood where inequity was obvious, saw through all the BS and PR. "The problem," he said, "is that I'm black. If I was white, it would be totally different." The Cowboys coaches, he said, treated black players "like animals." There were whispers in Dallas that Thomas was on drugs, that he was a Black Muslim, and when he admitted that he wanted to form a black players' association, local reporters began referring to him as "militant." He'd have been better off saying he wanted to join the KKK.

Boston had its own gifted yet perceived to be problematic running back in Carl Garrett, their most talented halfback since Ron Burton. Garrett, not Nance, was now

What's in a Name? By Vic Johnson

AFTER YOU, ALPHONSE

BUT, MY DEAR GASTON—

CARL IS A PRESTIGIOUS NAME IN BOSTON PRO SPORTS. CARL YASTRZEMSKI AND CARL REGINALD SMITH OF THE RED SOX ARE FIGHTING FOR THE A.L. BAT TITLE

...AND THE PATRIOTS' CARL GARRETT WAS AFL ROOKIE OF THE YEAR LAST SEASON

TOMORROW NIGHT, IN SHREVEPORT, HE GOES AGAINST THE PITTSBURGH STEELERS.

30

GARRETT 30

WITH SENSATIONAL TERRY BRADSHAW HURLING FOR THE STEELERS AND GARRETT THRUSTING FOR THE PATS...

...THE GAME COULD BE A SORT OF SPEAR VERSUS RAPIER DUEL.

The pride of New Mexico Highlands, running back Carl "Road Runner" Garrett was AFL Rookie of the Year in 1969 and led the Patriots in rushing yardage in 1971, their first season at Schaefer Stadium.

the Pats go-to rusher, but he was also prone to speaking out about the way black players were treated. Although Mazur provided a long leash, when Garrett showed up late or missed the occasional practice, the organization wondered if his production was worth the headache.

On July 31, the Cowboys and Pats exchanged their perceived problems. Bell sent Garrett and a first-round pick to Dallas for Thomas and two throw-ins.

In an understatement, it was not a good match. Mazur didn't want Thomas, and Bell felt that there

was real animus between some of Mazur's coaches and Boston's black players. Thomas spent all of about a day and a half as a full-fledged Patriot, most of it arguing with Mazur over the coach's insistence that he use a three-point stance. In a matter of minutes, Mazur kicked him out of his first practice, then told Bell to "get him the hell out of here," later adding, "I'm coaching a team, not a mob." Sullivan backed his coach. The team announced that Thomas refused to take a blood and urine test to complete his physical, which the press interpreted as confirmation that Thomas was on drugs. Upton Bell would later claim it was all untrue, that Thomas was never asked, though he told the press otherwise at the time. In the end, the league bailed everyone out when Rozelle convinced both parties to rescind the trade. Houston Antwine might have come closest to identifying the issue when he said, "We got too many flower children coming into the game looking for their Utopia . . . this isn't any kind of Utopia." It was the NFL, where the power balance has always been heavily tilted toward white management, then and now, no matter what.

Still, the Pats managed to go 6-8 in 1971, beneficiaries of a somewhat more favorable schedule than the year before. In fact, they scored several big upsets, including wins over the Dolphins, the Raiders, and, in the final game of the season, the Colts. They dumped the reigning world champs 21–17 in the season finale. According to some, it also ruined Bell's day. Had the Pats lost, he might have been able to fire Mazur, but at this point Bell already assumed that Sullivan had taken that authority back. A few days later, the coach received a one-year extension.

But if there was truly a season highlight, it came at the very start, when Gino Cappelletti retired on August 31, just before the start of the regular season. "I'd have to say," noted Cappelletti, after Charlie Gogolak beat him out for the kicking position, "the decision to retire is not all voluntary." He hadn't been a regular receiver since 1967 and hadn't caught a pass since 1969. "The luster of the game diminished when I had to give up receiving," he said. "Just kicking the ball isn't football." He then provided the best summation of his illustrious career: "I didn't have the burning speed. All I could do is get open and catch the ball."

That he did, 292 times, good enough to score 42 touchdowns and a total of 1,130 points, 872 with his right foot, and lead the AFL five times in scoring.

The 1972 season brought no relief for New England, and no further clarity over who was in charge. Bell wanted to dump Mazur again after the Pats went 1-4 in the preseason. Mazur coached as if looking over his shoulder, and the GM-coach split even affected the players—the veterans who knew Mazur, on one side, and those brought in by Bell, on the other. By midseason, the Pats were reeling. Week after week, Plunkett was being driven to the turf again and again, and his play suffered. For a time he was pulled, replaced by Yale's Brian Dowling; that gave him respite from the boo-birds, who'd begun blaming Plunkett for everything. But there was a reason Dowling hadn't been drafted until the eleventh round and then was cut before joining the Patriots. Still, he was no worse than Plunkett, who would wind up throwing for only eight touchdowns while finding himself flat on his back another 156 times over the course of the season.

The Pats went down like a dirigible in Miami's Orange Bowl on November 12. The Dolphins were on their way to an undefeated season, and the deflated Patriots were no match. The final score was 52–0. The next day, with five games left in the season, the board finally agreed with Bell. Mazur offered his resignation, and the Patriots accepted it.

In most such instances, an assistant would have taken over, but the obvious choice, Sam Rutigliano, had no desire for the position, saying, "That's not a job, it's a sentence."

Only the Patriots could have come up with the solution they chose. Instead of hiring a true replacement, the Pats hired San Diego personnel director and former Green Bay coach Phil Bengtson as a temporary coach and charged him only with "evaluating" the roster. After Carl Garrett skipped a practice a few weeks later and was suspended by the organization, Garrett appealed and Rozelle rescinded the suspension.

By now, the board was determined to wrest back control, embark on yet another fresh start, and clean house. Bell was let go, and Billy Sullivan was named to head a search committee to find a man to lead the franchise, both on the field and in the front office, a miracle

Quarterback Jim Plunkett is greeted by wide receiver Ron Sellers (34) and team PR executive Wally Carew following his first-ever regular-season NFL game, a 20–6 victory over the Oakland Raiders. The new stadium in Foxborough would both open and close with memorable wins over Oakland.

worker who could heal the organizational fractures, curry favor with Sullivan, build a winner, and be all things to all people. In the meantime, the Patriots finished the season 3-11, last again.

With Plunkett still on the roster, the smart choice probably would have been to select a coach who would finally try to build a team around him, starting with a strong offensive line and creating a passing game that could take advantage of his strength.

But Billy Sullivan—er, the Patriots—were ever occupied with the shiniest available object, which had already led them first to Rush, then to Kapp, Plunkett, Thomas, and Bell, all of whom had quickly lost their sheen in Foxborough. It also would have made sense to look to pro football for the solution, but that's not the way Sullivan's mind worked. Sullivan realized now that no one knew one assistant coach from another, that there was little PR benefit in hiring a name no one recognized. But big-name college coaches, well, *everyone* knew who they were.

Over a six-week period, during which he later estimated he sought advice from some forty coaches, including old partner Frank Leahy, Sullivan went down the list of current college coaching geniuses, starting with Penn State's Joe Paterno, USC's John McKay, and Nebraska's Bob Devaney. All were successful, and all were certain, more or less, to receive a welcome reception in Boston and Foxborough, at least initially.

But none of them wanted the job. For most, it was a step down every way but financially. Columnist Ray Fitzgerald summed it up when he wrote a tongue-in-cheek column treating the position like a want ad, writing: "Here are the pluses. Well, never mind, here are the minuses: We have no offense . . . we have no defense . . . and everyone says bad things about us, [but] the toilets are working." And that was just the perception in Boston.

Sullivan's offer to Paterno would have made the coach a millionaire, and McKay and Devaney would also have been handsomely compensated. Paterno initially accepted, famously telling his wife she was going to bed that night with a millionaire, only to have second thoughts and back out the next morning, while McKay and Devaney kicked the tires and withdrew on their own. Joining a dysfunctional organization at its nadir wasn't exactly a dream job.

Surprisingly, however, Oklahoma coach Chuck Fairbanks, whom Frank Leahy happened to recommend and whose team had just shut out Penn State in the Sugar Bowl, said yes.

In many ways he was a strange choice, for despite his success in college after taking over at Oklahoma in 1967, Fairbanks's personal coaching background was on the defensive side of the ball. Not that Oklahoma couldn't score: they put up 399 points in 1971 while shredding some of the best college defenses in the country. But they had done so using the wishbone formation, a run-first offense inappropriate for pro football. Oklahoma passed only ten or fifteen times a game. They were successful when they did, but most of the time a pass was for show.

Yet at the same time, Fairbanks, age forty-two and energetic, was extremely detail-oriented and innovative on defense. Bill Belichick still credits Fairbanks with creating the basic defense used today by most professional teams: "Some of the things he brought to the Patriots and the league in the seventies were things that stood the test of time and have been a big principle of this league for many, many years . . . such as the 3-4 defense, the way he organized the draft, personnel meetings, things like that." Those were all things the Patriots desperately needed. And in terms of personality, Fairbanks was not unlike Belichick. He

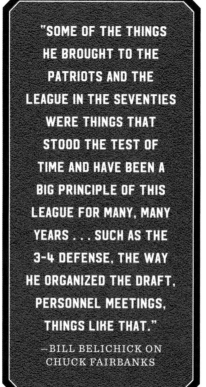

"SOME OF THE THINGS HE BROUGHT TO THE PATRIOTS AND THE LEAGUE IN THE SEVENTIES WERE THINGS THAT STOOD THE TEST OF TIME AND HAVE BEEN A BIG PRINCIPLE OF THIS LEAGUE FOR MANY, MANY YEARS . . . SUCH AS THE 3-4 DEFENSE, THE WAY HE ORGANIZED THE DRAFT, PERSONNEL MEETINGS, THINGS LIKE THAT."

—BILL BELICHICK ON CHUCK FAIRBANKS

talked only football, focused mostly on the task at hand, and, being unconcerned with social graces, managed to keep himself out of the crosshairs of the media in Boston, where sports talk radio was in its bawling infancy.

Fairbanks needed the Patriots at that point too. The NCAA was nipping at his heels over various infractions, including using players with falsified transcripts. Although Fairbanks pled ignorance, as head coach he was in the bull's-eye. He was also still under contract to Oklahoma, which he sort of failed to mention—the university only allowed him to leave because they thought it might help them escape punishment from the NCAA. Hoping to avoid the situation that had developed between Bell and Mazur, Fairbanks was officially named both head coach *and* GM on January 26, 1973, just before the draft.

He immediately proved his worth, or at least the value of having a consolidated authority in place. Fairbanks knew college personnel as well as anyone in the game, and with three first-round picks, the Patriots were in a position to help themselves for the first time in a long time . . . if they didn't screw up like they had so many times in the past.

This time, they didn't. In the first round, Fairbanks and player personnel director Bucko Kilroy were in agreement that Plunkett needed help, and they provided it, starting with Alabama offensive guard John Hannah with the fourth pick of the draft, then adding USC running back Sam Cunningham and wide receiver Darryl Stingley from Purdue. And in the fourteenth round, Fairbanks grabbed undersized defensive lineman Ray "Sugar Bear" Hamilton, who had played for him in Oklahoma and was overlooked by everyone else.

Had Fairbanks simply walked away after his initial draft, he still would have made a bigger impact on the franchise than any other Patriots coach in history to that point, save perhaps Mike Holovak. His astute eye continued to pay off in the off-season. He, Kilroy, and assistant GM Peter Hadhazy, who did all the administrative work Fairbanks despised, spoke as one. The Patriots scooped up the cream of the players who didn't make the cut with the teams that drafted them, such as tackle Leon Gray, and Fairbanks also hired a stable of competent coaches. His top three offensive assistants, Ron Erhardt, Sam Rutigliano, and Red Miller, would all

go on to head-coaching jobs in the NFL. Now at least the offense seemed to have a chance.

"My job is like that of any corporate leader," he said, leading columnist Leigh Montville to dub him a "football businessman." After the histrionics of the past few seasons, the players responded to a coach who was focused only on football. "He's the best thing that's ever happened to this place," said one player anonymously. "Never has this place been organized like this." Under Fairbanks, the Patriots would finally become a legitimate NFL team.

The NFL was maturing into a big business. By now, it had long since decided to share revenue among all its members. Staffs were expanding, scouting was becoming more organized, the influx of a more wide-open style of play was making the game more exciting, offenses and defenses were becoming more complex, and the expansion of color television and broadcasting innovations like instant replay were making the game ever more attractive to fans.

Of course, the Patriots' board of directors continued to be a mess, but under Fairbanks that didn't seem to matter quite as much, at least for a while. While Sullivan had been away looking for a head coach, New York board members Wetenhall and McConnell consolidated power by courting the ambitious new members of the board (up to sixteen members, as stock had been split among heirs) and ousting team president Sullivan, whom they blamed for all the fine messes of the past few seasons. They reasoned that, as the primary investors with the most at stake financially, they should control the direction of the franchise, not someone like Sullivan, who stayed afloat by indebtedness. Bob Marr, son of Daniel Marr Sr., one of the Pats' original owners, and brother of Dan Jr., also a member of the board, became the new team president. Sullivan bitterly accepted the new reality, agreeing to step down without a battle after being promised he'd eventually be named chairman of the board, essentially a ceremonial title. But remember, in Sullivan's world you were either for him or against him. He bided his time and plotted his return.

The Patriots were better in 1973, but their 5-9 record masked the fact that they went only 1-7 in their own division, they began the season 2-7, and those five wins came against teams that collectively won only 15

Running back "Mini" Mack Herron enjoyed a breakout season in 1974 while besting Sam Cunningham for the team lead in rushing yards with 824. His engaging personality endeared him to fans.

through the end of the season, the Patriots went through an astounding 168 players as Fairbanks and company threw everything they could up against the wall, hoping something, anything, would stick.

Entering the 1974 season, however, the NFL was worried about far more than the Patriots. The Rozelle Rule and other labor issues had so angered the players that on July 1, 1974, the NFL Players Association (NFLPA) called a strike.

It was one of the best things that could have ever happened to the Patriots.

Although members of the NFL Players Association couldn't practice, the strike didn't affect rookies and free agents, so in the off-season Fairbanks decided to make some changes to his defense. Although the offense was turning around ever so slowly, the Patriots, the worst run-defending team in the league, still had a hard time keeping the other team from scoring. Most teams didn't even feel they needed to pass to beat Boston. The problem was that the Patriots had neither size nor depth up front, nor in the middle, while their linebacking corps, though talented, lacked a true middle linebacker.

Fairbanks decided to go with the team's strengths and instituted the Oklahoma defense, first used by Bud Wilkinson. Instead of the standard 4-3 alignment, the Oklahoma used a 3-4: two defensive linemen and a nose guard, and four linebackers. With the additions of hard-nosed linebackers Steve Nelson and Sam Hunt in the draft, the Pats suddenly had a crew of young and mobile linebackers who were ideal for the new scheme, plus Ray Hamilton, who had played nose guard in college.

While the NFL vets were on strike, the rookies and rejects practiced and played exhibitions, allowing Fairbanks to drill his young charges in a defense little used in the NFL. By the time the strike ended on August 10, as the NFLPA decided to continue its battle against the Rozelle Rule in court, Fairbanks was committed not only to the new defense but to a host of new players. Seventeen new names were on the roster by the time the season finally got under way.

With the rest of the NFL unprepared for the Patriots' new defense, the team was able to jump-start the season, beginning with a 34–24 victory over Miami. In the next four games, the Pats defense only got better,

games, since the Patriots had the easiest schedule in the league. Plunkett rebounded to throw 13 TD passes and even won Player of the Week honors for his performance against Green Bay, but he also threw 17 interceptions and still found the ground 148 times, as Hannah and Gray couldn't block everyone. From the beginning of camp culminating in a 24–0 shellacking of the Jets to run their record to 5-0. Despite the fact that Plunkett was bothered by a balky knee and bad shoulder, the offensive line was finally able to give him some time while Sam Cunningham and Mack Herron—a Canadian Football League star who stood only five-five—provided an inside and outside running game. The offense was surprisingly potent—Herron eventually broke Gale Sayers's NFL single-season record for all-purpose yardage—he would run, receive, and return punts and kickoffs for 2,444 yards.

Unfortunately, the season was still fourteen games long. By midyear, the opposition began to adjust to the Patriots' new scheme, Plunkett's shoulder started acting up, and the club was hit with a rash of injuries. It was like someone turned the water faucet from hot to cold. After starting out 6-1 and looking like they might race into the playoffs, the Patriots lost six of their last seven to end the season 7-7. It was hard to tell if they were a good team that just ran out of steam or an overperformer that just got lucky.

One thing was certain, however. Jim Plunkett and Chuck Fairbanks just didn't see eye to eye. Or at least Plunkett didn't—Fairbanks's problem was that he just didn't notice much at all apart from the X's and O's. Plunkett was an employee, and CEOs didn't mingle with the workers.

Fairbanks was not a people person, and Plunkett needed reassurance and confidence-building, particularly when the team was losing, which was often. When he didn't get it, he thought the worst. And when, in 1974, Fairbanks brought in Jack Mildren, his old wishbone quarterback at Oklahoma who was now an NFL safety, Plunkett thought the worst. He was afraid that Fairbanks might have signed Mildren to try the wishbone, and in fact Fairbanks was considering it. By the end of the year, the shell-shocked Plunkett wanted out, and his agent told the Pats that he planned to play out his contract. A fishing and golfing trip to northern Michigan with the coach that was supposed to clear the air proved disastrous. Both men found that they had nothing to say to the other. As one player observed of Fairbanks, "He's a hard guy to get to know. You don't just sit down and talk with him." Three days of silence in the woods left Plunkett more eager than ever to leave New England.

Still, the Patriots seemed poised to compete in 1975. Another excellent draft landed tight end Russ Francis, linebacker Rod Shoate, and Kansas State quarterback Steve Grogan. The roster continued to be a revolving door as the coach added sixteen new names to the forty-three-man roster.

USC running back Sam Cunningham (*upper right*), the eleventh player selected in the 1973 NFL draft, soon became a folk hero in New England while leading the team in rushing for six of his first seven seasons in New England.

Wide receiver Randy Vataha was drafted out of Stanford and played for the Patriots for six seasons. He led the team in receptions in 1971 and 1975.

But a funny thing happened on the way to the playoffs.

Actually, just about everything happened, little of it positive. During the preseason, starting defensive lineman Arthur Moore was lost for the year with a knee injury, Julius Adams broke his foot, and offensive lineman Tom Neville broke a leg. Fairbanks installed a number of rollout passes before the season that Plunkett, who had already undergone three knee surgeries, was hardly capable of executing. Sure enough, on one such play in

a preseason game against San Diego, defensive end Coy Bacon blindsided Plunkett, separating his shoulder. "Plunkett getting hurt ruined the Patriots," said Buffalo head coach Lou Saban.

Then the Patriots players, some of whom were among the more activist members of the NFLPA, decided to strike.

Protesting the lack of a collective bargaining agreement, and frustrated with both their union and management, the Patriots thought a job action would push both to action. Just a few days before their final exhibition game against the Jets, scheduled for the Yale Bowl, the Patriots voted 39–2 to go on an unauthorized wildcat strike.

Union rep Randy Vataha expected to spark a revolution among other teams, saying, "We're trying to scare both sides into a settlement." But the NFLPA has never been particularly effective or united, and ownership has always been able to use that to their advantage. When no other team voted to support the Pats, they slunk back onto the field, having accomplished very little except thwart any momentum they had built up in the preseason.

Instead of challenging for the playoffs, the team McDonough had called "the best Patriots team in a decade" slid backwards. They started off by losing their first two games under quarterback Neil Graff and rookie Grogan, rushed Plunkett back too early, and then dropped two more. They seemed to right the ship when they won three of four, but along the way they lost Plunkett again—this time on an option, another play the offense had no business using with him in the game. The pin holding his shoulder together popped loose and had to be surgically reset.

It only got worse. Mack Herron held a party for teammate Leon Gray on a Friday, two nights before a game, and Boston television and radio stations reported that drugs had been present. The Patriots' front office, already dissatisfied with Herron's dwindling production in 1975 and grumbling over his contract, used the party as an excuse to ax him. After Herron was waived to Atlanta, the Pats stumbled through the final six games of the season, losing all six as Fairbanks vacillated between Plunkett, hurt and running an offense ill-suited to him while being booed unmercifully, and Grogan, who showed flashes of brilliance and ran with abandon, earning the cheers of the fans, but who was simply not ready. The "best Patriots team in a decade" finished 3-11.

But never fear: Billy Sullivan had made his comeback. He had spent his exile courting George Sargent's widow, Hessie, and her stake in the team, which, if she sold to him, would be just enough to put him back in charge. The only hang-up was the price, $112 a share, and the fact that according to team bylaws she'd have to make the same offer to McConnell and Wetenhall, who had the right of first refusal. Sullivan could once again be the man atop the Patriots franchise, but it would cost him $8 million, money he did not have.

That never stopped Sullivan, who hadn't had the money that put him atop the franchise the first time either. His oldest son, Chuck, now a New York attorney, was able to arrange financing for the amount of $10 million, enough

for Sullivan to not only gain majority control and abolish the board but to buy out the 2,500 public stockholders as well. He was in debt to the top of his balding head, but the Patriots, and their stadium, were now his and only his. "I had this thing lock stock and barrel for $25,000," said Sullivan in a bit of revisionist history, for although he had paid the initial franchise fee, he had never actually "owned" the team, except in his own estimation. "I ended up investing $10 million to buy back 75 percent of what I once totally owned. That's how smart I am."

If Billy thought that deal was smart, he outdid himself with what he came up with next. As future events would show, borrowing that $10 million would hardly be the last of his "smart" and terrible business decisions. But for now the New England Patriots, at long last, were the BS (Billy Sullivan) Patriots.

1976–1980

THE LONG GOOD-BYE

"Back then," remembered linebacker Steve Nelson, "the AFC was so much stronger than the NFC, with Pittsburgh, Miami, and the Raiders, and we beat them all." Said quarterback Steve Grogan, "If we'd won in Oakland, we had the perfect scenario. Pittsburgh was beaten up, and Minnesota never beat anyone in the Super Bowl. Coulda, shoulda, woulda."

IT'S AN ARTICLE OF FAITH AMONG PATRIOTS FANS of a certain age that the 1976 Patriots were a Super Bowl team, a powerhouse denied their destiny as a world champion by a conspiracy of the gods, a dynasty unfulfilled. There was already a long tradition of this kind of remote culpability in Boston sports history, particularly in regard to the Red Sox, whose fans always blamed one villain or another for their failure, from Harry Frazee to Johnny Pesky, Denny Galehouse, and Darrell Johnson. The end result is never viewed as just the loss of a game but as a universal affront, leaving an open wound to be touched over and over again in an unending tape loop that exposes a moral failure and traps the fans in a pitiful citywide wallow, feeling persecuted forever.

Within the next few years, Boston would experience several more such moments—Mike Torrez's pitch to

Head coach Chuck Fairbanks arrived in Foxborough in 1973 with a sterling college coaching résumé and a no-nonsense approach that quickly made a young, talented squad into championship contenders.

Bucky Dent that cost the Red Sox a win over the Yankees in the 1978 AL East playoff, and the infamous "too many men on the ice" call against Don Cherry's Bruins in the 1979 Stanley Cup semifinal between Boston and the Montreal Canadiens.

In 1976, that culpability would primarily take the form of NFL referee Ben Dreith, whose controversial "roughing the passer" call against Ray Hamilton was deemed the singular event that turned glory into infamy, a win to a loss, and ruined the Patriots for a decade. The roughing call would fall neatly on this continuum, extracting defeat from certain victory, as would the ugly divorce between Fairbanks and Billy Sullivan a few years later. The upshot was that, for the first few decades of their existence, Patriots fans rarely viewed themselves with much sense of pride. Oh, there were a hard-core few who stuck with the team regardless of what happened and wore every loss on their sleeve, but the rest were only along for the ride and jumped on and off the bandwagon according to the team's record, displaying little loyalty. In the larger Boston sports universe, before the 1976 season the Patriots had yet to really matter.

This sense of indignant righteousness among the most faithful is both true and not true. In fact, there is much more to the story of both the 1976 Patriots and the Patriots of this era. That they *could* have become Super Bowl champions once, if not twice, is legitimate, if far-fetched. That they *should* have won a Super Bowl if not for the interdiction of the universe is a far more complicated claim. "Coulda, should, woulda," indeed.

It began with the decision to trade Jim Plunkett—or rather, with whether Plunkett would decide to force a trade or sign a long-term contract, and with whether the Patriots would decide to let him go and rebuild or see what he could do if they finally gave him enough tools to work with. The protracted process that resulted—much like the decision whether to draft him in the first place—exposed the lingering uncertainty of the entire organization.

At the end of the 1975 season, with Plunkett's existing contract due to expire in May, the Patriots had to either re-sign the quarterback to an exorbitant contract or face the possibility that he would decide to play out his option in 1976 and then leave anyway, in which case their return on their investment would be minimal. Despite his injuries, and despite the punishment he endured as a Patriot, what in Boston were viewed as Plunkett's liabilities—a lack of mobility and his allegedly "mechanical" style of play (one observer described his style as "he liked to throw it up as long and as far as he could")—were not seen that way elsewhere. Plenty of NFL coaches saw Plunkett's failures as more organizational than personal. If he could just get healthy . . . well, they still believed Plunkett was the guy the Patriots first drafted, someone who could one day lead a team to a championship.

Plunkett himself had never been enamored of New England. He was a West Coast guy, and his desire to return to California was only reinforced by his devotion to his parents. While capable of taking care of themselves, they were still a point of worry.

The presence and performance of Steve Grogan were factors as well. The fifth-round draft pick had been selected primarily to serve as a backup. At Kansas State, he'd been known as a running quarterback, albeit one who, at six-four, possessed a strong arm that thrilled NFL scouts and reeked of potential. Grogan, went the thinking, was worth taking a chance on, a player who might one day develop into something more.

Going into the 1975 draft, the philosophy of selecting the best available athlete and Fairbanks's ability to spot them had already landed the Patriots tight end Russ Francis with their number-one pick, despite the fact that Francis, a free spirit, had sat out his senior year at Oregon after a coaching change. He'd dropped off everybody's radar, but before the draft Fairbanks sent assistant coach Red Miller out looking for him. Miller found Francis on a ranch, worked him out, and clocked him running a 4.6 forty-yard dash barefoot in the snow on a gravel driveway. At six-six and 220 pounds, he was an extraordinary athlete, a champion javelin thrower, a decathlete, and a close friend of collegiate running legend Steve Prefontaine. "If you were to pick a prototype tight end," said Fairbanks, "Russ Francis would be perfect."

Fairbanks also landed them Grogan, who despite throwing only 12 TDs and 26 interceptions in college in an option offense, could run and punt and had led both his high school track team and basketball team to state titles. Fairbanks had scouted him since high school, and

despite his dismal passing numbers as a college senior while he battled a neck injury, two separate scouting combines had rated him the top quarterback prospect in college football. When backup Dick Shiner retired and Neil Graff failed to perform, Grogan fell into the backup role behind Plunkett. Although unpolished as a passer and, in Fairbanks's words, "greener than a gourd," Grogan was far more adept at the rollout style of offense Fairbanks favored. The pro game of the mid-1970s was still run-first, and the thinking was that Grogan would grow into the position.

When Plunkett was hurt in 1975, Grogan received the opportunity to prove it faster than anyone had thought, and Pats fans, accustomed to seeing Plunkett on his back, responded to Grogan's daring runs. The wake of a 3-11 season made it possible for the Patriots to take a chance.

In April, they finally decided to trade Plunkett. Fairbanks reasoned: "He could bring the most in return, and we didn't have a good team. And the only reason I could make that trade was because we had drafted Grogan."

Denver and Los Angeles offered veterans, but the San Francisco 49ers offered the future. They first reached an agreement on a contract with Plunkett and then pulled the trigger, giving up two number-one picks in 1976, another number-one pick and a second-round pick in 1977, and backup QB Tom Owen. Five seasons after drafting Plunkett number one, the Patriots finally received what they might have had if they had chosen to trade the pick in the first place.

All of a sudden, the Patriots owned four of the first thirty-four picks in the 1976 draft. Fairbanks chose wisely, adding Arizona State cornerback Mike Haynes, Colorado center Pete Brock, Ohio State safety Tim Fox, and running back Ike Forte from Arkansas, shoring up the Patriots on both sides of the line.

Haynes, the best DB in college football, was also adept as a return man. The Patriots' defensive backfield, which for years had been a weakness, had become a strength.

So had the offensive line. With Plunkett, they'd been forced into pass protection, rarely the strong suit for an offensive lineman coming out of college. But with

Grogan under center, the Patriots became a run-first offense, which played to the strengths of linemen John Hannah and Leon Gray. And when they did pass, Grogan had the mobility to make pursuers miss, hit receivers on the run, or turn a broken play into positive yardage.

With the nation in the throes of the bicentennial celebration, there was optimism surrounding the Patriots, from the stands, the press, and the front office. Fairbanks told his club that for the first time since he had taken over, they had a "competent man" at every position. But in the opener against Baltimore, Grogan played like a guy drafted in the fifth round, tossing four interceptions as the Patriots lost. But then at home, the Patriots surprised the Dolphins as Grogan rebounded. A week later, they played the defending Super Bowl champion Steelers, who thus far had battled a championship hangover, losing to Oakland and struggling against Cleveland.

Although the headache continued against the Patriots as the Steelers fumbled six times in the first half, they still led, 13–9, as Grogan was terrible. But in the second half he threw for more than 200 yards, and the Patriots jumped ahead, 30–20, then hung on as a last-second field goal went wide to give New England a 30–27 win and all the confidence in the world. It carried over a week later versus Oakland at home as the Patriots steamrolled the previously undefeated Raiders 48–17. At 3-1, the Patriots were the surprise of the league—and the toughest part of their schedule was already behind them.

But neither the team nor Grogan was a finished product yet, as they fell to lowly 1-3 Detroit 30–10 after Grogan was intercepted five times. The loss proved costly: from that point on, the Patriots won every game they should have—often handily—but lost the one big game they needed, a road rematch versus divisional opponent Miami, losing 10–3 to finish the regular season 11-3. As a result, they made the playoffs only as a wild-card team, the fourth seed in the AFC, because the Colts' interdivision record of 7-1 bettered New England's 6-2 mark. Had they defeated either Detroit or Miami, the Patriots would have won the title outright and secured the home field for the first game of the playoffs. Playing on the road would prove costly.

Still, it was the Patriots' first winning season since 1966, and one of the most remarkable turnarounds in

league history. Along the way, they set forty-three team records, running the ball with abandon for 2,957 yards and averaging five yards a carry as Sam Cunningham took care of the inside, Andy Johnson picked through holes wide, and backup Don Calhoun led the team in average yards per carry. The defense collected 50 turnovers, Haynes intercepting eight passes himself and scoring two TDs on punt returns.

Yet Grogan received much of the credit. He earned most of it, playing with confidence and running, as Dan Jenkins of *Sports Illustrated* put it, "like a white tail buck" when he had to, setting an NFL record for a quarterback with 12 rushing TDs. In a sense, Fairbanks's use of Grogan as a primary runner was the offensive equivalent of using the 3-4 Oklahoma defense, a college strategy for which professional football was not prepared.

Yet underneath the numbers there should have been some caution. The Patriots were very good, but they were not yet a great team. They were young and undisciplined; one of the most penalized teams in the league, they took on 200 yards more in penalties than the opposition. And while Grogan proved adept at throwing the ball downfield—Stingley finally seemed to be delivering on his promise, averaging 21 yards a catch and scoring four TDs—he got Stingley the ball only 17 times and still threw 20 interceptions along with 18 touchdowns. Andy Johnson and Sam Cunningham led the team in receptions, with 29 and 27, but in the last half of the season Grogan averaged less than 100 yards passing per game. Of course, they were running the ball against the league's bottom feeders and didn't need to pass very much, but still . . .

The Patriots headed into the postseason knowing they'd be playing on the road, where they had barely outscored the opposition. Moreover, after a slow start, the Steelers had closed with a rush, winning their last nine. Oakland, after falling to the Patriots, had gone 10-0 to finish 13-1 and were salivating at taking another shot at New England. Winning a playoff game, much less reaching the Super Bowl and winning that, was anything but a sure thing for the Patriots.

Except in New England. In and around Boston, the fans and the press were drunk with success, lifetime teetotalers who had finally tasted liquor and decided they

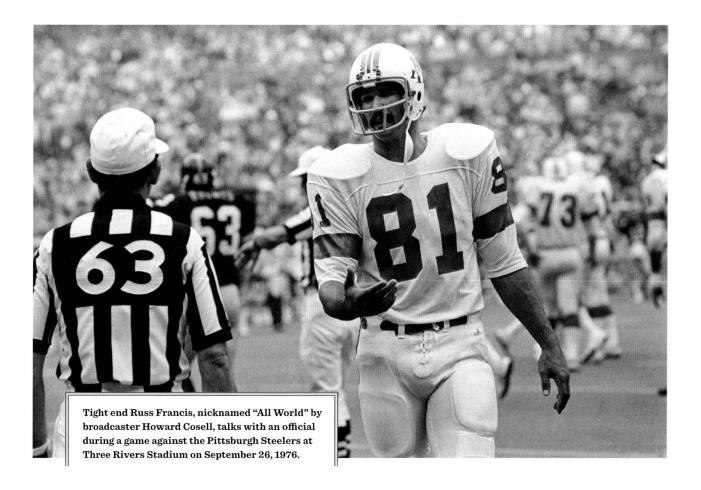

Tight end Russ Francis, nicknamed "All World" by broadcaster Howard Cosell, talks with an official during a game against the Pittsburgh Steelers at Three Rivers Stadium on September 26, 1976.

liked it. A lot. After all, they'd already beaten the Raiders 48–17. How hard would it be to beat them again?

Hard. And playing in Oakland? Very hard. There is a reason, after all, that the home field is valuable, and in 1976 it was even more so. The Raiders hated playing on artificial turf, and the field in Schaefer Stadium was widely thought to be the worst in the league. In Oakland, they played on grass.

In Las Vegas, the wiseguys installed the Raiders as six-point favorites. They not only had the home field but were healthier. Only Oakland cornerback and return man Neal Colzie, recovering from an ankle sprain, was less than 100 percent. Meanwhile, Patriots linebacker Steve Nelson would play for the first time in five weeks after dislocating his kneecap in Baltimore, Russ Francis was bothered by a bad hamstring and had caught only one pass in the previous month, and Sam Cunningham, who missed three games after bruising his right shoulder, also

against the Colts, had reinjured it against Tampa Bay in the regular-season finale. Don Calhoun was a more than adequate backup, but there was a reason Cunningham was the starter and, at $200,000 annually, the highest-paid player on the team. Before the game, he described his shoulder as "really sore," and there was some speculation he would not play at all. But Fairbanks was unbothered by the injuries, saying, "If they can walk, they'll play." Still, Cunningham and Francis were two of the Patriots' top three receivers. New England wasn't exactly limping into the game, but they weren't sprinting either.

And then there was the field. It had been a dry fall in Oakland, at least everywhere but the turf at Oakland Alameda County Coliseum, which was resodded after the baseball season and required extensive watering. Knowing the Patriots depended on the running game, Coliseum staff were particularly conscientious. By game time, the grass was long and lush and the field soft enough to slow New England's vaunted running attack. By game's end, the surface would be littered with chunks of soft turf.

The Patriots took the opening kickoff but failed to move the ball and had to punt, giving the Raiders good field position. Although Oakland stalled, Ray Guy's punt pinned the Patriots deep in their own end. New England responded with an 86-yard drive for a score, the key plays a remarkable 48-yard, one-handed grab of a Grogan pass by Francis and a 24-yard third-down pass to Stingley. The touchdown came on a one-yard run up the middle by

Andy Johnson, perhaps a sign that Cunningham's shoulder wasn't quite right. And Grogan wasn't running with his usual abandon either, as the Patriots seemed to realize their chances of going deep in the playoffs would go nowhere if he went down. Oakland came back to notch a field goal, and the two teams played to a standoff for much of the rest of the first half.

Late in the second quarter came a play that has been long overlooked in New England but may have been more important than any other. With just under three

Along with Leon Gray, the trio of Bob Cryder, John Hannah, and Pete Brock helped form one of the best offensive lines of the 1970s and early '80s.

minutes remaining, on second-and-6 on the Raider 36, almost within field goal range and with the Raiders on their heels, instead of driving the ball down their throats and potentially entering the half ahead 14–3, Fairbanks chose to get cute. He called a trick play, one the Patriots hadn't tried all year: an end-around pass featuring Russ Francis throwing the ball for the first time in his pro career, one of only two passes he would ever attempt.

Oakland was not fooled, and Stingley was covered by two men. As the *Globe*'s Bob Ryan noted the next day, Francis "should have put his head down and made it back to the line." But he didn't, probably because Oakland DB George Atkinson had already broken Francis's nose with a forearm smash, a noncall but still a dirty play. Atkinson used to say, "Football isn't a contact sport, it's a collision sport," and that was the reason the Raiders played the way they did—intimidation was effective. According to the rules at the time, forearms, spearing, and helmet-to-helmet contact were all legal. It's just that no other team had ever made them such an overt part of their arsenal before. The Raiders did.

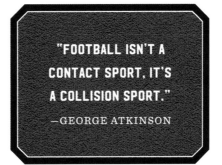

"FOOTBALL ISN'T A CONTACT SPORT, IT'S A COLLISION SPORT."
—GEORGE ATKINSON

Francis proved that his prowess with a javelin didn't extend to the pigskin. He threw off his back foot and got too much air under the ball. Oakland's Skip Thomas intercepted at the 6, returning the ball to the 24.

With only 2:27 left in the half, there was no quarterback in football better at running the two-minute drill than Oakland's Ken Stabler, who never seemed to panic. He needed barely half that time as Fred Biletnikoff snagged a 31-yard touchdown pass, outleaping New England's Bob Howard for the ball at the goal line and rendering both a "face mask" penalty and a "pass interference" call moot. Instead of leading 10–3 or 14–3, as they should have, the Pats now trailed 10–7. Of course, most Patriots fans today have no idea all this took place— neither a film or video broadcast remains available, and the papers the next day made little mention of this key turnaround.

It had been a bruising first half, and a heavily penalized one, particularly in the second period, which featured eleven infractions. Leonard Koppett of the *New York Times* observed that "the frequency and timing . . . made any real football continuity impossible." But so far, the two teams had played to a near standoff, the Patriots running effectively, Grogan maintaining his composure in the first playoff game of his career, and the Raiders, with Stabler, patiently able to move the ball downfield when they needed to. Only one thing seemed certain: this would be no repeat of the 48–17 blowout earlier in the season.

Then came the third quarter. During the Patriots' final drive of the first half, they'd been penalized five times. This period they would receive the benefit of the officials' flags. On their first drive of the second half, the Patriots were forced to punt, only to be saved by a holding call and given a first down. A few plays later, Grogan made it pay off when he hit Russ Francis over the middle on the 19 and the tight end rumbled in for a 26-yard score.

The Raiders failed to move the ball, going three and out, and the Patriots got it back at the 45. This time three Oakland penalties—including an offsides call on a punting down—helped New England to a first down at the 20. For all the complaints the Patriots and their fans would later level over the officiating, of the eleven penalties called on the Raiders that day, an NFL-playoff-record seven resulted in New England first downs. Neither team was happy—Raiders coach John Madden spent half the game stalking the officials down the sidelines and screaming his displeasure.

This time there was no trick play, and no penalties. Don Calhoun and Jess Phillips ran the ball on the next four plays, and Phillips finally punched it in up the middle from the 3. With a bit more than a quarter remaining, New England led 21–10 and seemed to be in control. If they could stop Stabler once more and then move the ball on the ground at all, Oakland seemed likely to run out of time.

But they called Stabler "the Snake," a nickname he had earned in high school for his ability to squirm out of trouble, and the Patriots let him slink away. With the game apparently in hand, New England's defense suddenly turned soft. Given both time and space, Stabler took full advantage, expertly moving the ball downfield, working sideline to sideline, completing all five passes he threw in an 11-play, 70-yard drive that ended when Mark van Eeghen scored from the 1 to make the score 21–17.

The Patriots got the ball back with 10:54 remaining and wisely stuck to the ground, burning almost four minutes off the clock before being forced to punt, pinning Oakland deep. This time the New England defense held firm and forced the Raiders to punt from their own end zone. The ball rolled out of bounds at the Oakland 48. Only 6:24 remained to play.

The goalpost had been moved back to the end line four years earlier, so the Patriots needed to get close to the 30-yard line to even think about a field goal, but either way, Oakland needed a touchdown. Keeping the ball was more important to New England. And with Oakland certain to be grabbing for the ball, no team in football seemed better prepared for this moment than the Patriots. It was football at its most basic: run the ball down Oakland's throat, stay in bounds, and work time off the clock. Either a touchdown or a string of first downs would put the game away.

Grogan first ran for 10 yards, and then Cunningham went up the middle for two. On second-and-8, Grogan handed the ball to Cunningham once more. He rumbled to the left behind Hannah and Gray, found some space, and turned upfield, looking for the down marker.

They called Cunningham "Sam Bam" for a reason. He should have lowered his shoulder, stayed in bounds, and smashed forward. But running to the left exposed his sore right shoulder to contact. He'd probably been reinjured earlier in the game—remember, Calhoun had already taken over for Cunningham on the first-half scoring drive.

Cunningham didn't stay in bounds and plow ahead. Appearing to eye the marker, he stepped out of bounds at the 28-yard line before taking a full hit, stopping the clock.

What really happened has been debated ever since. John Hannah has always claimed the official was holding the yard marker in the wrong spot, leading Cunningham to misjudge how much yardage he needed for a first down. Others believe Cunningham was short regardless and actually received a generous spot. Either way, the Patriots were a few inches short of a first down.

So what? The Raiders were known for their defense, but primarily because of their linebackers and defensive backfield. Their defensive front, while strong against the rush, wasn't imposing in a short-yardage situation. And the Patriots had Hannah and Gray. If those two couldn't make enough room to gain a few inches, no one could—Fairbanks had every option in the world: Cunningham, Johnson, Calhoun, or even Grogan on a quarterback keeper. After all, they needed only a few inches. And if they were still short? Well, the odds still favored New England. Fairbanks could go for it on fourth down, punt, and pin the Raiders deep in their own territory or call on kicker John Smith. Forty-five yards was near the outer limit of his range, but he'd made field goals from that distance before.

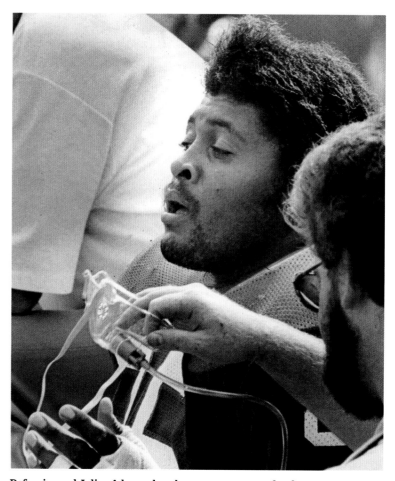

Defensive end Julius Adams played seventeen seasons for the Patriots, from 1971 to 1987, and is remembered for his uncanny ability to block field goal attempts, which he did on three occasions.

Fairbanks sent the play call in from the sideline: a run by Sam Cunningham, behind Hannah and Gray, with Jess Phillips as the lead blocker. But in the huddle, Grogan out-thought himself. All year long, the Patriots had generally snapped the ball on the first count. This time, hoping to draw the Raiders offsides, or at least give the Patriots' line the element of surprise, he called for the hike on three.

He bent under center and called out the snap, but after the first "hut" nobody moved—at least not on the Raider side of the ball. Then Oakland's linebackers started barking.

Finally the Patriots moved, or at least enough of them. Cunningham told the *Herald*, "Pete Brock moved and I went on his motion." Chuck Fairbanks said later that Phillips also jumped, and others remember Hannah and Gray flinching. A flag went in the air, and "illegal procedure" was called. The Patriots were pushed back five yards. Years later, Grogan told the *Herald*'s Michael Felger, "I should have known better."

Now it was third-and-5, not from the 28-yard line but the 33. Grogan hadn't thrown a pass since the third quarter, and it still made sense to call for a run. Even if they were short, it would burn another 30 or 40 seconds from the game clock, after which they could punt or kick or go for it on fourth down. Instead, he called for a short pass to Russ Francis.

Francis broke from the line, and Raider linebacker Phil Villapiano closed on him. The two had been going after each other all day, and in this era officials still allowed a lot of incidental contact between receivers and the defense. Francis tried to push off, ran a few yards downfield, and turned back for the ball. Villapiano was beat, so he held on, pulling Francis's arms down to his sides. Grogan threw, and Francis couldn't reach up to catch it—the ball bounced off his shoulder.

All across New England, potato chips and profanities went flying through the air as Villapiano feigned innocence, jumping around with, Will McDonough later wrote, "his arms outspread . . . saying 'not me,' like a kid caught with his hands in a cookie jar." The Patriots started screaming at the officials, who looked at each other. The down marker flipped from "3" to "4." No flag was thrown, although it appeared that Francis, even if

he had made the catch, might still have been short of a first down. The play was one reason the NFL would add another official in the off-season—it had taken place in a dead zone where authority for the call was uncertain. Each official had thought someone else was responsible for throwing the flag.

Now it was fourth down and a long five from the 33. Then came another fateful decision.

A 45-yard kick was pushing it for John Smith, but a 50-yarder was his absolute limit—the longest successful kick of his career had been 49 yards, and for the year he had only been seven of fourteen past the 40. Besides, the value of a field goal at the time was limited. Even if the Patriots missed, Oakland needed a touchdown. All a field goal would guarantee was a tie game if Oakland did score, forcing the Pats into a sudden-death situation on the road. There was no two-point conversion in the NFL—that had disappeared with the merger.

And if Smith missed . . . well, three years before, the NFL had adopted a rule change. Before then, missed field goals had been touchbacks, with the opposition taking over at the 20. But in a move to encourage offense, the opposition now took possession at the line of scrimmage. And who had pushed for that change? Oakland owner Al Davis. If Smith missed, the Raiders would be only 67 yards away from a winning score.

Were the Patriots to gamble, the smart play might have been to go for it on fourth down. Even if that failed, they'd have pushed the ball a few yards downfield and run some precious seconds off the clock. Or why not bring in punter Mike Patrick and try to pin Oakland back deep in their own territory, forcing them to drive 90 yards or more? The Pats even could have taken a "delay of game" penalty before the kick to run more time off the clock and give Patrick even more field to work with.

Fairbanks, however, chose to go for a field goal. Smith's kick was just short—it would have been good from the 45—but that didn't matter. Cunningham's bad decision, the spot, the penalty, an incomplete pass, and a field goal attempt had burned up precious little time. The Raiders took over with 4:12 still left to play.

Stabler hadn't panicked before, and he didn't panic now. He wasn't worried about the clock. Oakland still had time-outs plus the two-minute warning, and Stabler was

THE BRITISH INVASION

SUPERFOOT AND THE RETURN OF JOHN SMITH TO THE COLONIES

How're the birds there? —*The most commonly asked question among the 1,600 entries for "Superfoot"*

THE REAL-LIFE TALE OF SUPERFOOT COULD BE A GREAT HIDDEN MEL BROOKS SPORTS-THEMED SCRIPT, AND A CINEMATIC ADAPTATION OF THE SAGA OF JOHN SMITH COULD STAR EITHER THE ERUDITE HUGH GRANT OR THE GRITTY "OWS YUR MUM?" ACTION HERO JASON STATHAM—GUY RITCHIE MEETS EALING STUDIOS IN TWO REELS.

Superfoot got its start in 1970 as Boston's legendary trio of radio sports talkers known as "the Sports Huddle" (Eddie Andelman, Jim McCarthy, Mark Witkin) expressed their disgust as yet another Patriot placekicker underperformed in woeful fashion while shanking a chip-shot 14-yard field goal attempt. Always quick with a witty aside or an idea for a wacky promotion, the trio mused on the proliferation of foreign-born soccer-style kickers such as Jan Stenerud, Garo Yepremian, and the Gogolak brothers and wondered aloud why their Patriots couldn't secure the services of the next great foreign kicker.

They soon came up with the idea of hosting field goal kicking tryouts in England, the ancestral home of soccer, with the winner to receive a $1,000 prize and an expense-paid trip to Boston for the chance to try out for the Patriots. They dubbed their contest "Superfoot."

Soon BOAC Airlines, WBZ Radio, the Patriots, and London's *Daily Mirror* tabloid joined forces with the Sports Huddle to promote the contest. The *Mirror*, known for such headlines as "THE BIGGEST CAT IN ENGLAND" and "COP KILLER WAS SMOKING POT FROM AGE OF SIX," was proclaiming "WHO IS SUPERFOOT?" and "WHERE IS SUPERFOOT?" to its

expansive readership.

Thus, the promise of tabloid celebrity and American greenbacks lured some 1,600 would-be field goal kickers from pub and amateur teams across the United Kingdom to a series of tryouts culminating in a final session held at a US Air Force base in Oxfordshire. And true to any underdog script, the stuffy British sports establishment lent the contest even more promotional fuel when the august Football Association—the nation's governing body for soccer—announced that its members, including all of the country's professionals on ninety-two teams, were expressly forbidden from participating.

ON MAY 15, 1971, A WINDY DAY, A TWENTY-TWO-YEAR-OLD BRICKLAYER FROM LANCASHIRE NAMED MIKE WALKER BEAT A FIELD OF SIX OTHER KICKERS IN A COMPETITION THAT INCLUDED MAKING A SERIES OF KICKS FROM 40, 50, AND 55 YARDS.

Six weeks later, he and runner-ups Tug Wilson and Albie Evans were flown to Boston. After a night on the town that included a foray into the notorious "Combat Zone," they were brought to Bay State Raceway, a harness racing track adjacent to the construction site of the Patriots' new stadium. There they practiced

their new craft for the assembled media, then soon made their way to training camp at UMass–Amherst.

Only Walker made a lasting impression. He took a spot on the Patriots' taxi squad (and also moonlighted as a gardener for the new stadium). By the start of the following season, he'd replaced Charlie

Gogolak as the team's field goal, kickoff, and extra point specialist. And on September 24, 1972, in one of his last NFL games, Walker made good on the Sports Huddle's dream by kicking his third extra point of the day to lead the Patriots to a 21–20 upset win over the Atlanta Falcons.

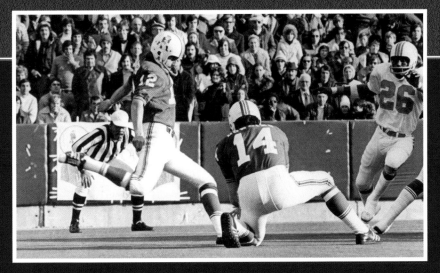

After winning the Superfoot competition, Mike Walker played in eight games for the 1972 Patriots, making two of eight attempted field goals but all fifteen extra points attempted, including a game-winner against Atlanta at Schaefer Stadium on September 24.

Just one of the little victories that serve as the charming and improbable backdrop of today's dynasty.

Less than two months before Mike Walker's winning kick, another Briton, John Smith, a graduate of Southampton University, was coaching soccer at Camp America in Lenox, Massachusetts, while seeking employment as a teacher in the United States.

It was here he had the luck of meeting Cleveland Browns executive Bob Griese (not the quarterback) after Griese's son asked Smith to try kicking an American football for the first time. After lofting several fifty-plus-yard kicks for both Grieses, the former Queens Park Rangers trainee was invited to a series of tryouts that never resulted in an invitation, though his prowess impressed.

After returning to England, Smith was contacted in 1973 by Patriots executive Peter Hadhazy, who invited Smith to a four-day tryout that coincided with the eve of his wedding. Thinking it would make a nice expense-paid vacation, Smith embarked on a trip that opened the door to both a lucrative career and a new home.

Before long, not only was John Smith kicking his first-ever field goal for the Patriots—in a helmetless scrimmage against the Redskins—but he also kicked in the first full game of American football he had ever witnessed, at the Hall of Fame exhibition contest in Canton, Ohio.

Despite making an impressive showing in training camp, Smith was traded in a paper deal with the Steelers that saw his return to Foxborough after he was cut by Pittsburgh and re-signed by the Patriots. He spent the rest of the 1973 season kicking for the minor league New England Colonials and perfecting his skills while attending a variety of regional college games.

English placekicker John Smith was discovered at a soccer camp and quickly learned his trade before joining the team in 1974. He retired in 1983 as the franchise's second-leading scorer, second only to Gino Cappelletti.

BY 1974, HOWEVER, HE'D MADE THE MOST OF HIS ARDUOUS APPRENTICESHIP AND WON A JOB HE'D KEEP FOR TEN SEASONS. AMONG HIS MOST FAMOUS KICKS WAS THE SNOW-BRUSH-ASSISTED BOOT IN 1982 THAT SAW HIS FIELD GOAL ACCOUNT FOR AN EPIC 3-0 HOME WIN OVER THE DOLPHINS. ON HIS RETIREMENT FOLLOWING THE 1983 SEASON, SMITH STOOD SECOND IN PATRIOTS ALL-TIME SCORING TO THE GREAT GINO CAPPELLETTI, WITH 692 POINTS, AND HE CURRENTLY RANKS BEHIND ONLY STEPHEN GOSTKOWSKI, ADAM VINATIERI, AND CAPPELLETTI.

Steve Grogan, shown here sporting a beard, held the Patriots' record for touchdown passes before it was broken by Tom Brady. He also is regarded as one of the NFL's all-time great rushing quarter-backs, having run for 35 career touchdowns.

adept at throwing to the sideline, where Biletnikoff was a ballet dancer. There was plenty of time, and in a perfect world, if the Raiders did score, they'd do so with little or no time left on the clock, leaving New England no chance.

All Patriots fans care to remember took place after Stabler moved the Raiders to the Patriots 21. On second down, he was sacked by Mel Lunsford, bringing up a third-and-18 situation with only 57 seconds remaining.

Stabler went back to pass once more. Nose guard Ray Hamilton stunted, charging around to his right, and beat Oakland guard Gene Upshaw. Stabler looked right and back to his left. Then, as Hamilton closed and Stabler started to throw to halfback Carl Garrett, who was turning toward the goal line on the left side, Sugar Bear launched himself as best he could toward the quarterback, raising his right arm to deflect the pass.

As film clearly shows, he reached Stabler at a 45-degree angle from the front just as the quarterback released the ball. Hamilton missed it, his right hand and forearm striking Stabler at the left temple. The hit wasn't overt or on purpose, but it was obvious he definitely made contact. Hamilton has always claimed that he tipped the ball, but the film says otherwise. At the moment of contact, Stabler's hand is free, and Hamilton's arm is striking Stabler's helmet. The ball sailed from the quarterback's hand, and Hamilton, airborne, collided with Stabler, driving him down and to the right.

As the ball fell short, New England defenders Willie Germany and Dick Conn rode former Patriot Garrett out of bounds, leading Garrett to hold his arms wide, begging for a flag—a call, Koppett of the *Times* noted, that would not have been "unlike some pass interference calls already made" in the game. But the actual flag thrown is all Pats fans recall. From about eight yards away, referee Ben Dreith called Hamilton for roughing the passer, giving the Raiders life—and a first down at the 13.

The Patriots acted as if they'd been mugged, and since that time the play has been draped in all sorts of mythology. Yes, it's true that there was no specific prohibition on striking a quarterback in the head at the time, but roughing calls were made at the discretion of the officials; unlike a punt, whether the ball was tipped or not—and it wasn't—was irrelevant to the call.

Was it roughing? That depends on perspective. A film of the play shot above it and from behind makes the contact appear incidental, while from field-level shots—Dreith's perspective—it's much more violent. At the time the pass was released and Hamilton struck Stabler, the quarterback was completely exposed. In the context of the game, did the hit stand out as particularly violent? No. Was it a legitimate call? Well, according to the rule, the quarterback can't be touched after releasing the ball unless contact is caused by momentum, and Hamilton's momentum clearly sent him into the quarterback. But Hamilton also clubbed Stabler after the ball was released. Was it understandable? In real time, as opposed to parsing a video for forty years, probably.

Whatever. No amount of protest was going to change it. It was yet another call in a game marked by penalties that had both teams howling all day.

The Patriots still led, but had lost their composure, something several of them later admitted. With a first down at the 13, a pass to a wide-open Dave Casper moved the ball to the 7 before Charlie Davis ran it to the 4, bringing up third down. Pete Banaszak dove toward the goal on the next play, but appeared short of a first down. After the officials spotted the ball, safety Prentice McCray moved the ball back, not once, but twice, and a flag was thrown for unsportsmanlike conduct, although reports differ on whether the guilty party was McCray or Hamilton, who was still barking over the call. Now the Raiders had a first down inside the 2, and the Patriots were on their heels.

Madden called for an option rollout to Casper, but Stabler overruled his coach and handed the ball to Banaszak again. He gained nothing. With only ten seconds left, Stabler went with the option, and seven Patriots played tight on the line. Casper couldn't get loose, Upshaw pulled to the left, and Stabler followed him.

Only Mike Haynes followed the flow on the right side. Upshaw sealed him off, and with Steve Nelson closing in from the middle, Stabler saw a path to the end zone and cut back to dive in a split-second before the gap closed.

Ball game. The extra point made it Raiders 24, Patriots 21. (For the record, the Patriots got off one more play after the kickoff, a Hail Mary intercepted by Oakland.)

"Livid" is too weak a word to describe New England's reaction after the game—Steve Nelson took his helmet to the Oakland locker room, while others seethed and screamed, Patriot broadcasters went ballistic, and the *Herald*'s Tim Horgan called the loss "as savage and obscene as the language the Patriots hurled at the officials." The Patriots lost, rightly or wrongly, but they lost. Although the "roughing the passer" call was unquestionably a key moment in that defeat, it was not the determining factor; every comeback takes place through a confluence of factors both accidental and not, and in that, this defeat was no different. If the loss to Detroit or Miami had not cost the Patriots a division title and a home-field first playoff game . . . if Francis had not thrown the interception . . . if Cunningham had not hurt his shoulder . . . if Fairbanks had called for a punt . . . if Grogan had just chosen to have the ball hiked on the first count . . . any of these plays or a dozen more could have changed the outcome. But they didn't. The Raiders would go on to beat first Pittsburgh and then Minnesota to win the Super Bowl.

For the first time in their history, a Patriots loss had really, really hurt. And that was significant, because for the first time in their history the Patriots had finally mattered in New England: they had finally become the equal or near-equal of the Red Sox, Bruins, and Celtics. They were a team that a new generation of fans had come to love and an older generation had seen come from nothing to become something, just like the 1967 Red Sox. The Patriots had at last captured the imagination of the fans in a way they never had before.

Just as Red Sox fans once cloaked themselves in the spurious "Curse of the Bambino" as proof of the world's injustice and an emblem of their pain, so would Patriots fans of certain generations use the name Ben Dreith. Enmity toward the referee became a test of whether someone was a "real" Patriots fan or not. But just as the Curse was used to explain away the later failures of the

BOSTON/NEW ENGLAND PATRIOTS

LESLEY VISSER

Even though I'm the only woman in the Pro Football Hall of Fame, people might be surprised to know that I went to many, many Red Sox games before I ever saw a football game. And the first football game I saw was in Fenway Park! In 1964, my father (who was a WASP from Amsterdam and knew nothing about American football) had somehow gotten tickets to the AFL game between the Patriots and the Oakland Raiders, being held at Fenway. The configuration of the ballpark was strange, laid out left to right to cover the infield. It was Babe Parilli throwing to either Jim Colclough or Larry Garron, then Gino Cappelletti kicking the extra point. The stripped ball would zing through the October air, and we got to see Cotton Davidson and Billy Cannon of the Raiders, along with my favorite, lineman Jim Otto.

It ended in a thrilling 43–43 tie, well before the merger and the endless discussions on overtime. The Boston Patriots, coached by Mike Holovak, wore red jerseys with blue and white stripes around the shoulders. It was well before Robert Kraft made the team the gold standard of the NFL. The bleachers were close to the field at Fenway, only two or three yards away, and I quietly walked down to stand near the end of the bench (my first sideline). I was next to Jim Otto, who seemed bigger than an Aztec statue, and apparently he would remember me. When I was enshrined in Canton (he and Al Davis were there for fellow inductee John Madden), Otto said to me, "You've done pretty well for a freezing little girl on the sideline at Fenway."

I loved the Patriots, even though they weren't easy to follow, moving from Fenway and Boston College to Harvard and even Boston University. By the time I won a Carnegie Foundation grant in 1974—which entitled me to work anywhere as a sportswriter—the Patriots had found a permanent home in Foxborough. Of course I chose the *Boston Globe*, which was considered the best sports section in the country, and they made me the first woman to cover the NFL as a beat. I was sickeningly nervous, but equally proud of the challenge.

My first day on the Patriots' beat, full of anxiety, I brushed my teeth as I drove from my apartment in Brookline Village all the way to the training camp at Bryant College in Rhode Island. I parked my Delta '88 (a huge monster of a car that I shared with my four roommates) in the back of the lot, so everything would be in front of me. The great

Will McDonough had told Billy Sullivan (then the owner of the Patriots) that the *Globe* was going to have a woman covering the team and that was that. Thank you, Will. My first assignments were features on players like future Hall of Famer Mike Haynes and running back "Sam Bam" Cunningham. I played pickup basketball with everyone from Carlo Emilio of the *Springfield Daily News* to tight end Russ Francis—anything to show that I belonged. I watched film with Sugar Bear Hamilton, and I ignored that everyone in the press box smoked, especially cigars.

It was a strange time, the midseventies. The credentials I wore around my neck to the game, printed right there for all to see, said, "NO WOMEN OR CHILDREN IN THE PRESS BOX"—kind of diminishing, no? Also, there were no ladies' rooms. I used to try to time it: when the Patriots had the ball first-and-10 on their own 20, could I get down the press elevator, across the field to the public ladies' room, and then back to the press box before they punted? After the games was just as difficult. Without provisions for equal access (called "Do you go in the locker room?" for everyone else), I used to wait outside in the parking lot, no matter what the weather, for the players to emerge. The worst predicament was when two players from one team came out together, then four from the other team. Where did I go? Whom did I lose? But the stress probably made me a better reporter.

John Madden later told me that I was caught in a "two-way go." I couldn't complain to the Patriots because I didn't want them to say that a woman couldn't cover the team, and I didn't want to complain to the *Boston Globe* for the same reason. So I stood out in the freezing parking lot waiting for the likes of John Hannah or Bert Jones of the Baltimore Colts. The second year I covered the team, Gayle Gardner joined me—she was from WBZ and really knew football. They would put us in the weight room until the players were ready for interviews, which we quickly dubbed the "wait" room because it took at least an hour after a game to get anyone to talk to us.

Of course, it was an awkward time—players and coaches weren't used to us, and we weren't used to them. I think I allowed for this unusual dynamic, so I let a lot of things slide. But I can tell you this:

I was not denied one assignment, in either print or TV, because of despicable behavior, and I covered thirty-five Super Bowls, thirty-five Final Fours, fifteen Wimbledons, and twenty-five US Opens, along with the World Series, the Olympics, the NBA Finals, and even box lacrosse! Okay, back to the Patriots.

I had known Billy Sullivan, a former newspaperman who founded the Boston (now New England) Patriots, for ten years. I went to Boston College with his son Patrick, now a multimillionaire on his own. In 1964, Billy Sullivan helped negotiate a five-year, $30 million television agreement with NBC to ensure the AFL's survival. And when the contract expired, and the AFL merged with the NFL, Sullivan helped get the antitrust exemption from Congress that the NFL enjoys today. He was devoted to his team but finally, for financial reasons, had to sell the team to Victor Kiam, for $83 million, in 1988. (Imagine—a group of us could almost put that together today!)

Sullivan was an optimistic and generous gambler, a founder of the famed Jimmy Fund, and a financier of Foxboro Stadium, which was once even named for him (Sullivan Stadium). He was a storyteller, an Irishman to the core, and fun to be around. His daughter married the mayor of San Francisco, Joseph Alioto, and his son Chuck served at the International Court of Justice in The Hague. The Sullivans were a great family, and Billy Sullivan was a great man.

Covering the Patriots was a blast. We traveled with the team at the time, even ate the same great food (which was a conflict of interest—most teams stopped traveling with the writers soon thereafter). I went fishing once with Abe Gibron, the legendary assistant at Tampa Bay, played the guitar on the beach with Russ Francis, and had too many drinks with Tom Neville. The Patriots treated me like part of the family; that would be unheard of today, but it was standard in 1976. Head coach Chuck Fairbanks, though, was never warm—he played at Michigan State and coached at Oklahoma. He was never a barrel of laughs, and I tried to stay out of his way unless I had to ask him a question. He and I finally hugged in 2010, a few years before he died.

People take the Patriots' greatness for granted now, but the years around 1976 were when they really came of age—before sliding back until the mideighties, when they lost to the Bears in the Super Bowl. Now, of course, they are the team everyone wants to be. In 1976, the Pats jumped off to a 7-3 record, crushing the Jets (yes, for a time the Jets were really tough to beat), 41–7. That game marked a turning point: the Jets had beaten the Patriots in all but two of the previous nineteen meetings. That year, 1976, the Patriots compiled an 8-3 record on the last Sunday of the season by beating the Jets again. Joe Namath was moving the team fairly easily, but quarterback Steve Grogan hit Darryl Stingley for a 14–10 lead and rookie Mike Haynes stalled a Namath drive with an end-zone interception. I'll never forget when a Randy Vataha reception in the fourth quarter took the Patriots to the Jet 6-yard line and Pete Brock—yes, the center!—doubled as a tight end and caught the winning pass. The play looked like early shades of Bill Belichick. It also led the Patriots to the playoffs.

The Patriots were for real. Left guard John Hannah turned out to be New England's Anthony Muñoz, and six-foot-six, 240-pound Hawaiian Russ Francis would yell "Kahuna" at his opponents, most of whom he rumbled over. The Patriots had beaten the Jets twice and the vaunted Oakland Raiders 48–17, and they had an offensive line that would challenge people today: Leon Gray, Hannah, Bill Lenkaitis, Sam Adams, and Bob McKay. The line didn't have a nickname, but they came to play. And because this was the era before zillion-dollar contracts, most of the players had second jobs. Lenkaitis was also a dentist, and he told me once that he couldn't schedule patients until Wednesdays because his fingers hurt too much early in the week.

New England drew a rematch with the Raiders in the playoffs, the AFC Divisional, but this time the game was in Oakland. And it changed both teams. With four minutes left in the game, the Patriots led 21–17 and New England fans were starting to celebrate. But with just a minute left, defensive tackle Sugar Bear Hamilton was called for roughing the passer when he sacked Oakland quarterback Ken Stabler. With ten seconds left, Stabler snaked into the end zone behind legendary guard Gene Upshaw, and the Raiders won, 24–21. No one from New England could believe referee Ben Dreith's call—we were collectively punched in the gut. The Raiders went on to win the Super Bowl, and Patriots fans were bitter for a decade. The "Spirit of '76," the newly installed 3-4 defense, and the unbridled confidence came crashing down.

I always say my career has gone from Jim Nance to Jim Nantz, but that year was the ultimate roller coaster.

LESLEY VISSER was the first woman to cover professional football full-time, as a beat reporter for the *Boston Globe*, before she became a broadcaster. She was the only broadcaster of either gender to work on the network broadcasts of the Final Four, the Super Bowl, the World Series, the NBA Finals, the Triple Crown, the Olympics, the US Open, and the World Figure Skating Championships. The author of *Sometimes You Have to Cross When It Says Don't Walk: A Memoir of Breaking Barriers*, Visser is a native of Quincy, Massachusetts.

Oakland Raider quarterback Ken Stabler (*on ground*) crashed into the end zone for a touchdown in the last seconds to score the winning TD against the New England Patriots in the 1976 AFC championship game. A happy Raider, George Buehler (64), raises his hands in jubilation. The disgusted Patriots are Steve Nelson (57), Pete Barnes (59), Ray Hamilton (71), and Mike Haynes (40).

Red Sox, the focus on this one play would come to obscure the larger reasons for the Patriots' later disappointments. The players bought in as well. Some, such as John Hannah, have since publicly and unequivocally stated that the game was fixed, and many other players never really got over their frustration, the loss becoming a defining stain on their careers. In hindsight, the 1976 Patriots would be seen as better than they ever really were. There is a reason why no team has gone from a record as poor as 3-11 one year to winning the Super Bowl the next. The gap is just too wide to close, the margin for error too slim, the line between very good and great too enormous.

Ever since Fairbanks was hired, Billy Sullivan had been something of an afterthought, the father of the franchise but no longer its face, and as the Pats surged his relative absence had been almost overlooked. Sullivan owned the team outright, but the club was still financially strapped, as Sullivan was heavily leveraged and forced to pay a heavy rate of interest on his loans. At the precise time the Patriots were surging on the field, the organization was pinching pennies. It had been no accident that his absence had coincided with the team's success. The impact of his return would not go unnoticed.

Hannah and Gray both made the Pro Bowl, played just after the Super Bowl. While there, the two Patriots took a measure of grief from members of the Raiders, who bragged not only of their victory but of how well they were treated by Davis and the Raiders. They started comparing salaries, something Gray and Hannah, cowed by the pro football experience, had never even done with each other. The two men were stunned to learn that their annual salaries negotiated with Pete Hadhazy, $38,500 and $40,000, respectively, were less than half of what their peers earned. Hannah realized that his contract, negotiated by an agent as naive as he was, was inadequate.

Now they felt taken advantage of. Hannah and Gray had long been promised that if they made the Pro Bowl, the team would renegotiate their contracts. As Hannah later wrote, "They had misled and used me, played me as a dumb redneck patsy, and undersold my contract by a proverbial country mile." The two players may have been naive, but they were not stupid. Hannah's family hog farm in Alabama—the source of his nickname "Hog"—was actually an agribusiness, Hannah Supply, and worth a small fortune. Gray had earned both an academic and a music scholarship to Jackson State. So in the spring, determined to be paid what they now knew they were worth, the two players signed with uber-agent Howard Slusher, who also represented Cunningham and Haynes.

In May, Slusher wrote the Patriots and said the men wanted to renegotiate. In effect, they were a package. More than a decade before, Los Angeles Dodgers Sandy Koufax and Don Drysdale had used a similar tactic and been handsomely rewarded.

"Renegotiate"? That was a dirty word to Billy Sullivan. He'd already given Fairbanks a new contract. The reported ten-year deal was actually five years at $150,000 annually, but it was still "long enough," as Fairbanks quipped, "to work on my New England accent." Sullivan also responded to Slusher by crying poormouth. "I used everything that belonged to me as collateral [to purchase the team] . . . the days of the Patriots throwing crazy figures around on contracts is over"—an admission that he had been the very one who threw those "crazy figures" at Plunkett and Joe Kapp.

But that had happened when someone else was paying the bills. Now it was a different story. Competition from the World Football League over the last few years had caused salaries to rise, and suddenly Sullivan had a super-talented team that expected to be paid like one.

A police officer confiscates beer in the end-zone stands during halftime of the game played between the New England Patriots and Buffalo at Schaefer Stadium on November 7, 1976.

The only renegotiation he wanted to do was on the terms of the loans he'd taken out to buy the Patriots. Depending on when you asked him, that was costing him either $2,000 or $3,000 a day, just in interest.

The team brushed Slusher off and said they expected the players to honor their existing contracts. Slusher responded by saying the players planned to walk out of camp on September 11, the date of the final exhibition game. The Patriots said they might discuss an extension, but Sullivan said that "under no conditions will I renegotiate." As camp approached he continued to brush the two men off.

Both sides dug in. The smooth machine that had been the surprise of the league a year before started to sputter. Sullivan went on a PR offensive, particularly against Slusher, and Patriots fans, egged on by talk radio, largely took Sullivan's side.

Fairbanks knew he needed Hannah and Gray, and now other players on the team were bitching about their contracts—they'd figured out they were underpaid as well. Fairbanks, still the GM, decided to intercede. With the final preseason game approaching, he met with Hannah, Gray, and their agent for a total of nineteen hours in the days before and immediately after the exhibition. He finally hammered out an agreement—but Sullivan had to sign off.

Uh-oh. Since taking control, Sullivan, with no board to answer to anymore, had consolidated power, turning the team into a family business. His two sons, Chuck and Pat, had been around the team since they were kids—Chuck had ferried players to the Patriots' first training camp and Patrick had been a ball boy.

Now he named son-in law Mike Chamberlain business manager. Chuck, the attorney and financial wizard who had bailed his father out, became team counsel and vice president, while Patrick, who had just graduated from—where else?—Boston College, was named manager of Schaefer Stadium. The sons became their father's closest confidants. It was the Sullivans against the world again.

The three Sullivans thought and acted as one, and no one else could object, at least not out loud, and not for very long. Chuck was reportedly present during Fairbanks's negotiating marathon, but refused to sit in the same room with Slusher.

As soon as the deal was made, Chuck squashed it, with his father and brother in agreement. Billy argued that he had taken all the risk and mortgaged his future to buy the team—he didn't owe the players "a dime"—while the sons were worrying that their family legacy could go bankrupt. What if other players wanted to renegotiate? Where would that leave the Sullivans?

Things had gotten ugly. Billy Sullivan's mother wrote John Hannah's mother and asked how she felt about her son "disgracing" his family, the local press hammered the players, and Billy filed a series of grievances with the NFL's Management Council and Player-Club Relations Committee (PCRC), charging the players with violating the latest collective bargaining agreement.

The players lost, sort of. Following an eight-hour hearing, the PCRC, to no one's surprise, sided with the Patriots. Hannah and Gray were ordered to return to the field and fulfill their contract or be placed on the retired list and get nothing. They had little choice. On October 5, when the Patriots gave a verbal but public guarantee that they would negotiate a contract extension at the end of the 1977 season, the players reluctantly returned.

But the Pats lost more. Against Oakland in the playoffs, all they had lost was a game. In this exchange, Sullivan and the Patriots lost a team. Ever so briefly, the Patriots had been out of Sullivan's shadow and had shone brightly. Now he was blocking out the sun again.

The Patriots had opened the season with a narrow win over Kansas City without Gray and Hannah, then lost two close games to the Browns and Jets. With Hannah and Gray, they bounced back with four straight wins, then lost two critical division games to Buffalo and Miami. They weren't the same team, going from very good to just pretty good. Everyone else got better and they did not. When the Patriots fell to Baltimore in the season finale, they ended the season 9-5 and were out of the playoffs. Moreover, the Sullivans had lost the trust of not only their players but also their coach. Although Fairbanks was under contract, he began looking for a way out. Far from being a martyr, he was looking out for himself. His coaching reputation had been enhanced during his years with the Patriots, and his earning power was at its peak.

On the field, the 1978 Patriots were still everything that everyone thought the 1976 Patriots could be, and the

Chuck Fairbanks's coaching staff in 1978 included four men who either had served or would serve as head coaches in the NFL. It also featured a young assistant named Ernie Adams, who prepared team scouting reports. (*Top row, left to right*) John Polonchek, Hank Bullough, Chuck Fairbanks, Ron Erhardt, Ray Berry; (*bottom row, left to right*) Ernie Adams, Charlie Summer, Tom Yewcic, Jim Ringo, and Fritz Shurmur.

Super Bowl the Patriots thought they should have won two years before could have been theirs. But winning games was no longer the primary priority of the organization. And there's an adage in sports: if you're trying to do anything else other than win, you're going to lose.

With Hannah and Gray back for the entire 1978 season, and with the help of some savvier draft picks such as defensive back Raymond Clayborn, wide receiver Stanley Morgan, tight end Don Hasselback, tackle Bob Cryder, quarterback Matt Cavanaugh, and trades, the Patriots were stronger and deeper than ever that year. Sullivan was even on the precipice of making money. The NFL's new television contract guaranteed him $5 million a year, and TV revenue, for the first time, eclipsed ticket revenue. From this moment on, the NFL is best understood as a television or broadcast league. TV ratings and whatever TV wanted were now far more important factors than the needs of the fans in the stands.

While Grogan still threw too many interceptions, he now appeared to have some dependable deep threats, and the rushing offense was better than ever. The team would eventually run for more than 3,000 yards.

But if there was a sign that 1978 would not go according to plan, it came on August 12 in a preseason game against the Raiders.

It was a nothing play in a nothing game. With the Patriots driving past midfield, Grogan dropped back and spotted Darryl Stingley on a slant-in from the right over the middle. He threw, and the pass was both wide and high. Stingley left his feet to try to make the catch but couldn't quite pull it in, the ball tumbling off his hand. As he came down toward the ground, stretching his right leg out, he bent at the waist and lowered his head, trying to stay on his feet.

Closing from the left, and running at not quite full speed, Oakland safety Jack Tatum, with Stingley in his sights from only two or three yards away, dipped to deliver a hit with his right shoulder. It was the kind of play Tatum had been making since he starred at Ohio State and earned a well-deserved reputation as, pound for pound, one of the hardest tacklers in football.

Stingley's upper body was almost parallel to the ground when Tatum struck. The top of the receiver's head collided with Tatum at the collarbone, between his helmet and right shoulder. It was a hard hit, a legal hit, and even a clean hit given that Stingley was still in the air and not in control of his body. It was the kind of contact one used to see a half-dozen times a game, the kind Tatum regularly delivered, and it was the reason receivers hate crossing patterns, which can put two players running in excess of 20 miles an hour on a collision course. The difference, of course, is that the receiver is looking for the ball and the defender is not. Even in today's game, the hit would likely be considered legal, since Tatum did not strike with his helmet or leave his feet.

Stingley went limp and fell straight down to the ground, landing on his back. Tatum staggered backwards, but stayed on his feet.

Darryl Stingley never took another step.

The collision broke Stingley's fourth and fifth cervical vertebrae. Although his spinal cord was not severed, the damage was extensive. He would spend the rest of his life paralyzed, with only nominal use of his right arm.

Stingley's son Derek later said, "Tatum was just giving him a hard hit. That was in the cosmos. That was in the stars that day."

Stingley would fight a long and courageous battle to live before passing away in 2007 from heart disease and pneumonia. Tatum, after suffering from diabetes for years—which eventually resulted in the amputation of his toes and a foot—died from a heart attack in 2011. Much to the dismay of New England fans, Tatum never apologized, and never visited Stingley in the hospital, telling the *Herald*'s D. Leo Monahan, "I can't get emotional about it, it's my job." Oakland coach John Madden, on the other hand, held a vigil at Stingley's side and later cited the violent incident as a reason he retired from coaching a year later.

. . .

The more immediate fallout for the Patriots, apart from the loss of a receiver, was yet another wedge between the team and ownership. Stingley had already agreed in principle to a new contract, but after the injury the team reneged on the deal. He would still be paid through his option years, but after that he was eligible only for the NFL's standard disability pension of $2,000 a month, plus workmen's compensation and Social Security. Any money the Patriots saved by reneging on Stingley's deal

Darryl Stingley is removed from the playing field after he suffered a broken neck in an exhibition game against the Oakland Raiders on August 12, 1978. Stingley was paralyzed from the head down after a collision with Raider defensive back Jack Tatum in the second quarter.

paled in comparison to the PR hit the Sullivans initially took. Eventually, they did the right thing. The Pats and Stingley came to what the *Globe*'s Bob Ryan called "an intricate financial settlement," which included a stipulation that the Patriots would pay for the college education of Stingley's two sons.

Although the Patriots played well in 1978, they were rarely dominant. They opened by losing two of their first three games, and although they bounced back to win nine of their next ten, the entire season was a grind, far more than anyone anticipated, with six games won by a touchdown or less. Still, with two weeks remaining, they controlled their fate. At 10-4, a victory over Buffalo on December 10 would give New England the division title.

But Chuck Fairbanks, despite being under contract, had other options. The Hannah-Gray affair had exposed the charade of his "total control" of the franchise: having realized that he was "totally controlled" by the Sullivans, he felt no loyalty to the team. And like almost every other head football coach, particularly at major college and pro programs, he was surrounded by sycophants and hangers-on. Most were moneyed business executives taking

Patriots linebacker Steve Nelson (57) looks on from the field during a game against the Cleveland Browns at Municipal Stadium in 1977. Named to both the Patriots' fiftieth-anniversary and All-Century teams, he was elected to the team's Hall of Fame in 1993.

advantage of the way cash provides access, often manifested in sweetheart deals delivered at the golf course in exchange for the status of being in proximity to celebrity. Oh, not that coaches don't get wealthy from their craft, they do, but few walk away from the kind of slam-dunk financial opportunities sent their way by well-meaning friends.

Fairbanks was no different. Two of his new best friends were Bob Six, a Continental Airlines executive, and Jack Vickers, an oilman. Both were based in Denver,

and both had a stake in making the University of Colorado a football power. As the Pats drove for the playoffs, the two men, after first tapping Fairbanks for "advice" in their quest for a new coach, put together a package worth $250,000 a year to entice Fairbanks himself to Colorado.

Six and Vickers didn't do a very good job of keeping it quiet: as the Pats narrowly defeated Buffalo to win their first division title, word began to leak out that Fairbanks was on the verge of leaving. He accepted their offer on December 13, although he later claimed it was conditional on Sullivan letting him out of his contract. Meanwhile, the Patriots were preparing to play Miami in the season finale, followed by a one-week layoff before the playoffs.

The next few days unfolded like a '70s afternoon soap opera, with Fairbanks playing the role of the ignored wife casting her lot with a youthful and wealthier lover, while Sullivan played the jilted husband suddenly turning vengeful and reminding his estranged spouse who had paid for all those fancy shoes and body work. Meanwhile, no one much thought about the impact on the children.

The players actually didn't much care, at least not at first, apart from the nuisance of being peppered with questions by the press. The Hannah-Gray holdout had underscored the fact that football was a business, and on the practice field the days before the Miami game unfolded as usual. But behind the scenes things were a mess, with Sullivan telling Fairbanks he'd suspend him if he didn't forget Colorado until after the playoffs and Fairbanks trying to have it both ways.

When everyone got to Miami, it all unraveled. Fairbanks met with his team that afternoon to tell them that he was taking the university job and that he'd been suspended by Sullivan. He then went to Sullivan and asked to be able to finish the season, which the players also wanted.

Sullivan wouldn't have it, saying, "I told him, long before Billy Sullivan or Chuck Fairbanks were around it was said, 'No man can serve two masters,'" later explaining that he did not think it was possible for Fairbanks to remain "mentally" focused on coaching the Patriots while calling high school football recruits. Funny, but that's what Sullivan himself had done for years, running Metropolitan Oil and the Patriots and the Stadium Authority simultaneously while still serving both the

Church and Boston College. Then Sullivan dropped the hammer: "The league will be informed and he [Fairbanks] will be suspended without compensation," which guaranteed the whole thing would end up in the courts.

There was more, and the "he said, she said" accounting of exactly what took place is still a matter of debate, but there was no turning back . . . or so it seemed.

To be fair, Fairbanks should have held Colorado off until after the season, but the school was eager to make an announcement and Fairbanks was eager to begin recruiting. And even after word of Fairbanks's departure leaked out, Sullivan probably should have swallowed his pride and let Fairbanks finish the year so the team could focus on the postseason as best it could. But despite what each man said, the team wasn't a priority to either—each thought mostly of himself and his own wallet, not the

Patriots. And when you're trying to do anything but win, you're destined to lose.

With Fairbanks gone, who would coach the game against Miami? Sullivan answered this question by making a bad and already confusing situation even worse. He named not one head coach but two, splitting the post between defensive coordinator Hank Bullough and offensive coordinator Ron Erhardt. In the Orange Bowl's cramped locker room, both men gave pregame pep talks, as did Sullivan, and even Fairbanks hung around for a while, not quite sure what his role was, where he should go, and how the hell he would get back to Boston—he finally begged a ride back on the Patriots' charter.

So of course, Grogan twisted a knee in pregame warm-up and the Patriots went out on the field and fell apart, losing 23–3.

The rocky "divorce" between head coach Chuck Fairbanks (*foreground*) and the Patriots came to a head just prior to the 1978 playoffs, when owner Billy Sullivan (*holding football*) barely spoke to his head coach, who'd already agreed to depart for head-coaching duties at the University of Colorado.

Chuck Fairbanks gives his final Patriots pep talk before the first home playoff game in franchise history—against the Houston Oilers at Schaefer Stadium on December 31, 1978. He and Ron Erhardt shared head-coaching duties in a disastrous game that ended in a 31–14 loss.

But it didn't stop there. Two weeks without football left plenty of time for telegrams and attorneys and threatened lawsuits with the word "breach" appearing in almost every sentence . . . and then suddenly all was forgiven. Fairbanks was back as head coach and everyone, at least publicly, tried to pretend that all was as it was before and the Patriots were still Super Bowl–bound.

The Super Bowl might have remained a possibility if Grogan had not been hurt, but it was the Oilers who,

with rookie running back Earl Campbell, beat Miami in the wild-card game and earned the right to come to Foxborough for the Patriots' first-ever home playoff game.

This game would prove not to be nearly as memorable or controversial as the Raiders game two years before. Grogan was ineffective, and the Patriots were never competitive. Houston led 24–0 before coasting to a 31–14 victory. Fans serenaded Fairbanks with a "Good-bye Chuckie" chant at the end, and then the Patriots and their former coach all went to court. Eventually, Colorado bought out Fairbanks's contract, and everyone just hoped the whole thing would go away.

In April 1979, after the Patriots flirted with USC coach John Robinson (to whom, GM Bucko Kilroy claimed, he'd offered the job, only to have Chuck Sullivan say he had not), Ron Erhardt was named head coach, his first head-coaching job since North Dakota State. Promising to "open up" the offense, Erhardt was a competent pick but not exactly an exciting one, a nice guy whom the players liked but who, after Fairbanks, just didn't have the indefinable "it" that all successful coaches seem to have. And with Sullivan back, Erhardt seemed to shrink in the position. In his defense, his situation was not unlike the one some poor coach will one day have to face when the Patriots replace Bill Belichick—remember the revolving door in Green Bay after Vince Lombardi retired?

In 1979 and 1980, Erhardt led the team to back-to-back second-place finishes in the AFC East behind a still-potent offense. Sullivan undermined the coach, however, by shedding big salaries to save money, beginning with Leon Gray, who was dealt away against Erhardt's wishes before he had even coached one game as a solo head coach. When Hannah found out, he announced, "We just traded away our Super Bowl." The move saved Sullivan about $500,000, and in later penny-pinching moves he also sent away such stalwarts as Russ Francis and Sam Adams, players who would go on to be productive with other teams. During each of the next two years, after a good start that put them in the playoff hunt, the club would collapse down the stretch and fail to make the postseason. A key loss each time took place during late-season trips to Miami, where the Patriots hadn't won since before Don Shula became coach in 1971.

Regardless, whatever door had been open for the Patriots began to close. Despite a collection of the best individual player talent in the history of the franchise with Grogan, Cunningham, Francis, Nelson, Hannah, Gray, and Haynes and a supporting cast that was more than adequate, the team just couldn't get past the dysfunction that permeated the organization. Although the door didn't slam shut, the end result was the same—the best Patriots team to date ended up with little tangible evidence of their glory, just a single division championship and two playoff losses, one utterly forgettable and the other ... well, that no one could ever forget.

Patriots backup quarterback Tom Owen, under heavy pressure from Bruce Radford (78), an unidentified teammate, and an inspired Bronco defense, throws an incomplete pass during the Broncos' 45–10 romp over the Pats at Mile High Stadium in 1979.

CHAPTER SIX

1981–1985

THE LAST SHALL BE (ALMOST) FIRST

A measure of just how far the Patriots fell, and how quickly, is that only a few years after being mentioned in the same sentence as the Super Bowl, their most memorable games of the 1981 season were not victories, or even tragedies, but unbridled embarrassments. For in 1981 the Patriots fell completely apart, both on the field and organizationally. Even worse, those humiliations played out in the open, for everyone to see.

Two-time Pulitzer Prize–winning photographer Stan Grossfeld of the *Boston Globe* captures the essence of the wildness that ensued when the Patriots clinched a wild-card berth on December 22, 1985, after beating the Bengals by a score of 34–23.

W HILE THE 1981 PATRIOTS were in some ways a better team than their record—they lost eight games by a touchdown or less and led the league in pass defense—even that small achievement came with a caveat. Against the Patriots' suddenly porous defense, other teams rarely found it necessary to pass. Any way you put it, 2-14 was still 2-14, and in some ways, it was even worse than that.

The Pats opened the season with two narrow defeats to Baltimore and Philadelphia, setting the stage for the first such indignity on September 21 in a *Monday Night Football* contest on ABC before a national audience.

It was bad enough that the Cowboys, on their way to an appearance in the NFC championship game with running back Tony Dorsett and quarterback Danny White, ran roughshod over New England to a 35–21 win. Dorsett alone ran for 162 yards, including a 75-yard touchdown run. But afterward there was far more talk about what had taken place in the stands than on the field.

Monday night games had always been problematic for the Patriots at home, particularly when the team wasn't doing well, the weather was poor, or the game was a blowout. Many season-ticket holders dumped their tickets for the weeknight contests, which didn't start till 9:00 PM and, given the stadium's access and egress issues, meant that a trip to Foxboro on the heels of Boston's rush hour traffic was an eight- or ten-hour commitment. So Monday night fans often showed up beginning in the late afternoon, not so much with the expectation of watching a football game but simply to extend the weekend. The late start provided fans with plenty of opportunities to "have more than one" while inching toward the stadium, tailgating in the parking lot, and watching the game, and then again in the parking lot before joining the raucous rolling bar careening back home.

The first Monday night incident had come in 1976 in the Pats' third appearance on the ABC prime-time broadcast. As the Patriots rolled up the score of a 41–7 blowout of the Jets, fans rolled out the barrel. Announcers Alex Karras, Howard Cosell, and Frank Gifford found more of interest going on in the stands than on the field, except when fans repeatedly ran onto the field—a total of thirteen were caught in the act.

• • •

The *Globe*'s Leigh Montville later aptly described the game as "a nationally televised nightmare . . . only it was for real." By daybreak, two men were dead of heart attacks, and a first responder was urinated on while giving one of the victims mouth-to-mouth resuscitation; there was a stabbing in the parking lot and random bombardments with cherry bombs; a police officer suffered a broken jaw after being punched in the face and then having his gun stolen; two men claimed to have fallen from the top of the stands; forty-nine arrests were made; and emergency room personnel treated so many patients at nearby Norwood Hospital that they lost track of the number.

The Patriots treated that game's mayhem as an anomaly, but similar chaos took place again in 1980 during and after a 23–14 victory over Denver, resulting in fifty-six arrests for various charges, including indecent exposure. That night two men were struck by cars in a running battle between groups of fans that extended from the parking lot out onto Route 1. Afterward the Patriots sort of said the right things, but took issue with media reports and blamed the troublemakers. The town fathers of Foxborough were not amused. Before the 1981 season, they threatened to ban alcohol sales at the stadium, but ended up only prohibiting beer sales fifteen minutes after the start of the third quarter—thus ensuring that fans crammed four quarters' worth of drinking into an even shorter time period.

By 1981, the Patriots knew what to expect and tried to head off trouble before the Dallas game. The team hired 300 security people—two-thirds of them "rent-a-cops" and 105 bona-fide officers from nearby towns. These were supplemented by another 20 plainclothes cops whom Billy Sullivan accurately but unfortunately referred to as "bouncers." His announcement that fans wouldn't be allowed to bring their own booze caused a run on flasks and an even more riotous drive to Foxborough. There the tailgating scene seemed scripted by Fellini as many fans arrived looking for and hoping for trouble. After all, they had a reputation to defend now as the most disorderly fans in pro football. They may have been less colorful and creative than Oakland's outlaws, but they were harder to control.

Three thousand guards would not have been enough. From the start, fans took efforts to subdue their menacing presence as a challenge, and for the third time in five years a national audience saw Sullivan Stadium turned into the NFL's version of Altamont. That's right: in 1981 the Sullivans, eager to have everything in the family name, bought out stadium shareholders for $12 a share. That was far more than the shares were worth,

and the sale increased the debt they were carrying to more than $30 million. The only tangible changes were the renaming of the stadium and the addition of luxury boxes, a new scoreboard, and other improvements . . . to the tune of another $15 million.

The first Sullivan Stadium riot was not quite as bad as the previous Schaefer Stadium rows. This time there was only one stabbing, a single hit-and-run on Route 1, and one assault on a cop. Foxborough police arrested thirty-eight, and the state police cuffed another twenty-one. Still, the town had had it: Foxborough banned *Monday Night* contests at Sullivan Stadium, and the NFL and ABC readily agreed to the sanction. The Patriots would not play another home game on Monday night until 1995.

> MONDAY NIGHT GAMES HAD ALWAYS BEEN PROBLEMATIC FOR THE PATRIOTS AT HOME, PARTICULARLY WHEN THE TEAM WASN'T DOING WELL, THE WEATHER WAS POOR, OR THE GAME WAS A BLOWOUT.

There would be one more mortifying moment during the season before the Patriots slunk off. As the losses added up, the team reached a nadir in the final game. The papers dubbed it the "Stupor Bowl" as the 2-13 Patriots faced the 1-14 Colts with the rights to the number-one draft pick at stake. The prize, which drew national press to the otherwise meaningless contest, was Texas defensive lineman Ken Sims. At six-five and 275 pounds, Sims had won the Lombardi Trophy as the best lineman in college football and was still considered by far the best player in a weak draft in spite of having suffered a broken ankle.

John Hannah noted before the game that "this one will show who has pride enough to win and who is dog enough to lose." As Kevin Mannix noted later in the *Herald*, the Pats were "the Worst in Show, a breed apart."

Charitably, it was one of the worst pro football games ever played. Each team barely and ineffectively disguised its desire to lose, leading Bob Verdi of the *Chicago Tribune* to call the game "a see-saw contest. That is, some of the things you did see, you really didn't believe you saw. . . . Both these teams were in a must-lose situation and they gave it all they had. . . . You could cut the suspense with a feather." Early in the game, the Patriots punted when the

New England Patriots owner Billy Sullivan pauses to reflect during a press conference called in Foxborough to announce the firing of coach Ron Erhardt on December 22, 1981.

Colts had only ten men on the field. Baltimore's return man conveniently fumbled, only to have the whole thing called back after the Patriots were flagged for having an illegal man downfield. Not to be thwarted, on the replay, as Verdi described it, Patriots punter Rich Camarillo caught the snap, "took one step forward, then dropped the ball." After all, if you didn't have the ball, you couldn't score, and if you couldn't score, you couldn't win. The game featured six turnovers, several fumbles that saw the wrong guy land on the ball, a missed extra point, one missed field goal, twelve penalties, and Camarillo averaging only 30 yards on six kicks. After the game, safety Tim Fox said, "Going into today, we really wanted to win. But now that we haven't, it's just as well."

Go, team. In the end, the Pats lost 23–21 after running out of time-outs with the ball on Baltimore's 15-yard line.

Now the door was not only closed but locked, the deadbolt slid in tight. The guts of Fairbanks's Patriots—Grogan, Cunningham, and the like—were beginning to show their age, and apart from the emergence of rookie running back Tony Collins, there was little help at hand. It looked like it was time to rebuild. Two days later, and just a week after saying he expected to retain Erhardt, Sullivan fired the coach and his entire staff, save for GM

Bucko Kilroy. Erhardt, Sullivan said, "was just too nice of a guy," and now he was looking for someone "like a military leader. . . . I think the old theory that if you spare the rod you spoil the child is true."

There was only one thing anyone knew with any certainty. The Patriots, long the laughingstock of the league, were right back to where they started.

With the opportunity to hire anyone in North America to coach his football team, Sullivan, as was his pattern, turned not to tried-and-true coaches with NFL experience, but to colleges, both established big-name coaches like USC's John Robinson (again) and Penn State's Joe Paterno (again) and the newest shiny bauble, Ron Meyer of SMU. The former Dallas scout was known as a master recruiter and had led a previously dismal program to a 10-1 record, albeit by violating a host of NCAA regulations. Meyer and his recruiting staff paid players, a scheme that in 1987 would eventually result in the dreaded death penalty for the Southwest Conference school. In 1982, SMU was already on probation and Meyer, like Fairbanks before him, was looking to get out before being hamstrung with penalties and losing his reputation for genius.

Kilroy led the search, which didn't mean much, because Chuck Sullivan was reportedly making inquiries of his own as well. Robinson was the first to rebuff the Sullivans, despite the fact that the Pats were ready to open the bank and give the new coach "complete front office control." Then Sullivan made a similar offer to Paterno, but Joe Pa also asked for a piece of the team, only to discover that his last name was not Sullivan.

Meyer, who had worked with Kilroy in Dallas, moved to the top of the list, and on January 15 he agreed to a four-year deal worth about $750,000 and giving him "full control"—except in regard to player movement, which remained with personnel director Dick Steinberg. Meyer brushed that off, saying he agreed with the "family approach" to management but not realizing that in the Patriots family he was only a foster child. The outwardly personable coach, who sported a Glen Campbell comb-over and a practiced Texas twang that disguised the fact that he was from the Columbus, Ohio, suburb of Westerville, promised a hard-nosed, if platitude-laden, approach. At his initial press conference, he likened his style to that of Dallas coach Tom Landry in terms of intelligence and Miami's Don Shula for his commitment to discipline and assertiveness, with the personality of Pittsburgh's Chuck Noll and the work ethic of Philadelphia's Dick Vermeil for good measure.

Oh boy. He somehow left out the piety of Frank Leahy and the wisdom of the Buddha. Nevertheless, Meyer, whom the Patriots compared to a more enthusiastic and sociable Fairbanks, took over.

With seven draft picks among the top sixty, there was plenty of opportunity—and need—to rebuild. That could have been enhanced had the Patriots considered trading top pick Sims; teams seemed to be ignoring the fact that his reputation as a world-class pass rusher had been earned in the SWC, a conference where most offensive linemen pass-blocked only a dozen or so times a game. Sims could have been swapped either for some established talent or for draft picks the following year. With luminaries like John Elway, Eric Dickerson, Jim Kelly, Kurt Warner, Dan Marino, and Todd Blackledge available, it was already being touted as the best potential draft class in years. But Meyer actually wanted to trade almost everyone else, including guys like John Hannah, and agreed with Steinberg. The Patriots drafted Sims, despite the broken ankle and rumors that he saved his best efforts for after the game.

Then again, it didn't matter much. Training camp opened under the specter of a potential strike, and Sims was virtually invisible from day one. The Pats first brushed it off by blaming his broken ankle, then a nagging back injury, and then the fact that he was being switched from inside tackle to defensive end, but by the first week of August they were wondering if it was more than that. Sims was pleasant enough, but said of training camp: "It's just been football, football, football . . . I really can't get into it . . . if I'm going to burn it, I'm not going to burn it in practice." His teammates were less understanding, one saying dismissively that "Mel Lunsford was a better defensive end than this guy." But Sims had an excuse for everything, promising twenty sacks for the year and claiming "I'll be there on game day. I always am."

The Patriots had yet to find out exactly where "there" was after only two games, a 24–13 win over Baltimore and a 31–7 loss to the Jets, when the players went on strike.

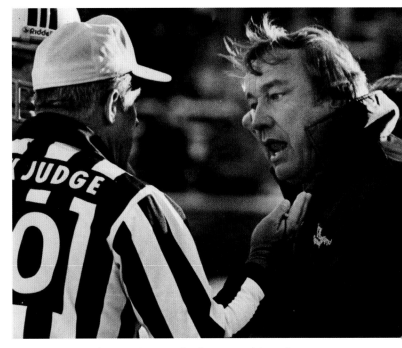

New England Patriots coach Ron Erhardt argues with a referee in his second-to-last game as head coach of the Patriots, a 19–10 loss to Buffalo on December 13, 1981.

There was already some dissatisfaction with Meyer, who had instituted a dress code and cut a host of veterans. He treated players dismissively, particularly guys like Hannah, whose football acumen was ignored. The glib bromides that worked so well in recruiting high schoolers and impressing their parents—such as "proper planning prevents poor performance," one of many maxims he cribbed from the kind of business textbooks favored by middle managers—sounded false to grizzled veterans of pro football. He delegated authority—a lot of it—and in a short time he was coming off as being about as genuine as the president of the local Optimists' Club who always tries to sell you some insurance on the side. The players wondered if he really knew the game and were already tuning him out. Now, with the strike, if they couldn't play, at least they couldn't lose and didn't have to listen to Meyer.

The reason for the strike boiled down to a demand from NFLPA president Ed Garvey that the players receive 55 percent of league revenues, an approach that some players, still submissive to management and susceptible to believing the propaganda that they were already over-paid, weren't completely happy with. But then again, in labor relations, pro football players, accustomed to the top-down structure inherent in the game, have always been behind the curve. The NFL is still the only major pro sport without universal guaranteed contracts. After the second game of the season, with little movement in negotiations, Garvey ordered a strike. In response, the NFL ordered the players locked out, stopping the season cold.

The players stayed out—except for two easily forgotten All-Star Games between strike-breakers that

Defensive lineman Kenneth Sims of the University of Texas poses with his new jersey, after being drafted with the number-one pick in the NFL player draft by the Patriots, at the Sheraton Hotel on April 27, 1982, in New York.

few attended or watched—for a total of fifty-seven days before the two sides reached agreement. The players received some concessions in benefits, minimum pay, and severance packages, while ownership failed to agree to the 55 percent figure and retained control. The 55 percent figure, however, eventually became the benchmark for future negotiations—and one the players have never reached.

In the short term, the strike made the Patriots a playoff team, or at least a potential one. Since the season would be shortened to only nine games, the league decided to hold a sixteen-team Super Bowl tournament that would guarantee playoff implications for nearly every remaining game, placating both players and fans and ensuring that every team in football, including the Patriots (despite all evidence to the contrary), were still in the hunt for the championship. Such a tournament would also give management and the television networks an opportunity to recoup some losses through an added round of playoff games. Although not everyone would get a trophy at the end of the season, almost everyone would have a chance at it. All the Patriots had to do to declare the season a success was win a few games and finish at .500, or close to it.

When the games resumed, the Patriots continued their unimpressive march to ignominy, losing to Cleveland, edging Houston, and then falling to the Bears, making their record 2-3. With the first-place Dolphins next up in Foxborough on December 12, and the potent Steelers also on the schedule, the Miami game became a must-win to keep New England's playoff hopes alive in what the press was already calling a "pseudo season."

But they hadn't seen anything yet.

The day before the game a storm swept into New England, first dumping sheets of rain before the temperature dropped, and then it started snowing enough for the Pats to offer a free ticket and ten bucks to anyone who helped shovel out the seats. By game time, conditions were brutal, with temperatures hovering around 20 degrees, a swirling wind, and still-falling snow on an icy field of Poly-Turf. Barely 25,000 fans shivered in the stands.

Players on both teams found it nearly impossible to keep their footing, and officials had to periodically stop the game to allow a guy driving a John Deere lawn tractor with a four-foot-wide spinning brush to clear the sidelines and 5-yard markers.

It was a war of attrition, as neither Grogan nor Miami quarterback David Woodley could throw the ball effectively, leading both teams to send running backs into the line over and over again on straight line plunges. Both Miami's Andra Franklin and New England's Mark van Eeghen gained over 100 yards for the day, but the most success came to the Patriots' Mosi Tatupu, a Samoan running back who, with his wide feet and low center of gravity, found conditions to his liking.

Still, neither team could score. Each tried and missed field goals when the kickers couldn't find secure footing. The game was still scoreless in the fourth quarter when the Patriots put together an 11-play, 77-yard drive, nearly all of it on running plays to the left side of the line behind center Pete Brock, Hannah, tackle Brian Holloway, and tight end Don Hasselback. When the drive stalled on the Miami 16, Meyer called timeout and sent for the field goal team.

John Smith and holder Matt Cavanaugh were digging at the field with their cleats, trying to clear the snow and chip through the ice, when Meyer had the most inspired moment of his coaching career. He spied the guy driving the John Deere tractor, a twenty-six-year-old prisoner on a work-release program from nearby MCI-Norfolk named Mark Henderson, standing alongside the machine clapping his hands and stomping his feet to keep warm. Meyer waved to him and yelled, "Get out there and do something!" As Henderson told the *Globe*'s Stan Grossfeld later, "I knew exactly what he meant, so I jumped on the tractor and proceeded to go out on the 20-yard line, where I was supposed to be."

Brush spinning, Henderson steered the machine onto the field, and Cavanaugh directed him to the appropriate spot on the 23-yard line. Henderson brushed the snow and loose ice away as Don Shula went ballistic, but there wasn't any rule that said you couldn't send a work-release prisoner onto the field with a John Deere tractor.

A moment later, Smith split the uprights, giving New England a 3–0 lead while Shula went from ballistic to apoplectic. The Patriots hung on for the next 4:45 and escaped with a 3–0 victory. Contrary to what Smith would later claim, he admitted the next day that Henderson "obviously helped me in my kick by clearing away the area where my first step was going to come through, so he did help me."

Henderson received a standing ovation from the crowd, saw his picture appear on the scoreboard, and was serenaded with chants of "MVP, MVP!" He was the man of the moment, his place in Patriots history secure for all time in what will forever be known, inaccuracy aside, as "the Snowplow Game." In the off-season, Shula spearheaded a rule change disallowing such shenanigans in the future, but for the moment the Patriots' playoff dream was still alive.

Henderson, a drug addict serving time for burglary, basked in the brief glow of notoriety, even being awarded his own game ball afterward. (To his credit, he did his time and went on to live an exemplary life.) The Patriots, while realizing they had gotten away with something—"They'll have to live with that," said a bitter Shula—used the win to slide into the postseason on their bellies, winning three of their last four, including a victory over Buffalo in the season finale, to finish 5-4 and earning a seventh seed in the AFC playoffs, ahead of only 4-5 Cleveland.

Ah, but these were the Patriots, and what goes around comes around. New England was sent to Miami, where they hadn't won a game in more than a decade, to face the vengeful Dolphins.

No one was very optimistic. Apart from the Snowplow Game, good teams had blown out the Patriots, who'd found most of their success against the bottom-feeders. For a mediocre team, the Pats played well, but they never really had a chance. The Dolphins almost doubled New England's total offensive output—Miami won, 28–13, in a game that wasn't as close as the final score.

> NO ONE WAS VERY OPTIMISTIC. APART FROM THE SNOWPLOW GAME, GOOD TEAMS HAD BLOWN OUT THE PATRIOTS, WHO'D FOUND MOST OF THEIR SUCCESS AGAINST THE BOTTOM-FEEDERS.

Ron Meyer, head coach of the Patriots from 1982 to 1984, looks on from the sidelines in the strike-shortened season of 1982.

The players were just glad it was over. On the plane trip back, the younger players serenaded the vets with the "Sha-na-na-a, hey hey, good-bye" song, knowing that some, like Cunningham, Andy Johnson, and Don Hasselbeck, were likely to leave as free agents—the new USFL was throwing a lot of money around—and that others, like Hannah and Stanley Morgan, whom Meyer had fined for making intemperate comments, wanted out.

So naturally Meyer was named AFC Coach of the Year for leading the Patriots to the playoffs. Few on the team felt that Meyer deserved the honor.

The Patriots were a team in flux and divided against itself, not just on the field but in the front office, where Meyer still wanted to clean house and Sullivan and Steinberg did not. In spite of the differences, the Patriots looked to the draft for redemption and a way to bring the factions together.

The big prize was quarterback John Elway of Stanford, whom Baltimore planned to select with the first pick, but between the New York Yankees, who had drafted

Elway to play baseball, and the USFL, the quarterback had options. He let it be known that he had no desire to play in Baltimore for hard-core coach Frank Kush.

Everybody made a play for Elway—the Patriots tried to package John Hannah—and the quarterback eventually went to Denver in a trade. But the Patriots needed everything. Dick Steinberg said they were looking for "another quarterback, a big running back, another super wide receiver . . . another inside linebacker and perhaps a defensive lineman to bring along." Was that all?

After being thwarted in their effort to get Elway, the Patriots' fallback pick was quarterback Jim Kelly, but he went to Buffalo with the fourteenth pick, one ahead of New England. So the Patriots drafted the next name on their chart, Tony Eason.

Eason looked the part of a quarterback, and he had set a host of records at Illinois, but he wasn't a consensus pick. He was a slow-twitch guy, effective in college but unexciting. Meyer later claimed that he'd had no input in the selection whatsoever and that "we weren't even allowed to read the [scouting] reports." He considered Eason "just another guy." Meanwhile, Pittsburgh QB Dan Marino, despite being dogged by rumors of drug use, fell to Miami as a total of six quarterbacks were drafted in the first round, an all-time record.

As Eason toiled behind Grogan, the Patriots were never in the race in 1983, starting off the season losing two, then winning two, only to lose the next two, win the next two, and . . . oh, you get the idea. The team never pulled itself above .500 and finished a deserved 8-8.

The real story that season had nothing to do with football—or it shouldn't have. In the end, the season would be brought down not by their coach, or by their quarterback, or by a gigantic lineman turning into a bust, but by a pop singer who stood five-nine, weighed 130 pounds, and never evinced any interest whatsoever in the game of football apart from the halftime show.

As a student at Boston College, Chuck Sullivan had dabbled in concert promotion, bringing in Duke Ellington and the Kingston Trio, and while in the service he had a hand in Bob Hope's 1968 Vietnam tour. After Schaefer Stadium opened, he worked with local promotor Don Law to bring a number of big rock acts to the stadium, the only venue of its size in New England.

In 1984, the biggest name in music was Michael Jackson, the King of Pop. In late 1982, he had released his album *Thriller*, which became the biggest-selling international album of all time, and his scintillating moon-walking performance of "Billie Jean" for the *Motown 25* television special on May 16, 1983, before an estimated audience of 47 million had rocketed all things Jackson into the stratosphere, grabbing the attention of Chuck Sullivan.

In the wake of his next album, *Victory*, Jackson planned to tour with his brothers in 1984, and Chuck Sullivan initially tried to secure a date in Foxborough. But when the original promoter backed out, Chuck, not just a Patriot VP but now also chairman of the NFL Management Council's Executive Committee, a position he gained owing to his presumed financial wizardry,

sensed an opportunity. He figured he could cut some sweet deals at stadiums controlled by his NFL brethren. It was bad enough that he had never promoted a major tour before, let alone anything on the level of what would become the highest-grossing tour ever to take place at the time.

But Sullivan was dazzled by the numbers and dollar signs. All he saw was the potential to make money, or at least get his family out of debt, a motivation that blinded him to the risks. There was a reason Jackson and his brothers weren't promoting themselves. Why put up their own money when someone else would?

Sullivan's first miscalculation was failing to account for the fact that the Victory Tour would include not just Michael Jackson but also the Jackson brothers, who had little following apart from Michael. Yet Sullivan,

Mark Henderson (*left*), a member of the Stadium Management Corporation maintenance crew, sweeps snow off the playing field at Schaefer Stadium during a snowstorm as the Dolphins (*background*) hold a pregame practice. Henderson drove the power brush onto the field and cleared snow prior to John Smith's field goal in the fourth quarter, allowing the Patriots to win by a score of 3–0.

through the Stadium Management Corporation, the legal entity that managed the football stadium, guaranteed the Jacksons 83.4 percent of gross revenues—about 25 percent higher than the industry standard—including a $35 million advance. It was all financed by using Sullivan Stadium as collateral and taking out an additional mortgage.

Chuck Sullivan tried to spread the wealth among his NFL cronies, booking about half the tour at other NFL stadiums, but few provided him with a discount. Within only a few weeks of the tour's start in July, it became clear that it would be a financial disaster for the Sullivans. Although the Jacksons played to sellout crowds almost everywhere, the shows were extremely pricey to produce. The incredible costs of transporting the 365-ton stage that took up one-third of a football field (cutting into available seating) hurt, not to mention paying for the thirty tractor-trailers to move it, the entourage of 250, insurance, and a host of other expenses. Overhead alone came to nearly $1 million a week for the nearly half-year tour. And then Sullivan made a bad situation worse by paying another $18 million in licensing fees for a line of clothing and other Jackson-related merchandise.

By the fall, audiences started to drop. They wanted Michael, not his brothers, and Michael wouldn't even do "Thriller"—he didn't like the way the song sounded when performed live. Then, at tour's end, the notoriously private Jackson withdrew from the public eye and his popularity slumped. It was like Sullivan had bought a house at the peak of the real estate market without doing a full inspection and then discovered that the septic system needed replacing.

The tour grossed $75 million and everyone made money . . . except the Sullivans. Even after negotiating some contractual changes in mid-tour, their losses were estimated to be $22 million. According to *Sports Illustrated*, over the next few years the cumulative debt—including the team's, Chuck's, Billy's, and the Sullivan-owned Stadium Management Corporation's—would mushroom to more than $100 million. And if that wasn't bad enough, the worst humiliation of all came when the Foxborough board of selectmen refused to approve any dates at Sullivan Stadium for the tour, citing murky concerns over "the unknown element" the concert would attract, which most interpreted in racial terms.

Going forward, the Sullivans' grip on the team would slowly loosen—they would come to own the Patriots in name only. The real owners were the banks that owned their debt. Eventually, the only way for the Sullivans to get out from under their debt would be to sell the team, but that solution would take years for them to admit. Only a few years before, Billy Sullivan had fired Chuck Fairbanks, saying it was impossible to serve "two masters." So it would be for the Sullivans—the team, and its performance on the field, would no longer be their first priority.

• • •

By now it was clear to all the players that Ron Meyer was a mistake, and the Patriots' front office was beginning to agree with them. But until the team's record suffered, his job was secure. In the off-season, the Patriots added Nebraska receiver Irving Fryar with the number-one pick of the draft, which they had acquired from Tampa—yet another instance where the team might have been better served by a trade. Meyer flexed his influence when he talked the team into signing free agent running back Craig James, who had starred for Meyer at SMU and found success in the USFL.

The Patriots started the 1984 season with a victory and actually won two of their first three, including a 38–23 win over Seattle in which they came back from a 23–0 deficit to ring up the greatest comeback in team history to date. The victory was keyed by Tony Eason, who came in to replace Grogan after the Pats fell behind and Grogan failed to complete a pass. Eason scored on a 25-yard scramble on his first possession and later threw two touchdowns to augment the win and secure his place in the starting lineup. It was the kind of performance that made the team believe that Eason could one day become a premier quarterback, but one that he would never duplicate with any regularity.

Eason's entire career would be an enigma. At Illinois, he was the most decorated quarterback in history and set NCAA records at the time in categories like total offense per game and passing yards per game, yet his personality never seemed to mesh with expectations in New England. He simply could never compare with the fiery Grogan and always acted, as one sportswriter noted, like "someone who had just gotten out of bed." Even his mother said of him, "He's never been one to get

Michael Jackson, his family, and Don King celebrate the 1984 Victory Tour, which just about bankrupted the Patriots and helped force the eventual sale of the team to Victor Kiam.

caught up in plans." When once asked about the burden of leadership, he responded, "I'm not looking at it like I have to be the guy more than anyone else." He shied away from the spotlight and, as his career continued, from all contact. Besides just not being a good fit from the start, Eason was saddled with expectations from the press, the fans, and the organization that were probably unrealistic. Moreover, it was always far too easy to compare Eason to other members of the 1983 draft class—Elway, Marino, and Kelly—and find him lacking.

Even though his tenure as a starter sparked a surge, after a 28–21 win over the Jets it all started coming undone. Only the Patriots could precipitate a crisis with a win.

Eason threw for three touchdowns, but after the game all Meyer could do was bad-mouth his own team,

saying he couldn't sleep afterward and "our inability to go for the coup de grâce turned the game into a cliffhanger. . . . We have no reason to be anywhere satisfied." Then he banned the media from both practices and the coach's area of the locker room. As one player wondered, "What would he have done if we lost?"

A few days later, stung by the public and private criticism from his team, Meyer benched Tony Collins and safety Rich Sanford, two of the more vocal players, then raced upstairs to Pat Sullivan's office and demanded that other "dissidents" on the roster—including Hannah, Grogan, Morgan, and Collins—be traded. Pat Sullivan (who, in replacing Bucko Kilroy as GM two years earlier, promised that, even though "I really don't know that much about the game of football," he would "work hard to learn the things that I should know") responded by deciding to hold a players-only meeting. To that point, he and Meyer had gotten along reasonably well, even attending Celtics games together in the off-season. But the players had been blaming Sullivan for the coach's growing impatience, thinking that he had given Meyer an ultimatum by telling him the club had to make the playoffs or else . . .

The gathering did not go well. Players were livid at Meyer for his public criticism and openly questioned his ability. When Sullivan reported on the meeting to Meyer, the coach felt undermined and reportedly threatened to quit.

The next few weeks were tense for everyone, with daily speculation on the status of both Meyer and a

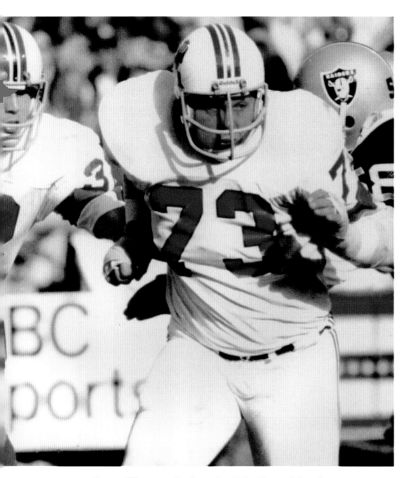

Sports Illustrated **referred to John Hannah in a famous cover story as the greatest lineman of all time. The Alabama graduate was nothing less than a legend in Foxborough, playing his entire career for the Patriots and becoming the first team member to be enshrined in the Pro Football Hall of Fame.**

number of players. It was obvious that the organization was being racked by a power struggle between the players and their coach. But even in this atmosphere, the Patriots managed to escape with two narrow wins, lifting their record to 5-2 and making Meyer feel secure. Then came the Miami game.

The Dolphins blew the Patriots away, winning 44–24, and this time Meyer blamed defensive coordinator Rod Rust, whom he had been praising only two weeks earlier for doing "a magnificent job." But Rust had disagreed with the benching of Sanford, and it leaked out that before the start of the season Meyer had tried to have Rust replaced. Three days after the loss to Miami, with both Pat Sullivan and Steinberg out of town, Meyer, claiming that he had "sole authority" to fire Rust, did so, citing "philosophical differences"—a strange decision to make in midseason.

The players couldn't believe it. "If it's not one thing around here, it's another," said defensive back Roland James. That line could have been permanently posted on the scoreboard at Sullivan Stadium. From the very beginning, having one man coach the team and others exercise authority over the roster and coaching staff had been an untenable situation, and it directly resulted in a divided team.

The next day Pat Sullivan fired Meyer, saying that the team had already decided to do so at the end of the season, no matter what (and in spite of the fact that Meyer had the highest winning percentage of any coach in club history), and that it had already been working on a list of potential replacements. But this time it was impossible to pick either a shiny new coach from college football or the hot assistant of the moment from another pro team—everyone was already under contract. Sullivan also didn't want to elevate any of Meyer's assistants.

Almost by default, his choice was former Pats assistant Raymond Berry, a Hall of Fame receiver and once Johnny Unitas's favorite target on the Colts. As a player, Berry fumbled only twice in a thirteen-year career, and no one could ever remember seeing him drop a pass. He earned a reputation for overcoming his physical limitations—he wasn't very fast or very big—through study and effort. He was constantly squeezing Silly Putty as a way to strengthen his hands and even practiced recovering fumbles, something unheard of at the time. But Berry was also a man who had been out of coaching for three years—he'd been selling real estate in Medfield, Massachusetts. Sullivan called him "a stable man for the moment," hardly a ringing endorsement. Most thought Berry would finish the season and then be replaced à la Phil Bengtson.

More often than not, when teams change coaches, they counterprogram, replacing young coaches with older coaches, defensive wizards with offensive geniuses, disciplinarians with players' coaches, and vice versa. By selecting Berry, they chose experience over youth and a low-key, steady, slow-twitch players' coach over the hardwired, hard-charging Meyer. Berry was nothing if not genuine. Columnist Jim Murray described him as "polite as a deacon, as quiet as a monk." As Steinberg later said of Berry, "He's an unusual person. Maybe one of the things that has made him successful is he's not like a coach. The guy has no ego at all. He doesn't care anything about getting any credit for anything."

The vets already knew and liked Berry from his time coaching wide receivers from 1978 through 1981, and they respected him for his accomplishments as a player. He had even babysat some of their kids. But apart from spending more than a decade as a receivers' coach, he had never served in any other coaching position. In the annals of NFL history, very few wide receivers have ever made a mark as a head coach, a position that favors ex-quarterbacks and those more intimately involved in game plans.

However, the great Unitas had often deferred to Berry in the huddle, not only for the play call but the blocking schemes. What few realized was that Berry's father had been his high school coach. He didn't know the names of many of the current Patriots players, or the coaches, but he knew the game and he knew people. His philosophy was simple: effort, execution, and conditioning, something he didn't try to distill to a bumper sticker.

For the moment, Berry seemed like the kindly uncle taking the kids away from their raging father, but he quickly impressed the players. When he rehired Rod Rust, Tony Collins said, "he earned more respect in one day than Ron Meyer had earned in three years." He also handed out Silly Putty to every Patriots receiver, which they studiously began squeezing.

Fired up by the change, the team responded with three straight wins before finding their level, finishing 9-7, and missing the playoffs by three games—nothing that hadn't been expected, even after making the change.

Still, the performance secured Raymond Berry's position into the 1985 season, and there was some reason for optimism. Collins, Craig James, Morgan, and Fryar gave the Pats plenty of weapons, Hannah was still one of the best linemen in the league, and the defense featured a blend of experienced vets like Steve Nelson and cornerback Raymond Clayborn in addition to emerging stars like Andre Tippett and Ronnie Lippett. They overlapped just enough to make a pretty good team.

Sticking with Eason at quarterback, Berry installed a new offense focused on running, not unlike one that Fairbanks had used. Like Plunkett before him, Grogan had broken down. Five knee surgeries, a broken leg, two shoulder separations, and other injuries had left him diminished, no longer able to outrace the defense. At the start of camp, Berry told him he was the backup, and Grogan accepted the role of mentoring Eason, even calling plays from the sideline.

Berry tried to keep it simple for the young quarterback. The Patriots used two running tandems, Collins and Craig James in one set, Tatupu and Robert Weathers in the other, ensuring that fresh legs were on the field at all times. And with the Sullivans distracted by their deteriorating financial situation, Berry was more or less left alone to make most decisions.

The team got off to a slow start as they adjusted, and with a 2-3 record, the season was at a crossroads. But in week six, Eason was sacked on three consecutive plays, the last resulting in a separated shoulder. Grogan stepped in and led the Pats to a 14–3 win. With the defense showing signs of getting better every week, Grogan followed up with some of the best sustained play of his career. Berry allowed Grogan to call his own plays, trusting him to make the right decision—Grogan was one of the last quarterbacks in the NFL to have that authority. The Patriots responded by winning six in a row and eight of nine, losing only to the Jets in overtime in Eason's first game back.

With two regular-season games left, the Jets, Dolphins, and Patriots were all 10-4 when New England made another trip to Miami. Although the Jets lost to the

Bears, the Orange Bowl and Miami proved to be too much for the Pats once again: the Dolphins edged them 30–27. Still, New England did manage to qualify for the playoffs with a season-ending 34–23 win against Cincinnati. True to form, this being the Patriots and the site of the win being Sullivan Stadium, the big story after the game wasn't the game but what took place after.

By midgame, dozens of fans were celebrating in typical Sullivan Stadium fashion by urinating, not in the restrooms, but alongside the concession stands and harassing female concession workers. By game's end, the celebratory spirit had spread to include thousands of revelers. When the clock reached 0:00, although Patriots fans had little practice celebrating making the playoffs, they made up for lost time and knew what to do next.

Most of the crowd swarmed the field. Then, not only did they tear down the goalpost, but the mob ("a bunch of drunken fans in a wild frenzy," as one state trooper recalled) proceeded to carry it out of the stadium and into the parking lot, where it was bent until broken into pieces. The mob then set off with a 20-foot section down Route 1. Where were they going? Who knew, who cared, and, more important, who was paying attention? The answer was "No one."

About a quarter-mile away, the metal post struck a power line and arced. Five fans were thrown to the ground, and only quick thinking by someone who used a sleeping bag as insulation in pulling the rest off the pole saved them from death. As it was, five fans were hurt, two seriously. They later sued the security company

Members of the New England Patriots celebrate. The Patriots began their march to the Super Bowl with a 26–14 win over the New York Jets in an AFC wild-card game at Giants Stadium on December 28, 1985.

hired by the Patriots and the town of Foxborough, winning settlements that totaled nearly $5 million. Only in Foxborough . . .

Although New England's defense had proven to be one of the best in the league, particularly in the second half of the season, few expected the Patriots to go very far. In a sense, they were not unlike the 1976 Patriots—a very good team, but not a great one. Expectations were low, for also as in 1976, the Patriots would have to play on the road. Only this time, they got on a roll. The first three weeks of the playoff run would provide the Patriots with the opportunity to exorcise almost every demon that had ever tortured the franchise.

If only they could have quit while they were ahead.

They started in New York, in the wild-card game against the Jets, a team they had played to a standoff during the regular season, splitting two close games. Anytime New York and Boston faced off in anything, there was more at stake, and this was no different. The Jets had become both a divisional and geographic rival. Although they weren't quite the Yankees, the meetings still conjured up the Boston–New York rivalry and all that it entailed—mainly providing Boston a chance to play the role of the snot-nosed kid who had been disrespected by the prep school scion who had every advantage.

The contest also featured a matchup between Eason and another quarterback from the 1983 class, Ken O'Brien, who, like Eason, had also been drafted ahead of Marino. Collectively, they were changing the game from one based on the run to one more oriented toward passing—particularly when rule changes meant to protect the investments in high-salaried quarterbacks and receivers made passing more efficient.

So far, O'Brien had the upper hand, outperforming Marino in 1985. The league's top-rated quarterback passed for almost 4,000 yards and threw 25 TDs with only 8 interceptions, albeit while being sacked 62 times. Eason, on the other hand, had thrown for barely half as many yards in 10 games, and his 11 TDs were offset by 17 interceptions. Playing on their home field, the Jets were favored.

Yet it wasn't even close. The Patriots played conservative, error-free football, while the Jets' sloppy play—fumbling three times and yielding two interceptions—fed into the Patriots' opportunistic defense.

New England led 13–7 late in the first half after two Tony Franklin field goals and a TD pass to Stanley Morgan on a fly pattern. There was less than a minute left in the half when the Patriots secured the win. O'Brien's receiver was covered on an option screen when Andre Tippett, rapidly becoming one of the best linebackers in football, burst up the middle and drilled the quarterback just after he released the ball. The helmet-to-helmet hit, compounded when O'Brien's head bounced off the ground, gave the quarterback a concussion. In an era when players were expected to "shake off" such injuries, O'Brien tried to return in the second half, but finally left the game. Replacement Pat Ryan, who had thrown only nine passes all year, wasn't O'Brien. Eason was an efficient 12 for 16 for the game, and New England won 26–14. "We just go out and fly around," said defensive back Fred Marion after the game. "Something will happen when you do that." And it did, giving the Patriots their first playoff win since 1963.

Of course, all that did was send the Patriots to the West Coast to face an even bigger nemesis, the Raiders, who had since relocated from Oakland to Los Angeles.

There was plenty of sniping before the game. Al Davis had denigrated the Patriots for not being very talented, and Raiders defensive end Howie Long, a native of Charlestown who had grown up in Milford, Massachusetts—not all that far from Foxborough—made the claim that if he had played for New England, he would not have been a very good player. But at the same time, the Raiders weren't playing very good football, particularly on offense. "That's what scares me," Al Davis said, "scoring points against that defense." With the specter of Ben Dreith and the "roughing the passer" call still lingering, the Patriots and their fans were pumped.

Davis was right to be scared of the defense. After bolting to a 17–7 lead, the Patriots' defense started flying around again and by the end of the game had intercepted Raider quarterback Marc Wilson three times and recovered three of five Raider fumbles, including one in the end zone for a touchdown. Meanwhile, Eason's Silly Putty–squeezing receivers caught everything they could

Patriots general manager Patrick Sullivan is punched in the jaw by Raiders linebacker Matt Millen following a verbal exchange in the aftermath of the Patriots' 27–20 upset win over the Raiders in Los Angeles.

touch, and Craig James ran for 100 yards. The Patriots' defense shut out the Raiders in the second half, giving the Patriots a 27–20 win and putting the team into the AFC championship game.

There was more to it, though, than just a win and a loss. There was no love lost between the two teams—Davis and Billy Sullivan had each testified against the other in various lawsuits, such as Sullivan's suit against the league over money and antitrust issues, the team stockholders' suit against Sullivan, and Davis's suit against the league for the right to move his team. As the two teams left the field through the same tunnel, the Raiders' Howie Long, hearing Pat Sullivan taunting him, faked a punch at the Patriots' GM. He told reporters later, "I kind of talked like I was going to hit him, but I just wanted to see him jump because I knew he was such a wimp. Spineless. That's pretty much what he is." Sullivan responded by grabbing Long's face mask. When Long's teammate Matt Millen saw that, the linebacker threw a punch—this one for real—that hit Sullivan on the jaw. The GM saw stars and later needed stitches.

Both sides probably should have let it go, but they chose to continue the skirmish in the press. "Let's just say that it hasn't been a very pleasant relationship," said Billy Sullivan of Davis and his club. "I'm not a saint, but I like to play by the rules. I mean, Al's 'Commitment to Excellence' makes me smile. I'd rather have a slogan that said, 'Commitment to Integrity.' Yes, I relish this victory more than anybody."

There would soon be little more to relish, the way things were about to go, both on the field and with his bankers.

• • •

The Dolphins beat the Browns to reach the championship game, setting up the finish every New England fan and player wanted. Fans and media at the time had elevated Miami's hold over the Patriots, at least in the Orange Bowl, to the near-equal of the hold the Yankees held over the Red Sox as archrival and ultimate antagonist. Time and time again the Dolphins had played Lucy to the Patriots' Charlie Brown, always pulling the ball away and leaving New England and its fans flat on their backs, usually uttering expressions far more profane than "good grief."

In the week before the game, the T-shirt catchphrase in New England became "Squish the Fish," a quest that seemed both unlikely and irresistible at once: the biggest victory in franchise history, one that promised to finally rid the team of the yoke of ineptitude. After all, they'd dumped the Jets and finally beaten the Raiders. Why not squish those swimming mammals from Miami?

Never before, not even in 1976, had the region been so consumed with Patriotic fervor.

Cue Irving Fryar. In his second season in the league, he was emerging as a top-rate talent. Fryar paired with Stanley Morgan gave the Patriots two bona-fide burners as receivers, even if Eason struggled to get them the ball as often as he should; their presence was much of the reason why the Patriots' running attack, paced by Craig James, had rushed for more than 2,300 yards. DBs couldn't cheat and had to play them close, leaving a running back plenty of room to run once he made it past the line. Moreover, Fryar also returned kicks and punts; earlier in the season, he had run back two for touchdowns.

But Fryar—who would later describe his early years with the Patriots as "dirty, filled with drugs, filled with lies, filled with alcohol"—was living large and taking advantage of being a first-round draft pick with fame and more money than he knew what to do with. And when the Patriots boarded their plane to Miami on Wednesday, after a rally before a crowd of 10,000 at Government Center, Fryar wasn't on board.

He had a good story. See, he'd been helping his pregnant wife, a former cheerleader for the USFL Breakers: "I was putting this knife away because I like to help around the house, and I had the blade in my hand. The tip caught on the edge of the counter because I wasn't paying attention." It had severed the tendon in his little finger, and he could not play.

That was the good story. In reality, after taking a late flight back from Los Angeles after the Raiders game, Fryar had stayed out all night. When he did get home, he told his wife she wasn't coming to Miami, sparking an argument. The next night, while having dinner at a restaurant on the South Shore, they kept arguing, his wife wanting to know just where Fryar had been two nights before. As the couple fought, Fryar knocked his wife to the ground and she stabbed him to defend herself from the act of domestic violence.

Boston talk radio erupted in a frenzy. This scandal was *so* Patriots, *so* Boston, the strangest kind of bad luck, like Ted Williams being hit on the elbow in a practice game before the 1946 World Series, only worse—and

Aboard Delta flight 257 bound for Miami and the AFC championship game were Patriots fans Brian Buck, Bob Ferzoco, and Doug Limone. New England did indeed "squish the fish," winning their first AFC championship by a score of 31–14.

certain to squelch any notion that the Patriots would ever, *ever* squish the fish.

But to their credit, the Patriots, taking a cue from their low-key coach, did their best to ignore the controversy. In reality, Fryar's issues were also the least of their concerns. That same week the Patriots learned that at least twelve team members had what were termed "drug problems." Five cases were deemed "serious," and most of them involved cocaine. For the time being, the organization chose to keep that issue in-house and look the other way. The *Globe*'s Ron Borges had the story, and Berry had confirmed it off the record. Both agreed to release the story at season's end.

One reason they weren't unduly concerned about the loss of Fryar was that he really wasn't part of the upcoming game plan, except as a decoy. The Patriots had no desire to test the Dolphins' "Killer B" defense and have Eason throw the ball thirty times. They planned to run and to try to keep the Dolphins' Dan Marino from throwing the ball forty times. If the Patriots could get some turnovers—which by now were an expected part of their game—and keep the ball out of Marino's hands, they liked their chances. Stephen Starring replaced Fryar in the lineup.

As John Hannah said later, "I think we only threw the ball like ten or twelve times. It was rock 'em, sock 'em football." On the first play from scrimmage, Dolphins running back Tony Nathan fumbled, and the ball-hawking Patriots recovered. The game was less than three minutes old and New England led 3–0.

That set the tone. The Dolphins couldn't keep control of the ball, and the Patriots wouldn't let it go, keeping the ball for an extraordinary forty minutes on a soft field and leaving little time for Dan Marino to work his magic downfield. Even when he did, the Dolphins either dropped the ball or fumbled it away, spitting it out six times. It was as if all the bad luck the Patriots had accrued over the decades in the Orange Bowl was swept away all at once. Eason, as Borges noted, "did a 1980s impersonation

Patriots running back Robert Weathers (24) races upfield against the Miami Dolphins in the 1985 AFC championship game at the Orange Bowl on January 12, 1986, to help seal a 31–14 triumph.

Longtime season-ticket holder Josh Crowley of Gardner, Massachusetts, shows off his Super Bowl tickets to the rest of the line after waiting hours at Foxboro Raceway in Foxborough on January 13, 1986.

of Bart Starr all afternoon by completing 10 of 12 passes for the paltry sum of 71 yards and the kingly total of 3 touchdowns," a performance as efficient as it was effective. Craig James ran for more than 100 yards and made it look easy. At the end of the game the Patriots, winners in Miami for the first time since 1966, carried Berry off the field like at the end of a Chip Hilton novel.

No team had ever gone on a better postseason run on the road than the Patriots. "We did it in the Meadowlands to the Jets, we did it in the Coliseum against the Raiders, we did it here in the Orange Bowl," said Pats tackle Brian Holloway. "We did it all to teams we had lost to. We have some magic. This is a different team from the past."

At last the Patriots were going to the Super Bowl. For Billy Sullivan, the win brought a brief instant of something that felt like vindication. For a moment, it had all been worth it. The *Washington Post*'s Tony Kornheiser captured the scene, noting that Sullivan spent the last moments of the game standing alone "in the steady, gloomy drizzle of the Miami evening, droplets of water landing softly on his bald head, and watched the numbers tick away. From five minutes, to four minutes, to three minutes. He saw the time remaining in the game continue to erode, and he saw the score—Patriots 31, Miami 14—continue to hold. And he knew the waiting was over . . . 'I never felt better,' he said looking up at the sky and smiling. 'I feel like I'm standing in glorious

sunlight. I don't even think it's raining out.'" Billy Sullivan was finally somebody—the owner of a Super Bowl team.

Squish the Fish shirts were rapidly exchanged for ones that optimistically read Berry the Bears. And for the first time ever, really, the Patriots bandwagon was not just full but spilling over. The economic revival known as "the Massachusetts Miracle" was in full swing, the city of Boston was rebuilding, the Celtics were in the midst of a run that would see them go 40-1 at home for the season and win a championship, the Red Sox were on the rise with the best young pitcher in baseball in Roger Clemens, and the Bruins were in a pitched five-team battle for a division title. And now the Patriots were part of it, the big story, above the fold and on the lips of every broadcaster in New England. Hell, they'd already won three straight on the road. Why couldn't they win just one more? It seemed like their time.

The thing about streaks, though, particularly the kind of streaks that haven't happened before, is that they always end, and when they do, the pendulum tends to swing the other way, and swing hard. While the 31–14 win swept away a lot of bad karma, Super Bowl XX and the Chicago Bears awaited the Patriots two weeks later at the Superdome in New Orleans.

The Patriots were a good team, and in recent weeks they had been an extremely fortunate one, winning by way of turnovers, ball control, field position, and a limited but surgical passing attack. But the Bears had been dominant all year. Paced by running back Walter Payton, flamboyant quarterback Jim McMahon, and an overwhelming physical defense that featured linebacker Mike Singletary and nose tackle William "the Refrigerator" Perry, who had become a cult hero after coach Mike Ditka used the 300-pound-plus lineman as a running back in goal-line situations, the Bears went 15-1 in the regular season and then won their two playoff games by shutout. If the Patriots were Cinderella, the Bears were Goliath, and there was a reason no fairy tale made use of that pairing.

The Pats' win in Miami might as well have taken place at midnight. Tony Collins would later note, "That was our Super Bowl." Unfortunately, it wasn't the real one, because the Patriots played that one as if it were an intrasquad scrimmage during the first week of camp. The sunlight Billy Sullivan imagined he felt on his face would soon be overtaken by darkness.

The Patriots had faced the Bears in the second week of the season and lost 20–7, but the game hadn't been a complete blowout. Then again, neither team had hit its stride. With both Holloway and Hannah out hurt, the Patriots ran for only 27 yards that day, but the Bears had improved since then as well. The fact that the Patriots entered the Super Bowl XX underdogs by nine and a half points should have been a sign.

Everything went according to plan . . . for about a minute and a half.

On the Bears' first possession, Walter Payton fumbled and the Patriots took over on the 19-yard line.

On the Pats' first offensive play, tight end Lin Dawson tore up a knee. On the second, Stanley Morgan dropped a touchdown pass. Two plays later, kicker Tony Franklin booted a field goal only 1:14 into the game to score the quickest points in Super Bowl history, giving New England a 3–0 lead. Too bad there were still nearly fifty-nine minutes to play. That would be the end of New England's highlight reel.

From that moment on, it was as if New England wasn't even on the field. The Bears took a 6–3 lead on two field-position field goals while the Patriots couldn't move the ball at all and were forced to throw. Eason had been protected in the game plans all year, but now that

Defensive tackle William Perry (72) of the Chicago Bears dives in for a touchdown during Super Bowl XX against the New England Patriots at the Superdome in New Orleans. The Bears won the game, 46–10.

he had to throw, he couldn't. His recent efficiency had been a mirage. Since mid-December, he'd thrown almost exclusively to running backs and tight ends, often with a lead, abandoning the middle of the field and deep throws. Every time he'd had to throw thirty or more times during the regular season, New England had lost.

He was pummeled, and when he wasn't, he turtled to avoid punishment. The *Herald*'s George Kimball accurately described the New England offense: "instead of three yards and a cloud of dust . . . three incompletions and a punt." Eason never even completed a pass, going 0-for-6 before being pulled and replaced by Grogan just before the end of the first half. The veteran was no better. He started off with five straight incompletions before the Bears went into the locker room with the safest 23–3 lead in football history.

The halftime show featured a performance by Up with People, the clean-cut, anti-counterculture quasi-cult, in a saccharine-coated, frozen-smiled extravaganza. They put on a far better performance than the Patriots.

Just how bad was it? Put it this way: in the first half, the Bears outgained the Patriots 236 yards to minus 19. A few days before the game, the *New Orleans Times Picayune* reported that the starters on Chicago's base 46 defense, which included five Pro Bowlers, were vastly underpaid by ownership, the penurious McCaskey family. Collectively, they earned a half-million dollars less than their Patriot counterparts. The Bears had a point to prove. They didn't just want to win—they wanted to grind the Patriots into the turf beneath their cleats.

New England took the second half kickoff and within two minutes faced a third-and-33 situation. Grogan had already been sacked twice and thrown two more incompletions. Rick Camarillo made the best play of the game for New England with a 62-yard punt, but in the next nine minutes the Bears scored three touchdowns, the last a kick-you-while-you're-down-and-rub-your-face-in-the-dirt one-yard plunge by the Refrigerator, William Perry. In the fourth quarter, the Bears were already celebrating as the Patriots finally scored a touchdown on a Grogan pass to Fryar, perhaps the most inconsequential score in Super Bowl history. The Bears ended the scoring with one final embarrassment as backup defensive lineman Henry Waechter sacked Grogan in the end zone for a safety.

Patriots fan Mike Rossini ponders his team's loss after the New England Patriots lost to the Chicago Bears in Super Bowl XX on January 26, 1986.

The end result was the worst defeat in Super Bowl history, 46–10. The game was never that close, and most Patriots fans didn't stick with it to the finish, even if they managed to make it through the halftime show. New England had hoped to run the ball, but ended the day with only seven yards rushing while losing 61 on seven sacks. In the aftermath, SQUISH THE FISH towels were sequestered in the back of the bottom drawer while those BERRY THE BEARS T-shirts were torn into shreds and used to mop up the mess of stale beer and sodden nachos. Afterward, Will McDonough wrote, "Once again, they were alone. Humiliated in front of the nation and most of the free world."

Three days after the game, the drug story became public. After all the good that had come during their remarkable run, the team was right back to where they began.

They were still the Patriots, and everyone was laughing again.

CHAPTER SEVEN

1986–1992

CLOSE SHAVES

Pick your metaphor. Train wreck? Car crash? Nightmare? Cataclysm? Act of God? Whatever phrase you choose, it was wicked awful. For every member of the Patriots organization, their fans, and even those who covered the team, the next few years were a careening disaster both on the field and off, a scorched earth of incompetence and ineptitude, a catastrophe unlike any other to befall an NFL franchise.

New England Patriots owner Victor Kiam stayed through a downpour as a thunderstorm hit the Patriots practice at Bryant College in Smithfield, Rhode Island, in 1989.

"We have a situation that exists that we feel is intolerable," explained Berry at the time. "It's been going on for a year and I had to weigh the damages of doing something about it immediately by going public. We felt with the season going the way it had . . . that's why we didn't do anything before."

It wasn't surprising, or it shouldn't have been. Playing football provides no immunity from drug use—if anything, it provides tacit approval. The culture of professional football has always encouraged players to take all kinds of drugs to counteract the effects of the game, and as Berry indicated, player health is usually secondary in importance to winning. Although the NFLPA opposed drug screening, after the scandal became public the Patriots reluctantly voted to approve testing. The team said the results would only be used for treatment, not for punishment.

By then, not only had the players turned against each other, but fans had turned against the team. A lot of Patriots fans thought drug use had cost the team a championship, and many black fans raised an eyebrow at the fact that only black players had been named publicly. The drug users were blamed disproportionately for the Patriots' failures, which for some made the loss to the Bears easier to explain, although in reality the Patriots' drug problem was little worse than that of any other club in the league, including the hard-partying champion Bears. Pot use was ubiquitous in the league, then and now. And this was the 1980s: cocaine in particular was widely available, its health impacts were little known, and it was a party drug attractive to young men with money in their pockets, which described most players in the league and an awful lot of other people around Boston at the cusp of the "Massachusetts Miracle." Coke was the drug of choice in the boardroom as much as the locker room. The revelations didn't end the careers of any of the six players named, or Berry, but in some respects the scandal remained a stain on their careers—particularly in Boston—that none of them could ever quite escape.

AND AS EXCRUCIATING AS IT IS TO RECOUNT, it was even more painful to experience as it wiped out a decade of relative success and left the franchise in ruins. But it is necessary to know what happened in the aftermath of Super Bowl XX in order to have a full understanding of how the franchise became what it is today. If you're much under forty, you may not even remember most of it.

Count your blessings.

Any shred of warm and fuzzy feelings remaining after the Super Bowl was erased a few days later when the drug scandal broke. Raymond Berry had been acutely aware of the team's drug problem since a postgame party it held after their regular-season loss in Miami. It was bad enough that as many as twelve players were said to be regular users of cocaine, marijuana, or both, but the scandal was made even worse when the only six names leaked publicly in the *Globe* were Fryar, Collins, Starring, Clayborn, Sims, and Roland James—all black. The anonymity of the other players involved cast a shadow over everyone, but particularly implicated the other black players on the roster. That didn't go unnoticed in Boston, where racial sensitivities always ran high. Team members started pointing fingers, trying to figure out who was the snitch and who had let Berry know what had gone on at that party.

• • •

The only people not making money during the Massachusetts Miracle were the Sullivans and the Patriots. During their Super Bowl run, the club reportedly lost $9 million, and while fans had been swept up in their race to the postseason, it had become ever clearer that Billy Sullivan was considering selling out. In August 1985, Sullivan had hired Goldman Sachs to broker a sale to include the stadium, the racetrack, and surrounding properties for somewhere around $100 million. All that fall and into the winter, reports of potential buyers and potential problems selling the team popped up in the press.

That was the first time the name of Robert Kraft, a native of Brookline, longtime season-ticket holder, and president and CEO of Rand-Whitney, a paper and packaging company, was mentioned as a potential suitor. If Boston sports fans knew his name—and few did—it was only because he had been floated a few times before as a possible buyer of the Red Sox and the Celtics, and because he'd owned the Boston Lobsters during the brief tenure of World Team Tennis. Now he joined the crowd pondering the Patriots, a dizzying array of dreamers and schemers, deal-makers and fakers, developers and bankers, people with connections but no money, or money but no connections. Over time that list would include former Red Sox trainer Buddy Leroux, sports talk host Eddie Andelman, hotelier Joe O'Donnell, shopping mall magnate Steve Karp, New York restaurateur and financier Jeffery Chodorow, Philadelphia-based businessman Fran Murray, Reebok head Paul Fireman, Wonderland dog-track owner Charlie Sarkis, New York businessman Ira Lampert, and assorted politicians, including former transportation secretary Drew Lewis, ex–postmaster general Robert Tisch, Donald Trump, and a dozen or so others who kicked the tires and then moved on or were booted out of the way as soon as their name hit the papers.

It would prove to be a messy transaction. Billy owned the team, the Stadium Management Corporation owned the actual stadium, and Foxboro Associates held the racetrack—a convoluted arrangement made more complicated by factors such as the shared parking situation, a court ruling that gave the racetrack control of scheduling, a variety of mortgages and loans taken out by various entities, and a basket of assorted lawsuits,

real, threatened, and imagined. Added to all this was the obvious fact that Billy Sullivan really didn't want to sell. Even though there was no other realistic way out, he still clung to the fantasy that he could somehow retain a role in running the team. All the while he was still hoping for a bailout and praying for a miracle, borrowing from Peter to pay Paul, signing players to contracts with deferred payments, and using any incoming cash as quickly as it came in to stave off debtors. According to some reports, interest payments alone totaled around $100,000 per day.

Given this, why, for God's sake, would anyone want to own this team? Well, in their own way, each man wanted to be Billy Sullivan—minus the mountain of debt—because if not for the Patriots, few would have continued to know Sullivan's name. He had been many things, but never a "non-entity." All interested parties thought they could make money on the deal just by not being named Sullivan—besides, owning a major sports team had already made someone who otherwise was just another sorta rich guy a very well-known rich guy. For most, simply buying an NFL team guaranteed healthy profits, celebrity, and access to the levers of power in politics and media, not just locally but nationally, and provided even more opportunities to accumulate wealth, power, and prestige. People would call you "Mister" who never knew your name before. And when you became a celebrity, well, you also suddenly got a lot better-looking.

The NFL had traditionally been something of a family business for many owners, but that was changing. Wall Street money was coming into the game, revenues were beginning to explode, and it was suddenly a lot more crowded at the trough. While old-timers in the league still looked at Sullivan with a kind of abject, nostalgic affection, the new breed of owners saw him as an anachronism. At various times, Kraft, Lampert, and Fran Murray emerged as the most serious suitors, but that list changed as often as the names on the team roster.

The on-field collapse wasn't instantaneous. Although the Patriots were clearly not a Super Bowl team, they were still talented. Before the start of the season, Berry was awarded a new five-year contract as coach, but Hannah and defensive end Julius Adams, both of whom had played their entire career with the Patriots, announced their retirement. Both were still able to play—Hannah had made the Pro Bowl the previous season, and Adams would eventually return after a one-year layoff—but the physical and psychological grind had become too much.

In 1986, Tony Eason seemed to rebound from his embarrassing performance in the Super Bowl, and after a slow start the Patriots ripped off seven straight wins to put themselves in the playoff hunt. Then they lost two in a row, setting up yet another trip to Miami with a division title on the line. Without Hannah, the Pats' running attack suffered, but Eason's arm made up the difference. This time the Dolphins, only 8-7, had little to play for in their final appearance at the Orange Bowl. The stadium-based curse was over, and after Eason was roughed up and knocked out of the game, Grogan came on to lead the Patriots to a 34–27 win, and their second consecutive division title.

Chuck Sullivan at the Dedham courthouse for hearings regarding the Patriots. Often criticized by fans for his handling of team legal matters, such as several noteworthy contract stalemates, Sullivan also forged a career apart from football as an attorney in New York.

Unfortunately, that gave the Pats the right to play John Elway and the Denver Broncos. Eason, back in the lineup, actually outplayed Elway statistically. The Broncos controlled the ball on the ground, though, and on the last play of the third quarter, Elway, even playing on a bum ankle after being crushed by Andre Tippett earlier, made the play of the game. On third down with the ball on the 48, the Pats' Don Blackmon jumped offsides. With a free play, Elway let it fly, and Vance Johnson made a tumbling catch in the end zone. The Broncos won 22–17, but the enduring image of the game for Patriots fans was Eason being dumped in the end zone by Rulon Jones for a safety to secure the loss.

In many ways, Eason never got back up.

• • •

Tony Eason had fallen deeply into a definition he would never escape, a player never measured by what he was, but by what he was not: he was neither Elway, Marino, and the other stars of the 1983 draft nor Grogan. Even in failure, the older vet looked like he was trying and took hits either standing up or running, while Eason (wisely) tried to protect himself and ducked before being hit. It didn't help that Hannah, after retiring, said that Eason "should have worn a skirt," but Hannah had not covered himself in glory versus the Bears any more than his quarterback. During Eason's tenure as starter, he had been sacked 130 times, including 59 in 1984. He had plenty of reasons to duck.

The 1987 season was no improvement. Eason signed late, but received only a one-year deal as the Patriots made it clear they'd decided to move on. A strike after only two games of the season—at which time New England was 1-1—helped mask their slide. Now the labor issue was free agency. The players hoped to break the onerous Rozelle Rule, which effectively neutered their power of free agency.

This time the NFL struck back, canceling the third week of games while teams assembled squads of replacement players and a fair number of regular-season players who chose to cross the picket line so they could continue to cash a check during the season. Among the Patriots who agreed to serve as scabs were Tony Collins, Andre Tippett, and Tony Franklin.

The Patriots went 2-1 during the strike, playing before small crowds and watching their TV ratings dwindle as the replacement players played like, well, replacement players. But they gained a quarterback when local hero Doug Flutie, the undersized Heisman Trophy–winning quarterback from Boston College, joined the team by trade from the Bears and crossed the line to lead them to victory in the final "strike" game. By then, the strike itself was over, because so many players had crossed the line that the Players Association essentially disbanded after gaining nothing. The regular players returned for week six, and the season continued as if nothing had happened, although some players, like Flutie, would have a hard time shedding the scab label. New England finished 8-7, out of the playoffs, in a season that in many ways was utterly forgettable as hardly anyone on the team had a year to be proud of. Eason went down again with a separated shoulder, and Grogan took the bulk of the snaps as quarterback, but it was obvious the Patriots were not going anywhere no matter who was under center.

All the while, the convoluted financial burden on the franchise grew even worse, and the predators circled as Billy and the other Sullivans tried to buy time and stave everyone off. In April 1986, Fran Murray, whose brother Jim had once been GM of the Eagles, signed a purchase-and-sale agreement to buy the leasehold on Sullivan Stadium for about $30 million, and in October Sullivan sold Murray's group, NEP Partners, an option to buy the team for $63 million. But within months, the group claimed the Patriots had violated terms of the option. By January 1987, it was revealed that the Murray group was offering the team to a group from St. Louis, where the Cardinals were in trouble, in a scheme both to help keep the Cardinals in St. Louis and unload the Patriots.

That didn't fly, so throughout the 1987 season one group after another raised their hands and tried to put together a bid while Sullivan grimly held on, but by January 1988 he was broke and couldn't meet the Patriots' payroll. The NFL stepped in and released $4 million in contingency funds to keep the franchise afloat. A month later, Stadium Management Corporation went bankrupt, drowning under a debt of more than $50 million.

The Sullivans were dead men walking. For the next six months, a variety of buyers looked over the rusting hulk of the Patriots like used-car dealers at an auction,

Former SMU "Pony Express" running back Craig James carries the ball in the Patriots' 33–3 win over the Indianapolis Colts in the 1986 season opener.

each thinking it was restorable, but one after another, either people like Trump chose not to make serious bids or guys like Fireman and Tisch tried and failed to put together an acceptable offer. The whole thing turned into a hot and very complicated mess.

"I liked it so much, I bought the company." That's all people knew about Victor Kiam, owner of the Remington Corporation, best known for its line of electric razors. Kiam was a guy who had parlayed an initial $500,000 investment into an eventual $700 million fortune and become the huckster for his own brand. He appeared on television commercials touting the shaver and presented himself as a Wall Street wunderkind in an era of entrepreneurial reverence, one of a generation of bean counters who thought being swept up in a suddenly roaring economy was a sign of unique financial genius. Kiam authored several treacly, ghostwritten accounts of "how I did it" and appeared on TV talk shows as an instant expert on everything. On July 29, 1988, he reached an agreement to buy the Patriots for $84 million, a transaction that did

In the 1986 AFC playoffs, John Elway celebrates as he crosses the goal line for a TD in the first half against New England on the way to a 22–17 Bronco victory at Mile High Stadium.

not include Sullivan Stadium. The deal became official on October 28, with Kiam as majority owner and chairman, minority stakeholder Fran Murray as vice chairman, and Billy Sullivan retaining the title of team president, a position with little remaining authority.

A month later, Robert Kraft and Steve Karp, through K-Korp, outbid Kiam to purchase Sullivan Stadium for what was variously reported as between $22 million and $25 million, and eventually they acquired the surrounding parcel of about 300 acres as well. Most thought they overpaid for the cursed stadium, but the team was tied to the facility by a lease that required the Pats to play at least ten games a year in Foxborough, including exhibitions, until 2001 while coughing up between $650,000 and $1.3 million in annual rent. Meanwhile, K-Korp would receive all the income from concessions and parking.

Kraft was taking a long view. His real goal was to own the Patriots, and he knew that any subsequent buyer would have to go through him, either to rid themselves of the lease or to build a new stadium on the land. It was all about leverage.

By this time, most Patriot fans didn't give a damn who owned the team or why, as long as it wasn't Sullivan. Although many appreciated Sullivan's initial effort that brought the franchise to New England and kept it there, as well as his role in the birth of the Jimmy Fund, younger fans found it hard to find much else very admirable in his twenty-eight-year tenure as owner. The team's record on the field simply did not support other conclusions—only Red Sox owner Tom Yawkey had owned a local franchise for longer without ever winning a championship. Over the previous decade or so, and particularly in the past few seasons, Pats fans had felt cheated as the constant financial Sturm und Drang made winning appear to be a secondary goal to the Sullivans.

But in the ways that mattered to Sullivan, he had succeeded. He had brought pro football to New England and by doing that had become somebody other than the non-entity he feared he might one day be. Yet in the end, that's what he became. Sullivan's flaw was somewhat similar to Yawkey's, minus the racial track record. For both men, retaining control and hiring friends and cronies—and in Sullivan's case, family—were in the end more important than wins or losses. But that came with a price. His final legacy was a team known for all that it was not, and for all the wrong reasons, rather than for any victories ever won on the field.

Rather remarkably, the new team owner made few changes when he took over. Kiam seemed satisfied simply with the added celebrity afforded by being an NFL owner. The Patriots opened the season with a win, but then lost three in a row, the only bright spot being rookie running back John Stephens. Grogan started the season as quarterback, but after game four, with the season already effectively over, he was replaced by Flutie.

The move was popular with fans—Flutie had long been revered in Boston for his last-second "Hail Mary" touchdown pass that allowed BC to beat Miami, 47–45, in 1984. Flutie himself recognized that the play had made him a national name and local legend, once saying, "Without the Hail Mary pass I think I could have been very easily forgotten." But at only five-nine—if that— he was considered too small to succeed in pro football and wasn't drafted until the eleventh round in the NFL. He signed with the USFL instead, struggled there, then joined the Bears and took his last chance to salvage a pro career in the United States by crossing the picket line.

He initially gave the Pats a burst of energy, and fans a reason to pay attention, and for a while, not unlike Tim Tebow's tenure with the Denver Broncos, it worked. The Patriots won six of their next nine with Flutie as quarterback, even as he often failed to throw for more than 100 yards. Berry, claimed Flutie, "had no confidence in me." He was beloved, but he was not a quarterback to build a team around. The Patriots finished 9-7, but all they had left was nostalgia.

In 1989, even that began to run out. Flutie started three games and was benched. Eason was done and eventually traded to the Jets. Grogan was worn out and worn down. Although they won five games—barely,

> "I LIKED IT SO MUCH,
> I BOUGHT THE COMPANY."
>
> —VICTOR KIAM

each victory was by a narrow margin—they weren't very good at any aspect of the game. Even worse, they had become boring. By the end of the year, crowds at Foxboro Stadium—the Sullivan name had been removed and "Foxborough" truncated to "Foxboro" to differentiate the stadium from the town—were less than half capacity. Boston was once again known for the Red Sox, the Celtics, and the Bruins. The Patriots barely mattered. They only seemed to make the papers for something bad. *Boston Herald* writer Michael Felger dubbed Irving Fryar "the human headline" for his continued run-ins with the law and other controversies, ranging from car accidents to brawls and other misbehavior.

Berry was fired at the end of the season, and longtime defensive coordinator Rod Rust—the man Ron Meyer had tried to fire—was named head coach, even though the Patriots defense was one of the league's worst. In an increasingly pass-oriented NFL, the Patriots had given up nearly eight yards per pass attempt in 1989.

Under Rust, the franchise reached a nadir: the Patriots won only a single game in 1990, finishing last in offense and next to last in defense in the NFL. How bad were they? That single victory proved to be the lowest point of the season for the 1-15 team.

The day after the Pats defeated the Colts, 16–14, *Boston Herald* reporter Lisa Olson went to Foxboro Stadium to do a story on the Patriots' injured linebackers. She had asked for the players to come to the media room, but they lingered in the locker room. She was on deadline, so she sought them out.

By 1990, the right of female reporters to enter a male locker room was well established. In 1976, the *Globe*'s Lesley Visser had become the first woman to serve as a beat writer for an NFL team when she began reporting on the Patriots. Denied locker room privileges, she was forced to wait for player interviews in the team's weight room while her male colleagues enjoyed full access. The NFL, following action by the NBA and NHL in 1980, finally extended locker room access to female reporters in 1985. By 1990, incidents of any kind were becoming isolated, although female reporters still faced resistance

In 1984, the Patriots scored the first overall pick in the NFL draft for the third time in their history and selected wide receiver Irving Fryar of Nebraska. In nine seasons with New England, Fryar seemed to make as many headlines off the field as on, while helping lead the Patriots to playoff berths in his first two seasons.

from some coaches and players. Olson wrote later that "ninety-nine percent of the time everyone acts like professionals and the arrangement works just fine."

This time the arrangement did not work fine. As she told Eileen Prose of Boston ABC television affiliate WCVB a few days later, as she spoke with defensive back Maurice Hurst at his locker about twenty feet from the shower area, she kept her back to the showers, because, as she said to Prose, "I hate being in there." From behind she heard a player saying, "Is she looking, is she looking? Go make her look." Then Patriot backup tight end Zeke Mowatt, towering over Olson, stood alongside her, exposed his genitals, and according to Olson said, "Is this what you want, is this what you're here for? Take a bite of this."

Mortified, Olson left and immediately reported the incident to her editors at the *Herald*. Not wanting to create a controversy or spark a war between the team and her paper, she and the *Herald* both wanted the Pats to handle the incident in-house, but even after the paper

contacted the team, it was several days before either Rust or owner Victor Kiam was informed. The *Globe* ended up breaking the story at the end of the following week, and Pat Sullivan, on behalf of the team, issued a statement that, while admitting Olson was harassed verbally, read, "My investigation has been unable to confirm the allegations that a player suggested physical contact with Ms. Olson," and stated that one player (who turned out to be Mowatt) had been levied a fine of $2,000. Then Kiam, asked about the incident by the *Herald*'s Kevin Mannix—who expected Kiam to make a statement, genuine or not, decrying the incident—said instead, "I can't disagree with the player's actions. Your paper is asking for trouble by sending a female reporter to cover the team." The *Globe*'s Will McDonough went on NBC and reported that Olson had embellished her account, saying the players "knocked down most of her story, okay?" Jim Baker of the *Herald* nailed it when he countered, "No. Not okay. In a word, wrong."

Still, in combination, Sullivan's and Kiam's statements and McDonough's defense hung Olson out to dry, called her account into question in the minds of some members of the public, and gave Patriots fans license to unleash their own form of harassment. Over the next weeks and months, some left crude messages on Olson's phone and broke into her apartment to scrawl LEAVE BOSTON OR DIE on the walls. Olson was reassigned to cover the Bruins and Celtics, but vile chants were directed toward her from the stands both at the Garden and on the road. Olson, easily recognizable due to her red hair and appearances on local media, was pelted in public with beer and food, and one fan even punched her in the face. Kiam himself proved to be utterly insensitive, calling her a "classic bitch" (Kiam later argued unconvincingly that he had said "classy bitch") and even telling an off-color joke about the episode at a banquet. The incident itself was bad enough, but the Patriots' and their fans' utterly inept and crude responses made it even worse and caused the fallout to cloud the entire season.

As the Patriots' season unraveled, the NFL conducted its own investigation of what took place, coming down as hard on the Patriots for the coverup as for the crime and condemning the team's resistance to taking definitive action. In November, the NFL accurately concluded in its report that Olson had been "degraded and humiliated." Their investigation confirmed Mowatt's actions, found his denials "not credible," and identified Michael Timpson and Robert Perryman as the two players who taunted her verbally. NFL commissioner Paul Tagliabue called the entire episode "distasteful, unnecessary and damaging to the league and others. It included a mix of misconduct, insensitivity, misstatements and other inappropriate actions or inaction, all of which could and should have been avoided." The league fined Mowatt $12,500, Timpson and Perryman $5,000 each, and the Patriots $50,000, half of that to go toward a leaguewide program for all league personnel on media relations. The report found Pat Sullivan's response "inadequate" and concluded that "no one tried to bring the humiliating activity around Lisa Olson to a stop. Neither players nor management personnel said or did anything."

For the organization, the weight of responsibility fell, rightfully, not just on the players but on management. Olson, alone among everyone involved, was the only person to act like a mature adult. She refused to let it thwart her career: she wrote for several of *Herald* owner Rupert Murdoch's papers in Australia before returning to the United States to write for other outlets. She eventually received a $250,000 settlement from the team, which she used to fund a scholarship program for young journalists. To this day, she refuses to use the incident for her own benefit.

The Patriots, meanwhile, lost their final fourteen games and tore themselves apart internally, since not every player on the team defended the actions of their teammates. As the season ended, the fallout continued. First Kiam tried to consolidate control by hiring Sam Jankovich, who had served as athletic director for the soon-to-be-scandal-ridden University of Miami, as team CEO, saying, "This is now the Sam Jankovich era." Jankovich moved into Billy Sullivan's old office, fired Rust as soon as the season ended, and three days later took a page from the Patriots' past by hiring another college coach. This time the choice was grandfatherly Dick MacPherson, who had recently led Syracuse back to national prominence. A month later, Pat Sullivan, sensing that he was no longer in a position of authority and feeling that he had been made a scapegoat over the Olson incident, resigned.

It was all just so much shuffling of the chairs on the deck. Kiam's continuing insensitivity made him persona non grata among other NFL owners and damaged the financial health of his company. His partner Fran Murray had an agreement that allowed him to opt out of the arrangement within a certain time period and sell his minority share to Kiam for the prearranged price of $38 million. Murray knew the Patriots' value had dropped and had his eye on St. Louis. He let Kiam know that when that date came in October, he wanted out, but now Kiam wasn't as flush with cash as before. Meanwhile, team "president" Billy Sullivan was suing the NFL, claiming that if they had just allowed him to sell 49 percent of the team to the public, he would have been able to keep the team for himself. The Patriots would endure yet another season with ownership in crisis.

The Pats were better under the ever-enthusiastic MacPherson, who hugged everybody but the line judge on the sidelines. But then again, it was hard to be worse. Retread quarterback Hugh Millen came in as a free agent and threw twice as many interceptions as touchdowns, and rookie running back Leonard Russell emerged as the feature back, but little else of consequence took place on the field. Crowds at Foxboro, where the artificial turf had finally been replaced with grass, remained sparse.

Kiam couldn't come up with the money to buy out Murray, and by the end of the season it was becoming increasingly clear that he would have to sell, something the NFL, desperate for some stability in such a potentially lucrative market, couldn't wait for. Kiam's financial genius with electric razors had not extended to the football field. In three years, he reportedly lost nearly $20

Patriot John Stephens (44) looks on during a 24–10 loss to the Miami Dolphins on September 17, 1989, at Foxboro Stadium. Stephens played for the Patriots from 1988 to 1992.

million atop the tottering and decaying Patriots empire.

The savior came that summer from St. Louis in the form of James Busch Orthwein, an ad man and investor with family ties and $70 million in stock alone of the Anheuser-Busch brewery fortune. He was also a friend of Fran Murray's and had helped him secure the loans for Murray's stake in the Patriots. Orthwein bought out both Kiam and Murray, but it was an open secret that his real interest in being involved was in bringing an NFL team back to St. Louis. Buying the Patriots was a way to buy goodwill among other NFL owners, the hope being that by straightening out the Patriots and giving them some stability, when the NFL decided to give St. Louis another try, Orthwein could recoup his investment in the Patriots. Or if that didn't work, maybe he would just move the whole franchise to the Gateway of the West, if he could ever figure a way out of the lease Bob Kraft held that still bound the team to Foxboro.

"It should be an interesting few years," he said at the time, making no one feel particularly secure. Still, after the last decade under first Sullivan and then Kiam, things couldn't possibly get any worse. This was not the first time, however, that had been said about the Patriots. "Even worse" always seemed to be right around the corner.

The Patriots shocked no one when they opened the season 0-9. Though scoring only 13 points over their first three games set a new low, it did set them up for the first pick in the 1993 draft. Two midseason victories under second-year quarterback Scott Zolak almost blew that opportunity, but the Patriots reverted to form to finish 2-14 and secure the number-one pick. The poor showing had the added bonus of giving the team a perfect excuse to buy out the last two years of Dick MacPherson's contract—he had missed part of the season because of colon surgery—and hire a new coach.

In early January, Jankovich, misreading his position in the organization, fired MacPherson. Two days later, Jankovich was half fired and half resigned himself after he jumped the gun and began making overtures to hire a new coach by planning to meet with the last coach he hired at Miami, Dennis Erickson. Orthwein made it clear that it wouldn't be a bad idea if Jankovich left too and offered a settlement.

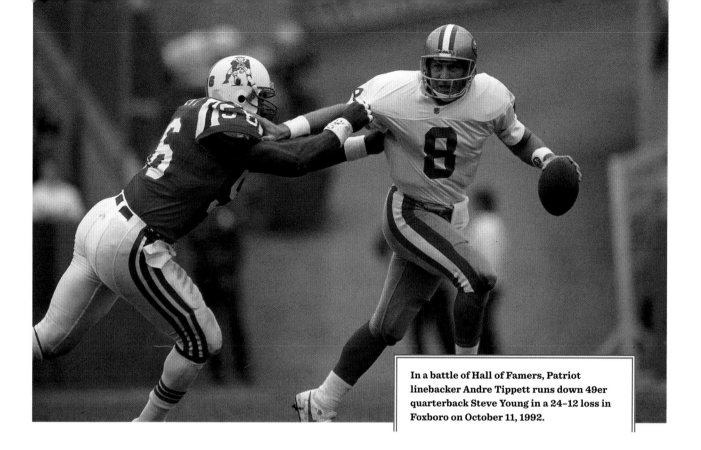

In a battle of Hall of Famers, Patriot linebacker Andre Tippett runs down 49er quarterback Steve Young in a 24–12 loss in Foxboro on October 11, 1992.

Orthwein was cleaning house, and it was looking increasingly likely that he wanted to pack up the team and move them to St. Louis, where the NFL was now dangling an expansion franchise. But first the Patriots needed a new coat of paint.

Orthwein had bought the team for $86 million, taken over $20 million of debt, and lost $4 million in two years despite having the lowest payroll in the league, and now, wanting to make sure he broke even at least, he went after the most attractive and available coaching names in pro football: former Bears coach Mike Ditka, former Giants coach Bill Parcells, and former Eagles coach Buddy Ryan. All three had stellar reputations as winners, and all three were out of the game but reportedly eager to get back in.

Of the three, Parcells already had a New England connection, having served as linebacker coach for Ron Meyer in 1980. From there, he coached Air Force before moving to the Giants and taking over as head coach in 1983. He had turned the once-proud franchise around, winning Super Bowls in 1987 and 1990 with "smash-mouth" football, an expression of his own personality: it was a game that relied on a tough physical defense paired with a grinding, run-oriented offense that wore the opposition down.

Parcells had retired after 1990 owing to heart trouble, but after spending two years in the broadcast booth and undergoing bypass surgery, he was cleared to resume coaching. Still, he didn't want to take the job unless he received assurance that he had both the financial means to build a team and the freedom to have final say on both the players and the coaching staff. Parcells was blunt and direct, a self-described "Jersey guy" who didn't want any interference and for whom the words "full control" had to mean just that. For Parcells, it was his way or the highway. After all, coaching under former Patriots head coach Erhardt, he'd seen the Patriots doing just the opposite.

It was almost as if Parcells was interviewing the Patriots rather than the other way around. He made it clear that he had no interest in simply making the Patriots competitive. He wanted to win a championship, and nothing less would do.

On January 21, 1993, Parcells was hired as the twelfth coach in Patriots history, and for the first time in that history they seemed to have gotten it right.

And everything changed.

CHAPTER EIGHT

1993–1996

ENTER THE TUNA

It was as if the ugly boy married the homecoming queen, the guy about to lose his house hit the Lotto, or the kid who expected only coal under the tree on Christmas morning found a brand-new bike. For the first time—the very first time in their entire thirty-three-year history—the Patriots actually hired a bona-fide professional football coach.

Not some college wunderkind, not the assistant of the moment, not a placeholder or the coaching equivalent of a temp, but a guy with stature, experience, and a record to match.

Tʜᴀᴛ ᴍᴀᴅᴇ ᴀʟʟ ᴛʜᴇ ᴅɪꜰꜰᴇʀᴇɴᴄᴇ. To a degree, Parcells cast a shadow over the franchise that has lasted ever since, neatly breaking the history of the team into two halves: Before Parcells and After Parcells.

When it actually happened, it seemed all the more unbelievable that the Patriots had taken so long to act like every other team in football—to stop rolling the dice over and over and actually go out and get a real coach. Rather incredibly, of all the Patriots coaches to date, only two, Lou Saban and (perhaps even more incredibly) Ron Meyer, had ever gone on to coach in the NFL again. For the others, coaching the Patriots (deservedly) marked the end of their NFL careers. But Billy Sullivan was no longer in charge; the Patriots no longer had an owner who made moves primarily in terms of his own security. Orthwein didn't want to own an NFL team anymore—he wanted to sell, and Bill Parcells was the best salesman out there, a guy who knew the product and the territory. "You are what you are, and Bill Parcells is a football coach," Parcells said of himself at the time of his hiring. "I don't envision myself as anything else."

He'd served a long apprenticeship after first starring as a running back at River Dell High School in Oradell, New Jersey, attending Colgate, and then moving on to Wichita State, where he played as a slow and undersized but overperforming linebacker. He was good enough to be drafted in the seventh round by the Detroit Lions, but smart enough to know he wouldn't make it in the NFL. Instead, he accepted an assistant's job at Hastings College in Nebraska and began climbing the assistant coaching ladder, first at West Point, then at Florida State, Vanderbilt, and Texas Tech, before earning a head-coaching job. He went 3-8 in one season at Air Force before joining the Giants as an assistant, then jumped to the Patriots for a year under Erhardt. That's where he earned the nickname "the Big Tuna." As Parcells later explained, "There was an old commercial from Star-Kist with Charlie the Star-Kist Tuna, so my players were trying to con me on something one time, and I said, 'You must think I'm Charlie the Tuna,' you know, a sucker." He was anything but. After one year in New England, he returned to the Giants as defensive coordinator. In New York, he received credit for helping focus linebacker Lawrence Taylor's immense talent, and

Robert Kraft of the New England Patriots and his wife, Myra, wave to the crowd as they are acknowledged by the public-address announcer during pregame warm-ups before the Patriots' 17–14 victory over the Cleveland Browns at Foxboro Stadium on September 2, 1995.

then he was offered the top job in New York in 1982. He'd thrived in the role.

Parcells was unique. He didn't BS his players but was still well liked—he tried to speak to every player every day—and the media found him refreshingly blunt and entertaining, with enough of an ego to enjoy the spotlight in a way that took the pressure off his players. He was the embodiment of the Sinatra standard "New York,

New York." He'd made it in New York and now believed that he could make it anywhere. The Patriots did too and gave him a four-year deal worth around $1.5 million annually. Although he wasn't technically the GM, in essence he was for everything but the paperwork, being free to hire and sign and draft anyone he wanted with a suddenly ballooning budget. TV revenue had escalated to more than $25 million a year, and Orthwein promised to open up his wallet as well.

Parcells surrounded himself with seven trusted assistants from New York and dove right in. The first major decision—and one he knew could make him or break him in New England—was what to do at quarterback and how to use the number-one draft pick.

Although Parcells had favored a running game in New York, he'd done so with a top-notch quarterback, Phil Simms. After two years of analyzing games on TV, Parcells knew that in Hugh Millen, Tommy Hodson, and Scott Zolak, he didn't have that guy in New England. "I have to sit down and see what we want to do quarterback-wise," he said.

All of a sudden, because of Parcells, players who had never thought about playing in New England not only wanted to be there but actually had a choice in the matter. While the Rozelle Rule that restricted player movement had been struck down, the NFL had replaced it with "Plan B" free agency, which allowed each team the right of first refusal for thirty-seven players on the roster and codified compensation. The result was the Rozelle Rule under a different name, the effects being much the same. But in 1992, in an antitrust lawsuit brought by eight players, Plan B was also stuck down. The outcome, at the precise time Parcells came to the Patriots, was somewhat less restricted free agency, albeit with a salary cap that required teams to spend a certain amount of league revenue on player contracts each year. Simms, at age thirty-seven, was a free agent and made public his desire to join Parcells, as did All-Pro defensive end Reggie White. Pats fans were pumped too. Parcells's hiring led to almost 4,000 season-ticket orders in the first week.

But Parcells had to rebuild, and it didn't make sense to waste money on players for a team that would likely struggle for a few years. He soon focused on the number-one draft pick.

This was not the year of the quarterback in the draft—or much of anything else—with only a few notable exceptions: quarterbacks Rick Mirer of Notre Dame and Drew Bledsoe of Washington State and Georgia running back Garrison Hearst.

The quarterback decision created an interesting dilemma that made it hard to choose between Mirer and Bledsoe. Both were the sons of high school coaches. The twenty-three-year-old Mirer had played for a winner and was athletic and charismatic, but Notre Dame's offense had focused on the run and Mirer, usually throwing from play action, averaged only 21 attempts per game. Still, that was enough to give him the team record in total offense and career TDs. Bledsoe, on the other hand, was only twenty-one and a prototype pocket passer for a team that favored a pro-style offense. Bledsoe averaged 34 passes a game for Washington State, but the Huskies hadn't been as successful as Notre Dame. He was also more low-key and, at six-five, not very mobile. "I think Mirer will develop faster, but Bledsoe will go further," said one pro coach. Seattle held the second pick, and most observers expected the two young men to go one-two in the draft.

Then Mirer decided to skip the NFL Combine, calling it "really sort of degrading," in favor of private workouts, took a trip to Europe, and in France visited the grave of rock legend Jim Morrison, which gave pause to some teams. Parcells and the Pats began to lean toward Bledsoe. Either way, it would be a new day for the Patriots, something the team underscored on March 31, 1993.

· · ·

"Pat Patriot" was out. In his place was a slick new logo designed by NFL Properties, one the press dubbed "Flying Elvis." Pat Patriot's designer, Phil Bissell, accurately called it "a good, slick commercial logo." The team also abandoned their old color scheme for silver pants and deep blue jerseys with red numbers. "We want to be historically accurate," said Orthwein. "The British Army wore red, not the Patriots." Although the red numerals would be abandoned as unreadable in favor of white in another year, the new logo and merchandise proved popular with fans. In the first two weeks, the team sold more merchandise than it had the previous year, although the excitement around Parcells also had something to do with that.

A SUNDAY MUG SHOT

GEORGE PLIMPTON

Just about every Sunday in the fall I spend my afternoons watching the football games on television in a melancholy saloon on the Upper East Side called the Mug Shot—so named because the walls are decorated with rows of criminal likenesses with identification numbers underneath. I thought they were jokes at first—regular customers who'd agreed to have mug shots taken of themselves in order to paper the walls with friendly faces of the bar's habitués. Not at all.

The mug shots are of famous people, celebrities, who have run afoul of the law and have been hauled down to the police station, mostly for minor altercations of one sort or another, and had their pictures taken—Don King, Dudley Moore, Jennifer Capriati, Joe Pepitone, Pee-wee Herman, Al Pacino among them. There are twenty or so mug shots on the wall so far, but Ken, who runs the place, has more in stock, and every day the newspapers with their stories on celebrity malfeasance suggest that he may well run out of room for his decorations. He has a framed O. J. Simpson mug shot stored away somewhere because he decided it was a bit out of tone to be up there with the others.

On football afternoons, the place is packed with fans. The television sets are arranged along the shelf above the bar and in the adjacent room; the billiard room in the back has a television set as well. Most of the crowd is packed under the sets showing the local teams, the Giants and the Jets, and from the rising tumult of either lamentations or exhalation going down the length of the long bar you can figure out how things are going for a local team. I go to watch the Detroit Lions. Their set is near the door and the street. The sound is off so that the commentary doesn't interfere with what's being said about the Giants or the Jets. There are three of us who meet in the Mug Shot to watch the Lions—a young electronics specialist who recently graduated from Amherst, a detective who once worked in Detroit, and myself. I am a Lions fan because as a participatory journalist back in the '60s I played with them during the exhibition season in order to write a book about the experience (*Paper Lion*).

I don't know anyone on the Detroit team anymore, and I don't learn very much about them from the TV commentary in the Mug Shot because the sound is always off. My heart sank when Barry Sanders resigned, because the one redemption, however badly the team was doing, was to see and marvel at those skittering runs of his. I hardly know one player from another. I am coached by the detective from Detroit.

If it weren't for my affiliation with the Lions I would be a Patriots fan. My forebears are New Englanders. My mother's family, the Ameses, are landowners in North Easton, just up the way from Foxborough. I went to schools in New Hampshire and Cambridge. I follow the Boston Red Sox in grim uncertainty. I once "played" (if that is the operative word) with both the Celtics and the Bruins.

So in the Mug Shot, when there's a Lions time-out, I invariably mosey down the length of the bar to see how the Patriots are doing. They have a larger group of supporters than the three of us. I join in their cheering when Bledsoe throws a touchdown pass. I linger to watch the Patriots' defense after the kickoff.

Frankly, I have always been vaguely unsettled by the Patriots' logo—the odd jut-jawed face that reminds me of the prows of those art-deco locomotives that were once on the New York–Chicago rail line. I would agree that it has been an improvement over the first Patriot logo, the crouched lineman wearing a tricorner hat—a slightly comic and unthreatening figure. If you opened up your door and saw someone like that crouched on the front porch you'd take him for someone who had arrived at the wrong address for a costume party.

Human representation on a football helmet doesn't seem to work very well, the downcast Indian logo of the Washington team being the exception. The Green Bay Packers were aware of this and resisted using anything to do with the packing industry as a logo. So have the Giants, the Steelers, and the Titans. The Oakland Raiders' helmets depict a face, but it has been so dehumanized with a black eye patch and so on as to be hardly recognizable. These things matter. I remember Alex Karras, the great Detroit defensive tackle, telling me that he had come home after a particularly bitterly fought game against the Pittsburgh Steelers to discover that his children were in fact Rams fans. "They liked the way the rams' horns curved back over the helmet. To think," Alex said, "that I've been out there on the field getting my thumbs pushed back, screaming with pain, while my children back home are supporting a team because of the artistic

Participatory journalist extraordinaire George Plimpton in action during Detroit Lions training camp in August 1963. He memorialized his experience in the classic book *Paper Lion*.

handiwork of some odd-ball decorator in Pasadena!"

In my own case, I recall despairing at the end of a Harvard-Yale game when I realized that my young daughter, age ten or so, had cast her allegiance to Yale because of its bulldog pacing the opposite sideline. The Harvard mascot, a Puritan with a conical hat, made no impression on her at all.

Perhaps all this is beside the point. If the Lions continue to flail around, I see no reason why I shouldn't join the Patriots' supporters in the Mug Shot at the beginning of the afternoon and stick with them throughout despite my problem with the team logo. Of course, from time to time I hope they won't mind if I sidle down the way to see how the Lions are doing.

GEORGE PLIMPTON, who attended Phillips Exeter and graduated from Harvard, was the founder of the *Paris Review*, a literary magazine. He was widely known for his participatory journalism and movie and television cameos in such works as *Good Will Hunting* and *ER*. He wrote this piece for the Patriots in 2000.

But since New England and Seattle weren't the only teams in need of a quarterback in a weak draft, Parcells entertained a variety of offers as the day of decision approached.

The most intriguing were packages offered by Indianapolis and San Francisco. The Colts dangled a portfolio of early draft picks and players, including one package that would give the Pats the Colts' top three picks and any other player on their roster, save from ten they chose to protect. The 49ers were even more generous. They wanted Mirer—badly—and offered the Patriots every single one of their picks in the draft, which included two number-ones, for the Patriots' first and second picks.

It was tempting—the bounty of picks could, in turn, have been traded for some established talent. But Parcells didn't like the talent pool in the draft and wasn't certain

the return would be worth it. He decided he wanted Bledsoe, and that was that—a decision made with little drama. But Parcells also knew he wasn't going to hand the rookie the job, and he let his displeasure be known whenever anyone referred to the potential draftee as a "franchise quarterback." Bledsoe would have to prove it.

The quarterback was quickly signed to a six-year deal worth $14.5 million, with a $4.5 million bonus, but as training camp approached Parcells wasn't done. Few of the Patriots were as tough, rugged, and committed as he preferred, and he quickly made a statement. When starting left guard Reggie Redding showed up to camp overweight, he was summarily cut, sending the message that no one's job was safe under Parcells. He expected you to be in shape and know your assignment. Performance was everything, and like Vince Lombardi a generation

Bill Parcells has some words with Drew Bledsoe during the Patriots' first-round playoff loss to the Browns on January 1, 1995.

before (of whom Packers lineman Henry Jordan once said, "He treats us all the same—like dogs"), Parcells was loud, in your face, and profane. But he wasn't a martinet. His style was to make practice harder and in many ways more stressful than the games, and players usually responded to his approach, even if they disliked him personally. Parcells didn't care if he was liked or not. A player rarely wondered where he stood with the coach—he'd let you know at high decibels. If you could survive practice, you could survive the league.

Bledsoe did win the quarterback job during training camp, and Parcells put his stamp on the team, turning over nearly 60 percent of the roster. But when the season began with a 38–14 loss to Buffalo, it became clear that this would be no instant turnaround. As *New York Times* reporter Frank Litsky noted afterward, "Bill Parcells returned to coaching today. He also returned to reality." The Patriots began the season with four straight losses and dropped eleven of the first twelve, the only win coming when Bledsoe was hurt and Scott Secules led the Pats to a 23–21 win over the Cardinals on a short last-second pass following a 69-yard run off a lateral by Leonard Russell. For much of the year, Bledsoe was inconsistent and often looked overwhelmed as he tried to adapt to both NFL defenses and Parcells's high expectations and abrasive personality. On defense, though, the team was substantially improved. With the exception of a few early-season blowouts, including an embarrassing 45–7 loss to the Jets, the Patriots, at least on one side of the ball, were beginning to display the hallmarks of a Parcells team.

The real turnaround began in the last month. With Bledsoe finally beginning to adjust, the team won four straight, including a stirring 33–27 overtime win in wintry conditions against the Dolphins that kept Miami out of the playoffs. Bledsoe engineered a late fourth-quarter drive while completing seven of nine passes to put New England in position to win in regulation before Miami tied the score with a late field goal. In OT, the Pats' defense forced a turnover, and Bledsoe tossed a 36-yard score to Michael Timpson to pick up the win and allow New England to finish 5-11.

Many fans thought the victory might be the last for the Patriots in New England. And even though the stands had not been full, thousands stayed long after the game ended, cheering and roaring, staking their claim to a franchise everyone knew Orthwein wanted to shuttle to St. Louis. While he had hoped to use the leverage and goodwill of owning the Patriots to help secure an expansion team, in November the league awarded an expansion franchise to Jacksonville and, a month later, Charlotte, leaving Orthwein and other suitors disappointed.

A lot of parties were newly interested in the Patriots, including those who felt jilted by the expansion decision, like Memphis and St. Louis—where it had been decided that the new club would be called the Stallions and a logo had already been designed—and groups from Hartford, San Antonio, and Baltimore, all of which had dangled dollars and stadium plans. With a new domed stadium going up in Orthwein's hometown, he didn't have the votes among his NFL brethren to move the team on his own. The new stadium was already an issue among the owners, as it would be the last closed-dome stadium built that utilized AstroTurf, which in recent years had been blamed for an uptick in knee injuries. Besides, other suitors might be willing to pay more, and every other NFL owner would get a cut of the franchise fee. Orthwein was already a leaseholder in St. Louis but was getting impatient—he wanted to retire. So he prepared to sell.

There was one more hang-up—the Foxboro Stadium lease, which ran until 2002 and was owned by Bob Kraft, who had bought out his partner Steve Karp a year earlier. In order for Orthwein to move the team, he had to get out of the lease, and that would be costly. Kraft and Karp had paid $25 million for the stadium initially and since that time had taken in some $3 million per year in lease revenue while making a host of improvements—such as putting in a small, covered practice facility. Most expected Kraft to accept a buyout, but he too announced his intention to bid for the team. That the property was also being eyed in nascent plans out of the State House for yet another megaplex including a domed stadium made it all even more complicated while simultaneously strengthening Kraft's position.

The lease was a hammer, and Kraft knew it. His lawyers thought that leaving him out of the bidding process might be a violation of the Racketeer Influenced and Corrupt Organizations (RICO) Act, a federal law regarding acts performed as part of an ongoing criminal organization. They believed any effort to prevent Kraft from making a bid could be seen as evidence of racketeering, and that fear percolated through the other potential bidders. While the media breathlessly tracked every move and countermove, fans didn't much care who owned the team, as long as they stayed in New England.

And then there was Billy Sullivan again. He had sued the NFL and won a $116 million judgment. That would eventually be greatly reduced in a settlement, but it still scared the NFL. As Bills owner Ralph Wilson said at the time, "Billy is a nice guy and I always tried to help him, but I never thought I'd end up paying him millions of dollars."

Late in the 1993 season, Orthwein and his attorney, Walter Metcalfe, kept pressing Kraft to name a price so they could let buyers know how much each had to factor that into their bids, but Kraft refused to do so, making the total bid package hard to figure. Kraft and his lawyers surmised that Orthwein, whether he wanted to or not, would have to sell to the highest bidder to avoid a raft of lawsuits from others if he tried to sell low to his pals in St. Louis. As *Buffalo News* reporter Larry Felzer noted at the time, the politics behind the sale was "just like the Balkans, except with a Boston accent."

Kraft had been underestimated from the start. Few realized that his plan all along had been to use the lease to put himself in position to buy the team, whether the league wanted him or not. Fewer still realized that he had been through this before and had learned some lessons along the way.

According to who is doing the talking, Bob Kraft is either an enlightened businessman whose approach is ruled by his adherence to the Jewish ethics he learned from his father or a genuine cutthroat who cares only for money. Beneficiaries of his philanthropy, like the Reverend John Brooks, the former president of Holy Cross College, have referred to him as "extraordinarily generous," while others, such as the union president of

> **"BILLY IS A NICE GUY AND I ALWAYS TRIED TO HELP HIM, BUT I NEVER THOUGHT I'D END UP PAYING HIM MILLIONS OF DOLLARS."**
>
> —RALPH WILSON
> ABOUT BILLY SULLIVAN

a Connecticut company Kraft acquired in a hostile take-over that cost 300 jobs, have called him a "taker."

Those people whom Kraft has made rich see him in altruistic terms. Those who have challenged him in business, like David Mugar, his onetime partner at Boston TV station Channel 7, believe that "he's only out for one person, and that's Robert Kraft." The truth depends on one's perspective and probably lies somewhere in between . . . but the victors tend to be those who write history. What is certain is that Kraft bought six Patriot season tickets in 1971—"section 217, row 23, seats 1 through 6," as he later recalled—and was a regular at the games with his sons and their friends.

Born in 1941, Kraft grew up in relatively modest circumstances in Brookline. His father Harry was a Chinatown dressmaker who wanted his son to become a rabbi. But Bob Kraft was a big sports fan who'd been crushed when his beloved Boston Braves moved to Milwaukee. At Brookline High, he desperately wanted to play football and other sports, but in his Orthodox household he deferred to his father's wishes to keep the Sabbath holy. Even practices clashed with Hebrew class.

The senior class president went to Columbia in 1960 on a scholarship and followed the Billy Sullivan model: he made connections and became something of a big man on campus, joining the Zeta Beta Tau fraternity and serving as class president. Finally freed from Hebrew studies, he tried out for the freshman football team but eventually landed on the lightweight football squad, a varsity sport for those who weighed less than 150 pounds. According to the Columbia student newspaper, Kraft, who played halfback and safety, was plagued by a leg injury and only played a handful of games across two seasons for the last-place lightweights.

On February 2, 1962, while drinking in a Boston deli called Ken's at Copley after watching a Columbia-Harvard basketball game, he met Myra Hiatt, a student at Brandeis. It was the pivotal moment in his life and one of the most important in Patriots history. For although Kraft and Myra had much in common, there was one big difference—she was rich and he was not.

They married in June 1963 and eventually had four sons. Kraft earned an MBA at Harvard and then gave Wall Street a brief whirl before accepting an offer from Myra's father, Jacob Hiatt, to join the family business.

Hiatt had been a judge in Lithuania before fleeing the Nazis. He made his way to Worcester, went to work as the second employee at a paper company, and grew the business into the Rand-Whitney Corporation, one of the biggest packaging firms in the country. At first, he and his son-in-law worked well together as Kraft learned the business, but Jacob Hiatt was beginning to focus his efforts on philanthropy and didn't share the same ambitions as his daughter's husband.

Impatient, in 1968 Kraft made his move. According to a 1997 profile by Charles Sennott in the *Boston Globe*, Kraft "acquired 50 percent of the company in a leveraged buyout," using company assets as collateral for the purchase. All of a sudden, the son-in-law was the boss, an arrangement that reportedly caused some acrimony between Kraft and his father-in-law. But under Kraft, the business grew and expanded rapidly. Today he's on the Fortune 500 list, his net worth estimated to be between $4 billion and $6 billion.

Kraft flirted with politics, serving as a Democrat on the Newton City Council and even pondering a run for Congress, but in 1975 he got a sniff of the sports world when he bought the Boston Lobsters franchise in the World Team Tennis league. As his fortune grew and he became a minority owner of Boston TV station WHDH, his name occasionally popped up as a potential buyer of the Red Sox or the Bruins. World Team Tennis failed, but Kraft learned a valuable lesson, later telling a reporter, "I was doing all the advertising and legwork . . . and Boston University was getting all the revenues from parking and concessions. I realized that, with a sports team, I had to do what I did with my business and control all the revenue streams."

That's what led him to acquire Foxboro Stadium and the surrounding properties. Later he said, "The option gave me ten years to figure out how to get the team." He knew that would eventually make him a player

and give him leverage whenever the team was sold. Having missed his first opportunity when Kiam stepped in, Kraft was determined not to make the same mistake twice. He might never have another chance.

While Kraft stood at the back of the line to kick the financial tires on the franchise, a third party apparently offered him up to $100 million for the property, but as Kraft told Will McDonough later, "I said no . . . the thing that made it possible to keep the team here, and for me to get the team, was my lease." Orthwein set a deadline for bids, and Kraft blew everyone away with an offer of $170 million, far more than anyone else, and $30 million more than the franchise fee paid by Charlotte and Jacksonville—the highest price ever paid for an NFL franchise. Orthwein had no choice but to accept, for as Kraft said later, his offer provided Orthwein and the NFL with "the cleanest, least complicated way to proceed." It also allowed Orthwein to walk away with an enormous profit.

A lot of people in the NFL were all asking the same question: he paid that much for the Patriots? But Kraft knew the Foxboro Stadium property was the logical choice if a new stadium was ever built, and that was invaluable.

The deal was announced on January 21, 1994, and approved by the NFL on February 25. And with that, Bob Kraft became "Mr. Kraft," achieving a stature and public profile he had never before held. Mrs. Kraft apparently wasn't very happy—in all those years she'd never attended a single Patriots game. Still, all the pieces were now in place for success—a first-rate coach, a potential franchise quarterback, and a local owner with deep pockets. Well, almost everything. Foxboro Stadium was still a subpar facility (other league members called it a "dump"), but Kraft was betting that a local owner not named Sullivan might prove more successful in getting a stadium built.

Now all the Patriots had to do was win. Yet all was not as straightforward as it looked.

Under Orthwein, Parcells had almost total control, but Kraft didn't feel encumbered by that agreement and Parcells grated at the way Kraft looked over his shoulder and talked and acted as if he knew more about the game than he did, a trait common to almost every NFL owner.

Robert Kraft is joined by his family on January 21, 1994, after signing papers with James Orthwein sealing his purchase of the New England Patriots football team for an estimated $170 million.

Almost from the start, Parcells treated Kraft as an annoyance and Kraft bristled at Parcells's dismissive attitude toward his boss. Over time Kraft came to believe that Parcells cast too large a shadow over all things Patriot. Eventually, that would prove to be a problem.

But not in 1994. For the time being, Kraft left Parcells more or less alone as he enjoyed local fame and adulation as the franchise's savior. In an ideal world, that's the role an NFL owner should take: hire the right people, provide adequate facilities and support staff, make wise financial decisions, and let football people run the franchise. Winning the last four games of the 1993 season earned the coach the space to continue to do things his way.

The Patriots added linebacker Willie McGinest in the draft, shoring up the defense, which had long been led by veteran Andre Tippett. Tippett had recorded the 100th sack of his career in the final game of the 1993 season and then retired, ending a fine career that included five Pro Bowl appearances. But for the second year in a row, the New England defense got off to a slow start. And although Parcells hoped to re-create the smash-mouth offense he'd had with the Giants, the Patriots didn't have a big running back or punishing line that allowed them to play ball-control football. All they had was Bledsoe and his arm, and Parcells had little choice but to let him use it. Even that was problematic, as the Patriot wide receivers, Michael Timpson and Vincent Brisby, were merely serviceable. But tight end Ben Coates was among the best in the league, and if the Pats couldn't run the ball, they could at least throw it to their running backs.

When Bledsoe was on target and the defense held, they were successful, but when he threw too many interceptions and the defense stayed too long on the field, they struggled. The team opened the season losing three straight shootouts, won three in a row when the defense stiffened, then dropped four straight when Bledsoe struggled again. The last was a 13–6 loss to Cleveland that the press played up as a personal battle between Parcells and a coach viewed as his protégé, Bill Belichick.

• • •

Steve Belichick had played fullback at Western Reserve, then one season with the NFL Lions, before joining the Navy. After the war, he served as coach at Hiram College and then as an assistant at Vanderbilt and North Carolina before joining the Naval Academy in 1956, where he spent much of the next thirty-three years as a scout, analyzing the opposition.

His only son, Bill, grew up watching Dad break down schemes and learning X's and O's the way other kids learned to build with Legos. He was just as disciplined and directed as his dad, his only distraction, apart from football, being lacrosse. He played both sports at Wesleyan College, then went straight to the NFL in 1975. He served a long apprenticeship as an assistant before joining the Giants in 1979, the same year Parcells became the Giants' defensive coordinator.

The pairing was accidental, but it worked. Even as the two differed in personality, Parcells as outgoing and bombastic as Belichick was taciturn and reserved, they shared one critical trait—neither cared much for anything else other than football and each was convinced he knew best. Both spent nearly every waking hour consumed with their jobs and evinced little knowledge of or interest in anything else. Belichick, asked in 2015 if he was ever recognized in the grocery store, responded by saying only, "Haven't been in the grocery store in a couple of years." More recently, he told a Boston radio station, "SnapFace and all that, I don't really get those . . . I'm not really too worried about what they put on InstantChat, or whatever it is."

When Parcells became the Giants' head coach, Belichick became his defensive coordinator, and when Parcells left, Belichick became head coach of the Browns. He had a rougher ride in Cleveland than Parcells in New England. The Browns were coming off a stretch of near-misses in the late 1980s, and Belichick was tasked with rebuilding a team that fans felt didn't need to be rebuilt, while owner Art Modell was struggling financially and the team was losing money. Belichick's inability to adapt to his role as the face of the franchise (his dry-as-dust, often dismissive answers to routine questions didn't play in the Midwest), coupled with his dumping of fan favorite Bernie Kosar as his quarterback in favor of Vinny Testaverde, led Cleveland fans to conclude that nothing the Browns did on the field was good enough. Fans raised on the offensive wizardry of Jim Brown, Leroy Kelly, and Brian Sipe found Belichick's defense-first philosophy unexciting.

No matter what happened, Belichick usually received the blame during this tumultuous time, but that didn't seem to bother him at all, which only further infuriated the fan base. After Modell announced he was moving the team, Belichick's final year there, 1995, had been excruciating to watch, the stands at Cleveland Municipal Stadium shaking with the chant "Bill must go! Bill must go!"

The Pats-Browns matchup in Cleveland on November 6 was viewed as a test between the two coaches, an answer to the question of whether the Giants' success was due mostly to Parcells . . . or to his trusted assistant.

Well, on this day it went to the trusted assistant. The Cleveland defense hounded Bledsoe into four interceptions, and although the Patriots' defense played well, the Browns won 13–6 as the Pats failed to score a touchdown. Cleveland improved to 7-2 and the Pats fell to 3-6, the playoffs apparently as far away as Lake Erie was from Foxborough. The *Globe*'s Ron Borges wrote, "Gray, wet, cold, drab Cleveland was the perfect setting for a gray, wet, cold, drab football game," while Bledsoe admitted, "This is not much fun at all. You lose like this, it starts piling up." Going into the game, there were more than a few whispers in the stands and on the airwaves that perhaps Parcells's reputation as a genius didn't extend past New Jersey, and those voices were getting louder.

But late in the game a funny thing went almost unnoticed. A few days before the contest, Parcells had been hospitalized overnight with lightheadedness, and there had been reports that Kraft was "meddling" with Parcells's authority. With nothing to lose, and after spending three quarters trying to run the ball down Cleveland's throat, Parcells had cut Bledsoe loose in the last twelve minutes of the game. In the fourth quarter alone, Bledsoe had thrown the ball 23 times. It hadn't resulted in a touchdown, since for the second game in a row they'd needed kicker Matt Bahr's foot to score, but Bledsoe, who in his previous four games threw only 3 TDs and 11 interceptions, had responded well. And the Cleveland game also marked the first start by McGinest—Parcells had a way with linebackers.

With the season on the line the following week at Foxboro against division-leading Minnesota, the first half was even more drab than the week before against Cleveland. Fifty-eight seconds before halftime the Vikings led 20–3, and it felt like 50–3. Minnesota had outgained New England 286 yards to 41.

Then—someone later said it was Scott Zolak's idea, and some said Ray Perkins, but in the end it was Parcells's decision—the Patriots went into a two-minute offense, marched down the field, and managed a field goal before the end of the half. Noticing that the Vikings seemed unprepared, Parcells decided to turn Bledsoe loose in the second half and essentially run their two-minute offense for a full thirty minutes. Why not? What did they have to lose? All Parcells said later was "I thought maybe if we could surprise them with that two-minute we might get something out of it quickly before they adjusted. Which we did."

It was the best thing that ever could have happened, at least in 1994. The Pats came out in the second half and went right to the two-minute, mostly no-huddle offense: essentially an endless variation of "Bledsoe looks downfield and throws," while punter Pat O'Neill kept the Vikings pinned back and Patriots defenders exhorted each other to "keep smashing them in the mouth."

Bledsoe ended up throwing an incredible 53 times after halftime. Boston fans hadn't seen such a high-volume performance throwing a ball since Luis Tiant in the 1975 World Series. More incredibly, he completed 37 of

those passes, tossing for two touchdowns before Matt Bahr kicked a late field goal to send the 20–20 game into overtime. "It was," said running back Leroy Thompson, "ridiculous." It was also effective.

It got better. When Viking Cris Carter muffed the coin toss, calling "heads" after the coin hit the ground, Patriot Vincent Brown noticed the infraction, causing the referee to flip the coin again. This time Carter called "tails," but the coin, unlike the Vikings, landed heads up.

Six pass completions later, Bledsoe surveyed the field one last time from the 14 and threw a perfect fade to Kevin Turner in the back left corner of the end zone. The back never broke stride as he headed straight into the tunnel for a stunning 26–20 victory. Bledsoe's 45 completions and 70 passes both set NFL records. "It's more fun for a quarterback if you throw," the quarterback said afterward, stating the obvious. Then he added, "I don't know about 70, though."

The win turned the season around and also gave observers a new appreciation for Parcells. Few had thought he was capable of adapting so dramatically, and so quickly. The Patriots raced through the second half of the season undefeated to finish 10-6 as five Patriots receivers caught 52 passes or more, led by Ben Coates's 96 receptions. New England finished second in the division, good enough to qualify for the wild-card game in the playoffs.

That meant going to Cleveland again, and this time local media built it up as a Parcells-Belichick grudge match, the NFL equivalent of the WWF. This time it didn't match the hype.

The Patriots' offense was good, but one-dimensional, while the Browns' defense in 1994 was the stingiest in pro football, giving up more than 20 points only once. And the "new" pass-oriented Patriots were nothing new to the Browns, who had plenty of time to prepare. They went after Bledsoe relentlessly, and when the Patriots fell behind and Bledsoe was forced to throw on almost every down, they were ready, intercepting him twice in the final quarter in the 20–13 New England loss. There was some bad luck involved too: Patriots receivers dropped several catchable balls, including one miss by Ray Crittenden that would have been a touchdown, and two of Bledsoe's three interceptions came on tipped balls. None of that, however, masked the fact that the Patriots

The fans go wild as Patriot Kevin Turner (34) gets hoisted triumphantly by teammate Ben Coates following Turner's overtime reception of a Drew Bledsoe pass that won Bledsoe's brilliant record-setting game versus the Vikings by a score of 26–20 on November 13, 1994.

were outplayed and that Bledsoe was only 21-for-50 in the air, including four straight incompletions in the final 19 seconds. As a not-so-philosophical Parcells said after the loss, "I don't see this as a great accomplishment."

With as many as seventeen potential free agents on the squad, the Patriots knew there would, by necessity, be plenty of changes before the 1995 season. But no one foresaw that the off-season would prove to be the beginning of the end of the Parcells era.

Like many other NFL owners, and like Billy Sullivan before him, Bob Kraft began viewing the Patriots as a family business of which he was the patriarch. He had already made his son Jonathan vice president and "owner's representative," a title that didn't really inspire trust among the coaching staff. And in February, after VP Patrick Forte was dismissed, Kraft chose to promote Bobby Grier from director of pro scouting to director of player personnel, making his guy, not Parcells, responsible for the roster.

Although it was said that Grier worked "with" Parcells, the coach didn't like the erosion of his authority. That wasn't what he'd signed on for two years before, and after making the playoffs, he took umbrage at the move.

On paper the Patriots should have been better in 1995, and in fact most observers had tabbed them for the playoffs without even factoring in the contributions of cornerback Ty Law (the number-one draft pick), linebacker Ted Johnson (the number-two pick), and Curtis Martin (a number-one talent who dropped to number three only because of a knee injury).

It took a while for Law and Johnson to find their place in the Patriots' young but erratic defense, but Martin was a revelation. He eventually ran for more than 1,500 yards as a rookie and was adept and reliable as a receiver. But much of his production as a rookie came in the second half of the season, and by then it was too late. The pass-happy Patriots could no longer surprise, and despite extracting some revenge by beating the Browns in the opener, they dropped their next five games, and six of the next seven, on their way to a disappointing 6-10 record. Bledsoe still put the ball in the air more than 600 times but rarely found the end zone. He ended with a pass rating of only 63.7. The defense gave up almost 400 points. It was hard to tell if Parcells's Patriots were just young or just not good enough.

Parcells hedged his bets. Over the course of the season, as the Patriots floundered, the relationship between Kraft and the coach had deteriorated. In midseason, at Parcells's behest, the team had released cornerback Maurice Hurst, previously a defensive stalwart, after a series of poor performances. That likely had something to do with the fact that he'd played all year with a bulging disk in his neck, an injury Parcells questioned even though the team doctor had noted the injury in September. Hurst would eventually fail physicals with other teams and sue the Patriots, receiving a $165,000 settlement a year later. After the surgery, he never played again.

The episode was yet another example of the distrust between Parcells and the coaching staff and the front office, and just before the end of the season Parcells told his staff that if he could arrange a buyout, he planned to coach only one more year. He almost quit, but didn't want to walk away from the money and be prevented from coaching elsewhere, or leave with a losing record. Kraft pondered firing him, but didn't want to pay off the final two years of the contract. Besides, if Parcells either quit or was fired, it would be a PR nightmare for the club, for the coach was still popular with fans, the media, and most of his players.

In the end, they compromised: in exchange for a $300,000 buyout and an agreement that prevented Parcells from coaching elsewhere in 1997, Kraft agreed to release Parcells from his contract at the end of the 1996 season unless both parties mutually agreed that he would stay on.

Fat chance. Yet as soon as the agreement was signed, Parcells was a lame duck. It all came to a head at the NFL draft, where the Pats held the seventh pick in the first round.

Parcells wanted help on defense, particularly on the defensive line. Opponents had shredded the Patriots in the air in 1995 and Parcells put the blame on the line, for while New England had led the NFL in offensive yardage in 1995, the defense had managed to give up even more to the opposition. Besides, in 1994 the Pats had turned to the air out of necessity. Now, with Martin, Parcells had a chance to put together a team more in the mold of the Giants, utilizing a more balanced offense. It was time to reassert smash-mouth football, and that required a tougher, stingier defense. To that end, Parcells added old friend Bill Belichick to his staff as assistant head coach and defensive backfield coach. With young talent in the backfield like Ty Law and linebackers Ted Johnson, Chris Slade, and Willie McGinest on the verge of reaching their prime, he believed that the line was the only thing holding the team back.

But Kraft, like so many other NFL owners, and like Billy Sullivan and Victor Kiam before him, equated business success with acumen in every other area. It was his team, and he wanted to put his stamp on it. The owner, whom one business acquaintance referred to derisively as a "jock sniffer," began to exert more control. As he became more familiar with football operations, he put more trust in the men he had hired or promoted in the front office than in the coaching staff. Kraft wanted help on offense, namely, a wide receiver who could provide Bledsoe with a dependable deep threat.

The best linemen and best wide receiver—Simeon Rice, Kevin Hardy, and Keyshawn Johnson, respectively—were expected to go in the first few picks, but each position was well stocked in the draft. Eight wide receivers picked in the draft would go on to earn Pro Bowl honors, and Parcells admitted that a "glob" of linemen was available just behind Rice and Hardy. In a sense, the Patriots couldn't go wrong.

The pick became a turf war, and parties on each side leaked their preferences to the press. The *Globe*'s Ron Borges noted just before the draft that the selection meant that "battle lines will be drawn. Owner Bob Kraft favors Ohio State wide receiver Terry Glenn, as does personnel director Bobby Grier. . . . Meanwhile, head coach Bill Parcells—a man to whom wide receivers have always been second-class citizens except when he has had to defend against them—favors defensive linemen Cedric Jones of Oklahoma or Duane Clemons of California, assuming Illinois pass rusher Kevin Hardy doesn't somehow slip through."

On draft day, Parcells still thought he was in control. No one had told him otherwise, which was a sign that Kraft was either not sure or intimidated—or more likely, did not want Parcells running to the press ahead of the draft. Everyone knew that Parcells and sportswriter Will McDonough, an increasingly visible presence on CBS, were close.

Parcells soon learned that he was just another employee. Minutes before the Patriots were scheduled to make their selection, Grier pulled Parcells into a side room and told him the team was selecting the talented Glenn, winner of the Fred Biletnikoff Award as college football's top wide receiver.

Parcells was bullshit at the news, reportedly telling Kraft, "If that's the way you want it, you got it," his voice dripping with disgust. He wanted to coach his way, with players he wanted, period, and the decision made it clear that Parcells was no longer in control. As he would later say, "It's just like a friend of mine told me, 'If they want

> "IT'S JUST LIKE A FRIEND OF MINE TOLD ME, 'IF THEY WANT YOU TO COOK THE DINNER, AT LEAST THEY OUGHT TO LET YOU SHOP FOR SOME OF THE GROCERIES.'"
>
> —BILL PARCELLS

you to cook the dinner, at least they ought to let you shop for some of the groceries.'"

That wasn't the end of it either. After drafting defensive back Lawyer Milloy in the second round when the linemen Parcells was interested in weren't available, in round five the Patriots selected Nebraska defensive tackle Christian Peter, a first- or second-round talent who had fallen due to what were then euphemistically referred to as "off-the-field issues."

In an era before 24/7 cable news sports coverage, digital media, and the instant dissemination of information, it was still possible for players and teams to bury with impunity any stories of drug and alcohol abuse, domestic violence and sexual assault, and other serious crimes. Fame, money, and a "boys will be boys" mentality protected players from paying a price for all but the most overt indiscretions. Red flags were already flying, for instance, from rumors of sexual indiscretions and assaults committed by Patriot running back Dave Meggett, a favorite of both Patriots fans and Parcells, behaviors that would eventually land him a thirty-year prison sentence for rape after he retired from the sport.

While at Nebraska, Peter had been arrested eight times, resulting in four convictions for various alcohol and assault charges, which included groping a young woman and grabbing another by the throat. Another woman claimed that Peter had raped her twice in 1991, and although no criminal charges were filed, she would later receive a settlement in a Title IX suit against the university.

Peter's selection did not go unnoticed, for Kraft had already said publicly that the Patriots would not consider Peter's teammate, running back Lawrence Phillips, who'd been put on probation for assaulting a girlfriend and suspended for fighting with teammates. When the press noted Peter's behavior, the Pats initially dismissed concerns—they said that they'd all discussed it before the draft, and that discussion had included Kraft. Bobby

Grier told the *Globe*, "We were well aware of his off-field problems. We did our normal investigation." He admitted that it was a "controversial pick for us, but Peter understands what this organization stands for, that we're not going to stand for any of those shenanigans off the field." Parcells added, "I think once he gets in a good, solid structure everything will be fine."

But after a *Sports Illustrated* story fleshed out the story, revealing more about Peter's legal and behavioral issues, the Patriots backed off, claiming NFL security had not made the magnitude of Peter's acts clear. Facing intense criticism, less than a week after the draft the Patriots waived Peter and discarded the pick, many observers believing that Myra Kraft, who inherited a

strong sense of social justice from her father, had been the driving force behind the decision.

Sadly, the judgment would not prove to be a watershed moment in the sport. Peter was snapped up by the Giants, underwent extensive counseling, and went on to play six seasons without incident, although he never admitted to the rape accusations. Meanwhile, teams throughout the NFL continued, more often than not, to turn a blind eye toward charges of assault and domestic violence against both prospects and players, particularly those veterans already under contract for big money, often blaming the victims. Player behavior off the field remains an issue that the NFL seems far less concerned about than it should be, and as later events would show,

Bill Parcells (*left*) on the field with Cleveland Browns head coach Bill Belichick before their AFC playoff game on January 1, 1995, at Cleveland Municipal Stadium. The former Giants assistant coach bested his old boss by a score of 20–13.

the Patriots have been little better than other teams in this regard. The NFL's policy to "defend the shield" remains in place. Accusers, forced to go up against the privilege that comes with money and fame, remain at a disadvantage.

After the draft debacles, Parcells reportedly mulled quitting once again, but ultimately chose to stay on, although the rift between owner and coach grew wider during training camp. When Terry Glenn was out with a hamstring issue and Parcells was asked about his status, he snidely replied, "She isn't ready yet." This time Myra Kraft went on the record, calling the comment "disgraceful" and saying of Parcells, "I hope he's chastised for that. It was the wrong thing for anyone to say." Her husband reprimanded Parcells for the remark, and the rift between the two men grew wider.

Some of the shine seemed to be coming off Parcells, and Kraft seemed over his head as the top man of an NFL franchise. The players knew what was going on, or at least sensed it, but the nature of the game makes football players seem better able to compartmentalize than athletes in many other sports. They mostly liked Parcells, and those who did not at least respected his record and his knowledge, but all of them knew who signed the checks. They stayed out of the drama.

The Pats got off to a rough start in 1996. After missing much of the preseason, Glenn sat out the first game with injuries, and even after he returned to the lineup the second week, the Patriots fell to Buffalo when rookie kicker Adam Vinatieri, whom Parcells had favored over veteran Matt Bahr, missed three field goals. The coach made it clear that was not acceptable. At 0-2, the 1996 Patriots season seemed on the brink of being over before it even started.

Fortunately, facing the 0-2 Arizona Cardinals in game three for the opener at Foxboro gave the Patriots a breather, and the team started to come together on both sides of the ball. The defense put up a shutout in the 31–0 win, the tandem of Glenn at wide receiver and Coates at tight end proved difficult to stop, Martin continued his solid performance out of the backfield, and the Patriots, for the first time, seemed to realize the type of team they could be. The following week Vinatieri got on board with five field goals, including the game-winner in an overtime victory over Jacksonville, and the Patriots were suddenly in a groove. Now that he didn't have to pass on every down and had more options, Bledsoe became much more consistent. A better-balanced offense gave everyone trouble, and the defense, young, quick, and opportunistic, improved every week. Milloy, Law, and Willie Clay formed one of the best backfield units in the game, Ted Johnson stuffed the middle, and McGinest emerged as one of the top linebackers and sack artists in football.

It slowly began to dawn on everyone that this was the best Patriots team in a decade. They won eight of ten, falling only to Washington and to John Elway and the Broncos, and clinched a playoff berth on December 8 and a division title a week later. But after losing to Dallas, they needed to beat Parcells's old club, the Giants, in the finale to avoid playing in a wild-card contest.

For the first thirty minutes, the Meadowlands looked to be the place where the legend of Bill Parcells might be buried, as the Giants took a 22–0 lead into halftime. The Patriots played as if looking ahead to a postseason they hadn't yet earned the right to play in. But in the second half, in a performance that later brought tears to Parcells's eyes, they responded.

The young team had grown up. Bledsoe was on target, and the much-maligned Glenn overcame a hip pointer to make several key catches and proved his toughness. Former Giant Dave Meggett returned a punt for a touchdown, overlooked wide receiver Troy Brown made a key catch, and Vinatieri made a clutch kick. The clincher came on a fourth-and-7, 13-yard touchdown pass from Bledsoe to Ben Coates with 1:23 remaining, giving the Patriots a 23–22 win and a bye in the first round of the playoffs.

"I didn't think we could come back," said Parcells afterward. "We may not be the best team, but this is as happy as we've been in a long time." Unfortunately, his happiness would be short-lived.

As the coach himself intimated, the Patriots weren't "the best team," and no one was penciling them in for the Super Bowl. The Western Division–winning Broncos, who had trashed the Patriots 34–19 in November, were odds-on favorites to make it to the title game against Green Bay. The Packers were the first team in the league to score the most points and give up the fewest since the 1985 Bears.

Bill Parcells congratulates wide receiver Terry Glenn on the sidelines during the fourth quarter of the team's blowout 45–7 road win against the San Diego Chargers.

But the Patriots got lucky, and even if they were not the best team, they were still pretty good. In the divisional playoff, the Broncos, in a huge upset, fell to the one-year-away-from-expansion Jaguars, and the Patriots rolled over the Steelers 28–3. For the Jacksonville Jags, beating Denver was like winning the Super Bowl, and they were greeted by 40,000 fans when they returned home. Foxboro Stadium, however, was not Florida, and in the conference championship, in conditions with zero-degree wind chill, Jacksonville shivered to a standstill. The Patriots weren't much better, but they scored an early touchdown after sacking Jacksonville's punter inside the 5, then put the game away late when Chris Slade knocked the ball out of the hands of Jaguar running back James Stewart and Otis Smith picked up the loose ball at the

47 and raced to the end zone. The Patriots won, 20–6, to make yet another improbable trip to the Super Bowl.

Parcells knew he was leaving, and so did the players. That wasn't anything new, even as the national media converged on the team and made it one of the story lines of the season. The others were Green Bay's first return to the Super Bowl since Vince Lombardi was coach and Packer quarterback Brett Favre's admission that in the off-season he'd overcome an addiction to the painkiller Vicodin.

The actual rift between Parcells and Kraft wasn't a distraction, but the constant questions about it in the two weeks before the game, and the way Kraft and Parcells and Parcells's agent Robert Fraley kept the story in the news, were. Fraley gave the *Globe* a scoop everyone already knew when he told the paper days before the game that Parcells would leave, and Parcells, after telling his team, "The Packers are here to make history, we're here to win a game," made it all about himself. He told his team that, now that they were at the Super Bowl, he would "show them what to do," since he'd already won two titles with the Giants. The disruption peaked a few days before the game when Kraft, as if unable to stand all the attention going elsewhere, held a news conference with Parcells to announce that he'd signed Parcells to a ten-year contract . . . to manage one of his paper mills. The joke fell like wet newspaper and angered the Packers. One assistant coach referred to Parcells as a "media ho'," and privately the Packers felt that their own coach, Mike Holmgren, was being overlooked, as were their already considerable accomplishments during the regular season.

Super Bowl XXXI at the Superdome began as if the rules had been changed. The Packers and the Patriots both played like the goal was to score the most points as fast as possible and then collapse exhausted on the living room floor to watch the halftime show featuring the Blues Brothers, James Brown, and ZZ-Top. Green Bay jumped out to a 10–0 lead and looked to have New England reeling, only to have Bledsoe complete six of ten passes on the next two drives and end each with a touchdown pass, first to Keith Byars and then to Ben Coates. At the end of the first period, the Pats led 14–10 and Green Bay suddenly looked overmatched. But the second quarter was all Green Bay and Favre, and the Packers went into halftime leading 27–14.

In the second half, the Pats stopped the rout with a seven-play, 53-yard drive, the score coming on a fine 18-yard run by Martin, and all of a sudden it was 27–21. "I guess," said one announcer, "it would be safe to say there's been a momentum change." The Patriots' sideline was rocking, Parcells was pumping his fist, and now the Patriots had a chance. Favre's magic suddenly seemed depleted, and the Patriots were brimming with confidence. They couldn't wait to get the ball back, confident they could catch Green Bay backpedaling and then surge ahead for one of the great comebacks in Super Bowl history.

But a funny thing happened on the way to taking that lead. There's a reason comebacks are rare—too many things have to go right. Green Bay return man Desmond Howard had already torched New England for two punt returns in excess of 30 yards, and earlier in the playoffs, against the 49ers, he'd scored a touchdown on a return.

The Patriots knew they'd have to control his kickoff returns and had a strategy to do so. Earlier in the game, Vinatieri's kickoffs had been high but not real deep, leaving Green Bay little time to set up a return—that had been the plan. But this time a pumped-up Vinatieri kicked it too hard, not quite as high . . . and long, leaving Howard, the only Packers return man, time to drift back and settle under the catch in the middle of the field, just shy of the end zone. It was just enough for him to take two or three extra steps and pick up some speed before the coverage team could converge.

He ran almost straight ahead, racing past the Patriots before they could seal off a crease left open in the middle of the field. A key block by Don Beebe allowed Howard to cut left, past the only man who even touched him, Mason Graham, leaving Vinatieri as the only white jersey between Howard and the end zone.

A few weeks before, against Dallas, Vinatieri had taken down a kick returner, earning high praise from Parcells, but Howard was another matter. Howard cut to Vinatieri's left and dashed by the kicker like a character from a cartoon, leaving Vinatieri chasing the air. A joyous Howard did the robot in the end zone, and Green Bay led 35–21.

That was it. Both teams knew the game was over. In five subsequent possessions, New England failed to move the ball at all, and Green Bay kept the ball on the ground, running down the clock.

One more time, a potential championship for the Patriots ended in something approaching embarrassment as what the Patriots did off the field overshadowed the game itself. As much as the hiring of Parcells, the drafting of Bledsoe, and the sale to Kraft had changed the arc of the franchise, for now the end result was the same as it ever was: another season ending with another team celebrating and the Patriots in disarray.

CHAPTER NINE

1997–1999

JACKED AND NOT SO PUMPED

The defeat was bad enough, but now came the divorce. Kraft and Parcells had kept it up for appearances' sake during the Super Bowl, but as soon as the game ended it was time to call in the attorneys.

It was as if, one last time, the Patriots had to remind everyone what they had been for most of their history: a team with a meddling, well-intentioned but sometimes vindictive owner, coached by someone who—even when successful—primarily looked out for himself.

THE PLANE HADN'T LANDED back in Boston before the Super Bowl seemed far, far back in the rearview mirror. That's because Parcells hadn't even been on the plane. In fact, he never even said good-bye to his team. He'd been in touch with the Jets for weeks. Four days after the game, on January 31, Parcells announced that he was through as coach of the Patriots.

In what the *New York Times* accurately described as "a distinct battle of ego and will," Parcells wanted to leave and Kraft didn't want him to stay, but Kraft also didn't want to let him go for free, any arrangement or understanding to the contrary be damned. In fact, even as Parcells was making calls to the Jets during the Pats' championship run, Kraft was thinking beyond the game as well, faxing Parcells's contract to the league

Patriots head coach Pete Carroll gives a hug to offensive lineman Dave Wohlabaugh following New England's 24–21 playoff-clinching victory over the 49ers at Foxboro Stadium on December 20, 1998.

and making his case for compensation in the event that Parcells tried to coach in 1997.

It wasn't quite Chuck Fairbanks redux, but once again New England fans were left with a bad taste in their mouths after a defeat that was already about as pleasant as acid reflux. It made everyone look small and petty, one more example of the kind of thing that *only* ever seemed to happen to the Patriots. Right and wrong, legal and illegal, honor and loyalty and dignity and everything else fell to the wayside in favor of the craven. The *Globe*'s Dan Shaughnessy called it "the Boor War."

When Kraft balked at releasing Parcells, the Jets tried an end run, hiring Parcells not as coach but as a consultant. Bill Belichick left the Pats to become the Jets' head coach, which, since it was a promotion, the Patriots were powerless to stop, although it was obvious the plan was that Belichick would only keep Parcells's seat warm until Parcells became free to assume the throne legitimately. Everyone knew it would be a title without a portfolio for Belichick. As Parcells dominated the press conference announcing the scheme, Belichick looked on like he was sucking a lemon. If the deal went through, it was clear that Parcells would be the head coach in every way but on the sidelines during the games. It was all about as believable as Parcells taking over that paper mill.

In the end, NFL commissioner Paul Tagliabue had to sort everything out. Parcells thought the buyout—which was actually a contractual agreement over a $300,000 fee requiring the coach to wear a certain brand of clothing—would leave him free and clear, but there's a cost to thinking about football all the time. He had signed it without consulting his attorney or reading the fine print about not being able to coach in 1997. Kraft, in a move as savvy and forward-thinking as buying Foxboro Stadium, had Parcells by the short hairs, his payback for feeling disrespected. He wanted a measure of revenge and needed to save face after losing a coach who had taken the team to the brink of its first championship.

In the end, Tagliabue gave both Parcells and Kraft what they wanted. Parcells would be free to coach the Jets, and the Patriots would receive a slew of draft choices—New York's third- and fourth-round picks in 1997, a second-rounder in 1998, and a first-round selection in 1999.

And New England fans and players got Pete Carroll as head coach.

Kraft had already been thinking for months about finding a new coach, and on January 31, 1997, when it first became official that Parcells would not return, he began the search in earnest. Initially, he seemed ready to do a full Billy Sullivan, with University of Texas coach John Mackovic, Green Bay offensive coordinator Sherm Lewis, and Auburn coach Terry Bowden apparently at the top of his list. But within a few hours he shifted focus and reportedly approached San Francisco coach George Seifert to gauge his interest. Seifert didn't want the job, but talked up his assistant, Pete Carroll. Kraft soon turned his attention to the 49ers' defensive coordinator.

Carroll, in just about every way possible, was the anti-Parcells. As Kraft noted at the time, that seemed about as important as anything else. "I think his style of motivation is probably right for coming into the age of the millennium and the Internet," said Kraft. "His style will help our younger players flourish to their ultimate potential." Carroll was only forty-six and looked younger, being nearly as fit as many of the players. For the San Francisco native, the phrase "youthful enthusiasm" seemed a mandatory part of his résumé and "jacked and pumped" a way of life. He had played safety at the University of the Pacific but was a World Football League washout. He spent the next fifteen years in football-coach apprenticeship school, putting in time at Arkansas, Iowa State, Ohio State, and North Carolina State before joining the staff of first the Buffalo Bills, then the Vikings and the Jets as an assistant, before being named head coach of the Jets in 1994. There he'd flamed out—after a quick start, the Jets had collapsed to finish 6-10. Carroll was fired, and Seifert then snapped him up to run the 49ers' defense.

Carroll came off as some kind of throwback from a more innocent time, all squeaky clean, rah-rah earnestness. You half expected him to wear a letter sweater, carry a megaphone, lead the cheer squad, and then take everyone to the beach, or at least that was the image presented by the press. In truth, many players both liked and respected him. When he took over, he met individually with every team member.

It wasn't that he was a bad coach—as his later performance at USC and Seattle would show, he is not—or necessarily a bad choice. He knew X's and O's, ran intense, highly organized practices, and impressed everyone with his football knowledge. But in the end, Carroll would prove to be the wrong choice for this team at this time, for these particular players. Over his four years in Foxboro, Parcells had surrounded himself primarily with players who responded to his kind of "tough love," guys who needed to be challenged, prodded, and pushed to perform. Even if they didn't like him, they'd played hard for him, and they missed that when he was gone. Carroll simply wasn't wired that way. He wanted to be your friend and was the kind of guy Parcells-type players didn't quite buy and younger players often took advantage of.

Carroll also wasn't meant for the Boston media. They liked jousting with Parcells, who gave as good as he got, and looked at cheerleaders like Carroll with typical New England suspicion. At his opening press conference, Carroll described taking over from Parcells in pop culture terms, saying, "It's like [when] Jay Leno took over for Johnny Carson. He was Jay Leno and he didn't try to be Johnny Carson. I'm going to be me." Then he played to the crowd, asking, "What's all this about groceries? All I know is when I go shopping with my wife, she makes me push the cart." It was funny, sort of, but it already seemed like he was trying too hard to be liked.

It wasn't his fault that he inherited a Super Bowl team and that his time in New England would play out between the tenure of two legends, Parcells and Belichick, who both blotted out the sun. He also didn't have anything close to full control. This was Bob Kraft's team, and with Bobby Grier elevated to general manager, Carroll was left to play the hand he was dealt. He was head coach, period.

Kraft wanted to run his team as a "business," and that meant "checks and balances," with no one having too much authority. That seemed fine with Carroll. Not many coaches had the opportunity to take over a team that had just made it to the Super Bowl. He didn't plan any big changes on either side of the ball and had no intention of trying to install the "West Coast" offense popularized by Bill Walsh and Seifert in San Francisco, saying, "Drew throws the football and he throws it extremely well to Ben Coates, and we found a great receiver and flanker in Glenn and there's just no way around getting the ball to Curtis, so this is everything you ever wanted in putting the offense together."

NO LOOKING BACK

HOWARD BRYANT

The last time the Patriots grabbed me, pulled me in, and reminded me that those Boston bloodlines were *who you were* wasn't during this current dynasty. It wasn't when the team of the Snowplow Game, the Stupor Bowl, and Irving Fryar nearly having his finger cut off before the Super Bowl turned into the Can't Be Killed, Get All the Breaks, Make All the Plays Joe Torre Yankees, but a few years before, in the year 1996—when it was just about time for me to say good-bye.

I was twenty-seven at the time, the appropriate age to retire the bedrock fan characteristics—rushing to Strawberries to buy Pats tickets, freezing your ass off on the metal benches of Schaefer/Sullivan/Foxboro Stadium. I was a professional now, covering telecommunications for the *San Jose Mercury News*, in the hotbed of Silicon Valley, two years away from covering the pros for the next twenty years: the Oakland A's, the Yankees, the Red Sox, the Pats and Celtics, the Washington football team, all of it. Since I wasn't yet covering sports, it was still all right to be a fan and not an Objective Journalist.

And it was then that I went all-in on the Bill Parcells Patriots. It really was, to me, the start of the change, when the Patriots were no longer a harmless mom-and-pop AFL stepchild, chum for the AFC Big Boys, the Steelers, Raiders, and Dolphins. It was then that the Patriots started having to be Taken

Seriously. And outside of the Pete Carroll blip, when both the players and the franchise thought they had arrived but hadn't, the 1994 to present-day New England Patriots have borne no resemblance to what they were in the first thirty-four years of their existence. With Parcells, they became a franchise to be feared.

At some point, every team in sports has its moment. The Buffalo Bills went to four straight Super Bowls and lost them all. As it turned out, those years were the aberration for what has been a mediocre franchise. The Michael Jordan Bulls from 1991 to 1998 were transformative—until Jordan left. Since then, the Bulls have been what they were before Michael arrived: not a JAG—Just Another Guy, in Parcells-speak—but a JAT (Just Another Team). The Minnesota Vikings of the 1970s were an outstanding, four–Super Bowl–reaching team, but haven't gotten back since 1977. And even

the legendary Dolphins, founded in 1966, owners of three Super Bowl appearances and two championships in their first ten years and five overall appearances in their first twenty, haven't reached the Big Game since 1985. There's a reason why the Packers, Cowboys, 49ers, and Steelers are the pillars of the sport.

What made 1996 different for the Patriots was, for me, the creation of a line of demarcation. There is a difference, however, between a Cinderella team that catches a wave and takes the whole region with it (like the 1985 team) or good playoff-level teams not spoken of in the same breath as the teams who would win championships (like the 1985–1987 teams), on the one hand, and *legitimate* teams without which the history of the league cannot be written, on the other. The Parcells Patriots were the forerunner to becoming Microsoft, Apple, and Duke basketball all in one. The leap to immortality was a shorter one because of them.

There was something transformative about the whole thing. It was cosmetic (the uniform, the colors, the logo change). It was stable: the end of the hapless Sullivans and the notorious Kiams of the world gave way to Kraft, whose "Aw shucks, I'm just a fan like you" approach was hardly believable but still contained no taint. You had to give the guy a chance.

And it was *talented*. Suddenly the Patriots were looking and acting first-class. In Parcells, they hired a hungry, Hall of Fame coach and not some college chump. They drafted a Hall of Fame–level quarterback (Drew Bledsoe), running back (Curtis Martin), tight end (Ben Coates), defensive end (Willie McGinest), wide receiver (Terry Glenn), safety (Lawyer Milloy), and cornerback (Ty Law), and New Englanders saw a team that looked like maybe it belonged. The Parcells Patriots looked like the Jimmy Johnson Cowboys: a young core of Hall of Fame or near-Hall-level talent at every key position on both offense and defense. I owned four jerseys: Law, Glenn, Chris Slade, and, of course, Martin. Like I said, I went all-in.

Was what was happening in New England really any different from the rise of any young team over the years? Or did it simply feel special because (1) Boston's collective ego cannot settle for simply being good, it must be extraordinary, and (2) it was finally

Patriots running back Curtis Martin (*left*) and quarterback Drew Bledsoe sign autographs on opening day of training camp at Bryant College. They were part of the core of star players led by head coach Bill Parcells who laid the groundwork for the team's dynasty.

happening to a team best known for being the laughingstock the good teams crunched in slow motion? It felt like the best *NFL Films* reels for the legends—the Dolphins, the Steelers, O. J. Simpson—came at the expense of the Patriots. If you only watched *NFL Films*, you might think *all* of Simpson's yards came against New England.

There were moments when you could see it coming: that Sunday afternoon in Buffalo two

years earlier when they went into Orchard Park and creamed that dynasty 41–17, putting a final cap to the Bills' four-straight AFC titles . . . or that Sunday night in 1996 when the Pats went into San Diego—who had been in the Super Bowl two years earlier—and demolished the Chargers 45–7. They had arrived.

Naturally, all the big thinking was a little premature. *Patriots gonna Patriot*, as the kids today would say. Parcells, secretly hired by the Jets, checked out during the Super Bowl against the Packers, and a winnable game turned into a Reggie White free-for-all. Martin followed Parcells to the Jets. The Patriots lost a playoff game 7–6 in Pittsburgh. Bledsoe never really got better, and suddenly they did what most teams do: they fell back to their old level . . . or so we thought. Then the next act came, and the Brady-Belichick combo avenged the Sugar Bear's 1976 pass interference call with the Tuck Rule for consecutive titles in 2003 and 2004. I remember puffing on that cigar at the Connecticut Yankee (San Francisco's Boston bar) after Willie Clay's end-zone interception sealed the AFC title game against Jacksonville, but by then I had left; now covering sports, I was no longer a True Fan but a Serious Objective Reporter. But 1996 remains for me the best year, and as the confetti flies, seemingly annually now, I go back to that year, when most people still saw the Patriots as the team whose fans once got so drunk the NFL banned the team from appearing on *Monday Night Football* for years. Since 1994, the Patriots have had two, just two, losing seasons. After 1994, they weren't a joke anymore. It wasn't a fluke. And they've never gone back.

Born in Boston, HOWARD BRYANT grew up in Dorchester and Plymouth. He covered sports and technology with the *Oakland Press* and *San Jose Mercury News* and the New York Yankees for the *Bergen Record* before joining the *Boston Herald* as a columnist. He then covered football for the *Washington Post* before joining ESPN in 2007. Bryant served as series editor of *The Best American Sports Writing 2017* and is the author of *Shut Out, Juicing the Game, The Last Hero*, and *The Heritage*.

It was still all smiles when the Patriots opened the 1997 season as favorites to win the division, and they started with a rush, blasting the Chargers and Colts to set up the game that, locally, was the near-equivalent of the Super Bowl: the first meeting between the Patriots and Parcells's Jets in Foxboro, a game already ripe with meaning for Carroll. The Jets had gone 1-15 in 1996. No matter who was coaching them, they had no business beating a team that had just gone to the Super Bowl. A loss would be a disaster.

It almost was. Only Curtis Martin prevented Carroll's tenure from ending almost before it started. The fired-up Jets, already 1-1 on the season, played the Patriots tough. Martin, a Parcells favorite, had one of the great games of his career, rushing for 199 yards, but it took overtime, and a great deal of luck, for the Patriots to prevail.

Late in the fourth quarter, with New England leading 24–17, Jets quarterback Neal O'Donnell led the Jets on a 12-play drive, culminating in a 24-yard touchdown pass to Keyshawn Johnson to tie the game. On the ensuing kickoff, the Pats' Derrick Cullors inexplicably ran the ball out of the end zone after the kicking team assumed he wouldn't. He fumbled on the 19, already within field goal range for New York. Moments later, kicker John Hall lined up for a 29-yard chip shot. New England was ready to erupt, and fans were putting sports talk radio on speed dial and preparing to sentence Carroll to a prolonged public flogging as Parcells partisans in the press sharpened their pencils.

But the new coach received a reprieve—several, actually. First, Hall kicked a line drive that was blocked, sending the game into overtime. And then Bledsoe, in New England's first possession, threw a pass right to Jets cornerback Otis Smith, a former Patriot, who had a clear path to the end zone, only to have receiver Troy Brown first tip and then rip the ball away. Bledsoe did throw an interception on the next pass, but the defense held.

Now the Patriots turned to the only strategy that had worked: Curtis Martin. They took over at their 21 and handed the ball to Martin on seven of the next eight plays, moving the ball to within field goal range at the 17. Vinatieri kicked a 34-yard field goal and New England escaped. Still, as Bob Ryan noted afterward, "Here was a long-downtrodden team coming into the home of the defending (and talent-upgraded) AFC champs and taking them to overtime." That shouldn't have happened.

One week later, the Patriots blasted the Bears 31–3. With one quarter of the season in the bank, the Pats were undefeated, leading the league in both scoring and scoring defense. Of course, three of the four teams they had played would finish last in their division. No one knew how good New England really was . . . or if they were any good at all.

They found out in week six. With a bye week giving them two weeks to prepare, the Patriots went into Denver's Mile High Stadium and got blown out. Falling behind early, they were unable to run the ball effectively and equally unable to throw. Meanwhile, Denver's Terrell Davis did whatever he wanted, running for 171 yards in the 34–13 thumping.

A big win over Buffalo, another subpar team, followed, but the Patriots couldn't play losing teams forever, and the rest of the season unfolded in Goofus and Gallant fashion as the Pats were alternately lousy and great. Most of that, however, was overshadowed by an incident in, of all places, the mosh pit in front of the stage at the Paradise nightclub on Commonwealth Avenue.

Two nights before the Tampa game, Bledsoe, Scott Zolak, and teammate Max Lane went out to see the post-grunge band Everclear, Bledsoe's favorite. Bledsoe and Lane climbed onstage, then stage-dived into the mosh pit, something that happened dozens of times almost every night in rock clubs all over the city.

Just days following his ill-advised mosh pit leap at Boston's Paradise Club, Drew Bledsoe was more animated than usual in his Wednesday press conference on November 19, 1997.

But Bledsoe wasn't just some anonymous BU student. He was also six-five and 235 pounds—and Lane weighed just over 300. They two crashed onto a young woman named Tameeka Messier. She left the club in an ambulance.

It was an accident, and a stupid one, but the reaction in Boston was as if Bledsoe had violated the Geneva Convention. More conservative and unaware members of the local press, utterly oblivious to Boston's music scene, were mortified. My God, not only was Bledsoe stage-diving with *punks* at a nightclub two days before a game, *but he left his wife and newborn home alone!* The uproar increased when the Pats fell to Tampa, 27–7, a few days later. The incident in the mosh pit was blamed for the defeat, one reporter writing that Bledsoe played "as though he were in a drunken hangover."

Tameeka Messier had to have two disks removed and sued the players, the band, and the nightclub, eventually receiving a well-deserved $1.2 million settlement. The episode lingered for the rest of the season, sparking questions about Bledsoe's commitment and maturity and, by extension, Carroll's control over his club. If Parcells had been in charge, went the thinking, the players wouldn't have dared to go out.

Nevertheless, the Patriots made the playoffs with a 10-6 record and played host to Miami in the wild-card game. But by then they were a diminished team, and the mosh pit had little to do with that. Curtis Martin separated his shoulder against Indianapolis in early December and didn't play another down for the rest of the season, leaving New England with a one-dimensional offense and no way to control the ball. The Patriots managed to defeat Miami, 17–3, but fell to Pittsburgh in the next round, 7–6. The only solace was that Bill Parcells's Jets failed to qualify for the postseason at all.

On February 23, 1998, Billy Sullivan died in a Florida retirement home after suffering from prostate cancer for eight long years. He'd spent the bulk of his time after selling the Patriots at his compound in Cotuit.

There, surrounded by his extended family and a pile of early Patriots memorabilia, much of which was lost in a fire, he spent his final years embroiled in legal disputes and trying to rewrite history. His passing was treated kindly, as he was rightly credited with bringing pro football back to the region and, against all odds and common sense, managing to hang on to the franchise for nearly thirty years. That said something, as did his role in starting the Jimmy Fund, the cancer charity that would raise hundreds and hundreds of millions of dollars over the years. Any history of professional sports in New England is impossible to write without Sullivan as a central character, a man who by turn was gregarious and glib, scheming and naive, stubborn and charitable, greedy and giving, as flawed as any of us. But this is sports, and like Tom Yawkey, longtime owner of the Red Sox, Sullivan ultimately failed to reach the critical goal in sports: winning a championship. In the end, however, he achieved his personal goal: Billy Sullivan was rarely a non-entity. Along the way he made it interesting, aggravating, and, let's face it, entertaining as hell.

• • •

It's a cliché to say that sports, politics, and revenge are New England's favorite pastimes, but in the case of Parcells and Kraft it's also true, and in the off-season Parcells soon got his revenge. Running back Curtis Martin was a Parcells favorite, New England's most important player, and someone whose performance on the field was matched by his character. By all accounts, he was a good, kind, pious, and decent man who the Patriots never had to worry might embarrass them; a role model for younger players dazzled by money and all that comes with fame, Martin was someone whose idea of fun was playing chess. It hadn't been easy, for Martin had grown up in horrific circumstances in Pittsburgh, where, as he admitted in his Hall of Fame speech, he had "many brushes with death." He went on to say, "I remember one distinct time a guy had a gun to my head, a loaded gun to my head, pulled the trigger seven times. God's honest

> IT'S A CLICHÉ TO SAY THAT SPORTS, POLITICS, AND REVENGE ARE NEW ENGLAND'S FAVORITE PASTIMES, BUT IN THE CASE OF PARCELLS AND KRAFT IT'S ALSO TRUE . . .

Patriots owner Robert Kraft and his wife, Myra, are jubilant and covered in confetti as the team goes up the ramp into the locker room following their 17–3 playoff victory over the Miami Dolphins on December 28, 1997. Kraft is about to high-five linebacker Chris Slade.

truth, the bullet didn't come out. He wasn't pointing the gun at me and pulled the trigger and a bullet came out." He credited first football, a sport he didn't even particularly like, and a religious conversion at age twenty for saving him. He adored Parcells, calling the coach "a life changer."

But after the 1998 season, Martin was a restricted free agent, meaning that the Patriots could match any offer or receive compensation. Parcells knew that adding Martin to the Jets and subtracting him from the Patriots would be a double win—a way to help his club and simultaneously hurt New England. Parcells also knew that, with yet another new TV contract, several Patriots, such as Willie McGinest and Ted Johnson, were due for big raises if they were to remain with New England, and that several more had contracts that would expire in another year. And he also knew that the Patriots didn't have enough room under the salary cap to sign everyone. The Jets offered Martin a godfather contract, one he couldn't refuse and wouldn't have anyway: a six-year deal worth $36 million that included an opt-out clause after one

season, meaning that even if New England matched the offer, in another year Martin could leave for New York anyway.

The Patriots let him go, and Martin, the best running back in Patriot history and one of the best in league history, signed with the Jets on March 25, New England receiving the Jets' number-one and number-three draft picks in return. The impact was similar to that of the Yankees signing Red Sox stalwart Luis Tiant after the 1978 baseball season. The ripple effect would last for years. As Bledsoe later told ESPN, losing Martin "was the pivotal thing for the Patriots," sparking the team's demise during Carroll's tenure.

In the NFL draft, with six selections among the first eighty-three picks, the Patriots looked to be in good position to plug some holes and rebuild while still winning. But it didn't work out that way.

The loss of Martin meant the Patriots needed a running back. They couldn't count on Dave Meggett, who had been arrested for beating and robbing a prostitute in what was the beginning of the legal spiral that would

Tight end Ben Coates looks on during a game against the Pittsburgh Steelers in Foxboro. In nine seasons with the Patriots, Coates was Drew Bledsoe's favorite receiver, while being named to five AFC Pro Bowl teams.

eventually lead to his imprisonment as a sexual predator. So the Patriots grabbed Georgia's Robert Edwards with the eighteenth pick of the first round. Their subsequent selections, however, were largely disappointing, as Grier's acumen in the draft proved faulty. Meanwhile, it was one thing after another in the off-season: Ben Coates was arrested on a domestic violence charge, and Glenn, out from under Parcells's thumb, started to fall to the back of the pack, beset by injuries and, as the season progressed, questions about his commitment.

Still, most thought the 1998 season would result in another playoff appearance for New England, a possibility the league recognized by giving the Patriots marquee billing in four nationally televised broadcasts. But there were unavoidable questions still to be answered: Could

Edwards make up for the loss of Martin? And could Bledsoe adjust to a new offensive scheme put in place by new offensive coordinator Ernie Zampese, a protégé of longtime San Diego coach Don Coryell? The answers to both, initially, seemed to be yes, as the Pats rebounded from a narrow season-opening loss to potent Denver to win four in a row. Then the Jets, struggling at 2-3, came to Foxboro for a game that could simultaneously vault the Patriots into first place in the division and bury the Jets. The press called it "World War Tuna."

It was clear that the game mattered more to New York than New England. In the Friday practice before the game, Parcells gathered his coaches and walked off the field in disgust, leaving his players speechless. The fired-up Jets then went out and simply outplayed the Patriots, grinding them down to win 24–14 as Testaverde bettered Bledsoe and Curtis Martin chalked up his third consecutive 100-yard performance.

That was the turning point of the season, or at least the first of two. The Patriots went into a tailspin, losing four of five, and then, just as they were showing signs of turning it around with a stirring comeback win over Miami, Bledsoe broke a finger in his throwing hand. He toughed it out for the next two games—both wins—but as the playoffs approached, he reinjured the finger in a loss to St. Louis. Scott Zolak, after seven years as the Patriots' backup, took over, but the already sputtering offense slowed to a crawl. The Patriots made the playoffs as a wild-card team, but fell to Jacksonville, 25–10. The Jets, meanwhile, made it all the way to the AFC championship game.

A disappointing season became disastrous just after the Super Bowl. In replacing Curtis Martin, Robert Edwards had earned Rookie of the Year honors while running for 1,115 yards, and he looked to be a back the Patriots could depend on for years to come. Invited to compete in a made-for-TV rookie flag football game on Waikiki Beach during Pro Bowl week, Edwards went out for a pass, collided with a defender, and fell to the sand.

All four ligaments in his left knee tore loose, and there was also nerve damage. The injury was so severe that for a time doctors thought he might lose his leg. Although he'd eventually return to the league after nearly three years of tortuous rehabilitation, he would never again be an effective back. In the end, the 1998 season had produced nothing positive for the Patriots . . . apart from the stadium issue finally being resolved.

All the while, ever since the Patriots' appearance in the Super Bowl, there had been another series of attempts to merge sports and politics and build a stadium for the Pats either in Boston proper or nearby. Urban sports facilities were the rage, and sites in Somerville, at South Station, and in South Boston were all floated as possible sites. Some plans touted a multi-use facility that might also house the Red Sox, who, under John Harrington of the Yawkey Trust, were claiming that Fenway Park was too decrepit to renovate. At the same time, Kraft was pondering building his own place in Foxborough and asking the state to kick in about $70 million for the much-needed highway and infrastructure improvements to make it easier to get in and out. That scheme also required the state to buy the land at Foxboro Stadium from Kraft for $20 million in exchange for a $700,000-a-year lease, something that would have freed the Patriots of a tax burden.

All year long, it was Lucy and the football with the stadium issue as the Democratic speaker of the Massachusetts House of Representatives, Tom Finneran—known as "King Tom" to his detractors—blocked the proposal. Meanwhile, Kraft entertained overtures from Hartford, Connecticut, leading Finneran to take umbrage at what he believed were Kraft's power plays, at various times referring to him as either a "whiney billionaire" or a "fat-assed millionaire," just in case his math was off. "Why are the owners of pro sports teams entitled to hundreds of millions of dollars?" he asked. "Entertainment is not a public responsibility."

Under Republican governor John Rowland (who, like Finneran, would later be convicted for illegal political activities, though on charges unrelated to the stadium deal), Connecticut offered Kraft just about everything to move to Hartford, where the state was unleashing an ambitious redevelopment program. They offered to pay for the entire cost of the stadium, even donating the land (the current site of a steam plant that would have to be relocated), a package that *Sports Illustrated* estimated to be worth a total of a billion dollars. That would make the Patriots—the Patriots!—the NFL's most lucrative franchise. According to *SI*, one league official called it "the greatest [stadium] deal I've ever seen."

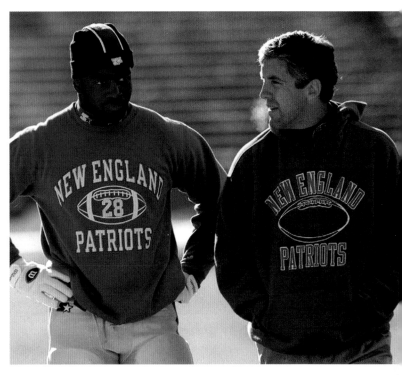

Patriots running back Curtis Martin and head coach Pete Carroll walk off the field at Foxboro Stadium a couple of hours before the start of the New England–Miami playoff game on December 28, 1997. Martin had gone out onto the field to test whether his various injuries were healed enough to allow him to play in the game. Carroll watched him work out, and after they talked briefly, the decision was made to hold him out of the game.

Kraft had publicly accepted the offer in November 1998, but then dallied on actually signing it until February because of concerns over whether the state could actually make good on its promises to meet deadlines. By then, Connecticut was so eager to claim victory that it agreed to sweeten the already sugarcoated deal and made even more concessions friendly to Kraft, essentially allowing him to call off the deal by May 2, 1999, if the state didn't make progress according to schedule. There were environmental issues with the site, and Kraft wanted to be in a new stadium by 2002. He knew that if he chose to leave, the franchise would be a lame duck in Massachusetts, and likely treated as such by fans and media, and despite sellout after sellout, the Patriots still weren't really making him any money. Connecticut even held a huge rally in Hartford to celebrate their potential coup, with state and city officials dancing in the end zone long before they had actually scored.

Connecticut governor John Rowland (*left*) and New England Patriots owner Robert Kraft (*right*) hold a press conference on November 19, 1998, at the State Capitol to announce that the Patriots have signed a deal to move the team to Hartford. Once the deal was approved by the Connecticut General Assembly, the team was scheduled to be in the new stadium (*shown in the drawing at left*) by the 2001 NFL season.

However, the concessions gave Kraft yet another hammer. Suddenly there was intense pressure on the State House to keep the Patriots, if not in Boston, at least in Foxborough. While Connecticut fiddled, the NFL, desperate for the Patriots to finally get a real stadium somewhere, stepped in and agreed to provide $150 million in loans so that Kraft could build his own stadium, effectively sidestepping a clause in Kraft's contract with Connecticut that prevented him from negotiating with another state. From the start, some wise Connecticut officials were worried that Kraft was simply using them for leverage, and the clause was designed to prevent that. Technically, it did. But now Kraft, technically, was negotiating not with Massachusetts but with the NFL. He already owned the land. The league was talking with Massachusetts about the infrastructure package and other issues, and the league had plenty of friends in high places. Suddenly—well, quickly enough, as nothing happened fast in the backrooms of Massachusetts politics—the $70 million infrastructure package was approved, making a new stadium in Foxborough tenable for the first time.

That's the thumbnail version of what could be a book in and of itself, but the end result was that on May 2, 1999, Connecticut failed to meet its deadlines, and on May 3 Kraft backed out of the Connecticut agreement.

On May 18, the Massachusetts state legislature approved the infrastructure package, and Kraft and the Patriots, backed by loan assurances from the NFL, began planning to build their own facility. In the end, it was a good deal for everyone but Connecticut. Massachusetts got to keep the Patriots, Kraft finally got a stadium, one he could build to his specifications, and Patriots fans got to keep their team.

Billy Sullivan had to be chuckling in his grave . . . or throwing up. For as historian David Welky noted in his essay in the book *The Rock, the Curse, and the Hub*, "Finneran's stubbornness, Boston's infighting and Kraft's blustering produced a stadium deal that cost taxpayers much less" than similar facilities in other cities. "Perhaps," added Welky, "the classic Boston triumvirate of sports, politics and revenge all worked out for the best."

The Patriots finally added some talent in the draft too, picking up center Damien Woody and running back Kevin Faulk. And with one of the highest payrolls in the league, on paper, the Patriots figured to make the playoffs. After an uninspiring preseason marred by a $100,000 fine levied on Terry Glenn for skipping mandatory workouts, the Patriots once again began a season under Carroll looking like world-beaters, ripping off four straight wins, including victories over the Jets and Colts. They weren't winning big, as Woody gave new life to the offensive line and Bledsoe got off to a quick start, but they were winning. Two losses were then followed by two wins, and the Patriots hit bye week at a surprising 6-2.

But their record was something of a mirage. Although they'd been winning, they weren't blowing anyone out. The illusion evaporated in their first week back, against—who else—the Jets, who stuffed the Patriots' offense and led 24–3 before New England scored twice late to make it look good.

The first half of the season had been a figment. The Pats now lost the kind of games they had won before, struggled to score, and were hounded by a series of distractions. Glenn played relatively well until Thanksgiving, but then, after a team party the night before the holiday, a woman said he groped her in the parking lot. He received a speeding ticket the next morning and then showed up three hours late for practice. "Holidays are very hard for me," explained Glenn. His mother had been shot and killed when he was twelve. "I have nobody to turn to this time of the year, nobody I can be with. That's why, even though some of my teammates don't realize it, they're like family to me. I went out with a bunch of them that night. I drank too much. I was hurting inside and I wanted to get rid of that."

All that may well have been the case, but it fueled tirades on talk radio and proved such a disruption that by the final weeks of the season, even his teammates were fed up. Carroll suspended Glenn for the final game of the season after he missed a game with an illness few believed was real. Meanwhile, unfounded rumors that Bledsoe was getting divorced and had an out-of-wedlock child swept through the tabloids, and Bobby Grier threw Carroll under the bus when he told a Boston TV station, "There's plenty of talent on this team," a reference to the players he'd supplied, not to their head coach. It all added up to the perception that Carroll was losing control, something the coach more or less confirmed when he held a closed-door meeting with his players. ESPN reported that Carroll's agent was already trying to get him another job.

With two weeks remaining in the season, the Patriots lost to lowly Philadelphia, a team with nothing to play for but pride, which seemed sorely lacking

in Foxboro. After the Eagles eliminated the 7-7 Patriots from playoff contention, the knives came out. "I'm not the coach, the quarterback, or the offensive coordinator, but there just seems to be no rhyme or reason to why we call certain plays," said tackle Bruce Armstrong. Carroll was also disgusted, saying his team "squatted" on the field and adding, "I'm sick about what we did."

In the end, the team with the third-highest payroll in football finished 8-8, which put them, technically, in last place in the division and marked the fourth year in a row under Carroll in which they had finished worse than the year before. The previous three seasons, making the playoffs had made up for that, but now there was no excuse.

Of course, much of that blame lay with the larger organization, first for overvaluing aging players and then for not replacing them with comparable talent. Carroll, the man at the top, took the fall, or at least took the fall first.

On January 3, 2000, Kraft fired Carroll, saying, "He is someone I have great respect for, but this is a business of accountability, and two years ago we won the division, last year we barely made the playoffs, and this year we're 8-8. We need a momentum change. Is it solely Pete Carroll's fault? No, I think we have to reassess the whole organization."

What would follow would be not so much a reassessment as a kind of return to the past, a rebooting of Bill Parcells in the form of Bill Belichick. But that would only happen after the entire episode was well drenched in the special kind of crazy sauce that only the Patriots could manufacture.

Kraft had already asked for permission to talk to a number of NFL assistant coaches about the opening, including Gary Kubiak and Mike Martz. Other reports indicated that Kraft also contacted Dom Capers, Marvin Lewis, Willie Shaw, Steve Sidwell, and Gary Crowton.

Under NFL rules, teams are not allowed to prevent an assistant from moving to another organization if the job is considered a step up. That's where things can get murky. Kraft had also asked permission to talk to Belichick, faxing a request to the Jets. The defensive coaching wizard still had a reputation as Parcells's most prominent protégé and had been on the short list for other head coaching jobs in the NFL over the last several

On May 24, 1999, Governor Paul Cellucci throws a football to Don Lowery (*right*), spokesperson for the New England Patriots, after he and Lieutenant Governor Jane Swift signed legislation keeping the NFL team's home in Massachusetts. Senate president Thomas Birmingham (*left*) looks on with (*left to right*) local businessman Paul Kirk, House speaker Thomas Finneran, and Republican representative Scott Brown (*obscured by the football*).

years. Holdovers on the Patriot defense from 1996, when Belichick had served in New England under Parcells, considered him a genius.

So did Kraft. Parcells had never really impressed Kraft. As a person, he found him boorish and loud, an attention-seeker who sought all the credit. Belichick, at least in Kraft's experience with him, was different, and a better fit for Kraft's corporate philosophy, a guy who always seemed to know everything about his department and everything about his aspect of the business, someone who kept his head down and thought only of results. In the corporate world, Kraft would have never hired a guy like Parcells in the first place. Belichick was a company man.

But the Jets turned down Kraft's request. They told him that Parcells was resigning and Belichick was their new head coach.

Under Jets owner Leon Hess, Belichick had signed a six-year contract that included an agreement that whenever Parcells stepped down, he'd get the Jets job. Hess had since passed away, but the agreement still held . . . or at least the Jets thought it did.

What followed was about something more than just

naming a coach. It was also about Kraft and Parcells and their egos as they went after each other like two sumo wrestlers shoving each other out of the ring, each determined to throw his weight around. By naming Belichick his successor, Parcells would secure his legacy in New York. But if Kraft could somehow pry Belichick away, it would be the ultimate revenge for the way Parcells had left New England, as well as a chance for addition by subtraction—harming the rival Jets in the process.

On the morning of January 4, the Jets had every reason to believe that Belichick would be their new coach. Belichick, however, had decided otherwise. With Hess no longer at the helm and the Jets for sale, Belichick wasn't sure he wanted that job—he didn't know whom he'd be working for. Who knew what they would be like, or how much control they would want, or how much they'd be willing to spend? He probably also felt some trepidation with Parcells still hovering around in the ill-defined role of team "adviser," sucking up the oxygen and much of the credit. And in a larger sense, the way the whole thing had unfolded was sort of like an arranged marriage—it just didn't feel right.

Belichick first told Parcells he didn't want the Jets job. Parcells felt betrayed, and he knew the Patriots' opening had something to do with Belichick's decision. Then Belichick scribbled on a sheet of paper and handed it to Jets president Steve Gutman. Never one to waste words—or ink—Belichick had written simply: "I am resigning as hc. of the n.y. js." With that, he went to the news conference and stunned the press, explaining that his agreement had been with Hess, Parcells, and Gutman and now that Hess was gone, well, so was the agreement. "I've been in the situation of a head coach of a team in transition," he said in reference to his tenure in Cleveland. "Frankly, it wasn't very good." In New York, they called him

"Belichick Arnold," an ungrateful backstabber. Reaction by the Boston media wasn't much better. The *Herald*'s Kevin Mannix famously referred to Belichick as "duplicitous pond scum" for double-crossing Parcells.

Of course, there's no telling what Belichick might have done had not the Patriots been waiting outside the chapel with the engine running. Had there been no other alternative, it seems likely that he would have taken the Jets job. As it was, two days after resigning, amid growing speculation that he wanted to go to New England and with the Jets refusing to free him from his contract, Belichick filed a grievance with the league against the Jets.

As Paul Tagliabue tried to sort things out, Kraft made his decision—the Patriots would not make a move to hire anyone else. On January 21, when Tagliabue ruled in the Jets' favor, that threatened to stop everything, but it wasn't that easy. Now the Jets (read Parcells) decided to let Belichick go, but this time they wanted compensation, payback for all the draft picks they'd had to give up when they hired Parcells. For a while, it looked as if that might nix the deal. Then Parcells caved, called Kraft, and after convincing him he wasn't joking, worked out a face-saving deal. For Belichick, New England would send their number-one pick in the upcoming draft to New York, along with their fourth- and seventh-round picks, a fifth-round pick in 2001, and a seventh-round pick in 2002.

Kraft agreed and formally offered Belichick the top job, saying, "He has an intimate knowledge of our team, intimate knowledge of our players and our division. People devise defensive schemes based on his success. He's the most capable person at this point to help us win next year."

Almost no one, however, thought it was a good idea, including Patriots fans, the media, and other NFL staffers. A *Globe* headline read, "Fans Weren't Bowled Over by the News." They saw Belichick as Parcells's lackey, and thus as someone who had already failed. Local media felt much the same way and bemoaned the loss of the draft picks, and others in the NFL questioned whether Belichick was right for New England, most thinking the price of that number of picks was too high. Belichick, after all, was no Bill Parcells.

And a lot of people thought that was important. Cleveland owner Art Modell, who had soured on Belichick during his tenure with the Browns, went so far as to warn Kraft that he was making a mistake. He even sent Kraft tape of Belichick's press conferences in Cleveland to underscore the point. "You're not getting Prince Charming," Modell told Kraft. He did admit that "give him some leeway and he'll deliver for you . . . but the other stuff, the human and public relations, is as important as a 3-4 defense."

In that respect, he'd been a disaster in Cleveland, by turns petulant and simply immature. At press conferences, Belichick acted like a kid forced to go to study

Running back Robert Edwards carries the football during the Patriots' 25–10 loss to the Jaguars in the 1998 AFC wild-card playoff game on January 3, 1999, at ALLTEL Stadium in Jacksonville, Florida. Within days, he sustained a devastating knee injury at a Pro Bowl rookie event that ended his Patriot career. He later came back to star in the Canadian Football League.

Kevin Faulk was one of the most versatile backs in Patriot history while also serving as a punt and kick returner. He's shown here in action against the Broncos in a 24–23 victory on October 24, 1999.

and O's went, the community of football minds considered Belichick a coaching savant. Besides, the last thing the franchise needed was to stretch out the excruciating process any longer.

· · ·

At his introductory press conference, Belichick tried to show a different side, referencing his awkward performance before the New York press, when he had "resigned as h.c.," by saying, "Hopefully this press conference will go better than the last one I had." For Belichick, that was the equivalent of doing about forty-five minutes of stand-up comedy.

He also took some responsibility for how things went in Cleveland, saying, "Previously, I think I maybe tried to do too many little things, too many things that maybe took away from bigger-picture things that I should've been doing. I've learned that as much as the game is played on the field—and it's extremely important to do everything right when you reach the football field in order to win in this league—there are also a lot of things on the periphery and outside, off the field, that are also important toward winning. I'll put more time and effort into making sure those things are right for the organization than maybe I did previously."

It was perfect Belichick-speak, for he never really admitted what any of those "things" were. But for now, it was enough. No one, not even Kraft, really knew what they had. As it turned out, Belichick's later success would not come as quite as big a surprise as Tom Brady's success—but Belichick still wasn't the equivalent of a number-one pick. His hiring was more akin to making a starter of a quarterback who'd been a capable backup, or elevating someone who had shown some promise as a starter when the number one was out with a sore arm. Think of Steve Young supplanting Joe Montana, or Aaron Rodgers taking over for Brett Favre. No one yet thought Belichick would be the equivalent of a Pro Bowler, much less a Hall of Famer.

Although Kraft had said that Belichick gave the Pats the best chance to "win now," that wasn't realistic, for the Patriots were something of a mess. As Ron Borges noted, "He joins a team that has had two straight lousy drafts, now has no No. 1 pick this year, is $10 million over the salary cap with nearly a half-dozen starting players eligible

hall, his contempt for sportswriters and broadcasters palpable. He routinely kept everything close to the vest and acted thin-skinned and defensive when he even deigned to entertain a tough question. And that was in Cleveland, not Boston, where press coverage was much more intense. Modell's advice had almost been enough to make Kraft change his mind, but in the end he went with his instincts. For all the red flags, as far as the X's for free agency next month, and must rebuild it while competing against the Colts, Dolphins, Bills, and most of all the Jets without sliding backward even for a year."

Borges had it almost right, but Kraft had apparently learned something during Carroll's tenure. He gave Belichick the authority he had taken from Parcells and that Carroll had never had, that all-important "control," and told him he wouldn't be judged harshly on the team's immediate performance. Belichick would have the luxury of time, or at least a little time. The Pats were about to break ground on the new stadium and Kraft expected them to be a winner when they moved in for the 2002 season.

Belichick, now not just head coach but also general manager, got to work, virtually cleaning house and bringing in a host of assistants from New York. He even dumped the Pats' popular strength coach Johnny Parker. Scott Pioli was elevated to assistant director of player personnel, but Belichick was the guy he was assistant to, and player moves would ultimately be the coach's responsibility. Then he made a couple of unpopular, but almost inevitable, decisions given the Pats' problems with the salary cap, choosing not to sign veteran free agents Ben Coates and Bruce Armstrong, who may have been two of the best players in Patriots history, but were both starting to slip. Bobby Grier was kept on through the draft, but it was clear that his role had been diminished, and he was let go in April.

And about that draft. It was almost a throwaway, considered by most all but inconsequential. Lacking a first-round pick, New England's first selection came in round two, the forty-sixth pick overall, at which point all the can't-miss prospects were certain to be gone. After that, New England had a three, a four, two fives, three sixes, and two sevens. At best, they hoped to find a starter with the number-two pick, maybe fill a few other roster slots, and find role players from the remaining flotsam. Before the draft, Belichick had already indicated that he hoped to get lucky with either free agents or draftees other teams might cut during the exhibition season.

They didn't get lucky with the second-round pick: the Pats selected offensive lineman Adrian Klemm, who for most of his career would be no better than a serviceable backup. Most of the later picks, including running backs J. R. Redmond and Patrick Pass and safety Antwan Harris, would fare little better.

But then there was that sixth-round pick, their second of the round, and the 199th pick in the draft. On April 16, 2000, the New England Patriots selected a skinny quarterback from Michigan, a guy who had split the job with a sophomore during his senior year.

Tom Brady.

Safety Lawyer Milloy during the pregame before the Patriots' 17–3 victory over the Miami Dolphins in the 1997 AFC wild-card playoff game on December 28, 1997, at Foxboro Stadium.

CHAPTER TEN

2000–2001

THE COACH AND THE QUARTERBACK

Pro Football Weekly's draft expert Joel Buchsbaum stood all of five-eight and weighed just a bit more than 100 pounds. Consumed by all things football, he lived in a small Brooklyn apartment surrounded by a mountain of media guides and videotapes. Although an amateur, the analyst was held in such high esteem that when Belichick was in Cleveland, he had tried to hire Buchsbaum as a scout. Buchsbaum turned him down, saying he preferred working for all thirty-two teams rather than just one.

IN HIS 2000 NFL DRAFT REPORT, Buchsbaum wrote this: "Positives: Good height to see the field. Very poised and composed. Smart and alert. Can read coverages. Good accuracy and touch. Produces in big spots and big games. Has some Brian Griese in him and is a gamer. Generally plays within himself. Team leader.

"Negatives: Poor build. Very skinny and narrow. Ended the '99 season weighing 195 pounds and still looks like a rail at 211. Looks a little frail and lacks great physical stature and strength. Can get pushed down more easily than you'd like. Lacks mobility and ability to avoid the rush. Lacks a really strong arm. Can't drive the ball down the field and does not throw a really tight spiral. System-type player who can get exposed if he must ad-lib and do things on his own.

"Summary: Is not what you're looking for in terms of physical stature, strength, arm strength, and mobility but he has the intangibles and production and showed great Griese-like improvement as a senior. Could make it in the right system but is not for everyone."

The subject was Tom Brady.

So why did the Patriots draft Tom Brady anyway? They already had Bledsoe, who at age twenty-eight seemed likely to hold the position for many more seasons. Belichick seemed satisfied, and John Friesz was considered an adequate backup, a safe step up from Scott Zolak. The nine-year veteran, also a sixth-round pick, had been a sometime starter over the course of his NFL career with San Diego, Washington, and Seattle. Although Friesz didn't throw a pass in 1999, he knew the offense and had seen action in sixty-eight NFL contests. And there was already a third quarterback on the roster, Michael Bishop out of Kansas State, a player who intrigued the Patriots and their fans with his running ability and possible future as a kind of "slash" quarterback, like Kordell Stewart in Pittsburgh and Ray Lucas with the Jets, although he had yet to do anything notable with the Pats outside of practices and exhibitions.

Well, one reason to add another quarterback to any mix is that during mini-camp and the first days of training camp, every team needs somebody who can throw the ball to make it possible to assess the pass-catching abilities of running backs and receivers. It's the same reason baseball teams invite so many pitchers to spring training every year: hitters need someone to take swings at. Having an extra quarterback can also help motivate the guys higher up on the depth chart—in this case, Bishop.

Add to the fact that it was considered a poor year for college quarterbacks. Only eleven were selected in the entire draft, the first being Chad Pennington with the eighteenth pick; it was the third round before another quarterback was chosen. The word around the league was that there were no draft-eligible quarterbacks likely to become stars in the NFL.

While in high school in California, Brady was considered a better baseball prospect than football player; as a left-handed-hitting catcher with power, he was an eighteenth-round pick by the Montreal Expos in 1995. Brady was a late bloomer as a quarterback, and in those pre-internet days he was not heavily recruited by colleges. He finally produced and distributed his own recruiting highlight film, which eventually drew the attention of college scouts. He settled on the University of Michigan, sat out his first year as a redshirt, and then served as a backup for two years before winning the starting job as a junior. But as a senior, Brady split time with Drew Henson, considered a super-prospect in both baseball and football. The two quarterbacks started alternate quarters. Although Brady put up solid numbers and the Wolverines won twenty of the twenty-six games he started, he was hard to assess. At the end of his senior year, he was considered perhaps a third-round NFL draft pick.

Then came the NFL Combine.

Brady scored a solid 33 of 50 on the Wonderlic personnel test used to assess the aptitude of prospective players for learning and problem-solving—an acceptable score for a quarterback. That was the good part. The bad part was everything else. He ran the 40-yard dash in a tick under 5.3—slower than many linemen—his vertical leap was only 24.5 inches, and his arm did not impress. On most teams' draft boards, Brady's stock dropped from a potential third-round pick to a guy a team might try to sign as a free agent.

But Patriot quarterback coach Dick Rehbein had scouted Brady at Michigan and came back raving. According to ESPN, he told his wife he thought he'd found another Joe Montana or Brett Favre. "Twenty years from now," he said, "people will know the name Tom Brady." Lloyd Carr,

Michigan's coach, had also once told Bobby Grier that if the Patriots drafted Brady, they would never regret it.

It was the sixth round, near the end of the draft's second day. Brady was the best player left undrafted on the Patriots' board. What the hell? So they drafted him, believing he was neither as bad as he had been at the Combine nor as good as Rehbein thought, with no idea whether Buchsbaum's positives would ever overcome the negatives. But he was a drop-back passer, and the Patriots used a drop-back offense. All he cost them was a minimum salary offer and a small five-figure bonus, pocket change in the NFL.

It was the kick upon which the fortune of a franchise hinged. Patriots placekicker Adam Vinatieri kicks the game-tying field goal out of the hold of Ken Walter against the Oakland Raiders to send the game into an overtime in which another Vinatieri kick would win the final game played at Foxboro Stadium, by a score of 16–13.

At mini-camp, Brady showed little that set him apart other than an arm a bit stronger than they expected to see. He was skinny, his body looking as if he'd spent five years at Michigan avoiding the weight room and eating greens. The *Globe* reported that "he will likely end up on the practice squad," a guy who might run the scout team when the Pats were due to face a drop-back QB. The Pats told him he needed to become stronger. Scarecrows didn't hold up under an NFL pass rush, particularly those who couldn't run.

Belichick's first New England training camp as head coach opened on July 16, and it immediately became clear that everything had changed. He wasn't out to make friends, and he had to know that if he failed in his second job as an NFL head coach, there would be no third offer. *Vacation's over,* thought Tedy Bruschi after the coach addressed the team. They hadn't seen anything yet.

The first day was marked by an interval running test—running twenty sprints with a brief break in between each one—to gauge each player's physical condition. Linemen had to run 40 yards in under six seconds. Linebackers, tight ends, fullbacks, and quarterbacks had to race 50 yards in under seven seconds, while backs and receivers had to dash 60 yards in less than eight seconds.

Belichick was not impressed. In fact, he was livid. "We've got too many players who are overweight, too many guys that are out of shape, too many guys who haven't paid the price.... You can't win in this league with forty good players when the other team's got fifty-three. You need fifty-three to match with them." Four players failed, and when one of them was number-two quarterback John Friesz, the coach had an excuse to look at the quarterback situation a little more closely. Friesz, who had undergone knee surgery a few years before, was perhaps acting a little too secure than the backup had a right to. The four were held out of workouts for the day and ordered to run extra laps and then ride stationary bikes. Belichick levied fines totaling $30,000, and at the end of the day even cut two players.

As camp went on, it became clear that no one's job was safe—Belichick was looking to create room under the salary cap. He was stingy with praise and used cuts to mete out criticism.

Brady hung on, completing three of four passes in mop-up duty in the first exhibition game against San Francisco, and then following up with a 10-for-15 performance against Detroit in Ann Arbor. He did just enough, week after week, to keep himself in the conversation and make it apparent that if he was placed on waivers, another team would be certain to snap him up.

What exactly was "just enough"? As Charles P. Pierce later wrote in his book on the quarterback, "Brady moves the chains. It's the first thing the New England Patriots and their coaches saw in him ... directing the scout team with players who hadn't been around long enough yet to be considered castoffs." It got him noticed. If nothing else, now he had value in a potential trade. For now, they'd keep him on the team.

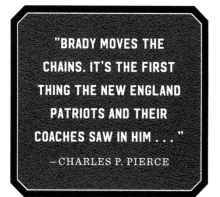

"BRADY MOVES THE CHAINS. IT'S THE FIRST THING THE NEW ENGLAND PATRIOTS AND THEIR COACHES SAW IN HIM . . ."

—CHARLES P. PIERCE

During the preseason, it became clear that the Patriots weren't Super Bowl contenders. They went 2-3 as offensive coordinator Charlie Weis installed a new offense more akin to the smash-mouth approach used when he had served under Parcells. A departure from the scheme used by Carroll, the new offense contained elements of the "Air Coryell" passing offense and required an entirely new nomenclature. Belichick didn't name a defensive coordinator: for the first year, that was his job. Rather than run a rigid base defense, like a 3-4 or a 4-3, Belichick's innovation, rare for the era, was to remain flexible and to adapt the defense—formation, scheme, and coverage—to the opposition according to the situation. His players had to know their roles in a wide variety of situations and sets, but when the coach made the right call, it would prove a challenge to the opposition's offense.

Of course, that also meant having a roster of players who could adapt and absorb the concept. In 2000, that wasn't quite the case. The players had to try to adjust to Belichick while the coach tested various combinations.

An often overlooked yet undeniable influence on Belichick's thinking is his background in lacrosse. Although Belichick played on the line for his college football team primarily in a backup role, he started on the lacrosse team. He was not a star, but Belichick had been a valuable role player with a reputation as a coach on the field. Lacrosse remains of intense interest to him. His daughter is a collegiate coach at Holy Cross, and as closed-mouthed as Belichick can be about football, he is sometimes effusive when discussing lacrosse.

Although the two sports are quite different, defensively they share some basic concepts, such as the use of man-to-man and zone coverage. Also, the dynamism of lacrosse requires that the defense constantly adapt to an ever-changing set of circumstances. Positions are more fluid than in football, and defenders must make decisions on the fly. The sport values speed, quickness, and team play over rigid, raw power and individual performance. In many ways, Belichick's constantly evolving defensive approach and roster strategy derive much of their elasticity from the influence of the stick-and-ball sport. His teams don't depend on star players but on depth, adaptability, and the capacity to fill a role and carry it out to perfection—"doing your job" is a favored Belichick phrase. A side benefit of not creating stars or being dependent on a select few performers can be a greater immunity to the impact of injuries and changes in personnel from year to year. In the long run, the approach also helps suppress salaries, giving a team continued flexibility under the salary cap. Consider this: since Belichick became the Patriots' head coach, only a single defensive player (Richard Seymour) and only three offensive players (Brady, Rob Gronkowski, and Wes Welker), apart from kickers, have earned first-team All-Pro honors more than once. By the start of the 2000 season, the Patriots' payroll, which had been third-highest in the league under Carroll, had fallen to twenty-ninth.

At the start of the 2000 season, the results on the field . . . were not good, at least as measured by wins and losses. The Patriots didn't lose badly, but they did lose, opening the season with four straight losses. They were followed by two wins over Denver and Indianapolis, both teams that would go on to win their division, but then a loss to the Jets sent the Patriots into another tailspin. They finished 5-11. The offense was a mess: without an effective running game, Bledsoe had to throw over 500 times while absorbing 45 sacks. The only bright spot on that side of the ball was undersized but sure-handed receiver Troy Brown, who at age twenty-nine led the team in receptions with 84, edging out the enigmatic Terry Glenn. Brown was becoming Bledsoe's favorite target as the opposition focused on the higher-paid Glenn. On the other side, the defense was much improved: the core, consisting of defensive backs Lawyer Milloy and Ty Law and linebackers McGinest, Bruschi, and Slade, all provided a bruise-inducing backbone that kept the Patriots competitive.

The best thing that happened in 2000 was that the Patriots' record set them up for a favorable schedule in 2001. The Patriots would play only a couple of games against teams that were .500 or better outside their own division. They also added University of Georgia defensive end Richard Seymour, a relentless pass rusher, and picked up free agent and former number-one draft pick Antowain Smith from the Buffalo Bills, who provided the Patriots with a solid running threat.

But Kraft and the Patriots made it clear that Drew Bledsoe was the most valuable player on the roster. Signing him to a ten-year, $103 million contract, the owner said, "He's 29 and at the top of his game and quarterbacks like this come around once in a lifetime."

Then there was Terry Glenn. They had hoped that Glenn, under the more disciplined Belichick, would respond as he had to Parcells. Belichick had promised to wipe the slate clean with the talented receiver, even signing him to a new six-year contract extension worth $50 million, including an $11 million signing bonus. But in the off-season Glenn raised concerns after being charged with domestic abuse, and on August 3 he was suspended for four games by the NFL after failing a drug test. It was just marijuana, but the NFL treated that drug like any other illegal substance. Although Glenn was still eligible to practice, he would go AWOL, reportedly because the Patriots had stopped paying his bonus. Two weeks later, Belichick suspended him for the season, and the players, who were tired of answering questions about Glenn, seemed to support that decision. Lawyer Milloy said, "It's just a cancer to us right now. As a whole that situation needs to die as soon as possible."

The dark cloud already hanging over the 2001 Patriots kept getting darker. On August 6, quarterback coach Dick Rehbein passed away due to cardiomyopathy, a heart condition. He would never witness the result of his trip to Ann Arbor, but Brady had already benefited from a year under his tutelage, gaining confidence each day.

• • •

The bright spot was the progress on the Patriots' new stadium. They'd started pouring concrete on June 15, 2000, and by March 2001 the final piece of structural steel had been hoisted into place. Later that summer, the Neponset River had been diverted to make way for related construction. The Patriots, unlike many other NFL teams, weren't requiring expensive and coercive seat licenses (fees for the right to purchase tickets). Although prices would go up—way up—and parking costs would prove onerous, this time Patriots fans would be getting something for their money, at least in terms of amenities. The 68,000-seat facility included 2,000 luxury seats and another 6,000 club seats. CMGI, a technology company, had agreed to fork over $7.6 million per year for fifteen

years in exchange for naming rights to "CMGI Field." The franchise had its eyes on a 2002 inaugural season.

Entering the 2001 campaign, the hope was that the Patriots, with twenty free agents on their roster, including receiver David Patten (who had already played in both Canada and the Arena League), might improve from a .500 team to one in the playoff conversation come December. But few expected much more. Las Vegas oddsmakers gave New England a 60–1 chance of winning the Super Bowl.

Then the Patriots opened with a 23–17 loss to Cincinnati, hardly a contending team, and those odds grew demonstrably longer. They still couldn't run and control the ball, and without Glenn as a target anymore, Bledsoe was forced to go searching for receivers, targeting nine different players during the contest. Troy Brown, who always seemed to catch any ball thrown his direction, was still the only receiver Bledsoe could depend on. Then came 9/11.

The terrorist attacks on the World Trade Center and the Pentagon rocked the nation and caused the NFL to postpone week two; those contests would be added onto the end of the season. Like many other NFL teams, the Pats were personally affected. Guard Joe Andruzzi, a native of Staten Island, was from a family of New York firefighters, and three of his brothers served on the NYFD. His brother Jimmy was in Tower One when Tower Two collapsed. He narrowly escaped with his life, and all three Andruzzi brothers participated in recovery efforts in the massive pile of debris.

The season resumed on September 23 with the Patriots playing host to the New York Jets in Foxboro. Pregame ceremonies included flyovers and the display of an enormous flag on the field held up by players and coaches and flanked by first responders, including the Andruzzi brothers. Briefly, the bitter and sometimes petty rivalry between the Patriots and the Jets seemed less important than a collective display of unity in the wake of a horrible event that still ripples through American life and culture. The nation needed to grieve, and the collective public gathering that sports often provides served that purpose. In another month, the World Series between the Arizona Diamondbacks and the New York Yankees would provide a similar opportunity.

Pro football analyst Joel Buchsbaum's encyclopedic knowledge was recognized by the likes of Patriots head coach Bill Belichick, who tried to hire him for the Patriots. Buchsbaum, along with Patriots quarterback coach Dick Rehbein, spotted the potential of Michigan quarterback Tom Brady as a future star.

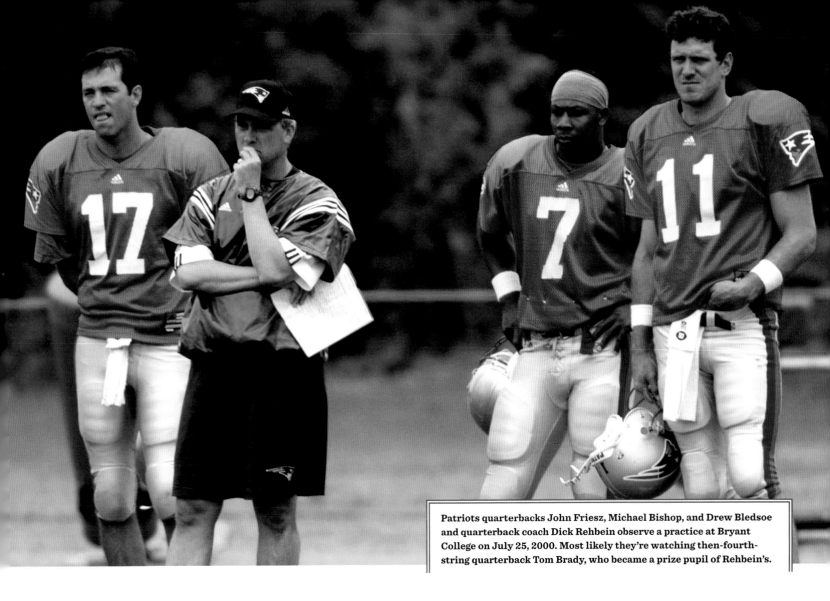

Patriots quarterbacks John Friesz, Michael Bishop, and Drew Bledsoe and quarterback coach Dick Rehbein observe a practice at Bryant College on July 25, 2000. Most likely they're watching then-fourth-string quarterback Tom Brady, who became a prize pupil of Rehbein's.

One can trace the increasing politicization of all things NFL to the league's initial response to 9/11. Over the ensuing years, professional sports, the NFL, and the Patriots would increasingly serve as a marketing arm for the military. That was not something done for reasons of altruism, as revealed in a report from Arizona Republican senators Jeff Flake and John McCain in 2015, but in exchange for money. McCain, a former POW, said, "I was appalled to learn last month that many of the ceremonies honoring members of our armed services at NFL games are not actually being conducted out of a sense of patriotism, but for profit in the form of millions in taxpayer dollars going from the Department of Defense to wealthy NFL franchises." McCain even cosponsored a bill to ban the practice and called for the league to hand over those fees to veterans' charities.

By 2015, the Pentagon had approved contracts leaguewide worth nearly $7 million for these scripted displays of patriotism. From 2012 through 2015, the Pats accepted $700,000 in such funds, second only to the Falcons. Something that was initially genuine and authentic became calculated and crass, patriotism used as a marketing tool. Given their name, few teams would prove more adept at this than the Patriots, as their actions bound the team and its moniker not to the Constitution or the Bill of Rights but to the armed forces. Few fans realize that until 2009, NFL players were never even on the field for the National Anthem, that such displays at NFL contests and other major sporting events had been both rare and understated.

Today most Patriots fans can hardly recall that first pregame display of unity on September 23, 2001. In

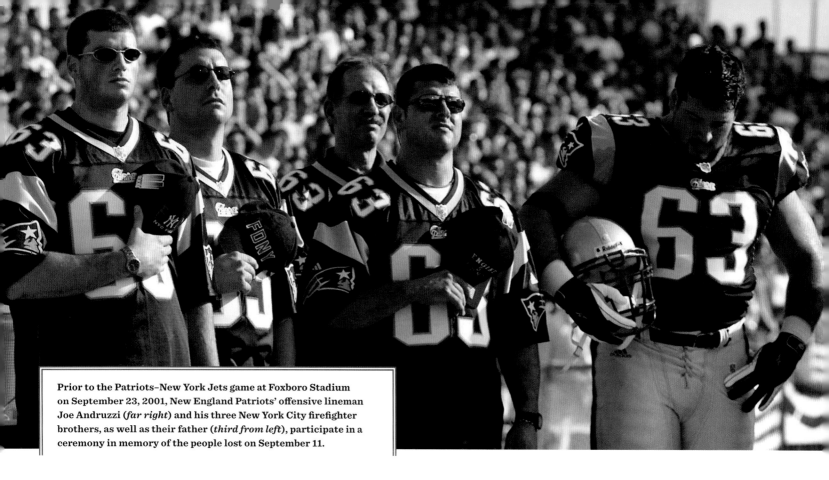

Prior to the Patriots–New York Jets game at Foxboro Stadium on September 23, 2001, New England Patriots' offensive lineman Joe Andruzzi (*far right*) and his three New York City firefighter brothers, as well as their father (*third from left*), participate in a ceremony in memory of the people lost on September 11.

the annals of Patriots history, that date is remembered instead for perhaps the most consequential single play in team history.

With 5:07 remaining in the game, New England trailed the Jets, 10–3. To this point, the game had been a tough defensive battle, and for the second week in a row, the Patriot offense sputtered, Bledsoe having already thrown two interceptions. With the ball on the New York 19, on third-down-and-10, and with a single blocker in the backfield and two receivers split on each side of the line, Bledsoe took the snap.

He backpedaled to the 10-yard line, and the Patriots' offensive line, despite facing only four rushing linemen against their front six, almost immediately collapsed. Bledsoe ran to his right, New York defensive end Shaun Ellis in pursuit, then turned upfield, taking aim on the first-down marker at the 29. He hesitated briefly at the 20, then cut up the sideline as Jets linebacker Mo Lewis, also noting the first-down marker, converged to a place just shy of the spot, hoping to knock Bledsoe out of bounds short of a first down. At the 25, Ellis dove, reaching for Bledsoe's legs, and the stumbling quarterback turned as Lewis lowered his shoulder and struck Bledsoe

at almost full speed, striking him with a combination of helmet, shoulder, and elbow along his left side and back. Bledsoe collapsed out of bounds, taking a hard hit, but not an illegal one.

Bledsoe remained on the ground for a full two minutes, then, remarkably, got back up and made his way to the sideline as the Patriots were forced to punt. Belichick asked him how he felt, and Bledsoe said, "I'm all right." The coach later said there was no sign of Bledsoe having a "significant concussion"—not a surprising statement for the era, when head injuries were often considered less serious than a twisted ankle. When the Patriots got the ball back for their next drive, Bledsoe returned to action for three more plays, even completing a two-yard pass to Marc Edwards before the running back fumbled the ball away. But Bledsoe *had* suffered a concussion, and as he later recalled about those plays, "I knew I had to go right or left, but I couldn't think of the words." His teammates, including Damon Huard, as Bledsoe said later, "ratted him out" to chief team physician Bert Zarins when he returned to the bench. In that pre-concussion protocol era, Bledsoe would watch the end of the game from the sidelines.

In a salary cap decision, 2000 backup quarterback John Friesz had not been re-signed, and Michael Bishop had been released to the Frankfurt Galaxy of NFL Europe to gain some experience, leaving Brady and Bledsoe as the Patriots' only two quarterbacks. So just before the start of the season, the Patriots signed former Miami backup Damon Huard to a three-year deal to serve the same role behind Bledsoe. Once the heir apparent to Dan Marino, he'd gone 5-1 as a starter in Miami in 2000. However, Belichick had decided that, for the first few weeks of the season, Brady would serve as the Patriots' number-two signal-caller, at least until Huard learned the offense. "I'm not saying that that situation will be that way every week throughout the year," said the coach, "but based on the preseason, we just feel like Tom, right now, is a little bit ahead of Damon in terms of handling the team."

Yet even though Huard now had several weeks of experience learning the system, when Bledsoe left the field after Edwards's fumble, Belichick turned to Brady and barked, "Drew is out and you're in." The young quarterback started warming up, and when the Patriots got the ball back with two minutes remaining, he trotted onto the field. Although Huard knew the offense, he had never run the Pats' two-minute offense in a game situation. During the preseason, Brady had. It was as much a situational decision as anything else.

To that point in his professional career—if one could call three plays at the tail end of a drubbing against the Lions in 2000 a career—Brady had completed only two inconsequential passes in an NFL game. For the record, his first was a four-yard gain to J. R. Redmond. But he had spent the past year and a half studying, practicing, working out, and impressing his teammates and coaches in exhibition performances while running the scout team. He'd bulked up and gained confidence. Still, had Bledsoe's injury come a game or two later, or if the Pats had gotten off to a better start, Huard may well have gotten the call and been handed the offense. Had that happened, the name Tom Brady might be no more important to Patriots fans than that of Michael Bishop.

With two minutes remaining in the game and the Patriots still trailing the Jets 10–3, Brady took the field and took command of the offense. Sixteen years later, he has yet to let it go.

The two-minute offense went into effect, requiring Brady to think fast. It was "spot a receiver, throw, and don't be in a hurry." In a funny way, it helped that Glenn was no longer available. Had he been, he might have drawn the attention of the defense, limiting Brady's choices. But without Glenn, defenses weren't quite sure who to cover. Brown did not yet attract the attention of a premier receiver, and no one else was considered a certain threat. Over time the relative anonymity of the Patriots' receiving corps, and the opposition's lack of any kind of "book" on Brady, would prove to be a benefit.

On Brady's first pass, he hit Patrick Pass out of the backfield for four yards. Next, he found Brown for nine. An incompletion followed, then another two completions to Brown, bringing the Patriots close to midfield before a holding call pushed them back 10 yards. Then Brady scrambled for nine, running out of bounds, and with only 33 seconds left, he spotted David Patten for 21 yards, moving the ball just short of the 28.

The Patriots needed to score a touchdown, and after another incompletion, Brady's next two passes were Hail Marys. Both fell incomplete, and the Patriots fell as well, losing 10–3. Brady's 5-for-10 performance for 46 yards went almost unnoticed, at least by everyone not named Belichick.

At the game's end, as Bledsoe left the field, team doctor Thomas Gill asked to take a look at him. Still woozy, Bledsoe said he wanted to attend the postgame prayer, but Gill saw that Bledsoe was pale and ashen and convinced the quarterback to head straight to the locker room. There he noticed that Bledsoe seemed strangely agitated, and the quarterback also complained about a sore shoulder, leading Gill to take a closer look at him. A quick check led the doctor to think that Bledsoe might have ruptured his spleen. He called for an ambulance to transport Bledsoe to Massachusetts General Hospital.

It was worse than a ruptured spleen. Although Bledsoe had felt no pain until the end of the game, he had suffered a hemothorax—a blood vessel behind a rib had ruptured. Bledsoe was bleeding internally: his abdomen was filling with blood, his lungs were starting to flood, and shock was setting in. In the hospital, doctors inserted a tube to drain the blood and Bledsoe's condition rapidly improved. If Gill had not sent Bledsoe to the emergency room and the quarterback had left Foxboro without seeking treatment, he might well have bled out and died.

He got lucky. After having the blood drained, Bledsoe stayed in the hospital and the vessel sealed itself. But he would be out of the lineup indefinitely until it healed completely.

For all intents and purposes, the season seemed over for the 0-2 Patriots, in the absence of their starting quarterback and best receiver. Borges suggested in the *Globe* that the Patriots let Brady "stay at it until something changes. Of course, if you believe in miracles, go watch the tape of the US Olympic hockey team beating the Russians in 1980, because it's not likely there will be a sporting miracle in New England."

But a miracle did happen.

Belichick surprised almost everyone by naming Brady to start the following week versus Indianapolis, saying, "I thought he did OK with what he had there. All things considered, I thought in that situation he threw the ball pretty accurately and made good decisions. I really don't think that I'm going to be standing here week after week talking about all the problems Tom Brady had." He also tamped down expectations by adding, "I don't think we're talking about John Elway here."

The coach had made his decision. He liked what he'd seen of Brady in practice, in the exhibition season, and in his brief appearance against the Jets. And at 0-2, he could afford to take a flyer. He knew what Huard could do—maybe Brady could do better. If he failed, well, that would be expected. But even at his first press conference as starting quarterback, Brady showed amazing poise, asking the press, when it was time to field his first question, "Who wants to shoot?" After one reporter asked if he'd be intimidated in his new role, he reminded everyone that he had played in front of 112,000 in Ann Arbor. He didn't expect to be nervous, he said. "Not a bit." Still, in the minds of most, the best they were hoping for was that the Patriots would somehow grind out a few wins under the second-year quarterback, make a run whenever Bledsoe was able to return, and then somehow turn a corner leading into the 2002 season in the new stadium.

In Brady's first start the following week, against Indianapolis, the Patriots kept it simple, running the ball with authority and throwing only when necessary—

mostly bubble screens, short flares, and crossing patterns underneath. The defense intercepted Peyton Manning three times, and New England plastered the Colts, 44–13. Brady went a quiet 13-for-23 with a touchdown, but he didn't throw an interception either, and he did nothing to lose his number-one status at quarterback. He had simply executed the plan he'd been given instead of ad-libbing, precisely as Buchsbaum's scouting report had said he would.

Brady's performance almost went unnoticed, but not quite. Writing in the *Herald* after the game, Kevin Mannix, his ear to the ground (or at least to talk radio), observed, "The Yahoos are out there already. Get rid of the overpaid statue who's been clogging up the pocket for years. Give the exciting, energetic young kid a chance. See if Brady can be the updated version of Steve Grogan to Bledsoe's Jim Plunkett." He concluded, one voice in the wilderness, "You know what? The Yahoos are right."

They were, but the strategy didn't work against the playoff-bound Dolphins a week later. Brady failed to throw for 100 yards in the 30–10 loss.

Terry Glenn's suspension had ended at that point, and as it proved more difficult for the Pats to suspend him for an entire season than let him play, he returned to the squad the following week against San Diego. Good thing too, because they needed him. Glenn's presence allowed the Patriots to open things up. With the score tied 3–3, just under four minutes remaining in the first quarter, and the ball on the 21, Brady went back while Glenn, with three receptions for the day already, worked his way across the field. Brady had plenty of time, and when the receiver got clear in the end zone, heading toward the left pylon, Brady threw a bullet. Glenn made a diving catch for the score, resulting in Brady's first career touchdown pass. Belichick and Weis then cut him loose, and Brady ended up throwing 54 times. He completed 33, including 25 to his wide receivers, as the Patriots won in overtime on a Vinatieri field goal. At the end of the game, Foxboro was abuzz with all things Brady. His counterpart on the field for San Diego that day, Doug Flutie, was an afterthought in a place where he had once been a legend.

New England won two of their next three, and Brady, while not exactly dynamic, proved steady, sticking to the game plan. He would go on to throw 162 passes before tossing his first interception, doing nothing to hurt his club.

With the Patriots' record at 5-4, Bledsoe was cleared to return to the active roster before their next game, hosting the St. Louis Rams. Under coach Mike Martz, the Rams' dynamic offense—behind quarterback Kurt Warner, a top-notch receiving crew, and multipurpose back Marshall Faulk—was known as "the Greatest Show on Turf." With a much-improved defense, and coming into the game with only one loss, the Rams were odds-on favorites to win the NFC and take the Super Bowl.

Bledsoe's return to the roster spawned a controversy. Although Brady had led a previously winless team to a 5-2 record in the seven games he started, conventional NFL wisdom said that quarterbacks don't lose their starting job because of injury, especially quarterbacks who have just signed a ten-year deal worth more than $100 million. All Belichick would say was that he'd give Bledsoe a chance to "compete" for his position, whatever that meant.

But there was more at stake than just wins and losses. Bledsoe's contract was an issue. So far, although Belichick was satisfied with Brady, he also knew that if the Patriots could get out from under Bledsoe's contract—which counted as $7.5 million against the salary cap in 2002—well, that would open up some room. The Patriots would have more flexibility in signing existing players to extensions or filling holes on the free agent market.

The decision would also be a test of Belichick's authority. It was no secret that Bledsoe was a Kraft favorite, but the coach had been given full control, and this would test just how serious Kraft was with that promise. As Borges noted, Belichick "walked the plank" with the decision, telling a local radio station that Brady was his quarterback for the rest of the year barring "unforeseen circumstances," without giving any indication of what those might be. There was no turning back, and it could well determine the rest of his tenure as head coach.

By then, the people's choice was Brady, a scrappy underdog to Bledsoe, whose absence had not made the hearts of New England fans grow fonder. He was considered even more wooden, mechanical, and immobile than before, and suddenly his bloated contract seemed a burden. Besides, Brady made a better story.

The Patriots lost to the Rams, 24–17. Warner and company put up nearly 500 yards of total offense, but the New England defense picked off Warner twice. They came away thinking that the Rams, for all their talent, weren't quite the same team playing on the road and on grass as they were in St. Louis. Brady was intercepted twice as well, but he'd shown poise, and the Patriots made a game most expected to be a blowout rather close. According to Rams receiver Isaac Bruce, "After the game our coaches told us we might have just played a Super Bowl team."

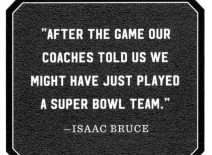

"AFTER THE GAME OUR COACHES TOLD US WE MIGHT HAVE JUST PLAYED A SUPER BOWL TEAM."

—ISAAC BRUCE

Although few agreed, Martz and his crew weren't just being nice. New England's defense had slowed the Rams, and the Pats had showed enough offense to be competitive.

This loss made the Patriots believers. If they could hang with the Rams, they felt they could hang with anyone. But there was also the question of Bledsoe. Afterward, some fans and members of the media wondered: if Bledsoe had played, might the Patriots have won?

New England fans will never know, because after the game Belichick didn't waste any time, announcing that Brady would start the following week versus New Orleans, a decision that could make or break his tenure in New England. If the Patriots, now 5-5 for the season, floundered, so would their playoff chances . . . and Belichick risked ending up in a quarterback controversy even more bitter than the one he'd faced in Cleveland. That week, it was all Patriots fans were talking about.

To their credit, both Brady and Bledsoe stayed out of it, at least in public, but Bledsoe was livid at being boxed out and let Belichick know it. Still, he played the good soldier and did what he could to help Brady succeed. Besides, he knew that if Brady went down, the job would go back to him, not Damon Huard. And in what had to be a first for a Patriots owner, Bob Kraft stayed out of it too. Having promised Belichick control, Kraft had had few expectations heading into the season anyway.

On September 23, 2001, Patriots quarterback Drew Bledsoe is attended to by team doctor Bert Zarins after being hit by Mo Lewis of the Jets in the fourth quarter. The injury proved a watershed moment in both team and NFL history when little-known backup Tom Brady was given a chance to lead the Patriots.

• • •

Brady shredded the Saints for four touchdown passes in a 34–17 win the next week, ending the controversy before it ever got much traction and winning the position for good from Bledsoe. And even though Brady was inconsistent for the remainder of the season as the opposition began taking away the short game he favored, the team still went undefeated. Suddenly, the Patriots were a playoff team, something few had expected to happen. There had been some luck along the way—namely, a late interception in their 17–16 win against the Jets and a timely 85-yard punt return by Troy Brown in a 27–16 victory over the Browns. But not everything had gone according to plan: Terry Glenn would play in only four more games, his last as a Patriot, as his personal issues finally sidelined his career in New England. The way things were going, though, his absence didn't seem likely to make a difference—at least not one with negative consequences.

Entering the playoffs, the Patriots got lucky again. First, because of the scheduling issues caused by 9/11, they ended the season with a bye in week sixteen before dumping the last-place Panthers in the season finale.

Until then, it had looked as if the Patriots would qualify as a wild-card team, but the Raiders collapsed in the final weeks, dropping two straight. In the tiebreakers, the Patriots earned not only a bye during the first playoff week but the second seed in the AFC to Pittsburgh, giving them the right to play the divisional playoff game at home, which meant one final appearance at Foxboro Stadium.

With only one game in the last month and two full weeks to prepare, the Patriots had plenty of time to get healthy and get ready. Brady was still learning, and the extra time gave him a chance to catch his breath and reset.

The Raiders beat the Jets and earned the right to travel to Foxboro—another instance of good fortune. Although the Raiders were considered the better team, they were also reeling, and now the warm-weather team had to contend with a January evening in New England. Facing the Raiders lowered expectations for the Patriots and also allowed them to avoid yet another round of the Jets-Patriots circus that had dominated so much of their recent history.

In a season when so much had already worked out in the Patriots' favor, they got lucky again for the Saturday night contest. A storm hit New England that afternoon, shrouding Foxboro Stadium in snow and slowing the Raiders' high-powered offense—which, behind quarterback Rich Gannon and wide receivers Jerry Rice and Tim Brown, had been the fourth-highest-scoring offense in the league. Conditions weren't quite as bad as those in the 1982 playoff against the Dolphins that made Don Shula come out against the work-release program—the field surface was now grass and, though snow-covered, clear of ice—but conditions were still tough, the kind of day kids hope to have for that backyard football game on Thanksgiving Day. Brady got stuck in traffic and had to call for a police escort to get him to the game on time. During stoppages, the grounds crew had to hustle to keep the sidelines and line markers clear.

Most of the game unfolded as a battle of attrition, both teams having a hard time mounting sustained drives. They played field position football and combined for a total of 17 punts.

Oakland was leading 13–3 when New England took over on their own 33 with just over 12 minutes remaining.

Until then, the Patriots had tried running the ball, but had little to nothing to show for it. Then Belichick and offensive coordinator Charlie Weis abandoned the running game, as the Raider defense lagged back, and went to the air—mostly short passes in front of the no-huddle offense. In fact, the next 26 plays the Patriots ran would all begin as passing plays, with Brady either throwing, being sacked, or scrambling. "Every quarterback loves the two-minute drill," he said later. "Once we went to the no-huddle, they had only three or four calls, and I knew what to expect."

The Patriots quickly found their rhythm and sound footing for Brady's receivers. Brady completed nine passes in a row—none of which went much more than about 20 yards in the air—and tight end Jermaine Wiggins was suddenly playing like John Mackey as the Patriots marched downfield to the 6-yard line. Then Brady, back to pass, saw that the middle was open, dashed for a touchdown, and dove over the goal line, making the score 13–10. In celebration, he tried to spike the ball, but lost his footing and took a pratfall. Bob Ryan wrote, in a line that could have also described the entire game, "There was nothing dazzling about it, but it got the job done."

The two teams traded punts, and the Raiders had a chance to run out the clock, but were forced to punt one more time. Troy Brown took the short kick, ran it back to midfield . . . then fumbled. The old Patriots would have lost the ball. But not this team. Larry Izzo recovered, and then Brady and the Patriots took over at the New England 46 with just over two minutes remaining.

All anybody remembers after that, particularly in Oakland, is a single play, one that has since resonated in their history the way Ben Dreith's "roughing the passer" call on Ray Hamilton resonated in New England's—as a travesty and something akin to a crime against nature.

After a short completion and a scramble to the sideline pushed the ball across the 50 to the 47, Brady huddled with Charlie Weis during the stoppage. Oakland cornerback Eric Allen, lingering by the sideline, heard the play call—a slant to the backside. He rushed into the huddle and alerted the defense so a linebacker would fill the passing lane.

The Patriots didn't have a clue. As Brady looked downfield, Oakland defensive back Charles Woodson came charging in on a blitz. Brady raised his arm, reared back to throw right, but saw the passing lane close. Then, like a batter checking his swing, he stopped his forward motion and began to pull the ball down and back toward his body as Woodson crashed into him, slapping the side of Brady's helmet and shoulder with his right arm and knocking Brady down. The ball fell loose, bouncing forward, and Oakland linebacker Greg Biekert smothered it.

Everyone watching thought it was a fumble, even Brady, his head dropped back to the ground in resignation, the great run having ended with only 1:43 remaining in the game as Cinderella stumbled down the snow-covered stands and slid into an embankment.

That was it, the season and the game were over. Referee Walt Coleman, closest to the play, ruled that it was a fumble, Oakland's ball, the same thing everyone in the stands and everyone on television thought. Woodson preened for the crowd, Oakland started thinking about next week, the Pats started thinking about next year, and the fans started thinking about the parking lot.

But . . . wait a minute. As a change of possession with less than two minutes remaining, the play underwent automatic video review. Time stopped, because no one on the field thought there was any way Brady was throwing the ball when he fumbled.

The videotape and the rule book said otherwise:

"NFL Rule 3, Section 22, Article 2, Note 2. When [an offensive] player is holding the ball to pass it forward, any intentional forward movement of his arm starts a forward pass, even if the player loses possession of the ball as he is attempting to tuck it back toward his body. Also, if the player has tucked the ball into his body and then loses possession, it is a fumble."

The camera angle from the front was clear. Brady had been holding the ball to pass and made an intentional forward movement, then lost possession as he brought the ball back down toward his body before he had tucked it in. The rule was clear, and Coleman spoke the sweetest words ever heard on the field at Foxboro: "After reviewing the play . . ." It wasn't a fumble. It was an incompletion. The Patriots still had the ball and still had a chance.

No one remembered at the time, but a similar play had taken place earlier in the season in the second quarter

of the first Jets game. Patriots defensive end Anthony Pleasant knocked the ball from the grasp of Jets quarterback Vinny Testaverde, an apparent fumble. Then, after review, the Tuck Rule was invoked. But that call had meant nothing. This one meant everything. Somewhere, Ben Dreith had to be screaming, "I'm off the hook!"

The Tuck Rule had been put in place in 1999 in an attempt to codify what, until then, had been a judgment call by the officials. It only came up a dozen or so times a year, and in most instances the ruling was obvious. This call, however, was right on the line—if the same play were to happen today, it would probably be ruled a fumble. The Tuck Rule would prove so controversial that it was rescinded in 2013.

But this was 2002. If they could get within field goal range, the Patriots still had a chance. With the ball on the 42, they needed at least another eight or ten yards to give Vinatieri, warming up on the sidelines, a chance. Even then, under these conditions, even with the wind at his back, no kick over 30 yards would be automatic. He'd made field goals as long as 55 yards, but never in a snowy environment like this, with so much on the line.

The game had been delayed several minutes, giving the Patriots time to regroup as the Raiders, like the Patriots after the Dreith call, came unglued, feeling as if something had been stolen from them. As Coach Jon Gruden berated the officials about the review, demanding an explanation, officials had to figure out where to spot the ball and how much time remained. Eventually they added four seconds back to the clock.

Then came the real key play of the game. If the Patriots didn't move the ball downfield, the Tuck Rule call would soon be forgotten, an interesting but ultimately insignificant play, a footnote in a narrow defeat. Brady's failure to convert after the review would receive all the scrutiny.

As it was, that's almost what happened. On the next play, Brady dropped back again, but this time, with no chance to eavesdrop, the Raiders didn't know what was coming. Oakland's backfield played a little soft, afraid that if they played tight under these field conditions, a slip could leave a receiver wide open. On the right side, David Patten raced downfield—or rather, he gingerly shuffled in

Patriots quarterback Tom Brady loses the ball after being hit by Oakland Raider Charles Woodson (*right*). The fumble was recovered by Raider Greg Biekert (*left*), but the Patriots would be given another chance when it was ruled an incomplete pass courtesy of the now-infamous Tuck Rule.

the snow, then found some space in front of cornerback Tory James at the 33 and turned back toward Brady. The pass was low, barely knee-high. Patten had to drop to the ground, but he made the catch, and then vaulted forward another three or four yards for a first down and a 14-yard gain to the 29, bringing the Patriots—barely—within field goal range.

They wanted to get closer, but Brady's next two passes, first to Brown and then to Wiggins, fell incomplete. On the next play, taking no chances on third down,

Brady, seeing no one open, pushed forward for a yard, clutching the ball to his chest and moving to the middle of the field before going down, doing his best to get his kicker the best angle. The Raiders called time-out in an attempt to freeze out the already frozen kicker.

That was a mistake. This time no Mark Henderson was available to brush the snow off the field, and footing was generally atrocious. But during the time-out, Vinatieri found his spot and a horde of teammates converged to scrape the snow clear and expose the grass, which was heated from below. Vinatieri had played college ball in South Dakota and kicked under worse conditions, but had the Raiders not called time-out, he would have had to approach the ball on a surface of snow.

Now he didn't have to, but he still stepped gingerly, to make sure he hit the ball square.

The kick was perfect. It sent the ball tumbling over the crossbar with perhaps a yard or two to spare, tying the game.

Then came the next key play: the coin flip before overtime.

It went New England's way, and after the kick the Patriots took over at the 34. Still throwing on every play, Brady played with confidence, picking the reeling Raiders apart, moving the ball to the 30. Then, after a run by Redmond—the first play since the third quarter that hadn't been either a pass or run by Brady—New England finally turned conservative. The ball went to Antowain Smith on four of the next six plays before Brady took a knee on the 7-yard line and Vinatieri came on the field one more time. From 23 yards away, his kick was good.

As the ball tumbled through the uprights, the old Patriots disappeared. The new Patriots were on their way to Pittsburgh. In a strange way, from here on, it would all feel strangely anticlimactic. The victory would also be the final game in old Schaefer/Sullivan/Foxboro Stadium, the last contest also one of the most memorable in franchise history, a fitting end to a place that, for too long, had been the site of more embarrassment than excellence.

There was no question now that in Tom Brady the Pats had not just an adequate quarterback, or a good one, but a potentially great one. His play in the fourth quarter and in overtime, in adverse weather conditions, coming from behind . . . well, that was positively Montana-esque.

> AS THE BALL TUMBLED THROUGH THE UPRIGHTS, THE OLD PATRIOTS DISAPPEARED. THE NEW PATRIOTS WERE ON THEIR WAY TO PITTSBURGH. IN A STRANGE WAY, FROM HERE ON, IT WOULD ALL FEEL STRANGELY ANTICLIMACTIC . . . THE LAST CONTEST ALSO ONE OF THE MOST MEMORABLE IN FRANCHISE HISTORY, A FITTING END TO A PLACE THAT, FOR TOO LONG, HAD BEEN THE SITE OF MORE EMBARRASSMENT THAN EXCELLENCE.

For while he lacked Montana's mobility, Brady had displayed a fine sense of knowing when to run, and his calmness under pressure and his touch on short to medium passes were impeccable. Even though his arm wasn't strong, unlike Bledsoe, his arm wasn't his greatest asset. He had presence and, like Montana, a supernatural calm that never made him seem rushed. The Raiders game had been a huge test. The Patriots had put everything on his shoulders and called on him to throw and make good decision after good decision. And he had come through, silencing forever any who doubted him.

But thank God for that Tuck Rule.

The Patriots faced the Steelers in the AFC championship game the following weekend. Pittsburgh, adapting the motto "One for the thumb" and in search of the franchise's fifth Super Bowl victory, had the league's best rushing offense and stingiest defense and were nine-and-a-half-point favorites. The Patriots just didn't seem to match up.

But they did, at least in some respects. If Pittsburgh had any weakness, it was special teams and the kicking game, and these flaws were underscored early. After both teams exchanged a series of punts over the first 11 minutes, Pittsburgh punter Josh Miller, kicking from the goal line, sent a rocket more than 70 yards downfield, over Troy Brown's head, where it took a freak bounce and finally rolled to a stop at the 23-yard line, giving the Steeler defense plenty of breathing room.

Except there was a flag. Pittsburgh wideout Troy Edwards inexplicably ran out of bounds and then back in—illegal procedure. The Steelers, winded after racing downfield and celebrating Miller's kick, had to do it all over again.

This time the kick was shorter, and Troy Brown was the only guy on the field not sucking wind. He took the punt at the 45, saw space in the middle, and ran straight up the field to score.

After a Pittsburgh field goal, Brady went back to pass and on third down hit Brown for a 28-yard gain. But as most eyes followed the ball, blitzing defensive back Lee Flowers hit Brady low, wrapping him up as he released the ball and pinning his left leg in the follow-through.

Brady went down, grabbed his lower leg, and stayed down. Cinderella had sprained his ankle.

Remember Bledsoe? The storybook tragedy now could have a storybook finish. The forgotten man, who'd kept his mouth shut during the last half of the season and taken one for the team, was ready.

It was as if two months of pent-up frustration was let loose all at once—or at least over the next 35 seconds.

Starting at the 40, Bledsoe first hit David Patten with a bullet for a 15-yard gain. On the next play, the protection broke down and Bledsoe scrambled. Just as he had done against the Jets in the last play he'd made on the field—one that could have killed him—Bledsoe floated to his right, then turned upfield and was blasted again.

Everyone held their breath. But Bledsoe bounced back up and high-fived his teammates, energized, ready to prove he belonged back on the field. On second down, he found Patten on the sideline for a 10-yard gain, and then, in only his fourth play back, threw a perfect pass to Patten in the far right corner of the end zone. Touchdown. In 35 seconds, he'd *almost* made everyone forget about Tom Brady.

The Patriots now led 14–3, and that was essentially the game. In the third quarter, the Pats added another touchdown on a blocked punt scooped up by Troy Brown, who, after returning it 11 yards, alertly lateraled the ball to Antwan Harris, who ran another 49 yards for a touchdown. The Steelers finally answered, scoring twice, but after they made it 21–17, Vinatieri kicked another field goal to put the Patriots ahead by a touchdown, and Pittsburgh's Kordell Stewart, in a panic, threw two late

interceptions: the first by Tebucky Jones and the second by Milloy.

Meanwhile, after his stunning return, Bledsoe effectively managed the game with a workmanlike, mostly mistake-free performance that provided just what the Patriots needed at just the right time, but nothing more. His play was admirable, but after his initial series, he'd been a bit erratic and avoided a pick-six only because a Pittsburgh defender dropped the ball. Although there were still a few Bledsoe partisans in the media, nearly everyone else was praying for Brady's ankle to heal. The sprain was bad, but Belichick later said that Brady could have returned to the game if he had to. That may not have been true, but it helped diminish everyone's concerns.

For the third time, the Patriots would head to the Crescent City and the Superdome with a chance to become the champions of the NFL, this time facing the St. Louis Rams. Of course, their first two appearances in the championship game had proven to be utterly disastrous, not just defeats but losses that reverberated for years. They hoped the third time would prove to be the charm ... or at the very least, not a resounding embarrassment.

What the Patriots did not need, and ultimately did not get, was a controversy like those that had marred so many other potential championship seasons. This time, for once, no coach threatened to quit and no player got arrested or assaulted his partner or went on a drug binge. The usual two-week break before the Super Bowl was cut to only one week as a result of the post-9/11 schedule shift. Although Belichick knew at this point that Brady would probably play, he delayed announcing the decision throughout the week, keeping the Rams guessing and forcing them to prepare for both quarterbacks. If Bledsoe started, the Patriots were far more likely to try to throw the ball downfield.

In the meantime, most fans patted the Patriots on the head and told them they had a lot to be proud of, congratulations for a good season. Hardly anyone expected them to win.

HOW DID THESE GUYS WIN?

RON BORGES

S ometimes a quarterback tries to throw the ball away and it backfires. Same can be true of a throwaway line. It was January 31, 2002, four days before the birth of one of pro football's greatest and longest-lasting dynasties. The gestation period for this dynasty was standing at forty-two years, though, so few New Englanders expected the delivery date to be so near. In fact, truth be told, they weren't expecting a dynasty at all. They were expecting the worst because, well, look at the history.

The 2001 Patriots had already given their long-suffering fans an unexpected thrill ride to Super Bowl XXXVI, surviving, among other travails, the stunning loss of franchise quarterback Drew Bledsoe, who in March had signed a ten-year, $103 million contract that led nearly everyone to believe that his future and the Patriots' were entwined.

"I've expressed over and over again my desire to play my entire career with the New England Patriots," Bledsoe said at the time of the signing. "It looks like that is a very real possibility."

Or maybe not.

Patriots owner Bob Kraft said then that Bledsoe had a chance to be remembered in Boston like Ted Williams, Bill Russell, and Larry Bird, each of whom played his entire career in the city. No one thought Bledsoe would end up as the football version of Wally Pipp, who caught a cold, turned first base over to a kid named Lou Gehrig, and never returned.

When New York Jets linebacker Mo Lewis leveled Bledsoe on September 23, 2001, at 5:03 of the fourth quarter, in the Patriots' first home game since the 9/11 terrorist attacks were launched from Boston, it changed Patriot history and NFL history, although no one sensed anything quite so dramatic at the time.

That day Patriots offensive lineman Joe Andruzzi led the team out of the tunnel at Foxboro Stadium, carrying huge American flags honoring his brothers and other New York City firefighters who had fought to save lives amid the rubble of the fallen Twin Towers of the World Trade Center in lower Manhattan.

In an odd way, the dynasty that has ruled the NFL ever since was born that evening courtesy of Lewis's crushing hit, which sheared a blood vessel behind Bledsoe's ribs and left it pumping blood into his chest cavity. As things turned out, that terrible injury pumped new life into the long-dormant Patriots.

Up to that moment, the Patriots were one of the most star-crossed franchises in NFL history. They had played in only six playoff games in thirty-four years prior to Kraft buying the team in 1994, and they had hosted only one, a 31–14 debacle of a loss to the Houston Oilers in the final game of Chuck Fairbanks's NFL coaching career. It was his final game because he'd already jumped ship to coach the University of Colorado and been suspended by Billy Sullivan when the team owner learned of Fairbanks's imminent departure late in the season—only to be reinstated by Sullivan just long enough to be embarrassed by the underdog Oilers.

And that wasn't the worst of it.

The Patriots had also sustained the worst loss in AFL championship game history (51–10 to the San Diego Chargers in 1963) and the second-worst in Super Bowl history (46–10 to the 1985 Chicago Bears). So even though these Patriots had made a spirited run to Super Bowl XXXVI led by Tom

Brady, a second-year quarterback not yet in need of a daily shave, and an opportunistic defense, there was only minimal reason for optimism.

Many felt that the team had gotten this far on a fluke—the infamous and now-legendary Tuck Rule call against the Oakland Raiders in the midst of a play-off-game blizzard. Maybe that actually should have been the warning that something special was going on, but it eluded all but the most avid supporters because now they were facing the most feared offense in football, the St. Louis Rams' "Greatest Show on Turf." Quite frankly, no one gave them a chance.

The Rams were making their second Super Bowl appearance in three years and had put up over 500 points for the third straight season, an NFL record. They finished 14-2 with a perfect 8-0 road mark that included a win over the Patriots, so when all this was factored in, the Las Vegas oddsmakers made New England a 14-point underdog, one of the widest spreads in Super Bowl history.

Bledsoe was back by then, but this was now Brady's team. They would sink or swim with a sixth-round draft choice out of Michigan who had been forced to share the quarterbacking duties there, although at the end of the game he always seemed to be the one under center. Despite their success and the outpouring of emotion and patriotism that swept the country after 9/11, it just seemed too much of a fairy-tale ending for the underdog Patriots to win on February 3.

That was the conventional wisdom, and it's what was powering my own thinking when a reporter from *USA Today* began circulating through the media center in New Orleans several days before the game asking for predictions. I was in a rush to leave the room in pursuit of a story when he asked, "Who you picking?"

Naturally I said, "The Rams," and headed on my way, but he needed a bit more information than that. You know how those damn reporters can be.

"I need a score," he said.

Never one to miss a chance for a wiseacre remark in a historical context, I said, "73–0," and didn't think a thing about it until my phone started ringing the next morning. New England fans were furious, and talk radio had its knickers in a twist because they get paid to wear them that way.

Everyone seemed to miss this reference to the most one-sided loss in NFL championship game history: the Chicago Bears' 73–0 pasting of the Washington Redskins on December 8, 1940. That was the day the Bears' Bill Osmanski ran 68 yards for a touchdown on the second play of the game. Washington drove back downfield but missed a chance to tie the score when Charlie Malone dropped Sammy Baugh's perfect touchdown pass in the end zone. Asked if the game would have been different if Malone hadn't dropped that pass, Baugh quipped, "Sure. The final score would have been 73–7." My kind of guy, Sammy Baugh.

There were few Sammy Baughs in New England that week, though. The fan base was hot, talk radio was fulminating, and I was an enemy of the state. All I could say was "It seemed like a funny idea at the time."

Every Patriots fan knows what followed, and I should have seen it coming. The Rams' offense was introduced individually, as had always been done, but when it came time to introduce the Patriots, they refused to conform, instead rushing out as one team. They were a team of Patriots at one of the most fervently patriotic moments since World War II.

Soon Ty Law had picked off a Kurt Warner pass and returned it 47 yards for a touchdown and a 7–3 lead that would swell to 17–3 before the Rams made a furious fourth-quarter rally to tie the game with only 90 seconds left in regulation and the Patriots without a time-out.

Hall of Fame coach and Fox broadcaster John Madden blustered that the Patriots should run out the clock and take their chances with overtime, but as Brady was turning to go back out with the offense, the last words he heard came from Bledsoe.

"Sling it!" Bledsoe hollered to the man who had replaced him.

Sling it he did, moving the Patriots 53 yards in nine plays before Adam Vinatieri trotted out to attempt a 48-yard field goal as time was expiring. Sitting next to me was my friend and longtime colleague Will McDonough, the greatest sports reporter who ever lived. He had seen every failure and faux pas in Patriots history, and I had shared the past nineteen years of them with him.

He looked at me, and I looked at him, and neither one of us said a word. We just leaned forward and watched that ball sail high and straight, and as it flew we both stood up, disbelief in our eyes. As it crossed between the uprights, we spontaneously did what sportswriters are not supposed to do.

We high-fived each other as if that victory was our own. It was not, of course. It was a victory that belonged to the Patriots and to America. Maybe a little piece of it was ours too.

Once we realized what we'd done, though, we sat down in a hurry and sheepishly began to type. Duty called. It was now a time for hosannas and a mea culpa.

It was also the happiest I'd ever been to be wrong.

RON BORGES wrote for the *Boston Globe* before joining the *Boston Herald* in 2008. Known primarily for his writing on boxing and football, Borges has been named Massachusetts Sportswriter of the Year by the National Association of Sportswriters and Sports Broadcasters five times and was a recipient of the Nat Fleischer Award for boxing journalism from the Boxing Writers Association of America. He coauthored Upton Bell's *Present at the Creation: My Life in the NFL and the Rise of America's Game.*

It's impossible to overstate just how few people—apart from Patriots zealots who probably still thought the Patriots should have won their first championship game against Sid Gillman's Chargers—thought the Patriots had any chance to beat the Rams. The Pats' seven-point loss earlier in the season to the Rams was considered by most to be an anomaly, and Rams coach Mike Martz's faint praise a class move without meaning. The Rams had the league's best player, running back Marshall Faulk, who was as effective a receiver as he was a runner and had been named the league's best offensive player for the third year in a row. They also had the best quarterback in Kurt Warner, who was armed with a story even better than Brady's (he'd been bagging groceries before starting his pro career in the Arena League); not one but two premier receivers in Isaac Bruce and Torry Holt; and a total of six receivers who had caught 38 passes or more. The Rams had led the league in yards and scoring, and their defense, paced by All-Pro end Leonard Little and linebacker London Fletcher, had given up the third-fewest yards. Hell, even their return man, Aeneas Williams, was an All-Pro. In the playoffs, the Rams had smoked Green Bay 45–17 and then dumped the Eagles 29–24 in a game they had dominated statistically.

Everyone from rapper LL Cool J to NFL Hall of Famers Emmitt Smith and Nick Buoniconti and ex-Bills coach turned broadcaster Marv Levy picked the Rams to win. Only in New England, where local scribes had to play to their base, were the Patriots favored, and then usually by less than a touchdown. Will McDonough offered that "most of America feels the trophy will be riding on the backs of the Budweiser Clydesdales in St. Louis." Las Vegas installed the Rams as 14-point favorites, the same margin they'd picked for the Bears over the Patriots in 1985 and a bit more than for the Packers over the Patriots in 1996, and everyone knew how those games had gone. Like the Bears and Packers in those seasons, the 14-2 Rams were considered a dynasty in waiting, a super-team whose style of play and swagger was a template for a new way to play the game. Only twice before had a team been favored by more—the 49ers over the Chargers by 19 in Super Bowl XXIX and the Colts over the Jets by 18 in Super Bowl III. Of course, the Jets had won, but still . . .

The Patriots? They were the beneficiaries of an easy schedule, dumb luck, a weak division, some late breaks, lousy weather, and a bad call against Oakland. They were a team you expected to fail. As Bill Simmons wrote for ESPN, "You bleed for your team, you follow them through thick and thin . . . and there's a little rainbow waiting at the end. You can't see it, but you know it's there. It's there. It has to be there. So you believe. Of course, there's one catch: You might never get there. . . . Season after season, no championship . . . and then you die." That's exactly how longtime Pats fans felt: like Red Sox fans, they'd probably die before their team ever won. That was such a certainty that by game time scalpers on Bourbon Street were selling tickets below face value. No one wanted to watch a drubbing.

Belichick waited until Friday before making it official that, to use Mannix's phrase, "the Yahoos were right." Brady had gone through practice with his ankle wrapped and wearing a brace and showed no ill effects. He would start, with Bledsoe in reserve.

Before the game, 9/11 tributes dominated the extended pregame show at the stadium and on TV as the NFL wrapped the entire game in a flag-draped package called "Heroes, Hope, and Homeland." Keith Lockhart led the Boston Pops in Aaron Copland's "Lincoln's Portrait," a host of present and past NFL players and coaches read from the Declaration of Independence, Fox cut to US servicemen on duty around the world, and No Doubt, the Barenaked Ladies, and Paul McCartney all gave performances. Just before the coin toss, Mary J. Blige and Marc Anthony performed "America the Beautiful," and Mariah Carey sang "The Star-Spangled Banner," backed by the Boston Pops.

In the locker rooms, none of that really mattered. 9/11 was there, but it wasn't present. Players on both teams knew they had to play football, and thinking about much of anything else was a luxury they could not afford to indulge.

Since the two teams had played each other earlier, they held few secrets, but the Pats did make one change in their approach. All year long, teams had tried to stop Warner, but for most of the year the big quarterback's quick release had made those efforts fruitless. The Patriots decided that stopping Marshall Faulk, not Kurt Warner, was the key to slowing the Rams' offense. As defensive coordinator Romeo Crennel said later, "I told our players we had to keep Marshall Faulk from getting to the outside, we had to keep him in the middle of the field . . . we had to jump on their receivers and play them

Quarterback Drew Bledsoe of the New England Patriots hoists the AFC championship trophy after coming off the bench to lead the Patriots to a 24–17 victory over the Pittsburgh Steelers at Heinz Field.

tight . . . and we wanted to make it a physical game. We thought our guys on defense could outhit them." During practice, to help the defense get ready to jam the Rams at every opportunity, scout team receivers standing in for their Ram counterparts started two yards downfield to prepare them for their opponents' speed. Comparing the Rams to a fast-break basketball team, Belichick noted that such teams "usually don't want to play a half-court game." For the last time in a Super Bowl contest, the game would be played on AstroTurf, an unforgiving surface neither team was accustomed to, but one that promised to give St. Louis, a team built around speed, more trouble than New England.

On offense, the story was told in the first line of Weis's game plan: "Take Care of the Ball. No Turnovers."

That had been the approach ever since Brady took over: nothing fancy, spread the ball around, take what the defense gives, keep it simple, involve all the receivers, don't force anything, run when you can, *but protect the ball at all costs.* Give the defense a chance, hope for turnovers, slow the opposition down, and make them kick field goals.

That's how they drew it up, because if the Rams had any weaknesses, it was playing on the road (where, although undefeated, they'd been tested by the Pats, Eagles, 49ers, and Panthers), playing against very physical teams (New England, Philadelphia, the Bucs, the Giants), turnovers (Warner had thrown 22 interceptions for the year, albeit in 546 attempts, and the Rams had fumbled almost twice as often as their opponents), and their kicking game (Jeff Wilkins was automatic under 40 yards, but barely .500 beyond that distance).

The Patriots eschewed the traditional individual player introductions and came out as a team, just as they had done all year. When the game finally began, the Rams got off quick, returning the ball to near midfield, but then quickly stalled.

The Patriot defense did exactly what they said they would: they contained Faulk and knocked the snot out of Rams receivers anytime they got close to the ball, making sure they knew they'd be hit on almost every play. But three minutes in, Jeff Wilkins knocked through a 50-yard field goal to put the Rams up, 3–0. And as the first quarter moved into the second, Warner and the Rams started to find their rhythm, though Wilkins missed on a 52-yarder that would have given them a 6–0 lead. Warner wasn't connecting a lot, but when he did the Rams flashed the brilliance that had gotten them there. Then, with 8:49 remaining in the half, Warner dropped back to throw and linebacker Mike Vrabel hit the quarterback just as he released the ball, helmet to helmet, a penalty in today's game. But this was 2002. The ball floated past Rams receiver Isaac Bruce and Ty Law caught it running the other direction, not stopping for 47 yards until he gave the Patriots a surprising, and most thought temporary, 7–3 lead.

The Patriots weren't completely stopping the Rams, but they were making the contest a half-court game. On almost every series when the Rams had at least one play that made everyone think, *Here it comes . . .* , a broken-up pass or a hard hit would stop them in their plastic cleats.

The Patriots were like a swarm of bees the Rams couldn't quite outrun.

Then, with just over a minute left before halftime, Antwan Harris put his helmet on the ball after a reception by Ricky Proehl. The football took a crazy bounce downfield and Terrell Buckley scooped it up and ran it back to the 40. Patriots' ball.

What followed wasn't quite a two-minute drill, but it was close. Throughout his career, Brady has never looked more comfortable than when his decisions are limited by the clock and the situation, when what has to be done is clear and his options are clearly defined. A pass to Brown, then an eight-yard completion to Wiggins and an eight-yard run by Kevin Faulk, all sandwiched around two incompletions and two time-outs, brought the ball to the 8-yard line. With 31 seconds left, Brady found Patten on an out pattern in the right rear corner of the end zone. At halftime, the Patriots led by a shocking 14–3. Guys who'd bet big on the Pats started flipping through boat catalogs.

After a halftime extravaganza by U2, both teams struggled in the third quarter to move the ball effectively. The only score came on a 37-yard field goal by Vinatieri after an Otis Smith interception, putting the Patriots up 17–3. Patriots fans almost started to believe.

Their increasingly dire situation seemed to energize the Rams, and they took over just before the end of the quarter, virtually abandoning the run and depending on Warner's arm to move them down the field. The result was their best drive of the day, moving from the 23 all the way to the 9 on a nine-play drive.

All year long no team in the league had been better at converting scores in the red zone. A pass took the ball to the 3, and then New England stiffened: on back-to-back plays, Milloy and Law nearly intercepted Warner in the end zone. It was now fourth-and-goal.

Warner dropped back again, looking for Faulk on the left side, but the running back was jammed by McGinest. Warner floated to the right and then took off, seeing a clear lane to the pylon. But Warner was a throw-first quarterback, and on the 5-yard line, still looking for a receiver, he hesitated, the ball held by only his right hand. The hesitation allowed McGinest to close on Warner at the 2, where McGinest hit him and the quarterback lost the ball. Tebucky Jones fielded it like a bunt and then

The Patriots break precedent by entering the field as a team before their Super Bowl XXXVI game against the St. Louis Rams at the Superdome in New Orleans.

took off, racing 97 yards for an apparent score, a dagger that would give the Pats a 24–3 lead.

Apparent score. There was a flag. McGinest hadn't jammed Faulk; he'd held him with both arms just as surely as the Raiders' Phil Villapiano had held the Pats' Russ Francis back in the playoff versus Oakland in 1975. This time, however, the referee made the call: holding,

first-and-goal for the Rams. On the next play, Warner went up the middle almost untouched—it was 17–10.

If you were a Patriots fan with a sense of history—or that guy looking at the boat catalogs—you could see the heartbreaking loss lingering on the horizon. It seemed only a matter of how and when. A bad call? A stupid play? An act of God? The two teams exchanged punts, and with just under two minutes left, after a poor punt, the Rams took over on the 45.

For the first time all game, New England seemed tired, beaten, and confused as "the Greatest Show on Turf," also for the first time, finally showed up. Three crisp passes, the last a 26-yard toss to Proehl, tied the game. The drive took all of 21 seconds. Overtime seemed as inevitable as another eventual Ram score and a Kurt Warner photo op with Mickey Mouse.

One minute and 21 seconds. That's all the time that remained after Brown returned the kickoff to the 17. Everything everyone thought they had ever known about football, from Pop Warner League through decades spent coaching from the couch, said it was time for the Patriots to take a knee, run the clock out, and take their chances in overtime. Don't push it, and for God's sake, don't do anything that might turn the ball over. Don't you remember what has always happened to the Patriots at times like this? On the last drive the Rams had finally hit stride, and you could see it coming: if they somehow got the ball back, there'd be some way a blue-and-gold jersey would streak down the field, some way the ball would cross the goal line or tumble through the uprights as time ran out, some way to crush the hearts of New England in a dramatic and unexpected way. Was Ben Dreith pulling on a striped jersey? Chuck Fairbanks stalking the sidelines? Desmond Howard putting on a helmet? Billy Sullivan pushing up from the earth?

Belichick and Weis didn't look to the past, but to the present. After a short conversation, the head coach made the call, as *Sports Illustrated* reported later, saying, "OK, let's go for it." All they needed was 50 yards and Vinatieri, only 150 feet—a couple of New England backyards, from the clothesline to the dieffenbachias. Then Weis told Brady. The quarterback's eyes registered surprise for half a second, and then his head went back into the game. Besides, if the young quarterback showed any nerves, or if New England couldn't stop the clock . . . well, as long as Brady didn't throw an interception, as long as no one dropped the ball on the ground, they could still call the whole thing off.

There was no panic. On the first play, Brady checked down and dumped the ball off to Redmond. Five yards and out of bounds. Second play, same thing, throwing under the coverage, which tightened at midfield, only this time Redmond gained eight but stayed in bounds, forcing Brady to spike the ball and stop the clock. Then another dump-off to Redmond, who now fought and clawed for 11 yards, dragging his way out of bounds to stop the clock.

They were only at their own 40; they still needed 30 yards more and had only 29 seconds to get there.

Brady dropped back, looked downfield, felt some pressure, stepped up, and waited. Troy Brown cut across the field, then found some space, a narrow seam in the zone, with three St. Louis defenders just three, four yards away—behind, in front, and trailing. The ball was a little high, and Brown jumped in stride and caught it with both hands across midfield at the 45. He turned north and gained six yards more before stumbling out of bounds at the 38, taking no chances.

Vinatieri was almost in range . . . 48 yards from the line of scrimmage plus another seven, 55 total. He'd made field goals from that far before. But now? They needed another play, another few yards. There was just barely enough time.

Brady in the shotgun. Tight end Jermaine Wiggins floated to his right, under the coverage, an otherwise pedestrian receiver playing the best stretch of football in his life. The ball hit him on the numbers, and he turned and fell upfield, landing at the 30. Then the Pats rushed to the line, where Brady spiked the ball at the right hash mark. Seven seconds remained. Redemption and joy or disaster and embarrassment was only 48 yards away.

On came Vinatieri, and all over New England people inhaled, held their breath, remembered Oakland, and then the ball was snapped and the past slipped away.

Entering the game, Vinatieri had made his last six last-second kicks—he was almost perfect under a dome. With each tumble of the ball, exhalations turned to shouts and screams and finally, "YEEESSS!!!"

Down the middle. Perfect. Absolutely frigging perfect. And when the referees' arms went into the air signaling the kick was good, the scoreboard froze:

20 17

0:00.

They'd always remember that.

"That's the way you should win a Super Bowl," said a flabbergasted John Madden on the Fox broadcast. He'd spent the last five minutes wondering why the Patriots hadn't just run out the clock, but now . . . "You come in here against all odds, they were backed up, they had no time-outs and got in field goal position. That was a great, great drive."

No kidding.

It was almost beyond metaphor, as if the 1967 Red Sox had defeated the Cardinals in the World Series or the British had run for cover after the first bale of tea splashed into Boston Harbor. As if Charlie Brown had split the uprights and this time sent Lucy home crying. Men wept, women gave each other high-fives and hugs, friends called friends, and family feuds were forgotten. From Bangor to Brockton, Northampton to Roxbury, from Lake Champlain to Buzzards Bay, forty years of frustration ended and in some instances forty years of frustration they didn't even realize they had—for expectations had been so low, for so long, and so much had gone wrong in almost every way possible that it was like awakening to

a new world. Everything was in hyperfocus, smiles were exchanged for no reason, all those traffic jams on Route 1 were suddenly not a bother, not for a second, but now a badge of honor. Remember when . . . ? Knew it all the time.

After forty-two years, the scowling face of old Pat Patriot turned to Flying Elvis winked and finally cracked a smile.

Tom Brady, Super Bowl MVP, went to Disneyland and got to meet Mickey. Of course, he had to ask Belichick for permission to miss the plane ride home. "Of course you can go," the coach said. "How many times do you win the Super Bowl?"

The quote, which appeared in a *Sports Illustrated* story by Michael Silver, was followed by this comment: "The answer, for as long as Brady plays and as long as Belichick coaches, will always be this: at least one more than anyone ever imagined."

At least. Because, to this very day, the final answer to that question is still being written.

Adam Vinatieri breaks into celebration after kicking the game-winning field goal against the St. Louis Rams during Super Bowl XXXVI at the Superdome in New Orleans. The Patriots defeated the Rams by a score of 20–17.

CHAPTER ELEVEN

2002–2004

BACK-TO-BACK

No place in America celebrates its championships with quite the same zeal as New England. Neither does any place turn on those champions quite as quickly. The Patriots' first championship would eventually put both behaviors on display.

In the wake of their victory in Super Bowl XXXVI, for the rest of the winter, spring, and early summer it seemed as if the Patriots and their trophy were everywhere, with rallies held throughout the region and in every state.

Photographs of fans standing before the trophy were suddenly as ubiquitous as those of JFK on the mantel a generation before. The Patriots were even part of the opening day ceremonies at Fenway Park, leaving long-suffering Red Sox fans to wonder if their time would ever come. New England experienced an extended lovefest, one that even included the Patriots' new home, CMGI Field, where the finishing touches were being put in place as Foxboro Stadium underwent the wrecking ball.

COMMEMORATIVE EDITION
NEW ENGLAND PATRIOTS
GAMEDAY
NFL
Grand Opening

HOME OF THE SUPER BOWL CHAMPIONS

Fleet

$10.00
**Patriots
vs. Steelers**
September 9, 2002 · 9:00 p.m.

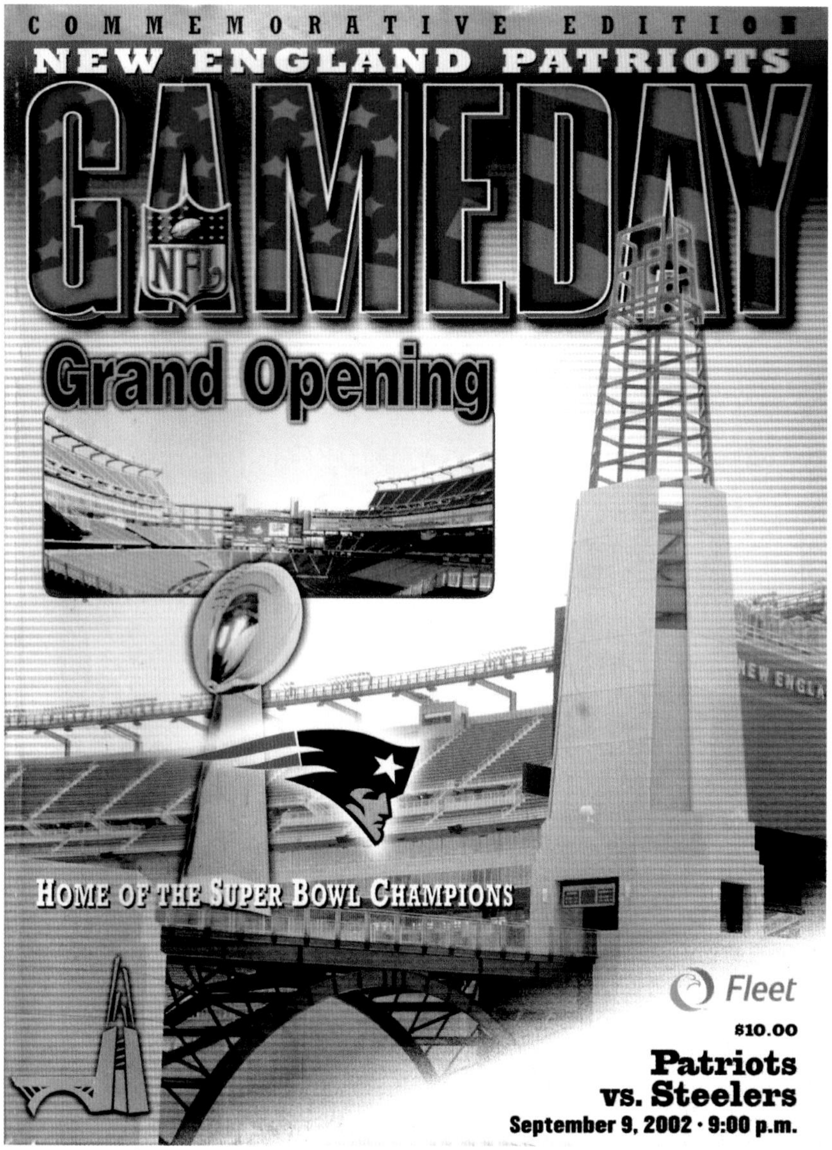

After years of attempting to move the Patriots to Hartford or even back to Boston, the Krafts settled on staying put. They opened their state-of-the-art stadium, sponsored by Gillette, on the night they flew their first Super Bowl banner.

Few football stadiums have the same romance attached to them as ballparks, and although no one had any aesthetic reasons for bemoaning the demise of Schaefer/Sullivan/Foxboro Stadium, its mere existence had been some measure of achievement. Had it not been built, the Patriots might have ended up elsewhere—or just as unfortunately, in some concrete megaplex mausoleum that would have saddled the Commonwealth with debt and perhaps precipitated the demolition of Fenway Park.

Foxboro Stadium bought the franchise time—time for a new owner and, finally, time for a new facility.

Designed by the well-known stadium architectural firm HOK, the new stadium went through some 200 renderings before a soft opening on May 11 for a New England Revolution soccer game. At the cost of some $325 million, it was—and mostly remains—a state-of-the-art football stadium. Unencumbered by a roof, the basic open horseshoe bowl contains every possible amenity and a few New England–esque flourishes, such as the twelve-story lighthouse beacon and footbridge that echoes Boston's Longfellow Bridge. John Powers wrote in the *Globe* that in comparison to Foxboro Stadium, CMGI was "what the Taj Mahal is to the Clam Box . . . a Calvinist's nightmare," with almost too much of everything—too much comfort (87 luxury suites), too much parking (17,000 spaces), too many TVs (1,000), and even too many bathrooms (which actually worked the first time they were used). Everything was peddled in sponsorship deals, from the parking lot gates to the road signs and concessions, every seat was sold before the Patriots even played a game, and already there was a waiting list of more than 50,000—some of whom are still waiting on an even longer list today. In every possible way, the stadium has proved to be a ringing cash register for Kraft and the Patriots.

Also the home of the Revolution, the stadium has hosted men's and women's World Cup soccer matches, concerts, pro hockey, college lacrosse, Supercross, and dozens of other events. Eventually, in 2006, Patriot Place, which the team refers to as a "super regional lifestyle and entertainment center," was built next door.

Sullivan's folly was in the right place. It just wasn't the right building, or the right time.

Of course, that popularity has all come with a price. The average ticket price today is $300, plus parking, and the fan base, once decidedly working-class, has become decidedly more affluent, suburban, and corporate, but then what isn't in pro sports these days? Now, for the first time, the Patriots team had a facility at least on par with and usually far better than those of other NFL teams, though CMGI itself never benefited. Before the Patriots ever played a game, financial issues sank the internet darling, and stock shares fell from a high of $164 to 40 cents. Gillette picked up the sponsorship deal and changed more than 2,000 signs.

No one would ever mistake Gillette for a high school stadium. With a championship trophy, a brand-new field, a bright young quarterback, and a coach who seemed to know what he was doing and didn't mind staying around, the 2002 season opened with nothing but unbridled optimism. Most Patriots fans had already circled the date of the next Super Bowl on their calendar, many blocking out vacation time well in advance.

So what went wrong? How did the Super Bowl champions become so damn average so damn quick? In a funny way, that was almost the plan. Or rather, the blueprint that has made the Patriots champions under Belichick is, in a sense, not always sustainable from one season to the next. It's a blueprint that takes a longer view, one that inoculates the Patriots from collapse but also makes it really hard to stay at the very top season after season after season. Even after a championship, the plan doesn't stand pat. Regardless of the team's record, it enforces change. As team personnel fluctuates, a certain amount of ebb and flow is guaranteed. When it works, the

approach makes the Patriots playoff contenders on an almost annual basis, but it does not attempt to preserve a Super Bowl team under glass for the following season. The Patriots simply don't pay tomorrow for what happened yesterday. And to be fair, it's not possible to stay at the very top anyway. Few other organizations seem to recognize that championship teams have a limited shelf life, and many have ended up paying a premium for champions past their prime. The Patriots' longer-term approach helps explain why no other team this millennium has come close to New England's sustained level of performance, but also why, as of 2017, the Patriots have won back-to-back Super Bowls only once.

Much of the credit for the success of this approach goes to the salary cap strategies and resulting roster maneuverings first perfected by Belichick with VP of Player Personnel Scott Pioli. Everything is subservient to their unsentimental approach, a team concept that bends for no individual. Although the particular genius ascribed to Belichick and Pioli's cap manipulation may be overstated, they were among the first in the league to realize the strategic opportunities the cap could help create. The cap was supposed to enforce parity, but it doesn't really do that, for it does nothing to control other expenditures beyond player salaries. High-revenue teams, like the Patriots, are free to spend whatever they want on the coaching staff, front office, scouting, facilities, and other perks, all of which have helped to make the Patriots a more attractive destination for players than many other franchises.

Not surprisingly, then, as soon as the Super Bowl trophy began its New England tour, the Patriots sought to dump Drew Bledsoe and his contract. Although potentially worth $100 million, no NFL contract is fully guaranteed, and Bledsoe's also provided an out after four years. So while dumping Bledsoe would save the Patriots about $8 million for the season, it also wouldn't unduly burden the team that accepted him in trade.

For the time being at least, Belichick and the Patriots were betting on Brady, even though a closer look still showed some reason why he might not be a sure thing. After all, in three playoff contests during their Super Bowl–winning season, the Patriots had scored only three offensive touchdowns, and one of those was on a throw by Bledsoe. They'd won with defense, Adam Vinatieri's right foot, and their ability to get within field goal range. Had the Tuck Rule call gone the other way, who was to say that another quarterback might not have proven just as successful, at least in the short term? To this point, in Belichick's system, skill position players—quarterbacks, running backs, receivers—were fungible, parts to be used and discarded as necessary. Brady was their guy for now, but he too might still be disposable.

On April 21, Bledsoe was dealt to Buffalo, ending his Patriots career as the team's all-time best passer to date, with 4,518 attempts, 2,544 completions, 29,657 yards, 166 touchdowns—none bigger than his last—and 138 interceptions. In exchange, they received the Bills number-one draft pick in 2003 and considerable room under the salary cap. That allowed the Patriots, who had added thirteen free agents in 2001, to add a similar number in 2002. Huard remained as backup quarterback.

Kraft went along, even though his emotions said otherwise, and everyone said the right thing about the trade, the owner noting in a statement that "Drew Bledsoe is a special player . . . and there will always be a special place reserved for him in the hearts of Patriots fans." Belichick added, "Drew's a great player and a tremendous person on and off the field . . . I have respect and personal admiration for Drew. I don't look forward to facing him." That wasn't true, for he'd have never dealt him within the division if that were the case, but it was a nice thing to say.

After winning the Super Bowl, the Patriots drafted last and received little. They also took on a much tougher schedule. From the start, their task in 2002 would be more difficult. Ron Borges and many other NFL observers already saw them as "accidental Champs, a good-but-not-great team that had gotten hit squarely on top of the head by the Lucky Stick." Still, due to a change in the playoff format in 2002, the champions should have had an easy time making the playoffs.

In their never-ending lust for TV dollars, and with the addition of the expansion Houston Texans, the league had reconfigured, going from three divisions in each conference to four. Instead of three division winners and three wild cards advancing to the postseason, now four division winners and two wild-card teams from each conference would advance. In theory, the Patriots now had

only to defeat three division foes, not four (Indianapolis moved to the AFC South). But even if they still looked like a lock for a wild-card spot, it didn't quite work out that way. The 2002 season would prove to be a reckoning.

At first, the Pats seemed to be riding the momentum of the Super Bowl, blasting their way to a 3-0 start by powering over the Steelers 30–14 in the CMGI—er, Gillette—opener, burying the detestable Jets 44–7, and then outlasting the Chiefs 41–38 in a little overtime magic. New England was rolling, Richard Seymour saying "It's very realistic" to think that the Patriots could go undefeated. Others weren't quite that certain, but Patriots fans were giddy. They liked being top dogs for a change. The transformation from long-suffering to smug was lightning-quick.

Then came reality. Brady was not yet a finished product. Screens, quick slants, and curls weren't enough, particularly when the opposition knew that was all he could throw with confidence. As the season went on, the Patriots couldn't run the ball and Brady had to throw, leading the conference with 28 touchdown passes, but it took him more than 600 attempts to do so. In the long run, this served him well, for if there was anything Brady still needed, it was in-game reps and experience.

At the same time, the defense, which really had been the backbone during the championship run, getting better every week, now went the opposite direction. The opposition ran with abandon and controlled the ball, converting third downs against the Pats more than 40 percent of the time. In 2001, nearly every free agent Belichick brought in had worked out. In 2002, few did, most turning into a JAG (Just Another Guy), the derisive term first coined by Bill Parcells. The starters were virtually unchanged, but all were a year older and a touch less motivated, and many went backwards. That was a mistake Belichick would not make again. The 2002 season, in many ways, turned out to be the most consequential of his tenure: he learned something.

Good teams, winning teams, were more than the Patriots could handle, and they followed the 3-0 start by dropping four in a row. Still, a late-season run put them in position to make the playoffs in a year when it seemed like anyone could win the AFC East. Then, with one week left in the season, the Patriots fell 30–17 to the same Jets they had earlier beaten 44–7. Brady passed for only 80 yards in the first three quarters before putting up some numbers while the game was out of reach. Had they still been playing in the old stadium, fans would have been chanting epithets and pissing in the concourse. As Brady noted afterward, "When teams come in here, they're not thinking they're playing the Super Bowl champions. They think they're playing a team that's 8-6." In other words, the Patriots unquestionably were what their record said they were: not all that good.

Despite everything, in the final week a stirring 27–24 overtime win over Miami nearly put them into the playoffs anyway. The Dolphins, Jets, and Patriots all finished 9-7, but the Jets beat the Packers to win the division based on the fourth tiebreaker (best record in common games), and the Patriots lost the wild card to Cleveland based on conference record. And who was New York's quarterback during a 7-2 late-season run that pushed them past New England? Chad Pennington, chosen ahead of Brady in the draft and now considered the Tom Brady of 2002.

At the end of the season, Belichick pretty much said it all: "We executed to a 9-7 level." Remember, Pete Carroll had been fired for missing the playoffs three years after the Super Bowl. Belichick wasn't at risk—yet—but something had to change.

The poor performance gave license for wholesale changes in personnel. The same approach that led them to the middle of the pack would soon lead them back to the front. Belichick, from the very start, displayed little loyalty to anything but the final score.

In training camp, he brought in eighty players to compete for fifty-four roster sports, not allowing anyone to feel very comfortable. And the message that change was in the air was leveled at the end of camp when Lawyer Milloy, long a stalwart of the defensive backfield, was released.

Released? Milloy had been an All-Pro in 1999, made the Pro Bowl in 2001, and in 2002 had been third on the team in tackles. But as the regular season approached and last-minute roster decisions were being made, the Patriots were over the salary cap. They asked Milloy, in the fourth year of a seven-year, $35 million contract, to take a pay cut to help out. He refused, and it was "thanks for the memories."

His teammates in the locker room were stunned. "Has it ever been this quiet in here?" asked Tedy Bruschi after the team found out. "I think 'shocked' is the word. . . . You sort of just shake your head." Belichick said only that Milloy was "a casualty of the way the system is now," but one NFL observer noted at the time that "the Patriots believed that Lawyer Milloy wasn't worth the money they were paying him . . . they didn't believe he was that important a player on their team." Milloy turned around and signed with the Bills, the Patriots' first opponent in the upcoming season, joining Bledsoe.

Coming out of the 2002 season, Belichick decided to remake the secondary, trading Tebucky Jones, waiving Otis Smith, and not re-signing several others. Like baseball's Branch Rickey, he calculated that it was better to get rid of a player a year too soon than a year too late. The shock wave continued in the 2003 opener against the Bills as the Patriots played like petulant teenagers in a game most had penciled in as an easy win. ESPN analyst Tom Jackson reported afterward: "I want to say this very clearly; they hate their coach." Drew Bledsoe picked apart the "Cover 5" defense that Milloy had backed up in the last 106 regular-season games, Brady threw four interceptions, and both Bledsoe and Milloy played as if out to prove that the Patriots had gotten rid of the wrong guys. Even Brady didn't escape criticism, as the *Herald*'s Michael Gee wrote, "No team could survive a game from its QB like the one Brady had," which resulted in a quarterback rating of, gulp, 20.4. New England fell, hard, losing 31–0.

But releasing Milloy had the desired impact, even if "hate" was too strong a word for it. The message was received loud and clear that yesterday was gone—all that

> THEN CAME REALITY. BRADY WAS NOT YET A FINISHED PRODUCT. SCREENS, QUICK SLANTS, AND CURLS WEREN'T ENOUGH, PARTICULARLY WHEN THE OPPOSITION KNEW THAT WAS ALL HE COULD THROW WITH CONFIDENCE.

Pro Bowlers defensive end Willie McGinest, cornerback Ty Law, and defensive lineman Richard Seymour pose for a photo on Media Day, January 27, 2004, at Reliant Stadium before Super Bowl XXXVIII against the Carolina Panthers in Houston, Texas.

mattered was what you did today. In a sense, the release clarified exactly what the Patriots were there for, and it also put the fear of God, or at least of unemployment, in players worried about their future. It also brought the team together, not in opposition to their coach, but to the task at hand. They knew to a man—at least those who were left—that they hadn't played as hard or as well in 2002 as the year before, and they knew that if they didn't improve, they'd soon be following Milloy. If a player wanted to stay, wanted to receive the adulation of the region and play in arguably the best facility in the league, there were many incentives to play hard. With a game coming up against the Eagles, who'd suffered an opening game loss themselves and were equally pissed off, there was little time to mope.

Few teams have ever turned around faster. The hurt the Patriots were feeling going into the Buffalo game was channeled toward Philadelphia as the defense harassed Donovan McNabb into a terrible performance, sacking the mobile quarterback eight times and forcing six turnovers. Meanwhile, Brady rebounded to throw three touchdown passes. Bledsoe and Milloy faded into the rearview mirror. Thanks, guys.

It would have made a nice story line had the Patriots rolled through the rest of the season, but they didn't. After the emotion of the first two games, over the next two they had to settle down and find out what they were without the adrenaline. First they barely beat an undermanned Jets team 23–16, and then they fell to Washington 20–17. The Pats were 2-2, the season hung in the balance, and the casualties were adding up. Rosevelt Colvin broke his hip, nose tackle Ted Washington fractured his leg, Ty Law was hobbled by a bad ankle, Mike Vrabel broke his arm, David Patten sprained a knee, McGinest hurt his neck, and Brady, who'd battled a sore shoulder since the end of the 2002 season, now had a sore elbow. A headline in the *Globe* summed up the way most were looking at the rest of the season: "Hoping for a Repeat? Forget It."

Injuries either tear a team apart and expose them or create opportunities and pull them together, and that's another part of the Patriots strategy. With few exceptions—Brady being one of them—they rarely depend on a single player. In theory, if Belichick and company are doing their jobs, a replacement is already on the roster.

For the rest of the 2003 season, the Patriots may not have been dominant, but they were determined. Every game was a battle and a grind, almost every one of them requiring a confluence of luck and opportunity and creativity to either hang in or win late. That's how any winning streak works, really. The Pats went undefeated the rest of the way, but they rarely won by a lot or very easily: they won twice in overtime and twice in low-scoring standoffs, and they never won by more than two scores. Yet they still won, whether the games were shootouts, wars of attrition, or turnover-laden laughers. It wasn't always artistic, but Rodney Harrison made up for the loss of Milloy, Brady returned to form, and the linebacking crew led by Bruschi and Ted Johnson swarmed over everyone funneled their way. As the *Globe*'s Michael Smith wrote, "There are at least 1,000 ways to win a football game, and the New England Patriots obviously intend on sampling every one."

Perhaps no victory was more creative than their 30–26 win over Denver on November 3, none luckier than their overtime win over Houston on November 23, and none more emblematic than their win over the Colts on November 30, at least when viewed from the Patriots' sideline.

The winning streak was four in a row when the Patriots went into Denver to face the Broncos in a back-and-forth contest in which neither team was able to pull away. A Denver punt return for a touchdown put the Broncos up late, 24–20, even though the Patriots had stymied them on offense in the second half. A Vinatieri field goal made it a one-point game at 24–23, and with just under three minutes left, with the ball at their own 1-yard line facing a fourth-and-10 situation and any chance of victory a desperate prayer away, the Patriots lined up to punt.

Which they had no intention of ever doing. But neither did they plan for a fake and a try for a first down.

Instead, Belichick called for the Patriots to snap the ball out of the end zone and give the Broncos a safety, increasing their lead to 26–23.

Huh?

It's the reason the rest of us aren't football coaches, for the ploy made little sense except to Belichick and the Patriots. Going for it on fourth down was insane, but a punt was risky too—it might be blocked, and even if it wasn't, it would guarantee the Broncos good field position and a chance to either run out the clock or score. But the safety allowed the Patriots to take a free kick from the 20-yard line. The Broncos would get the ball back, but if the Patriots' defense held, they'd get possession in far better field position, giving Brady, and perhaps Vinatieri, a chance.

That's exactly what happened. The free kick punt pinned the Broncos back, Denver eventually punted from the 19, and the Patriots returned it to their own 42, the two-point exchange having netted them 41 yards. Then Brady picked the Broncos apart, throwing the winning TD to David Givens and giving New England the win. How about that?

You want luck? As Kevin Mannix wrote in the *Herald*, "The Patriots keep losing everything but the games." Three weeks later in Houston against the Texans, the Patriots ran all over the upstarts, who had no reason to be in the game, until the Pats started stepping all over themselves. First Vinatieri, who would go 25-for-34 in field goals in 2003, missed his first field goal attempt ever inside a dome. Meanwhile, the defense allowed Tony Banks to throw two second-half touchdown passes, one after a fumble and another after an interception, and in the waning seconds the expansion-team Texans led New England 20–13. Brady saved the day—sort of—when Daniel Graham bailed him out by catching a bad pass for the tying touchdown in the last minute. But in overtime, Vinatieri—for whom Houston's Reliant Stadium was anything but reliable—had a winning kick blocked. Brady finally got them downfield in time for Vinatieri to try another, and this time it was good. Belichick wasn't impressed by the quality of his team's play, but admitted afterward, "We talk a lot on our team about hanging in there, about playing 60 minutes of football. Today it was 74 or 73." In other words, it was just enough.

And that game against the Colts? It depended on who you rooted for.

Although Brady and Peyton Manning had faced each other twice before, the matchup marked the first time the game mattered to both teams, and the first real contest in what would be one of the great quarterback rivalries in NFL history. In this game, for the first time, football fans saw the quarterbacks who would come to dominate the league for the next decade go head to head, each leading a team with championship aspirations, both 9-2 for the season. And this game would demonstrate just how close the margin between the two quarterbacks would be.

How about one yard?

Brady started out like the best quarterback in football, Mr. Accuracy, completing 20 of his first 23 passes, while Manning, Mr. Arm, looked overmatched. But then, as Nick Cafardo noted in the *Globe*, "in the second half Tom Brady looked like the second coming of Joe Kapp." He wasn't talking about the Kapp who led Minnesota to the Super Bowl either.

After leading the Pats to a 17–0 start and taking a 31–10 lead early in the second half, the Joe Kapp who had once played for the Patriots showed up. Brady didn't take care of the ball and threw a series of interceptions, giving Manning a chance to show what he could do. He did, leading the Colts on an epic comeback and tying the game at 31–31 before Brady Goofus became Brady Gallant and put the Patriots up again by a touchdown.

After a field goal, Manning then led the Colts on a "take that" drive. Working out of the no-huddle and forcing the Patriots to scramble to match up, it was all Manning and momentum. The Colts, taking a cue from Tom Brady Super Bowl hero, seemed determined to end the game with a drive that would leave no time on the clock for New England.

Then, with 1:09 remaining and the Patriots out of time-outs, Willie McGinest went down and did not get up very fast. "My leg got caught in the turf," McGinest told ESPN later. Officials awarded the Pats a free time-out as McGinest limped off the field like the last soldier on the

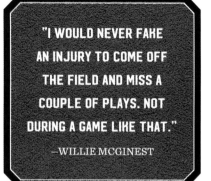

"I WOULD NEVER FAKE AN INJURY TO COME OFF THE FIELD AND MISS A COUPLE OF PLAYS. NOT DURING A GAME LIKE THAT."
—WILLIE MCGINEST

battlefield, conveniently giving the gassed Patriots time to regroup and swap in some fresh legs.

At least that's what it looked like. When McGinest returned two plays later, the Colts thought they'd been played. "I would never fake an injury to come off the field and miss a couple of plays. Not during a game like that," said McGinest later. The Colts begged to differ, because on fourth-and-1, with the game on the line, Manning, baited into an audible by McGinest, swapped a pass play for a run. Then 365-pound Ted Washington and McGinest—allegedly sprained knee and all—stuffed Edgerrin James on fourth down short of the goal with 11 seconds left. Brady took a knee, and New England won 38–34.

The Pats then raced through the remainder of the season, running their win streak to twelve and ending with a 31–0 win over Buffalo, the same score they'd started off the season with. By now, no one missed their former quarterback and safety. Entering the playoffs, the 14-2 Patriots were the hottest team in the league.

They would need the heat, because in the first round versus Tennessee it was all of 3 degrees, with a wind chill of minus 12, at Gillette. The saving grace was a close game that kept fans warm and frostbite to a minimum, albeit at the cost of a few heart attacks, as the Patriots played brinksmanship once again and escaped with a 17–14 win on a late Vinatieri field goal and a final stand by the New England defense. The game ended when the Titans' Drew Bennett outjumped Tyrone Poole on a touchdown pass, only to bobble the ball and then have Asante Samuel knock it away.

That set up another matchup between Brady and Manning, for the AFC championship. Like the Rams a few years before, the Indianapolis offense looked unstoppable, and thus far had scored 10 touchdowns on 17 playoff possessions. Their finely tuned passing game, built around timing, seemed a step ahead. Yet like the Rams, the Colts were a dome team: they were most effective indoors, on artificial turf. And in a season in which the Patriots seemed to have won in every way possible, they found yet another way. Although Manning entered the game with eight TDs and a rating of 156.9 in the 2004 postseason, he left it with his reputation in shreds. He may well still be having nightmares about Ty Law.

Back in 1978, the NFL instituted what became commonly known as the Mel Blount Rule, named after the Pittsburgh cornerback. Before then, defensive backs were allowed to make contact with a wide receiver at the line of scrimmage; utilizing so-called bump-and-run coverage, they could jam the receiver at the line and make continued contact as the receiver made his way—or tried to make his way—downfield. Blount was so physical, so good, and his style so effective that the new rule limited such contact to the first five yards. After that, any contact could result in a penalty. Combined with a 1978 rule change that allowed pass blockers to extend their hands, the change opened up the passing game and led to a revolution in offense.

Yet enforcement of the rule waxed and waned. Like the hand check used by basketball defenders, over the years officials had slowly allowed incremental increases in contact. And in the AFC championship game, Ty Law took full advantage of the increasingly lax prosecution, doing his best to administer what Belichick called—ahem—the "re-routing" of Colts receivers. It was the same approach they had used against the Rams in the Super Bowl, only turned up exponentially in order to take whatever the league would give now that league officials were loath to make calls that would bring attention to themselves. Thanks, Ben Dreith.

The Pats' entire backfield used the strategy, but none more effectively than Law. On a sloppy field at Gillette, under swirling snow, he played up and tight, usually matched up against wide receiver Marvin Harrison. If Manning didn't have nightmares after playing the Pats that day, Harrison most certainly did. Law shut down the slipping and sliding Harrison and thwarted three separate drives with interceptions due to his aggressive play. Time and time again, Colt receivers were hit as they tried to pick their way downfield, and Manning's passes ended up where the receivers were not just as often as where they were. It wasn't bump-and-run so much as bump-and-shove, push-and-nudge, and do-whatever-you-can-get-away-with-and-if-that-includes-holding-well-okay.

The vaunted Brady-Manning matchup ended up no contest as New England won easily, 24–14.

After the game, through gritted teeth, Colts president Bill Polian would only say, "I give the Patriots great credit for what they did. I won't go beyond that."

But after the season, Polian, an influential member of the league's rules committee, convinced his cohorts to order the Blount Rule enforced as written. As a result, ever since the 2004 season, the passing game has come to dominate the NFL as quarterbacks and receivers put up gaudy numbers unthinkable in the past. The reason is not that players have become exponentially better or that offenses are so much more sophisticated, but that the rules have made passing more efficient than running the ball. Comparing passing and receiving stats before and after the rule changes is like comparing baseball stats for the Deadball and Live Ball Eras—it's a different game entirely.

In 2004, Law's aggressive approach helped put the Patriots back in the Super Bowl for the second time in three seasons. Their opponents, the Carolina Panthers, were an utter surprise, only two years removed from going 1-15. With an offense built around running back Stephen Davis, who rushed for nearly 1,500 yards, and quarterback Jake Delhomme in his first season as a starter, and under coach John Fox, the Panthers were overperforming. Like the Patriots, they played a physical defense and had proven adept in close games, winning nine times by a touchdown or less and making it into the playoffs as a wild-card team, then playing their best football of the season.

Almost everyone had expected a close game at Houston's Reliant Stadium, a defensive battle, but what took place shocked everyone.

Before the game, Fox admonished his team to take the Patriots to some "dark places," while Belichick denigrated Carolina, telling his team, "They'll never be champions." For most of the first half, both were accurate.

For the first 27 minutes of Super Bowl XXXVIII, the Patriots and Panthers circled each other like two boxers, as if each was too afraid to make a mistake and get taken out. The Patriots moved the ball, but couldn't kick, Adam Vinatieri apparently being determined to ruin his reputation as the best money kicker in the game. And the Panthers couldn't do anything on offense as Delhomme

Nose tackle/defensive end Richard Seymour sits on the sidelines at Network Associates Coliseum in Oakland, California, and watches his future team defeat the Patriots by a score of 27–20 on November 17, 2002.

was all sound and fury, but accomplishing nothing.

Three plays later, Mike Vrabel, one of Belichick's first and best free-agent pickups earlier, swooped in behind Delhomme and swiped the ball loose. He'd been mostly a special teams player in Pittsburgh before signing with New England, his only suitor, saying later it was either that or "sell insurance in Ohio." Richard Seymour fell on the ball at the 20, and Patriots fans hoped Vinatieri stayed on the bench. So far, the Panthers were minus-nine yards on offense and had been playing like they didn't want the ball. Maybe the Patriots could eventually get a safety.

Only this time, with only 20 yards to go, the Patriots got across the goal line. A Brady scramble took it to the 5, and then the Panthers fell for a play action. Brady found Deion Branch alone in the back of the end zone in the middle of the field. Vinatieri finally made a kick and the Pats led, 7–0. At least the game wouldn't be scoreless.

Then came the wild punches. It was as if each team suddenly decided the other couldn't hurt them. It was one wild shot after another as the most boring and lowest-scoring Super Bowl in history suddenly turned into a fight between two schoolyard rivals behind the town library, all haymakers and flurries and windmills. Then it morphed into Ali versus Frazier in the final round. In the end, it was perhaps the best Super Bowl game to date (at least until Super Bowl LII)—and if it wasn't that, it was certainly the most entertaining.

The Patriots started pinwheeling, and the law of averages spun Delhomme's way as he responded with some wild blows of his own. He completed four passes on the drive, the last 39 yards a strike to Steve Smith on a go route down the sidelines. The score was tied.

Not to be outdone, with 59 seconds left in the half, Brady punched back. There was no one better in such

seemed determined to make everyone forget about Tony Eason.

From the start, the Patriots shut down Davis, who everyone knew was the key to their attack. Forced to throw, Delhomme looked harried, scared, and rushed as he ended up flat on his back three times and completed just one of his first nine passes.

Brady was better, but Vinatieri wasn't. When a Patriots drive stalled after reaching the 9, Vinatieri, in a dome, under perfect conditions with no pressure or snow flying in his face, shanked a chip shot from 31 yards. Another drive put the Pats in range, only to see Troy Brown stuffed on a reverse as Will Witherspoon stood him up and dropped him like he'd hit a force field. New England drove down the field yet a third time, but once again couldn't push it in, and this time, with six minutes left in the half, Vinatieri kicked low. Shane Burton got enough of the ball to keep the game scoreless. One announcer said the game was like "Yale versus Harvard in 1938 with leather helmets. It might end 6–0 today." It a situation—a flurry of combinations at the end of the round that ended with tight end David Givens making his fourth reception of the drive in the end zone, a drive that took all of 36 seconds. Now New England led 14–7, and with momentum swinging their way, fans headed to the concession stand before the halftime show. But those who left their seats to stand in line made the biggest mistake of their lives.

Belichick made a bonehead call, calling for a squib kick to run down the clock and keep the Panthers from a long return. But the first half did not belong to Vinatieri. He "hated" making squib kicks, and with good reason. He kicked it straight into the arms of Kris Mangum, who returned it past midfield. Then Coach Fox fooled everyone: Delhomme, instead of passing, handed the ball off to Davis, who burst up the middle for 21 yards before Rodney Harrison brought him down, preventing a touchdown. That was just close enough for kicker John Kasay, who nailed a 50-yarder. The field goal was the wild punch at the end of the round that kept the fight close.

By the time fans started returning to their seats with a brat and beer, asking, "What'd I miss?," they couldn't believe the answer, or the 14–10 score. And if they stopped for a bathroom break, well, they also missed the most infamous moment in Super Bowl halftime history, Janet Jackson's "nipple slip," with an assist from Justin Timberlake. Somewhere the Up with People crowd started to prepare a bid for the next halftime show.

In combination, the flurry of points—24 in the last three minutes of the half—and the split-second of indecent exposure made the whole experience surreal. *Did that just happen?* If the pace of scoring continued in the second half, the final score would end up like something from Australian Rules football, 157 to 135 maybe.

• • •

The third quarter unfolded like each club was still trying to catch its breath. As both defenses showed up again, the two teams exchanged a series of punts before the Patriots put together a long drive that ended with Antowain Smith rumbling into the end zone, making the score 21–10 New England with just under a quarter remaining.

All season long, Belichick's defense had excelled at making the most of matchups as he shuffled players in and out according to the situation. That's what their personnel decisions were designed to do; it was a lot easier to find and utilize players who could do a few things well than find players who could do everything. His strategy has always been about getting the right players on the field at the right time.

But now Carolina went to a hurry-up offense, thwarting the Pats' substitution pattern and leaving them little time to make changes. Delhomme suddenly had the Patriots backpedaling again, and from the 33-yard line Deshaun Foster, on a screen play, burst up the middle,

BELICHICK'S DEFENSE HAD EXCELLED AT MAKING THE MOST OF MATCHUPS AS HE SHUFFLED PLAYERS IN AND OUT ACCORDING TO THE SITUATION.

broke two tackles, and sprinted into the end zone. Carolina went for two, trying to get within three points, but failed, and it was 21–16.

Now the pendulum had swung back toward Brady, and the Patriots should have put Carolina away, a "down goes Frazier" moment. By this time, the Panther defense had been on the field way too much, and it started to show as New England stormed down the field to the 9 on their best drive of the day. Then Brady, under pressure, floated a pass instead of throwing it, and didn't see Reggie Howard. The defender caught the ball in the end zone and returned it to the 10. It was Carolina's ball, and suddenly a touchdown would give them the lead.

They got it. Three plays later, Muhsin Muhammad ran past Ty Law. Safety Eugene Wilson was slow to pick him up, and Delhomme lofted a pass that Muhammad caught in stride before stiff-arming his way into the end zone. But another try for two failed, making the score 22–21 in favor of Carolina. New England fans hoped they wouldn't need Vinatieri, not today.

It was like *Back to the Future* as both teams went back to playing like it was the end of the first half. By now, both defenses were gassed, and no one was leaving their seat. It was flip-a-coin time: whoever had the ball last would win. You could see it coming.

It was also shaping up as a Tom Brady moment. For as the *Herald*'s Karen Guregian had previously noted, "What he's able to do is something that can't be taught or imitated. You can't reach the level of calmness and the cool he has amid the pressure.... Either you have it or you don't. And Brady definitely has it." At twenty-six, he was already a quarterback whose reputation for late-game heroics in big games was as well established as that of any quarterback who had ever played. He proved it again, smartly moving the Patriots down the field, the key plays two catches by David Givens.

At the 1, the Patriots brought in their short yardage offense, subbing in Seymour and Vrabel as pass-eligible blockers on the ends. Vrabel was already having the game of his life with two sacks and a forced fumble. But the ex-Steeler wasn't finished yet.

In a game this crazy, it was time to up the stakes and go for the KO. Everyone expected a run up the gut, but the Patriots' call was for a "136-X-Cross-Z." In other words, not what Carolina expected. Brady faked and then

threw to Vrabel, crossing left to right just inside the goal line for a touchdown, the second of Vrabel's career. The previous season, versus San Diego, the Pats had used a similar play. In fact, over the course of his career, Vrabel, normally a linebacker, would eventually catch 14 passes in comparable situations—10 for touchdowns.

The Patriots weren't done. Now they decided to go for two, to make it a seven-point lead. This time the call was for Brady's favorite play, a straight snap to Kevin Faulk, lined up as a blocking back in what otherwise looked like a running play or a sneak. At the snap, Brady spun away from his center as if he'd lost control of the ball and it had sailed over his head, pirouetting like a ballerina. Instead, the center snapped directly to Faulk, who charged ahead. Now New England led 29–22.

Big mistake by New England. Well, not by scoring, but in this game, by scoring so fast. There were almost three minutes left in the game, time enough for, what, another two or three or four touchdowns? All New England needed was a stop, but the Panthers hadn't

Quarterback Tom Brady speaks with rival Peyton Manning after the Patriots defeated the Colts, 24–14, in the AFC championship game on January 18, 2004, at Gillette Stadium.

punted since midway through the third quarter. All they had done was score.

And here they came again, Delhomme and Ricky Proehl, Deshaun Foster, Muhsin Muhammad, and a cast of seeming thousands, all throwing punches from every direction. This time it took all of a minute and a half. For the second time in three years, with McGinest in Delhomme's face, Proehl caught an apparent late-game touchdown pass to win a championship and become a legend, only this time for the Panthers from 12 yards out with just over a minute remaining. The Panthers didn't go for two this time, kicking the extra point instead to tie the game at 29–29, daring Brady and the Patriots to try what they had pulled against the Rams.

Big mistake by Carolina. They left Brady his very favorite situation—just enough time. Afterward, he said he wasn't nervous, "not at all." This was something he knew he could do.

It came down to a kick. Well, actually two kicks. On the kickoff, Panthers kicker Kasay, incredibly, shanked it out of bounds, giving the Patriots the ball at the 40, which left Brady needing only 30 or 35 yards to gain with three time-outs and a little over a minute to get there and hug Vinatieri . . . if he could make it this time. With the ability to stop the clock, the whole field was available. The Patriots could even run the ball if they wanted, forcing the Panthers' defense, which had already been on the field for almost 38 minutes, to defend everything.

They couldn't defend everything, and even when they did, Brady made the play anyway. After an incompletion, he turned to Troy Brown and found the receiver twice, sandwiched around an interference call, the second catch a thread through traffic in midfield. Then a catch by Daniel Graham delivered the ball to the 40. The Patriots still needed more, though, and there were only 14 seconds left.

But remember, the whole field was open, and New England still had two time-outs. Brady went back, looked right, waited, waited, saw the Panthers bite on a short route to Brown, and went instead to Deion Branch, who went up in the air and held on at the 23-yard line. "I think," said Brady, "we had the perfect play called for that coverage." You think? Then Brady waited some more and, with eight seconds left, called time.

Vinatieri, who'd spent the last five minutes kicking into a net, was waiting too. Now all he had to do was the one thing he'd had trouble with all day, and trouble at Reliant Stadium with all year—kicking it between the posts.

But if Brady was made for the last-minute drive, Vinatieri was made for the last-second kick. If either man was not, their reputations today would be far different. Suffice to say, each has earned the other a lot of money, as well as for their teammates, their coach, and their owner. Vinatieri's kick, this time from 41 yards, was pure money.

A kickoff and short return later, the Patriots were champions again, 32–29. Brady—who else?—was named MVP, only this time he turned down Disneyland for Pebble Beach. "If someone were to sculpt a Mount Rushmore of Boston sports legends," wrote Guregian, "prior to last night there would be no Patriots etched in stone." Brady had just carved his face in granite.

With two titles in three seasons, the Patriots had the hardware as the Lombardi Trophy made its way back to Gillette. The only thing they didn't have was respect, something Belichick even alluded to when he received the award after the game, saying, "You win 15 in a row and win a Super Bowl championship, that's pretty good. I think you're going to be talked about with so many of the other teams that have had great accomplishments."

• • •

Well, everyone agreed with that in New England, but despite their performance, outside the region there was still the lingering feeling that the Patriots, in some ways, were not quite all that. Yes, they'd won two Super Bowls out of the last three, the only team to do so without winning two consecutively, and they'd won fifteen games in a row and counting, but their street cred didn't match the accomplishment. Some still viewed the win in XXXVI over the Rams as almost some kind of fluke, and the Panthers, well, no one thought they were a *truly* great team. There was a lingering suspicion that the Patriots had lucked out both times by winning late and making it to the Super Bowl without playing one of the league's true powerhouses at the top of their game along the way. They were champions, sure, but champions by way of parity. They'd won both Super Bowls on field goals, for crying out loud, defense, and, as *Sports Illustrated* described it, an offense "more efficient than dominant, mixing a vanilla running game with multiple short-pass packages."

Ouch. They just weren't sexy and, outside of Brady, didn't have a real star, a dominant wide-out à la Jerry Rice, a bone-crushing linebacker in the mold of a Dick Butkus, or a Hall of Fame running back like Franco Harris. Even Belichick lacked the élan of a Lombardi, Tom Landry, Bill Parcells, or Bill Walsh. The Patriots' earlier history tainted their achievement—the lingering perception of fans elsewhere that New England was a second-rate franchise still cast their accomplishments in shadow. Sure, they'd won, but . . .

• • •

Although the Patriots already had the trophy everyone wanted, that wasn't enough. The theme song for the 2004 season might as well have been R-E-S-P-E-C-T. They needed victory worthy of Aretha to drive the point home.

They took a major step toward that in the off-season. Corey Dillon, the Bengals' premier running back, had worn out his welcome in Cincinnati, once saying that he'd rather "flip burgers" than play for the Bengals. Yet despite the fact that they'd won only 34 games during his time there and never finished above .500, he'd still run for more than 1,000 yards in six consecutive seasons before falling to less than half that in 2004, owing to injury and the emergence of Rudi Johnson. Still, Dillon was the rare running back who provided both power and speed, adept at running and receiving. The Patriots of recent vintage had only accomplished that in tandem—guys like Kevin Faulk providing the speed and receiving skills, while Antowain Smith and Matt Luke brought the power. The result, while unquestionably efficient, was also predictable, and put more pressure on Brady. In Dillon, the Patriots potentially had their best all-around back since losing Curtis Martin.

They would eventually need him, though at the start of the 2005 season Dillon was a luxury, an add-on to an already very good team. He gave them a runner they could more or less depend on for somewhere around 100 yards a game (his lowest game total for the regular season was 79 yards, and he'd top 100 nine times), and he could keep defenses honest and the focus off Brady and the passing game.

The result was a balanced offensive attack that maintained control of the ball and kept the other team's

offense off the field. After beating the Jets 13–7, the Patriots were 6-0, winners of an NFL record 18 regular-season games in a row—21 including the postseason.

Not that everyone recognized the achievement. The Miami Dolphins, who went undefeated for the entire 1972 season, were among those who scoffed at the Patriots' record. Asked if the Pats compared to the Dolphins, linebacker Nick Buoniconti dismissed the query, saying, "You don't want me to dignify that by answering the question, do you?" Streaks just didn't count unless they lasted for a season. Even Ty Law noted, "If we don't make the playoffs, who's going to remember the team that won 18 games?"

Still, that was the record they were shooting for before week seven against Pittsburgh. With a victory, they could tie the Dolphins' record, which had extended into 1973. Unfortunately, it was Halloween night and the game turned into a horror movie.

Pittsburgh rookie Ben Roethlisberger had taken over at quarterback after Tommy Maddox was injured and proved to be a revelation, going 4-0 as a starter. The Patriots were considered his first big test.

He passed. And passed and passed, sloughing off blitzes like a veteran, throwing for two first-quarter TDs, then protecting the football as the Steelers raced to a 24–3 lead and eventually coasted to an easy 34–20 win in a game that was never close. Even with Corey Dillon out with an injury, no one had expected a blowout. But it was worse than that.

On only the third series of the game, Ty Law left the game with what would eventually be diagnosed as a broken foot. The secondary was already down a man because of an earlier injury to Tyrone Poole, and the Patriots, who had looked to be unbeatable, suddenly seemed anything but. Rookie Randall Gay had been burned after stepping in for Law. The winning streak was over, and now it seemed as if Law's earlier observation might prove to be prescient.

Entering the season, it was already likely that Law was seeing his last season as a Patriot. He was making too much money, and just as Milloy had been let go to make room under the salary cap, there was open speculation that the Patriots would soon do the same with Law, no matter how well he played. That was the plan after all—to create a team not dependent on any one piece. They'd already been thinking about how to adapt, and the signing

Rodney Harrison, Bill Belichick, Robert Kraft, Jim Nantz, former Dolphin great Larry Csonka, and Antowain Smith await the awarding of the Lamar Hunt Trophy. The Patriots won their fourth AFC championship over the Colts by a score of 24–14.

of Gay, a nondrafted free agent, was part of that. They just hadn't expected to depend on him so soon.

Now, with the pass-happy Rams due next, they had to move more quickly. The patchwork on-the-fly approach against Pittsburgh hadn't worked. Rather than try to pick up another DB who would have to learn the defense from scratch, they looked internally . . . to the offense. Troy Brown, after being drafted out of Marshall University as a return man, had evolved into a backup receiver who then became a valuable slotback and now, after a decade in the league, was primarily a passing down receiver and return man again. But there was probably no one on the team who knew the Patriots' defense better, at least from an offensive perspective. He was already one of Belichick's all-time favorites, not a JAG but "some football player. . . . You have to love guys like that on your team. He puts the team first."

It wasn't quite the equivalent of the Colts shifting running back Tom Matte to fill in for injured quarterback Johnny Unitas in 1965, or Magic Johnson replacing Kareem at center in the 1980 NBA playoffs, but with a week to prepare, defensive back coach Eric Mangini and Brown made it work. Another player might have backed off, afraid of failure, but Brown, like Brady a late-round pick, had never played that way.

Incredibly, it wasn't even a total surprise. As far back as mini-camp, the Patriots had discussed just such a role for Brown. Belichick admitted as much, saying, "The coaches do a good job of looking ahead and not just seeing what the next day is going to bring, but trying to anticipate your needs through the course of the season." Another GM called the ploy "brilliant," the coaching equivalent of the Derek Jeter flip play—being prepared for the most unexpected event.

Losing Law to injury was no excuse for losing, and as Brown filled in capably, New England surged through the remainder of the season, losing only once more, by a single point to Miami, and finishing 14-2 to secure second seed in the AFC East division. But their success did not mean their path to a third Super Bowl was without challenges.

This time they'd have to go through the best of the best. The Pittsburgh Steelers, behind Roethlisberger and a punishing defense that gave up the fewest points in the league, had finished a gaudy 15-1, while the Indianapolis Colts, behind Manning, had scored a remarkable 522 points. Manning set a record with 49 touchdown passes, earning league MVP honors. No matter who won, Super Bowl XXXIX would be a title well earned.

But if the Colts were the NFL equivalent of a flashy Porsche Carrera, and the Steelers an armor steel–plated

Hummer, then the Patriots were a superbly tuned Subaru Impreza—smooth shifting and dependable, good in all conditions, ideal for New England winters, yet faster and more powerful than they looked. Sure, the Patriots had won 21 games in a row, but that was yesterday. In the minds of most, this was the Colts' year—the overdue Manning was having the season of his life, and this time New England's now-no-name defensive backfield wouldn't be allowed to mug Manning's receivers. He'd already shredded the Broncos for 49 points in the first playoff round. And if it wasn't Manning's year, well, Roethlisberger was the future. He hadn't lost a game as a starter, going 14-0. Brady, despite the rings on his fingers, wasn't even considered the best quarterback in the playoffs.

But the one thing no one could account for was the Patriots' twelfth man: the weather conditions in Foxborough. The game started under wet snow, on a muddy field, and amid swirling winds. In other words, it was nothing like playing in the dome in Indianapolis.

The Patriots adjusted, handing the ball to Corey Dillon, but the Colts did not. Manning, throwing his coaching staff under the bus, would later say: "We just didn't have the plays called at the right time." It took a quarter for New England to gain traction, but once they did, Dillon plowed through the snow time and time again while Brady contributed the occasional safe pass. That kept Manning and the Colts off the field and spinning their tires. When they did get traction, the Patriots' defense hit them immediately and sent them into the ditch, forcing two key fumbles. New England controlled the ball for an incredible 37 minutes and 43 seconds and drove to an easy 20–3 win as Dillon ran for 144 yards. Over the game's final minutes, the crowd chanted his name, his teammates chiming in and calling him "Clock Killin' Dillon." After the game, Manning looked like he'd spent 60 minutes standing along the road waiting for a tow truck that never showed up. He had failed not only to throw for a touchdown, but to complete a pass for more than 18 yards. Brady didn't either, but then again, the Patriots hadn't needed him to.

In the meantime, the Steelers had struggled to defeat the Jets but escaped with a 20–17 win, which sent the Patriots to Pittsburgh for the NFC championship. They were greeted with New England weather: a wind chill of near zero made it the coldest home game in Steeler history and an amped-up crowd waved bright yellow "Terrible Towels" in a frenzy.

Tom Brady warmed up before the game wearing shorts and a T-shirt.

And once again, the race was over early. New England's game plan was to put pressure on Roethlisberger. They did so from the start. His first pass went off the hand of receiver Antwaan Randle El, was tipped by Asante Samuel, then intercepted by Eugene Wilson, leading to a Vinatieri field goal to put New England up 3–0. On Pittsburgh's next series, Coach Bill Cowher chose to go for it on fourth-and-1. Jerome Bettis fumbled, Vrabel recovered, and on the next play Brady hit Deion Branch in stride on a go route up the middle for a 60-yard touchdown pass. It was 10–0 New England and in the stands everyone's coffee was still piping hot.

Although Brady has never had quite the arm strength of some other quarterbacks in the league, after the conservative game plans of his first few years, the Patriots increasingly began to ask him to throw deep. And he could. They just picked their spots, and with a receiving corps that never had an obvious premier target, when New England did choose to go deep, they didn't aim for the same receiver time and time again. From one year to another, Brown, Branch, Patten, Givens, and a host of tight ends all found themselves as favored targets according to the opponent and the situation. In a sense, not having an evident Pro Bowler worked to New England's advantage: the opposing defense never quite knew which receiver to focus on, and over time, as they tried to shut down the control passing game, that left the deep ball available more and more often. Brady was like a hitter using the whole field—he could slap at the ball, pull it, hit a line drive into the gap, yet still pop the occasional ball over the outfielder's head for a homer. Putting a number on the scoreboard was all that mattered.

The Patriots put up another seven points after a 45-yard completion to Branch between defenders in the middle, scoring on a short sideline pass to David Givens. Now trailing 17–3, the Steelers had to throw and New England knew it.

With the ball on Pittsburgh's 20-yard line, Roethlisberger was supposed to look off safety Rodney Harrison but made a rookie mistake and did not. Harrison jumped the route, intercepting the pass on the run at the 13, and racing down the sideline. The only player in his way was Roethlisberger, and the rookie made perhaps the most pitiful attempt at a tackle in NFL history. By the time Harrison crossed the goal line, he had slowed to a walk, and with the score 24–3, the stands started to empty. When the game ended 41–27 in New England's favor, the stands were littered with more Not-So-Terrible-Anymore Towels than Steelers fans.

· · ·

So far, the Pats' two playoff wins had come by way of cool efficiency on offense and a hard-nosed, ball-hawking defense, the way they had played all year long. But that was also the approach of the Philadelphia Eagles, another team with something to prove. After reaching and losing the NFC championship game three years in a row, the Eagles were eager to shed their reputation for folding every January. Sensing that they needed a change, in the off-season they'd added a controversial free agent to the roster, receiver Terrell Owens, adding octane to an already high-performing engine. Owens, who thought he should be the target on every pass play, seemed worth the risk.

But the risk was considerable. As *Sports Illustrated*'s Peter King noted, "Owens can be a hopeless me-first guy who in the midst of consecutive two-catch games might erupt in a coach's face on the sideline. He'll use the media to snipe at the play-calling or the quarterback's performance." Some of that had already taken place, but so far the positives had outweighed the negatives. With Owens as a target, McNabb enjoyed his best season as an NFL quarterback.

Philadelphia had rolled through the regular season, reaching 13-1, and with home-field advantage through the NFC playoffs secured, Coach Andy Reid shifted to neutral and coasted, resting players in the season's final two games, both losses. He'd faced criticism for that, but when the playoffs resumed, the Eagles hit the accelerator and easily dispatched the Vikings and Falcons. They were easily the class of the NFC and featured a quarterback who, on paper, had a better year than Brady. Owens finished with 14 TDs as quarterback McNabb threw for 31 scores with only 8 interceptions, and Philadelphia's scoring defense was second in the league to Pittsburgh.

Offensive tackle Matt Light celebrates after the Patriots win the 2003 AFC championship game at Gillette Stadium.

Owens had suffered a severe ankle sprain late in the season, tearing ligaments, but managed to make it back for the Super Bowl. Yet his absence had emboldened other Eagles receivers—a few days before the game, Freddie Mitchell piped up that that he didn't even know the names of the defenders in New England's patchwork secondary. In particular, when asked about Rodney Harrison, he scoffed and directed his answer to the safety, saying, "I got something for you."

That provided any extra motivation the Patriots' defense needed. Winning would be nice, but shutting up Mitchell would be sweet. "We don't worry about what he's saying," said McGinest in response. "He will have to deal with that on the field." They knew they'd been challenged.

The Patriots were seven-point favorites at kickoff time in Jacksonville, so the only real distraction for New England at the time was the open secret that both offensive coordinator Charlie Weis and defensive coordinator Romeo Crennel would leave the fold for head-coaching jobs elsewhere. No one felt the coaches were abandoning them, and if anything, the Patriots wanted to give them a memorable send-off. In the event that this wasn't motivation enough, at a team meeting Belichick read aloud the route of the Eagles' proposed victory parade through the streets of Philadelphia, page one from the motivational book of coaching clichés.

The Eagles learned early that the Patriots were determined to stop the parade. After using a 3-4 front all year, the Pats changed it up in the Super Bowl, asking McGinest to play end in a 4-3 alignment designed to put pressure on McNabb and keep the fleet quarterback from running. It immediately paid dividends as McNabb fumbled on the first series. The call was overturned, but the tone was set. Both teams punted twice, but on the Eagles'

Quarterback Tom Brady spots teammate Mike Vrabel in the end zone for a touchdown reception during the fourth quarter of Super Bowl XXXVIII at Reliant Stadium in Houston, Texas. The versatile Vrabel, a linebacker by trade, proved the perfect foil for the cagey Patriots.

next drive, McNabb was intercepted in the end zone. Once again the call was overturned, but with the Patriot defense hounding him, Rodney Harrison picked him off on the next play.

After the Eagles scored on a long drive to take a 7–0 lead—the only time the Pats had trailed in the postseason—and after Brady fumbled on a botched handoff at the Philadelphia 4-yard line, the Eagles had the opportunity to take control. But they failed to move the ball, botched a punt, and with 1:10 left in the half, Brady hit a wide-open David Givens in the back corner of the end zone. He celebrated by mocking the Eagles, flapping his arms.

To the great relief of the NFL, Paul McCartney didn't expose himself or anyone else during the halftime show. In the third quarter, the two teams traded touchdowns, the Patriots apparently taking control, only to have the Eagles tie the game late in the third quarter. For the first time in history, the fourth quarter of a Super Bowl began with a tie score—a potential classic in the making.

But the classic went as flat as the tires on the floats for the Eagles' postgame parade. The Patriots opened the final period with a workmanlike nine-play, 66-yard drive that ended with Corey Dillon surging into the end zone. On the next drive, a circus catch by Deion Branch, who was the best receiver on the field that day and the eventual Super Bowl MVP, set up a Vinatieri field goal to put the Patriots ahead 24–14.

The game was all but over. The listless Eagles played the remainder of the game with precious little urgency. With 5:40 remaining, Philadelphia coach Andy Reid didn't even try going to the no-huddle offense, coaching as if it were a preseason game. It was later revealed that McNabb, sick all week with a cold, simply ran out of gas. A teammate said, "He could hardly call the plays—that's how exhausted he was trying to give it his all.... He exhausted everything he had." On one occasion, Freddie Mitchell had to finish the play call in the huddle.

That was the only thing Mitchell finished that day. He ended the game with only one reception, one fewer than Rodney Harrison, whose two interceptions included the one that ended the game. A late score had made the Eagles look good, but New England's 24–21 win was as dispassionately efficient as the entire season had been.

It was, wrote Michael Silver in *Sports Illustrated*, "great in the way that a chocolate milk shake is great, as poised and proficient as the Beach Boys doing background harmonies onstage." The game would hasten the departure from Philadelphia a year later of Terrell Owens, who delivered a bitter last shot at McNabb: "I'm not the one who got tired in the Super Bowl." Thanks, T.O.

The Patriots had simply done it all, in every way possible—setting a record for consecutive wins during the regular season, then dispatching the team with the best regular-season record, the team with the best record in the NFC, the quarterback with the best regular-season record, the MVP quarterback who'd just set a regular-season record for touchdowns with the best passing rating in the league, and then defeating the two teams with the lowest-scoring defenses in each league during the playoffs. They became the second team, after the Cowboys, to win three Super Bowls across four seasons, going back-to-back in the last two.

There really wasn't anything left, or much left, for them to do. Respect had been earned, no Aretha needed, just a chorus in harmony. They hadn't needed a last-second field goal, or a late call by an official, or a miracle play. They had just won, coolly, relentlessly, no matter who was hurt or who they played, executing the plan, adjusting as needed, putting Brown in the secondary, handing off to Dillon, placing their trust in Brady, distributing the ball to everyone eligible to catch it. They didn't make headlines or give the other team bulletin board fodder, create any drama or depend on stirring comebacks. They were as bland as their coach, not even saying anything after the game that was particularly memorable or profound.

Despite winning a Super Bowl by only three points, the victory felt inevitable, almost unavoidable, the predicted outcome of the plan, nothing more, nothing less. The victory wasn't an exclamation point, but a simple declarative statement, an exercise in proper grammar. In only a few short seasons, they'd gone from underdogs to overlords. The view was intoxicating, and there seemed to be no end in sight.

A few months before, the Red Sox had finally won a world championship, shedding the yoke that had followed that franchise for decades. It was as if all of New England had suddenly forgotten how to lose.

CHAPTER TWELVE

2005–2008

ALMOST PERFECT

In most of the country there was unbridled joy. It was a classic scene for the last moments of a Super Bowl: a quarterback scrambling, his team trailing, and a long, wobbling, near-desperation pass downfield. Then a receiver and a defensive back both in the air, fighting for the ball. The receiver, some-how, some way, pinning the ball against his helmet with one hand, falling to the turf, and then hanging on—the key play on another championship-winning drive.

Only this time the devastating, last-minute, game-winning drive was not delivered by Belichick and Brady and the Patriots but by quarterback Eli Manning and the New York Giants in Super Bowl XLII, where receiver David Tyree miraculously made a catch in what then was immediately called the greatest play in Super Bowl history, followed by Manning calmly tossing for the winning score a few plays later, the third straight year the Patriots' season had ended in defeat.

Nearly everywhere but in New England fans slapped hands, screamed, "YEAH!," and started celebrating with a vengeance. The mighty New England Patriots, undefeated for the season and on the verge of making history, the team that had got caught cheating, was vanquished. Again!

It was 2007, and outside New England, watching the Patriots lose at the end of the season had become the next best thing to seeing your home team win. In the

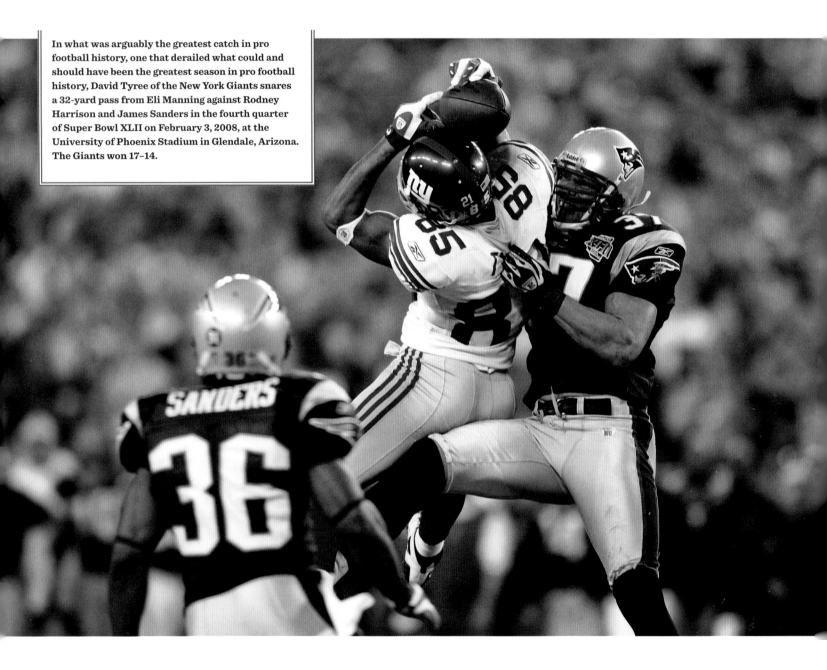

In what was arguably the greatest catch in pro football history, one that derailed what could and should have been the greatest season in pro football history, David Tyree of the New York Giants snares a 32-yard pass from Eli Manning against Rodney Harrison and James Sanders in the fourth quarter of Super Bowl XLII on February 3, 2008, at the University of Phoenix Stadium in Glendale, Arizona. The Giants won 17–14.

wake of the Patriots' victory in Super Bowl XXXIX, the plucky little Patriots were officially no more. They were now a verified dynasty, their bandwagon full to overflowing with fans who didn't know the difference between a cover-2 and a covered wagon. People were suddenly sporting Brady jerseys as sleepwear and espousing the banal bromides of Bill Belichick as wisdom akin to the Dalai Lama's. And with that "dynasty" designation came not just jealousy but, over time, something closer to hate—or at least a great aversion for everything the Patriots were and everything they had come to represent. For the past three years, the Patriots' season had ended with a painful loss and the Lombardi Trophy being paraded around another city. Your team may not have won, but the Patriots—the hated Patriots—had lost, and that was the next best thing . . . everywhere *but* in New England.

Knowing that was how the rest of the country felt had become a point of pride among Patriots fans, because the next best thing to being loved is being hated with equal passion. Patriots fans responded with a middle finger, a heavily accented rejoinder, and a profane reminder that Brady and Belichick and Kraft still sported three gaudy Super Bowl rings. After being kicked while they were down for so long, loyal Pats fans enjoyed being on top and let everyone know it. It wasn't just that the Patriots were "wicked awesome," but that your team "sucks!"

Then three straight seasons ended in painful losses—first in the divisional playoff, then the AFC championship game, and now the Super Bowl—and that had taken some of the shine off not only all the trophies but off Belichick, Brady, and the vaunted plan. Fans elsewhere were enjoying these moments of schadenfreude. The team that didn't know how to lose now didn't seem to know how to win the big one anymore. The reasons were obvious and subtle, circumstantial, situational, and self-imposed, and an awful lot of stuff never noted on the timeline on the Patriots' official website. Still, the results were absolutely irrefutable.

For years, occasionally coming close to a championship had been enough to sustain the franchise. But after dispatching the Eagles in the 2004 season, nothing but the Lombardi Trophy would ever suffice again.

By the time the plane landed back at Logan Airport with the newly anointed champions after Super Bowl XXXIX, the Patriots were already a changed team. Success had created opportunities and the chance to cash in. As soon as the game ended, both Romeo Crennel and Charlie Weis left, Crennel accepting a job as head coach with the Browns and Weis with Notre Dame.

There was never a better time to leave. As Kevin Paul DuPont of the *Globe* had written, "The winning has become so facile and expected, so routine, so just the way it is, that sometimes it seems as if Bill Belichick has unearthed the long-lost tome, 'The Secret Coaching Treasures of the NFL.'" Few industries play "follow the leader" more than professional sports teams, and his assistants basked in the afterglow. The Patriots way was seen as the key to success, and teams throughout football hoped to capture the team's magic by hiring away Belichick's foremost lieutenants. Belichick called it "sort of a perfect ending."

Few worried about the transition to new coordinators, since the plan accounted for that too. Michael Gee of the *Herald* called the Pats "Charles Darwin's team" for their ability to "adapt to their environment better than any species in the NFL." The transition simply required another adaptation: defensive back coach Eric Mangini slid into Crennel's role and . . . well, no one took over for Weis. The Patriots would move forward as a team, the offensive game plan now a group effort managed by Belichick. Such was the faith in what they had created. If they retained the same approach that had gotten them there, continued success seemed inevitable. The names of the individuals, whether on the field or the sideline, did not seem to matter. The plan accounted for everything. Almost.

Less than two weeks after the Super Bowl victory, the first unforeseen incident took place. Ever since arriving in New England as a third-round pick in the 1996 draft after overperforming as an undersized lineman, Tedy Bruschi had played his way into a key role as inside linebacker and defensive captain, a go-to guy for the media and acknowledged team leader. Despite being a protégé of Pete Carroll, Bruschi had bought in completely to Belichick's method, and the coach responded in kind, later saying, "If you ask me to sum up how I feel about Tedy Bruschi in five seconds: He's the perfect player."

On February 16, 2005, just a few days after appearing in the Pro Bowl in Hawaii, Bruschi experienced headaches, blurred vision, and weakness. After reaching the hospital, he was diagnosed with a mild stroke. Although he was released a few days later and soon began rehabilitation, his future was uncertain. Football, at least for 2005, seemed out of the question. Among fans and within the burgeoning online blogosphere, there was rampant speculation that his condition might have been caused by steroid abuse, which Bruschi always denied, once saying that steroids "scare me to death." Neither the word "steroid" nor the phrase "PEDs" even appears in his biography.

Although the NFL had tested for the drugs since 1987, the program had little bite. But concern over steroids and other performance-enhancing substances had received increasing scrutiny ever since the home run spike in major league baseball during the late 1990s. Unlike baseball, the public didn't seem to care whether football players juiced or not—suspensions were treated with an eye-roll by both the public and NFL teams. Remember, as far back as the early 1960s, pro teams distributed steroids, and NFL doctors and training staff had been known to hand out all sorts of drugs, from amphetamines to painkillers, to keep players on the field, often in dosages far above those recommended and for purposes not covered by medical protocols. The "whatever it takes" culture of the game made drug abuse—of some kind—almost obligatory. To date, beginning with Rodney Harrison's 2007 suspension, at least five Patriots have been suspended for PEDs, about the average for an NFL team, plus several more caught during periods of free agency between contracts.

The loss of Bruschi had not been anticipated, really, but if there was one position where the Patriots were well stocked, it was linebacker, with Ted Johnson, Larry Izzo, Rosevelt Colvin, Mike Vrabel, Willie McGinest, and others still on the roster. For the time being, the team was more concerned about Bruschi's long-term health than anything else.

Only ten days later, however, came another loss. On February 25, to little surprise, the Patriots released ten-year veteran Ty Law, tied with Raymond Clayborn for the most interceptions in team history.

The decision was clinical. Although Law was still among the best defenders in the league and his broken foot no concern, cutting him saved the Patriots $12 million against the salary cap in 2005 and $9 million in real money. Law knew it was coming, but was still incensed. When Belichick called him to try to smooth over the release, Law cut him off, reportedly saying, "Hey, forget that stuff. We won together. And now I'm gone." It was pure Belichick, a calculation made without sentiment. As Ted Johnson later characterized the coach, "Belichick does it in a way I've never seen it. He's established this culture. He doesn't ask about my family, he doesn't ask about my personal life. He doesn't care. He doesn't have an emotional attachment to his players. . . . You wonder, how does the guy get guys to play for him when you're like that?"

The answer, presumably, is because they won. But now, less than a month after winning the Super Bowl, and after losing not only its defensive and offensive coordinators but two of its best defenders, apparently the team felt able to move forward without skipping a beat.

Before the season began, there would be one more unanticipated loss: on July 28, linebacker Ted Johnson abruptly retired.

In the Patriots' defensive alignment, Johnson played what is known as the "Mike," an inside position, even in a 3-4 alignment. His job was not so much to make tackles, although he made plenty, but to occupy and tie up the other team's inside lineman, usually a guard, freeing his teammates to make tackles. This is a thankless task best appreciated by the men around him. Said Izzo, "He was such a physical, hard-nosed style of player, a throwback to the old days of smash-mouth football. . . . He attacked the line of scrimmage, identified the play, and attacked blockers." That often put Johnson, no slouch at six-four and 250-plus pounds, head-to-head against interior linemen who outweighed him by as much as 100 pounds.

Johnson, who played in every Patriot game he was physically able to after being drafted out of Colorado, paid a price for that. Over the course of his career, he suffered a torn left biceps, a broken foot, and a torn right bicep, underwent surgery on both shoulders, and tore what he claimed was "every tendon imaginable." But that was just what showed up on the injury reports. There was more. In the off-season after the Super Bowl, an annual physical with his regular physician raised concerns when Johnson cited symptoms that included irritability, difficulty sleeping, and memory loss. His doctor told him these symptoms were likely due to concussions. "It was strongly urged and suggested that I not play; that I should consider the ramifications," Johnson said at the time. "I can still play, but I open myself up to potentially some very damaging long-term health issues." He then admitted that he'd played most of the 2004 season while suffering those same symptoms.

The long-term impact of concussions suffered while playing football was just beginning to be recognized by the general public, although in 2001, after suffering a reported nine concussions, Dallas quarterback Troy Aikman had retired for the same reason (and faced questions concerning his "toughness" for doing so). Johnson was one of the first players to retire for that reason

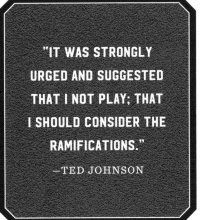

"IT WAS STRONGLY URGED AND SUGGESTED THAT I NOT PLAY; THAT I SHOULD CONSIDER THE RAMIFICATIONS."

—TED JOHNSON

after Aikman. As health issues suffered by players like former Pittsburgh center Mike Webster, NFL Hall of Famer John Mackey, and others began to be recognized by doctors as concussion-related throughout the 1990s, the NFL continued to look the other way.

The Patriots organization said the right things at the time. Bob Kraft had learned a lesson after the disastrous departure of Parcells, and now few organizations in sports were more PR-conscious than the Pats. Belichick said that Johnson retired "as a champion," but there was little expression of concern or accountability for his health, and Johnson seemed to accept that responsibility himself. But over time, as his symptoms increased and it became known that more players were impacted, Johnson was led to reassess the role played by the Patriots and their coaching staff in his deteriorating

health. Meanwhile, the league, and every team in it—including the Patriots—did their best to slough off any measure of responsibility beyond what was legally required, either moral or financial. That attitude continues to this day, even after the NFL concussion settlement went into effect in 2017. That settlement includes hundreds of players who spent at least a short time with the Patriots. (Johnson declined to sign on to the settlement.)

Over the next few years, Johnson's symptoms became more debilitating. He divorced his wife after being charged with domestic violence and withdrew from public life as depression took hold. Suffering from incapacitating headaches and fatigue, he left a job as a TV analyst because he couldn't take the bright lights. In 2007, Johnson went public, telling his story to Alan Schwarz of the *New York Times* and Robert Sanchez of *5280* magazine. Among other revelations, Johnson told of a time during the 2002 preseason when he suffered a concussion and was supposed to be withheld from contact, only to be pressured by the coaching staff to participate in a full-contact drill. "I knew I shouldn't be hitting, but I was afraid if I didn't get in there and hit, maybe I'd get cut. So I got in there, our offense ran a play up the middle and the fullback blew me up. I had a concussion again. From then on, I never felt right." He specifically blamed Belichick for forcing him back into action prematurely, saying the coach later told him, "I had to see if you could play."

Public reaction in Boston—at least among the fan base—was unsympathetic. Johnson eventually became a pariah, someone who had "betrayed" the Patriots. He hid from the public, lived in a hotel, became addicted to amphetamines, and eventually sought treatment at both the McLean and Spaulding Hospitals, where he finally came to understand just how much damage he had suffered. Although Johnson has since returned to Gillette and participated in team events, he later told CBS Sports Radio, "I knew that was a big thing I did with the Patriots because I broke Robert Kraft's heart. We were very, very close, and I think he felt I betrayed him by telling that story because it brought negative energy and attention to his program. I didn't mean it to do that. I just wanted guys to get help. . . . I did it for the bigger picture, but that hurt our relationship in a big, big way."

Everyone involved in the NFL in any capacity—owner, coach, player, broadcast entity, media member, sponsor, or fan—must one day reconcile their relationship with a game that by its very nature leaves so many severely and permanently debilitated. A game that has made coaches and owners and executives and players and media companies wealthy and provided jobs for journalists and hours of entertainment for the fans in the stands and sitting on the couch has also exacted a steep human price, paid by nearly every man who has played the game at any level. Over the last few years, increasing numbers of players have retired prematurely, and a growing number of fans have abandoned the game over these concerns, as have some media members who, in protest, refuse to cover football any longer.

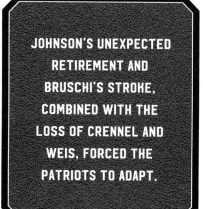

JOHNSON'S UNEXPECTED RETIREMENT AND BRUSCHI'S STROKE, COMBINED WITH THE LOSS OF CRENNEL AND WEIS, FORCED THE PATRIOTS TO ADAPT.

A report by Bob Hohler in the *Boston Globe* in March 2018 entitled "The Cheers Fade but the Damage Lingers" underscored just how dramatically Patriot players have been affected by repetitive head impacts. Of the 100 players on the roster during the Pats' first three Super Bowl wins, 42—many of them under the age of forty—joined a class-action lawsuit against the NFL and helmet-maker Riddell. Hohler went on to identify at least 340 Patriots or their estates "who allege they suffered brain injuries on the job since the franchise was founded in 1960," including 90 since 2000 alone.

It is interesting to note that despite increasing evidence of the dangers inherent in professional football, not a single coach or owner in the NFL has made a similar decision to leave the game. It is hard to come to any other conclusion than that, to them, financial gains, social stature, and power—and perhaps the narrow belief

that football plays some intangible role in the building of "character"—have rendered concern over the physical health of the game's players less important.

• • •

Johnson's unexpected retirement and Bruschi's stroke, combined with the loss of Crennel and Weis, forced the Patriots to adapt—Vrabel was shifted from outside to inside linebacker, for one—but the Patriots entered the 2005 season changed in ways they had not expected. At the same time, other teams played follow the leader and began aping the Patriots' approach, becoming more adept at playing the salary cap game and looking to free agency to provide solutions. The special edge the Patriots had enjoyed over the past few seasons began to erode, as did the veneer of their invincibility.

They suffered across the board. After being the fourth-highest-scoring team in the league in 2004 and giving up the second-fewest points (tied with the Eagles) in 2005, the Patriots slipped to tenth and seventeenth, respectively.

It didn't help that Corey Dillon, after running for more than 1,600 yards in 2004, seemed a step slower and was hobbled by nagging injuries for much of the year, or that tackle Matt Light and safety Rodney Harrison were both lost early due to injuries. The Pats opened the season a desultory 4-4, but then Bruschi, cleared by his doctors, miraculously returned. Over the second half of the season, the Patriots stiffened; finishing 10-6, they edged out Miami for the division title and qualified for the playoffs' wild-card round.

The reason was Brady. No longer a kid but a finished product, he sometimes could make something out of nothing and was always trying to be the best quarterback on the field—the motivation that had driven him since he first stepped behind center in Ann Arbor as a freshman, the sixth or seventh quarterback on the depth chart, determined to prove others wrong. That's how he looked at it, and so far, when it mattered most, he had been just that: the best quarterback on the field.

Brady hit a career high in passing yardage in 2005, passing the 4,000-yard mark for the first time. Despite the drop-off in the running game—or perhaps because of it—he continued to show incremental progress in all aspects of his game, completing passes to a remarkable seventeen receivers. Even though the team had troubles in the regular season, Patriots fans and the organization alike had come to believe that if they could just keep it close and get into the playoffs, Brady, somehow, some way, would lead them to victory. "In Brady We Trust," a phrase first coined in print by the *Globe*'s Jackie MacMullan in 2004, could have been embossed on the 50-yard line at Gillette.

The quarterback did it again in the playoff opener versus Jacksonville. All was right in New England, for as Jerome Solomon wrote in the *Globe*, there was still blind faith that the quarterback "gets hotter when the temperature gets colder and better when the stakes are higher." After a sluggish first half, in the second half Brady—with an assist from the return game and the Patriots' defense—came alive, and New England rumbled to a 28–3 win that wasn't quite as easy as the final score made it appear.

No matter. For Belichick, Brady, and the Patriots, it was their tenth consecutive postseason victory, eclipsing a record set by Vince Lombardi's Packers in the 1960s. The win also lifted Brady's record at Gillette to a gaudy 20-1, and Belichick was being hailed as a genius. That fall he had even been the subject of a book that burnished the coach's reputation to a high gloss, *The Education of a Coach,* by the esteemed journalist David Halberstam, a neighbor of Belichick's on Nantucket.

Unfortunately, the shine quickly tarnished. The win sent them to Denver, where Brady's performance was merely human. Since Belichick had taken over, the Patriots had taken advantage of 27 turnovers during the playoffs and given up only six. Against Denver, the Pats turned the ball over five times, and Brady's two interceptions, one a pick-6, offset his 341 yards in the air. It was Broncos quarterback Jake Plummer—Jake Plummer!—who in the fourth quarter, with the game on the line, had led his team to scores and Brady who, with time running out and in need of a miracle, had thrown an interception. Patriots fans and local media were stunned by the

27–13 loss. Such was the level of their disbelief that one local writer insisted that the Patriots were "still one of the best teams ever assembled. Nothing the Broncos did to them at Invesco Field at Mile High, nor anything they did to themselves, will change that." The score said otherwise, as did media in other cities, with John Branch writing in the *Times*: "So this is how a dynasty ends, or at least how it is interrupted," citing New England's turnovers and the failure of calls to go their way. It was the first time in years that Pats fans had witnessed both in a game that really mattered.

The 2006 season unfolded differently but was the same in the end, and more deck chairs were shuffled in the aftermath. Defensive back coach Eric Mangini, who had become football's "It girl" assistant, left the Pats to join the Jets as head coach. And then, finally, salary cap maneuvers, both expected and unexpected, would cost them.

The organization concluded that Willie McGinest, after twelve years as a Patriot, cost too much and provided too little, so he was released. In 2005, David Givens and Deion Branch were, pound for pound, the most productive and least expensive wide-out combo in the league, and the Patriots smugly hoped to sign one or both players, thinking that at least one of them, surely, would choose to earn less for the right to play for Bill Belichick rather than opt for mere filthy lucre elsewhere. After Givens received an offer from Tennessee for far more than the Patriots were willing to pay, the Pats made a contract extension offer to Branch, who was signed through the season. His contract was back-loaded, however, and wholly in the team's favor; he had little assurance that he would actually receive most of what was on offer. He balked at signing, and the two sides dug into a protracted standoff that lasted a week into the regular season. In the end, the Pats traded Branch to the Seahawks for a number-one draft pick in 2007. And Adam Vinatieri, the franchise's all-time leader in points with 1,156, was allowed to leave for cap reasons as well; he eventually signed with Indianapolis. To date, in recognition of Vinatieri's role in their first three championships, the Patriots have yet to reissue his number, in anticipation of retiring it if the ageless kicker ever, ever retires.

JUST ONE KICK . . .

HAD SCOTT NORWOOD BEEN NEW ENGLAND'S KICKER, THIS BOOK MIGHT NEVER HAVE BEEN WRITTEN. AND IF ADAM VINATIERI OR HIS EQUIVALENT HAD BEEN KICKING FOR BUFFALO, THIS BOOK MIGHT HAVE BEEN ABOUT THE BILLS.

Norwood became notorious, of course, for missing "wide right" at the end of Super Bowl XXV, costing Buffalo its first chance at a Super Bowl victory, after which the team went on to lose another three Super Bowls in a row.

But in New England, beginning in 1996 and for the next ten seasons, there was Adam Vinatieri, widely acknowledged as the best and most clutch placekicker of all time. Vinatieri is as responsible for the success of the franchise as anyone else, including Brady and Belichick. And his is the most unlikely story imaginable. It started with a single kick.

In college, after washing out as an undersized quarterback and linebacker, Vinatieri kicked for South Dakota State, hardly a football hotbed. To say Vinatieri kicked might be generous. He *tried* to kick, connecting on only 27 of 53 field goal attempts in his career, including only four of 12 as a senior, a season in which he lost his job to a defensive lineman who kicked in a straight line, like Lou Groza. It wasn't entirely Vinatieri's fault, as kicking conditions in South Dakota were hardly ideal and success as a kicker is also dependent on the snapper and holder, but still . . .

Undrafted by the NFL, Vinatieri bet on himself and traveled to Virginia after the draft to work under wheelchair-bound kicking guru Doug Blevins, a man who had never played the game. Vinatieri waited tables while remaking himself as a kicker in an eight-month boot camp with Blevins to earn the slimmest chance at pro football: kicking for the Amsterdam Admirals of the now-defunct World League of American Football. In Europe, Vinatieri nailed nine of ten field goals, none longer than 43 yards, and that was *just enough* to earn an invitation to training camp with Bill Parcells's Patriots in 1996. Then, by the slimmest of margins, he beat out veteran Matt Bahr for the job, as much due to his lower salary as to his performance.

And then, well, he became Adam Vinatieri of South Dakota State again. In his first two weeks kicking in the NFL, Vinatieri converted only three of his first seven kicks as the Pats lost two close games. Ouch.

Parcells, never known for his patience, made it clear that there were other options. When the Pats rebounded against the Arizona Cardinals and took a 28–0 lead into the game's last 36 seconds, Parcells, with no need for another score,

Gulp.

Yet, as noted before, although the Patriots' approach doesn't guarantee a Super Bowl win, it does seem to protect against utter collapse. The personnel losses, as dramatic as they were, opened up opportunity. The draft provided running back Laurence Maroney, who would help take the load off Dillon, and kicker Stephen Gostkowski as a replacement for Vinatieri—roles both filled admirably.

In the end, nothing really went dramatically wrong during the 2006 season. In fact, an awful lot went right as the Patriots, as had been the recent pattern, overcame a slow start to close the season in a rush: they rebounded from back-to-back losses in midseason to the Colts and Eric Mangini's Jets to finish by winning six of their last seven, including several blowouts. They won the division with a 12-4 mark, the second half of the season marred only by an uncharacteristic 21–0 shutout on December called for Vinatieri to attempt a 31-yard field goal, a kick that meant nothing in the game but everything to Vinatieri. If he missed . . . well, there were other kickers on speed dial. Parcells reportedly told him that if he shanked the kick, there was no reason to return to the locker room. The coach had to find out something about his kicker.

This was pressure. Make the kick and stay. Miss it and go back to waiting tables. "Would you like ketchup with that?" Vinatieri, with more hanging on the kick than he could ever imagine, made it, and afterward Parcells gave him the weakest vote of confidence ever, saying, "He's week to week." Matt Bahr still didn't have a job and was waiting by the phone, after all, but that week his phone did not ring.

In that next week, on a slick field at Foxboro and in the wind and rain, the 1-2 Patriots took the Jaguars into overtime with the season on the line. If they won, the Pats would go to 2-2 and still have a chance for the playoffs. If they lost, well, at 1-3 the season would effectively be over. They moved the ball down the field and Vinatieri, who had already made three field goals that day, now lined up to try one that would mean everything—a missed extra point in the first quarter was the only reason the game was tied in the first place. As the *Herald* noted later, "He could be the hero or he could be among the unemployed. Vinatieri knew that if he didn't convert the 40-yarder, his Patriot career was in for a sudden end."

But he had made that kick the week before, under even more pressure. Now, after the Jags called a time-out to try to freeze him out, Vinatieri pounded and prodded the ground with his foot to give himself a firm surface, lined up, took a deep breath, watched the snap taken by Tom Tupa, kept his head down, stepped forward, and kicked.

It wasn't pretty, and it wasn't perfect, sneaking in just inside the upright, but he raised his arms in the air when he saw that it was good, the first game winner of his career, Patriots 28, Jacksonville 25. And in the *Herald* the next day, the headline read: "No Boot for Now."

Over the course of his Patriots career, Vinatieri would go on to convert another 17 of 19 kicks that meant either a win, a loss, or a chance at a tie or overtime, including, you might recall, a spectacular 45-yard kick in a snowstorm against Oakland in the 2002 AFC championship game to force overtime and then a 23-yard kick to end that game; a 48-yard field goal as time expired to beat St. Louis in the 2002 Super Bowl; and a 41-yard kick with four seconds remaining to beat Carolina in the 2004 Super Bowl, kick-starting the dynasty.

The rest, as they say, is history.

10 delivered by the Dolphins in one of Brady's worst performances ever. They made the playoffs once again, but had to play in the wild-card round, which meant the path to the Super Bowl was not only a bit longer but would have to go through several other cities besides Foxborough.

Just as success seems to focus all the attention on the ultimate victory, defeat draws attention to the most devastating loss, and the 2006 season would end with the most painful defeat in the Belichick and Brady era to date. But first came revenge against the Jets and Mangini for the 17–14 loss in week ten. This time the Patriots allowed the Jets to hang around until midway through the third quarter before finally taking command to win going away, 37–16.

Yet once again, the story became not so much what took place during the game as what took place around it. In their last meeting, Belichick had drawn attention by barely acknowledging his former assistant coach's

Patriot Doug Flutie executes the first NFL drop-kick since 1941 for a two-point fourth-quarter conversion as the Patriots' defeat the Dolphins at Gillette Stadium on January 1, 2006.

presence after the game, acting as if he wanted to avoid the traditional midfield greeting between the two head coaches. As Belichick avoided eye contact, Mangini finally reached out to force what had to be the least generous handshake of the coach's career. As Borges had noted, "This time there was no escape for Bill Belichick. The 'no-look handshake,' just like everything else the Patriots coach tried yesterday, was foiled by his former student."

It was no better after the playoff win. Belichick had not been pleased with the attention surrounding the earlier handshake and seemed determined to get it over with this time as quickly as possible. At the same time, his earlier behavior made it almost as significant as any play of the game. As Brian McGrory described it in the *Globe*, as Belichick and Mangini approached each other in a "media scrum" near midfield, one that included longtime *Globe* photographer Jim Davis, "Belichick could have done a lot of things. He could have let his security detail clear a path. He could have paused and said something uncharacteristic like, 'Excuse me.' He could have jostled through the photographers. He did none of the above." Instead, as Davis focused his camera on Mangini, Belichick reached past Davis from behind, shoved the camera into Davis's face, then shook Mangini's hand before briefly embracing. Although Belichick later apologized to Davis, it was a bizarre finish to what should have been an opportunity to end the nonsense.

A week later, the Pats won in classic fashion in the divisional playoff against the Chargers. San Diego, building its game plan around premier running back LaDainian Tomlinson, controlled the first half as Brady was, well, awful, completing only four of his first 12 passes, and the Chargers surged to a 14–3 lead. But with only a few minutes left in the half, the Pats turned the clock back to what had gotten them there in the first place. In a two-minute drill, Brady drove them down the field and hit Jabar Gaffney for a short TD pass to make it 14–10 at halftime. Then, in the second half, the Patriots stayed in the air and mostly stayed in the hurry-up. Meanwhile, as John Clayton of ESPN noted, the Chargers "played not to lose," trying to control the ball and play field position. But late in the game, as had happened so many times before, field position didn't matter much to Brady. With the score tied and only 2:37 remaining, Brady hit Reche Caldwell for a 49-yard strike, setting up Gostkowski to perform a perfect imitation of Vinatieri as he drilled a 34-yard field goal to win the game, 24–21. Tomlinson ran for 123 yards, and Brady threw three interceptions, but the Patriots had prevailed.

That set up the game everyone really wanted to see, particularly in Indianapolis—the Colts versus the Patriots for the AFC championship. Indianapolis, like the Pats, had also struggled through the first two rounds of the playoffs, beating the Chiefs 23–8 and the Ravens 15–6. Most observers thought it was a case of both teams looking past their opponents and toward each other.

Who could blame them, and the Colts in particular? Perhaps no opposing player's reputation had suffered more during the Patriots' rise than that of quarterback Peyton Manning, the best quarterback in the world until he faced New England. Now, at age thirty and in his ninth season in the league, Manning had done almost everything, setting records and winning MVPs and taking the Colts to the postseason seven times, but he had yet to either beat the Patriots in the playoffs or win a Super Bowl. Now he'd have no chance to do the latter if he

didn't do the former. If he couldn't find a way to dispatch the Pats, he seemed destined to have an otherwise fine career besmirched by his seeming inability to win the big one and find himself relegated to a pile of almost legendary quarterbacks like Fran Tarkenton and Jim Kelly, guys whose careers would forever be defined by what they had not done rather than what they had.

In week nine, Manning had at long last defeated Belichick and Brady in a 27–20 win at Gillette, but Pats fans nervously sloughed it off as sort of meaningless— New England was coming off a short week after blasting the Vikings, and a potential game-tying drive by Brady had been thwarted only because Kevin Faulk tipped a pass that ended in a cheap interception. In an increasingly data-driven time, a lot of Patriots supporters muttered that the loss was more about "returning to the mean" and "the law of averages." If anything, the Patriots now had something to prove and could adopt the approach of the underdog, which made fans more certain of victory.

For the Colts, a chance to beat New England again made the game, in effect, as big as the Super Bowl. But for the Patriots there was more at play. Everything may not have been as it seemed. To date, Tom Brady had managed to avoid the pitfalls of celebrity. There were no scandals or missteps or stage dives into a mosh pit, and his image remained as squeaky clean as that of the saccharine TV sitcom that had earned the Patriots the nickname "the Brady Bunch." Oh, there had been a night of bump-and-grind on the dance floor with the singer Mariah Carey and a few other brief dalliances with models and actresses, and he'd even hosted *Saturday Night Live* and done a voice-over on *The Simpsons*, but thus far Brady had escaped falling into what football players refer to as "the life," where every desire is easily fulfilled and instant gratification the goal of every day. He even kept his endorsements low-key, and his craziest ambition was reportedly a fantasy about running for the US Senate.

For now, football seemed to be enough, and for the last several years he had been occupied with long-term girlfriend, actress Bridget Moynahan. She'd grown up in Longmeadow, Massachusetts, almost a local girl, an all-Irish pairing that only burnished Brady's image in Hibernian Boston. He was everybody's big brother, still the guy fathers wanted their daughter to marry.

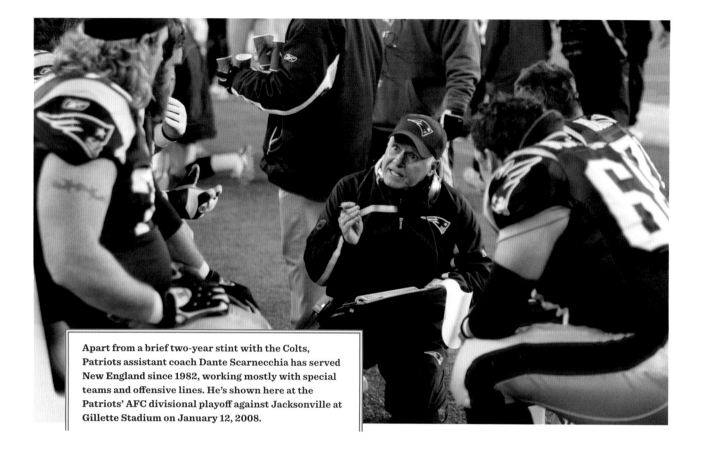

Apart from a brief two-year stint with the Colts,
Patriots assistant coach Dante Scarnecchia has served
New England since 1982, working mostly with special
teams and offensive lines. He's shown here at the
Patriots' AFC divisional playoff against Jacksonville at
Gillette Stadium on January 12, 2008.

But in mid-December, Moynahan had announced by way of *People* magazine that "several weeks" earlier she and Brady had come to an "amicable" split-up, which might have explained Brady's subpar performance in the Miami shutout. He'd thrown for only 78 yards in a 12-for-25 performance, leading Miami's Vonnie Holliday to note that Brady had been yelling at teammates throughout the game: "It was a little bit uncharacteristic of Brady—he's usually so cool and calm." Perhaps he was human after all.

After the game, the newly single quarterback had gone to New York for his first date with Brazilian supermodel Gisele Bundchen. The two had been introduced by a mutual friend whom *Boston* magazine later identified as Will McDonough, Brady's little-known personal assistant and former player liaison with the Patriots' marketing department (no relation to the sportswriter of the same name). By Christmas, the two would be publicly linked, and they married in 2009. But in February 2007, Brady would learn that Moynahan was pregnant with his

first child. When the Pats faced the Colts, for once, football might not have been the only thing on his mind.

The same thing could be said for Bill Belichick. A midsummer story in the *Boston Herald* entitled "Belichick Named 'Other Man' in Nasty NJ Divorce" revealed that Belichick, reportedly separated from his wife Debby since 2004, had allegedly been having an affair with a New Jersey woman, Sharon Shenocca, whom he had known since she was a receptionist for the New York Giants while Belichick served under Parcells. Shenocca and her husband were divorcing, and Vincent Shenocca, charging that "his wife and the coach have been involved for several years" and that Belichick had been supporting her financially, wanted the coach deposed.

Through the remainder of the year and into the following spring, the story wouldn't go away. Belichick eventually divorced his wife and reportedly reached a settlement with Vincent Shenocca to avoid the public airing of private business, but like Brady's relationship issues, it had to be a distraction. Belichick's testy behavior over the course of the season, showing few signs of ending after Handshakegate, had in fact been something of a concern and had not gone unnoticed. Apparently, both Belichick and his quarterback had trouble exerting the same amount of control over their private lives and behaviors that they brought to the football field.

Suffice to say that on the cusp of the AFC championship game against the Colts, there was a lot going on off the field for the Patriots coach and his quarterback. It was, as Kevin Faulk described it, as much a "soap opera" as a football game, with Brady trying to retain his aura of invincibility as Manning tried to create his own aura in what was essentially a Super Bowl before the real one.

And at first, it went the way Super Bowls had recently gone for the Patriots. A long opening drive ended with a fumble in the end zone recovered by Patriots lineman Logan Mankins, followed by another lengthy drive for a score. Then Asante Samuel jumped a route at the Colts' 40 and went in untouched for another touchdown. Leading 21–3 before Indianapolis fans even had a chance to raise their voices, the Patriots had history on their side—no team had ever come back from such a deficit in a conference final. On New England's next possession, they were driving for yet another score before penalties stopped them. Manning finally responded with a must-have drive, but all the Colts came away with was a field goal. By halftime, it was 21–6 and maybe time to see what else was on TV.

But in the second half, the two quarterbacks and the two teams switched roles: Manning was unstoppable, leading his team on one long drive after another. The Colts converted on trick plays and dumb luck, one score coming on a TD pass to lineman Dan Klecko, another on a fumble recovery by center Jeff Saturday. Hell, even Manning, hardly the most nimble guy on the field, snuck in for a score.

Still, when Stephen Gostkowski kicked a field goal with less than four minutes remaining, the Patriots were leading 34–31. After forcing the Colts to punt, for once

> THE TWO QUARTER-
> BACKS AND THE TWO
> TEAMS SWITCHED
> ROLES: MANNING WAS
> UNSTOPPABLE, LEADING
> HIS TEAM ON ONE LONG
> DRIVE AFTER ANOTHER.

Brady, with the chance to run out the clock, couldn't convert on a third-and-4 pass that could have cut off the Colts' chances. New England was forced to punt, giving Manning one final opportunity with just over two minutes left.

It took him all of four passes, three of them completions, and 16 seconds to move the ball from his own 20 to the New England 11. And then, with Belichick and the entire New England defense absolutely certain that Manning, who had already thrown 47 times for 349 yards, would do so again, Manning handed the ball off to Joseph Addai on the next three plays. On the third, he ran three yards up the middle to make the score 38–34.

Brady had the Colts right where he wanted them, right? After all, with a minute still left to play, there was no one better in this situation. On first down, with two time-outs remaining and the Colts expecting a patented controlled Brady drive, Reche Caldwell, New England's number-one receiver by default, who had already made two brutal drops in the game that likely cost the Patriots at least one touchdown, streaked down the left sideline with a chance for retribution.

That was totally unexpected. But then Caldwell turned in, never turning around, and the pass fell to the ground. But this was Brady, and two more passes took the Pats to the Colts' 44. Manning sat on the sideline, head down, looking to the ground as if he couldn't stand to see what was coming next. Brady, with one time-out remaining, would have at least four shots to get to the end zone, as sure a thing as there ever was. On the next play, he spied tight end Ben Watson over the middle, 20 yards downfield.

But he did not see Marlon Jackson. The Colts' defensive back caught the ball and hit the ground. One knee by Manning later, the Patriots were defeated, 38–34.

It was precisely the kind of game New England usually won . . . but not this time. Belichick at least greeted Colt coach Tony Dungy at midfield, but when Manning approached, the Pats' coach brushed him aside as if he had an infectious disease, a petty move that made the loss loom even bigger and made the coach look like a sore loser. Any fans around the country still indifferent to the Patriots landed heavily on the other side.

Broadcaster Bob Costas summed up the feeling of many when he said, "I would hope Bill Belichick's personal graciousness could approach his personal greatness as a coach."

The previously unbreakable Brady-Belichick bubble had burst, and in the weeks that followed, as the Colts went on to win the Super Bowl over the Bears, it just kept bursting. Moynahan went public with her pregnancy, and everybody who had wanted Brady to marry their daughter now wanted to greet him with a shotgun to "do the right thing." Then Ted Johnson's concussion story broke, as well as more tawdry stories about Belichick's tawdry private life. The man some considered a coaching idiot savant now seemed more like just another idiot. He and the Patriots sensed his public image was slipping, and the coach agreed to a rare interview for a touchy and touchy-feely profile, not to a sportswriter but to the *Globe* feature writer Bella English. Belichick contributed little of note beyond making it clear that he "hadn't asked" for the story to be done and chose not to comment on almost everything. As sports talk radio's Michael Holley noted, "I don't think people would say Bill Belichick is a great man," adding, "He's a great coach" but only "an interesting man"—and one who, for the first time since coming to New England, was showing visible cracks in his public facade.

That may well help explain Belichick's and the Patriots' approach to the 2007 season. He and Brady had something to prove. The guys who couldn't lose had lost, and now they were losing just as much off the field as on it. So for the first time, instead of filling out the Patriots' roster and staying under the salary cap with spare parts, the Pats went big. After losing Givens and Branch, the receiving corps had been an issue in 2006, and Troy Brown told ESPN that had angered Brady, saying, "We had receivers coming in on Monday or Tuesday, we'd pick them up that week, and they'd be playing 40 snaps on Sunday."

Flush with draft picks, the Patriots created some cap room by releasing and re-signing Dillon for a pay cut and by dumping Tebucky Jones and several others. Brady even restructured his contract to free up more money, angering the players' union. But the moves allowed the Patriots to go after some bona-fide talent. First came Broncos receiver Wes Welker, a quick if undersized receiver adept at finding space in the middle who had impressed the Patriots whenever they played Denver; the price was two draft picks and a new contract for Welker. Next came Randy Moss, both the best and the most problematic receiver in the NFL. He was so eager to leave Oakland for New England that he took a pay cut.

Packers quarterback Brett Favre accurately said of the receiver that "there is no one in this league who puts fear in people more than Randy Moss." That was true, however, for both those on the field who had to cover the rangy receiver with sprinter's speed and those who manned NFL front offices, who found Moss hard to handle, questioned his commitment, and were troubled by his repeated run-ins with the law over marijuana possession and assault (even before he pulled his pants down and mooned Packers fans). His talent was undeniable, but many around the league thought he was more trouble than he was worth.

It was a measure of the Patriots' desperation that they made a deal for Moss with the Raiders, trading a fourth-round draft pick, since Oakland was anxious to unload him and his contract. Ever since their experience with Terry Glenn and the drafting of Christian Peter, the Patriots had tended to steer clear of players with personal issues, but losing to the Colts and subsequently losing their allure caused the Pats to lower the bar. And they weren't done either. In signing yet another talented receiver, Donte Stallworth, and several other key free agents, including star veteran linebacker Junior Seau, they made it clear that they wanted to win now and would worry about the implications later.

After struggling through the preseason as Brady tried to adapt to the bounty of having too many receivers to throw to instead of not enough, the Patriots opened the regular season against the New York Jets and blew them out, 38–17. But it would prove to be a costly victory.

During the game, the Jets noticed that the Patriots were filming the hand signals they used to send the plays in to the quarterback. It was a clear violation of league rules, which stated: "Any communications or

Junior Seau reacts after sacking New York Jets quarterback Chad Pennington for an eight-yard loss during second-quarter action at Gillette Stadium on December 16, 2007.

information-gathering equipment, other than Polaroid-type cameras or field telephones, shall be prohibited . . . including without limitation . . . any other form of electronic devices that might aid a team during the playing of a game." Mangini informed NFL security, later saying, "I didn't think it was any kind of significant advantage, but I wasn't going to give them the convenience of doing it in our stadium, and I wanted to shut it down. But there was no intent to get the league involved." Right.

The league acted swiftly, citing a 2006 memorandum meant to clarify the rule that stated: "Videotaping of any type, including but not limited to taping of an opponent's offensive or defensive signals, is prohibited on the sidelines, in the coaches' booth, in the locker room, or at any other locations accessible to club staff members during the game." In theory, analysis of the film, either during the game or in advance of subsequent meetings, could yield opponents' play plans and audible calls, providing a significant advantage. Only a few days later, the league levied a record fine of $500,000 on Belichick and $250,000 on the team and stripped the Pats of their 2008 number-one draft pick. Publicly, Belichick pled ignorance and called the snafu an issue of "interpretation of the rule."

The players mostly thought it was BS, but the team, admitting only that they might have stretched the rules, told everyone to keep their mouths shut. Outside the locker room, reaction split along partisan lines. In New England, fans mostly took Belichick's explanation on its face, choosing to believe that this was an instance of "everybody does it and we just got caught," even if local media wasn't quite as gullible. Kraft later told an interviewer that when he confronted Belichick about the taping, the coach admitted to the ploy. Kraft then asked, "How much did this help us on a scale of 1 to 100?" Belichick replied, "One," and Kraft said, "Then you're a real schmuck."

It was a rare moment of discord between the two men. Since taking over, Kraft had primarily played the benevolent face of the front office, freeing Belichick from doing much of the PR work. Compared to many other NFL owners, like Dallas's Jerry Jones, Kraft was low-key and, if not behind the scenes, generally not much of a scene-stealer. But he didn't like being embarrassed either, and neither did Myra Kraft. The controversy would mark the beginning of a long slow reemergence of the owner as a more publicly active force in the organization. Over time it would no longer be just Brady and Belichick who got the credit, but Belichick, Brady, and Kraft. They were like a law firm, a partnership, yet one in which each partner believed he was the key man.

Elsewhere, however, was a different story. The taping was widely seen as evidence of a pattern of breaking the rules the Patriots had indulged in ever since Belichick became head coach. There had long been unsubstantiated rumors that the Patriots illegally filmed the Rams during a walk-through before Super Bowl XXXVI, not unlike the spying that many Patriots thought took place before the AFL championship game against the Chargers decades before. Over the next few years, more scrutiny would come the Patriots' way as others made similar charges. It was eventually revealed by ESPN's Don Van Natta Jr. that the Patriots had illegally taped as many as forty games between 2000 and 2007 and that, in what appeared to

be an attempt to suppress a larger scandal, the league had ordered the evidence destroyed. Any impact the taping may have had on games and their outcome remains uncertain, but the impression that the Patriots cheated gained credence in light of an earlier statement by former linebacker Ted Johnson. In 2005, he had claimed that "every now and then I'd get a sheet, one hour before the game, with a list of audibles for our opponent. I don't know how, but they just showed up."

The punishment stung and left no one on the Patriots very happy, seeing another layer of polish stripped from their veneer. But Belichick and company tried to turn the incident to their advantage. For the remainder of the 2007 season, the Patriots adopted an overt "us against the world" approach, Belichick telling his team, "Winning cures everything." By then, there was an awful lot of everything to be cured. Belichick was

Corey Dillon carries the ball against the Pittsburgh Steelers at Heinz Field on September 25, 2005, as the Patriots defeated the Steelers 23–20.

determined not just to win but, whenever possible, to win big, run up the score, shove it in everyone's faces, and punish the Patriots' detractors at every step.

And it almost worked, for if the 2007 season had ended with the Patriots undefeated and hoisting their fourth Super Bowl trophy high above their heads in Phoenix and then parading it through the streets of Boston and throughout the region, the details of that season would probably have been worth a chapter all to itself, if not an entire volume, with each game of their inexorable march into the record books described in detail. No team but the 1972 Dolphins has ever completed a perfect season, and nearly fifty years later, that record—17-0, including the postseason—makes them the consensus choice as the greatest team in NFL history. The Patriots were oh-so-close in 2007 to taking their place. Only the final few seconds of the 2007 Super Bowl prevented them from usurping the 1972 Dolphins. In the end, however, a season that ended not in glory but in defeat would also forever change the narrative.

• • •

But let's get the good stuff out of the way first. For all but the final few seconds of the season, the 2007 Patriots were the best team in football history. Incremental rule changes continued to favor the passing game, and the Patriots were right in step. There really hasn't ever been a team more explosive on offense. Moss and Welker made the Patriots' passing attack almost unstoppable, Welker catching 112 passes and Moss's 98 going along with a record 23 touchdowns. Four other Patriots receivers— Faulk, Gaffney, Stallworth, and Ben Watson—caught between 36 and 47 passes each. The Pats went nearly exclusively to the shotgun, spread their receivers like a college team, dropped the fullback almost entirely, and left it up to Brady to survey the defense and make the call at the line of scrimmage, depending in turn on his receivers, particularly Welker, to choose the correct option among several potential routes. The result was that Brady threw for 50 touchdowns and more than 5,000 yards, with only eight interceptions; this worked out to 80 more yards passing per game than in 2006, an increase of 36 percent. The average score for each regular-season game was a gaudy 37–17 in New England's favor as they scored 30 or more points nine times, topping 50 twice.

ESPN'S Seth Wickersham called the 2007 Pats both "the most entertaining team of the 21st century" and the "most dominant . . . you had to appreciate them, even if you hated them, because you can't discuss the greatest teams in NFL history without mentioning them." All true. Elements of the offense New England unveiled that season have since been copied by every team in the league.

They were seriously challenged only a few times: in week nine by the Colts, necessitating a comeback from a ten-point deficit with ten minutes left; in a grind-it-out victory over the Eagles in week twelve; and in week thirteen when they escaped with a three-point win over the Ravens on a controversial touchdown catch by Gaffney. Then there was the regular-season finale against the Giants. The Pats' approach to that game may well have cost them a championship and their place in history.

At 15-0 entering the final week of the season, the Patriots and their fans all knew they were chasing history. National interest in the game was so intense that it was broadcast nationally not only on the NFL Network but on CBS and NBC. But in the Patriots locker room, it was even bigger. The opportunity to go undefeated *and* win the Super Bowl in the process became a greater goal than winning the championship itself. Yet again, the Patriots found themselves squarely up against one of the age-old adages in sports: if you are trying to do anything other than win, you are destined to lose. When the Patriots chose to make going undefeated and extracting revenge on their detractors more important than the championship itself, they set a dynamic in motion that, in the end, prevented them from reaching either goal.

The final game versus the Giants tapped into the age-old Boston versus New York rivalry, because in Boston, the only thing ever better than winning was beating New York in anything. The 2004 Red Sox had proven that. After the Sox won their first championship in eighty-six years, that season is remembered today not so much for the way they steamrolled the Cardinals in the World Series, but for their comeback in the championship series against the Yankees.

For the Patriots' undefeated season to go through New York in the final week of the regular season, in front of a hostile New York media, was an opportunity not to be missed. It was New York, for crying out loud, and the

Giants, the team that, before the Patriots were anything more than a distant dream in Billy Sullivan's bosom, had once been New England's team. And then there was the Parcells factor, still looming over all things Patriot out of proportion to its historical significance. Parcells's success with the Giants—with Belichick at his side—had eventually propelled the Tuna to New England and then created a border war with the New York Jets. Whether Belichick would admit it or not, that was important. Squashing Parcells's old team to go undefeated in the regular season would crush that bug forever. And the Giants were even led by Manning-lite—quarterback Eli Manning, the younger brother of Peyton, who represented yet another rivalry to be vanquished. The loss to the Colts in the AFC championship a year before still stung, and although the Pats had since beaten the Colts and older brother Peyton earlier in the season, kicking sand in Eli's face presented an opportunity to add yet another exclamation point.

And let's not forget the personal issues that had hounded Belichick in 2006 and 2007, which had taken some shine off the coach's only-interested-in-football image. A final victory—an undefeated season and a fourth Super Bowl—would compel history, forever and always, to anoint not just the Patriots as the greatest team of all time and Brady as the greatest quarterback, but Belichick as the greatest coach. Arguments, Spygate, divorce courts, and handshakes be damned. There was an awful lot of vindication at stake.

Entering the regular-season finale, the seemingly cold and calculating coach who cut valued players or risked their health if it meant improving the team was thinking as much with his heart as his head for perhaps the first time ever. For once, Belichick was focused on his ego more than on what was best for his team. Backup quarterback Matt Cassel has since told reporters that initially the plan was to have Brady and other key starters sit out the game, but they resisted and Belichick caved.

There were plenty of good reasons to lift the foot from the accelerator against the Giants in the finale—at least a little. Like the Eagles a few years before, after a grueling, pressure-filled season, key players could use a break. Tedy Bruschi later noted that "he [Belichick] has coached us harder this year than he has ever done in previous years," and by that he meant during practice, which as the season went on remained tough and rigorous. Although Belichick wasn't talking about running the table, he was clearly thinking about it.

There seemed little risk once the playoffs started that the Patriots could depress the accelerator once more. Besides, there was some chance that they might meet the Giants, at 10-5 already a playoff team, in the Super Bowl. Why provide them with any more insight or motivation for a potential later meeting? This is not to say that the Patriots should have tanked the final game, but it might have been wiser to leave a little in reserve, strategically and emotionally, in the event it was needed later. And if they lost their chance to make history and finish the season unbeaten, well, what was more important, an undefeated regular season or a championship? Their stated goal each year was to win the Super Bowl, nothing else. This was the first year they wanted more.

> IT WAS ALL THERE FOR THE TAKING. HISTORY, RETRIBUTION, REVENGE, AND SO MUCH MORE WERE RIDING ON A SUPER BOWL WIN . . .

The Giants made it clear that the only thing they wanted was to beat the Patriots in the finale, to shred the veneer of invincibility, and to use that as motivation for their own march to the title. Like Belichick, Coach Tom Coughlin was a protégé of Parcells's—he had coached the receivers for the Giants when Belichick was in charge of the defensive backfield. Well known in New England, where he had served as Boston College's head coach, Coughlin was a successful pro coach in his own right, though not quite at Belichick's level—no one was. And for Eli Manning, there was considerable family pride at stake. Peyton had defeated the Patriots in the AFC championship the year before and captured a Super Bowl title. This was Eli's chance.

The Patriots won, but it wasn't easy. The team trailing 28–24 late in the fourth quarter, Moss dropped what looked like a sure touchdown pass from Brady. But the

Patriots rewound the tape and tried it again—this time Moss held on to give the Patriots the lead. An interception put the Patriots in position for a second score and the eventual, hard-earned 38–34 win.

The Giants lost, but they learned something too. For much of the game, they'd slowed the Patriots' offense, and their own offense hadn't been intimidated. No other team scored so many points against New England all season.

Not only did the Giants outplay the Patriots for the first three quarters, but as Christopher Gaspar wrote in the *Globe*, they "played fast, fierce, and with a purpose . . . part of the Giants' game plan was to bully the NFL bullies," and they succeeded. It was a chippy game, with lots of jawing and late shots and shoving after the whistle. The Giants lost, but they had frustrated the Patriots with verbal salvos and borderline play. The adjective "undefeated" had not been intimidating, and Coughlin said afterward, "I don't know of any other way of being better prepared for the playoffs than to go against a team that is 15-0." As New York's Michael Strahan noted later, the loss gave the Giants a valuable "gauge" by which to measure what they needed to do next time.

Meanwhile, the Patriots mostly felt relief. "I'm glad the regular season is over, to tell you the truth," said Bruschi. But Donte Stallworth later told Wickersham, "In hindsight, I wish we would have lost that game."

For now, though, there was glee. The Patriots had *arrived*. In *Slate*, Charlie Pierce captured the chest-thumping taking place around the region when he wrote of the Pats: "They're bullies now, it seems. And targets. Everyone's against them. They've got the world right where they want it. Deal with it, world."

Most expected the Patriots to end up meeting either the Cowboys or Packers in the Super Bowl, each of which finished the regular season 13-3, but the newly confident Giants upended both teams to reach the title game as a five seed. Meanwhile, the Patriots had it rather easy as Jacksonville upset Pittsburgh in the wild-card game and the Chargers knocked off the Colts. The Patriots more or less cruised into the Super Bowl, beating Jacksonville 30–21 and the Chargers 21–12 in the AFC championship game. Neither contest really pushed them.

It was all there for the taking. History, retribution, revenge, and so much more were riding on a Super Bowl win that winning seemed almost an afterthought. Belichick, Brady, and the Patriots wanted it—bad. During the bye week before the game, when most teams take a bit of a break to allow players time to heal and then build toward the game, Belichick kept pushing, breaking protocol by holding three straight full-contact practices—which turned out to be three not particularly impressive practices that left some players wondering. Tight end Kyle Brady told Wickersham, "We had to put

New England's twin nemeses meet as Peyton Manning of the Indianapolis Colts is greeted by Bill Polian, the team's president, before the AFC championship game against the New England Patriots at the RCA Dome on January 21, 2007. The Colts defeated the Patriots 38-34.

out so much energy to get to that point . . . maybe we had peaked and maybe we were physically and emotionally drained. The crispness and the sharpness were lacking." It was the first time all year, he confessed, that he had felt that. Little things that never bothered the Patriots before suddenly did: the hotel, the beds, the food. Trying to win the Super Bowl was hard enough, no matter who they were playing, but trying to make history was something else again. The whole city was swept up in the quest. The *Globe* was already accepting orders for the planned quickie book commemorating the historic season, one that would include a Super Bowl win.

But that's not what happened. For the first time all year, the Patriots were out-hit and outplayed. The Giants changed up their defensive front for the game, employing different looks that gave the Patriots fits, moving Justin Tuck all over the place while keeping everyone else back in coverage. The Giants stopped New England's running game in its tracks, and for the first time all year Brady often found his receivers covered as the line hounded him all game long, sacking him five times (twice by Tuck), knocking him down a half-dozen times more, and almost sacking or knocking him down another half-dozen times. It was old-school, smash-mouth football, and at this stage of the season the Patriots, after eighteen high-octane performances, seemed to shy away from the hits. All season long, the offense had set the pace, but on this day they were a step behind.

Vince Wilfork (*left*) and Tedy Bruschi, the heart and soul of the Patriots' defense, face the Miami Dolphins at Gillette Stadium on December 23, 2007. The Patriots won by a score of 28–7.

Still, the Patriots almost won. After Manning threw a touchdown pass to Tyree with 11:05 to play to put the Giants up 10–7, Brady finally got untracked, completing eight of 11 on an 80-yard drive and finishing with a six-yard TD pass to Moss that put New England ahead 14–10 with 2:42 remaining.

Every victory—and every loss—has a hundred moments that could have gone another way, and in a close game those that take place at the end loom large. In this one, it came with under two minutes remaining.

On the Giants' final drive—with 1:20 on the clock and the ball on the New York 44, two time-outs left, second-down-and-5, and Fox announcer Joe Buck preparing his "close but no cigar" obituary for the Giants—Manning threw to Tyree on the right sideline, but the receiver cut the route short. New England's Asante Samuel jumped up to make the game-clinching interception . . . and it slipped through his hands, leaving the cornerback screaming and holding his helmet with his hands in frustration.

The door to imperfection had cracked open.

Third down, 1:15 remaining. Manning took the snap in the shotgun, and almost immediately the pocket began to collapse. Patriot lineman Jarvis Greene grabbed at the quarterback, Manning's jersey pulled away, then more hands were on him before Manning reappeared and spun to his right. With Vrabel charging into his face, he slung the ball down the middle of the field. David Tyree was there at the 24-yard line, the only white jersey surrounded by four Patriots, wearing one of them, Rodney Harrison, like a shirt.

Tyree then made the catch of a lifetime—of every lifetime of every man to ever play in the Super Bowl to that time—outleaping Harrison, snagging the ball with one hand, then pinning it against his helmet as he fell to the ground, improbably and impossibly holding on.

Now the door was wide open. A sack on the next play gave New England hope, but also gave Manning a chance to regroup. An incompletion made it third-and-11, but a pass down the right sideline to Steve Smith gave New York a first down.

Thirty-nine seconds. On a simple slant and go, Plaxico Burress faked inside, Ellis Hobbs bit, and then Burress broke for the corner, turning around and catching the ball in the end zone with 36 seconds remaining. The extra point made the score 17–14.

After the final kickoff, Brady had 29 seconds and three time-outs and needed only 40 yards to get within field goal range.

It wasn't enough. An incompletion was followed by a sack and then a desperation pass way, way downfield toward Moss, who had a step on the defender. But a pass that needed to go 70 yards went only 65, and then fell incomplete. All the Patriots had needed, really, was another 40 to kick a field goal and tie the game, but the play was emblematic of the way they had approached the entire season—trying to do more than just win. On the last play of the game, Brady threw another pass down the sideline, almost as long, again toward Moss, but he was tightly covered and the pass was broken up.

The game wasn't even officially over when Bill Belichick jogged out to midfield, found Coughlin, shook his hand, and then walked off, the photographers abandoning him for the champions. Manning took a final knee to make it official.

The perfect season, lasting only 18 games, 59 minutes, and 39 seconds when it needed 21 more seconds to be preserved forever, was over.

CHAPTER THIRTEEN

2008–2011

NO EXCUSE FOR LOSING

Excruciating last-minute defeats generally cause one of two outcomes. They can either be used as inspiration going forward or have a lasting impact that takes years to overcome.

For the Patriots, the loss in Super Bowl XLII would linger. In 2008, the Patriots, a team that had been less than a minute shy of becoming the greatest team in NFL history, failed to qualify as one of the twelve teams in the thirty-two-team NFL to make the playoffs.

IN THE WAKE OF THE DEFEAT, Brady's and Belichick's public reputations continued to take hits, as did the organization's when three Patriots—Willie Andrew, Kevin Faulk, and Nick Kaczur—were arrested on separate drug charges. To stay under the salary cap, the Pats cut Asante Samuel, Randall Gay, and Eugene Wilson, three veteran defensive backs who had combined to start 122 games for New England. The draft provided little help, and after losing all four preseason games, the unstoppable Patriots of 2007 had yet to make an appearance.

They disappeared for good halfway through the first quarter of the opener against Kansas City. Just as Brady released a pass to Moss and his weight landed on his front leg, he was hit below the knee by Bernard Pollard. His left leg buckled, tearing both the ACL and MCL ligaments in

his knee. Brady had to undergo surgery and would miss the rest of the season.

Matt Cassel, who in three years with the Patriots had completed all of 22 passes, was suddenly the Patriots' quarterback. For the remainder of the season, Brady became, as Guregian noted, "the proverbial elephant in the room," his absence looming over everything. Cassel wasn't bad. In fact, he was far better than expected, responding with the best season of his NFL career and earning himself an extended livelihood in the league.

But he was no Brady, and the Patriots were not nearly as potent as the year before. Moss was wasted as the offense played conservatively to minimize mistakes and take the pressure off their inexperienced quarterback. Those who hoped for a miracle akin to what had

On a day when New England held its collective breath, Tom Brady is helped off the field after sustaining a season-ending injury in the 2008 season opener versus Kansas City.

taken place when Brady replaced Bledsoe were disappointed. Although the Patriots still went 11-5, it wasn't enough to make the postseason.

Almost without noticing, the notion of a Patriots dynasty was becoming an anachronism. The Super Bowl suddenly seemed a long way off. After three straight season-ending postseason losses and then missing the playoffs entirely, the Patriots were gaining a new reputation—as a team that could no longer win the big one. They were still a premier franchise, one that other teams still sought to emulate, and Patriot fans still enjoyed their status as supporters of the team everyone else loved to hate, but their gloating was taking on a disheartened edge.

Belichick, although in no danger of losing his job, was no longer being lauded as the greatest coach in NFL history. Oh, he was in the conversation, but he no longer set the story line. The same went for Brady. His year-in-year-out excellence was unquestioned, but whatever special magic he possessed during his first years with Belichick seemed to have passed. The late-game, no-doubt-about-it comebacks were no longer a given, and teams facing the Patriots no longer expected to lose. Somehow, even as Brady and the Patriots had become more talented, championships got harder to come by.

It didn't get any easier in 2009. Key members of the organization reasoned that it was better to leave sooner rather than later. Scott Pioli became GM in Kansas City, and offensive coordinator Josh McDaniels took over as head coach of the Dolphins. Cassel parlayed his performance into a trade that reunited him with Pioli, Bruschi retired, and just before the start of the season half the defensive backfield left. Richard Seymour, two years removed from knee surgery and with another year remaining on his current deal, became a victim of his contract and the plan. Although he was one of the best linemen in team history, he was traded to Oakland for a first-round draft pick. Seymour, who had even accompanied Myra Kraft on an off-season trip to the Middle East, felt "blindsided" and disrespected, but he shouldn't have been surprised. Under Belichick, no Patriot is ever in a more precarious position than a veteran with a big contract headed into his final season.

The whole year was a scuffle. Brady was back, apparently little worse for wear, for mobility had never been a strength. Apart from a few blowouts, the Pats seemed oddly out of sync, as if uncertain how to move forward. Welker and Moss combined for more than 200 receptions, but the Patriots' offense, while still prolific, was more predictable than usual. Belichick chose to go through the season without naming an offensive coordinator, and as Welker and Moss went, so went the Patriots.

On defense, they missed Seymour's presence up front and Bruschi's leadership. Slow starts were something of a Belichick trademark; each year he and his staff and his team recognized that, in his words, they had to "figure out who we are," what worked with the personnel at hand, and what did not. But in 2009, they never quite seemed to gel into anything more than a faceless collection of players with little personality. Worst of all, the Patriots didn't intimidate or scare anyone on either side of the ball anymore. They never won more than three games in a row and failed to build any momentum over the course of the season. Although they still finished 10-6, whatever advantage their reputation had given them was gone. They managed to win the division title, but a final-game loss to the Texans cost them a possible three seed in the playoffs and forced them to play in the wild-card game against the always tough Baltimore Ravens.

It was an ugly end. Adam Kilgore summed it up in the *Globe*: "Disaster always had stayed foreign to these Patriots, some evil force that only other teams needed to worry about. They might not win. They never would collapse and embarrass themselves. . . . And then yesterday came. . . . In their first playoff game of the new decade, the Patriots may have lost the final bit of the dynastic mystique they created in the last one."

The Ravens thoroughly dominated New England, Ray Rice scoring on the first play from scrimmage. The Ravens raced to a 24–0 lead in the first quarter and then laughed themselves silly to a 33–14 win. By the end, Pats fans were even booing Tom Brady. "The final three quarters," wrote Kilgore, "were little more than calisthenics."

Desperate times led to desperate measures. Before the spying scandal, the Patriots' record in the playoffs under Belichick had been 12-2, but since then, it was 2-2. Although many other things could and would change, the only certainties were that Belichick and Brady weren't going anywhere, the fortunes of each man tied to the other. But going forward, the Patriots had to do something different.

The change began in the 2010 draft when the Patriots made an uncharacteristic move. Receiver Randy Moss, displeased with his contract, was making noise about wanting an extension, which the Patriots were loath to give him. They could have done so—theoretically there was no salary cap in 2010 because after the 2008 season the NFL had pulled out of the collective bargaining agreement—but the league warned teams to stay inside the parameters that existed in 2009, and most did, including the Patriots. Realizing that Moss's days in New England were numbered, Belichick seemed to conclude that the competitive advantage of providing Brady with a premier deep threat had passed. After all, where was the Super Bowl ring they had expected Moss to deliver? He'd put up numbers and would end his Patriots career with 259 catches, but he hadn't delivered the expected championship. Belichick seemed more comfortable with a more controlled passing game anyway, one that called for Brady to select from a number of shorter passing routes designed to enable him to hit receivers on the move. It was cheaper too. Superstars like Moss were costly.

On the other hand, Wes Welker had been a revelation to Patriot fans. Before he arrived in New England by way of a trade with the Dolphins, he was little known. In New England, he flourished as the Patriots tailored their offense to take advantage of his strengths—his quickness and his hands—rather than cover for the weakness posed by his short stature, which made it problematic for Welker to work the sidelines downfield against taller defensive backs. Instead of stretching the field, as they had done with Moss, the Patriots spread it out, using crossing patterns and slants over the middle so that Welker, working from the slot, could choose his own routes. If the linebackers played tight, Welker would find space between them and the defensive backs. If they dropped back, well, he could cut his routes short and stay underneath. He played like the smallest kid in the backyard football game,

the one who could catch the ball between the bushes: he was fast enough to beat most linebackers to the ball and adept enough to find the seams between deeper coverage.

The approach tended to put the ball in Welker's hands on a dead run in the middle of the field, where he had room to move after the catch—more than half his yardage came after making a reception, a category in which he was usually among the league leaders. Of course, it also exposed him to more punishment. The *Herald*'s Gerry Callahan accurately described Welker's role as running across the middle catching passes "while

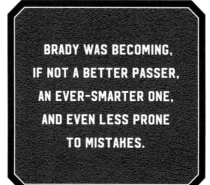

BRADY WAS BECOMING, IF NOT A BETTER PASSER, AN EVER-SMARTER ONE, AND EVEN LESS PRONE TO MISTAKES.

avoiding the assorted 270-pound sociopaths who would like nothing more than to knock him into the nearest head-trauma unit." That was why so few teams tried the same approach—and none nearly as often as New England—but that didn't seem to concern the Patriots.

And Brady? Well, Brady was becoming, if not a better passer, an ever-smarter one, and even less prone to mistakes. The game never seemed too fast for him. Besides, shorter throws were less risky, harder to intercept, and allowed him to get rid of the ball more quickly. Besides making it easier for the line to provide protection and prevent him from receiving too much punishment, the approach also led to longer, more sustained drives that kept the opposing team's offense on the sideline. Ever since Brady took over as quarterback in 2001, he has benefited from a Patriot offense that's designed to enhance what he does best and has evolved as Brady has evolved, not one that has ever required him to try to do what he cannot.

But as Moss moved toward the exit ramp, Brady would need options other than Welker. With the Patriots at their usual draft disadvantage, there was no obvious solution.

But there were some intriguing possibilities. University of Arizona tight end Rob Gronkowski played as if football were another version of the WWF. Tall, faster than he looked, and incredibly strong, Gronkowski came from an uber-athletic family (brothers Dan, Chris, and

Former New England Patriots video operator Matthew Walsh (*center*) leaves NFL headquarters in New York City with his counsel, Michael N. Levy (*left*), following a meeting with NFL commissioner Roger Goodell on May 13, 2008. Walsh was there to discuss the Patriots' videotaping practices in the Spygate controversy.

Glenn all would play in the NFL, brother Gordon played pro baseball, and their father had tried out for the USFL) and created matchup problems wherever he was lined up. He was faster than the linebackers generally assigned to cover him, taller than the defensive backs, and stronger than them all. Like Moss, Gronkowski could go up and get balls no one else could reach. Although his NFL pre-draft assessment cautioned that he "lacks the elusiveness to make people miss after catch," that didn't matter much—at six-six and 265 pounds, Gronkowski was hard to tackle one-on-one, usually staying on his feet until the accumulated weight of several pursuers brought him down.

He shouldn't have been available to the Pats, but after catching 16 TD passes his first two years at Arizona, a back injury early in his junior year caused him to miss the 2009 season and his pro prospects dropped. But then he showed 4.6 speed in the 40-yard dash and a 34-inch vertical leap in the NFL Combine, leading several teams to consider him the best athlete in the draft, not unlike the previous generation's Russ Francis, another player who missed his final season of college football. Still, concerns over Gronk's back lingered, causing him to slip to the second round, and when the Patriots saw he was still available, they traded up to grab him with the forty-second pick.

In any other year, they probably would have passed on selecting another tight end in the same draft. But anxiety over Gronkowski's back—and another intriguing uber-athlete falling through the cracks—caused the Patriots to reassess.

While Gronkowski sat out the 2009 collegiate season, Florida tight end Aaron Hernandez had emerged as the best in the nation, a first-team All-American and winner of the John Mackey Award as the premier college tight end. Although not as big as Gronkowski, Hernandez, six-two and almost 250 pounds, was every bit the athlete Gronkowski was, smaller but also faster. But if Gronkowski exuded a frat boy, hard-partying, but essentially goofy persona, Hernandez was a mercurial, brooding, and occasionally menacing presence who gave many teams pause. His college career had been marked by trouble off the field and behavior that teammates and coaches often found troubling and sometimes frightening. One-on-one, Hernandez could be charming, doing and saying all the right things, but once he got off the field, it was as if he had to prove his street cred. He constantly put himself in situations that intersected with gangs, crime, and drugs.

Quarterback Matt Cassel, faced with the impossible task of filling Tom Brady's shoes, performed remarkably and led the Patriots to eleven wins.

Normally, the Patriots wouldn't have been interested. Myra Kraft hadn't let her husband forget the drafting of Christian Peter, and in the wake of that fiasco Kraft had told his coaching staff, "I don't want thugs and hoodlums here." But Myra Kraft, recently diagnosed with ovarian cancer, was less involved now, and over time the Patriots had become a little less concerned with what football people euphemistically call "character issues," such as drug use, assault, and domestic violence. Five years without a title made it a lot easier for the Patriots to overlook such concerns.

And in Hernandez, the Patriots knew exactly what they were getting. He had tested positive for marijuana use at Florida, and in predraft testing he'd failed several more drug tests. But as many as one-third of draftees that year tested positive for pot, and before the draft, at his agent's behest, Hernandez had sent teams an apparently heartfelt letter promising to wise up: "My coaches have told you that nobody worked harder than me . . . the only X-factor is concerns about my use of recreational drugs." He then volunteered for extra testing and promised to give up a portion of his salary if he failed. It was an empty promise the NFLPA would never allow, but it left an impression.

Smoking pot, however, was the least of the Patriots' worries with Hernandez . . . or at least it should have been. Hernandez had grown up in Bristol, Connecticut, a Patriots fan who wore Bledsoe's number 11 jersey. He followed in the footsteps of his older brother, Jonathan, who played quarterback for UConn. Aaron, a receiver, became one of the greatest high school players in Connecticut history. But after his father died unexpectedly in 2006, Aaron Hernandez's behavior began to change. He was well known in Bristol, where others basked in his celebrity and took advantage of the fact that authorities tended to look the other way when he was around. Heavily recruited, he went to Florida under Coach Urban Meyer, a place where he was surrounded by temptation of all kinds and even more sheltered, as a pampered college athlete, from the consequences. There Hernandez had ever more serious run-ins with the law.

In the spring of 2007, after drinking at a restaurant and refusing to pay the bill, Hernandez was thrown out. On his way to the door, he punched an employee in

Patriots Andre Tippett, John Hannah (*right*), and owner Robert Kraft (*center*) pose with Tippett's bust after his induction with the Class of 2008 at the Pro Football Hall of Fame Enshrinement Ceremony at Fawcett Stadium.

the head, rupturing the man's eardrum, but a potential charge of felony battery was settled on deferred prosecution. Later that year, he was implicated and investigated in regard to a shooting at a stoplight after leaving a nightclub, but he refused to cooperate and was never charged.

The NFL had looked into Hernandez's past and found it full of red flags, including a penchant for hanging out with what they later described as "unsavory characters," in both Florida and his hometown. A predraft psychological assessment gave him the lowest possible score in social maturity, describing him as prone to "challenge acceptable behavior." There was a reason, after all, a first-round talent was still available in the fourth round. Several teams were so concerned that they had dropped him from their draft boards entirely—which isn't to say they might not still have been willing to sign him as a free agent and take their chances.

But Belichick, who later called Hernandez "a player that we, quite frankly, were surprised to have the opportunity to draft," looked past his reputation. Where others saw potential trouble, Belichick saw only potential. Of course, no one could have predicted that Hernandez would become a murderer, but Kraft's later claim that the

Patriots were "duped" by Hernandez isn't truly accurate. His selection was emblematic of the anxiety surrounding the franchise at the time, and their resulting willingness to take a risk. The Patriots needed to win, and Hernandez could help—it was that simple.

In training camp and during the 2009 exhibition season, the Patriots began to figure out what they had. Rather than have Hernandez and Gronkowski compete for the same position, they began to use them simultaneously, sometimes splitting Hernandez out and sometimes utilizing him as an H-back, allowing the Patriots to expand the number of options available to Brady and giving opposing defenses matchup problems. As former Ravens coach Bill Billick later explained to the *Herald*'s Dan Ventura, "Rob Gronkowski is a transformational figure at the tight end because of the size, athleticism, the speed and the ability to catch the ball," and pairing him with Hernandez put everyone else's defense in a quandary. As Billick put it, if defenses responded with a nickel package of five defensive backs, Hernandez and Gronkowski made it possible to "run the ball down your throat, [and] if they put in their big people, I'm gonna throw the ball on every down." In tandem, with the best quarterback in football wisely distributing the ball, the two players gave the Patriots options they previously did not have. In 2009, the Pats had used a two–tight end setup on only 38 percent of offensive plays, near the league average. Over the next two years, that figure would almost double, to far and away the greatest percentage in the NFL.

Once they figured that out, the Patriots didn't wait around. Running back Laurence Maroney, an oft-injured disappointment, was dealt away on September 24, 2010. One week after Randy Moss caught two touchdown passes against Buffalo to earn Player of the Game honors from *Boston Herald* readers and become only the second receiver to score 150 or more touchdowns in a career, he was never a target and didn't catch a pass in a 41–14 win over Miami. If the receiver was being sent a message, he got it. Moss, thirty-three years old and in the final year of a three-year, $27 million contract, demanded a trade.

The Patriots soon accommodated him, sending him to the Vikings for a third-round pick. On October 12, they traded for Moss-lite, bringing back Deion Branch from the Seahawks for a fourth-rounder. After a few weeks getting to know each other again, the Patriots offense took off. They not only went undefeated for the rest of the season after a 34–14 loss to Cleveland on November 7, but scored more than 30 points in eight consecutive games. As the season wound down, the defense began to match the offense in dominance, holding four of their last five opponents to a touchdown or less.

In this new two–tight end configuration, Brady was magnificent. He didn't throw any interceptions after the Moss trade and connected for a total of 36 touchdowns, including 22 in the second half of the season. Just as Billick noted, when the defense chose to cover the pass, Danny Woodhead and BenJarvus Green-Ellis found plenty of room to run. And when the defense played tight, Brady shredded them, peppering the field with passes to Welker over the middle, Branch downfield, and his two new tight ends everywhere else.

The Pats began the postseason as the number-one seed in the AFC. The odds-on favorites to make the Super Bowl, they had become an unstoppable force and, in recent weeks, an immovable object as well. When the Jets dumped the Colts in the wild-card round to earn the right to travel to Gillette for the divisional playoff, Pats fans began salivating. Although the Jets had topped the Patriots earlier in the season, in a later meeting New England had lashed New York 45–3 as Brady threw for four touchdowns and the Patriots intercepted quarterback Mark Sanchez three times. That game left the Jets thinking the Patriots deliberately ran up the score. "I came in to kick his butt and he kicked mine," Jets coach Rex Ryan said afterwards. "Obviously we got outcoached, got outplayed, got our butt kicked. I don't know what else you can say about it." In New England, everyone was saying the Super Bowl was almost a given.

Then it turned comical. In an only-because-of-the-internet moment, in late December the *New York Daily News* discovered that photos of Rex Ryan's barefoot wife appeared on a foot fetish website. The Jets coach apparently had, well, a thing for feet.

What could possibly be better than to see the Pats' rival in such a humiliating posture? All New England fell over itself making jokes at Ryan's expense, fueling sports talk radio for days. Ryan called it a personal matter, but in the runup to the game, Patriots fans became experts in jokes made at the expense of pedicures and podiatry.

The Patriots as an organization prided themselves on being above such matters, but Welker blew that out of the water at a pregame press conference when he made at least ten foot references at Ryan's expense, describing other receivers as having "great feet" and saying things like "you have to be on your toes" in the playoffs. That had the unintended consequence of making the issue not so much about Ryan as Welker's cruel lack of discretion.

> THE PATS BEGAN THE POSTSEASON AS THE NUMBER-ONE SEED IN THE AFC. THE ODDS-ON FAVORITES TO MAKE THE SUPER BOWL, THEY HAD BECOME AN UNSTOPPABLE FORCE AND, IN RECENT WEEKS, AN IMMOVABLE OBJECT AS WELL.

The Jets responded by circling around their coach, and when a New York player threatened to target Welker during the game, the league ordered everyone to knock it off. It all became a distraction the Patriots did not need. Belichick was so ticked off that he benched Welker for the first series of the divisional playoff game.

He may as well have benched the whole damn team—or benched no one at all. Either way, it would have made little difference. For the second year in a row, the Patriots were eliminated from the playoffs by losing the opening game at home. New England scored only three points in the first half, and after Patrick Chung botched a fake punt by fumbling the snap, the Patriots never really recovered. The Jets' pass rush hounded Brady all day, forcing them to use Gronkowski in a more traditional role and keeping Hernandez off the field. Trailing 21–11 early in the fourth quarter, the Pats played with all the urgency of an honor student taking an open-book test. They inexplicably chose to run and chewed eight valuable minutes off the clock without scoring. A late touchdown made the final a slightly more respectable 28–21. The Patriots ended the season with one foot in their mouth and another kicking their rear end.

That ran Belichick's record with the Patriots to 126-50, a winning percentage of .716, by then ranking eighth all-time, tied with Hall of Famer Paul Brown. The AP still named him Coach of the Year, but it was an empty title that meant nothing really, sort of a lifetime achievement award. Meanwhile, the only award that mattered, the Lombardi Trophy, was won by Green Bay.

Most off-seasons the Patriots looked to load up on free agents, sort them out during mini-camp, and move forward. By the start of official training camp, they generally had a pretty good idea whether or not they had found a gem or two among the free agent scrum. In March 2011, however, a labor dispute resulted in a lockout, halting practices until late July and leaving the Patriots uncertain. They needed help on defense, particularly on the line with the pass rush and in the defensive backfield, but they started out behind and never really caught up. That was a problem leaguewide, as defenses everywhere were left scrambling. Although the *Globe* noted at the start of camp that "it's a safe bet he [Belichick] has a carefully constructed plan for how his team will approach the preseason and prepare for the regular season," that really didn't prove to be the case.

Fortunately for the Patriots, their high-powered offense—at least as good as the 2007 version, if not better—was little changed and came together quickly. At the start of the season, they were already operating at high efficiency. But the defense? Not so much. The Patriots started the season racing to outscore the opposition and hoping that, somehow, their defense would eventually catch up. It never really did, but the offense was more potent than ever.

They were helped again by a series of rule changes. The NFL, too late in the estimation of many observers, began to recognize the danger of concussions and attempted to make a few adjustments to limit risk. Rule changes moved the kickoff from the 30 to the 35 to cut down on the number of returns and high-speed collisions. Another change determined that any hit to a quarterback's head, even accidental, would result in a personal foul. In addition, any defensive player caught leaving his feet and making contact with an offensive player's head or neck would be flagged for unnecessary roughness and could be ejected from the game. Officials were told to err on the side of caution and, when in doubt, throw a flag.

The changes were welcome, long overdue, and unfortunately far too late for many players. Concussions had started to spike in the 1970s when increases in player size, the proliferation of unforgiving artificial playing surfaces, and an increase in the number of games played each season, in both professional football and college football, combined to escalate the risks of playing the game. The number of players who have either died prematurely or suffered emotional or behavioral issues after retiring from the game during this era is vast. Although, as of April 2018, Aaron Hernandez, Ronnie Caveness, Junior Seau, Chuck Osborne, Dennis Wirgowski, Bill Lenkaitis, Mosi Tatupu, and Kevin Turner are the only former Patriots players known to have suffered from chronic traumatic encephalopathy (CTE), that's solely because diagnosis can only be confirmed after death. One hundred and ten of 111 players so far tested have been confirmed to have had CTE, with fifty-one the average age of death. In researching the biographies of dozens of former Patriots, one cannot help but be struck by the number of

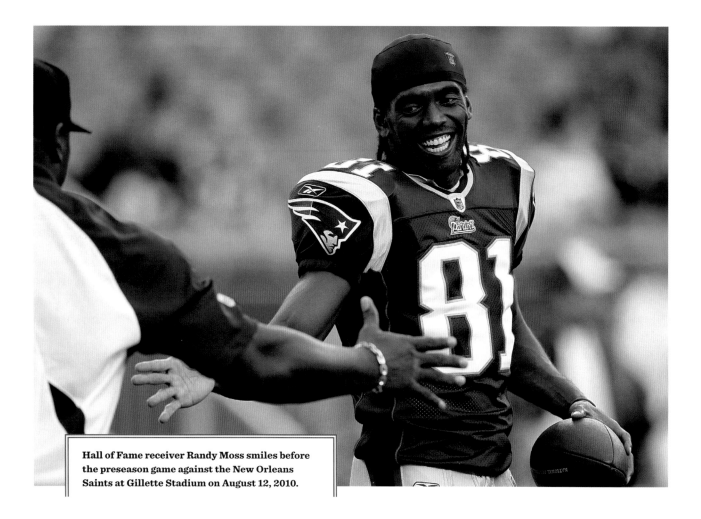

Hall of Fame receiver Randy Moss smiles before the preseason game against the New Orleans Saints at Gillette Stadium on August 12, 2010.

them who built careers and lives away from football but then suffered setbacks that now appear concussion-related. Players like Ted Johnson, Nick Buoniconti, Jim Plunkett, and Tim Fox—who describes himself as "a living, breathing petri dish for CTE research"—are just a few of the many who now suspect that they suffer from the effects of CTE, and that number is destined to grow with the passage of time.

These rule changes also helped Brady, who is fortunate to have played his entire career during an era when protecting the quarterback from contact has become increasingly important, a boon to not only his numbers but his longevity. The new rules, plus one more year with Gronkowski, Hernandez, Green-Ellis, and the others working together, made a huge difference for the quarterback.

The Patriots started the 2011 season in a sprint that left defenses gasping. The old adage that "defense wins championships" was fading—and quickly. The end result would be a few super-teams and a whole lot of others scrambling to keep up and stay around .500.

The Patriots' approach to the season was as simple as it was predictable: jump ahead, try to outlast the opposition, and hope the defense slowed the other team down.

On July 20, Myra Kraft had passed away from ovarian cancer. The organization dedicated the season to the owner's wife, whose family fortune had provided the fuel for the franchise and whose moral code had, at times, influenced the team's approach. Although she'd warmed to the game over the years and served as something of a mother figure to some players, she still saw it as more of a diversion from the more important things in life rather than a metaphor for life itself. Her legacy would not be the football team as much as her philanthropy, through which she'd often used access to the Patriots as leverage to extract even more dollars from well-heeled donors to the dozens of organizations she supported. The Patriots would play the season with her initials, MHK, emblazoned on their uniforms.

His wife's death also led Robert Kraft to begin to take a more active public role and take more credit for his team's success. While Myra was alive, her presence and public commitment to philanthropy and social justice had helped him keep the Patriots in perspective. She had never felt that football was the most important part of their lives. It has been said that becoming an owner in the NFL today is the American equivalent of royalty—to this point, Kraft had generally been far more understated

than most other NFL owners. But in Myra's absence, Kraft seemed to embrace the role of an NFL owner with increasing zeal and act with more of the swagger of his peers.

For most of the season, the Patriots' opponents saw Myra Kraft's initials on a dizzying array of receivers as Brady threw early and often. Although Gronkowski played the majority of downs as the primary tight end, he was joined by Hernandez on almost 75 percent of all plays. Welker remained Brady's primary target, the object of no fewer than 173 pass attempts, but Hernandez and Gronkowski weren't far behind, Hernandez being targeted 113 times and Gronkowski 124, each man catching around 70 percent of those attempts.

It was a revolutionary approach, which the Patriots seemed to realize as the season unfolded. With one tight

Tight end Aaron Hernandez makes a catch over the middle as New York Jets cornerback Dwight Lowery defends. Hernandez, a Connecticut native, later was tried and convicted for murder and took his own life while in prison.

end on the field, Brady and the Patriots' offense were average at best, Brady throwing only eight touchdowns and getting intercepted eight times. But when both tight ends played, paired with Welker and Branch, who was targeted 90 times himself, they were nearly unstoppable. Brady threw for 31 touchdowns with only four interceptions as Gronkowski and Hernandez combined for 169 receptions. In the red zone, Gronkowski became a favorite target, catching a remarkable 17 touchdowns as defensive backs simply found it impossible to outleap him for the ball. A player and personality almost beyond description, Gronk quickly became a fan favorite and cult hero, a kind of postmodern Babe Ruth: guileless and almost impossible not to like, no matter how over the top he acted off the field, where his one-man party persona found plenty of companions. *Sports Illustrated*'s Chris Ballard called him "a Yeti loosed . . . the best tight end ever; an overrated

product of the Patriots system; a breath of fresh air; just another attention-seeking athlete. He is idiot, jester, hero, foil, buffoon and prodigy, the embodiment of a pathetic bro-centric fraternity culture, a regrettable symbol of the TMZ age." And that wasn't the half of it.

The Patriots blasted through the regular season, losing only three times: in week three to the Bills, when Brady uncharacteristically threw four interceptions and Hernandez sat out with a knee injury; then to the Steelers, a game in which Pittsburgh managed to hold the ball for almost 40 minutes; and finally, to the Giants as New York's rush kept Hernandez off the field for long stretches and Brady had his worst game of the year. But after those last two losses in weeks eight and nine, the Patriots were overpowering during the second half of the year, going undefeated and scoring more than 31 points in all but one contest.

Patriot Niko Koutouvides celebrates after Billy Cundiff (*center*) of the Baltimore Ravens misses a game-tying field goal late in the fourth quarter during the AFC championship game at Gillette Stadium on January 22, 2012.

In the divisional playoff, they faced the Denver Broncos, who were riding high on the magic of quarterback Tim Tebow. The fan favorite had somehow managed to be absolutely dismal for the first three and a half quarters of every game and then sensational in the final minutes, leading the Broncos to a series of stirring wins. The league hadn't seen anything like it since Brady took over for Bledsoe.

The Patriots, having none of it, started out as if the postseason would simply provide another venue for their stellar play. On only the fourth play from scrimmage, New England came out in a no-back package; Belichick later explained, "We didn't have any backs in the game in that personnel grouping; we just had the three receivers and the two tight ends. You see all those receivers on the field, and you're not really thinking too much about the running game defensively, so we tried to pop a couple runs in there just to keep them honest." That they did: Hernandez, given the ball from a deep slot, ran for a 43-yard gain.

Hernandez set the tone as the Pats utterly obliterated Denver and Tebow. Brady was magnificent, throwing for six touchdowns, three to Gronkowski and one to Hernandez, as the two tight ends completely befuddled the Broncos. Hernandez finished with 61 yards on the ground to lead New England on only five carries and added another 55 in the air.

• • •

If there was any team that seemed capable of thwarting the Patriot offense, it was the Ravens, their opponent in the AFC championship game. Baltimore had allowed fewer than 700 yards in passes to tight ends all year long—together, Hernandez and Gronkowski had more than 2,200. Baltimore simply took a different approach than most other teams, which usually added a fifth defensive back against the two–tight end package. The Ravens stubbornly stuck with their usual 3-4 alignment. Of course, when one of those defenders included Ray Lewis, widely considered the best linebacker of his generation, the Ravens could do things on defense that few other teams could do—Lewis was almost the equivalent of two defenders in one. Despite missing four games to injury that season, the sixteen-year veteran had still led the Ravens in tackles and led a bone-crushing defense

After the Patriots defeat the Baltimore Ravens to win the AFC championship, owner Robert Kraft gestures skyward in tribute to his late wife, Myra, upon being presented with the Lamar Hunt Trophy.

that Footballoutsiders.com ranked the best in the league. Yet as the *New York Post* noted, "The fate of the Ravens in Sunday's AFC Championship is tied directly to how their dominating defense handles the Patriots' two game-changing tight ends."

In a tight contest, that turned out to be true, but not in the way anyone had foreseen. Although it had not bothered him against Denver, Brady had injured his throwing shoulder in the final game of the regular season and then sat out most of practice in the week before the AFC championship. From the start, it was obvious that he was a little off, and Baltimore's defense was able to take advantage, bottling up the Patriots' attack.

Baltimore, in fact, should have won the game. Forced to run, the Patriots were able to move the ball, but found it difficult to find the end zone. After a Ravens touchdown in the third quarter gave them a 17–16 lead, Danny Woodhead fumbled the kickoff and the Ravens cashed in with a field goal to make the score 20–16. Then, late in the third quarter, after Gronkowski hauled in a pass from Brady and fought to stay upright, the Ravens' Bernard Pollard pulled him to the ground and Gronk twisted his right ankle and was forced from the game. Nevertheless, the Patriots were able to grind it out and punch the ball in, Brady scoring on a quarterback sneak to put the Pats ahead 23–20.

More than eleven minutes remained, and for the rest of the game both teams seemed to be doing their best to lose, Joe Flacco throwing an interception on the next drive and then Brady giving the ball back with an interception of his own.

The outcome came down to a final drive by the Ravens. With less than a minute remaining and the ball on the New England 14, the Ravens, out of time-outs, had to go for a score. On back-to-back plays, the Patriots' Sterling Moore just managed to break up a potential game-winning pass. Then, as overtime looked inevitable, Baltimore kicker Billy Cundiff missed a 32-yard chip shot that would have tied the game and the Patriots were headed to the Super Bowl.

The Ravens hadn't managed to shut down the two tight ends—Hernandez had collected four first downs—but they'd knocked Gronkowski out of the contest, which proved to be the biggest play of the game. Pollard, who'd made the tackle, secured his title on the play as all-time Patriots killer. He'd also been the tackler when Brady injured his knee and when Welker went down with a similar injury. Gronkowski made him three-for-three.

This was no "tape it up and get out there" type of injury. It was a high ankle sprain that probably included ligament damage, an injury that usually took four to six weeks to heal. But this was Gronk, football's Incredible Hulk. With two weeks to heal, most Pats fans, if not the Patriot coaching staff, expected him to play.

Over the next two weeks it was easy to feel confident, because the Pats' Super Bowl opponent would be Tom Coughlin and Eli Manning's New York Giants,

a team few had expected to make the playoffs in 2011, much less the Super Bowl. They'd appeared to be the Patriots' equal with their 24–20 win in week nine, but they'd lost five of their next six, squeaking into the playoffs as a wild-card team after winning their division with a victory over Dallas in the season's final week. Their defense, led by Jason Pierre-Paul, the league's best pass rusher, made them a dangerous opponent, but Manning had been maddeningly inconsistent all year before gaining traction late, finally finding wide receivers Hakeem Nicks and, most notably, Victor Cruz.

Still, after the Giants beat Atlanta in the wild-card game, observers were shocked when they dumped both the Packers, 15-1 in the regular season, and the 49ers to earn the right to travel to Houston for the Super Bowl.

Most felt that the Patriots got off lucky in the pairing, as they avoided both Aaron Rodgers, the Packers quarterback who set a host of records in 2011, and the rugged 49ers, the NFC equivalent of the Ravens. The Giants? Well, among other things, they were the worst rushing team in the NFL, and no team had ever won the Super Bowl after winning only nine regular-season games. Besides, the Patriots were playing for Myra Kraft and history, with a chance to join the 49ers, Cowboys, Steelers, and Packers as the only teams up to that point to win at least four Super Bowls. Of course, a defeat would put them on another list, one with Minnesota, Denver, and Buffalo, as the only teams to lose four Super Bowls, but no one was talking about that. There was something to be said for consistency—either way, no team had ever played in so many Super Bowls. But the NFL is a zero-sum league, and Belichick and Brady had set a standard for a franchise that measured success in Super Bowls, nothing else. They were now like baseball's Yankees: anything less than a title was, well, just another loss.

Brady's shoulder remained sore, but Gronkowski proved to be almost superhuman: he was able to play, although not to his usual standard. He became just another guy, still six-six, but unable to get free or do much once he did. In combination, those factors were just enough to give the Giants a chance.

New York got off fast, knowing that the way to get to Brady, particularly a diminished Brady forced to play without his usual arsenal, was to put on the pressure. They delivered early, forcing him into an intentional grounding call in the end zone for a safety, then scoring on a touchdown pass to Victor Cruz on a do-over after Cruz fumbled the ball away but the Giants retained the ball when the Patriots were flagged for having twelve men on the field. The Giants led 9–0, and New England was reeling.

But these were still the Patriots, right? After a Gostkowski field goal, with only four minutes remaining in the half, Brady went 11-for-11 on a drive that included four completions to Hernandez and ended with a four-yard pass to Danny Woodhead to give New England a 10–9 lead.

That's just how the Patriots draw it up. When given the opportunity, they usually defer to the opposition on the opening kickoff, reasoning that if they can score late in the first half, getting the ball back to start the second half can provide a devastating dose of momentum.

So it was again. Brady continued to click on the opening drive of the second half, with Hernandez scoring on a 12-yard pass and giving Myra Kraft's initials on his

Lightning does strike twice: New York Giant Mario Manningham makes a 38-yard catch versus Patriots Patrick Chung and Sterling Moore to help lead the Giants to a 21–17 victory at Lucas Oil Stadium in Super Bowl XLVI.

chest a pat afterward. With a 17–9 lead, Pats fans began to relax. All was right with the world.

Until it wasn't. Just when everyone expected the Patriots to continue to roll, they rolled to a stop. Their next three possessions ended in two quick punts and then an interception. Meanwhile, the Giants controlled the ball for minutes at a time, knocking down two field goals to make the score 17–15.

With just over nine minutes remaining, the Patriots got the ball back once again and smartly moved it down the field to the Giants' 44. One more pass could put them within field goal range or keep the drive going for a touchdown.

To this point, Welker had been targeted seven times by Brady and caught all seven—not unexpected after 122 regular-season catches. On the next play, he burst downfield, then cut across the middle on a slant, wide open. Brady threw, a touch behind him, but the kind of catch that Welker would later call one that "I never drop."

He did this time, his error such a surprise that referee John Parry was heard exclaiming, "Whoa, that was the game." After another incompletion, the Patriots had to punt.

Still, with 3:46 remaining and the Giants pinned on their own 12, all the Patriots had to do was hold on. According to the *Daily News*, before the Pats took the field for that series, Belichick had gathered his defense together and reminded them: "This is still a Cruz and Nicks game . . . those are still the guys. Make them go to Manningham, make them go to Pascoe, all right. But let's make sure we get Cruz and Nicks." Unless Manning hit a big play to either of his two main targets, Belichick was confident his defense could stop New York.

Maybe the Giants heard him, because on first down Manning dropped back and saw the Pats in their Cover-2 alignment, with both Nicks and Cruz covered to the right. Then he spotted Mario Manningham darting

past rookie cornerback Sterling Moore on a go route as Patrick Chung scrambled to get over from his position in the middle of the field.

The ball dropped in a perfect arc to the perfect place, Manningham's fingertips, with his feet barely in bounds, just before Chung could get there. It was a 38-yard completion, the longest play of the game. With Belichick standing only a few yards away, it was an in-your-face moment.

Patriots fans went from a combination of exultation and expectation to barely being able to exhale. All the Giants needed was another 20 yards or so and they could take the lead with a field goal. The Patriots might still have a chance for a last-minute drive, but only if they got the ball back with time on the clock.

Manning moved New York down the field, targeting Manningham on the next three plays before a completion to Nicks pushed the Giants even closer to the goal line. With 1:09 left, it was first down and goal to go. Ahmad Bradshaw pushed forward for a yard as it suddenly seemed obvious that the Giants could run the clock down and kick a last-second field goal, leaving New England no time to respond.

Finding themselves in a quandary, the Patriots called a precious time-out, which left them only one more for the rest of the game. They needed the ball with some time left on the clock. So the Patriots made the kind of call that only a Belichick team dares to make: let the Giants score a touchdown. Now. They reasoned that it would be better to have a minute remaining and the whole field available to Brady to get the Pats into the end zone for a tie than to allow the Giants to hold the ball and try a no-doubt-about-it field goal with little or no time left. At least this way gave them a chance.

Bradshaw took the handoff on the next play . . . and no one wanted to tackle him. He picked his way to the goal line, arms wrapped tightly around the ball, and

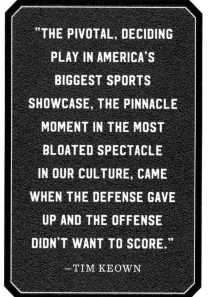

"THE PIVOTAL, DECIDING PLAY IN AMERICA'S BIGGEST SPORTS SHOWCASE, THE PINNACLE MOMENT IN THE MOST BLOATED SPECTACLE IN OUR CULTURE, CAME WHEN THE DEFENSE GAVE UP AND THE OFFENSE DIDN'T WANT TO SCORE."

—TIM KEOWN

then stopped short of the line, as if uncertain what to do. As Tim Keown accurately described it for ESPN, "The pivotal, deciding play in America's biggest sports showcase, the pinnacle moment in the most bloated spectacle in our culture, came when the defense gave up and the offense didn't want to score." No Patriot rushed in to take Bradshaw's head off. Instead, they pulled up short, even shielding him from contact. Bradshaw finally turned and, as if uncertain he was doing the right thing, sort of fell backwards into the end zone. With the easiest and least enthusiastic touchdown run in Super Bowl history, the Giants took a 21–17 lead. Had Bradshaw not made it in on his own, Patriot linebacker Jerod Mayo later said, "We were going to drag him into the end zone."

That gave Brady time and a chance to turn back the clock, but those patented comebacks had been increasingly rare in January and February. And this time he had a sore arm and a limping tight end, and they needed a touchdown, not a field goal.

New England took over at the 20, but eight plays moved the ball only to the 49. With five seconds remaining, it was time to send up a prayer. Brady scrambled and, standing on the 40, threw the ball almost 70 yards downfield where four receivers and five defenders gathered in a scrum in the end zone. The high-arching pass seemed to stay in the air forever and then dropped nearly straight down, giving New England a chance as the ball momentarily bounced free. Gronkowski, playing on one leg, stretched out to pull it in, but even if he'd had two good legs and stood seven-six, it still would have eluded him.

The ball touched the ground, and the clock read 0:00, the final score 21–17. The Patriots had made history not for winning the most Super Bowls in NFL history, like they'd hoped to do, but for losing the most.

For a lot of other teams in a lot of other cities, that didn't sound bad. But not in New England, not anymore.

In New England, well, it *sucked*.

CHAPTER FOURTEEN

2012–2014

PATRIOTS RISING

In her 2012 AFC East preview in the *New York Times*, Judy Battista wrote: "Until Tom Brady and Bill Belichick retire, the only question is how deep the New England Patriots can go in the playoffs." A variation of those words appeared in many other prognostications.

Tom Brady and Julian Edelman celebrate after defeating the Seattle Seahawks 28–24 to win Super Bowl XLIX at University of Phoenix Stadium on February 1, 2015, in Glendale, Arizona.

EVEN AFTER THEIR LOSS TO THE GIANTS in Super Bowl XLVI, the Patriots remained favorites to win their division and make the playoffs, a virtual given in the Belichick-Brady era. Those words underlined both their greatest strength—consistency—and their greatest weakness—being a playoff team but not necessarily a Super Bowl championship team. Those words also reflected the Pats' greatest concern: just how much longer could the Belichick-Brady era continue, and what might follow it?

For all their success, the Patriots found themselves in an uncomfortable place, not unlike that of the Dallas Cowboys a generation before: a premier franchise, they were a championship-caliber team that, despite a string of Super Bowl appearances and titles, had gained a reputation as mere contenders. And underlying it all were the unanswered questions: Who was responsible for that success? Belichick? Brady? Both, or neither? And what

about Bob Kraft? Who was he without his coach and quarterback? Each of the three men had to wonder whether if not for the other two, he might be Just Another Guy.

Thus far, the Pats had shown themselves to be unusually adept at adapting to a changing NFL. Belichick had arrived in the league as a defensive wizard, but in his thirteenth season as head coach, he now found himself leading one of the most potent offenses in NFL history. Brady, too, had proved to be a master of evolution, transitioning from a conservative, safety-first quarterback into one of the most prolific and effective passers in the game. But in August 2012, he would turn thirty-five years old—ancient for an NFL quarterback. Was that still the way to win a championship?

Entering the 2012 season, the Patriots had little choice but to continue to go all in with their focus on offense, even as they were well positioned in the draft for a change. They added two defensive stalwarts, defensive end Chandler Jones and Alabama linebacker Dont'a Hightower, spending all but one draft pick on defensive players. At the same time, faced with the possibility of losing Wes Welker to free agency, the Pats designated Welker, whose 554 receptions over the last five years made him the most productive receiver in the NFL, with their franchise tag. That allowed both sides more time to reach a long-term agreement while still guaranteeing that the wide receiver would receive a hefty raise, to almost $10 million, albeit for only one year. Welker agreed, confident that he and the team would eventually reach a long-term deal, and tweeted, "Glad that I will be a Patriot in 2012, and hopefully '13, '14, '15, '16, '17, '18 . . ." While their two tight ends set them apart from other teams, it was Welker who made it impossible to key on only Gronkowski and Hernandez.

In midsummer, Gronkowski signed a six-year contract extension worth $54 million, including an $8 million bonus, and just before the start of the season Hernandez signed a five-year extension worth $40 million, including a $12.5 million bonus. For at least one more year, it appeared as if the key members of the Patriots' receiving corps would remain in place.

But the Patriots were also thinking past their wide receiver and envisioning the day when Welker would either leave or be injured. In 2009, the Pats had drafted Kent State quarterback Julian Edelman, not for his arm but for his legs, and over the past four seasons they had used the versatile player as a return man, a defensive back, and increasingly as a receiver, a clone of Welker. Beginning in 2012, Edelman's role would increase.

In recent years, every Patriots season had been following the predictable pattern of a slow start followed by a strong finish. Since 2001, they were a remarkable 73–15 in the second half. One reason for their slow starts, apart from their roster approach, was the game of musical chairs played each year with the coaching staff, which was in a kind of constant state of creative disruption.

In the NFL, even if a coach is under contract, he must be allowed to leave if he's offered a job with another team that would be considered a promotion—thus, Pats position coaches were poached to be coordinators, and coordinators to become head coaches, as other pro and college teams came calling in search of some Patriots

magic. Many also found success elsewhere as assistants, including those who had worked under Belichick when he was in New York as a coordinator or in Cleveland as head coach. But since Belichick joined the Patriots as head coach, not a single branch of his coaching tree had found his own resounding success as a head coach, particularly in the NFL. Eric Mangini failed with both the Jets and the Browns; *Sports Illustrated*'s Joe Posnanski called him "the worst NFL coach hire in 25 years." Josh McDaniels started off 6-0 with Denver, then went 7-22 and, in a not-so-shocking development, became embroiled in a videotape scandal of his own. Romeo Crennel enjoyed only one winning season in five years as coach of the Browns. Bill O'Brien, after going to Penn State, has spent four years as coach of the Texans, reaching the playoffs twice, but never winning more than nine games, accumulating a record of only 31-33. And Charlie Weis, widely credited with being an offensive coaching genius with New England, failed as head coach at both Notre Dame and Kansas and is no longer in coaching.

Some would eventually return to the Patriots, as McDaniels did in 2011, taking over as offensive coordinator a year later. But the end result has been that almost every year Belichick has been forced to promote an assistant coach into a new role from within or grab someone outside the organization. The transitions have almost always resulted in a feeling-out process for both the coach and the team.

Belichick is certainly not the only head coach whose protégés have failed to thrive. The assistants to vaunted Green Bay Packer coach Vince Lombardi, for instance, left a scant mark on the game as head coaches. It's not thoroughly surprising. Assistants are not hired for their head-coaching potential but for their teaching skills, work ethic, and subservience to a system. Patriots coaches are expected to be as focused as their boss and to do their job, not his. Belichick tends to hire what former assistant Mike Judge referred to as those with a "clean mind"—not former head coaches but younger assistants untethered to their own ideas, the coaching equivalent of the player free agents ignored by others, people Belichick can indoctrinate into his system.

Belichick's assistants usually start at the bottom, doing the grunt work of coaching—studying film and doing whatever else they're asked to do before slowly earning more responsibility and larger roles. They're never taught to be head coaches, which may explain their failure rate when they try: elsewhere, they inherit teams and systems not of their own making and usually lack the near-bottomless resources of the Patriots organization.

Their aspirations, first and foremost, are just to be in the game. For instance, 2017 Pats defensive coordinator Matt Patricia played guard at the Rensselaer Polytechnic Institute, hardly a sports powerhouse. He earned a degree in aeronautical engineering and worked as a sales rep selling industrial blowers before deciding that what he really wanted to do was stay in football. He worked a few years as a graduate assistant and assistant collegiate coach before taking a nondescript entry-level assistant job with the Patriots in 2004. Since then, he has worked his way up in the ever more specialized coaching

environment of the NFL, becoming, in turn, offensive line coach, linebacker coach, and safety coach before being named defensive coordinator in 2012. In that season, Patricia's promotion was one of at least six changes to the coaching staff, which also included the return of McDaniels to run the offense. Patricia has never been a head coach at any level but has already turned down one opportunity, with Cleveland, and after Super Bowl LII he accepted the top spot with the Lions.

This also may explain Belichick's earlier failure in Cleveland. He knew how to coach—his father taught him that—but he did not yet know how to be a head coach. Former Patriot punter Ken Walter, who served as a ball boy while Belichick was with the Browns, once said that while he was in Cleveland, "Don't think I didn't see a locker room that hated their coach there." Belichick learned to be a head coach under Parcells, not by emulating Parcells

For the five seasons Wes Welker was a Patriot, there may have been no more courageous player in the NFL as he sustained numerous hits serving as Tom Brady's go-to short-yardage receiver.

directly, but by learning how to impose his very different personality on an organization. Consider Belichick's management of press conferences. He is very different from Parcells, who became something of a profane yet unquestionably authentic entertainer, but the result has been the same. In a very different way, using his relative lack of personality as skillfully as Parcells used his own oversized persona, Belichick is always as much in control and in command as Parcells was.

The *Globe* has accurately noted that "the Patriots have seamlessly overcome numerous coaching changes." They're like a long-running play: the script and director stay the same, but the cast and crew constantly change. In the long run, that's worked about as well for Belichick and the Patriots as it has for Lin-Manuel Miranda and *Hamilton*.

The 2012 season began with one other disruption: the use of replacement referees as the NFL's usual complement of officials went on strike. The Pats also started the season a bit out of sync after Hernandez suffered a bad ankle sprain in the opener and would go on to miss six games.

"THE PATRIOTS HAVE SEAMLESSLY OVERCOME NUMEROUS COACHING CHANGES."
—BOSTON GLOBE

They weren't helped by the officiating. In week three, the Pats lost 31–30 to Baltimore on a controversial last-second field goal that officials determined went over the upright. The whole game had been teetering on the brink of anarchy because of the inconsistent officiating—television commentator Cris Collinsworth called it "ridiculous," and late in the game the Ravens crowd taunted the refs with a profane chant. After the game-ending field goal, Belichick confronted one replacement, screaming at him and physically trying to grab him as left the field.

The nadir came in week six when New England was defeated by none other than Pete Carroll's Seattle Seahawks and rookie quarterback Russell Wilson, 24–23. Like Belichick, Carroll had shown that perhaps he was not quite prepared in his first head-coaching jobs with the Jets and New England. He returned to the college ranks, where he turned around a once-proud University of Southern California program (albeit by

way of infractions that resulted in the school later being stripped of its 2004–2005 Bowl Championship Series title). But he did learn to be a head coach, and a wiser and now gray-haired Carroll rapidly found success upon his return to the NFL in Seattle.

Early on, the Pats' offense was out of balance as they tried to adjust to a hurry-up style designed to create favorable matchups, and the secondary was in its usual early season state of flux. But for the first time, blame began to be directed toward Belichick and Brady. In his weekly report card in the *Herald* after the Seattle game, Ron Borges gave both a C-minus. The whispers weren't very loud, but the math was irrefutable: the Patriots were 3-3, and both Brady and Belichick were getting older.

Fortunately for Belichick and Brady, the Pats would play the Jets the following week, and the release of a new book, Bryan O'Leary's *Spygate*, got a lot of play in New York before the game, providing the team with some extra motivation. O'Leary used statistical analysis to argue that the Patriots were still cheating, not only by illegal videotaping but also through a secret second radio frequency the Patriots allegedly used to communicate with Brady on the field.

Brady's horse whisperer was allegedly the mysterious Ernie Adams, who held the title of "research director" for the Pats. Adams, who has known Belichick since high school at Phillips Andover Academy, has been at the coach's side for nearly his entire career, and no one, except for Belichick, knows precisely what that role entails. In 1975, Adams worked as a scout for the Pats under Chuck Fairbanks, then joined the Giants organization, where he convinced Coach Ray Perkins to hire Belichick. He followed his classmate to Cleveland, where Art Modell reportedly offered $10,000 to anyone who could tell him what Adams did. Even longtime Patriots players don't really know what he does; Matt Light, who retired after the 2011 season, admitted to ESPN, "I'm not sure what Ernie does, but I'm sure whatever it is, he's good at it." All anybody ever really seems to know is that

Adams wears a headset in the press box with a direct line to Belichick and is heavily involved in scouting and draft preparation. Over the years, he has been the one constant in the ever-changing makeup of the team's staff. David Halberstam called him "Belichick's Belichick."

In any case, having the opposition think the Patriots might be cheating has proven to be as much of an edge for the franchise as actually cheating itself. Word of the book provided just enough extra "Pats versus the world" inspiration to get the team to the postseason. After Brady led the Pats to a late score to tie the Jets in regulation, Gostkowski kicked a field goal in overtime, and then, with the Jets driving, quarterback Mark Sanchez fumbled to deliver the Pats from the ignominy of falling below .500. The victory vaulted them into first place and allowed a reset to the season. New England took advantage of a weak schedule to go on their patented second-half surge, with Steve Ridley giving the team a running game while Welker, Edelman, Brandon Lloyd, and the returning Hernandez proved to be nearly as prolific as they were in 2011.

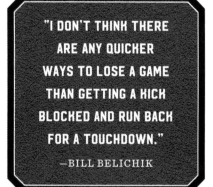

"I DON'T THINK THERE ARE ANY QUICKER WAYS TO LOSE A GAME THAN GETTING A KICK BLOCKED AND RUN BACK FOR A TOUCHDOWN."
—BILL BELICHIK

The Pats once again were racing through the second half, despite the fact that Gronkowski broke his arm in week eleven while blocking on an extra point late in a blowout 59–24 win over the Colts, a time when he probably shouldn't have even been on the field. Belichick tried to explain why the tight end was still in the game, saying, "I don't think there are any quicker ways to lose a game than getting a kick blocked and run back for a touchdown," but given the score, his reasoning sounded hollow. Gronkowski would not return until the final regular-season game, just in time to resume his pairing with Hernandez, albeit wearing a heavily padded brace and playing virtually one-handed, causing some to wonder if he was being rushed into action too soon.

The Pats finished 12-4, winning the division and earning a bye in the first playoff round. They ended with the league's most potent offense, worth 557 points and 6,846 total yards as their hurry-up approach took hold. But that offense also inspired controversy. Opponents claimed, once again, that the Pats pushed the rules as far as possible and then a bit more. The Patriots often used a flurry of replacements that made it unclear to the opponents exactly which players were eligible in each formation to run or receive the ball, using defensive tackles as tight ends and other players out of position. It was legal—the subs always reported to the officials—but no team had ever used the ploy so, well, offensively.

The Patriots' big worry was on the other side of the ball. They featured a bend-not-break defense that, despite giving up 400 or more yards six times, had been stingy giving up points. As Guregian wrote, "The Pats seem to have misplaced the formula that established them as a dynasty and allowed them to rule the early part of the decade. . . . The defense, usually dependable with the game on the line, hasn't always made that critical stop." The question entering the playoffs was whether or not the constant bending might cause a break.

It didn't do either in the divisional playoff against the Texans, who had been 11-1 before being blown out in week 13 and then losing three of their last four regular-season games. The Pats blew them out again, racing out to leads of 17–3 and 31–13 on their way to a 41–28 blowout. And as the Pats dashed ahead, Super Bowl dreams started dancing in the heads of fans like holiday sugarplums.

But, yet again, the dream burst short of a title. Because so did Gronkowski's left forearm. While the defense proved firm, Gronkowski, who had returned to the playing field only five weeks after first being injured, broke his arm again in the first quarter when he landed on it trying to catch a pass along the left sideline. Belichick dismissed questions about whether Gronk had returned too quickly, saying, "The doctors handle the medical decisions."

The Ravens, playing in Ray Lewis's final year, were not the least intimidated by the Patriots and in the days before the AFC championship game openly sparred with their opponents. "New England does some suspect stuff on offense," wrote linebacker Brendon Ayanbadejo on Twitter in regard to their substitutions. "Can't really respect it. Comparable to a cheap shot [before] a fight."

For the first half of the championship game, the Patriots looked like winners, bolting out to a 13–0 lead, and they were on their way to taking command when Welker dropped a key third-down pass. Then Baltimore quarterback Joe Flacco began playing like Brady often did, and Brady unfortunately started playing like Flacco when he was playing any team other than the Patriots. Steve Ridley suffered a concussion, and as he departed from the field, so did the Patriots' number-one rushing threat. Without Ridley and Gronkowski, Brady was without weapons, and New England went scoreless in the second half. The Ravens wreaked revenge for their losses in the previous years and walked off with a dominating 28–13 victory.

As bad as that was, it would soon get worse. The Patriots suffered one of the worst off-seasons in pro football history.

First, freed from the burden of playing, a shirtless Gronkowski had partied through the Super Bowl, including being filmed body-slamming at a nightclub. And then his oft-injured left forearm failed to heal correctly. He developed an infection, underwent surgery again in late February—his third since first breaking his arm—then underwent surgery on the arm a fourth time in May and had back surgery in June. He was proving to be remarkably fragile, but it was hard not to fault the Patriots for the lingering arm issue. Broken bones, like concussions, simply can't be played through.

While all this was taking place, negotiations between Welker and the Patriots broke down. When the Broncos offered him a two-year deal with $6 million annually, the Patriots chose not to match it and allowed him to leave. Although he'd again caught more than 100 passes, their decision to let him go was a simple calculation: he was reaching the end of his useful life. In fact, he would only have one more year as an effective receiver before retiring after the 2015 season, having suffered several concussions and failing a drug test for amphetamines. The Pats had already decided on an alternative when they signed veteran Danny Amendola—who, like Edelman, was something of a Welker clone—to a five-year deal worth $28 million. The parts and pieces would

change, but the show would go on and, in another victory over the salary cap, at a lower pay scale at that.

Ever since first signing Aaron Hernandez, the Patriots had told themselves and everyone else that, despite his issues coming out of college, in their system, under their supervision, he would be a changed man. That hadn't quite happened. Although Hernandez had performed on the field, he rarely interacted with teammates off the field and ran with a crew of hangers-on, wannabes, true gangsters, and drug dealers. He spent much of his free time partying, smoking blunts and chronic, high-powered weed or synthetics, often mixed with other drugs.

After Hernandez signed his big contract, trouble found him ever more easily. A searing report for *Rolling Stone* by Paul Solotaroff and Ron Borges later revealed that Hernandez had probably been involved in several shootings after joining the Patriots, including the killing of two men in a car in Boston's South End following an altercation at a nightclub. After another argument with his friend Alexander Bradley at a strip club, he also reportedly shot him in the face, costing Bradley an eye. Bradley refused to ID the shooter to police, but later filed suit against Hernandez in civil court.

As a variety of media reports would later reveal, the Patriots really didn't want to hear any bad news about their tight end prodigy, and when they did, they tended to look the other way. Solotaroff and Borges called the drafting of Hernandez part of the Patriots' growing "stoop-to-conquer" approach. They also wrote, "According to a source close to Hernandez, he flew to the NFL Combine in Indianapolis this past February and confided to Belichick that his life was in danger." One of Hernandez's attorneys even said that he asked to be traded to someplace where he'd be safer, only to be told that wasn't possible at the moment. After all, Gronkowski was hurt. Solotaroff and Borges wrote that Belichick admonished the tight end to "lay low, rent a safe house for a while," and told Hernandez that if there were "any more disruptions," he would be "traded or cut at the end of the 2013 season." Contacting the authorities might have saved a life, but hey, there was a football season to think of.

It did no good. Six weeks before training camp, Hernandez got into what appeared to be a minor argument at a nightclub with Odin Lloyd, the boyfriend of Shaneah Jenkins, who was the sister of Hernandez's fiancé, Shayanna Jenkins. The reason for the argument has never been ascertained for certain. According to some reports, it stemmed from one of Lloyd's friends apparently eyeballing Hernandez after learning from Lloyd that Hernandez might be bisexual.

Lloyd, a linebacker for the semipro Boston Bandits, was one Hernandez's more recent acquaintances, not a member of the problem crowd of lowlifes who usually ran with the rich young football star. He was just a guy from Dorchester who loved football and had knocked around, climbing utility poles for a power company before circumstance brought him into contact with Hernandez and gave him a glimpse of a lifestyle he'd never before experienced, full of girls, partying, and assorted drugs. He had been both amazed and mightily impressed one night when Hernandez dropped $10,000 on a night of clubbing.

A few days after their argument, on June 17, 2013, Hernandez used a pretext to lure Lloyd out and then

Former Patriot Aaron Hernandez stands in the courtroom in Attleboro District Court in Attleboro, Massachusetts, on July 24, 2013, to face charges of murder.

drove him to an industrial park, where Lloyd was shot and killed. A police investigation immediately focused on Hernandez.

Even before Hernandez was charged, the Patriots rapidly cut him off, banning him from their facilities, blocking his Twitter feed, and erasing his presence on the team's website. (As of this writing, many links lead to "404" or "page not found" messages, although some highlight videos and interviews remain accessible.) Otherwise, the organization stayed silent, and his teammates were admonished to make no comment.

Hernandez was arrested on June 26 and charged with murder. He would be convicted two years later, on April 15, 2015, the only NFL player known to commit murder while still an active player. (In 1999, Panther wide receiver Rae Carruth hired a hitman and was later convicted of conspiracy to commit murder, but not the crime itself.) On April 19, 2017, Hernandez hung himself while in prison. In September of that year, researchers at Boston University determined that Hernandez, who had played contact football beginning in the Pop Warner League (from which he received the organization's Inspiration for Youth award only three weeks before committing murder), suffered from CTE. Hernandez's attorney Jose Baez said researchers described Hernandez as having "the most severe case they had ever seen in someone of Aaron's age."

The Patriots' reaction to Hernandez's initial arrest was, well, muted at best. They expressed little compassion or concern over the death of Lloyd and distanced the team from the event as fast as possible. Every statement sounded as if it had been deliberately scrubbed of both moral and legal responsibility.

Kraft was out of the country when the crime took place. When he returned on July 8, he read a statement: "Today is my first business day back in the country since Aaron's arrest; I arrived back in the country on Saturday. I want to establish up front that I have to be limited in what I talk about today as there is an ongoing criminal investigation, as well as other potential civil proceedings." He went on to say very little else other than to explain why the tight end had been cut before being arrested.

Brady spoke to *Sports Illustrated* on July 23 and gave new meaning to the word "circumspect," saying, "I have moved on. I'm focusing on the great teammates I have who are committed to helping us win games. The only thing I care about is winning. Nothing is going to ever get in the way of that goal." In a later statement, he only described the murder as "sad" and a "terrible thing."

Belichick, too, was on vacation when the arrest took place and didn't address what had happened until just before the start of training camp, one day after his quarterback's remarks. At a brief press conference, he read an 848-word statement, said, "Our thoughts and prayers are with the family of the victim," without ever mentioning Lloyd's name, and deflected any organizational accountability before admitting, in an understatement, "My comments are certainly not in proportion to the unfortunate and sad situation that we have here." He then turned to what was really important: football. "I've been advised to address the subject once," he said, "and it's time for the New England Patriots to move forward. Moving forward consists of what it's always been here: to build a winning football team."

That was pretty much it, and for most Pats fans, that was enough. The past was past. Aaron who? Right now, they were more concerned about replacing the 175 receptions and 18 touchdowns Hernandez had delivered. After Spygate, Belichick had said, "Winning cures everything." In the wake of the murder, the Patriots would adhere to that logic and approach. It would prove to be a struggle.

The local press, too, mostly gave the Patriots, their owner, and their coach a pass when it came to Hernandez, but that kind of deference was becoming the norm in regard to professional sports almost everywhere. For just as Brady has benefited from rule changes over the course of his career that have helped make it possible for him to entertain the notion of spending twenty years in the NFL, both Belichick and Kraft have benefited from an increasingly friendly and more cooperative press environment. In the last few decades of the last century, the Boston media market was hypercompetitive, with two vital newspaper behemoths, the *Herald* and the *Globe*, vying for scoops. Nearly a dozen other daily newspapers in New England covered the Pats with ferocity, and a local broadcast market, in both radio and television, also looked to break news. All that has changed, particularly in the last decade, as newspaper readership has eroded

and both the NFL and the Patriots have taken over management of their own news through team-owned websites, social media, and cable outlets. The various digital media entities, from ESPN all the way down to those that employ amateurs to write for free and from afar, simply don't provide the same kind of constant, vigorous, probing coverage as in the past. Access to players, coaches, and the front office is far more controlled now, resulting in coverage that is often less critical, more sympathetic, and more prone to take its cues from those in the front office, particularly since the team has become a perennial winner. Belichick and Kraft simply don't have to face anywhere near the same direct media pressure as their predecessors, a change that has served both men and their team well. Older media members bemoan the changes that now leave them virtually cut off from the players they cover, while younger reporters are often blind to the way in which their access is managed and controlled to the benefit of the team.

. . .

For the 2013 Patriots, the line between winning and losing would be much thinner than in any recent season. They finished 12-4, winning another title and a second seed in the playoffs, behind only the Denver Broncos, but they could have easily finished below .500. They won six games by a touchdown or less as the defense propped them up early, the offense came on late, and no other team in their division finished above .500. They didn't replace Hernandez, but they did manage to adapt, spreading the receptions that once went his way between Amendola and running backs Shane Vereen and Brandon Bolden, while Edelman made everyone forget about Wes Welker. Gronkowski, although missing half the season, was his usual monstrous self when he did play. But they won the games they had to and, when playing one of the league's powerhouses, managed to up their game and give fans hope for another appearance in the Super Bowl.

Much of that sentiment stemmed from a furious comeback against the division-leading Denver Broncos in week twelve. Peyton Manning had joined the Broncos a year earlier, and the matchup opposite Brady was the fourteenth in the history of the quarterback rivalry.

It was the kind of magical win the Patriots seemed to pull off once or twice each season (just not in the recent playoffs), a "there's no way we can win now" contest that Brady somehow inexplicably managed to pull off.

Actually, these wins weren't really inexplicable, but Brady's comebacks, unlike those of other quarterbacks who have had to do something really special, unique, and out of the ordinary to pull out such victories—Brett Favre's "go for it" bombs after a scramble, Aaron Rodgers's back shoulder sideline throws, Cam Newton's or Russell Wilson's brazen sprint-outs—are different. He doesn't really do anything special at all, but for a drive, a quarter, or sometimes a half, he is just simply perfect, making no mistakes and helped out every once in a while by a catch from an unlikely source that leaves fans gasping. Apart from that, he just reaches a place where, in the end, you don't celebrate his athleticism or his heart or any cliché attribute he may possess as much as you celebrate his decisions, his skill at taking advantage of what is offered. Brady has always realized that when ninety-nine other options are closed, there is one that is not, and he finds that one option time and time again with precision, leaving the entire team knowing that if they can just get the ball, he'll take care of the rest. In those moments, he almost seems to be playing another game, one that often results in a transfer of the magic to someone else, the key play not so often a brazen throw by Brady but a simple run, kick, or shorter controlled pass. As Ted Johnson once said of Brady, "He can do it with his mind. If you keep him clean, he doesn't need to be running around making plays. He quarterbacks from his mind."

So it was against the Broncos. On a blustery cold night at Gillette, with a wind chill of only 6 degrees, the Broncos barely needed Manning in the first half as they jammed the ball down New England's throat for a 24–0 halftime lead and the Pats fumbled the ball six times. Meanwhile, Brady was throwing for less than 100 yards in an invisible 11-for-17 passing performance that left Patriot fans clinging to a hope, as Borges wrote, for a "resurrection that by halftime seemed less likely than Lazarus'."

Then, after halftime, Brady rose and lifted those around him. In the opening drive, he was perfect, peppering the secondary with seven straight completions, none spectacular, and ending the drive with a beautiful five-yard fade to Edelman. It took all of three and a half minutes.

The Broncos fumbled shortly after the ensuing kickoff, New England recovered, and boom, Brady delivered a missile to Gronkowski at the 1 and Vereen tumbled in, making the score 24–14. It was a new game, one that, Borges noted, "began to make you think you'd seen this movie before." Before the quarter ended, Brady found Gronkowski in the end zone. An interception and two completions later led Borges to write that "pigs were flying, hell was frozen over as Gillette and the Patriots led, 28–24."

He had taken them back, quarterbacking with his mind, and then he handed the game over to everyone else: the defense, special teams, and the kicking game. A field goal made it 31–24, Manning tied it with a late touchdown pass, but in overtime the Pats hung around until the Broncos fumbled a punt at the 13. After two quarterback sneaks, Gostkowski made the comeback official. The Pats walked off with a 34–31 win and the Super Bowl within sight. But only a few weeks later, against Cleveland, Gronkowski went down with a torn ACL and MCL, ending his season. Making it to the Super Bowl didn't seem so certain anymore.

They faced the Colts in the divisional round, but Indianapolis quarterback Andrew Luck was neither Peyton Manning nor Tom Brady, despite his temporary anointment as the next big thing. He threw three interceptions, and Brady was able to take the week off in the Pats' 43–22 win.

That brought up a rematch with the Broncos in Denver to decide the conference championship, and despite their earlier loss, the Broncos were heavily favored. Yet again, it was Manning versus Brady's brain. This time, however, it was another brain that would let them down—Belichick's.

More than one sportswriter noted that, as he stood at the podium for the postgame press conference after the Broncos' workmanlike 26–16 win (the Patriots only making it look close late), Belichick resembled Manning in his befuddled look after so many losses to the Patriots. New England's defense—Belichick's defense—had let them down. Manning threw for more than 400 yards as Denver gained more 500 total yards, rendering the mind of Tom Brady, who had missed a midweek practice for an undisclosed reason, moot. "I wish we could've done a

Patriots head coach Bill Belichick talks to defensive coordinator Matt Patricia during first-half action against the Miami Dolphins at Gillette Stadium on October 27, 2013.

little bit better job today—especially me," said Belichick at the presser. "Lose a game like that, you certainly think there were things you could've done better." The *Herald*'s report card gave the coach an "F," noting that "Belichick's team was outplayed and he was out-schemed." And for the Patriots, another season ended in a loss. No one bothered to bring up the name of Aaron Hernandez.

It had been nearly ten years since the Patriots had last hoisted the Lombardi Trophy. There had long been speculation that Belichick, now sixty-one years old, and Brady, at age thirty-seven, might choose to leave the Patriots for retirement at the same time. Now it appeared that might happen sooner rather than later, and that perhaps that would not be such a bad thing. Not that there was anything wrong with the Patriots, or with Brady, or with Belichick, for New England was still inarguably one of the best franchises in the league. Yet many were beginning to

wonder if time was slowly passing the Patriots by, if just making the playoffs had become the goal.

They were led by a defensive-minded coach in an increasingly offensive league, and by a traditional pocket passer at a time when the flavor of the moment as quarterback seemed to be a guy who could throw *and* run—like Robert Griffin III, Colin Kaepernick, and Russell Wilson. Hell, even the Packers' Aaron Rodgers looked like Usain Bolt compared to Brady. Of course, Brady isn't expected to run. After taking hundreds of thousands of snaps, he seems to have a preternatural sense for skipping and sliding just enough to avoid the rush, using his eyes to magically misdirect defensive backs away from his target. Still, in the Super Bowl, Wilson led Pete Carroll's Seahawks to one of the most dominant victories in Super Bowl history, a 43–8 thrashing of the Broncos, the same team that had dominated the Patriots.

Quarterbacks like Wilson who provide the occasional running option give defenses fits: who covers the QB? And the ability to roll out and throw on the run, or from outside the pocket, provides still another option. The Patriots, well, they just weren't that special or distinctive anymore. They weren't quite as predictable as three yards and a cloud of dust, but there was the unmistakable hint of mildew beginning to show. Every recent season had been more or less a replay of the last, and there were kids entering their teens, Patriots fans their whole lives, who couldn't remember seeing the Patriots win a Super Bowl. Their parents were beginning to wonder if they ever would.

The most interesting occurrence took place in the draft. Since the Patriots drafted him in the third round in 2011, Ryan Mallet had served as Brady's backup, sharing the spot with Brian Hoyer for a year before taking over in 2012. Now the Patriots ran the actuarial tables and seemed to realize that maybe Brady couldn't play forever. Sure, the loss of Hernandez and then Gronkowski for part of the season had hurt, but Brady seemed to be starting to slip, particularly on longer throws, completing only 17 of 68 throws beyond 20 yards for the season.

So with their second-round pick in 2014, they picked up Eastern Illinois quarterback Jimmy Garoppolo, the team's highest quarterback selection since Belichick had arrived in New England. The message was subtle, but unmistakable. New England fans and even the organization were beginning to envision a day when Tom Brady might not be their quarterback. The pick allowed them to trade Mallet to Houston before the start of the season as Garoppolo became the heir apparent.

The pick also lit a fire under Brady. Since 2006, he had been working with a man named Alex Guerrero, a somewhat shadowy figure who at various times has claimed to be a medical doctor and who ran afoul of the Federal Trade Commission for selling "Supreme Greens," a product with questionable medical benefits. Even Guerrero admits that some physical trainers consider him

"a kook." The *New York Times* described him as Brady's "spiritual guide, counselor, pal, nutrition adviser, trainer, massage therapist and family member." He's even the godfather to one of Brady's children. With the stated goal of being able to play well into his forties, Brady apparently redoubled his efforts and became ever more committed to what *Boston* magazine termed Guerrero's "New-Agey ideas"—a "blend of supplemental nutrition, massage, resistance training, and other hands-on techniques." In 2013, Brady went into business with Guerrero as "TB12," selling their own supplements and opening their own training facility in the shadow of Gillette Stadium. Guerrero's methods might serve as the world's greatest placebo, and it may be Brady's DNA or plain dumb luck, but whatever Brady has been doing apparently seems to work, at least for him, at least for now. Against the odds, he seems to have gotten better at a time when most athletes get worse and start breaking down.

> THE PATRIOTS WERE PAYING ATTENTION TO WHAT WAS GOING ON IN THE LEAGUE, BUT THEY REALLY WEREN'T THINKING OF CHANGING THEIR OFFENSIVE APPROACH.

The Patriots were paying attention to what was going on in the league, but they really weren't thinking of changing their offensive approach. What had impressed them most about the Seahawks was not their offense but the defense, which had clamped down on the Broncos. Although the rules made it ever easier to pass and harder to hit the quarterback, the Seahawks seemed to make the adjustment. Speed on defense was the great equalizer, with defenders flexible enough to fill multiple roles and close on the ball. On defense, Seattle looked as if they were playing in hyperdrive.

To that end, the Patriots pumped up their own defense, signing Darrelle Revis, bringing back Patrick Chung, and poaching Brandon Browner from Seattle. Although they also provided Brady with another target, Brandon LaFell, they seemed to realize they would rise or fall in 2014 with their defense. For now, the offense, under Brady, could still take care of itself, particularly given that Gronkowski would return.

Again, the result was another relatively slow start. The Pats dropped the 2015 opener to Miami as the defense introduced themselves to each other, followed by two drab wins over the Vikings and Raiders. Brady was ranked just twenty-eighth among NFL quarterbacks. Former teammate Ross Tucker, a commentator at Sirius XM, said, "He used to be automatic, one bad throw every few games. Now it's like one bad throw every quarter. . . . I know nobody ever wants to hear that Tom Brady is a descending player, but he is." Then came the Chiefs in week four, and Brady and the Patriots responded with arguably their worst performance of the Belichick era—the defense fell apart and Brady was terrible. With the score 41–7, Belichick even pulled Brady from the game in favor of Garoppolo, something that just didn't happen.

In the wake of the defeat, the obituary writers got busy. "It's time to start wondering if the clock is running out on Brady's Patriots tenure a lot more quickly than we thought," wrote the *Globe*'s Ben Volin. "Thus began the Jimmy Garoppolo era," added Borges in his summation of the game.

The wheels seemed to be coming off. There were reports of dissension and dissatisfaction with offensive coordinator Josh McDaniels, and everyone teed off, including guys like former NFL quarterback Trent Dilfer, who said the Pats were "not good anymore." Even Jonathan Kraft, Bob Kraft's son and heir apparent, chimed in. When asked about discontent percolating among Patriots fans, he said, "I'm right there with them."

The Patriots' apparently impending demise would have been an even bigger story had it not been for the release of a video that showed Ravens running back Ray Rice punching his girlfriend in an elevator, sparking a long-overdue debate within the league on player behavior, particularly in regard to domestic violence and violence toward women. For years the NFL had tried its best to ignore what it called "off-field issues," rarely taking any effective punitive action against players for their personal behavior, but in the internet age, and in the wake of the Hernandez murder, it was becoming a lot harder to look the other way.

• • •

With the undefeated Bengals due up next and the Patriots playing lost on defense and impotent on offense, it seemed as if the time everyone had feared was finally at hand. But these were still the Patriots, and over the remainder of the season they would explore precisely what that meant, for better and worse.

The organization's greatest strength has always been its focus, its ability to take the long view and never panic; this tone, set by Belichick and Brady, has long percolated through the organization. And the next week in Cincinnati it was that team that showed up—they were as good against the Bengals as they had been bad against the Chiefs.

What changed? Well, nothing, really, only the results. Nothing ever much changes with this team, not anymore. There's little a team can do in midseason anyway except do what they're trying to do better, and that's what the Patriots did against Cincinnati, winning 43–17. Maybe they just needed a kick in the rear. Whatever it was, it worked.

They surged through the rest of the season, particularly on offense, and lost only twice—in a potential Super Bowl preview to Green Bay, and then to Buffalo in the season finale. In that meaningless game, Brady sat out the second half and a number of other players, including Gronkowski and Edelman, didn't play at all. It was the first time in the Belichick era the Pats ever coasted into the postseason. Then again, it was the first time when it seemed they might need to coast, if for no other reason than to protect Brady and his many weapons.

In any other season, the Patriots' two comebacks against the Ravens in the divisional playoff would have been the story of the postseason, for the Patriots recovered from not one but two 14-point deficits during the game. The Ravens led both 14–0 and then, after the Patriots tied the score, 28–14 before the Pats came roaring back to take their only lead with only five minutes remaining, winning 35–31 on a 23-yard pass from Brady to LaFell.

That game, not the conference championship—a 45–7 pounding of the Colts—should have been the lingering story before the Super Bowl, but even in recent years the Patriots have tended to find themselves in the middle of stories and controversies of their own making; this is the single franchise trait that has never really changed, no matter who has owned the team, coached it, or played quarterback. Just when it looks like they won't, the

Stephen Gostkowski celebrates his second-quarter field goal against the Denver Broncos during the AFC championship game at Sports Authority Field at Mile High Stadium on January 19, 2014.

Patriots always seem to manage to step into something they just can't get off their shoes. It would all prove to be, well, deflating.

In a week-eleven matchup against the Colts, following a couple of interceptions, the Colts had apparently noticed that the football used by the Patriots was underinflated and felt tacky to the touch. During the championship game, after another interception, the Colts notified the league that there might be an issue with the footballs the Patriots were using. Game officials checked the balls at halftime and found one underinflated. According to the rule, each ball is supposed to be inflated to between 12.5 and 13.5 pounds per square inch, and since 2006 each team is responsible for its own footballs.

Why does it matter? Well, theoretically, an underinflated football gives a bit more when squeezed, making it a little bit easier for the quarterback to throw the ball and for receivers and running backs to maintain their grip. And like baseball pitchers, quarterbacks depend on using balls that all feel the same. So in theory, using underinflated footballs could be an advantage.

How much of an advantage? Well, that depends. Depending on when it takes place in a contest, a pass completed that otherwise might not be, or a fumble avoided, can be a game-changer. The outcome of any contest, even a blowout, can hinge on the smallest, most insignificant play, causing a change in momentum or a score that changes the game entirely. It's impossible to gauge, like disproving a negative, although in New England it later became gospel among Pats fans that, even if the balls had been doctored, it clearly had no impact on a game that ended in a blowout.

It's specious logic. No one can say with any certainty whatsoever that the Colts might have scored first—instead of the Patriots bolting out to a lead—if, for instance, a Patriots player had fumbled on the first series with a properly inflated ball, or Brady, instead of throwing a completion, had lost his grip and thrown an interception. Then, armed with confidence, perhaps the Colts would have gone on to win. Maybe Brady would have blown out a hamstring trying to make a tackle on a Colts defensive back after an interception. Or maybe he'd have destroyed his knee and never played again. That's why playing fields are supposed to be level.

Still, it probably shouldn't have been a big deal, except that these were the Patriots, who were always under suspicion for pushing the rules to the very edge, whether for illegal taping or the way they toyed with offensive eligibility during substitutions. There was also the way the story, first reported by Bob Kravitz, a reporter for an Indianapolis television station, found its way to the press. ESPN's Chris Mortensen turned it into a national story in two tweets by misreporting that officials found eleven of twelve Patriot balls to be underinflated. The entire incident was soon under more scrutiny than the Zapruder film after the Kennedy assassination, and the Patriots didn't help matters by doing their best to obscure, obfuscate, and complicate the league's inquiry and acting guilty as hell whether they were or not. It soon went into Oliver Stone territory—"a mystery wrapped in a riddle inside an enigma."

At first, the Patriots pled ignorance, yet promised to cooperate with the league, Belichick saying, "I had no knowledge of the situation until Monday morning [after the game]. . . . I think we all know that quarterbacks, kickers, specialists have certain preferences on the footballs. They know a lot more than I do." Brady called the controversy "ridiculous" and denied any involvement in or knowledge of the situation before downplaying the whole thing: "This isn't ISIS. No one is dying."

The media always looks for stories during the two-week layoff before the Super Bowl. This year, the Pats' victory had earned them the right to face the defending Super Bowl champion Seattle Seahawks while becoming only the third team to reach the ultimate game eight times. Again, they had a chance to win their fourth title,

to cement Brady and Belichick, nearly a decade after their last championship, as among the best quarterbacks and best coaches of all time, in the same company as Chuck Noll, Bill Walsh, Joe Montana, and Terry Bradshaw, at least when measured by Lombardi Trophies. But the controversy, immediately dubbed "Deflategate," quickly took on outsized importance.

It wasn't helped by the fact that the NFL embarked on a kind of ad hoc initial inquiry that only served to create more questions. The league hired Ted Wells—an attorney who had helped it with an earlier inquiry, into Miami offensive lineman Richie Incognito's bullying of Jonathan Martin—to conduct what the league called "a thorough and objective" investigation. Meanwhile, Patriots partisans and critics chose sides, and everyone else just wanted to get on with the Super Bowl. The Patriots and Seahawks looked like one of the best matchups in recent history and a study in contrasts: Seattle's number-one defense versus New England's offense; an opportunistic defense created by a genius against one of the game's most dynamic attacks; Brady, one of the game's greatest quarterbacks, versus Wilson, one of the game's best young quarterbacks; Pete Carroll looking for redemption and Belichick trying to make history; East Coast versus West Coast; new age versus old school—it was a battle for the ages.

If the Patriots had a concern entering the game, it was that Seahawks defense. They had given up the fewest points in the league, rarely giving up more than 100 yards on the ground, or 200 in the air, and they only improved as the season progressed; in five of their last six regular-season games, they'd given up only a touchdown or less. The Seattle backfield, led by cornerback Richard Sherman and safety Kam Chancellor, earned the nickname "the Legion of Boom." Not that the Seahawks were without offensive weapons. In addition to Wilson, running back Marshawn Lynch was probably the best power back in football. In one word, he was a load—when Lynch went into what they called "beast mode," he was almost impossible to stop on short yardage.

The most important play in that Super Bowl may have been one that hardly anyone remembers today. It took place on New England's first long drive. For eight long minutes, Brady expertly led the Patriots down the field. Then, from the 10, he dropped back and threw a terrible pass from his back foot, straight into the hands of the Seahawks' Jeremy Lane, who was just inside the end zone.

Lane returned the ball, zigging and zagging and breaking one tackle before Edelman cut him down, sending Lane out of bounds at the Seattle 14 and causing his helmet to fly off when the two made contact. As the defender hit the ground, he landed on his left hand, breaking his wrist. Tharold Simon took his place, but the loss of Lane disrupted the Seahawks' nickel pass coverage for the rest of the game.

No one needed to alert Brady, who seized on the opportunity. For the rest of the half, it almost wasn't fair. The Seahawks could do nothing, and Brady and the Patriots could more or less do whatever they wanted, putting together three long drives. One ended in an interception, but two others ended in scores—a short pass to LaFell as Simon broke the wrong way on a move, and then, with only 36 seconds left in the half, a 22-yard bomb to Gronkowski in the corner of the end zone. Seattle had scored once, set up by way of a long pass to Chris Matthews in the first reception of his career, but

Jermaine Kearse of the Seattle Seahawks makes a circus catch against Malcolm Butler and Duron Harmon in the fourth quarter during Super Bowl XLIX at University of Phoenix Stadium, evoking bad memories for New England fans of similar past Super Bowl catches by David Tyree and Mario Manningham.

Malcolm Butler intercepts a pass by Russell Wilson of the Seattle Seahawks intended for Ricardo Lockette late in the fourth quarter during Super Bowl XLIX to seal the Patriots' fourth Super Bowl title.

the Patriots prepared to go to the locker room with a 14–7 lead that felt larger.

They forgot that the half wasn't over. If you got off the couch to get to the chicken wings early, you missed it. A run up the middle, a Wilson scramble, a pass to Ricardo Lockette down the right sideline, and a penalty brought the ball all the way to the 11-yard line with six seconds left. The already surprised Patriots were surprised again when Carroll decided to go for a touchdown and Wilson found Chris Matthews at the goal line. New England had dominated the first half, but somehow the score was tied, 14–14.

Seattle scored on their first two possessions of the second half to make it 24–14, while the Pats punted and Brady threw an interception. The fourth quarter began with New England trailing by 10, a deficit no Super Bowl team had ever overcome so late in the game.

But though it had been a long, long time since Brady had been in this position in the postseason, he knew what to do and how to do it: time to be perfect.

The Patriots forgot about the run, forgot about everything but Brady. In the next two series, sandwiched around a Seattle punt, Brady spread the ball and worked Simon to death, making it all look easy, playing with video game precision. He threw sixteen times and completed all sixteen, two ending in short touchdown passes, the first to Amendola, and the second to Edelman, covered ineffectively by Simon. With just over two minutes left, the Seahawks got the ball back trailing 28–24.

But Wilson wasn't done. A short pass to Lynch went for 31, and then, from the New England 49, Wilson lofted a pass deep down the right sideline to Jermaine Kearse.

The Pats' Malcolm Butler, an undrafted free agent rookie, was beaten, just barely. Kearse turned to make the catch. It bounced off his hands, and as he fell to the ground the ball bounced from his left calf to his right shin, to his right foot, to his right hand again . . . and into his arms.

Then Butler made a game-saver, beginning the best minute of his life. Kearse, only eight yards shy of the goal, got up and started to run, but Butler alertly knocked him out of bounds.

It was over, and when Lynch ran it down to the 1, it was more than over. The Seahawks had three plays, Marshawn Lynch, and almost 30 seconds to gain one long yard and keep the Lombardi Trophy for the second year in a row.

Pats fans couldn't help it—the flip book of excruciating defeats started riffling past: Ken Stabler, Ben Dreith, David Tyree. And now, unquestionably, Marshawn Lynch. The Patriots' obituary was 36 inches away, which would make the franchise the first to lose five Super Bowls, putting Bill Belichick and Tom Brady on the short list of coaches and quarterbacks, joining Bud Grant and Fran Tarkenton and Marv Levy and Jim Kelly, to have lost the game three times or more. Sure, they'd won three times too, but that was a long time ago.

The Seahawks broke from the huddle. On the right side, Seattle stacked two receivers, Jermaine Kearse and Ricardo Lockette. Wilson was in the shotgun, Lynch by his side.

Perhaps no team in football is more prepared than the Patriots. That's where their organizational advantage comes into play—in the technology and brains they're able to unleash in preparation. Hours of film breakdown,

> **PATS FANS COULDN'T HELP IT—THE FLIP BOOK OF EXCRUCIATING DEFEATS STARTED RIFFLING PAST: KEN STABLER, BEN DREITH, DAVID TYREE.**

beginning with the coaches, then more film study by the players. One of the things the Patriots look for when setting their roster is players who, in addition to their physical skills, are adept at film study and can recall and recognize what every formation tells them to do.

That, in fact, was why Malcolm Butler was on the squad. He'd played collegiately for West Alabama, a D-II school, and had gone undrafted. Invited to mini-camp, he impressed not just with his athleticism but with his ability to interpret film and formations, making him a quintessential Patriots-type player. He made the team, but had played only about eight or ten downs a game all season, mostly on special teams. He had gained much of his experience on the scout team, playing against the best quarterback in football as he matched his brain with Brady's.

In the first half, he'd barely played, but in the second half he found more reps, often as the third corner on passing downs.

The call for the Pats' goal-line defense was for something called a "goal-line corner 3." That meant Butler, moments after Kearse's catch, was back on the field.

Everyone sitting on their couch at home and in the stands just knew that the Seahawks would hand the ball to Lynch and watch him plow into the end zone. And if that failed, they'd call time and he'd try it again. Good luck stopping him twice.

Ah, but Pete Carroll had to be the smartest guy in the room. He decided he wouldn't give the ball to Lynch—that's what everyone was expecting. Instead, he called a slant in, a pick over the middle, a quick pass before the Pats could react. The result is now known as the worst play call in Super Bowl history.

Butler saw the formation. Kearse split out to the right, Lockette behind him. All those hours of study and repetition told him that Lynch wasn't getting the ball, that the Seahawks were going to pass.

As ESPN later reported, three days earlier, in practice, Butler had seen this formation. And at the snap, he'd stepped back, and then been beaten.

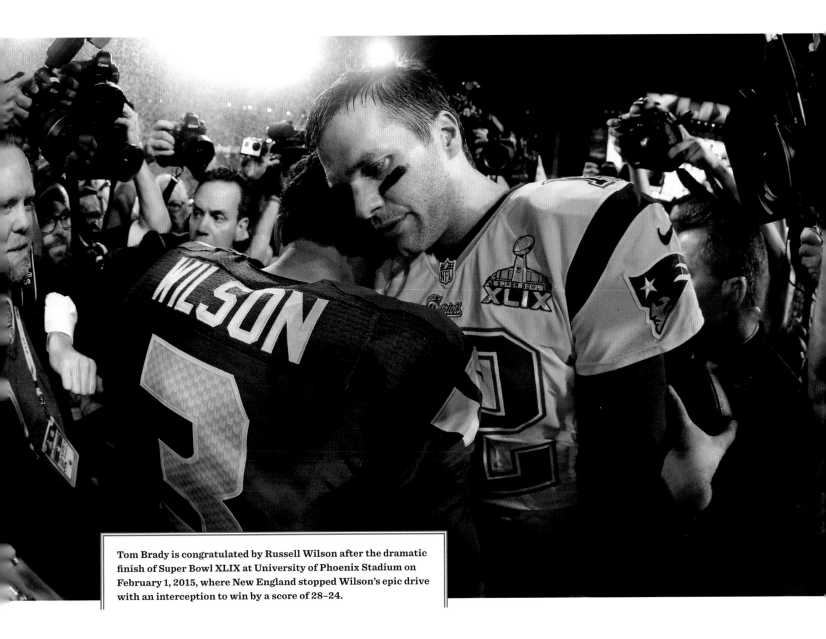

Tom Brady is congratulated by Russell Wilson after the dramatic finish of Super Bowl XLIX at University of Phoenix Stadium on February 1, 2015, where New England stopped Wilson's epic drive with an interception to win by a score of 28–24.

Belichick had noticed. He told Butler, "Seattle's going to run that play, Malcolm. Don't get beat on it."

Now was the time. Butler had seen this before. He remembered: "Don't get beat on it." If he was wrong, if they handed the ball to Lynch, it was probably a touchdown. But in this formation, which Seattle didn't often run, they'd throw a quick slant, a pick, using Kearse to tie up Browner and allow Lockette to break over the middle while everyone else was keying on Lynch.

Butler was lined up deep. At the snap, he did not step back. Instead, he broke in. Browner tied up Kearse, and Lockette slanted across the goal line. Wilson threw, Lockette turned back for the ball . . . and it wasn't there. Butler had beaten him to the spot and snapped the ball out of the air before Lockette's arms could reach it. Butler stepped forward and fell to the ground, holding the game in his hands, squeezing it tight, waiting for the Lombardi Trophy to find him.

In this game, the Patriots hadn't won because of the ball, or because of their brawn.

They'd won because of their brains.

CHAPTER FIFTEEN

2015–2016

DEFLATED...
AND ELATED

Remember, as Bill Belichick said in the aftermath of Spygate, "Winning cures everything," and in the wake of their Super Bowl win over the Seahawks, that's exactly the approach the Patriots took. In the minds of Patriot fans, finally winning another title justified just about everything. The same people who in late September had been calling talk radio and blathering that the coach was out of touch and the quarterback was too old were now naming their kids Brady and their new puppy Belichick.

STILL, THE MARGIN HAD BEEN SEE-THROUGH THIN. Had Butler not intercepted that pass, or if Pete Carroll had just called for Wilson to hand the ball to Lynch, Belichick and Brady and the Patriots would have been the objects of the kind of pity that only takes place in sports, where almost winning but still losing is worse than not even

coming close. But Butler caught the pass, and the world shifted into a different focus.

The Patriots had never really gone away, yet years of coming close had taken a toll. Now they were back, and so were their fans, with all the attendant joy and elation and smugness that inspired. It felt good to be a Patriots fan again.

"BEST TEAM EVAH!" became the motto of the moment.

In the meantime, as everyone basked in the glow of the off-season, the Patriots and their followers did their best to brush off the ongoing investigation into Deflategate. Armed with another Super Bowl win, the Patriots acted as if they could bluff and bully their way past the whole thing, acting like the high school football star caught smoking in the boys' bathroom. Locally, it was considered a nonstory, a waste of time and energy, an unfair assault fueled by jealousy. In the minds of Patriots fans, the whole thing was a witch hunt bred by the Patriots' success, a reaction the team did little to discourage

But far more was going on behind the scenes than anyone imagined. Ever since Spygate had first been revealed, there were those in the league who thought the Patriots, far more than any other team, had contemptuously pushed the boundaries of the rules. This included not only illegal taping but testing ethical boundaries in other areas, such as allegedly stealing their opponents' play calls from emptied locker rooms before games. Many even questioned whether the last two of the Patriots' three Super Bowl wins were legitimate. As ESPN's Don Van Natta Jr. and Seth Wickersham revealed in a 2015 report, "The Patriots Way," staffers from both the St. Louis Rams and the Philadelphia Eagles remain convinced that illegal taping done by the Patriots contributed to their defeats. Though it received scant attention in New England, former Ram Willie Gray and some fans even went so far as to file suits against the Patriots. The suits were dismissed by the courts, but still . . .

Critics believed that Commissioner Roger Goodell, in an effort to protect the integrity of the league in the minds of the public, had done the Patriots a huge favor by allowing them to skate in regard to Spygate and other alleged indiscretions. Bob Kraft had also become friendly

Matt Ryan of the Atlanta Falcons looks to get his pass off under pressure from Dont'a Hightower during Super Bowl LI at NRG Stadium on February 5, 2017, in Houston, Texas. It proved to be a key play in the Patriots' remarkable comeback.

with Goodell and emerged as a key supporter of the commissioner during the frequent internecine wars between NFL owners and the league. All were alpha-type CEOs who thought they knew best and grated against anyone— even the commissioner they'd hired to serve as their boss—who dared tell them otherwise.

For many NFL owners, Deflategate was an opportunity for a do-over, a chance to punish the Patriots for more than a decade of unethical behavior. It didn't matter whether or not the wrongly inflated football had impacted a game: it was time for the Patriots to pay.

By outsourcing the investigation, the league gave the inquiry a veneer of impartiality, but they also lost control over the process when the inquiry outcome turned into a legal battle. During the rest of the winter and spring, Ted Wills and his investigators spent about $5 million and conducted dozens and dozens of interviews with various members of the Patriots organization.

Wells's 243-page report was made public on May 6. Citing cell-phone records and text messages, Wells came to the conclusion that it was "more probable than not" that the Patriots intentionally deflated footballs. The report laid specific blame on Patriots locker room attendant Jim McNally and assistant equipment manager John Jastremski—exonerating Belichick and the coaching staff while implicating Tom Brady, who they claimed was "at least generally aware." The report left its conclusions less than certain by including a complicated, confusing, and perhaps inaccurate and incomplete scientific discussion of the various factors that influence the inflation of footballs. If the science was suspect and it couldn't be definitively proven that the "crime" had taken place, what was the point?

The point was control. The investigation was as much political as it was substantive. Initially, the Patriots seemed to accept the

conclusions of the report, and they suspended both Jastremski and McNally. But that changed a few days later when the league dealt out punishments. The Patriots were fined $1 million and ordered to forfeit their number-one pick in the 2016 draft and their number-four pick in the 2017 draft. Then, to the horror of the Patriots and their fans, Tom Brady was suspended for the first four games of the 2016 season. A letter to Brady from the league stated that "your actions as set forth in the report clearly constitute conduct detrimental to the integrity of and public confidence in the game of professional football," citing his "failure to cooperate fully and candidly with the investigation" and the fact that he had provided "testimony that the report concludes was not plausible and contradicted by other evidence."

With that, Brady went to court, represented in an appeal by the NFL Players Association. He took particular umbrage at the intimation that he had destroyed a cell phone that might have included texts that could show his

Tom Brady (*center*) exits federal court in New York City on August 31, 2015. Brady would ultimately serve a four-game suspension and the Patriots would forfeit a first-round draft choice as the result of the Deflategate controversy.

culpability in the deflation of the footballs. Brady claimed that in the interests of privacy he regularly changed phones and gave the old ones to an assistant to destroy. The Patriots, however, accepted their punishment, angering their fans, and Bob Kraft tried to walk a line between the fans' outrage and the league's desire to protect the shield, saying, "Although I might disagree [with] what is decided . . . I don't want to continue the rhetoric that's gone on for the last four months. We won't appeal." He was acting, he added, in the best interests of the league. "I know a lot of Patriot fans are going to be disappointed in that decision," Kraft said, "but I hope they trust my judgment and know that I really feel, at this point in time, that taking this off the agenda is the best thing for the New England Patriots, our fans and the NFL."

Pats fans, like fans just about everywhere else, are usually more than willing to back their players for behavior they would attack in others—witness Red Sox fan reactions to the PED charges leveled against their players versus their reaction to players like Alex Rodriguez. It was no different in regard to Brady. Had Eli Manning and

the Giants been the target of such a report and their Super Bowl victory called into question, Patriots Nation would have reacted with glee and taken the Lombardi Trophy by force. But when Tom Brady was the target, they held a "Free Brady" rally in Foxborough, the Patriots footing the bill for security as more than 100 supporters mugged for television cameras, one referring to their beleaguered quarterback as "half God, half man, Tom Brady."

As the appeal wound its way through the courts, it provided fuel for the unending blasting of Goodell and the NFL by local sports talk radio and bloviators and provocateurs of all stripes. Some took issue with the science, some filed legal challenges of their own, and nearly everyone involved grappled for their five minutes of self-flagellating fame as some kind of wronged party. Openly mocked and held in contempt, Roger Goodell became the most hated sports figure in New England in generations.

When Brady's appeal was denied, he reacted with a Facebook post saying: "There is no 'smoking gun,' and this controversy is manufactured to distract from the fact they have zero evidence of wrongdoing." Kraft then

Ryan Desilets and Jon Harmon, both from Milford, Massachusetts, show support for Patriots quarterback Tom Brady at the "Free Tom Brady" rally at Gillette Stadium on May 24, 2015. The rally was held in protest of Brady's four-game suspension for his role in the Deflategate scandal.

backtracked, saying, "I was wrong to put my faith in the league," and apologized to the fans for agreeing to the "harshest penalty in the history of NFL for an alleged ball violation." The whole thing finally found its way into district court. Then, on the cusp of the season, Brady's suspension was vacated pending an appeal by the NFL.

The entire affair had been nothing short of embarrassing for everyone involved, an unnecessary exercise from the start, and all involved parties bear some responsibility for the way things played out—the Patriots for mucking around with the ball in the first place, the NFL for embarking on an investigation out of proportion to the offense, and both sides for letting their own bloated sense of self-importance turn an event that could have, and should have, been handled in a twenty-minute meeting into something more. Had the Patriots admitted to smoking in the boys' bathroom at the time and accepted some equivalent of detention and public shaming, that would have been the end of it. Instead, the end result satisfied no one and made everyone involved look petty and small, and none more than the triumvirate atop the franchise: Belichick, Brady, and Kraft.

In the meantime, the 2015 season wasn't going to wait. The Pats adopted a "we wuz robbed," "Patriots versus the world" mind-set and milked it for all it was worth, both in the locker room and as a marketing tool. They began the season trying to provide evidence of Belichick's cure-all philosophy: the Patriots were determined to win their way past the problem and use victory as evidence of their moral certitude.

Eleven weeks into the season, the Patriots were 10-0 and rolling, the division title in their pocket, their ticket to another Super Bowl appearance virtually certain. So far they had barely been tested and led the league in almost everything, including arrogance. "The best," wrote Albert Speier in the *Globe*, "appear to be getting better." Readers didn't need the headline to know what he was referring to. An undefeated season was not just in sight but almost expected, and praise came from all directions. On ESPN, former Patriot Damien Woody summed up the consensus: "Belichick is the brains, the one voice behind the whole thing, and he has everybody on the same page . . . that's what separates the Patriots from everyone else—the ability to identify certain players," citing running back Dion Lewis, who had been cut by Cleveland—Cleveland!—and the Colts before joining the Patriots, and Deion Branch, a star in two tours with New England but a dog in Seattle. "What does that tell you?" said Woody. "They know how to identify players and know how to use them."

But the test of a season is often who survives it, and in the final weeks the Patriots proved that the one thing they couldn't account for, injuries, could take its toll. First Lewis and then Edelman went down, and then, in a 20–13 win against Buffalo, Amendola and running back James White were hurt.

The invincible Patriots were suddenly . . . is "vincible" a word? They fell first to the Broncos—playing without Manning—and then the Eagles. The offense sputtered, the defense began to be exposed when left on the field too long, and the team lost four of their last six games. The goal suddenly became to survive the season, then hope to get healthy for the playoffs and make a run. And while it was true, as Steve Buckley noted in the *Herald*, that "even if the Pats fell backward into the tourney as one of those phony-baloney 7-9 playoff teams, opponents would still be a-scared of lining up against them so long as Bill Belichick and Tom Brady were still breathing," the problem was that the 12-4 Patriots entered the playoffs playing even worse than the phony-baloneys, losing the number-one seed in the final week when they were beaten by the lowly Dolphins. They began the playoffs, as Borges put it, "battered and beaten down. They are tired, they are aching and they have too many guys who need to get better to believe too strongly that better days are coming soon."

They couldn't run the ball, and when forced to pass for an entire game, even Brady couldn't succeed without enough targets. The Patriots still managed to upset the Chiefs in the divisional playoff, and though there was some excitement over the seventeenth installment of the Brady-Manning rivalry in the championship game against Denver, it would fall flat. Playing on the road, where the Patriots had been a mortal 3-3, the mistake-prone New England team trailed the entire game in the 20–18 loss—a late comeback fell short when a try for a two-point conversion failed, as did a subsequent onside kick.

Prepped as Tom Brady's understudy, Jimmy Garoppolo made the most of his starting role in the 2016 season. He is shown here a year earlier, running out on the field before playing against the Houston Texans at NRG Stadium.

It was a deflating end to a season that had started off with such promise, and in a rare move, the Pats immediately fired offensive line coach Dave DeGuglielmo, sending a message that injuries were no excuse for a team that started the season 10-0 yet finished by losing five of eight. The injured would heal and the same mindset that had resulted in a 10-0 start was still in place, but the Patriots had some rebuilding to do before the start of the 2016 season. They'd soon find out that would entail far more than they thought.

While the Patriots first marched and then limped through the 2015 season, the wheel of inflated football justice ground merrily along according to its own schedule. In late October, the NFL had filed a 61-page brief appealing the decision that had set aside Brady's suspension. In essence, the league argued that the court had no right to interfere with the commissioner's power as outlined in the collective bargaining agreement and that the commissioner's authority wasn't subject to due process. On March 3, 2016, a three-judge panel of the US Court of Appeals held a hearing to consider the argument.

Legal minds warned that, short of a possible appeal to the Supreme Court, the NFL was likely to win the case, which boiled down to a simple labor issue that didn't

DEFLATED . . . AND ELATED | 2015–2016

have anything to do with whether or not the balls had been doctored with, or whether Brady knew anything about it. All that had already been determined in the Wells report. The appeal was just about Goodell's right to impose punishment, and on April 25 the court upheld the suspension. As *Globe* columnist Dan Shaughnessy noted, the sensible conclusion was that the Patriots "don't need to engage in dirty tricks to win, but they do it anyway, and they are paying the price."

But Brady and the NFLPA fought on, filing a petition before the full court. On July 13, the petition was denied, and not a single one of the fourteen judges issued a dissent. There was little chance of success in taking the case forward, and even less chance that the suspension would be stayed in the interim. Even if it was, the Supreme Court might still refuse to hear the case, or a ruling could come in midseason and cause an even bigger disruption.

Brady gave up the fight. It was better to get the suspension over with. Besides, back in March he had signed a contract extension that guaranteed he'd be with the team through 2019. For now, the Patriots' quarterback was Jimmy Garoppolo.

In the annals of Patriots history, there is perhaps no more bizarre episode than the year-and-a-half Deflategate saga. Given all the mind-bending and befuddling things that have happened to this franchise, from players being called in to play from the stands, fans running onto the field to break up plays, convicts running snowplows, phantom kitchen accidents, and coaches being fired in the middle of the playoffs, that's saying something. And in many ways, it was also the most avoidable and embarrassing. In the long run, it remains to be seen whether the fallout from Deflategate might yet inspire another episode of retribution by the league or another act of arrogance by the Patriots, an organization that in recent times seems determined to test the limits of hubris.

Opening the season with Garoppolo would prove to be the ultimate test of the Patriots' approach. To this

point, really, it was impossible to separate the team's success from the two-headed hydra of Belichick and Brady. Apart from 2008, when Brady was hurt, Cassel played quarterback, and the Patriots missed the playoffs, both Belichick's success and Brady's have been inextricably linked. Neither knows, with any real certainty, whether he would have enjoyed success without the other, or whether the team's success stems only from some organizational alchemy that requires both of them. Never before in professional sports have one coach and one key player been codependent for so long, and so successfully. And let's not forget Bob Kraft, who managed to keep the pairing together.

Fortunately, although Brady was suspended for the first four games of the regular season, he was not banned from training camp. Had Brady been barred from practice but not the regular season, the punishment might have been greater, for it would have required Brady to jump into the season cold. But Brady was even allowed to play in the exhibition preseason. After sitting out the first two games because of some private issues and to allow Garoppolo time on the field, he appeared in the last two contests as the Patriots went 3-1.

By the start of the regular season, the Pats had worries beyond Brady. Halfway through training camp, Gronkowski pulled a hamstring. Although he expected to return for the season opener, the injury would be slow to heal, and he started the season on the sidelines, as did two other members of the offensive line: left tackle Nate Solder and backup guard Jonathan Cooper.

Expectations for Garoppolo were already low, the bar set at "don't screw up." The Pats were expected to take much the same approach they had with Brady when he took over for Bledsoe: keep it simple, and don't ask him to do too much. "We don't need anybody to be somebody else," said Josh McDaniels. "We're not going to ask any more than that." In other words, no one was expecting Garoppolo to become the next Tom Brady and Brady to play the role of Bledsoe. But without Gronkowski, and

> IN THE ANNALS OF PATRIOTS HISTORY, THERE IS PERHAPS NO MORE BIZARRE EPISODE THAN THE YEAR-AND-A-HALF DEFLATEGATE SAGA.

with a beat-up line, expectations dropped even lower. The hope was, of course, that Brady would return in time to lead the team to the postseason again, but a 1-3 or 0-4 start would be disastrous and put that at risk. Most Pats fans hoped the team could split the four games. Anything better would be gravy. Garoppolo's job was to make sure he didn't mess up too badly and stay healthy—to that end, Garoppolo didn't even play in the final preseason contest.

The schedule didn't help, as the Pats opened against the Cardinals, who had finished second in their division in 2015 with the NFL's fifth-ranked defense. Garoppolo would be tested right away.

He passed the test, throwing for more than 100 yards in the first quarter as the Pats surprised the Cardinals. Martellus Bennett filled in admirably for Gronkowski in New England's 23–21 win, but the Pats also got lucky: Chandler Catonzaro missed a 47-yard field goal at the end that would have beaten them. Then, with five minutes left before halftime of game two, against Miami, no one could have blamed Brady if he was checking the back of his shirt to see if it suddenly read BLEDSOE. Garoppolo had thrown three touchdown passes on 18 of 27 passes good for 234 yards. New England led 21–0, and he had the Pats driving downfield once more.

Then Dolphins linebacker Kiko Alonso drove him to the ground. Garoppolo landed on his shoulder, spraining his AC joint. Casual Pats fans began thumbing through their programs to figure out who would play quarterback.

It was Jacoby Brissett. About the only accommodation the Pats made to Brady's absence was drafting Brissett from North Carolina State in the third round to provide quarterback depth. Although he had performed relatively well in limited duty in the preseason, no one had really wanted to think about what might happen if the Patriots were forced by circumstance to play a rookie.

Fortunately, a 21–0 lead made his job a lot easier, and the Pats kept the game plan even simpler for Brissett. They ran the ball for all but nine plays the rest of the way, and when they did pass, they helped out the young quarterback by calling mostly screens and play-action passes. He was good enough, the running game got untracked, and the Pats coasted to a 31–24 win. Even better, Brissett stayed healthy. If he'd been injured, the emergency quarterback was Julian Edelman, the pride of Kent State, who

would have quickly learned what it was like not to have himself available as a receiver.

In some ways, the injury to Garoppolo might have been the best thing that happened—or at least the best thing until Brady came back and Gronkowski returned to form. More than ever, the Patriots had to play as a team. The following week, Brissett became the first black quarterback ever to start a game for the Patriots, and only the third, after Rohan Davey and Michael Bishop, to appear in a regular-season contest. A fired-up defense gave Brissett the cushion he needed, and the Pats' ground game continued its improvement in the 27–0 shutout win over the Texans. They were 3-0, with Brady due back in two weeks. Although the Pats were shut out by the Bills the following week, 16–0, that wasn't Brissett's fault. They had survived Brady's absence.

All was suddenly right with the world. Gronkowski was already back, and now Garoppolo returned as well. A team that was 3-1 was adding the best quarterback in football and an All-Pro tight end to their roster. In the meantime, they had become a better team than the one that ended the 2015 season in defeat.

In any other season, for any other team, the story of the remainder of the season and the first two games of the playoffs would be worth a blow-by-blow account detailing Brady's return to greatness and the Patriots' drive to their eighth Super Bowl appearance in fifteen seasons:

Brady not only didn't miss a beat, he barely missed a receiver, throwing for 28 touchdowns and only two—*two!*—interceptions the rest of the year. The Patriots were rarely tested, falling only once, in week ten, to the Seahawks 31–24. And it didn't even seem to matter much when Gronkowski, who took a massive hit from Seahawks safety Earl Thomas while going up for a pass, came out of the game injured again. He missed the next game with a chest injury, then returned against the Jets and blew out his back. He would sit out the remainder of the year after surgery for a herniated disk, but Brady and the Patriots didn't miss a beat as a conga line of receivers stepped forward, took up the slack, and Brady found them again and again. The Pats won the division and the right to play at home and took full advantage of both, slamming first the Texans, 34–16, and then the Steelers, 36–17, both games just close enough to keep fan interest

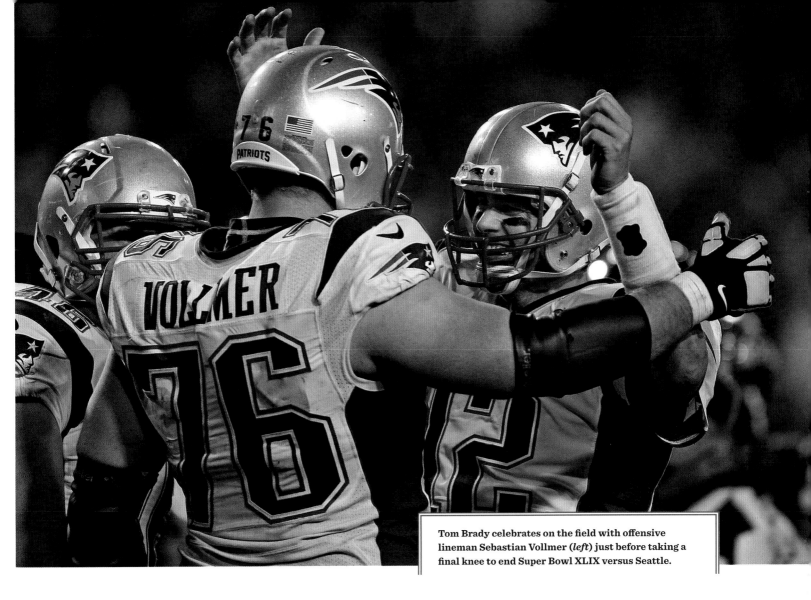

Tom Brady celebrates on the field with offensive lineman Sebastian Vollmer (*left*) just before taking a final knee to end Super Bowl XLIX versus Seattle.

into the third quarter and the networks happy. There's all the blow-by-blow necessary.

Because this wasn't any other season, and this wasn't any other team, and what took place next, in Super Bowl LI in Houston, was so unexpected, unforgettable, and, even today, unbelievable that it renders everything that took place before it in the postseason almost immaterial.

Super Bowl LI was a great black hole of a football game, one that sucked up everything around it and made it appear insignificant. If New England fans have long enjoyed the sadomasochism of touching the raw nerves that excruciating defeats have so often exposed, well, this game was the payback, the glorious victory to be relived in perpetuity.

It was the kind of game that made every second of the whole twisted and sometimes tortured history of this franchise worth it, one that justified every previous embarrassment, a game that made the past, well, finally the past.

If you're a Patriots fan, the first two and a half quarters of Super Bowl LI have probably been erased from memory, an attack of transient global amnesia not worth recalling. Because for two and a half quarters, the Atlanta Falcons were the best team in football and the Patriots didn't look like they even belonged on the field. Or in the league.

That's because, after a scoreless first period, Atlanta quarterback Matt Ryan was near-perfect, running back Devonta Freeman ran at will, Tom Brady was playing like he was thirty-seven going on forty-seven, and Bill Belichick's game plan seemed to indicate the game had passed him by. Throw in a fumble by LeGarrette Blount, a pick-six by Brady at the end of the half that was run back 82 yards for a touchdown, and an 85-yard scoring drive by the Falcons on their second possession of the second half, and with just over 23 minutes remaining in the game Atlanta was completely in control, leading 28–3 and looking like they might win 58–3. The Patriots seemed as out of place as Lady Gaga did catching a football at the end of the halftime show.

The Patriots were finished, done, cooked. Every metaphor meant the same thing. Few teams ever recover from 25-point deficits midway through the third quarter in any game in any league, fewer still in the NFL, even fewer against one of the best teams in the league, and in the Super Bowl . . . none. It appeared as if the curtain on the dynasty was at least being tested, if not quite drawn.

To this point, the Falcons' front four had dominated New England's line, pressuring Brady and making

Always the life of the party, Rob Gronkowski poses as he arrives at the 2016 *Vanity Fair* Oscar party on February 28, 2016, in Beverly Hills, California.

him play like an aging quarterback racing to retirement. And the Pats had no answer to Atlanta quarterback Matt Ryan—none whatsoever. To this point, his passer rating was 158.3, the highest possible.

And there really seemed to be nothing they could do about it. As the *Globe* noted, the Pats "were outmanned and outclassed in every facet of the game," and getting beat in just about every way possible: in the air, on the ground, on special teams, on both sides of the ball, mentally, physically, spiritually. At this stage of the game, it wasn't like they could change their defensive scheme or put in some secret weapon or special series of special plays. And no matter what, they weren't going to pull Brady in favor of Garoppolo. Seventeen years in the league had earned Brady the right to play to the end, no matter how badly he had played up till now. As running back James White put it later, "If we play that game 100 times, we probably lose 99 times."

All they could do was all they have ever done since Belichick and Brady first found each other on the same sideline. The one change—the only change—they have ever made when falling behind is both deceptively simple and, as proven over time, deadly efficient. Or at least more efficient than any other approach. From the moment they got the ball back after the ensuing kickoff, the Patriots would use the one advantage that no other team has ever enjoyed—Tom Brady's singular brain.

Belichick and McDaniels made the decision (or rather, the 28–3 score made the decision for them) to speed things up, to hurry up and pass. That would pit Brady's greatest strength—his ability to process what was happening before him, to slow down a game that seemed to speed up for everyone else—against the Falcons' defense.

Perhaps no quarterback in football history has ever taken so many snaps, seen so many defensive schemes, or made more decisions in his career. Since first taking over as Patriots quarterback to the time he took the field down 28–3 with only 8:31 remaining in the third quarter of the Super Bowl, Brady had taken the snap on the field nearly 20,000 times, and he had looked downfield and made a decision about who to throw the ball to about 10,000 times. And that was just in games. Add practices to that and the number probably triples. And when one includes the hours spent gazing at film and breaking that down, well, how high is up? Over those thousands and thousands of repetitions, the decisions that other quarterbacks grapple and struggle with, that cause them to hesitate before taking action, have become automatic to Brady. When the ball is snapped, time slows, the play unfolds, and a series of options appears before him. Brady sees, processes, and seamlessly acts. It is not done without thought, but in a sense it is done beyond thought. Brady's decisions on the field have become nearly instinctual, pure reaction, as automatic as a hitter in baseball reacting to another pitch, all that preparation put into practice in the moment, as deadly and accurate as a snake strike: see and react, see and react, see and react . . .

At these times, it doesn't seem to matter much to Brady who is playing with him, who his receivers are, where they line up, what the blocking scheme is, or who is on the other side of the ball. There are no deviations he has not already encountered, no aberration he has not dealt with. He has seen it all a hundred or a thousand times before.

Of course, that doesn't mean that Brady cannot be beat or that the ability he displays on the football field endows him with any special prowess or wisdom off it, but on the field he has few peers. He is no perfect automaton, and on this day he had already failed again and again. But by speeding everything up and just letting him go, the game plan be damned, the Patriots put their faith in his brain, dared the Falcons to keep up . . . and hoped like hell that, at the same time, their defense could get a few stops or turnovers, that someone would make a miracle catch, that the Falcons would make a mistake or two or three. All Brady could provide, at best, was hope, a chance to slip through whatever small window might still be open. The rest was up to the universe—all the dominoes had to drop precisely in line, one after the other.

It started slow, the Falcons still confident, still aggressive, but maybe, just maybe, starting to relax, to see the celebration they felt certain would soon take place.

The Patriots took over at the 25, and Brady took his time, starting the drive with a short pass up the middle to Dion Lewis, knowing full well that if they were stopped, well, that would be the game. For the next quarter and a half, the Pats would be playing a zero-sum game.

Friends since their days as football teammates at Phillips Academy, Bill Belichick and Patriots football research director Ernie Adams also worked together for both the New York Giants and the Cleveland Browns before coming to New England. Adams, one of the truly legendary students of the game, is often referred to as "Belichick's Belichick."

The Patriots went quickly, but did not rush, mixing it up, but still taking chances. Brady threw 17 yards to Amendola on fourth-and-3 for a first down. And then, on third-and-8 from the Atlanta 35, Brady, seeing no one open but sensing space in the middle of the field, ran for a first down, sliding in safe at the 20. Four plays later, James White caught a short pass out of the backfield just shy of the goal line, spun to avoid a tackle, then dove in across the goal as New England scored its first touchdown. The drive had taken more than six minutes, which in one sense was good: for the first time the Falcon defense had been forced to stay on the field and expend some energy. But at the same time, there were now only a few seconds over 17 minutes remaining in the game.

Something snapped in over the course of that drive—the mystery of Atlanta's defense had begun to unravel, not just for Brady but for the Patriots' play-calling. Every defensive scheme decides who to stop and, conversely, who must be left alone. And on this day, with Gronkowski out, the Falcons had left one man unaccounted for: running back James White. Before the touchdown drive, he'd touched the ball only eight times. But three of those touches, all completed passes, had come in the Pats' final drive of the first half. Now, in the scoring drive, he was still unaccounted for, getting the call time and again over LeGarrette Blount. During the remainder of the game, White's number of touches would more than double, and he would play nearly every down. The running back from Wisconsin, drafted in the fourth round in 2014, was a quintessential Patriots pick: unassuming, undersized, and thought by almost everyone else to be too small and too slow for the NFL.

In college, White had usually been overshadowed by another back and was never even thought of as a receiver until his senior year. In his rookie year with the Pats, he'd caught only five passes and been left off the Super Bowl roster. White had never rushed for more than 26 yards in a pro game and had caught more than five passes only four times. He was a role player. Of all the offensive weapons the Falcons had game-planned against, White was way down on the list; Atlanta was far more concerned about Edelman, Amendola, Bennett, Dion Lewis, and virtually everyone else. But on this day White suddenly found himself thrust into the spotlight as he went from a secondary option to a primary one—sometimes split wide, sometimes coming out of the backfield, and almost always open. The Falcons never figured that out.

As Josh McDaniels admitted later, even the Patriots hadn't prepared for White, saying, "We didn't practice some of those plays with James White in the game." How then could the Falcons have done so? On this day, White would make history.

But not quite yet. After the touchdown, Gostkowski shanked the automatic extra point, hitting the upright, and the glimmer of hope seemed to subside. Instead of the score being 28–10, it was 28–9—a somewhat tougher climb even if everything broke right. A tie or even a victory had been within reach on three scores—two touchdowns and two-point conversions plus a field goal. Now a win would require another score, either a third touchdown or another field goal. The brief moment of optimism felt by Patriots fans faded. Well, at least the final score wouldn't look completely embarrassing.

The situation was still dire when the Patriots went for an onside kick, only to have Gostkowski flagged for running into the ball before it traveled the requisite five yards. The Falcons took over at the New England 41, needing only ten yards or so to reach field goal range and stick a sharp pin into the distant bubble of a comeback.

But they didn't. After a nine-yard pass to make a field goal nearly automatic, a holding call, an incompletion, and then a "delay of game" call, the Falcons were forced to punt. They'd had a chance to end it and let it slip away. Had that not happened, and had the Falcons kicked a three-pointer, it would have meant the ball game. Now, barely two minutes after scoring a touchdown, the Patriots had the ball back, and Atlanta's defense back on the field.

Now Brady moved faster, throwing controlled passes as he moved the ball down the field, while the Falcons' linemen began gasping a little more after pass rushing on nearly every play. After Brady took a sack at the Atlanta 15, Gostkowski was called to kick. This time he nailed the 33-yard field goal, and now the score was 28–12. In theory, the Pats could still tie with two touchdowns and two two-point conversions, but there were less than ten minutes remaining in the game. To even entertain the thought of victory, the Patriots needed a break.

They got it. On third-and-1 on Atlanta's next possession, even though they'd been running effectively all day, the Falcons chose to pass. They'd run this play before, and the Pats had gambled, sending Dont'a Hightower around from the left on a blitz. The last time the end had picked him up and Ryan had stepped forward to deftly complete the pass over the middle. But this time the end released, Freeman missed the block in the backfield, and the quarterback never saw Hightower. The linebacker had survived Tuscaloosa tornadoes in college, huddling in an apartment with his roommates, and knew all about fine lines and survival.

As Ryan pulled his arm back to pass, Hightower stripped him of the ball. Had Hightower arrived only a split-second later, had Ryan had time to move his hand an inch forward, it would have been an incomplete pass. Instead, it was a fumble, and Alan Branch fell on it at the 25.

Now Patriots fans could feel that once-familiar surge beginning to swell in their chests—they'd finally gotten a break. And the Falcons' defense, still huffing, was back on the field, pass rushing now on almost every down and expending their dwindling supply of energy.

Brady's pace increased. After a sack, four short passes—the first to White—ended with a score on a pass to Amendola crossing to the left at the goal line. Prepared, the Pats lined up immediately for the conversion, giving Atlanta no time to adjust, and Belichick and McDaniels called Brady's favorite play: the fake fumble direct snap to the running back. As Brady pretended the ball went over his head, James White—there's that name again—stormed up the middle for two points. Suddenly, somehow, it was 28–20 and a one-touchdown game. Patriots fans began looking at each other, wide-eyed, maybe smiling, without saying anything, all thinking, *Maybe . . .*

But then the game was over.

New England's last touchdown woke the Falcons, who finally seemed to realize that, yes, perhaps they had started celebrating too soon and needed to start playing again. After taking over with just under six minutes remaining, Ryan, who'd completed only two passes since the Falcons last scored, suddenly found range.

First he found Devonta Freeman on a play action. Freeman, wide open on the left side as the Pats blew coverage, scooted 39 yards to midfield, each step squashing the Patriots' hopes. Anxious Falcons fans, who had begun to move nervously to the edge of the couch, slid back and started to relax, while Patriots fans suddenly found their

AT LEAST THE PATRIOTS' SURGE HAD MADE THE SECOND HALF WORTH WATCHING, BUT LET'S FACE IT, THE GAME WAS *OVAH.*

throats getting tighter. If Atlanta could kick a field goal, it would be a two-score game again, a two-score game with barely enough time for one score. One play later, Ryan, under pressure, scrambled free and threw a prayer on the run, a high arcing pass for 27 yards that somehow found Julio Jones's hands, the receiver stretching out nearly parallel to the ground, his toenails somehow staying in bounds, to give the Falcons a first down on the 22.

That was the play, the sign from the gods that in Atlanta meant they had weathered the comeback. Falcons fans started hugging each other. Now, with only 4:40 to go, all the Falcons needed to do was run the ball up the middle three times and kick a field goal. Everybody coaching from an easy chair knew that. From that range, it would be only about a 40-yard kick, at most, and Atlanta kicker Matt Bryant, a Pro Bowler, was as automatic as any kicker in the game: he had missed only one field goal all year from less than 50 yards. Oh, the Patriots would try to stop the clock and use up their time-outs, but at best, the clock would still tick down to less than three minutes by the time of the kick, giving New England the ball with no time-outs and needing two scores with three minutes left. It might still be nerve-wracking, but not even Tom Brady could score points with no time on the clock.

In a few minutes, New England's furious comeback would be forgotten and the franchise's Super Bowl record would tumble to 4-5 (4-3 with Belichick and Brady). Well, hell, for Falcons fans that made it even better. They'd taken everything the Patriots had, with Tom Brady at his best, and *still* managed to beat New England.

In New England, the mood was grim and getting ugly. At least the Patriots' surge had made the second half worth watching, but let's face it, the game was *ovah*. A lot had already gone right to bring the Patriots this close and make a game of it—Brady's scramble, Hightower's strip sack, the Falcons' weird play-calling, White's conversion—but it just wasn't possible to expect much more. The Pats' last Super Bowl win had been crazy enough.

By now, the luck tank had to be bone-dry. What was Matt Ryan going to do—get confused and start running the wrong way?

Well . . . not quite. But almost.

On the next play, Falcons running back Freeman, still winded after his 39-yard dash a moment before, raced to the left side, losing a yard as he fought to keep time ticking off the clock. After he went down, there was no reason to rush.

The Falcons lined up, but on the sidelines Atlanta offensive coordinator Kyle Shanahan, the man responsible for calling the play under Coach Dan Quinn and expected to take the 49ers head-coaching job as soon as the game ended, hesitated. He was already kicking himself for the way the offense had stalled earlier in the half, and now he wanted more. Instead of playing it safe and calling for another run, he called a pass play, explaining later that "we were just trying to play smart and do what we thought was the best chance to move the chains, get us some more yards, an easier field goal, hopefully even a touchdown, not giving the ball back to them."

What's that old adage again? If you're trying to do anything other than win, you are destined to lose? Sure, Shanahan wanted to win, but like Pete Carroll in the last moments of Super Bowl XLIX, he also wanted something more—more yards, more points, more proof of genius before he arrived in San Francisco as a savior. But as Al Davis, the former owner and coach of the old AFL Raiders, once said, the name of the game is unalterably simple: just win, baby!

As Ryan dropped back, taking five, six, seven steps, scanning the field for a receiver, he should have had only two overarching thoughts in his mind: Number one—do not get sacked. Number two—do not throw an interception. There was no number three.

New England's line pushed forward, Trey Flowers lined up against center Alex Mack, and the two men got tangled. Flowers didn't even look as if he was trying for a sack, only to contain Ryan in the pocket. Mack spun and pushed Flowers around until the lineman, improbably, found himself in the backfield with Mack shoving him toward the quarterback.

All of a sudden, there was Ryan over his left shoulder and no one in the way. Flowers reached out with his left arm, grabbed at Ryan, and the quarterback, holding the ball in his right hand, inexplicably did not throw. The player whose composure had earned him the name "Matty Ice" in Atlanta went from cool to frozen solid. He turned back inside and . . . just fell over.

On the New England sidelines, Brady threw his hands up in the air. He knew. He'd seen this, all of this, before. The Patriots called time.

The 12-yard loss still made a put-the-game-away field goal only slightly less likely, a kick that would be 53 yards now but still almost automatic for Bryant, well within his range. Now, after screwing up the call once, Shanahan would surely keep the ball on the ground, calling for a safe run that might pick up a few yards or, if they got lucky, a few more. Every inch made a field goal and victory more likely. It was third-down-and-23.

Nope. Shanahan still wanted more. Now he had to make up for his mistake. The call was a flare to Mohamed Sanu, who gathered the pass and then, stupidly, ran out of bounds at the 25, stopping the clock.

But it would've stopped anyway because of a flag: holding was called again on the Falcons' Jake Mathews, who had ridden Chris Long to the ground in an obvious chokehold. That made it third-down-and-33, the ball on the New England 42—*way* out of field goal range, or at least far enough out that to try one now would have made about as much sense as trying to throw the ball when you were already in range at the 22. Atlanta called time, and on the next play, with everyone knowing the Falcons would throw, they played it safe: this time, finally, Ryan threw the ball away. Incredibly, after reaching the 22-yard line, the Falcons had not only gone 20 yards backwards but run only a bit over a minute off the clock. Now the Falcons had to punt, and Edelman called for a fair catch at the 9-yard line.

Brady still had more than three minutes and two time-outs. Of course, the Patriots needed a touchdown and then a two-point conversion just to tie. According to the statisticians, the Falcons had a 93 percent chance of winning the game—despite all that had happened, the odds for a Patriots win had risen only from .05 percent to 7 percent.

But that was according to the statisticians, whose calculations didn't factor in that Brady was playing quarterback. With Brady behind the center, that 7 percent chance almost seemed like a sure thing.

Perfect doesn't always mean being successful in every instant. But it does mean not making any mistakes. Over the next three minutes, Brady didn't make a mistake, or at least not any that cost him. When he was pressured, he threw the ball away. When a receiver was covered too close, well, he got lucky, and the ball bounced to where no one could catch it. And then, on first-and-10 from the 36 with 2:28 remaining, he got *really* lucky.

Edelman curled to the middle 20 yards downfield. The ball was tipped by cornerback Robert Alford, and suddenly Edelman and three Falcons backs were scrambling for it, Edelman trying to catch the ball while the Falcons fell all over each other and the ball followed the inexorable laws of gravity. Between the ball and the ground was the hand of Falcons safety Ricardo Allen, but Edelman grabbed it, lost it, and then, with a scant inch remaining between the ball and irrefutable physical rules of the universe bringing it down to earth, grabbed

Julian Edelman makes a miraculous catch while covered by Keanu Neal and Ricardo Allen of the Atlanta Falcons during Super Bowl LI. His catch was but one of the benchmark plays in the Patriots' 34–28 comeback overtime victory.

it again—along with Alford's foot—squeezed all of it to his chest, and began screaming, "I caught it, I caught it, I caught it!"

He did, moving David Tyree's catch in Super Bowl XLII down on the list of remarkable catches and causing Dont'a Hightower to call him "Julian Incredibleman." The Falcons were now officially reeling.

Brady found Amendola for 20 yards, James White (who else?) in the middle for 13, and then White again for 7—quarterback calculus. Then, with the Falcons finally thinking "Hey, maybe we better cover this guy," the Pats handed White the ball, and he burst through the middle from a yard out with 57 seconds left to play. You could almost see Atlanta's coaches on the sidelines asking, "Him again?"

Of course, that still left the two-point conversion, but the game wasn't as much in Brady's hands anymore as everyone else's.

James White scores the winning touchdown in overtime against the Atlanta Falcons during Super Bowl LI to cap one of the greatest games in NFL history.

A short screen to Amendola to the left, and he was stopped . . . six inches over the line.

Impossibly, the score was now tied, 28–28. A kickoff, and an excruciating minute and one punt later, the fourth quarter ended, the game tied. For the first time ever, a Super Bowl would end in overtime.

• • •

The most important call in overtime was the first: the Pats' Matt Slater calling "heads" on the coin toss. It came up for New England. According to overtime rules, if the receiving team scores a touchdown on its first possession, the opponent does not receive a chance to respond. However, if the Pats kicked a field goal, the Falcons would have the opportunity either to match it or to win with a touchdown of their own.

Brady's brain went into overdrive. Five straight passes, all perfect, two of them to White—inexplicably left too much alone and too open, he hauled in his 13th and 14th receptions of the game—brought the ball to the 25. Then it was time for a changeup: this time they gave the ball to the running back, and White went for 10 yards.

And then Brady was not perfect. An interference call on an incomplete pass to Bennett moved the ball to the 2, and on the next play Brady nearly made a mistake on another pass to Bennett, almost throwing an interception in the end zone.

Whoops. This was no time to fool around. Keep the ball, kick a field goal if you have to, but just keep the ball. Just win.

By this point, the Falcons were spent. The call came in from the Pats' sideline, a safe call to the man of the moment, the only guy on the field as flawless as Brady had been—a pitch to White. He ran right, turned in, picked and plowed and dove and clawed for the goal line, and then the final improbable domino—the most implausible one yet—fell to the ground, just barely over the line.

Touchdown. 34–28 New England. A split-second of silence, and then a roar spread west from the Gulf of Maine and Massachusetts Bay, finding the throat of every Patriots fan in the country.

A pause for the replay . . . then the game was history. The Patriots were champions again.

CHAPTER SIXTEEN

2017

DYNASTY'S END?

Well, that didn't take long.

In the wake of the Patriots' remarkable comeback victory in Super Bowl LI, the standard response, particularly in New England, was that the Patriots were invincible, that every obstacle could be overcome, and that Bill Belichick was light-years ahead of every other coach in football, Tom Brady was ageless, and the organization was incapable of failure.

The Patriots had somehow cracked the code that had thus far eluded every team in professional football history and were impermeable to everything that every other team in football was susceptible to—age, errors of judgment, bad luck, bad karma, you name it. The Patriots weren't just a dynasty but the dynasty of all dynasties, not just in football but in all sports, and better than not just the Yankees but all previous dynasties of any kind: the Greeks, the Romans, the Ming . . .

Enough already. What no one recognized was that, just as a comeback is due to a confluence of factors that cannot be anticipated, so too is a winning team. It's a Venn diagram overlap of so many factors that it is almost impossible to control or predict or create according to some design. There is, after all, a reason they still play the games with actual people: people must be found who can execute a game no matter what a plan says, but human

beings are also fallible creatures. If there is any lesson in recent Patriots history, it is that success takes time and, despite the best efforts, is still not really a choice. The Patriots were due for a reckoning.

It began in the 2016 off-season after Kraft, Belichick, and Brady misread their own team and fan base and made the Patriots a political football. At a time when most fans just wanted to bask in the glow of a world championship run, the most powerful members of the Patriot organization all cozied up to Donald Trump. Belichick wrote Trump a treacly letter of support during the campaign that called Trump's leadership "amazing" and praised him for dealing "with an unbelievable slanted and negative media, and [coming] out beautifully—beautifully," Brady hung a MAGA hat in his locker, and Kraft sent Trump $1 million for his inauguration. But when the Super Bowl–winning team was invited to the White House on April 19, more than two dozen members of a team that refused to be introduced individually before the Super Bowl voted with their feet and for a variety of reasons didn't show up for the photo op, a rare display of public disunity. Among those who skipped the event were Brady, citing "family matters"; Amendola, who said he was attending a funeral; and Chris Long, one of the most vocal supporters of Colin Kaepernick's sideline protesting of police brutality. But many of the other players who skipped out were black, some citing political differences with the president, including team captain Devin McCourty, who said, "I don't feel accepted in the White House." Kraft, who famously lost a 2004 Super Bowl ring by showing it to Vladimir Putin (Putin put it on and never gave it back), gave Trump a 2016 Super Bowl ring of his own and lauded the president as a "great man." The visit, which took place on the same day Aaron Hernandez committed suicide in prison, underscored an issue not often examined in regard to the Patriots. In a league in which 70 percent of the players were black, ESPN noted that Belichick's coaching staff (which includes Belichick's own son, Steve, the safeties coach), was the least integrated in the league. Among the fourteen on staff, there were only two minority coaches: running back coach Ivan Fears, a member of the staff since 1999, and linebacker coach Brian Flores, who began serving as a scout in 2004 before becoming an assistant in 2008.

As part of a gala ceremony at Gillette Stadium prior to the Patriots' 2017 home opener, the team unveiled its fifth Super Bowl banner.

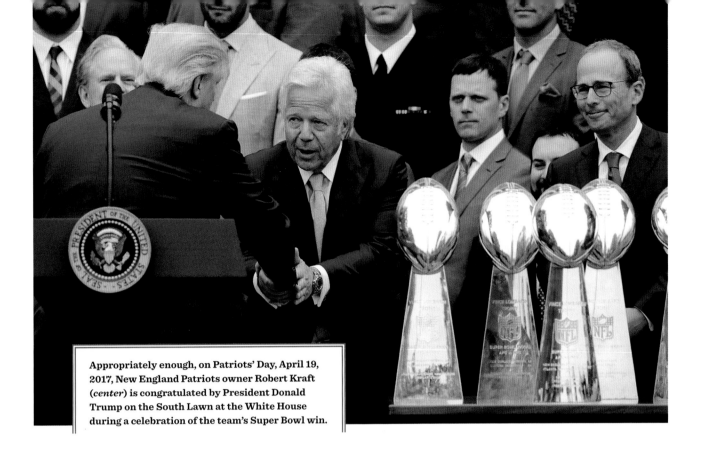

Appropriately enough, on Patriots' Day, April 19, 2017, New England Patriots owner Robert Kraft (*center*) is congratulated by President Donald Trump on the South Lawn at the White House during a celebration of the team's Super Bowl win.

The Patriots had also allowed several key players to leave (among them tight end Martellus Bennett, Chris Long, and LeGarrette Blount, with Long not even receiving a contract offer), thinking it would be just a matter of plugging in other assets to achieve the same result. Then the loss of Julian Edelman in a preseason game to a season-ending knee injury forced the team to abandon the plan they had to pair him with free agent receiver Brandin Cooks, a bona-fide deep threat.

And then there was Brady, suddenly forty and playing like it at the start of the season. The quarterback had already taken nearly 800 serious hits as a professional, and his wife admitted that he had suffered not only a concussion during 2016 but a series of concussions as a pro. The cumulative effects of age and more than two decades of pounding finally appeared to be taking a toll on his performance, at least at the start of the season: his passes were less crisp, his reactions less definite, and the results less certain.

The Patriots' opening night 42–27 loss to the Kansas City Chiefs was both a slap in the face and a wake-up call. Following a pre-program extravaganza at Gillette that featured five ersatz giant Lombardi Trophies—and a gigantic, crowd-sized raspberry from the home crowd directed toward Roger Goodell—the Patriots suffered what was arguably their worst and most surprising defeat of the Brady-Belichick era. The Pats gave up more points (42) and more yards (537) than at any time in the coach's and his quarterback's tenure, while Brady completed only 14 of 36 passes and failed to put the ball into the end zone. *And* they lost receiver and return man Danny Amendola in the fourth quarter to a concussion when he was struck in the head by a knee—at least the third such event of his career—as that unavoidable and inevitable consequence of football took its first victim of the regular season, leaving the Patriots' receiving corps undermanned.

A week later against New Orleans, the previous game looked like an anomaly as Tom Brady played perhaps the best first quarter of his career, staking the Pats to a 20–3 lead. Drew Brees and the Saints couldn't keep up, and everyone exhaled again. But the early surge masked the fact that the Saints still gained more than 400 yards and that, from the midpoint of the second quarter forward, the Patriots were no better than they had been in their opener.

Members of the New England Patriots kneel during the National Anthem before a game against the Houston Texans at Gillette Stadium on September 24, 2017.

Comebacks were key in the next two games, the first in the Patriots' favor against Houston. Brady, with 2:24 remaining, led a patented surge, with Brandin Cooks catching a 25-yard touchdown pass with 29 seconds left and then adding an exclamation point by catching another toss for a two-point conversion. But the second comeback fell the other way: when the Panthers scored on a late field goal for a 33–30 win, making the Pats 2-2 for the year, the season was already hanging in the balance.

New England, a team many expected to go undefeated, was winning and losing with all the consistency of a ten-year-old playing a pinball machine for the first time—in both the Houston and Carolina games, the Patriots seemed to land on one side or the other of success as more a matter of when the clock stopped than of anything based on how well, or badly, they played. The defense quite simply was one of the worst in the league, giving up an average of nearly 450 yards a game. And although the team had previously recovered from 2-2 starts to win the Super Bowl twice, in 2003 and in 2014, in neither case had they done so with a defense quite so porous.

But the split did do one thing: it bought the franchise time to find out both "who they were" and who the other teams that had dashed out of the gate, like undefeated Kansas City, were, as well as to consider whether they could maintain their pace regardless of injuries and the inevitable distractions that come with success.

While the Patriots were floundering, much of the focus around the rest of the league centered on the player protests against police brutality and societal inequity inspired by Colin Kaepernick's stand in 2016 when he took a knee in protest during the National Anthem. The protest spread after the American president decided to make this expression of a First Amendment right an issue, calling the protesters "sons of bitches" during an Alabama rally. Before the game against the Texans in Foxborough on September 24, 2017, seventeen Patriots players had knelt in solidarity.

After Trump's divisive pronouncements about protest in the NFL, Bob Kraft, now facing some public pressure for cozying up so close to Trump during the presidential campaign, released the following statement in an attempt to placate his critics: "I am deeply disappointed by the tone of the comments made by the President on Friday. I am proud to be associated with so many players who make such tremendous contributions in positively impacting our communities. . . . Our players are intelligent, thoughtful, and care deeply about our community and I support their right to peacefully affect social change and raise awareness in a manner that they feel is most impactful."

The following day, Belichick refused to address the issue, saying, "I'm just gonna talk about the game."

Then, only a few hours afterward, the Patriots released Belichick's official statement.

It was hardly a profile in courage. In fact, it was hardly a statement at all—just an inchoate series of nearly meaningless platitudes that said nothing about the issue at hand. It read, in part:

"I have immense respect and admiration for our players, for how they conduct themselves professionally as New England Patriots and for how they represent themselves, their families and community as men. . . . As with any large group of people, there is a variety of perspectives and opinions on many topics."

Following his coach's lead, Brady issued a statement that echoed his empty response to the death of Aaron Hernandez, mentioning neither the issues nor the personalities directly, but pushing it all into the past and leaning forward:

"I've got a lot of love for my teammates. I mean, we go through a lot together. There's a lot of blood, sweat and tears. I don't think it's easy to play this sport. I mean, there's a lot of guys that sacrifice a lot. I think you have a lot of respect for the guys who play, not only your own teammates but guys you play against. I mean, without them, it's not a great game. So, it's like I said. I believe in all of us coming together."

In week five, the Patriots beat the Buccaneers, 19–14, but it was a distinction without much of a difference. Although the score indicated a resurgent Patriots defense, it was misleading: Buc quarterback Jameis Winston had missed wide-open receivers all night and kicker Nick Folk missed three field goals, two from distances that generally cost you your job in the NFL. Patriots defenders still gave up in excess of 400 yards. Meanwhile, New England's offense—minus Gronkowski, who was out with a thigh injury—was generally inconsistent and struggled for most of the game.

The Bucs were hardly the 1985 Bears. Nevertheless, the victory lifted the Pats to 3-2, putting them in a virtual tie for first in a suddenly competitive division in a conference marked by parity. If the Patriots weren't going to be a super-team per expectation, the lack of another super-team in the conference kept all the doors open despite their disappointing start.

"Make the playoffs and see what happens" became the mantra of the season, and in the back of everyone's mind was the knowledge that this team might suddenly put it together at a moment's notice. It had happened before—all one needed to do was revisit Super Bowl LI to make that case. A matchup with the Jets in week six that no one had expected to matter at the start of the season suddenly loomed large. New York, which almost as many people had expected to go winless as those who had expected New England to go undefeated, had won three in a row. Suddenly they would be playing for the division lead.

Yet, like so many other teams, New York had no real answer to the return of Gronkowski. Midway through the fourth quarter, with the Patriots leading 24–13, Jets quarterback Josh McCown hit his tight end Austin Seferian-Jenkins on a slant at the 5-yard line. Seferian-Jenkins then turned upfield and aimed for the pylon. With Duron Howard and Malcolm Butler hanging on, he stretched out over the orange-colored marker for an apparent touchdown.

But there are touchdowns, what the NFL considers touchdowns, and apparently also what the NFL considered touchdowns when scored against the Patriots in 2017. At least that's what others in the league would soon come to believe.

In an utterly befuddling call to everyone outside New England, upon review officials ruled not only that Seferian-Jenkins had not scored, but that he had fumbled—it did seem that he had briefly lost his grip on the ball. They took away the Jets' touchdown and gave the ball to New England.

Referee Tony Corrente later explained:

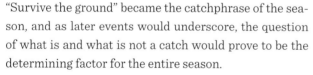

The final shot we saw was from the end zone that showed the New York Jets' runner, we'll call him a runner at that point, with the football starting to go toward the ground. He lost the ball. It came out of his control as he was almost to the ground. Now he re-grasps the ball and by rule, he has to complete the process of recovery, which means he has to survive the ground again. So in recovering it, he recovered, hit the knee, started to roll and the ball came out a second time. So the ball started to move in his hands this way . . . he's now out of bounds in the end zone, which now created a touchback. So he didn't survive the recovery and didn't survive the ground during the recovery is what happened here.

"Survive the ground" became the catchphrase of the season, and as later events would underscore, the question of what is and what is not a catch would prove to be the determining factor for the entire season.

The play deflated the Jets, and despite what in many ways was a bad start to the season, the Patriots were suddenly 4-2. After that, every time the Patriots were challenged, the ball, the calls, and everything else that seemed to threaten the Patriots would fall their way . . . including the loss to injury of other premier quarterbacks around the league who could have led their team to a championship. In quick succession, the Packers' Aaron Rodgers, Houston rookie Deshaun Watson, the Cardinals' Carson Palmer, and the Eagles' Carson Wentz all fell to season-ending injuries, either taking their team's playoff hopes with them or at least dramatically damaging their likelihood of playing into February. NFL owners, cowed by Trump but mostly unconcerned about politics to begin

with, chose not to compete for anything but draft position. They would sign guys who had barely played quarterback in college to replace these quarterbacks, while keeping the utterly healthy Colin Kaepernick, who had played well in San Francisco in 2016 before becoming a free agent, frozen out of the game.

• • •

Several years before, Belichick—accepting the reality that as Brady entered his late thirties the Patriots would have to plan for the future and develop a quarterback to play Brady to his Bledsoe—had drafted and then groomed Jimmy Garoppolo to take over. And when Brady was suspended, Garoppolo's performance had done nothing but underscore the wisdom of that decision: he seemed ready to be a very good starting NFL quarterback, and other NFL teams took notice. In the off-season, the Patriots were peppered with trade offers for Garoppolo, only to turn them all down.

But when Brady's resurgence in 2016 was followed by a slow start in 2017, it caused a quandary. Keeping Garoppolo was expensive, and the young quarterback was understandably impatient: he had turned down long-term deals worth as much as $18 million to stay in New England while Brady tested the quarterback actuarial table. It was becoming clear that to retain Garoppolo through the 2018 season, the Pats would have to designate him as their franchise player, a costly move that could also hamper the team in its roster flexibility.

As the season unfolded, the behind-the-scenes drama around the Garoppolo decision exposed fractures in the organization. It was all a little bit of the old Patriot way, the kind of organizational schizophrenia that once happened with regularity but in recent years had dwindled and become masked by the glow reflecting off all those Lombardi Trophies.

On one side was Belichick. Unsentimental to a fault, he wanted to keep the young quarterback, knowing it was inevitable that Brady would one day falter, from either age or injury, and Garoppolo would take over. After all, they'd invested years in his tutelage, and starting over with another young quarterback might not make for a seamless—and winning—transition. On the other side was Brady, who made it clear that he didn't think he was even close to being finished and had no intention of stepping aside, joined by Kraft, who now felt about Brady the same way he had once felt about Drew Bledsoe. Back then, he had swallowed his pride and allowed Belichick to make a quarterback change. But this was different. Brady was no Bledsoe—Brady was uninjured and a living legend.

How do you replace a legend? Particularly one who, despite his slow start, still seemed to be a premier quarterback? That question, in fact, could be applied to the entire organization: the sixty-six-year-old coach had a host of assistants, including his own son, who lay in wait to take his job, and the owner also had a son, Jonathan Kraft, who had long been preparing to take over for his now-seventy-five-year-old father. If the Patriots of recent vintage have been characterized by stability at the top, at some point in the not too distant future the transition after the loss of Brady, Belichick, and Kraft will inevitably present challenges to that stability.

The Patriots' slow return to form continued as they ended October with wins over the Falcons, still flailing after the Super Bowl loss, and the Chargers. They entered bye week at 6-2 and on a secure path to the playoffs.

One day after beating Los Angeles, they traded Garoppolo to the 49ers, a deal that had been in place for some time at that point, only to be held up by trying to get everyone—read Belichick—on the same page. In the end, the coach did as he was told by Kraft, but wasn't happy about it. Now he'd have to acquire and develop another quarterback, all the while hoping that Brady stayed healthy and productive and that the next quarterback's success would overlap with Brady's. For all that to happen, it looked like Belichick would have to keep coaching a bit longer than he might have wanted to. By year's end, there were credible rumors that if the Patriots won another championship, he might retire.

They received relatively little for a player they considered so valuable, dealing Garoppolo to the 0-8 49ers for only a second-round draft pick and the release of former New England backup Brian Hoyer; in effect, they traded Garoppolo for a player they desperately hoped they'd never have to play. But Hoyer knew the system, having spent parts of three seasons in New England from 2009 to 2011 and throwing 43 passes before going on to play, mostly without distinction, in Arizona, Pittsburgh, Cleveland, Houston, Chicago, and San Francisco. Of course, Kaepernick was still out there, willing, available, and easily the best quarterback in the world not playing and the best equipped to take the Pats to the postseason if Brady were hurt. But he received no consideration whatsoever from the Pats, who, like every other team, seemed content to risk losing with someone else than winning with a player who asked uncomfortable questions. Meanwhile, when Garoppolo took over the 49ers, they finished the year winning five in a row.

Belichick, who had apparently raved about Garoppolo to 49er GM John Lynch, saying he was "special . . . you're gonna love the player, guys respond to him," was typically taciturn and obtuse when asked about the deal, publicly said only, "Unfortunately it just wasn't sustainable" for the Pats to keep him. It was for the 49ers, who after the Super Bowl signed the quarterback to a record-high $137.5 million five-year contract, although only $48.7 million was fully guaranteed.

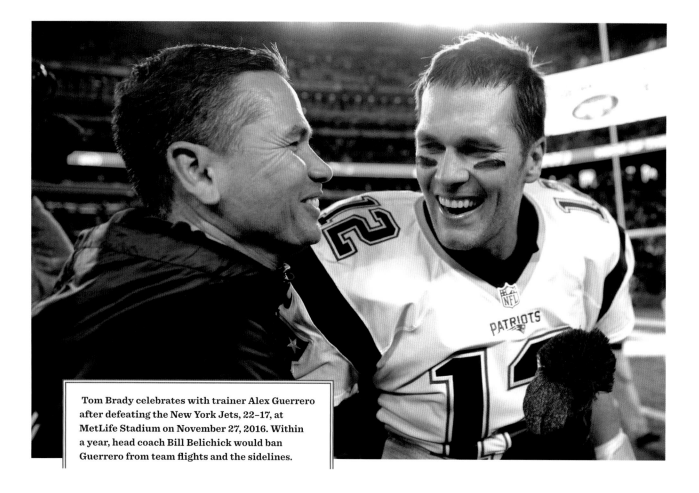

Tom Brady celebrates with trainer Alex Guerrero after defeating the New York Jets, 22–17, at MetLife Stadium on November 27, 2016. Within a year, head coach Bill Belichick would ban Guerrero from team flights and the sidelines.

The plan, or at least Brady's plan, was that the Pats wouldn't need a backup quarterback. Over the past several seasons, Brady had become an even more devoted adept of his private health guru Alex Guerrero, who enjoyed Brady's utter faith. In the off-season, Brady had published a best-selling book, *The TB12 Method*, labeled "short on science" by the *New York Times*. It contains his training and lifestyle regimen based on Guerrero's concepts, which Brady believes somehow protects him from the risks of concussions. The two men opened their own TB12 training center adjacent to Gillette Stadium in Patriot Place, and a number of Brady's teammates, particularly his receivers, also adopted "the Method." Gronkowski was working out at the TB12 facility during the off-season, and as the season progressed as many as twenty other players followed suit.

TB12's popularity, of course, raised problems with the Patriots' own medical and training staff and created divisions within the team between those who followed TB12, those who did not, and those who felt pressured to do so. It wasn't long before Guerrero's advice (among other things, he reportedly tells followers to avoid lifting heavy weights, long a staple of the NFL) and that of the training staff were reportedly in conflict. A falling-out became inevitable.

• • •

The Pats put the bye week to good use and came back humming, opening the second half of the season with three big wins over the Broncos, Raiders, and Dolphins that made the loss to Kansas City seem like something from another era. A third straight appearance in the Super Bowl suddenly seemed a near-certainty, the only possible impediments being injuries, acts of God, and the Pittsburgh Steelers.

They didn't get an act of God, but they did get an act of Gronk, one that could prove to be even more devastating. In week thirteen, the Patriots played the Bills in a chippy game as Buffalo played surprisingly tough. All game long the Bills' defense pushed and shoved Gronkowski, and the receiver became frustrated over the lack of calls by the officials. Late in the fourth quarter, with a safe 23–3 lead, Brady threw to Gronkowski on the sideline. Bills back Tre'Davious White pushed past Gronkowski for the interception, then fell to the ground out of bounds.

Gronkowski came unglued and responded like some professional wrestling heel. He launched himself in the air toward the prone player and landed on top of White with his full body weight, slamming his left arm and shoulder onto the back of White's head and driving it into the ground, a vicious, unconscionable act impossible to justify. White had to leave the game with a concussion, and Gronkowski was flagged for roughness. Even Belichick was upset, calling the premeditated act "bullshit."

Although Gronk later apologized—he had little choice—the expectation was that he'd receive a suspension, the only question appearing to be its length. Most thought he got off easy when the league followed with a suspension of only one week, costing him $281,250 in salary but also many times more than that by putting several contract incentives out of reach. A week later, without him, the Pats fell flat and lost to Miami.

That set up a long-awaited Sunday night contest in Pittsburgh versus the Steelers, the one team that seemed able to stop the Pats in the AFC. The game was also likely to determine the ever-important home-field advantage in the playoffs.

It was a great game, as the two teams threw everything at each other, but what took place in the last minute also made it the most memorable game of the regular season.

Earlier in the back-and-forth contest, Pittsburgh's premier receiver, Antonio Brown, was lost to an injury, and now a Gostkowski field goal with just under four minutes remaining had made the score 24–19, pulling the Pats to within five points. The defense held and set up a patented last-minute Brady comeback, which the quarterback made good on three minutes later when

Rob Gronkowski leaves the field at Gillette Stadium after being placed in observation for the NFL's concussion protocol following a helmet-to-helmet hit from Jaguars safety Barry Church in the 2017 AFC championship game.

Dion Lewis burst into the end zone from eight yards out. Then Brady made the two-point conversion on a pass to Gronkowski to put New England ahead. Now trailing 27–24, Pittsburgh had only 56 seconds to respond.

From the Pittsburgh 20-yard line, JuJu Smith-Schuster caught a short pass from Ben Roethlisberger on a crossing route and seemed to be heading to the sidelines to stop the clock only to see the Patriots' Jordan Richards and Devin McCourty colliding with each other. Smith-Schuster then cut back to the middle before finally being brought down at the 10.

On the next play, Roethlisberger found Jesse James two yards shy of the end zone, and James lunged in untouched for what are the two most frightening words in the NFL, an "apparent score," and was mauled by his teammates, the game seemingly over, Heinz Field erupting with Terrible Towels waving in frenzy.

Then came the review, followed by the next-most ominous words in the NFL: "survive the ground." According to the rule, after a catch, until the receiver becomes a runner, he must retain possession when landing in the end zone until he "survives the ground"—in other words, hits the ground still holding the ball firmly. It doesn't matter if the ball is wrapped in the receiver's arms with the ball past the goal line—that's only the rule for runners. Receivers are held to a higher and far more difficult to determine standard, and when James hit the ground, the ball had wobbled. The catch was ruled incomplete. Despite running two more plays, the stunned Steelers failed to score, and the Pats escaped—that's the only right word for it—with a 27–24 win, securing home-field advantage in the postseason.

Then, incredibly, it happened again the following week against Buffalo. The fired-up Bills were playing New England tight when, at the end of the first half, the Bills' Kelvin Benjamin outjumped Stephen Gilmore to catch a pass in the end zone that would have put Buffalo in the lead. Then the officials ruled, once again under replay, that Benjamin's foot hadn't touched the ground, an assessment that almost everyone else watching the replay violently disagreed with. The Pats went on to win, 37–16. It seemed as if everyone knew what a catch was except the NFL rule book, and the fact that the Patriots benefited from the calls three times in the season, helping them to three wins, made fans in other cities feel like the fix was in. Many speculated that perhaps the NFL was now trying to make up for suspending Brady the previous season.

In the meantime, as the Pats dispatched the Jets in the season finale to secure a 13-3 record, a number-one seed, and home-field advantage, not all seemed to be well behind the scenes in Foxborough. First Belichick, after hearing complaints from his staff, banned Brady's guru Alex Guerrero from the sidelines and decided that other Patriots could no longer receive treatment from him at the office he'd been given at the team's facilities.

That was a direct affront, and a rare one, to Brady, and it led to further scrutiny of the relationship among the coach, his quarterback, and the owner. Then a report from ESPN by Seth Wickersham appeared to reveal that all sorts of palace intrigue had been taking place over the entire season, beginning with Belichick's desire to retain Garoppolo, Brady's failure to provide the younger quarterback with much help, splits among the team along generational lines, and Bob Kraft's escalating attempts to rein in Belichick's authority and reassert control. Wickersham termed it "the beginning of the end," and while that might have overstated the situation a touch—for that had been the case even before the season started—it did identify the fact that all three men were having difficulty imagining and coming to terms with life without the Patriots and each other. All three appeared to be looking toward the postcareer evaluation of who would receive credit for the team's success and to be starting to jockey for their own standing in that accounting rather than letting results on the field speak for them.

Remember that when Kraft first took over as owner, Bill Parcells had been promised full control by James Orthwein, only to have Kraft withdraw it, saying he preferred a system of "checks and balances." That would be a significant factor in Parcells's decision to leave the Pats. After he left, Kraft hired Pete Carroll, but divided his authority. After firing Carroll, the owner admitted that "hamstringing" his coach, not giving him enough leeway and authority, had been a mistake. He hadn't placed the same restrictions on Belichick and had almost always deferred to him, which was made clear when Kraft, albeit reluctantly, went along with his coach's decision first to play Brady over Bledsoe and eventually to trade Bledsoe, the owner's favorite.

Kraft had more or less maintained that level of detachment ever since, but over time incidents like Spygate, the drafting of Aaron Hernandez, and Deflategate had left him to clean up messes he felt weren't entirely of his own making. In combination, it appeared that the Guerrero and Garoppolo situations had exposed a possible waning of Kraft's faith in his coach, the likelihood that Belichick was beginning to grate under the erosion of his authority. At the same time, Brady's increasing stature and power within the organization further complicated the relationship among the three most important figures in the franchise. Increasingly, none of the three seemed to much like either of the other two telling him what to do or taking credit for his achievements.

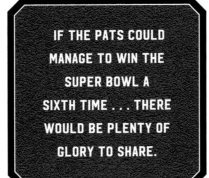

IF THE PATS COULD MANAGE TO WIN THE SUPER BOWL A SIXTH TIME . . . THERE WOULD BE PLENTY OF GLORY TO SHARE.

Now Kraft turned back the clock. In an August interview with the *Globe*'s Ben Volin, when asked if Belichick had his full trust, he said, "Well, yeah—with checks and balances," using the phrase in regard to Belichick for the first time. He also began overtly reminding people that he owned the team, after all, implying that he didn't appreciate being overlooked either by the press or by people in his own organization.

So what was the solution? Well, the same as it's always been: winning cures everything. If the Pats could manage to win the Super Bowl a sixth time, a record for a quarterback, coach, and owner, the question of who got the credit and who was in control would become a lot less important. There would be plenty of glory to share.

And winning that next Super Bowl suddenly didn't seem that far-fetched. In fact, it began to seem inevitable. Apart from the Steelers, no team appeared to be a lock in the postseason, mainly because no one else had a quarterback to compare with Brady, who had rebounded after a slow start to put together an MVP season. The Saints had Drew Brees, but the others in the playoffs— the likes of Blake Bortles, Marcus Mariota, Nick Foles, and Alex Smith—didn't exactly strike fear in the hearts of the Patriots. And then the Saints fell to the Titans on a last-second desperation pass and Brees was knocked out of the equation. New England's path to the Super Bowl seemed to only get even easier.

The Pats dispatched the Titans like a minor annoyance, 35–14, and a day later the Jaguars upset the Steelers in a wild game, 45–42. Few gave the Jaguars and their erratic quarterback, Blake Bortles, much of a chance against the Patriots and their MVP Hall of Famer in waiting. The NFC championship would be played between the Minnesota Vikings and Philadelphia Eagles, both manned by quarterbacks who only had the job because the starter had been hurt. Case Keenum and Nick Foles were little more than journeymen, quarterback JAGs, players the Patriots could have signed as backup to Brady at some point but had passed over.

Each of these quarterbacks, if given the opportunity, was expected to melt before the specter of facing Brady and the Patriots. After all, that's what had happened to Matt Ryan in Super Bowl LI and even Roethlisberger at the end of the recent Pittsburgh game. The thinking went that the Patriots were now in everyone's head and their defense, despite its early struggles and the loss of Dont'a Hightower, was now a strength, among the stingiest in the league. In the final weeks of the season, they'd received a boost by picking up veteran linebacker James Harrison, who'd been dropped by the Steelers, and were now playing their best football of the year on that side of the ball. How could they lose?

After the AFC championship game, the answer seemed obvious: they couldn't. Because even though the Jags pushed and shoved the Pats around like a kid on the playground for three quarters, the Patriots, when it mattered, played like these Patriots had always seemed to play in the postseason in recent years. In pursuit of an upset, Jacksonville would not survive the ground.

But for a while, Jacksonville looked good. With Tom Brady wearing a glove for the first time in a game since 2002—he'd suffered a cut on his throwing hand in

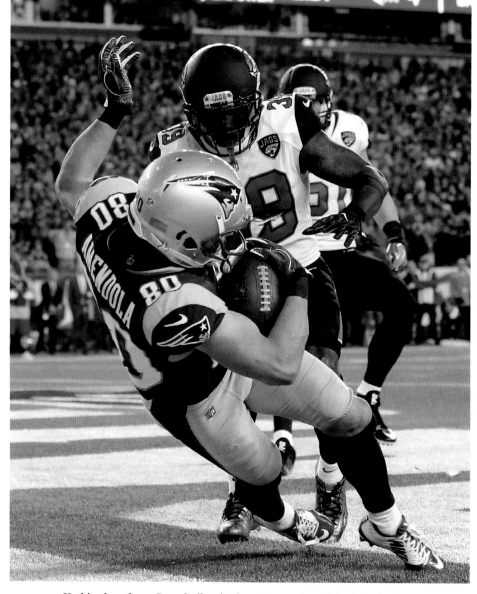

Nothing less than a Baryshnikov in cleats, Danny Amendola, defended by Tashaun Gipson of the Jacksonville Jaguars, catches a touchdown pass in the fourth quarter of the 2017 AFC championship game at Gillette Stadium.

had given the Patriots trouble all year. Then, after another Patriot punt, the Jags drove 77 yards for another score and the Pats were forced to punt again. All of a sudden, with Jacksonville driving, this game was looking a lot like the first half of Super Bowl LI.

Which was true in more ways than one. With the Patriots on their heels and less than two minutes left in the first half, the Jaguars crossed midfield, and on a third-and-7, Bortles, playing more like Matt Ryan than himself, hit Mercedes Lewis for a gain of 12, giving the Jags a first down at the 32, well within field goal range. It seemed likely that Jacksonville would enter halftime leading 17–3 at least, if not score a touchdown and then take possession after the second-half kickoff with a chance to increase their lead even more before the Pats had a chance to respond. It wasn't unthinkable, with just over two minutes remaining in the half, that if they worked the clock, the score could be 28–3 before New England even got the ball back.

That, of course, had once been the score in Super Bowl LI, but what were the chances of New England overcoming a deficit like that again in the postseason? Yet this game would continue to resemble that one, soon in an even more significant way. Just a split-second after the snap, a flag was thrown. Despite having two time-outs remaining, Bortles had taken too much time, calling for the ball a split-second after the play clock had run out. Instead of a first down, the Jags were assessed a five-yard "delay of game" penalty. Bortles was sacked on the next play, pushing them back another six yards, to the 49. Instead of kicking a field goal, the Jags had to punt. Somewhere, the Falcons knew just how they felt.

That's all Brady needed. Over the next minute, he completed four of six passes, drove the Pats down the

a collision during practice with Rex Birkhead—the game matched the Jaguars and their league-best pass defense and second-best pass rush against the Pats with their league-best passing offense.

The Pats opened the game, which took place on the twenty-fourth anniversary of Kraft's purchase of the team, with a long drive that culminated in a field goal as Brady seemed unaffected by the cut or the glove. After an exchange of punts, the Jaguars responded with a touchdown drive of their own, mixing runs and short passes out of a run-pass option offense. This scheme, in which the quarterback reads the defense and decides after the snap on almost every play whether to hand the ball off or pass, field, and then James White turned back the clock and ran in from the 1. At halftime, the score wasn't 17–3, or 21–3, but 14–10, the "delay of game" call responsible for a point swing of at least 10 points, if not 14 or more. Like Atlanta, the Jaguars missed an opportunity to put their foot on New England's neck and apply the pressure. Of course, this opportunity had come in the second quarter, not the fourth, but the result would be the same as it had been in Super Bowl LI. They'd blown it.

It was a mistake they would regret.

In the second half, the Pats still had a hard time stopping Jacksonville, and the Jags' defense, known as "Sacksonville" to their fans, kept the pressure on. With just over 12 minutes left, Jacksonville was leading 20–10 when the Pats took over, at which point their chance of victory was calculated by ProFootballReference.com at less than 10 percent. If Jacksonville could stop Brady one more time and put together any kind of drive of its own, a New England victory would become even less likely.

But they could not. With 12 minutes left, Brady suddenly became unstoppable, the mission clear. Over the next three minutes, he completed five of seven passes, three to Amendola, the last from nine yards out. Suddenly it was 20–17, and you could tell what would happen next.

One of the keys to a Brady-led comeback is that the Pats' defense always, always, seems to get the critical stop, and they did so again. Jacksonville couldn't move the ball and had to punt, and the Pats didn't panic. When their own drive stalled, they punted and pinned the Jags back, forcing another Jacksonville punt a few plays later, and Amendola tricked the Jags into thinking he would call a fair catch, then returned the ball 20 yards, giving Brady the ball with five minutes remaining and victory only 30 yards away. In the exchange of punts, the Pats had gained almost 20 yards. It wasn't quite like taking that safety against the Broncos, but it provided a similar opportunity.

It was becoming monotonous. The Pats had the Jaguars right where they wanted them—time running out, the ball in Brady's hands, the game on the line, Jacksonville knowing what would happen next and all but powerless to stop it. For most of the game, the Jaguars had fiercely held the upper hand. Now the Jags became a team of JAGs—just another bunch of guys knowing they were going to lose.

It almost wasn't fair. Brady and company might as well have been lining up opposite a Pop Warner team. Brady took his time, a pass here, a run there, then Danny Amendola, cutting across the back of the end zone, reached for a pass only he could catch. As he completely stretched out, first his right toes and then his left toes came down just inside the end line, the ball in his hands, held firm, for a touchdown.

The crowd at Gillette erupted. A year before, most had seen this on TV against Atlanta. This time they got to watch it at home, up close, and feel the vibe themselves. Brady had led the Pats to comebacks in the playoffs before, most notably in 2001, 2004, and 2006, then in the Super Bowl, but this felt like a command performance.

It's not luck when it happens time and time again. A few minutes later, the Pats walked off with a stunning 24–20 win in a game they probably should have lost, one in which they'd been dominated for more than three quarters. Later that night, the Eagles smoked Minnesota 38–7 to win the right to play in the Super Bowl. But if they saw New England's performance in the final 12 minutes, every Eagle with a breath in his body had to be asking, "How do you beat this team? Is any lead safe, ever?"

The Patriots had history and everything else on their side. It was there for the taking, all of it, an opportunity for the franchise to achieve things no other team had ever done. With another victory, the Patriots—the Pats!—would be anointed as the greatest dynasty in football history. While other teams—the Packers and Bears—have won more championships, only the Steelers, with six titles in eight tries, have won more Super Bowls. However, none have approached the Patriots' recent record of success, with eight Super Bowl appearances across the last sixteen seasons, appearing in the postseason nine straight years and fifteen out of the last seventeen (and beginning in 1994 under Bill Parcells, nineteen of the last twenty-four). Over that time period, the Pats have had only one—one!—losing season.

But for the franchise's dominant personalities, Belichick, Brady, and Kraft, there was even more at stake.

Among NFL coaches, only George Halas and Vince Lombardi had ever won six championships, but Halas never won a Super Bowl. Only two of Lombardi's rings were earned in a Super Bowl; the others had come in a league less than half the size of the current NFL. The Packers had won the NFL championship three times in a row twice, but no team had ever won three Super Bowls in four seasons with the same coach, much less six under his tenure. If Belichick and the Patriots could beat the Eagles, it was not unthinkable that his name might one day appear on the trophy along with Lombardi's, if not by itself.

Similarly, no quarterback had ever matched Brady's achievement, making his eighth appearance in the NFL's premier game in his eighteen-year NFL career, with the opportunity to win for the sixth time. One more win would put even more distance between Brady and every other championship quarterback. Only Joe Montana and Terry Bradshaw had won the Super Bowl as many as four times, and only Bart Starr had as many as five championship rings. With six wins, Brady would stand alone and prove the wisdom of his "Method."

For Bob Kraft, the stakes were comparable. George Halas of the Bears, who owned the team he also coached, was the only NFL individual owner in history with six championships, but it had taken him more than forty years to accomplish that. (The Packers are owned collectively while the Steelers have been owned by various members of the Rooney family.) With a victory, Kraft would have done something infinitely more difficult, and in only twenty-four seasons. Moreover, it would come in a season in which he had reasserted his authority. A win would justify that move.

These three men had never before had so much personally at stake as there would be in Super Bowl LII. And maybe that was the problem, for the pressure had already caused each to behave, whether they recognized it or not, in ways they would not have in the past. Winning the Super Bowl is hard enough, but when you're trying to do more than that, the challenge is even greater. Repeat after me: if you are trying to do anything more than win, you are destined to lose.

And maybe the Patriots weren't just looking to win. Maybe they were looking to make a statement.

How else can Super Bowl LII be explained? If one is a Patriots fan or a member of the organization, how else can one accept the inglorious, agonizing mess that was Super Bowl LII, simultaneously the most entertaining and aggravating Super Bowl of all time, a game that history will debate and replay just as much as it will continue

to celebrate Super Bowl LI? The difference between the two games is both infinitesimal and enormous, and the consequences of loss hard to comprehend.

How else to fathom a game in which the Patriots never punted and gained more than 600 yards, yet lost—something no NFL team had ever done—while also allowing the other team to hold the ball for more than 34 minutes? What can one say about a game in which Brady threw for a postseason-record 505 yards and yet was outplayed by his counterpart, a game in which Brady dropped a potential touchdown pass and Eagles quarterback Nick Foles caught one? Who could have foreseen a game in which the two teams combined gained the most yards in NFL history and went up and down the field for 60 minutes like they were playing Aussie Rules? In which two guys cut by the Patriots after 2016 over money came up big for the Eagles and two touchdown-catch reviews went against the Pats? In which their defense turned in the worst performance in Super Bowl history and a player who had started 17 of 18 games and played a central role on the defense since becoming the hero in Super Bowl XLIX was inexplicably benched by the coach? And after all that, how did the game *still* come down to the very final play, a last chance at victory hanging in the air and everyone, everyone, holding their breath because, after all, these are the Patriots?

• • •

There were signs from the start that something never seen before was about to take place. The Patriots' defense seemed incapable of stopping Philadelphia—just as in the AFC championship game, the run-pass option seemed to befuddle the Pats. But neither team played the first quarter with much authority, first trading field goals before the Eagles scored the game's first touchdown, a pass to Alshon Jeffery over Eric Rowe—Belichick's surprise choice to start instead of Malcolm Butler—only to miss the extra point.

Belichick's decision to start Rowe over Butler—and to stick with that decision throughout the game—would prove to be controversial and would expose him to blistering criticism. Butler, who had earned All-Pro status in 2016, admitted to slipping in 2017, but he had still taken 97 percent of the snaps at his position, finishing fourth on the team in tackles. Moreover, no one on the team apparently knew of the change until just before game time, and

Tom Brady fumbles against the Philadelphia Eagles during the final minutes of the fourth quarter in Super Bowl LII at US Bank Stadium.

the news reportedly caused disbelief and anger among both players and coaches. Butler stood for the National Anthem looking utterly crushed, with tears running down his face. After the game, he responded to rumors and vehemently denied that he had committed any kind of infraction warranting being benched, saying, "They gave up on me." Responding after the game to the criticism, Belichick offered only that he thought Rowe "gave us the best chance to win." In all Boston sports history lore, only Red Sox manager Joe McCarthy's choice of Denny Galehouse to pitch the 1948 playoff game against the Cleveland Indians has proven to be as inexplicable—and consequential. Said one Eagle afterward, "We had Rowe on our team here in Philly, we knew that was a mismatch." The Pats would later have to change coverage assignments to protect Rowe.

When New England tried to respond to the Eagles' first touchdown, a bad snap and hold caused a rare Gostkowski miss of a field goal, the line drive thudding off the left goalpost. Then the defense stiffened, forcing what would be the only punt of the game. This would also

be the only time Malcolm Butler appeared on the field the entire game.

Still, when New England took over with 13 minutes remaining in the first half, trailing 9–3, it seemed as if both teams had settled in and the real game was about to start. On the first play, Brady found Brandin Cooks in between defenders 20 yards downfield, and after the catch Cooks cut and twirled and pivoted, looking to gain a few more yards. He did not see the Eagles' Malcolm Jenkins, closing fast, and Cooks was blindsided by a helmet-to-helmet hit, legal but still dangerous. Everyone recognized that he'd suffered a concussion before he hit the ground. Cooks walked off the field but would not return.

That may have been the most consequential play of the game, for it removed Brady's deep threat from New England's arsenal. Phillip Dorsett, with only 12 catches for the season, took over for Cooks.

The loss of Cooks seemed to unnerve the Pats. Only three plays later, on third-and-5 from the 35, the Patriots uncharacteristically tried a flea flicker. It was the kind of play you draw on dirt and call in the backyard, a double-fake reverse from the shotgun. James White took the handoff and ran left before flipping the ball back to Amendola, the ex–college quarterback. Meanwhile, Brady circled out to the right, all alone, and Amendola lofted a pass his way.

For anyone else, it might have been a touchdown. Even for the slow-footed Brady, it would have at least been a first down, but the quarterback let the ball drift off his fingertips for an incompletion—after all, on a team whose mantra is "do your job," Brady's job was to throw passes, not catch them. But it was a strange play for New England to call in that situation, wasted in an attempt for a first down, a sign perhaps that the Patriots were already feeling a little desperate.

They failed to convert on fourth down on the next play, and from that point forward, slowly and inexorably, the game began to get away from the Patriots. The Eagles and their quarterback Foles dictated the pace, remaining patient, mixing runs and passes, and forcing the Patriots to react to them rather than the other way around. As the Eagles played with increasing confidence, the Patriots, even when succeeding, seemed a little out of sync: Brady missed short passes he usually made, tacklers reached for air, and Gronkowski, back after his concussion two weeks earlier, was almost invisible as he played a quiet first half, as if still in a fog. For the rest of the game, there was a feeling that something was not quite right, though it didn't seem reflected in the stats, or even in the score. The Patriots were usually behind not by much, but it always felt like they were barely hanging in, even when they would later, briefly, take the lead.

If there is anything that has characterized the Patriots' approach, particularly in big games and in the postseason since their run to the Super Bowl in 2014, it's that even when they have trailed, they always seem to be in the game and in control. Beyond the X's and O's, within the context of the game and in the moment, they have always been able to play their way. Then, when the game comes to them, they exert pressure and force the other team to react. But on this day, even as they moved the ball almost at will, that never seemed to happen. On offense, they gained yards and made plays, but they always seemed to be counterpunching, playing catchup, while on defense they could slow the Eagles down but never really stop them. In the playoffs, the Patriots' defense had

always been able to make the big stop when they needed it, forcing a turnover or getting a call that Brady and the offense, sensing a way to win and forcing their will upon the other team, could take advantage of.

On this day, that never happened, and the Eagles didn't flinch. Unlike Pete Carroll, Matt Ryan, and the Jaguars, Philadelphia coach Doug Pederson didn't overthink things, Nick Foles didn't take the critical sack, and the Eagles didn't sit on their lead.

The path the Patriots expected to follow never appeared, and they were not prepared to take another. And the Eagles never played scared, were never intimidated over facing a *dynasty* and all the extra baggage that comes with that. They were just playing the team on the other side of the ball, play by play, and more often than not they simply outplayed the Pats.

Four plays really made the difference. The first came after a 26-yard dash by James White drew the Patriots close to the Eagles, leading only 15–12. On fourth down-and-goal from the 1, with 38 seconds remaining in the first half, common sense said that Philly should play it safe, kick a field goal, and take an 18–12 lead into the locker room. But the Eagles had a special play, one they had practiced the week before, not on the field in Minneapolis, but in their hotel. With the Pats' reputation for spying still in the back of their minds, they called it the "Philly Special." Foles suggested it on the sidelines, and Pederson agreed.

Tight end Trey Burton lined up in the backfield. Then he shifted next to Foles in the shotgun, and Foles went up to the line, barked, and shifted to the slot, as if communicating with his line. The ball was snapped directly to Burton, the entire defense charged, expecting Burton to thunder into the line . . . and Foles drifted to the right, to the goal line in the flat, wide open. Burton threw the perfect pass, raising his arms to call for a touchdown before Foles even caught the ball.

The play was a slap in the face, a "take that" call after the Pats failed to pass to Brady, an "anything you can do we can do better" moment. It not only gave the Eagles a 22–12 lead, it gave them belief.

In the second half, the calls fell Philly's way. The first came after the Eagles took the kickoff and drove 75 yards for a score, a catch at the back of the end zone by Corey Clement, who appeared, just barely, to lose control of the ball, then step on the line. It was called a touchdown on the field, but that was the kind of call the geniuses responsible for replay had ruled incomplete all year, the kind of call that had fallen the Patriots' way. But on this day, on the big stage, it was as if the league had decided that the Super Bowl would not be determined on an overturned call. The touchdown stood, putting the Eagles up 29–19.

The killer came in the fourth quarter, after Brady, incredibly, drove the Patriots on two more 75-yard scoring drives, sandwiched around a Philadelphia field goal, to put the Patriots nominally ahead, 33–32. Since halftime, the game had felt like whoever had the ball last would win, and with 9:22 remaining, the Eagles seemed to sense that and began a relentless, seven-minute march down the field,

knowing they not only had to score but had to leave Brady little time to mount a comeback. Foles never panicked. He made safe, short passes and occasionally handed the ball off to former Patriot LeGarrette Blount, who had been called "the Closer" by his teammates in New England. On the way, Foles completed a key fourth-down pass to tight end Zach Ertz, and with 2:25 left in the game, he found Ertz at the 5. The tight end turned toward the end zone, took two steps, and lunged, stretching the ball out over the goal line. When he hit the ground, the ball bounced free, but Ertz caught it again while on his back.

Again, the call on the field was a touchdown. It was another play that on review during the season had often been ruled incomplete, but not this time: officials determined that Ertz had made the catch and become a

In Super Bowl LII at US Bank Stadium, Eagle Zach Ertz dives into the end zone for a fourth-quarter, 11-yard touchdown that clinched Philadelphia's first-ever Super Bowl title.

runner, rendering control of the football moot once he crossed the line. A two-point conversion failed, but the Eagles led 38–33.

The Patriots, of course, still had Brady and, needing a touchdown, still had a chance. And after all, every time Brady won a Super Bowl in the past it had required a comeback, so maybe this was finally the situation the Pats needed—comeback was a game they knew how to play. Anyone not thinking that was out of their mind. Hell, Brady had more than two minutes and a time-out to play with. There was still plenty of time.

All day long, the Pats' line had kept Philadelphia's vaunted line at bay, allowing Brady to throw 38 times to that point without being sacked, usually facing little pressure. But not this time. On the second play after the kick, Philadelphia finally put on the pressure: ex-Patriot Chris Long and Brandon Graham crashed in from the right side, and as Brady lifted the ball to throw, Graham reached out and slapped it from his hand. There was no Tuck Rule now, and even if there had been, it was a clear fumble. The ball bounced free, the Eagles recovered, and they soon kicked a field goal to increase their lead to 41–33.

But these were still the Patriots, and their quarterback was still Tom Brady, and even on this day, even after all that had happened, Pats fans still believed. Philly kicked short, forcing a return, and a desperate try for a reverse return failed, pinning the Pats back at the 9. Eight plays brought the ball only to midfield, and the Pats were out of time-outs.

With nine seconds remaining—time for just one more play—the ball was on the New England 49-yard line. Fans in Philadelphia and New England and everywhere else were on the edge of their chairs, holding good luck charms, with the champagne chilled and four hours of gut-wrenching anxiety waiting to explode. Because after all, as Belichick always says, you have to play all 60 minutes, every tick of the clock for every one of the 3,600 seconds of the game and sometimes even more.

And when your quarterback is Tom Brady, anything can happen—because it has so many times before.

Not a Patriot living thought a white shirt wouldn't catch the ball, that a two-point conversion wouldn't be next, and then, like so many teams so many times before, that the Eagles wouldn't fold as the Pats marched down the field to history and exultation, with two Super Bowl wins in a row, three of four, six of ten, more than anybody, waiting in the end zone.

Brady dropped back, waited, waited, wound up, and stepped forward to the Philadelphia 45 . . . and threw a prayer.

Patriots fans had seen all this before, or some version of it. Dozens of times dreams had become flesh, the seemingly impossible improbably coming true. Of all their comebacks, this would be the best *evah*, the final exclamation point, an even-better-than-Doug-Flutie-"Miracle in Miami"-Hail-Mary of a play, the ultimate stamp that would prove that, yes, Tom Brady *was* more god than man, that Belichick had once again gotten his team to play to the finish, and that Bob Kraft and his belief in both men, despite the sniping of the last few weeks, was complete and whole and total, an article of faith fully justified.

> IT'S A MEASURE OF SOMETHING THAT EVERY SINGLE PERSON WATCHING THE GAME, UNTIL THE FINAL WHISTLE SOUNDED, BELIEVED THAT IMAGINED OUTCOME MIGHT TAKE PLACE. WHEN IT DID NOT, IT WAS EVEN MORE SHOCKING THAN IF IT HAD.

In the end zone, Gronkowski waited, with Amendola and Dorsett and Hogan crashing in on both sides and in front, surrounded by five Eagles, then six and seven. The ball dropped down, Gronk leaped, the Eagles all went up, and Gronk got a hand on it, keeping the ball alive. The Eagles all fell away, a hand in a white jersey stretched and reached out and pulled the ball from the air, and then the referees' hands shot in the air and the roof came off in what will forever be known as the Miracle in Minneapolis . . .

. . . except that's not what happened. Gronk did get a hand on it, the ball did come free, hanging a moment in the air, but no hand was there to catch it. That dream did not survive the ground. The ball bounced off the turf, and the final second ticked off. No miracle, no overtime, and for the first time in a long time, nothing for New England to celebrate.

It's a measure of something that every single person watching the game, until the final whistle sounded, believed that imagined outcome might take place. When it did not, it was even more shocking than if it had.

In the end, it was 41–33 Eagles. History was made, but not in a way anyone expected.

And then the Patriots were the Patriots again, not the unbeatable team of recent vintage but that other one, because for the first time in a long time there were questions and a lot of sniping. The loss hurt, and somebody had to take the blame. The venting lit up Twitter, and phones rang off the hook, a thousand voices on hold ready to take to the radio: *Where was the defense? What was Belichick thinking? Why'd he bench Butler? They've ruined our winter!*

And the questions were justified, because neither Belichick nor anyone else could give a straight answer: MassLive later reported forty-one non-answers to the Butler question from Patriots personnel after the game. Was he benched because he was a free-agent-to-be who had resisted a management-friendly salary offer, or was he being punished for some minor infraction, discipline delivered at the most inopportune time imaginable due to an outsized sense of authority? Did Belichick just think he knew better? Was it that he needed to prove he could win his way and would risk losing rather than compromise some private conviction? In other words, was this the time to try to do more than just win?

To no one's surprise, rifts appeared in the wake of the loss as the defeat shuddered through the entire organization. After the game, Gronkowski muttered that the season hadn't been any fun and he was pondering retirement. Defensive coordinator Matt Patricia immediately accepted a head-coaching position with Detroit, leaving Lions fans, in the wake of the pathetic performance of the defense in the Super Bowl, wondering what he'd done to deserve the job. Then offensive coordinator Josh McDaniels, with a press conference scheduled in Indianapolis to announce his appointment as coach of the Colts, abruptly changed his mind, fueling speculation that he'd soon take over for Belichick. As Brady, Belichick, and Kraft all took another step toward the natural end of their individual careers, the loss made it seem even more likely that each was approaching a new role, one that, maybe not this year, maybe not next year, but

soon, would not include the others, unknown territory for all three. Belichick, Brady, and Kraft have long been inexorably tied to each other, and there is no way of separating them. Each man has no way of knowing definitively how much of his success has been truly his own or simply situational. Each has had little individual control.

Is Bob Kraft the greatest NFL owner, Bill Belichick the greatest NFL coach, and Tom Brady the greatest quarterback? Maybe, but maybe not if they hadn't been together. Like a three-legged stool that falls over if one leg is removed, Kraft, without Belichick and Brady, might have shifted and slammed the gears from coach to coach like virtually every other owner in the league. Without Brady and Kraft, Belichick might never have found the player to execute his plans or the owner to provide the resources. And without Kraft and Belichick, Brady might never have had not only the chance to prove himself but the surrounding cast, an offense uniquely tuned to the precise skill set he needed to succeed.

The dynasty had come together by accident. Kraft acquired the team only after outlasting, outmaneuvering, and overpaying the competition to gain control of the club, and only then because Billy Sullivan was the only guy in pro football who couldn't get local government to build a stadium. Bill Belichick could have easily stayed with the Jets, Parcells might have decided to remain with the Patriots, or Kraft might have listened to all those who warned him that Belichick was something of a cipher. And Tom Brady might be the most fortunate of all—after all, NFL teams had said, "There's someone better," and ignored him 198 times before one did not. And even then, if Drew Bledsoe is a half-step faster—or slower—Mo Lewis makes just another tackle, the Pats miss the playoffs, Brady sits on the bench another season, and then likely leaves as a free agent to be a backup someplace else and maybe never gets a chance.

These things we will never know, but what we do know is irrefutable: if winning is the goal and the only thing that matters, in recent years the Patriots have been one of the most efficient teams of all time. It's hard to argue with that. Yet all of pro football is at a kind of crossroads, and over the next few years everyone involved will have to reckon with a sport in transition and come to terms with that. Great wealth and prestige have been gained by the men who own and coach the teams, but it is becoming

HOW IT HAPPENED

SUPER BOWL LII

QUARTER	TIME	TEAM	SCORING PLAY	EAGLES	PATS
1	7:55	Eagles	**Jake Elliott,** 25-yard field goal	3	0
	4:17	Patriots	**Stephen Gostkowski,** 26-yard field goal	3	3
	2:34	Eagles	**Alshon Jeffery,** 34-yard pass from Nick Foles (kick failed)	9	3
2	8:48	Eagles	**LeGarrette Blount,** 21-yard rush (conversion pass failed)	15	3
	7:24	Patriots	**Stephen Gostkowski,** 45-yard field goal	15	6
	2:04	Patriots	**James White,** 26-yard rush (kick failed)	15	12
	0:34	Eagles	**Nick Foles,** 1-yard pass from tight end Trey Burton (Elliott kick)	22	12
3	12:15	Patriots	**Rob Gronkowski,** 5-yard pass from Tom Brady (Gostkowski kick)	22	19
	7:18	Eagles	**Corey Clement,** 22-yard pass from Nick Foles (Elliott kick)	29	19
	3:23	Patriots	**Chris Hogan,** 26-yard pass from Tom Brady (Gostkowski kick)	29	26
4	14:09	Eagles	**Jake Elliott,** 42-yard field goal	32	26
	9:22	Patriots	**Rob Gronkowski,** 4-yard pass from Tom Brady (Gostkowski kick)	32	33
	2:21	Eagles	**Zach Ertz,** 11-yard pass from Nick Foles (pass failed)	38	33
	1:05	Eagles	**Jake Elliott,** 46-yard field goal	41	33

SUPER BOWL RECORDS SET IN SUPER BOWL LII

Most games	8	Tom Brady
Most games, head coach	8	Bill Belichick
Most passes, career	357	Tom Brady
Most completions, career	235	Tom Brady
Most passing yards, career	2,576	Tom Brady
Most passing yards, game	505	Tom Brady
Most touchdown passes, Super Bowl career	18	Tom Brady
Most Super Bowl appearances, team	10	New England
Most points, game, losing team	33	New England
Most first downs passing, game, both teams	42	
Most total yards, game, team	613	New England
Most total yards, game, both teams	1,151	
Most passing yards, game, team	500	New England
Most passing yards, game, both teams	874	
Fewest punts, game, team	0	New England
Fewest punts, game, both teams	1	
Most missed PAT conversions, game, both teams	4	

ever clearer that those benefits have been earned only at the cost of the long-term health and well-being of the players, without whom there is no game at all. It's telling that while more and more players retire prematurely due to concerns over the long-term health of their brains, not a single head coach or owner has left the game citing their own culpability in that all too common outcome.

The accounting of wins and losses is neither the full story of this team nor their entire history. And despite recent events, the future of the team does not reside in the fates of three men named Belichick, Brady, or Kraft, nor in the debate over some specious notion of "legacy."

The most misused phrase in sports, "legacy" is not an accounting quantified by numbers, money, victories, awards, or even championships. It is, by definition, not something that one possesses, but a gift one leaves behind for the next generation. And in this context, the lasting legacy of the Patriots belongs not to anyone who has ever owned or coached or played for the team, not to Billy Sullivan or Bob Kraft, not to Mike Holovak or Bill Belichick, and not to Steve Grogan, Curtis Martin, Drew Bledsoe, or Tom Brady.

No, the lasting legacy of the Patriots, the true gift, resides with their fans, from the first few who traipsed down Commonwealth Avenue to watch a team they'd never seen before, in a league they'd barely heard of, to the ones who screamed themselves hoarse over Jim Nance barreling over tacklers, who waited in traffic on Route 1, pulling on a tallboy, who huddled in the snow on aluminum bleachers. From the fans who booed Chuck Fairbanks to the ones who laughed with Billy Sullivan, listened to Gil and Gino on the radio, sneered with Bill Parcells, cheered with Adam Vinatieri, and cried with Malcolm Butler. Since 1960, the fans have been the only constant in this franchise, no matter who has owned it, coached the team, or played on the field. They are the true legacy of the Patriots, which at its heart is all about loving something enough to care what happens, no matter what happens.. You're either in or out, win or lose, and long-time fans know that.

In 1958, time in New England stopped for a few hours as fans watched the Giants and the Colts play a football game on television, one of the best ever—a shared experience they talked about at work the next day and a game still talked about today. More recently, in Super Bowl LI and LII—both classic, unforgettable contests, albeit with very different outcomes—the common experience first kindled that cold December afternoon continues. Some sixty years from now, those games, too, will still be part of New England's story.

This is the legacy of this team: for nearly sixty years, no matter where they have played or how many games they have won or lost, the Patriots have mattered to the fans in the stands and those who sit at home. Since 1960, for better and worse—and few teams in sports have, at various times, ever been much better or ever much worse—the Pats have helped define a region and meant something important. And that's why winning brings elation, why losing hurts so much, and why, no matter the outcome, you return each year. In the end, that's the only legacy that really matters.

• • •

History teaches us that every dynasty rises and falls, and, yes, that the most joy comes during the rise and the brief time at the top and not in the inevitable fall. But it is also true that it is only possible to see a dynasty in its full dimension from a distance, after the passage of time reveals it fully, in perspective. Dynasties are not made up only of their best moments: the struggle is just as important and gives meaning to a dynasty's success.

Talk to any old-time Patriots fans or players, even from a time when victories were few, defeat was expected, disappointment and occasional dismay were almost compulsory, and championships were the most distant dream imaginable . . . and they do not shake their heads in anger, dwell in sadness, or revisit (at least not too often) the bitterness of loss. Instead, they smile, laugh, and slap each other on the back, share memories, tell stories, and then tell another and another. Yes, for many years the Patriots were awful, and often laughable. But had they been any other way, would what they have recently become been half as enjoyable? No.

So if this is the start of a fall, the dynasty's end, that means it is also a beginning. Such is the nature of things. Thirty-one other teams and their fans are jealous as hell.

All in all, it's been a wicked good time.

SEASON BY SEASON WITH THE PATS

SEASON	RECORD	POSTSEASON
2017	13-3-0, 1st—AFC East	Lost Super Bowl to the Philadelphia Eagles, 41–33
2016	14-2-0, 1st—AFC East	Won Super Bowl over the Atlanta Falcons, 34–28
2015	12-4-0, 1st—AFC East	Lost conference championship
2014	12-4-0, 1st—AFC East	Won Super Bowl over the Seattle Seahawks, 28–24
2013	12-4-0, 1st—AFC East	Lost conference championship
2012	12-4-0, 1st—AFC East	Lost conference championship
2011	13-3-0, 1st—AFC East	Lost Super Bowl to the New York Giants, 21–17
2010	14-2-0, 1st—AFC East	Lost divisional playoffs
2009	10-6-0, 1st—AFC East	Lost wild-card playoffs
2008	11-5-0, 2nd—AFC East	
2007	16-0-0, 1st—AFC East	Lost Super Bowl to the New York Giants, 17–14
2006	12-4-0, 1st—AFC East	Lost conference championship
2005	10-6-0, 1st—AFC East	Lost divisional playoffs
2004	14-2-0, 1st—AFC East	Won Super Bowl over the Philadelphia Eagles, 24–21
2003	14-2-0, 1st—AFC East	Won Super Bowl over the Carolina Panthers, 32–29
2002	9-7-0, T2nd—AFC East	
2001	11-5-0, 1st—AFC East	Won Super Bowl over the St. Louis Rams, 20–17
2000	5-11-0, 5th—AFC East	
1999	8-8-0, T4th—AFC East	
1998	9-7-0, 4th—AFC East	Lost wild-card playoffs
1997	10-6-0, 1st—AFC East	Lost divisional playoffs
1996	11-5-0, 1st—AFC East	Lost Super Bowl to the Green Bay Packers, 35–21
1995	6-10-0, 4th—AFC East	
1994	10-6-0, 2nd—AFC East	Lost wild-card playoffs
1993	5-11-0, 4th—AFC East	
1992	2-14-0, 5th—AFC East	

1991	6-10-0, 4th—AFC East	
1990	1-15-0, 5th—AFC East	
1989	5-11-0, 4th—AFC East	
1988	9-7-0, T2nd—AFC East	
1987	8-7-0, T2nd—AFC East	
1986	11-5-0, 1st—AFC East	
1985	11-5-0, T2nd—AFC East	Lost Super Bowl to the Chicago Bears, 46-10
1984	9-7-0, 2nd—AFC East	
1983	8-8-0, T2nd—AFC East	
1982	5-4-0, 7th—AFC East	Lost round 1
1981	2-14-0, T4th—AFC East	
1980	10-6-0, 2nd—AFC East	
1979	9-7-0, 2nd—AFC East	
1978	11-5-0, 1st—AFC East	Lost divisional playoffs
1977	9-5-0, 3rd—AFC East	
1976	11-3-0, 2nd—AFC East	Lost divisional playoffs
1975	3-11-0, T4th—AFC East	
1974	7-7-0, T3rd—AFC East	
1973	5-9-0, 3rd—AFC East	
1972	3-11-0, 5th—AFC East	
1971	6-8-0, T3rd—AFC East	
1970	2-12-0, 5th—AFC East	

PATRIOTS JOIN THE NFL AS A MEMBER OF THE AFC EAST

1969	4-10-0, T3rd—AFL East	
1968	4-10-0, 4th—AFL East	
1967	3-10-1, 5th—AFL East	
1966	8-4-2, 2nd—AFL East	
1965	4-8-2, 3rd—AFL East	
1964	10-3-1, 2nd—AFL East	
1963	7-6-1, 1st—AFL East	Lost AFL championship to the San Diego Chargers, 51–10
1962	9-4-1, 2nd—AFL East	
1961	9-4-1, 2nd—AFL East	
1960	5-9-0, 4th—AFL East	
TOTAL	**489-386-9**	**34-20**

INDEX

Page numbers in *italics* indicate illustrations.

A

PHOTO CREDITS

Arthur Anderson/Getty Images: 237

Mike Andersen, Courtesy of The Sports Museum: 60

Brian Bahr /Allsport-Getty Images: 188, 228

Al Bello/Getty Images: 217, 221

Bettmann/Getty Images: 115, 119, 133

Phil Bissell: 14, 16, 21, 34, 35, 36, 37, 38, 39, 42, 45, 71

John Bohn/The Boston Globe via Getty Images: 192

Courtesy of the Boston Globe: xii (top), xvi, 9, 20, 66, 77, 140, 202, 322

Courtesy of the Boston Public Library, Leslie Jones Collection: viii

Bill Brett/The Boston Globe via Getty Images: 6

Yoon S. Byun/The Boston Globe via Getty Images: 290

Rob Carr/Getty Images: 264, 276

Barry Chin/The Boston Globe via Getty Images: 203, 313

Timothy A. Clary/AFP/Getty Images: 190

Jim Davis/The Boston Globe via Getty: v, 158, 164, 171, 176, 180, 187, 189, 199, 204, 208, 211, 266, 277, 311, 329

Denver Post via Getty Images: 98, 123, 146, 152

Albert Dickson/Sporting News via Getty Images: 254

Ted Dully/The Boston Globe via Getty Images: 85

Mike Ehrmann/Getty Images: 298

Gin Ellis/Getty Images: 142

Elsa/Getty Images: 234, 282, 286, 296, 328

Ed Farrand/The Boston Globe via Getty Images: 87

Focus on Sport/Getty Images: 132, 151, 156, 302, 304, 317, 318

Hannah Foslien/Getty Images: 320, 337

George Gojkovich/Getty Images: 103, 120, 130

Bill Greene, Courtesy of The Boston Globe: 143, 150

Bill Greene/The Boston Globe via Getty Images: 145

Stan Grossfeld, Courtesy of The Boston Globe: 126, 129, 141

Tom Hauck/Getty Images: 232

Harry How /Allsport-Getty Images: 194, 258

John Iacono /Sports Illustrated/Getty Images: 174

Collection of Richard A. Johnson: x, xi, xiii, xiv, 2, 11, 17, 18, 27, 40, 52, 53, 57, 58, 64, 67, 69 (top), 71, 80, 82, 86

Cartoon by Vic Johnson, Collection of Richard A. Johnson: 90

Rich Kane/Icon SMI/Icon Sport Media via Getty Images: 275

Allen Kee/Getty Images: 178, 193, 195

Matthew J. Lee/The Boston Globe via Getty Images: 222, 240, 257, 293

The LIFE Picture Collection/Getty Images: 135